YOUNG INDIA

1927-1928

YOUNG INDIA

1927-1928

MAHATMA GANDHI

GYAN

Published by

Gyan Publishing House
5, Ansari Road
Daryaganj, New Delhi-110002
Phone: 011-47034999, 9811692060
E-mail: books@gyanbooks.com

Distribution Network
gyanbooks.com
India, USA, Canada, UK, Australia

ISBN: 978-93-7225-342-9 (PB)

First Published, 1935

2nd Impression 2025

Printed at: Gyan Press, Delhi.

YOUNG INDIA 1927-1928
Author: MAHATMA GANDHI

YOUNG INDIA

1927–1928

YOUNG INDIA

1927–1928

By

MAHATMA GANDHI

1935

CONTENTS

PREFACE

The period with which this volume treats was one during which the country was mentally in a very depressed state. The Non-co-operation Movement had been in full swing for some time, but had not yielded the results which those who misconceived the nature of its working had expected of it. Those who took Gandhiji's dictum about "Swaraj within a Year" literally found themselves in deep disappointment. The movement towards co-operation began to gather momentum as was evidenced by the fact that resolutions began to be moved in the legislatures demanding "Dominion Status" and enquiry into the Indian Reforms question. The Government, on their part, were not slow to exploit the situation. The notorious "Dual Policy" was put in operation, and while repression had not been given up, the foundations were being laid for a policy which resulted in the setting up of the Simon Commission.

The period was in every way a trying one for Gandhiji. He was riddled with questions about the efficacy of his policy. Was his political philosophy consistent with the teachings of the *Gita* that it was the duty of God and the Great Ones to put down the wicked and protect the righteous? How could he expect masses of ordinary mortals to withstand the attacks of unscrupulous enemies without retaliating? Had not all his talk of "Swaraj within a Year" proved vainglorious? Had not his "somersault" in the Bardoli affair worked untold havoc among the people of Guntur who had withheld payment of taxes in pursuance of his programme? How was Hindu-Muslim unity furthered by his "playing into the hands" of a handful of fanatical Muslims? Far rather, had not communal feuds increased since the advent of Gandhiji in Indian politics? Had he not alienated, by his obstinate adherence to an inane philosophy, leaders like Malaviya, Das, Lajpat Rai? Was he not weakening the already docile and timid Hindus by his anti-untouchability campaign? Had not the charkha proved its untrustworthiness in this age of science?

The publication which is placed before the public provides answers to these and other similar questions. The doctrine of Ahimsa is so great, its bearing on the multitudinous situations that arise in the course of human affairs so close and yet so subtle that there is little to be surprised at that, to its exposition, Gandhiji has devoted many of his most valuable articles. So are his other teachings—the value of handspinning from the spiritual no less than from the economic standpoint; the need for purging the country of the evils of drink and of untouchability that corrode Hindu society; the paramount necessity of bridging the gulf that exists between community and community, between those who believe in Hinduism and those who profess Islam, between the rich and powerful and the poor and lowly, between Capital and Labour.

Above all, Gandhiji's treatment of the many problems that have arisen for solution from time to time not only in the political, social and economic affairs of the nation, but in the lives of individuals as well in so far as they have been referred to him, is of such universal interest and value that it cannot be allowed to lie imprisoned in the stray volumes of a weekly periodical. Hence this publication—this "guide to perfect life", if we may so call it, for bringing which out the Publishers need not make any apology.

RAJENDRA PRASAD.

YOUNG INDIA

6th January, 1927

THE CONGRESS

BY M. K. GANDHI

When in Cawnpore the Assam delegates gave the invitation to hold the Congress of 1926 at Gauhati and the Congress accepted the invitation, I was filled with misgivings. I felt that Assam was too far away, too unorganised and too poor to shoulder the heavy burden of holding a Congress session. Gauhati has a population of only 16,000. No place with such a small population has before Gauhati had the temerity to invite the Congress. Gauhati, however, beat all previous records, and in an incredibly short space of time erected, in the midst of surroundings of great natural beauty on the banks of the great Brahmaputra, a city under Khadi canvas. The huge Congress pavilion itself was made of pure Assam Khadi. The Reception Committee had to import material and men from outside in order to provide for the varied tastes of delegates and visitors from different provinces. Leaders' quarters were isolated from the delegates' quarters. When I resented the isolation, I was told that it was not done intentionally, but it had to be done because there was not enough ground available in one single spot to provide accommodation for all. The construction of the cottages was incredibly simple: Assam bamboo, Assam mud, Assam straw, Assam Khadi and Assam labour were responsible for the very simple but artistic huts erected on the Brahmaputra bank. And as Mr. Phookan led me to one of these beautiful huts, he said, 'Now it must delight your heart in that we are giving you, not a palace miscalled hut, as you had remarked in Belgaum, but we are giving you a proper hut, only we cannot claim any merit for it because it is a virtue of necessity; for we could have given you nothing more, nothing less.' I was, however, more than glad for this virtue of necessity. Let not the reader, however, imagine for one moment that there was in any degree whatsoever less comfort in these artistic huts than in the palatial-looking structure that was provided in Belgaum. All the other arrangements, so far as I gather, were in keeping with this artistic simplicity.

The address of the Chairman of the Reception Committee was equally simple and equally artistic, and, therefore, naturally brief.

Proceedings commenced punctually at the advertised time. No time was lost in ceremonial functions. In a few minutes Mr. Phookan's brief address was finished, the President amidst shouts of applause walked to the rostrum and read his address. The suppressed gloom cast over the assembly through the news of the assassination of Swami Shraddhanandji was no doubt there, but it was not allowed to be made visible. The delegates knew that Swamiji had died a hero's death and it therefore demanded no tears but action, and so the business part of the Congress went on as if nothing had happened. The ceremonial was severely cut off, including the usual presidential procession. The address of the President for the matters it covers is brief enough. I pass by the references to the Councils and the defence of the Swarajist attitude, which occupies half of the address.

The constructive programme has its due share given to it. The place of honour is assigned to Khaddar. The President trusts that the All-India Spinners' Association will become a nation-wide labour organisation which, if it cannot be identical with Swaraj, will go some way towards it. It can become that, if every Congressman and every Congresswoman will do his or her duty. "The spinning wheel," says Sjt. S. Srinivasa Iyengar, "has by its persuasiveness affected to a visible extent the national psychology and has lent a new dignity to our manhood and womanhood." This was more than exemplified by the enthusiastic manner in which the amendment in the franchise clause regarding Khaddar was accepted by the Congress in spite of stubborn opposition offered to it. No wonder that the President considers that "Khaddar is at once the radiant symbol of our self-reliance and of our power of resistance."

In the constructive programme the second place is given to Prohibition, and the President correctly pleads guilty to the charge that we have not lately paid much attention to the question of total prohibition. "The movement," he says, "will gain in moral grandeur, if we successfully organise the will of the nation in that behalf." He remarks that "no minister has during the past six years been found, and I doubt whether a minister will now be found, to be courageous enough to bring in a bill for total prohibition and to resign his office on its rejection or disallowance." There is something somewhere utterly wrong, if in a place like India, which is overwhelmingly dry, ministers are unwilling to provide what is the nation's due, namely, total prohibition. There is as much flaw in the argument that it is an interference with the right of the people as there would be in the argument that the laws prohibiting theft interfere with the right of thieving. A thief steals all earthly possessions, a drunkard steals his own and his neighbours' honour. It surprises me to discover that the President has failed to suggest the obvious method of providing for the deficit of revenue. There is a huge military expenditure, so much of which is utterly useless and based upon distrust of the nation. It is capable of reduction by more than 25 crores, which is the revenue from drinks and drugs.

Untouchability comes next. He does not think that it is necessary to wait for Swaraj till untouchability is removed. He cites the capital instance, in his favour, of the United States of America achieving freedom long before the abolition of a very real and widespread slavery. But he hastens to add

"We must all agree that we must make an end of untouchability, apart from any question of Swaraj and whether we ever win Swaraj or not. And then this Brahmin philosopher lays down that "the higher philosophy of Hinduism as well as the history of the religious dissidence in our country emboldens me to claim that the rule regarding untouchability has neither part nor lot with the indestructible soul of Hinduism. Judged by any test humanitarian, rational or spiritual, patriotic or democratic, we cannot with decency uphold in Hinduism the dogma of an immutable untouchability. It clouds our vision, limits our experience, hardens our heart, narrows our sphere of responsibility and prevents our ideals of justice, love and sincerity from being perfect." I congratulate the President for this eloquent and severe condemnation of the curse that has descended upon Hinduism.

The next heading is labour and unemployment. I am inclined to think that this needs more diligent study than it appears to have been given to it. It requires, in my opinion, considerable revision. I suggest that the Charka movement with all its implications provides the largest form of relief to the unemployment of millions.

The currency policy of the Government has also claimed a paragraph in his address. The President 'cordially' welcomes the formation of the Indian Currency League and trusts that it will adequately educate public opinion on the question of the ratio, the gold standard, gold currency and other cognate questions. "But I am certain," he says, "the League will be able to achieve nothing, either by debate and vote in the Assembly or by protest outside, unless it comes into line with the Congress and unless its members harness themselves to the dynamic politics of the Congress."

Indian States have also found a paragraph in the address.

Greater India naturally follows the paragraph on Indian States. "The status of Indians abroad, whether in South Africa or Kenya, in Fiji or Guiana, in Ceylon or Malaya, in America or Australia, depends inevitably upon the status of

Indians in their own land; and Swaraj for India depends in its turn upon the brave and unfaltering spirit of our kith and kin across the seas."

I suppose the presidential suggestion "of the holding once in a way of a session of the Congress in South Africa" is merely a pious wish. The subject deserves better examination than it has received. I presume the absence of any reference to Mr. Andrews' signal services is an unintentional oversight due to the many local pre-occupations of the very busy President.

Asiatic Federation comes in, too, for a few lines. Mr. Iyengar deplores that "we have too long neglected the possibilities of a cultural and business union with all Asiatic countries." I venture to suggest that the cultural union is being sufficiently attended to by our great Poet and the business union by the great commercial firms.

The irrepressible optimism of the President is to be observed in the paragraphs upon Communalism and Nationalism. "I am confident," says he, "that, wherever intensive propaganda, sincere and persuasive, clearly analyses the fallacies underlying it, communalism will go to the wall. Happily, prejudice and suspicion are not deep-seated amongst Indians and communalism is but their off-spring."

Under the heading 'Plea for Tolerance,' one reads the following pregnant sentence: "Though each community should be free to make conversions, no resort to conversion is really any longer useful or necessary. For the lives of the best and most pious men in each community are a fitter and more effective propaganda in that behalf than definite missionary effort. But wherever the latter is made, it should be open and general, and neither secret nor directed to the converting of particular men or women. Let us realise that no great and long-established religion gains in truth, beauty or spirituality with any increase in its census figures." He winds up the paragraph by quoting the following beautiful passage from Ashoka's inscriptions: "He who does reverence to his own sect, while disparaging the sects of others wholly. from attachment to his own, with intent to enhance the splendour of his own sect, in reality by such conduct inflicts the severest injury on his own sect."

The President is evidently against communal representation. He says. "That much abused expression 'communal representation' is a misnomer; for all the communities are equally interested in all public questions and in the country's problems and in the particular solutions of them" Again he says. "Let us realise clearly that to uphold justice between man and man is to uphold justice between community and community. As a safeguard, a negative rule against members of any community or caste monopolising offices is all that is required."

"The intrusion into politics of religion," the President remarks, "and very often of dogmatic religion, must be resisted as a primitive or mediaeval idea, born of theocracies and disastrous alike to religion and to politics." But he adds, "I do not speak of morality or of that spiritual quality which is common to all religions; for thereby politics and organisations are cleansed and made sweet and wholesome."

"Let us not forget," Sjt. Iyengar adds, "in the fever of political controversy, that the strength of each religion is derived from God and rooted in the souls of Prahlads. Not all the tortures of a Torquemada, nor all the burning at the stakes, nor all the forms of persecution have been able to destroy the mystic quality of the human soul. Neither Hinduism nor Islam derives or requires strength either from the present or from any future Government. Both stand far, far above Swaraj, which is not comparable to them. Neither foreign governments nor self-governments, neither democracies nor autocracies, can destroy that seed of faith which is in every one of us, that inspired interpretation of the universe to which one clings for guidance and solace in this world and for salvation in the next."

The last three pages of the address are devoted to a fervent appeal for unity." There can be only two parties in India, the party of the Government and its adherents that obstruct Swaraj, and the party that fights visibly and unceasingly for Swaraj. I deprecate the philosophy of individualism in a supreme struggle for freedom against a powerful people with their trained bureaucracy and with unlimited, material resources. On a question whether a particular course is wise or unwise, will succeed or fail, will accelerate Swaraj or retard it, to make one's opinion or judgment or feeling a matter of conscience is false philosophy. On a point of religion, of morality, of honour, one's own conscience must be the arbiter, but in transacting the affairs of a country, when a decision is not irreligious, immoral or dishonourable, I fail to see how we may rely on our right to differ from one another and yet uphold the discipline necessary for an organisation fighting for Swaraj."

The conclusion is in keeping with the fervency of the appeal and the deep emotion that underlies every line of this address. He says, "Swaraj is not an intellectual but an emotional proposition. We must cherish it in our hearts with unquenchable faith. We must become possessed by a passion for Swaraj that is not warped by fallacies and impulses, that will stand for a uniform and rapid corporate advance in serried masses, that will know no obstacles, that will not wax and wane with the seasons, that will not be daunted by imprisonments or depressed by failures."

Let me hope that the appeal will find an echo in the hearts of us all.

The resolutions do not require an elaborate examination. Besides the condolence resolutions, there is, of course, the Council resolution for the guidance of Council-wallas, then the resolutions about South Africa and Kenya, the Bengal detenues and the Gurdwara prisoners. The Khaddar clause in the constitution is, in my opinion, altered for the better. The ceremonial wear had become the laughing stock of all. Habitual wear of Khaddar is the right, thing if Khaddar wear should find a place in our franchise qualifications. It is to be hoped that every Congress worker will enforce this resolution in his own person and induce others to do likewise. But I must deal more fully in a subsequent issue with many other things that were discussed in the Subjects Committee in connection with the resolutions withdrawn or rejected.

6th January, 1927.

WEEKLY LETTER

I am writing this on my way back to Calcutta from Gauhati. Never before one went to the Congress with more reluctance, and less hopeful of the Congress week than this time. And yet several happenings conspired to give the Gauhati Congress an unexpected importance and made the Congress week more eventful than one had expected. Gandhiji himself was not sure if he had any work at Gauhati, and would not have gone but for Pandit Motilalji's and Sjt. Aiyengar's urgent and imperative telegrams. The worst one expected to happen at Gauhati was miserable wrangles between the Responsivists and Swarajists, and the best that could happen nothing more than a peaceful ending of the quarrels between the two contending sections. But Lalaji refused to disturb the atmosphere and did not proceed beyond Calcutta. Providence had meant him for another and far more urgent duty. Who knew the dark day that would dawn on India on the morning of the 24th?

* *

The stunning news of Swamiji's assassination was received by Lalaji on the evening of the 23rd and he forwarded it to Gandhiji on the 24th. It was delivered at a wayside station — Sorbhog. According to his wont, Gandhiji was going to the carriage door to appeal to the surging crowds crying '*Mahatma Gandhi ki jai*' to pay their mites for Gandhi's work, rather than raise those empty cries, when the telegram bearing the terrible news was delivered to him. For a moment he could not believe his eyes as he read it, but he was soon sure that there could be no mistake about it. Friends who were immediately informed saw him, every one refusing to believe the contents and trying to read in the language something less terrible than it indicated. But Gandhiji had no doubt in his mind. He immediately wired to Lalaji asking him to proceed to Delhi to pacify the public, and to Indra, the Swamiji's son to say that the death was a hero's death.

* * *

And so the leaders who met at Gauhati found themselves faced with a catastrophe they were totally unprepared for. Shrimati Sarojini Naidu began the proceedings of the last A. I. C. C. meeting of her regime with an appropriate reference to the event of the week, and summoned Gandhiji to voice the Hindus' feelings in the matter and Maulana Mahomed Ali the Musalmans.' At the open Congress, too, the resolution of the day was the one about 'the treacherous and cowardly murder of Swami Shraddhanandji.' In his speeches on both the occasions, Gandhiji described the death as a privilege and a portent, if I may summarise his sentiments in two words. A privilege, inasmuch as for a fighter like Swamiji there could be no nobler consummation. His Guru—Swami Dayanand—was also treacherously murdered and the Arya Samaj lived all these years in his death. The disciple had now cemented the foundation of that religious organisation with his noble blood. But in Gandhiji's sense, it was a greater privilege, privilege not for the Hindus to be proud of, but a privilege for both Hindus and Musalmans to chasten themselves and cement their unity with. And yet what could be a more terrible portent, looking to the surcharged atmosphere of today? To those who are living in that atmosphere and to those responsible for it, he addressed words of warning. 'Repent, repent,' he seemed to say:

'Though ye have trod
Through paths of wickedness and woe,

And though your sins be red as scarlet,
They shall be white as snow.'

* * *

A unanimous manifesto by the Ulema and leaders present at Gauhati, condemning the deed as not sanctioned by Islam, was appropriate. At the Hindu Mahasabha Special Session, though every one spoke from a lacerated heart, no unguarded word escaped the lips of the least of the speakers, to say nothing of the greatest, *i. e.* Pandit Malaviyaji, whose speech was one of the most remarkable I have heard for restraint and sobriety. A Maulvi from Mymensing, it seems, specially attended the session and asked to be allowed to speak. Panditji allowed him and he said that from the point of view of Islam the act was most reprehensible. 'Are you sincere? cried some one from the audience. 'I am, if you please,' said the Maulvi, 'I am voicing the feelings of my heart.' Towards the end of the proceedings Dr. Rajaballi Patel, a Bombay Musalman, who happened to be present, was the first to subscribe to the Fund started in memory of Swami Shraddhanandji. He earmarked his contribution of Rs. 100 for untouchability work and Panditji accepted it gratefully as a fine expression of good-will.

* * *

The other work for Gandhiji was the opening of the Swadeshi Exhibition. There was nothing unusual in the Exhibition. Gandhiji formally declared it open with a speech which was a passionate utterance from beginning to end. The reference to the poverty in the land was touching. The illusory character of the wealth in the country he summed up in a sentence or two. 'Every 5 millions in the hands of a millionaire means 95 millions sent out of India. Like the old man of the sea, we are a perpetual burden on the poor taxpayer.' How could a return be made? Khadi was the only means. No programme had surer results. The Spinners' Association had to-day 50,000 women spinners who supplemented their daily earnings or earned a couple of annas each where formerly they earned nothing But who would listen to their cry? Who would listen to his cry? 'Draupadi, when she found that not even her five husbands could help her, cried out in agony to Krishna, the only help of the helpless, and he heard her prayers. Even so shall I work away to-day and cry in the name of the dumb millions of India, and I am sure my prayers will be heard one day.'

* * *

When one whole day was being spent in discussing numberless amendments to the resolution on the Councils programme, one felt as though Gandhiji's cry was no more than a cry in the wilderness. But as though in response to that cry, came up before the Subjects Committee a resolution from the Working Committee making habitual wearing of Khaddar compulsory on every one who sought to exercise a vote as a Congressman. Mr. Aney stoutly opposed it. He opposed it as one who had no faith in Khaddar. Another member supported him and appealed to Gandhiji's sense of justice and fairplay. Gandhiji, who was specially requested by the President to be present on the occasion, dealt with this in a few sentences which should have gone home. 'Let me say my sense of justice will be reconciled only by the restoration of the spinning franchise. If a stiffening of the franchise is, as I think it certainly is, necessary for national growth, am I not justified in laying down conditions for it? If any member should charge me with motives to exclude any party, I should feel deeply sorry, if not insulted.' But more necessary than this answer to the objections was the warning to those who with eyes open wanted to pass the resolution, knowing that they themselves did not want it a year ago. 'This amendment is a plea for purification. If you feel that it is to be observed in its breach, if you are going to pass it here and defy it as soon as you leave the Congress, I ask you to reject it. As the rule at present stands, it is most humiliating and must be removed or radically changed. Khaddar must stand on its own bottom. . . . If you carry the resolution, I want you to do so with all the implications I have mentioned. . . . I do not want any patronage, as I do not give any. I am a lover of my own liberty and so I would do nothing to restrict yours. I simply want to please my own conscience, which is God.' The resolution was passed with an overwhelming majority both in the Subjects Committee and at the open Congress. It was the only right and proper thing to do, as it followed as a necessary corollary to the resolution about 'work in the country,' which, besides, would have remained a pious wish but for the change about habitual wearing of Khaddar.

M. D.

6th January, 1927

SWAMIJI AS I KNEW HIM

By M. K. Gandhi

My first acquaintance with Swamiji was when he was Mahatma Munshiram, and that by letter. He was then Governor of Kangdi Gurukul, his great original contribution to education. He was not satisfied with the orthodox Western method. He wanted his boys to be saturated with Vedic teaching, and he taught through Hindi, not English. He wanted them to be and remain brahmacharis during their training He had inspired his boys to contribute to the fund that was then being collected for the Satyagrahis of South Africa. And he wanted them to do so by themselves labouring as coolies for hire; for, was it not a coolies' fight in South Africa? The boys rose to the occasion, earned full wages and sent them to me. The letter he wrote to me about this incident was written in Hindi. I was addressed as 'my dear brother.' It endeared me to Mahatma Munshiram, we had never met each other before.

Andrews was the link between us. He was anxious that, whenever I returned home, I should make the acquaintance of what I used to call his trinity—the Poet, Principal Rudra and Mahatma Munshiram.

From the time of the receipt of that letter, we became

brothers in arms. We met each other in 1915 at his favourite Gurukul and with each meeting we came closer and knew each other better. His love of ancient India, Sanskrit and Hindi was remarkable. He was undoubtedly a non-cooperator before non-cooperation was born. He was impatient to gain Swaraj. He hated untouchability and was anxious to raise the status of the 'untouchables.' He could not brook any restriction upon their freedom.

When the Rowlatt agitation was started, he was among the very first to hail it. He wrote a very warm letter to me. But the suspension of Satyagraha after the Amritsar and Viramgam tragedies he could not understand. From that period our differences commenced, but they never once disturbed the brotherly relations that subsisted between us. The difference showed to me his childlike nature. He blurted out the truth as he knew it, without regard to consequences. He was daring to a fault. I observed more and more the temperamental differences between us as time progressed, but they only proved to me the goodness of the soul in him. To think audibly is no crime, it is a virtue. It is the hall-mark of truth. Swamiji thought audibly.

The Bardoli decision broke his heart. He despaired of me. His open protest was most energetic. His private letters to me were still more so, but with the emphasis on the differences, there was an equal emphasis on love. He was not satisfied with an avowal of love in mere letters. He sought me out as opportunity offered and explained his own position, tried to understand mine. But the real reason, as it seems to me, for seeking me out was to assure me, as if any such assurance was necessary, of undiminished love for me as for a younger brother.

My remarks about the Arya Samaj and its great author and my references to him hurt him deeply; but our friendship was strong enough to bear the strain. He could not understand that it was possible to reconcile my general estimate of the Maharshi with the quality of forgiveness that he had in a boundless measure for personal injury. His devotion to the Maharshi was too great to brook any criticism of him or his teachings.

He has been severely criticised and maligned in the Musalman press for his Shuddhi movement. I myself could not accept it even now. But, in my opinion, he had a complete defence of his own position from his own standpoint. Shuddhi is entitled to the same toleration that is claimed for Tabligh, so long as either remains within moral and legitimate bounds. But this is not the occasion for entering into an examination of that highly controversial question. Both the Tabligh and the Shuddhi, which is a reply to the former, have to undergo a radical change. Progress of liberal study of religions of the world is bound to revolutionise the existing clumsy method of proselytising which looks to the form rather than the substance. It is the transference of allegiance from one fold to another and the mutual decrying of rival faiths which gives rise to mutual hatred.

Swamiji's assassination can be turned to good account by us, if we both Hindus and Musalmans could possibly realise the deeper meaning of Shuddhi.

I cannot close the reminiscences of the life of a great reformer without recalling his last visit to the Satyagraha Ashram only a few months ago. Let me assure my Musalman friends that he was no hater of Musalmans. He undoubtedly distrusted many Musalmans But he bore them no ill-will. He thought that Hindus were cowed down and he wanted them to be brave and be able to defend themselves and their honour. In this connection he told me that he was much misunderstood and that he was absolutely innocent of many things that were said against him. He told me he had several threatening letters. He was warned by friends not to travel alone But this man of faith said, 'What protection shall I seek but of God? Not a blade of grass perishes without His will. I know, therefore, that nothing can happen to me so long He wishes me to serve through this body.'

During this stay of his he spoke to the boys and girls of the Ashram school. He said the best protection of Hinduism must come from within, from self-purification. He put the greatest emphasis on the need of Brahmacharya for the building of character and body.

6th January, 1927.

SHRADDHANAND MEMORIAL

BY M. K. GANDHI,

It is in the fitness of things that there should be an appeal on behalf of the Hindu Mahasabha for funds to perpetuate the memory of the late Swami Shraddhanandji. I congratulate the Sabha on having decided upon inviting collections for carrying on the work for which the Swamiji chiefly lived after his *Sannyasa.* This was removal of 'untouchability,' Shuddhi and Sangathan. The appeal has been made for five lakhs for 'untouchability' and as many for Shuddhi and Sangathan. For my own part, I still remain unconvinced about the necessity of the Shuddhi movement, taking 'Shuddhi' in the sense it is generally understood. Shuddhi of sinners is a perpetual inward performance. Shuddhi of those who can be identified neither as Hindus nor as Musalmans or who have been recently declared converts but who do not know even the meaning of conversion and who want to be known definitely as Hindus is not conversion but *prayashchitta* or penance. The third aspect of Shuddhi is conversion properly so-called. And I question its use in this age of growing toleration and enlightenment. I am against conversion, whether it is known as Shuddhi by Hindus, Tabligh by Musalmans or proselytising by Christians. Conversion is a heart-process known only to and by God. It must be left to itself. But this is no place for airing my views on conversion. Those who believe in it have a perfect right to follow their own course without let or hindrance, so long as it is kept within proper limits, *i. e.,* so long as there is no force nor fraud nor material inducement and so long as the parties are free agents and of mature age and understanding. Those, therefore, who believe in Shuddhi have a perfect right to subscribe to the appeal.

Sangathan is really a sound movement. Every community is entitled, indeed bound, to organise itself if it is to live as a separate entity. I have kept myself aloof from it because of my peculiar ideas of organisation. I believe in quality rather than quantity. The fashion now-a-days is to rely upon quantity even at the cost of quality. Quantity has its place no doubt in social and political economy. Only I am ill-fitted for organising quantity in the way it is done at present. Therefore, for me, only the appeal for funds for the removal of untouchability has a value. It comes with a force all its own. For reform of Hinduism and for its real protection, removal of untouchability is the greatest thing. It is all-inclusive, and, therefore, if this, the blackest spot on Hinduism, is removed, you have automatically all that Shuddhi and Sangathan can be expected to yield. And I say this, not because of the vast number of untouchables whom every Hindu should seek to embrace as one of his own, but because consciousness of having broken down a barbarous and ancient custom and consequent purity it necessarily implies gives a strength which is irresistible. Removal of untouchability, therefore, is a spiritual process. Swamiji was a living embodiment of that reformation, because he had no half measures about it, because he would not compromise, he would give no quarter. If he could have had his way, he would have made short work of untouchability in Hinduism. He would have opened every well and every temple to every 'untouchable' on conditions of absolute equality and he would have braved all consequences. I can conceive no more fitting memorial to Swami Shraddhanandji than that every Hindu should henceforth purge his heart of the uncleanliness, which untouchability undoubtedly is, and deal with the untouchable as with his own kith and kin. His monetary contribution to the memorial, therefore will, in my opinion, be merely an earnest of his, irrevocable resolution to root out the evil and cast it away once and for all from Hinduism.

The 9th day of January is the day appointed for doing public and religious reverence to the memory of the Swamiji. I hope that the ceremony will be performed in every city and every village. But the ceremony will lose its real significance, if at the same time those who take part in it do not purge themselves of the taint of untouchability. Every 'untouchable' should, therefore, take part in the ceremony; and what a great thing it would be if every temple were thrown open to the 'untouchables' on that day. If an organised effort is made, the collections could be finished without the slightest difficulty before the sun sets on the 9th January.

6th January, 1927

"GIVE BACK TO THE VILLAGE"

By C. Rajagopalachar

Diwan Bahadur R. Ramachandra Rao is a retired Government servant. He was Collector and District Magistrate in several districts. He filled the post of Registrar of Co-operative Societies in the Presidency of Madras at a time when that department had to be built up and societies organised and developed. He rose to be a Secretary to Government in one of the most important 'reserved' departments. The Government appreciated his services by conferring on him first the title of Diwan Bahadur and then a C. I. E. As a district officer with ample opportunities to come in direct touch with the rural cultivating classes, he must have seen enough with his own eyes to convince him of the poverty and helplessness of the masses. The opinion of this ex-Government servant, after long and varied experience, in support of the Charkha as a supplementary occupation for the families of poor cultivators, and his earnest appeal on behalf of Khaddar, as a bond of co-operation between rich and poor, must strengthen the

Khaddar worker who wavers and be food for serious reflection on the part of sceptics. In a remarkable address which he delivered at Tinnevelly on the co-operative movement, he has made a vigorous appeal on behalf of Khaddar. Referring to Mahatmaji, he showed an extraordinarily fine appreciation of the essential principles underlying the movement of Non-co-operation. He said.

"I would then cite the instance of a far greater name, that of Mahatma Gandhi. His message to the world is one of Ahimsa, and co-operation. It is very unlucky that the policy with which his name is associated has got the name of Non-co-operation. If closely analysed, his policy is one of love and a call for the rich and the poor, the educated and the unlettered, the higher and the lower castes, *to co-operate.*" Referring to Khaddar in particular, he said: "His Khaddar movement is one of profound significance. The man who wears one bit of Khaddar thereby shows the sympathy and fulfils the duty which he owes to the poor."

There cannot be a finer or clearer exposition of the ethics and the economics of Khaddar He further elaborated this in his speech and showed how Khaddar was true co-operation, of which the work done by the "co-operative societies" was only one part or phase. He said:

"Co-operation is an all-embracing subject. We have at present something to do with one branch of it. The educated classess have received their education cheaply at the cost of the poor. The rich and the middle classes owe a duty to the poor tiller of the soil and the labourer, and this can be concretely shown by Khaddar."

Diwan Bahadur Ramachandra Rao was grieved to find that the Central Bank at Madras had accumulated large deposits without finding a proper use of the money. "The movement has absorbed a lot of money, which has not been utilised. The Central Bank has got one crore of rupees, which has not found its way into the primary societies. There, on the one hand, are the poor indebted villagers that are very badly in need of money, there, on the other, is the Central Bank that has plenty of money. But no method of intensive work has been devised to absorb this money for the spread of the movement. It should be the duty of all to see that ryots get the full benefit of every available pie that flows into the Co-operative movement."

The best form of intensive work which would circulate the savings among the tillers of the soil is Khadi work. Khadi work in Tamil Nadu is being done in a most businesslike and satisfactory manner. With one lakh more of capital, we could greatly increase the production of Khadi in the South. An investment of one lakh out of an accumulation of a crore to which the Diwan Bahadur refers would hardly be felt as a serious risk undertaken in a new kind of venture, but the money would return to our villages and circulate among the poorest and greatly help to revive the lost industry of hand spinning, thereby premanently improving the economic condition of the villages.

He deprecated hesitation in investing deposits in rural work:

"In whatever way we may draw our money, either as salaries in service or as profits in trade, remember that money ultimately comes from the cultivator of land. Any development of co-operation that ignores the ryot and the tiller of the soil is bound to fail."

There can be no better expression of a courageous and patriotic sense of duty to the masses by a man of long experience than the exhortation by Diwan Bahadur Ramachandra Rao to "Co-operators" to throw off timidity and launch on a programme of investmet in rural work.

The support of this high ex-Government officer with a long record of active service and rural experience is a remarkable testimony to the value of the Charkha in the solution of the problem of our rural poverty, and to the validity of the claim of Khadi on the patronage of the middle and upper classes.

13th January, 1927.

HERO AMONG HEROES

The following is a free translation of Gandhiji's Hindi speech with which he moved the resolution on the death of Swami Sharaddhanandji at the last session of the Indian National Congress;

"You must have noticed that the resolution I have moved originally stood in Maulana Mahomed Ali's name. But I am here to move it in obedience to the President's summons. We see from the newspapers that the assassination of Swamiji has evoked grief and horror throughout the land. I said, speaking on the same subject at the All-India Congress Committee, that we should not mourn over the Swamiji's death. He had died the death of a hero, and every one of us might wish for such a death. But I want to make a slight correction in that last statement. Every brave man welcomes such a death whenever it comes to him. He greets it as a friend. But let no one, therefore, invite or hanker after such a death, let no one desire that some one else should be in the wrong and err against God and man, so that he might become a martyr. It is wrong to wish any one to go astray. Let us all be brave enough to die the death of a martyr, but let no one lust for martyrdom.

"Swamiji was a hero among heroes, the bravest of the brave. He had astonished the nation with an unbroken record of bravery. I am witness of the pledge he had taken to sacrifice himself at the altar of the country.

"But need any one speak at length on the Swamiji's services to the nation? Swamiji, as every one knew, was the help of the helpless, the friend of the weak and the oppressed, and the work he had done for the untouchables was unsurpassed. I well remember his having told me once that, unless every Hindu member of the All-India

Congress Committee had an 'untouchable' servant in his home, the work of the Congress for the uplift of the untouchables would not be complete. This may sound as an impracticable proposal, but it shows his unbounded love for the untouchables.

"I shall not refer here to his many other services. Whilst the assassination of such a great hero and patriot, such a servant and devotee of God as the Swamiji can be made to serve the country's cause, imperfect men as we are, it is natural for us to mourn over his sad death. And when one thinks of the circumstances under which he met his death one is naturally filled with horror and indignation. The assassin sought an interview with the Swamiji to have a discussion on Islam. His faithful servant refused to admit him as he had Dr. Ansari's orders to allow no interviews so long as Swamiji was seriously ailing. But God had evidently ordered otherwise. Swamiji, when he overheard the request, asked Dharmasingh to let the man in. Brother Abdul Rashid was shown in. I purposely call him brother, and if we are true Hindus, you will understand why I call him so. Swamiji asked his servant to admit Abdul Rashid, because God had willed to show there through the greatness of Swamiji and the glory of Hinduism. Swamiji was, of course, too ill to discuss religious topics and he asked the stranger to seek another occasion. But he would not go. He said he was thirsty and asked for water. Swamiji asked Dharmasingh to fetch water for him and taking the advantage of his absence, the man deposited bullet shots in Swamiji's breast.

"This is a thing which should not have happened in India—India, where both Hindus and Musalmans are proud of other faiths. I have studied the Koran with the same reverent attention as I give the Gita, and I say that the Koran nowhere sanctions or enjoins such murders. The murder has been possible because the two communities look upon each other with feelings of hatred and enmity.

Many Musalmans believe that Lalaji and Malaviyaji are the sworn enemies of Islam, as was Swamiji in their opinion. On the other hand, many Hindus regard Sir Abdur Rahim and other Musalmans as the enemies of Hinduism. To my mind both are wholly wrong. Swamiji was no enemy of Islam, nor are Lalaji and Malaviyaji. Lalaji and Malaviyaji have a right to express their opinion freely and, even if we disagree with them, no one may excite feelings of hatred against them. And yet what do we see today? There are few Musalman papers today which do not use foul language against these patriots. Now, I ask in all humility what is the wrong they have done. We may not see eye to eye with them in their methods of work. But I am sure that it his great service that has earned for Malaviyaji the name Bharata Bhushan. Lalaji, too, has a great record of service. Then, take the Musalman leaders. Sir Abdur Rahim may think that Hindus are in advance of the Musalmans in every respect, that they are rich, they are educated, and the Musalmans are poor and uneducated. Sir Abdur Rahim thinks that his community should have a preference in the services. It is open to us to feel and say that he is mistaken in his views, but why should we abuse him for his opinions? If Maulana Mahomed Ali says that, although he has respect for Gandhi, he holds that the faith of a Muslim who believes in the Koran is greater than the faith of Gandhi, why should we be angry? Do not some Christian clergymen say that a Christian regularly going to church and serving Jesus is better than a Hindu, however pious he may be? What does that matter to us? I, therefore, appeal to you that, if you hold dear the memory of Swami Sharddanandji you would help in purging the atmosphere of mutual hatred and calumny, you would help in boycotting papers which foment hatred and spread misrepresentation. I am sure that India would lose nothing, if 90% of the papers were to cease today. Many Musalman papers today subsist on hatred of the Hindu and many Hindu papers subsist on hatred of the Musalman.

Swamiji has left for us a rich lesson written in his blood. 'Do you know the liberality of the Arya Samaj?' he once asked me. 'Do you know how Maharshi Dayanand forgave the man who poisoned him?' I knew it. How could I be ignorant of it, knowing as I did that the Maharishi had before him the example of Yudhishthira and the teaching of the Gita and the Upanishads? But Shraddhanandji, in his overflowing reverence for the Maharishi, dilated upon his forgiveness. I tell you the disciple had no less of that noble quality than his great master. Speaking once about the implications of 'Shuddhi', he told me that his 'Shuddhi' excluded any feeling of ill-will for the Musalman, that it meant purification of self and the great community to which he belonged and that his ideal was the ideal of the Gita—'See thyself in every one of the created beings'. But he emphasised that the Hindu also was no less a friend of his than the Musalman and that it was his duty to serve him. Even if the whole Muslim world were to turn against me, I would declare that Malaviyaji is my friend and elder brother. I declare also in the same breath that none of the Musalman leaders is an enemy of Hinduism. Sir Abdur Rahim is not an enemy of the Hindus, nor is Mian Fazli Hussain. When I met him, he assured me that he was an old Congressman, that he loved the Hindus no less than the Musalmans, but that as a Musalman he wanted to serve the latter. We may disagree with him in his views, we may not like his demands for the Musalmans, but why should we, therefore, swear at him and say that he is an enemy of the Hindus? Why should we not express our dissent from his views and fight them, if necessary, even as I do with Malaviyaji, in many respects, in a Satyagrahi way? I repeat, therefore, with all the emphasis I can command that Sir Abdur Rahim or Mr. Jinnah or the Ali Brothers are no enemies of the Hindus. Let not the lesson of Swami Shradhanandji's death be lost on us. You will all be accepting this resolution standing, while at this moment, perhaps, there are Hindu-Muslim disturbances going on in Delhi. But I tell you that, if every one of you understands and lays to his heart the lesson that Swami Shraddhanandji has left for us, it is again possible to win Swaraj in no time. I am a mad man, you will say, accustomed to giving rash promises. Well, I tell you I am not mad, I am still as much in earnest about my programme as I was in 1920, but those who made pledges in 1920 broke them and made Swaraj impossible then. We are all children of the same Father, whom the Hindu and the Musalman and the Christian know by different names. What if Shankara declared his faith in one God in his formula *Ekamevadvitiyam,* or Ramanuja in his dual doctrine or Mahomed in his *La Ilaha Illillaha?* All meant one and the same thing. If we cleanse our hearts, we shall be able to see that Swamiji has served us in his death as much as he served us when living. Let us purify our hearts with his blood and fight, if need be, for our rights in a peaceful and Satyagrahi way. Let every Musalman also understand that Swami Shraddhanandji was no enemy of Islam, that his was a pure and unsullied life and that he has left for us all the lesson of peace written in his blood.

"Now you will perhaps understand why I have called Abdul Rashid a brother, and I repeat it. I do not even regard him as guilty of Swami's murder. Guilty, indeed, are all those who excited feelings of hatred against one another. For us Hindus, the Gita enjoins on us the lesson of equality, we are to cherish the same feelings towards a learned Brahman, as towards a *chandala*, a dog, a cow and an elephant.

"This is no occasion for mourning or tears, it is an occasion that should burn on our hearts the lesson of bravery. Bravery is not the exclusive quality of the Kshatriyas. It may be their special privilege. But in our battle for Swaraj bravery is essential as much for the Brahman and the Vaishya and the Shudra as for the Kshatriya. Let us not, therefore, shed tears of sorrow, but chasten our hearts and steel them with some of the fire and faith that were Shraddhanandji's."

13th January, 1927

INDEPENDENCE

BY M. K. GANDHI

Year after year a resolution is moved in the Congress to amend the Congress creed so as to define Swaraj as complete independence, and year, after year happily, the Congress throws out the resolution by an overwhelming majority. The rejection of the resolution is proof of the sanity of the Congress. The moving of the resolution betrays the impatience (pardonable in the circumstances) of some ardent Congressmen who have lost all faith in the British intentions and who think that the British Government will never render justice to India. The advocates of independence forget that they betray want of faith in human nature and, therefore, in themselves. Why do they think that there can never be change of heart in those who are guiding the British people? Is it not more correct and more dignified to own that there is no change of heart because we are weak? Nature abhors weakness. We want from the British people and the world at large not mercy but justice that is our due. And justice will come when it is deserved by our being and feeling strong.

I am sure that the staunchest votary of independence does not mean that he will not have any British association on any terms whatsoever. Even when he says so, he means, as one of the supporters of the resolution admitted in answer to my question, that the British people will never accept association on equal terms. This is totally different from rejecting British association on any terms.

Indeed, the word Swaraj is all embracing. It does include complete independence as it includes many other things. To give it one definite meaning is to narrow the outlook and to limit what is at present happily limitless. Let the content of Swaraj grow with the growth of national consciousness and aspirations. We may be satisfied today with dominion status. The future generations may not be, may want something better. Swaraj without any qualifying clause includes that which is better than the best one can conceive or have today. Swaraj means even under dominion status a capacity to declare independence at will. So long as we have not achieved that capacity, we have no Swaraj. This is the least it should mean. South Africa has achieved that status today. It is a partnership at will of free peoples. Between Britain and the dominions, there is a partnership at will on terms of equality and for mutual benefit. What India will finally have is for her and her alone to determine. This power of determination remains unfettered by the existing creed. What, therefore, the creed does retain is the possibility of evolution of Swaraj within the British Empire, or call it the British Commonwealth. The cryptic meaning of Swaraj I have often described to be within the Empire if possible, without, if necessary. I venture to think that it is not possible to improve upon that conception. It is totally consistent with national self-respect and it provides for the highest growth of the nation.

After all, the real definition will be determined by our action, the means we adopt to achieve the goal. If we would but concentrate upon the means, Swaraj will take care of itself. Our explorations should, therefore, take place in the direction of determining not the definition of an indefinable term like Swaraj but in discovering the ways and means.

13th January, 1927

LOOK ON THAT PICTURE AND THIS!

By C. Rajagopalachar

Ontario is one of the important provinces of British America. Every province in Canada has its own Lieutenant Governor, with a ministry and one or two Houses of Parliament, and is practically a self-governing unit. In the province of Ontario with its capital Toronto, is also Ottawa the capital of the whole Dominion of Canada. Most provinces in Canada have, like the United States, been battling against Alcohol curse. They try to meet the evil by a system of Government control. Officers of the Government are in charge of liquor stores and sell regulated quantities. The province of Ontario, however, is a "Prohibition" province, after the fashion of the neighbouring States of America, not controlling but under total prohibition of liquor.

The liquor interests will not let Ontario have peace. They are ever trying to get the province to fall in line with the other provinces and repeal Prohibition. Since 1918, the question was made the subject of referendum three times and now it is fought over a fourth time. On all the three previous occasions, the electors returned an answer in favour of retaining the Prohibition Law. The present conservative Premier of Ontario has brought forward again a plan of licenses.

As against the Alcohol forces, the great point in favour of the prohibitionists is the decrease of crime that has taken place since the introduction of Prohibition. Statistics show that, although the population of the chief city Toronto has largely increased, the figures for drunkenness have been reduced by the same percentage. The battle, we are told by a *Times of India* correspondent, promises to be more bitterly fought than the recent Federal election.

Liquor interests have a strong selfish motive to fight for a return to License from Prohibition. They are ever, therefore, busy to adduce proof that men will not be controlled and will drink whatever you may do. They assert that Prohibition will not succeed, but yet they want it to be repealed. They have good reasons to invest plenty of money in this game of defeating or repealing Prohibition. But as against this, on the other side nothing but patriotic and philanthropic fervour, backed by a keen realisation of the national benefits of Prohibition, has to furnish the fighting strength of Prohibitionists. Yet we find that Ontario gave strong and successful battle each time the Liquor forces gave the challenge. This shows how clear the proof must be of the advantages of saving the people from Drink.

While the American people, in the United States as in Canada, have so clearly realised the benefits of Prohibition, in our country, where religion, customs, manners and everything else favour the introduction of Prohibition and where the chronic and widespread poverty of the people calls for it, at least as a measure of economic relief for the poor, much more urgently than in wealthy Canada or America, we have not thought it time yet to take up this question as seriously as we should. May we hope that along with poultry-farming, basket-making and other subsidiary industries, about which we hear so much as occupations for relief of the poverty of the masses, the proposal of saving them from the waste and the curse of Drink may also be considered? The suffering women and children of India are inarticulate and helpless. If only we think about it, there can be nothing more wicked than to have the toddy shops and country liquor shops with which the Government have studded rural and urban India, nothing more immoral than to draw high salaries out of the proceeds of the suffering of the victims of Drink and to talk of financial difficulties, nothing so disgraceful as to get cheap education for our children, so to say on scholarships founded on the robbery of the down-trodden and the ignorant whom we can successfully tempt with liquor. Yet this is what is going on and what is meant by squaring the Budget with Excise Revenue!

Instructive Omission.

Sir Henry Rew has contributed to the *Hindu Annual* an interesting article on "Indian Rural Revival." According to him, a large proportion of Indian land holdings are "uneconomic and, even in favourable circumstances, are too small to support a family. The consequence is that the agriculturist must find some other occupation, and rural life is complicated by the necessity for providing subsidiary or supplementary means of livelihood for the agricultural population." Sir Henry Rew thinks that this is one of the main obstacles to agricultural progress and constitutes in itself a problem the solution of which is not easy. He refers to the official report of the moral and material progress and condition of India (1923-24) and quotes from it to confirm the fact that the cultivator in many provinces of India is compelled by climatic conditions to remain idle for more than one-third of the year. Therefore, it is deplored he does not busy himself with poultry-farming, pig-keeping, fruit-growing and seri-culture, on which small holders in other countries largely rely.

Why do all these writers omit hand-spinning? There may be some subtle, self-protective instinct which makes these and other such writers and thinkers omit the one supplementary occupation which will help the cultivators' families and which will not be open to the objection of "social tradition which checks the employment of female labour," or the other objection of reluctance to take to new ways to which they make constant reference. "His forefathers" *knew* this thing, and what is more, the surplus product of such supplementary occupation reached and clothed people in Europe after supplying all the needs of India. C. R.

13th January, 1927

AFTER THE CONGRESS

At a public meeting held in the Mahesh Prangam at Comilla on the 5th January, after a brief speech in Hindi on 'the work before us', Gandhiji made the following speech in English;

"You have been so kind to me in giving me permission to speak in Hindi. If only because I want to show you my appreciation of your kindness, I propose to say a few words to you in English. Every time that I am obliged to speak in the English language before an audience of my countrymen, I feel humiliated and ashamed. I have urged upon Bengali audiences several times not to put an undue strain upon my loyalty, not to put an undue strain upon Bharatmata herself. It is the easiest thing possible for every Indian north of the Vindhya range to pick up Hindi inside of a month, Try it and tell me if what I say is not true. Let us not say that our mother tongue is only Bengali or Gujarati or Punjabi, as the case may be. These are provincial languages. When we sing that ode to the Motherland—*Bande Mataram*, we sing it to the whole of India. When Bankim wrote the inspired song, he said *Saptakoti bhujaih*. But you and others deliberately said *Dwi-Trimshatkoti bhujaih* and it was proper. It was proper and dignified on your part to sing of *Dwi-Trimshatkoti bhujaih*, and it was proper and dignified for the whole of India to accept that magnificent ode. Shall we not then live up to it and sing with all our hearts and say we are sons of Mother India, not merely sons of Bengal? I ask you, therefore, next time I happen to come here or you invite me to come, to insist upon my speaking to you in Hindi and Hindi alone. That is one thing.

"We have seen the last of the last session of the Congress. On the sacred banks of the Brahmaputra, in the midst of that magnificent foliage and scenery almost unrivalled in the world, our leaders deliberated. They have evolved a Councils programme. But how many of us can take a direct part in the working of that programme? How many of us can enter Councils and the Legislative Assembly? How many of us are entitled to elect members to these legislative bodies? Are the millions of the villagers of India enfranchised? Is India living in her 10 or 20 cities, or is she living in her 700,000 villages? What, then, is the programme that can weld together the 30 crores of people scattered on a surface 19 hundred miles long and 15 hundred miles broad in 700,000 villages? What is it that every villager, man woman and child, Hindu and Musalman, can do with profit and at the same time uplift the whole of India? The one and unequivocal answer is the spinning wheel and Khaddar. The message of Khaddar can penetrate to remotest villages, if we only will that it shall be so. The spinning wheel can be turned by millions of the villagers of India who have been reduced to pauperism, who have been ground down to dust, not merely under the foreigners' heels but under your heels, under my heels. We, the city-dwellers, are living upon the labour, upon the wealth of these millions of villagers; not like the Americans, not like the Englishmen, who live upon the exploitation of Asiatic races or the so-called weaker races of the earth. Even they would be obliged to take up the spinning wheel or any equivalent, if they were not able to exploit India, China, Africa and other parts of the earth. We do not exploit them, because it is a virtue of necessity with us. But I hope that a time is coming when, out of the fulness of our hearts, out of a wider national outlook, we shall disdain of our own free will to exploit a single nation of the earth, no matter how weak. I hope that in your life-time and mine that time is coming when we shall reach our freedom and, having reached it, we shall say to all the nations of the earth, that they need not fear us, as we have lived in perpetual fear of the so-called civilised races of the earth. You may not believe me to-day. You may call me, if you like, a mad man. But the time is coming when you will say that what that old man said was right and that, if India was really to prosper in her villages and not in her cities, the spinning wheel was the only instrument of India's prosperity and India's freedom.

"And hence it was that you saw the phenomenon at Gauhati, which I did not expect, which I had not asked for, however much I desired it. But you saw at Gauhati the extra-ordinary phenomenon of the Congress franchise being improved along Khaddar lines. I know there were bickerings about it. But I also know that it was the pressure of the popular mind that exhorted that improvement in the franchise. The leaders made that important improvement, because they saw that *Khaddar and Khaddar alone was the only passport to the hearts of the villagers.* Let me assure you that it was Khaddar that won the elections for the Swarajists. You may not know, or perhaps you know, that in Madras even those who were otherwise opposed to Khaddar were obliged to take it up at the time of appealing to the electorate, and as days roll on, you will find that Khaddar will gain in importance, because it has intrinsic worth about it, because no national popular organisation contains for its working so many self-sacrificing, able, young educated men as the Khaddar organisation, because no other organisation is capable of giving employment to an almost unlimited number of patriotic youths who will be content with an honourable livelihood and who will be content to pass their lives in the closest touch with the villagers and share their food, their sorrows and joys. I invite you to show me a single other organisation which has that capacity in it.

"Believe me, Khaddar is not a dying cult. There is no fall in the barometer of Khaddar. Five years' experience shows that it has been an undoubtedly gradual, but a steady and hopeful, rise. It could not have been otherwise. Because India wants it, because India's millions require full meals in order to sustain their energy, therefore the Congress has passed the resolution making it necessary for Congressman to wear Khaddar habitually and not merely on ceremonial occasions. They may wear mill cloth on rare occasions, when it is absolutely necessary for their bread and butter; but they dare not, if they are honest Congressmen, habitually wear anything but handspun and handwoven Khaddar.

"And now a word about untouchability. A great hero and patriot, Swami Shraddhanandji, died for the sake of the untouchables. He loved them as dearly as his own life. He regarded them as his own children, and if it was in his power, he would have banished untouchability from the shores of India. And what does that banishment mean? It means universal love. It means translating into action the great message of the Bhagavad Gita which is: Treat the Brahman and the Bhangi alike, if you would but know God. But how are they alike? A Brahman is any day superior to the Bhangi in learning, and how am I to treat both alike? The Bhagavad Gita says that you should treat them even as you would wish to be treated by them, or even as you would treat yourself:

आत्मवत्सर्वभूतेषु यः पश्यति स पश्यति ।

"That is the teaching of the Bhagavad Gita. That hero and martyr translated this teaching into action in his own life, and he has sanctified it and sealed it with his blood. Let that blood purify us and let it remove the last taint of any isolation or aloofness that we may be harbouring against those brothers of ours whom in our arrogance we call 'untouchables'. They are not untouchables, we are untouchables. Let them have every attention, every kindness that they deserve from us. During my Comilla visit I have seen two villages which are predominently occupied by the so-called untouchables. Had I not been told, I should not have known that the people I saw were untouchables. I could see no difference between them and the others who were standing with them there. They eat and drink and think and feel even as we do. If a sum total of their virtues and vices and the privileges they are denied were to be made and compared with our virtues and vices and the privileges we enjoy and deny to them, I am sure in God's books we should find our debit side far heavier than theirs. Let us, then, think no more of any single person on earth as an untouchable. That is the lesson that comes down to us from South Africa too. A just Nemesis has descended upon us there. Just as we are treating our brothers here, our kith and kin are being treated as Pariahs and Bhangis in South Africa. The moment we purge ourselves of the sin, the moment we are free from the curse of untouchability, you will find the shackles dropping off our countrymen in South Africa.

"I dare not touch the problem of Hindu Muslim unity. It has passed out of human hands and has been transferred to God's hands alone. Even as Draupadi, forsaken by her husbands, forsaken by men and gods alike, asked God and God alone to come to her help and God gave her unfailing help, so it is with me and so should it be with every one of us. Let us ask for help from God, the All-Powerful and tell Him that we, His tiny creatures, have failed to do what we ought to do, we hate one another, we distrust one another, we fly at one another's throat and we even become assassins. Let our hearts' cry, then, ascend to His throne, and let us wash His feet with tears of blood and ask Him to purge our hearts of all hatred in us. We are disgracing His earth, His name and this sacred land by distrusting and fearing one another. Although we are sons and daughters of the same motherland, although we eat the same food, we have no room for one another. Let us ask God in all humility to give us sense, to give us wisdom.

"You have listened to me with the greatest attention. I have given you also what I don't willingly give to the audience —an English speech, and that also at some length. I now want my reward. I want you to-morrow to come to the Abhoy Ashram and denude it of every yard of Khaddar in its store, if my message, the message of the paupers of India, has gone home to you. There you will see a band of workers working for them and for you. They are the link between you and the villagers. They are trying to do their level best to serve the motherland. I want you to put your hands into your pockets and give me what you have and what you can and what you will, not out of shame, not out of any pressure that you may feel because you are in this meeting, not out of patronage for me or affection for me. I shall use your affection for other work, if you will give me your affection. But I want you to give me what you can and what you have for the sake of paupers, for the sake of those who do not even get one square meal a day. If you are satisfied that this organisation is being worked well, and with ability and self-sacrifice, and if you are convinced that it is not sinful to wear Khaddar and it cannot be wrong to wear Khaddar woven and spun by your starving countrymen and that it is right and proper and necessary to do so, you will give your coppers and silver and gold, whatever you may have.

"If you have any suspicion about it, any doubts in the matter, I ask you to restrain your hands and not give me a single pie. If not today, at least on some near date, you will be convinced of the message. But if you are convinced that this is the right thing—although you may not have the strength to carry out the message fully into practice—you will support this great, aye the greatest, national industry. There is no better way of industrialising the villages of India than the spinning wheel. No man has yet been able to show a better or more effective substitute—I say even an equal substitute—than the spinning wheel for the millions of Indians who are idle for at least four months in the year, who are starving for want of a square meal and for whom even one anna a day means a fortune. I plead on behalf of them. May God help you to understand this simple message.

"You will recall that last time I was in Bengal I collected for the All-Bengal Deshabandhu Memorial. That was for what is now the Seva Sadan. I announced then that in due course I would collect for the All-India Deshabandhu Memorial. You know that its object was to promote the message of the spinning wheel. You will thus be contributing to the Memorial by contributing to Khaddar."

20th January, 1927

ALL-INDIA DESHABANDHU MEMORIAL

By M. K. Gandhi

I hope the readers of *Young India* have not forgotten the All-India Deshabandhu Memorial. When I suspended touring after the Cawnpore Congress for one year, I knew that the collection of funds for the All-India Deshabandhu Memorial to which I had pledged myself would be suspended. But it was inevitable. At the time of suspension I had stated that, if God willed it, at the end of the year I would resume my tour for the collection. I resumed it at Calcutta, and all the collections that I am now making will be for the All-India Deshabandhu Memorial, except where the donors otherwise specify the object of their donations. And since the object of the All-India Deshabandhu Memorial is village organisation and that through the spinning movement, all these collections automatically become part of the All-India Spinners' Association which is the agency through which the Memorial collections are to be utilised for the purpose. A resolution to this effect was passed by the All-India Deshabandhu Memorial Committee at Cawnpore in 1925. I trust, therefore, that those who are in charge of the organisation of meetings in connection with my tour will take good care to inform those who may attend meetings of the object of the tour. There should be no desire to spring a surprise upon those who attend meetings by asking for subscription. The honest course is to let them know beforehand that they will be asked to pay. No one need pay, unless he believes in the Memorial and its object. I know, too, that a man may revere the memory of Deshabandhu and still not believe in the spinning movement. But I would venture to remind such people of what were Deshabandhu's last wishes expressed to his wife, his sister and his trusted lieutenants and Satis Chandra Das Gupta of Khadi Pratishthan and to me almost exactly 7 days before his death. He said that, as soon as he descended from Darjeeling, he would throw himself heart and soul into the spinning movement. He could see that that was the greatest constructive movement we could undertake and that it was the most effective method of village organisation and village reconstruction. It was for that reason that he had asked me to send for Satis Babu with whom he had discussed the plan of working the spinning movement, and it was for the spinning movement that he had intended to spend the largest part of the the money that had been collected for village reconstruction. The Spinners' Association, therefore, is the natural outcome, if I may say so, of Deshabandhu's wishes.

20th January, 1927

TO ORGANISERS

BY M. K. GANDHI

If all goes well, I hope during the year to cover, besides Bihar, part of Maharashtra, Madras Presidency including Karnatak, U. P., Bengal and Orissa. I should love to visit the other provinces also, if time and health permit and if they intend to subscribe to the Memorial, that is, Khadi work.

To Orissa I have promised to go and pass there, so far as it is humanly possible, the month of November, not because I expect to make large collections but because it is to my mind an epitome of our distressful condition. Orissa regenerate is to me the regeneration for the whole of India. It is a land which need not be the poorest in the country. Its people are in no way inferior to those of the other parts of India. They have a fine history all their own. They have magnificent temples. They have the Lord of the Universe in their midst, who knows no distinction between his creatures. And yet, sad to relate, under the very shadow of the mighty temple people die of hunger in their thousands. It is a land of chronic poverty, chronic famine and chronic disease. Nowhere have I seen in the eyes of people so much blankness, so much despair, so much lifelessness as in Orissa. I, therefore, look forward to my stay in November with sad pleasure.

It is a province that can be, ought to be, easily organised for spinning, because the people have no work. The whole of Orissa cannot be transplanted to the factories of Bengal or the factories of all India put together. It would be wrong, even if it was possible. Happily it is not possible. The people must live on their own land, learn to be resourceful, industrious and learn even to be happy. They have forgotten what happiness can be. Let the workers in Orissa, therefore, understand their responsibility. I expect them to throw themselves heart and soul into the spinning movement. Let them not think of the whole of Orissa. Let them think of single villages where they will establish themselves and where they may by prayerful and persistent effort lift the people out of the slough of despond into which they have sunk.

And though, as I have said, I do not expect to make large collections, I shall welcome the pies of the people who will attend meetings, even as I welcomed them when I travelled in 1921. The sight of old people with their trembling fingers untying the knots which firmly held their pies and willingly surrendering them to me is never to be forgotten I want to see it again and renew, if a renewal is necessary, the determination that this winter of despair is to be changed into the summer of hope and happiness within a measurable distance of time.

May I ask the organisers also to bear in mind that the tour is to be almost incessant and that I must do my editing and attend to my correspondence during the hours they may leave for me and in the trains? Besides Mondays, at least three hours should be left for me in addition to the time required for ablutions and meals. All night demonstrations must be avoided. It is impossible after a strenuous day's work to stand the strain of disturbance during sleeping hours.

And as this is to be a purely business tour, the meetings should be so arranged and the audiences should be so seated as to leave passages for collectors to pass to and fro. All shoutings and noises should be avoided. I have observed that, where management is efficient, collections mount up. The audiences have invariably been found by me to be responsive. Though the thousands of the rich are welcome, I know that it is the coppers and the single rupees of the poor people that bless the movement. It is theirs, and let them freely contribute to it their mite.

20th January, 1927

THE CENTRAL FACT

By M. K. Gandhi

During my tour in so far as it has progressed up to now, I have observed that spinning organisations have not an accurate register of spinners and that the figures supplied and published by me from time to time in these pages were based upon the deductions drawn from the actual wages paid to the spinners. For statistical information, the calculation is sound enough, because it must err on the right side, *i.e.* of understatement. But it is not good enough for the movement itself. The spinning movement depends for its permanence upon a vital and direct contact being established between the workers and the spinners; for then and then only shall we be able to understand the wants, aspirations and limitations of the spinners. The object is to penetrate the remotest Indian homes in the innumerable villages of India and to introduce a ray of hope and light into these homes. This we shall never do, if we do not establish a living touch with the spinners. We cannot, therefore, be satisfied with the work of middlemen whom we may not and do not know. We must be able to trace the course of every pie till it is safely deposited in the hands of the spinners. And let it be remembered that spinning is the central fact of the movement, not weaving, not dyeing, not printing, not even carding and ginning, anterior though the last two processes are to spinning. For, the economic solution depends upon a supplementary employment being found for the largest number of the semi-starved millions. Of such employment by far the best is spinning and that alone, as will be seen by a study of the figures for the various provinces given in these pages.

The Bihar figures* show 489 weavers against 2,698 spinners. My own observation is that ten spinners are required to feed one weaver both working for the same length of time. The ultimate ambition is to teach the

* See page 49.

spinners carding and ginning, so as to enable them to increase their earnings as spinners without much effort and without much training. This is being done on a fairly large scale in Bihar, Bengal and the Madras Presidency. The Spinners' Association can justify its existence, therefore, only upon its achieving a progressive amelioration in the economic condition of the vast masses who can be reached in no other way in a shorter time. The movement depends also for its increasing influence and vitality upon this fact of its tender care for the millions of whom it has as yet only touched but a small part.

Workers have suggested to me that, if an accurate register is to be kept of every spinner, it would involve extra cost. Possibly it will. Not being in charge of a single centre, I am unable fully to understand the difficulty of keeping such registers. But I can say without any fear of challenge that, whatever the cost may be, a complete register of spinners is an absolute necessity until spinning has become an automatically working movement beyond risk of destruction. The extra cost that the keeping of such a register may involve will be worth undertaking, if we are to put the movement on a stable foundation. What an accurate and simultaneous entry of every pie received and spent in a banking corporation is to its honest existence and steady growth, an accurate register of spinners is to the honest existence and steady growth of the spinning movement. I hope, therefore, that every spinning organisation will without any loss of time set about keeping a full and up-to-date register of its spinners. Needless to say that the workers who will be in charge of the registers and who will come in contact with the spinners must be men—and how nice if they were women?—of unimpeachable character and purity. The discovery of this flaw in the movement was made by me through the hypersensitiveness of the workers of Bengal. In my notice of the Abhoy Ashram report, I made an incidental observation that our statements of figures must not contain "abouts' and "nearlies", and then I made a general observation about the necessity of purity of character. I had in making that observation no one in particular in mind, but owing to the juxtaposition of the general remark to the mention of the work of the Abhoy Ashram, some of its inmates suspected that my remarks were aimed at them. I had no difficulty in disabusing their minds of the suspicion ; but the conversation enabled me to understand and convince the members of the Ashram of the necessity of keeping an accurate up-to-date register of spinners. I am, therefore, not sorry for the paragraph that I wrote in my notice of the Abhoy Ashram, if only because it has led to the discovery of the flaw in our human account-keeping. But let me reiterate for the information of all concerned that in this spinning movement, which is fraught with tremendous consequences, we cannot put too much stress upon the absolute necessity of members of our organisations being and remaining beyond suspicion, and if we are to attain this standard of purity, we will have to develop a skin thick enough to stand and take in good part well-meant suggestions, criticisms and observations.

20th January, 1927

A CANDID CRITIC

BY M. K. GANDHI

I must not withhold the following letter from the readers:

"I have perused your article 'Swamiji, the martyr' with the care and reverence it deserves. I have read it five times before attempting to criticise it. This is to avoid hasty criticism.

"The article is undoubtedly written in fascinating language. I envy your style. It attracts, but to me it appears that it is rather dangerously attractive.

"My criticism is based on my estimation of your character. I have often debated with some friends on this subject. They hold that you are a statesman in the garb of a saint ready to forego truth in the cause of your country. I have, on the contrary, maintained that you are a saint—who has entered politics in fulfilment of your mission, to practise truth in the face of most trying and perplexing circumstances. I shall be very obliged to know if my estimation is correct. For, if it is not, the criticism that follows has little value. I am of the opinion that a man of policy is within his rights to write in the manner you have done.

"You will agree with me that to suppress truth is a form of falsehood; to refuse to call a spade a spade when you feel it like that is cowardice; and that fearlessness and truth go together.

"Do you feel, Mahatmaji, that the murder of Swamiji was an inhuman, barbarous and cruel act of a Muslim ruffian and that the entire Muslim community should be ashamed of it? Why do you refuse to characterise it as such? Instead of condemning the deed and the doer and those who are responsible for this act (those who describe Hindu leaders, as Kafirs—the hot Muslim propagandists and the mad Muslim priests), you have begun to defend the murderer and hold an apology for the community. You never defended Dyer. Is not a European a brother, too?

"You say further, Islam means peace. Is this truth? Islam as taught by the Koran and practised by Muslims ever since its birth never meant peace. What makes you write a thing so patently wrong? Buddhism, Christianity, Hinduism, of course, teach peace, but not Islam. May I know what makes you think and write like this?

"You never minced matters when condemning the wrongs of the Government, you never minced matters when you condemned Arya Samaj, why fear to condemn Muslims for even proved wrongs?

"I am sure that, if such a black act had been committed by a Hindu against a Muslim leader (which Heaven forbid), you would have condemned the murderer and the community in unsparing terms. You would have asked Hindus to repent in sack-cloth and ashes, to offer fasts, hold hartal, raise memorial to the departed Muslim and many other things. Why do you accord preferential treatment to your 'blood brothers', the Muslims?

"A truth-teller knows no fear, not even of the sword of Islam, and I trust you will oblige me by giving reply to above in the columns of your esteemed weekly."

The writer is frank and obviously in earnest and reflects the prevalent mood.

To clothe me with sainthood is too early, even if it is possible. I myself do not feel a saint in any shape or form. But I do feel I am a votary of Truth in spite of all my errors of unconscious omission and commission. The correspondent has judged rightly that I am not "a statesman in the garb of a saint." But since Truth is the highest wisdom, sometimes my acts appear to be consistent with the highest statesmanship. But I hope I have no policy in me save the policy of truth and *ahimsa*. I will not sacrifice truth and *ahimsa* even for the deliverance of my country or religion. This is as much as to say that neither can be so delivered.

In writing about the assassination of Swamiji, I have not suppressed truth. I do believe the act to be all that the correspondent describes. But I feel pity for the murderer even as I felt for General Dyer, Let not the correspondent forget that I refused to be party to any agitation for the prosecution of General Dyer. I do claim that a European is just as much brother to me as a Musalman Indian or a Hindu.

What I do feel about the assassin is that he is himself a victim of foul irreligous propaganda in the name of religion. Hence it is that I have held the newspapers that have corrupted the public mind to be responsible for the murder. I do hold the maulvis and all those who have indulged in exciting hatred against Swamiji to be responsible.

But I do regard Islam to be a religion of peace in the same sense as Christianity, Buddhism and Hinduism are. No doubt these are differences in degree, but the object of these religions is peace. I know the passages that can be quoted from the Koran to the contrary. But so is it possible to quote passages from the Vedas to the contrary. What is the meaning of imprecations pronounced against the Anryas? Of course, these passages bear to-day a different meaning, but at one time they did wear a dreadful aspect. What is the meaning, of the treatment of untouchables by us Hindus? Let not the pot call the kettle black. The fact is that we are all growing. I have given my opinion that the followers of Islam are too free with the sword. But that is not due to the teaching of the Koran. That is due in my opinion to the environment in which Islam was born. Christianity has a bloody record against it, not because Jesus was found wanting, but because the environment in which it spread was not responsive to his lofty teaching.

These two, Christianity and Islam, are, after all, religions of but yesterday. They are yet in the course of being interpreted. I reject the claim of maulvis to give a final interpretation to the message of Mahomed, as I reject that of the Christian clergy to give a final interpretation to the message of Jesus. Both are being interpreted in the lives of those who are living these messages in silence and in perfect self-dedication. Bluster is no religion, nor is vast learning stored in capacious brains. The Seat of religion is in the heart. We Hindus, Christians, Musalmans and others have to write the interpretation of our respective faiths with our own crimson blood and not otherwise.

20th January, 1927

WEEKLY LETTER

The main object of the visit to Benares during the week was to attend the annual function of the *Gandhi Ashram* as Professor Kripalani's co-workers in and about Benares call themselves. But before I write about the Ashram, I shall briefly refer to Gandhiji's talk to the students of the Hindu University, arranged at the instance of Pandit Malaviyaji. It seems Panditji was very much struck with the Khadi Exhibition at Gauhati and expressly desired that Gandhiji should give the message of Khaddar to the students of his University when he visited Benares. Nearly two thousand students had gathered to listen to Gandhiji under a spacious shamiana specially erected for the viceregal visit, which had preceded Gandhiji's just by a week. He had addressed them last six years ago; then he had gone with a more difficult message. This time he delivered the simple message of Khaddar and purity. "You have had your say now. No one is listening to you. Why not stop talking of Khaddar?" That was the advice that was being given him in some quarters. "But why should I stop reciting my favourite mantra," said Gandhiji, "when I have before me the example of Prahlad of old refusing to give up *Ramanama* in the teeth of tortures worse than death? And I have not had to go through any tortures yet. How can I give up the only message that the condition of my country has been whispering to me? Panditji has collected and has been still collecting lakhs and lakhs of rupees for you from Rajas and Maharajas. The money apparently comes from these wealthy princes, but in reality it comes from the millions of our poor. For, unlike Europe, the rich of our land grow rich at the expense of our villagers, the bulk of whom have to go without a square meal a day. The education that you receive to-day is thus paid for by the starving villagers, who will never have the chance of such an education. It is your duty to refuse to have an education that is not within the reach of the poor, but I do not ask that of you to-day. I ask you to render just a slight return to the poor by doing a little *yajna* for them. For, he who eats without doing his *yajna* steals his food, says the Gita. The *yajna* that was required of the British civic population during the War was for each household to grow potatoes in its yard and for each household to do a little simple sewing.

The *yajna* of our age and for us is the spinning wheel. Day in and day out I have been talking about it, writing about it. I shall say no more to-day. If the message of the poor of India has touched your hearts, I want you to raid Kripalani's Khaddar stores to-morrow and denude it of all their stock and to empty your pockets to-night. Panditji has cultivated the art of beggary. I have learnt it from him, and if he specialises in laying the princes under tribute, I have learnt to be equally shamelesss in emptying the pockets of the poor, for the benefit of those who are poorer than they."

That summarises the first part of his talk. The second was a fervent plea for purity. "Malaviyaji's one object in begging millions for you, in raising these palatial buildings, is to send out to the country gems of purest ray, citizens healthy and strong to serve their motherland. That purpose will be defeated if you allow yourselves to be swept with the wind that comes today from the West—the wind of impurity. Not that the methods have the general sanction of Europe. There are friends in Europe, a very few, who are fighting hard to counteract the poisonous tendency. But if you do not wake up betimes, the immoral wave that is fast gathering strength might soon envelop and overwhelm you. I cry out to you, therefore, with all the strength at my command: Be warned, and flee from the fire before it consumes you."

Malaviyaji in a stirring speech associated himself with every part of Gandhiji's appeal, and asked the students to respond to the best of their power to what he called the fourfold demand; (1) spinning religiously; (2) wearing Khaddar; (3) contributing to the fund; and (4) *brahmacharya*. The response to the third part was prompt, nearly Rs. 850 being collected on the spot. The response to the other items only the future can show.

On the morning of the 9th—the Shraddhanand Day—Malaviyaji and Gandhiji walked in procession from Gandhi Ashram to Dashashvamedh Ghat, performed ablutions there, offered *jalanjali* to the departed martyr and then went and offered prayers in Kashi Vishvanath Temple. A few yards from the temple the gathering formed itself into a meeting, *Mahimnah Stotra* (verses in praise of Shiva) was recited, Devadas conducted congregational repetition of *Ramanama*, and Gandhiji delivered a brief speech emphasising the outstanding significance of Swamiji's martyrdom, viz., purification of self and of religion and ceaseless striving after self-control and *brahmacharya*, which summed up Swamiji's life. All who come under the comprehensive term 'Hindus' as defined by the Hindu Mahasabha joined in the prayers at the Vishvanath temple—even Buddhism being represented by a German lady. I say it on Malaviyaji's authority that even untouchables were to be found in this procession and prayer.

To come now to the Gandhi Ashram. It has had a chequered history, beginning with the withdrawal from Hindu University College of 200 students, formation of the Vidyapith, a further increase in numbers, to the depletion in ranks due to the depression in the country and concentration of the few determined souls, left after the ebb and flow, on Khadi work. The tenacity, the will, the courage, the intrepid and undimmed faith with which these few have pursued their task have been worthy of soldiers in any battle for freedom. I visited the Ashram nearly four years ago, when the inmates were struggling with unfavourable conditions. I saw them then, with Proof. Kripalani at their head, doing all their tasks themselves, including the drawing of the *mhote* from the well for the garden and the scavenger's work, and subsisting on Rs. 7-8-0 per month. Their determination won the day, and whereas then they satisfied themselves with some literary education and spinning and weaving and a little carpentry on the premises, they have today a successful Khaddar organisation with centres at Dhamhara, Akbarpur, Kulpahad, Milki and Muzaffarnagar. In some centres spinning and weaving is done under the exchange system, and in one or two Khadi is taken straight from the weavers who themselves get the yarn spun from the vicinity. Close control is exercised by the Ashram workers over this spinning and weaving, and the report of work is a record of steady progress in quantity and quality and in reduction of prices. The following tables give in a nutshell the result of 5 years' work.

	Production Rs.	Sale Rs.
1921	48	3,011
1922	4,759	23,156
1923	23,123	23,115
1924	16,000	21,577
1925	36,157	32,769
1926	65,312	71,805

Price in annas per yard at the centres

Width	21	'22	'23	'24	'25	'26
36"	9	8	7½	8	7½	7½
42"			7¾-8¼	8¼-8¾	8½	7¼-8
45"			9-9½	8½-9½	8½-9	7½-8¾
48"				9¼-10½	9-9½	8½-9

It should be borne in mind that the reduction in each case has been in spite of the improvement in quality each year. There was a pretty little exhibition arranged in the Town Hall which was open to all and where the arrangement itself was an eloquent record of progress from year to year. The figures of sale cover sale of Khadi from other provinces also, and the response from the province in respect of the Khadi produced in the province itself is very small. The Benares visit will have borne some fruit, if it stimulates local demand for the Khadi manufactured by the Gandhi Ashram.

M. D.

20th January, 1927

KHADI IN BEHAR

BY M. K. GANDHI

Sjt. Rajendra Prasad has sent me the report of the work of the Bihar branch of the A. I. S. A. for the year ending September 1926. It is a record of steady progress. After mentioning the vicissitudes the organisation had to pass through in the early stages, the report says:

"The following figures will show the progress of work since the work was centralised under the Khadi Board and later under A. I. S. A.

	April 1924 to Sep. 1924	October 1924 to March 1925	April 1925 to Sep. 1925	Oct. 1925 to March 1926	April 1926 to Sep. 1926
Production Rs.	21,588	35,273	47,031	51,080	96,723
Sale "	17,479	27,784	33,335	51,865	59,678

"This statement does not include the figures for production and sale of Khaddar by the Gandhi-Kutir, whose work till the beginning of 1926 was on a more extensive scale than that of the Provincial Khaddar Board and, latterly, the Bihar branch of the A. I. S. A."

There are 8 production and sale centres and 11 sale depots. Besides these, there are sale agencies at 6 places and more are being established. The agency has 65 whole-time workers including two honorary workers. Their average earnings are Rs. 25 per month. During the year under review, 2,698 spinners earned Rs. 29,519; 489 weavers, Rs. 36,862; 6 tailors, Rs. 230 during two months; 8 dyers and printers Rs. 2,273 including the cost of dyes (during six months); and 40 washermen Rs. 1,951 during six months. It goes without saying that the spinners and weavers, too, were not whole-time workers. They worked only during their spare time and irregularly.

The report then says:—"The progress that has been made is not only in regard to increased production and sale but also in regard to the quality of Khaddar and reduction in its price." The average price in 1923 was Rs. 1-0-5 per yard of fine cloth. It was reduced to As. 13 in 1926. When the yarn was very weak, the weaving charge was 3 annas 3 pies per yard of 45 inches width. On account of the improvement in the yarn, it has now been reduced to 2 annas 3 pies per yard of the same width. Nor is there any difficulty about getting sufficient weavers to weave handspun yarn. Some of these weavers weave even up to 72 inches width, and the variety of weaving includes twills, coatings of various designs etc Dyeing and printing is being developed under the special care of a graduate of the Bihar Vidyapith.

The report after mentioning the work in different branches of the organisation says: "If we could dispose of our present stock, it is expected that we shall be able to reduce our prices still further by about 10 p. c."

It naturally dwells upon the successful peripatetic exhibitions that were held during the year, of which a detailed account has appeared from time to time in these pages. The interesting report contains the following pregnant reflections:

" The province of Bihar is particularly suited for Khaddar work. The population is agricultural; there is no industry in the province worth the name, outside the coal-fields of Chota-Nagpur and apart from the great Tata Iron and Steel Works at Jamshedpur. The tradition of spinning is still extant in most parts of it and the number of weavers and looms is large enough to supply almost the entire requirement of cloth of the province Cotton, though of an inferior quality, is also produced in many parts of it. The work of production of Khaddar is, therefore, not very difficult, although it requires organisation and technical skill to improve its quality. It can be extended almost indefinitely, if sufficient capital and organising and technical skill are forthcoming."

"The above narrative will show the progress made in

reviving the ancient but practically all but dead industry of spinning in Bihar. We have succeeded in touching but the merest fringe of the vast area in which spinning can be revived and made to furnish a much needed occupation for the idle hours of our great agricultural population. That its possibilities are vast can hardly be denied. That some supplementary occupation, not to speak of income, is necessary for the population will be apparent from the fact that the average quantity of land actually cultivated with food and non-food crops is less than three quarters of an acre per head. It is the yield of this small quantity of land, nearly four-fifths of which are unirrigated and depend upon the freaks of the monsoon, that is expected, not only to keep the body and soul together of every individual, but also to supply him with cloth and other necessaries of life and to meet, among others, all demands of the Zemindar, the society and the state. Looked at from this point of view, the admittedly scanty earning of 7 pies per day by Charkha is not, after all, so small and does afford, as experience has shown, substantial relief to a class of people who need such relief but cannot get it through forced unemployment. It is believed that agriculture does not require more than a hundred days' labour in the year, but the work is so distributed that the agriculturist cannot leave his farm and seek work elsewhere at a distance. In fact, the nature of the work is such that it allows plenty of leisure but at short intervals, and a supplementary industry, which is not capable of being taken up aud put aside to be resumed later at the stage at which it was left, cannot be usefully taken up. Experience has shown that the Charka alone can serve the purpose."

It is hoped that the appeal made in the report to the public for the purchase of Khaddar will meet with the liberal response it deserves.

20th January, 1927

HINDI v. ENGLISH

BY M K. GANDHI

Organisers of meetings seem to require constant reminders that not English but Hindi or Hindustani is the common medium of expression among the masses. I have observed that, unlike as in 1921, the addresses hitherto presented to me during the tour have been in most cases in English. The absurdity became patent when an address in English on behalf of the employees of Jharia collieries was sought to be read to me and that at a big mass meeting attended by thousands, hardly firty of whom could possibly understand English. The vast majority could have easily followed Hindi and a very large number could have understood Bengali. The officers of the association were from Bengal. If the English drafting was meant for me, it was wholly unnecessary. They might have written the address in Bengali and given me a translation in Hindi or even in English. But to inflict English on that big audience would have been an insult to them. I hope that the time is coming when, if the proceedings are conducted in a language the majority cannot understand, they would leave such meetings. Be it said to the credit of the chairman at this meeting that he saw the absurdity as soon as I drew his attention to it and very courteously allowed the address to be taken as read. May the incident serve as a warning to all the organisers, but more especially those in the Andhradesh, Tamil Nadu, Kerala and Karnatak. I know their difficulty. But they have had now for six years in their midst an efficient organisation for the spread of Hindi. Their addresses should be in the vernaculars of their respective provinces with Hindi translation for my benefit. I have always made an exception in Dravida land and delivered my speeches in English wherever they have so desired. But I do think that the time has come when they should dispense with English for big public meetings. Really it is the English-speaking leaders who are blocking the way to our rapid progress among the masses by their refusal to learn Hindi, which can be easily picked up inside of three months even in Dravida land, if the learners will give three hours per day. Let those who doubt give a trial to the Hindi Prachar Karyalaya conducted in Madras under the aegis of the Hindi Sahitya Sammelan, Prayag. They will find at the head office in Triplicane and the branches in Andhradesh and elsewhere books and teachers that will satisfy them. There is no excuse save idleness or disinclination for not knowing Hindi which is understood by over twenty crores of the people of Hindustan.

27th January, 1927

WEEKLY LETTER

'I have come here to do business—to collect money for Charkha and Khadi and to sell Khadi. Who knows this may be my last visit to Bihar! Let me do as much business as I can.' This was the brief one-minute speech that Gandhiji addressed to a crowd gathered at a railway station in Bihar, and business visit it has been, indeed, in right earnest. We began with places south of the Ganges, Daltonganj in Chota Nagpur being the first place, thence to Gaya through the coalfields, and then we crossed the Ganges at Patna and, having been right through the rich alluvial tracts of Chapra District, had a quiet day at Jiradehi, a place of pilgrimage for us, being the village in which Rajendra Babu was born. Since then it has been a rush through space—some more subdivisions in Chapra district, studded at every half a mile with emeralds of mango-groves and carpeted with fields smiling with green *tuar* and wheat and gram and peas, and then again to East and North to Darbhanga.

It has been a very strenuous time, what with noisy crowds and motor journeys over bad roads and what with friends' anxiety to cover as many places as possible in the shortest possible time. At Daltonganj the villagers from the hillsides had come from distances of twenty to thirty miles and mustered in their thousands. One speech or one speaker could not reach them at a time, so Gandhiji first addressed the people in front, then those in the rear and then on the sides. This was sufficient to restore quiet and they responded wonderfully to the appeal for collections which has now become a permanent feature at all meetings. The collections at Daltonganj were so successful that, though the bulk of the contributions were in copper and nickel, the total collected was Rs. 526, *i.e*, as much as one third of the purse collected from the select rich. The meetings at Ekma and Maharajganj were nearly quite as big as at Daltonganj, but there was no organisation and they could be managed with very great difficulty. The meeting, however, that was at once a model of orderliness and the biggest that we have yet had was at Mairwa. Over thirty thousand people had seated themselves, almost in battle array, the vast mass, including the huge elephants that had brought some of them to the meeting, having an appearance of a peaceful military camp. There was not a stir when Gandhiji came and none even when it was announced that he would first give a few minutes to the women who had a *purdah* meeting in a corner, and then come and address them. A long speech was out of the question here. They did not want a speech either. They knew what they were to be told and what was to be expected of them. But Gandhiji addressed them a few words from several places in the meeting and asked them to empty their pockets for the poor. And the response that they made has been something unique in our memory The coins did not rain, they poured Men and women (who had now broken through their *purdah*), young and old, vied with one another to contribute their mites and paid ringing testimony to the fact that it was a poor man's movement. The run on the dais was just like a run on a bank, not in this case to embarrass the Khaddar bank, but to enrich it. The pile of coins collected required three men to carry, and it is estimated that it will amount to nothing less than Rs. 1,000 Mairwa has a Khaddar depot in charge of the A.I.S.A. and an army of volunteers who had evidently done their duty. The meeting at Gopalganj was nearly quite as big, but the realisations were much less, as the meeting was tightly packed and there was sacrcely any room for the collectors to go about with their bags.

The collections at other places were no less significant, those at women's meetings easily exceeding a hundred and even a couple of hundreds if the ornaments were taken into account. But one thing is clear. The countryside is still instinct with life, no matter how many 'ups and downs' the movement might have undergone. There is much more pure Khadi in evidence than in the towns, and one hears of a number of people everywhere who spin and weave their own cloth for themselves. The upper classes have, as everywhere, suffered from the so called 'depression', with the result that the response of the city and town dwellers has been far from satisfactory. Jharia, which topped the list in the province in 1921, wil probably be among the lowest this time, chiefly no doubt due to many of the Indian collieries lying idle, thanks to the South African coal, which is suffered to maintain a successful competition with the Indian coal by means of heavy railway freights. At Gaya the purse collection might well have been better if it had been better organised. But even here the the collections at the meeting were good. A gentleman gave away his Ford which was sold to the highest bidder at Rs. 750. The response at Chapra and Sewan has been the poorest, though even there the poor men's mite was commendable. The day on which the largest business has been done during the tour was the 18th—about Rs. 7,500 having been collected from Dalsingserai, Samastipur and Darbhanga.

The women's meetings have been very good everywhere though they might have been better, if they had been less noisy and more orderly. A special feature at these meetings has been the collection of ornaments, a good beginning having been made at Sonepur. There was a quieter little meeting of women here whom Gandhiji exhorted to relieve themselves from the encumbrance of heavy ornaments. 'Think of Sita,' he said, 'Do you imagine she went about with Rama in his 14 years' forest wanderings with heavy ornaments like you? Do you think they add to your beauty? Sita cared for the beauty of her heart and covered her body with pure Khaddar. The heavy ornaments you wear are not only ugly, but harmful inasmuch as they are the permanent receptacles of dirt. Free yourselves of these shackles and relieve the poverty of people who have no clothes, much less ornaments, to wear.' The heavy ornaments collected here served as eloquent speeches at other meetings.

At Sonepur one more new departure was made by Gandhiji taking a stock of Khaddar with himself and selling it at every station and every meeting. The response has been uniformly satisfactory, hundreds of Rupees worth of Khadi being sold at every meeting.

I summarise here the result of the collections:

	Purse	Collections at meeting
Daltonganj	1,500	754-4-9
Coalfields	2,263	743-10-9
Aurangabad	2,501	225-0-9
Gaya	1,795	350-0-3
Sonepur	431	205-12-0
Chhapra		358-10-4½
Ekma		352-12-4½
Maharajganj	575	372-11-9
Dalsingsarai	2,000	310-14-10½

I am not able to make the list up to date, as the collections are in many cases being counted. The collections at meetings include those at women's meetings also.

The provinces which have been already booked for Gandhiji's visit and have an ample margin of time left to prepare for the visit will, it is hoped, not let the grass grow under their feet. Let them organise their meetings well, both for collections and sale of Khadi. Let them have ample walking spaces, in case of big meetings, for Gandhiji to address them from any point and for collectors to move about, and let them have at the meetings Khadi of all varieties and texture to suit all purses and tastes.

I have done with the business part of the visit. I shall briefly dwell on items of incidental interest. The Gaya municipal address, out of all addresses, was frankly sceptical about Khadi and untouchability programme, and Gandhiji wondered and asked why an address was voted to him at all and why he was not previously favoured with a copy of the interesting address. At Gaya, again, there was an address given by the Hindu Sabha, which expressed heartiest sympathy with the Khadi and untouchability programme—I wonder if the gentleman who read the address was not also a municipal councillor—and asked Gandhiji to bless their Shuddhi work. The reply is worth recording: "I have made no secret of the fact that I did not approve of all aspects of the 'Shuddhi' work. After much prayerful study of the Hindu Shastras I have come to the conclusion that there is no room in them for conversions such as they have in Islam and Christianity. I am also certain on a prayerful reading of the Koran that there is no warrant for the *tabligh* that is being promoted today. It is possible that I may be mistaken. Let God correct me in that case. I for myself would love to protect my religion with *tapashcharya*—the way of prayerful suffering, which is the royal road to success in any noble object. The real memorial that the Hindus can raise to Swamiji is to rid Hinduism of the curse of untouchability. Let both Hindus and Musalmans cleanse their hearts with the purifying blood of Swamiji's sacrifice. I must be free to read the Gita or the Koran of my own accord. Why should a Hindu compel me to read the one or a Musalman to read the other? Why should I need a Christian to compel me to read the Bible? No one may stand between a man and his religion or God. He who has no inkling of religion, whose heart is arid and unpurified—how dare he purify (by proselytising) others? But that is my opinion. And as I am a votary of liberty, I have, in spite of my opinion, insisted that Shraddhanandji had as much right to propagate the Vedic Dharma as a Musalman to propagate that of the Koran. And if Shraddhanandji was assassinated for his Shuddhi work, it did no credit to Islam. Hinduism is proud of the sacrifice and has been enriched by it.

Let no Musalman secretly approve of the act or believe that it has done any good to Islam. Let not a single Hindu harbour any thought of retaliation. If the Hindu and the Musalman rid themselves of mutual distrust and fear, there is no power that can stop their freedom. We are the makers of our own slavery. I had sealed my lips up to now on this burning topic. It is Shraddhanandji's sacrifice that has compelled me to open them to a certain extent. But I can give no guidance in this atmosphere. I shall only send my prayers to God that he may rid us of fear and hatred and distrust, and make us rely solely on the strength of love."

But I must conclude this letter which has already exceeded its usual length. I send a fairly long condensed summary of Gandhiji's speech at Sewan*, where he was particularly requested to address himself to Hindu-Muslim unity. M. D.

27th January, 1927

NATIONAL SCHOOLS

By M. K. Gandhi

During my Bihar tour I come in touch with national schools which continue to flourish in spite of obstacles. But these schools demonstrate to me the reason for the apparent failure of the educational programme of Non-co-operation, for they prove, at least for me, beyond a shadow of doubt that the thousands of boys who left Government schools went back, not because they were weak, not because the parents were weak, but because the school-masters and professors lacked the necessary dynamic faith in their own programme. But as I have said, even they could not very well be held blameworthy.

* *See Page 65.*

They were themselves products of the vicious educational system and they could not be expected to throw off all on a sudden all the effects of their old environment. The marvel is that in spite of tremendous odds so many still remain staunch to the ideal and manage to live in the face of over-whelming difficulties. But to the few who still remain staunch, I would make an earnest appeal to be absolutely truthful. Non-co-operation in every one of its branches had its positive aspect, just as much as its negative. Indeed, the positive aspect was the most permanent. The negative was useless without the positive. Mere withdrawal from Government schools was nothing, if the withdrawal did not mean some corresponding constructive educational programme. Every unaffiliated school is not a national school simply because it is not affiliated and because it does not receive a grant-in-aid. Thousands of missionary schools could be called national, if mere non-affiliation and non-acceptance of grant-in-aid was the one test. We have the definition of National educational institutions given to us by the Congress. The definition includes among other important things, spinning as a compulsory subject. At one of the national schools in Bihar, I discovered that the Charkha existed only in name and for show indifferently staged, and the school-masters were themselves indifferent spinners. They hardly knew carding. They did not know a good Charkha from a bad one. They did not know the qualities of a straight spindle. They did not know that it was necessary to have finer spindles in order to draw finer counts and to have a larger output. Almost every wheel that I examined produced a foreign and jarring sound. The head-master of a school whom I examined critically bravely admitted all the defects and has promised to remedy them. The lesson I should like to draw from this instructive experience is that national school-masters, if they are to make good their double claim, should live up to it, that is, be truthful. If they do not believe in the Charkha, they must say so and leave their employers; if the parents who send their children do not believe in the Charkha and do not want them to learn and practise spinning, the school-masters must refuse to take such children. But if they believe in the necessity of spinning as a necessary part of the curriculum, they must themselves master its science and technique and teach it to their pupils as they are expected to teach any other subject. It is not for them to say their pupils do not like it. It is for the teachers to make the subject they teach interesting. I hated chemistry which I subsequently learnt and appreciated as a most interesting study, only because my teacher did not know his subject sufficiently to make it interesting. Hundreds of boys will not take to geometry, a most fascinating recreation, simply because the teachers have no interest in their work and they have themselves not developed enough interest in it. Similarly for spinning. I know of no accomplished spinner who has not acknowledged spinning even as a pastime to be an interesting and uplifting study. A mere thumping on the piano would give a headache to a most willing listener, but the exquisite touch of a master would convert even one who has no ear for music. Even so with spinning. My proposal, however, at the present moment is, not to demonstrate the entertaining power of the spinning wheel, but to drive home the truth that, if it has to be taught in national schools, it must be by teachers who know it thoroughly and who have patience with their pupils. Let us not by our own ignorance or indifference be guilty of producing in our pupils a nausea for an occupation which is generally acknowledged as one of primary national importance.

Honesty demands that school-masters who do not know spinning or have no faith in it should, even though their refusal may cost their dismissal, refuse to have anything to do with it in their schools. If we are truthful, it will be well with us in the end. If we are untruthful, nothing will save us. And such a tremendous movement like handspinning, which depends for its success solely upon the character of the workers in it, has no chance of success if the workers resolve to camouflage. Let me incidentally remind managers of national institutions that it would be also better and more profitable in the long run to introduce *taklis* instead of the spinning wheel. The best spinners among the boys may have good spinning wheels, and that also, so long as they undertake to spin per month a minimum amount of yarn of uniform kind and strength.

27th January, 1927

PROHIBITION NOTES

The Devil Can Quote!

Everybody knows that powerful organisations have sprung up in America whose object is to nullify and force the repeal of Prohibition. These organisations are a part of the programme of the strongly organised international liquor traffic of the world. They have enormous wealth and influence and are determined that Prohibition shall fail in the United States. They are also carrying on subtle propaganda in other countries where anti-drink efforts are likely to be made. In India, too, this kind of work has now begun. I have seen a bunch of leaflets purporting to be isued from Delhi by a body called the "True Temperance Publicity Bureau." The sort of stuff that this body is circulating may be sampled by an extract or two.

Bhagavad Gita supports drink! "In the Bhagvadgita, known as the Lord's Song", says one of the tracts of this Publicity Bureau, "are several references to Soma juice, the favourite drink of those times, and the Soma drinkers are spoken of highly. For instance, in the Bhagavad Gita, Krishna says: "The knowers of the three Vedas, the Soma drinkers, the purified from sin, worshipping me with sacrifice, pray of me the way to heaven". Krishna again says:. "Permeating the soil, I support beings by my vital energy and, having become the delicious Soma, I nourish all plants." "How can Krishna call Soma juice delicious, unless he has drunk it?" asks this triumphant defender of Drink,

From the Gita to the Itihasas! "In the Mahabharata,

there is abundant evidence to show that most of the leading characters in that great epic were addicted to strong drink." "Krishna and Arjuna are described as having wine-inflamed eye." "The Ramayana, too, frequently refers to the drinking of spirits." "Bharata returning from his ineffectual mission to bring back Rama mourns the lost glories of the capital in these words: 'No longer the exhilarating aroma of arrack now wafts through the city'. Thus are quotations taken from our most holy books and authority shown for keeping up the Drink evil.

The argument is that India was even in ancient times indulging in strong drink, so do not try to fight Alcohol now. It is decent and respectable to drink. Indra drank, Vishvamitra drank, Vasishtha feasted. Krishna and Arjuna had wine picnics! The old rule that uninstructed people should not read holy book was not made without reason,

Then we are treated to quotations from modern writers. It is surprising to see how quotations from very eminent modern European writers, thinkers, statesmen and doctors of religion, too, could be culled and pressed into service by the liquor propagandists. It is a common thing to find sentiments like the following in English speeches and writings, which are made full use of in the "True Temperance' tracts.

"Wine, beer and spirits have their place in the world. When taken in excess they do harm". "The spectacle of over-indulgence and its consequences should not be used as an argument to deprive the whole race of the 'kindly blessing that maketh glad the heart of man, saint and sinner alike."

It is inconceivable that such pleas on behalf of intoxicating liquors may be put forward by similar writers or thinkers in India. Of course, a new band of paid poets and moralists may be created by 'wet' organisations even in India in the future, who may sing the praises of moderate drinking. The whole difference between India and Western countries in the attitude towards intoxicating liquors is brought out by this, that, while it is possible to get pro-liquor passages from Charles

Dickens, Professor Blackie, the Dean of St. Paul's and others like them, it would be impossible to find pleas for the moderate use of Alcohol in the non-mystic literature of any Indian language of any period.

Decent life in India does not permit the use of spiritous drink at all. Indulgence in it is treated as an indecent act to be permitted, if at all, only in privacy and away from the house, and that, too, only for classes admittedly below the standard of national culture and refinement. Arguments, by good men in Europe, based on the respectability and tolerance of drink, have no place or relevency in dealing with the question in India.

As against the outstanding fact that America has adopted Prohibition, reliance is placed on the opinion of eminent men of America. Sir Basil Blackett quoted Abraham Lincoln, the liberator. These citations prove, indeed, too much. We need not attempt to be more loyal to Lincoln than Americans themselves. America could not have adopted the amendment in the constitution with all the difficult procedure prescribed, if wise Americans had been so clearly against Prohibition. Either modern Americans think differently from people of the time of Abraham Lincoln, or present day America considers herself free to root out an evil which she had before no time to attend to on account of her pre-occupations with other aims and ideals. Or it may be that the liquor evil has grown to be a far greater menace to public welfare now than in the older days. Whatever it may be, the fact cannot be disputed that the Americans, a cultured and democratic modern people, have, by a free and elaborately safeguarded procedure, voted for and adopted, and are enforcing, total Prohibition on a stupendous scale, in a country many times bigger than India and among people much more addicted to the evil.

Has Prohibition Failed?

We are constantly told that drink has not gone down in America in spite of Prohibition. Deleterious concoctions, it is said, have taken the place of 'good' liquors; secret unrestrained indulgence has replaced moderate public drinking; and the nation is no better for the new laws. One wonders why, if Prohibition has not succeeded in reducing the consumption of liquor, the liquor interests are so eager to get a repeal. While it may be admitted that Drink will offer the utmost resistance before yielding to the laws of Prohibition and that many years of hard persevering work will have to be gone through before full enforcement of Prohibition can be expected in a country like America, the very propaganda and the organised efforts of the Anti-prohibitionists are a sufficient proof that Prohibition has materially decreased consumption and will one day bring to an end the liquor trade. Any one can get liquor if he likes, say they. And they contradict themselves the next minute and deplore the fact that men are driven to all sorts of shifts to procure some poisonous substitute for good liquor. The argument that laws are ineffective to stop drink is no more sound than an argument that laws cannot altogether stop theft or adultery and, therefore, let us repeal the Penal Code.

Rich people in America may take advantage of the cupidity of importers of liquor and for some time procure what they wish to have. But as a result of Prohibition the poorer people are saved from the temptations of Drink. What Sir T. Vijayaraghavacharya, a high Government official, said after his Canadian visit, and what the Holt Ladies said to Mahadev Desai prove this. No one can deny that it would be a blessing to save poor men from the temptation of Drink. It is no sound argument to contend that, because some men can pay heavy prices and take great risks and get what they want, every one should be provided with temptations.

The talk about impure liquor being indulged in, because 'good' liquor is not available, is again a curious instance of spacious exaggeration to serve selfish ends. Such evasions of the law and indulgence in poisons have their own automatic checks. Those men who will take poison because no liquor is given to them may well be left to themselves. We need not stop our attempts at reform because some men will rather die than give up liquor.

C. R.

27th January, 1927

PRAYER THE ONLY WAY

Challenged at Sewan (Bihar) to say something on Hindu-Muslim unity, Gandhiji delivered a Hindi speech of which the following is a condensed summary:

"I am glad you say that your subdivision is better than other parts so far as Hindu-Muslim unity is concerned. But can you say that you are so united that your unity will stand the strain of anything happening elsewhere? I wish there can be at least one province, one district, one subdivision in this vast land which can proudly say that no power on earth can foment a Hindu-Muslim quarrel there. We may think we are living, but disunited we are worse than dead. The Hindu thinks that in quarrelling with the Musalman he is benefiting Hinduism, and the Musalman thinks that in fighting a Hindu he is benefiting Islam. But each is ruining his faith. And the poison has spread as among the members of the communities themselves. And no wonder. For one man cannot do right in one department of life whilst he is occupied in doing wrong in any other department. Life is one indivisible whole.

"I said at Comilla that the problem has passed out of human hands, and that God has taken it into his own. May be the statement springs from my egotism. But I do not think so. I have ample reason for it. With my hand on my breast I can say that not a minute in my life am I forgetful of God. For over twenty years I have been doing everything that I have done as in the presence of God. Hindu-Muslim unity I had made a mission of my life. I worked for it in

South Africa, I toiled for it here, I did penance for it, but God was not satisfied; God did not want me to take any credit for the work. And so I have now washed my hands. I am helpless. I have exhausted all my effort. But as I am a believer in God, as I never for a moment lose faith in Him, as I content myself with the joy and sorrow that He wills for me, I may feel helpless, but I never lose hope. Something within me tells me that Hindu-Muslim unity must come and will come sooner than we might dare to hope, that God will one day force it on us, in spite of ourselves. That is why I said that it has passed into the hands of God. This, I said, might be taken to be an arrogant utterance—arrogant inasmuch as it implies that it is not in the power of any other man to achieve the work, as if no one has worked for it more than I. But there is no arrogance in the statement. Hundreds may have done the work, with the same earnestness, love and energy, but none with more. And I believe that all of them must be feeling as helpless as I. In 1920 I said that not even the British Empire with all the resources of its armed strength, diplomacy and organisation could efface us, make us slaves, or divide Hindus from Musalmans. But that was because I thought we were God-fearing then. We trusted one another and we relied on one another's strength. But how am I to prevail upon you to day to cast off all fear, hatred and distrust? Shraddhanandji was not the enemy of Musalmans. He was a warrior, he had the courage of his conviction. Assassination was not the way to fight him. Let us Hindus and Musalmans both wash the sins of our heart with his blood.

"And what is it that we should be fighting for? We Hindus may be idol-worshippers. We may be mistaken. But when God gave every man the right to make mistakes, when God suffers us to live although we are idol-worshippers, why should not the Musalmans suffer us too? And if a Musalman thinks that he must slaughter the cow, why should a Hindu stay s hands by force? Why should he not fall on bended knees before him and plead with him? But we will do no such thing. Well then, God will one day make the Musalman and the Hindu do what we will not do to-day. If you are believers, I beseech you to retire into yourselves and pray to the Indweller to stay your hands from wrong and to make them do the right thing. Let that be our prayer every morning and evening. There is no other way."

A Good English Woman

In India, with the exception of a few who came in personal touch with that good Englishwoman, no one knew anything of Miss Florence Winterbottom, who, a friendly message from England tells me, has just died. She was among the rare men and women who find service its own reward, and she belonged to that class amongst the English who seek out and befriend forlorn causes in the teeth of odium, ridicule and opposition. She was a leading light of the Ethical movement and was for some time president of the Union of Ethical Societies. She was Secretary of the Emerson Club. I had the privilege of coming in touch with her when I went to England in charge of the first South African Indian Deputation in 1906. I knew nothing of her, but, by reading in the papers about the doings of the Deputation, in out-of-the-way corners of the leading dailies of London, she sought us out, she offered me a platform, she studied the question and, in a variety of ways, helped the cause that at that time had only a few chosen friends in England. She became from that time one of the most constant and painstaking supporters of the cause in South Africa. No one who came in contact with her failed to recognise in her fearlessness, honesty for the sake of honesty not merely as the best policy, and a capacity to take an exceptionally detached view of all things. Though intensely English, she was equally intensely international. Her patriotism never took the shape of justifying everything English whether good, bad or indifferent. When people tell me that non-violence is of no effect so far as English people are concerned, I renew my faith in non-violence and in English nature, or better still human nature, by thinking of instances like those of Miss Florence Winterbottom. May her soul rest in peace.

M. K. G.

3rd February, 1927

OUR HELPLESSNESS

By M. K. Gandhi

So the fiat has gone forth that India is to send Indian soldiers to China, in reality to aid in suppressing China's bid for freedom, ostensibly to protect the foreigners. The Legislative Assembly had no voice in the matter. It had not even the power to express its academic opinion. The Viceroy considered it inexpedient for the Assembly to do so. That was enough to prevent the Assembly from voicing its feelings.

And yet it is as vital a matter as could be imagined for the members of the Assembly not merely to discuss but to direct India's foreign policy. Our helplessness becomes never so apparent as when Indian soldiers are shamelessly used to crush other people's freedom. Indeed, India is the key to the exploitation of the Asiatic and other non-European races of the Earth. She is held under bondage not merely for the sake of her own exploitation but that of her neighbours near and distant

No wonder the Viceroy was emphatic and unequivocal in his pronouncement that for any advance upon the so-called reforms, India had to wait on the British Parliament on bended knees. She is to expect nothing as of right. Historical events have given Britain the mastery over India and she means to retain it so long as she can. Every reform has to be subject to that one supreme condition.

Here then there is an outlook which no self-respecting

Indian can accept. British mastery is the one thing that India cannot tolerate. It was to make this position absolutely clear that the 'Independents' fought at Gauhati for unequivocal independence for the country. That it could not be had for the moment did not matter much to them. They wanted the nation to realise that goal and no other.

Men like me cling to their faith in human nature and expect to bend even the haughty English spirit, all appearances to the contrary notwithstanding. But whether it be Dominion status or any other, they do not want to be *under* the British Government; they want absolute equality. They, not the English Government, should be able to say what their soldiers will do, where they will go.

This real vital power is not to be had through working the reforms *now*. That power has to come from within and from the bottom. It is then possible to work any constitution. Today it is impossible to work any constitution with effect. We have not the internal capacity. We have not got the needed influence over the people. That influence can only come through real selfless service. So long as we fail to realise this central fact, every one of our activities must ultimately turn to nothingness.

Let not the impatient reader laugh when I mention the spinning wheel in this connection. I hold that it is impossible for us to establish a living vital connection with the masses unless we will work for them, through them and in their midst, not as their patrons but as their servants.

Let the impatient reader know that these masses for whom he is called upon to work, in whose name he would like to speak, are underfed, underclothed and living for the most part in enforced idleness. Let the Viceregal embargo on the Chinese resolution and His Excellency's frank pronouncement about reforms open our eyes to the stern reality.

It is well that the Working Committee of the Congress has washed its hands clean of the immoral transaction which the impending departure of Indian soldiers for China is. Let the struggling Chinese know that our soliders will go to China only because we are, if possible, more helpless than they. This is not the first time that Indian soldiers will go to China to suppress her freedom. Lowes Dickinson by his immortal letters of John Chinaman has shown us how Indian soldiers were taken to China to impose opium upon her. We know what the powers miscalled Christian have done in China. But no nation that is prepared to pay the price can be baulked of her freedom for ever. And it is well with China, as she seems to be prepared to pay the price required.

3rd February, 1927

INSANITARY GAYA

By M. K. Gandhi

I have no desire to advertise the insanitation of Gaya, a prince among the holy places of Hinduism. It was because my Hindu soul rebelled against the stinking cesspools I saw in a principal street of Gaya that I was obliged to draw pointed attention to it in my reply to the address of the Gaya municipality. I am aware that there are many holy places which are insanitary enough. But I do not remember having seen anything like what I saw in Gaya. It is possible that I have not been taken to the dirty places in other sacred places. But insanitation need not be weighed in golden scales. Gaya I am using merely as an example in order to draw the attention of all municipalities that sanitation of their cities must be their first care. This one thing must be above municipal politics, parties and intrigues. Just as it must be the care of every party in a municipality to keep its finance pure and above suspicion, so must it be the sacred duty of every party in a municipality to keep the sanitation of its city in perfect order and above suspicion. Every municipality should constitute itself a model school for teaching the science of sanitation. Of city sanitation we have not yet much knowledge. We do not mind what happens to our neighbours, so long as our own houses are in fair order. We do not know the use of city latrines. We do not know how to use our drains. It has to be admitted, therefore, that our municipalities have an arduous task before them in handling this great and important problem. But handled it must be whatever the difficulties. It becomes much more important in sacred cities which are visited by lacs of people from year to year. There was no reason for the foul cesspools I noticed in Gaya. There is no reason why people should be allowed to dirty river banks. There are many things which municipalities can, if they will only treat the cities under their care as if they were their own houses, remedy without much difficulty or hindrance from the citizens.

But the difficulty comes from within. Municipal councillors are often indifferent and sometimes obstruct their own elected chairman. Sometimes they are absorbed in internal quarrels and neglect sanitation. It is high time that we developed a healthy sense of civic duty. In this matter we have much to learn from the West. People of the West are builders of big cities. They know the value of fresh air, clean water and clean surroundings. Any city that would attend to its sanitation in a proper spirit will add to both its health and wealth. Sacred cities ought to lead the way in this matter. They have opportunities which other cities do not possess. There is a great deal of wisdom in the English proverb 'Cleanliness is next to godliness.' Manu, Moses and Mahomed have laid down laws of sanitation suited to their times. These have to be elaborated in keeping with the modern requirements. It is enough to know from these ancient lawgivers that they held cleanliness to be part of a truly religious life.

3rd February, 1927

TEAR DOWN THE PURDAH

BY M. K. GANDHI

Whenever I have gone to Bengal, Bihar or the United Provinces, I have observed the *purdah* system more strictly followed than in the other provinces. But when I addressed a meeting at Darbhanga late at night and amid calm surroundings free from noise and bustle and unmanageable crowds, I found in front of me men, but behind me and behind the screen were women of whose presence I knew nothing till my attention was drawn to it. The function was in connection with the laying of the foundation-stone of an orphanage, but I was called upon to address the ladies behind the *purdah*. The sight of the screen behind which my audience, whose numbers I did not know, was seated made me sad. It pained and humiliated me deeply. I thought of the wrong being done by men to the women of India by clinging to a barbarous custom which, whatever use it might have had when it was first introduced, had now become totally useless and was doing incalculable harm to the country. All the education that we have been receiving for the past 100 years seems to have produced but little impression upon us, for I note that the *purdah* is being retained even in educated households not because the educated men believe in it themselves but because they will not manfully resist the brutal custom and sweep it away at a stroke. I have the privilege of addressing hundreds of meetings of women attended by thousands. The din and the noise created at these meetings make it impossible to speak with any effect to the women who attend them. Nothing better is to be expected so long as they are caged and confined in their houses and little courtyards When, therefore, they find themselves congregated in a big room and are expected all of a sudden to listen to some one, they do not know what to do with themselves or with the speaker. And when silence is restored it becomes difficult to interest them in many everyday topics, for they know nothing of them having been never allowed to breathe the fresh air of freedom. I know that this is a somewhat exaggerated picture. I am quite aware of the very high culture of these thousands of sisters whom I get the privilege of addressing. I know that they are capable of rising to the same height that men are capable of, and I know, too, that they do not have occasions to go out. But this is not to be put down to the credit of the educated classes. The question is, why have they not gone further? Why do not our women enjoy the same freedom that men do? Why should they not be able to walk out and have fresh air?

Chastity is not a hot-house growth. It cannot be superimposed. It cannot be protected by the surrounding wall of the *purdah*. It must grow from within, and, to be worth anything, it must be capable of withstanding every unsought temptation. It must be as defiant as Sita's. It must be a very poor thing that cannot stand the gaze of men. Men, to be men, must be able to trust their women-folk, even as the latter are compelled to trust them. Let us not live with one limb completely or partially paralysed. Rama would be nowhere without Sita, free and independent even as he was himself. But, for robust independence, Draupadi is perhaps a better example. Sita was gentleness incarnate. She was a delicate flower. Draupadi was a giant oak. She bent mighty Bhima himself to her imperious will. Bhima was terrible to every one, but he was a lamb before Draupadi. She stood in no need of protection from any one of the Pandavas. By seeking to-day to interfere with the free growth of the womanhood of India we are interfering with the growth of free and independent-spirited men. What we are doing to our women and what we are doing to the untouchables recoils upon our heads with a force thousand times multiplied. It partly accounts for our weakness, indecision, narrowness and helplessness. Let us, then, tear down the *purdah* with one mighty effort.

WEEKLY LETTER

3rd February, 1927

The surging crowds and stupendous meetings make one wonder whether the organisers of the tour could not have done anything better than this heavy programme to be performed at breakneck speed. And yet they could not have done anything better, for we find that in spite of their anxiety to satisfy all, they have not been able to include all places that wanted to be on the programme. And when we reach the end, the feeling will not be so much of relief as of thankfulness that Gandhiji has stood the strain fairly well—not a sense of relief, for the thousands of people that for a moment overwhelm you fill you with hope of the tremendous possibilities of a movement the magnitude of which newspapers retailing gloomy reports of communal disturbances and division among Congress ranks have failed to gauge. Let the doubter and the sceptic go to Bihar and see that the province watered by the mighty rivers Ganges and Sarayu, Gandak and Sone, is watered no less by the mighty Ganges of faith which will never dry.

Darbhanga, Champaran, Monghyr and Arrah—four districts in the course of a week! It is impossible to gather one's impressions and arrange them however briefly within the scope of a weekly letter But I shall try to give a sketch as hurried as the tour.

Darbhanga is the land of modern *tirthas* if I may say so without offending orthodox susceptibilities. For *tirthas* are holy and purifying, and whereas the squalour and cupidity and hypocrisy that reign in our orthodox *tirthas* stink in one's nostrils, a pilgrimage to the modern ones—the Khadi depots—chastens and uplifts. 'You must not accompany me,' said Gandhiji. 'You will see nothing today in the rush and hurry. Go to these places to-morrow and study them to your heart's content.' And I willingly obeyed. The visit was not only a study, but a revelation, a feast for the eyes and solace for the soul. Pandaul, and Madhubani and Sakri and Kapasi conjure up visions before you. In beautifully swept courtyards those women were sitting—all Musalmans, it will gladden

Maulana Shaukatali's heart to know—working out of their wheels a music of which the echoes still resound in the ears Not ten or fifty, but three hundred giving a wonderful demonstration of the art to which they were born. As we paused and wondered at every stage at the dexterity of these mothers and grandmothers, one of the men who showed us round said: 'There are not less than a thousand, sir, in this locality. They spin and we weave These are all women from weavers' families.' And as you proceed you notice a sister young, but awfully humpbacked, and you seem to melt with pity at her misfortune But no! She laughs at your pitying look, and the gossamer yarn running out of her proud fingers seems to tell you that God has not deprived her of the cunning of her fingers and she can earn therewith a living possibly more honourable than the spectators.' A few yards from her is a dame, whose silver hair, wrinkled forehead and crumpled cheeks tell you her years. She is spinning away her fine *Kokti* yarn without caring to notice you. 'How long have you been doing this?' 'Since morning,' she replies. 'No, I mean, how many years?' 'I cannot say, exactly.' She smiles wondering at the question. 'But you can imagine, I began it ever since I was married when I was that age', she says, pointing to a tot who might have been her great grand-daughter. 'And how much do you earn out of this?' the irrepressible economist in you asks. 'Well, that is the sole means of our livelihood,' she says, and when pressed to be more definite she gives you details which the weaver friend clad in fine homespun has to help you to understand. 'That means 7 to 8 rupees a month earned in your spare hours?' you ask almost envying her wage, though you earn ten times as much with less labour. 'Well, yes,' she modestly admits, not willing to proclaim her high wage. And lest you should run away with a hasty inference she adds, 'Not all earn so much. All have not as much time as I, and all do not spin so well. And then you do not get as much out of ordinary yarn as from *Kokti* yarn'

At the depot you meet women with their bundles of yarn anxious to tell the visitors that the fall in the cotton prices have adversely affected them. How? They take away a pound and a half of cotton and return a pound of yarn, the price of half a pound of cotton being their wage. It was a commentary on the exchange system of getting yarn that obtains in these parts. At Belwar there is a colony of Brahmin women-spinners, girls spinning on their neat little *taklis* and elderly women on their wheels. Their hands do not show the cunning of their Musalman sisters, but the boundless enthusiasm of a sixty years old virgin widow who has brigaded them tells you what the Charkha means to them. Among these, too, there are spinners, though not many, whose art you pause to admire The modest mother spinning away with the baby at her breast has no proud tale of a heavy wage to tell you. But more proudly still, because unselfishly, she says: 'My yarn went to make Mahatmaji's garland yesterday' Kapasia is a village where nearly all the weavers weave handspun yarn. We visited a number of houses and found men, women, and children working and not a soul idle It was, again, a Musalman village organised by Hindu youths. Let the Musalman sceptic visit one of these centres and learn the lesson of patriotism and perseverance from these Musalman men and women. We sat and talked with the weavers It was no use talking to them. Their spokesman was far more able to give you a business-like speech. He knew both the economics and politics of his trade. 'Do you ever fight as Hindus and Musalmans do in other parts?' 'No, sir, we do fight amongst ourselves, as the Hindus do amongst themselves, but never the one community with the other. We have no time left. Our women spin and we weave. The Musalman weaver and the Hindu spinner are as brother and sister. I do wish our Brahmin brethren also were doing something when their women spin away at their wheels,' he said casting a just reflection on the idle Brahmin.

But I must pass on. Darbhanga and Monghyr have been the best in point of contributions too. Some of the monster meetings in Muzaffarpur district were as big as, if less organised than, the Mairwa meeting. The demonstrations in Champaran have been very noisy—they seem to have a special claim on Gandhiji, feeling as they do that they made him famous—and those in Monghyr and Arrah have been the rowdiest, possibly because Gandhiji visited some of these places for the first time And yet the response everywhere was heartiest, collections having been quite in proportion to the crowds, excepting at Motihari, where not much could be collected, for no fault of the crowd, but because of the faulty arrangement of the meeting.

In this connection let me make an observation or two. I have said something in my last as to the arrangement of the meeting Particular care requires to be taken in the construction of the platform It should be not less than six to seven feet high and broad enough to seat five or six people, with enough space on all sides. That will ensure collections by Gandhiji without danger of a rush or accident (so many people being anxious to hand the money to Gandhiji himself). At Begusarai in Monghyr the arrangement in this respect was perfect, the platform being something over six feet supported on four strong pillars, between which men could come and go. And as Gandhiji bended to receive the money, men at the rate of 14 per minute passed through his hands, so to say, having satisfied themselves that they paid the money to Gandhiji himself, and yet being successfully prevented from touching his feet—a thing which always gives rise to terrific rush and crush. We escaped accidents in Bihar only by a fluke. Let us, however, make accidents practically impossible, by better organisation and arrangement

It must be said that during the short time at their disposal the workers succeeded in getting together fair purses at most meetings. The collections at meetings have, as I have pointed out, a lesson all their own. Taking the Mairwa meeting to have numbered 32,000, the collection there worked out at two pice per head That was the result of nothing but fine organisation Organisers in other provinces will please note

I must mention in brief some of the items of interest. Amongst the purses and collections must be mentioned one little purse at Muzaffarpur It was presented on the occasion of Gandhiji's visit to the local Khadi Bhandar by the dyers, washermen and printers who serve this A.I S A. branch. It was handed to Gandhiji by a washerman clad in homespun 'How much is it?' asked Gandhiji 'Rs 150, sir' 'I appreciate it very much, but you must have made a lot of money too?' asked Gandhiji. 'Yes,' said the washerman. 'Thanks to your movement, our hands are full.' 'Well, then,' said Gandhiji, 'know that even this purse that you are presenting will go to add to your income' 'We know, sir. Nearly twenty *dhobis* here refuse to wash anything but Khaddar, and two of the best *dhobis* in the town are Khaddarites. Some of the fashionable gentry wearing foreign clothes feel the pinch of our vow, but how can we help it?' 'Certainly not,' said Gandhiji with a hearty laugh 'Let them beware.' The Khadi in the shop was tastefully arranged, there were all varieties, and some of the finest specimens of printing and dyeing were there to satisfy the most aesthetic taste. Let aesthetes and people with houses to furnish ask for whatever variety of cloth they want and they shall have it.

At Muzaffarpur the students also surrounded Gandhiji There are a thousand belonging to schools and a college. Every place in Champaran is full of happy memories and Gandhiji began his speech to the students by narrating one of the sweetest. 'You students—I wonder if there is still any one of those old boys at college—with Kirpalani at their head were the first to welcome and harbour me in Champaran Your response during the years that followed was no less remarkable Will you not do today the little that I am asking of you?' The rest of the speech was an impassioned utterance—a plea for Khadi-wearing and Brahmacharya couched in the same tone as the speech at the Hindu University They offered a slender purse but responded heartily to the call for purchasing Khadi.

10th February, 1927.

The last day in the Bihar tour was given to the students and professors of the Vidyapith and to the Khadi workers. Rajendrababu as Vice-Chancellor gave away the degrees to nine Snatakas and Gandhiji delivered the Convocation address. But before I come to that let me dispose of another interesting item I think it has been known by now that Bihar enjoys a unique place in all the provinces for the mutual goodwill and even friendship that subsists between the non-cooperating workers and the official and the semi-official world. It was not difficult, therefore, for Rajendrababu to invite the Vakils, Barristers, Members of the Councils, Ministers and Government officials, to a special Khadi Exhibition - arranged in an institution which is the Hon. Mr. Sinha's gift to Bihar. The meeting was very well attended, but the quiet nature of the function which the organisers had intended it to be was spoiled by crowds who raided the Shamiana. Gandhiji would have loved nothing like a discussion on Khadi with the members of the audience, but as it was not possible he gave them only a talk, of course in Hindi. He had with him charts of daily income per head in different countries of the world, and of production and sale of Khadi during recent years prepared by the students of the Vidyapith. 'Look,' said he, 'how this long strip of red representing the *per capita* income of U. S. A. compares with the little speck which represents that of India. Whereas the one is over Rs. 14 per day the other is 1½ anna per day! Compare the incomes of other countries—England, France, Japan, which are respectively Rs. 7, 6, and 5 per day. And even this 1½ anna per day is the average The actual income of the vast majority of our poor people would be still less, if you were to keep out of account the income of salaried ministers and executive councillors, of a few barristers and fewer millionaires. I ask you in all humility to suggest some way wherewith you can supplement this scanty income. I have been asking one and all but without avail As a result of hard thinking and living contact with the millions during recent years I have suggested the Charkha as the only means calculated to supplement this income' He then took the Khadi production and sale charts and showed the steady and rapid increase in production in Bihar and drew attention to the slow pace at which sales were going up. This production means Rs 30,000 distributed to 3,000 of the poor women of Bihar Come with me to the Khadi centres of Darbhanga and see the joy and happiness the Charkha has brought to those Hindu and Musalman women. If I cannot give work to more it is not my fault, but yours. If you do not care to purchase the products of their hands the work cannot progress. Every yard of Khaddar you purchase means a few coppers in the hands of those women.' 'A few coppers,' he added, 'and not more.

But it means a few coppers where none was carried before. I saw the fallen women in Rajahmundry and Barisal. A young girl came and said to me, 'Gandhi, what can your Charkha give us? The men who come to us pay us Rs 5 to 10 for a few minutes.' I said to her the Charkha could not give them that but if they renounced the life of shame I could arrange to teach them spinning and weaving and help them to earn a decent living As I listened to that girl my heart sank within me and I asked God why I was also not born a woman. But if I was not born a woman I can become a woman and it is for the women of India, a large number of whom do not get even an anna per day, that I am going about the country with my spinning wheel and my begging bowl'

The talk had its effects. Owing to tremendous rush every one could not see the exhibition as well as he wanted, but ministers and barristers saw the exhibition the next day and over Rs 2,000 worth of Khaddar was sold in a day and a half.

I come now to the Convocation. The Registrar's report gave the following figures of educational institutions and students: 1 College with 32 students; 9 high schools with 797 students; 16 middle schools with 1,285 students and 30 primary schools with 1,019 students. In all the institutions the medium of instruction is Hindi, spinning is compulsory and weaving is also taught in some of them. Some of the special features of the report are worth noticing. It traces in brief the history of the different high schools, mostly maintained by public funds, and in some cases from the income of lands donated to them Whereas the number of students in 3 out of the 9 schools has considerably gone down, in three the number continues as before, and in three the number has been steadily increasing The College is residential, located in a beautiful mango grove on the bank of the Ganges, and the students' monthly food charges are probably the lowest in the whole of India, i.e., Rs 8 to 9. Twenty-four have up to now taken their degrees The report gives interesting details of their post-collegiate career; one of them is preparing for a diploma of the College of France, one has found an important place in a business firm in Japan, one has studied dairying and cattle-farming and has a dairy of his own, two are engaged in journalism, eleven have taken up service in the national schools, one is doing business in Calcutta and one is doing Congress work.

The very large number of people from the city who attended the Convocation testified to the public attention the institution has succeeded in attracting.

Gandhiji's Convocation address was more a long heart-to-heart chat than a speech, although it was addressed not only to the students, but to the public at large. But it was a public whom he well might have taken into confidence, who understood not only the spoken word, but the unspoken language of the heart. It was a talk full of colour and passion and replete with autobiographic references.

He hoped at the outset that the Snatakas would live in their lives the vows they had solemnly taken that day and said, as he did at the time of the Gujarat Vidyapith Convocation, that the Vidyapith would have more than justified its existence if it turned out even one ideal student and one ideal teacher. For what was the function of these institutions? To discover gems, no matter how few, 'of the purest ray serene.' And he proceeded to give a reminiscence of his South African days. "I lived in South Africa for 20 years, but never once thought of going to see the diamond mines there, partly because I was afraid lest as an 'untouchable' I should be refused admission and insulted. But when Gokhale was there I felt it my duty to show him the chief industry of the place. There was no fear of his being insulted. So we went to the biggest mine there, and saw scenes which I have not forgotton. Mountains upon mountains of excavated earth and stone and no diamonds! It was after millions were sunk in excavating millions of tons of earth and stone that a handful of precious stones could be discovered. And when Cullinan, the owner, discovered the stone named after him—a stone larger than the one which adorned the crown of the Czar and the Kohinoor—after years of labour and millions of pounds had been spent on it, you might imagine his joy. He felt that his lifework was done. If we should not grudge to spend any amount of labour and capital on a thing which had but an artificial value, how much should we spend on excavating jewels from the human mine? Let us work away in that spirit' That was an apt simile apter than Ruskin used when he coined that phrase 'manufacture of souls.' That manufacture is only in God's power. We human mortals have but to discover what is already there hidden by God

Ha then referred to the positive and negative aspect of all non-co-operating institutions. The negative which consisted of withdrawal of all connection with Government had been already achieved by the existing institutions When he thought of the number of students and teachers that he had called out, he felt not the slightest egret. Nor did he feel repentant for the fact that many of these had gone back, that many were discontented and unhappy. He felt sorry for them, they had his deep sympathy, but regret or repentance he had none. 'These troubles and sorrows are our daily lot, should be our daily lot. If observance of truth was a bed of roses, if truth cost one nothing and was all happiness and ease, there would be no beauty about it. We must adhere to truth even if the heavens should fall. What matters it, if, by following truth, we were to lose the whole world including even India? We shall be true votaries of truth only if we follow it to death, in the conviction that under God we will get back the things we hold dear including India I know that a large number of our teachers and professors are restless, a few are starving. That is true penance necessary for a proper cleansing of the national atmosphere.'

That was the negative aspect and he was glad it had been carried out and a fair share of penance had been gone through. But this dual world had a positive aspect too, and one which was more difficult is also more permanent Where else was it to be fulfilled except in institutions like the Vidyapith? And he drew a contrast between the method of education followed in Europe and that followed in India. 'In Europe the education follows the peculiar genius of the people. One thing is taught in three different countries in three different ways according to the varying culture and genius of each. Only we delight in slavishly following the English model.

The whole objective of the present system was to make us faithful imitators of the West. There is nothing novel in this, it is but the natural outcome of our having entrusted our affairs to those who never cared to know us Poor Macaulay! What could he do? He sincerely believed that our Sanskrit literature was all superstition and he seriously thought he would give us something wholesome in the shape of Western culture! Let us not abuse him for having unintentionally worked our ruin. As a result of English being the medium of instruction, we have lost all originality. We have become birds without wings. The most we aspire to is a clerkship or editorship. One of us may under the system be a Lord Sinha, but every one at best is designed to be part of the huge foreign machine. At Muzaffarpur a boy came and asked me if by going to a national school he could one day be a *Lat* saheb. I said, 'No, you can be a village *Lat*, but not a Lord Sinha. Only Lord Birkenhead can make you that.'

He referred to the craze for more and more palatial buildings raised out of the money of the poor, and raised for the purpose of giving an education which was denied to the poor. 'I had an occasion to visit the Economic Institute at Allahabad. As Prof. Jevons showed me over it and I was told that it had cost Rs. 30 lakhs (if my memory serves me right), I shuddered. You could not raise those palaces but by starving millions. Look at New Delhi which tells the same tale. Look at the grand improvements in first and second class carriages on railways. The whole trend is to think of the privileged few and to neglect the poor. If this is not satanic, what is it? If I must tell the truth I can say nothing less. I have no quarrel with those who conceived the system. They could not do otherwise. How is an elephant to think for an ant? As Sir Leppel Griffen once put it in his speech as member of the South African Deputation, only the toad under the harrow knows where it pinches. The arrangement of our affairs is in their hands and with the best will in the world, the best of them could not order our affairs as well as we could For theirs is a diametrically opposite conception to ours They think in the terms of the privileged few. We must think in the terms of the teeming millions.'

And that naturally led him on to the Charkha, which he said should be the very pivot and centre of all our arrangements

'Let the Snatakas take their degrees, learn anything they like, but let it centre round the Charkha, let their economics and their science subserve the purpose of the Charkha Do not relegate the Charkha to an old corner. The Charkha is the Sun of the solar system of our activities. Without it Vidyapiths are Vidyapiths in name. Lord Irwin told God's truth, when he said, that for any advancement through the Councils we should look to the British Parliament. Let us not be angry with him. He cannot think but in the terms of the Parliament The Sun of his system is London, the Sun of our system is the Charkha. I may be mistaken in this, but, so far as I am not convinced of the mistake, I shall treasure it The Charkha at any rate is incapable of harming anybody and without it we, and if I may say so, even the world, will go to rack and ruin. We know what Europe has been feeling after the war in which lies were propagated as the highest religion. The world is weary of the after-effects of the war and even as the Charkha is India's comforter today, it may be the world's tomorrow, because it stands not for the greatest good of the greatest number but for the greatest good of all. Whenever I see an erring man, I say to myself I have also erred; when I see a lustful man I say to myself, so was I once, and in this way I feel kinship with every one in the world and feel that I cannot be happy without the humblest of us being happy. It is in this sense that I want you to make the Charkha the centre of your studies Just as Prahlada saw Rama everywhere and Tulsidas could see nothing but Rama even in the image of Krishna, let all your learning be directed to realising the implications of the Charkha. Our science, our carpentry, our economics should all be utilised for making the Charkha the prop and mainstay of our poorest. I know in Gujarat Vidyapith we have not yet succeeded in doing it, you are not doing it. I am not saying this in a spirit of complaint. I am simply pouring out the agony of my heart. May you all understand it.'

The rest was an appeal for helping the Vidyapith and it evoked a hearty response from all present. Rs. 2,000 were promised and over Rs. 600 were collected on the spot. M. D.

10th February, 1927

BE IN TIME

By M. K. Gandhi

The eventful month of April will be soon on us with its memories of the birth of the nation accompanied by unparalleled rejoicings in which lakhs upon lakhs of people took part and which showed the possibilities of what the nation, if it could only act with one mind, could do. It is a month which showed also what haughty, revengeful and merciless Imperialism could do to save itself. The 6th and the 13th of April are never-to-be-forgotten days in the life of the nation. Since then the nation has been struggling not to return evil for evil, not to act in a spirit of retaliation, but to use for self-purification the mingled crimson stream that flowed in Jallianwalla. The nation has been struggling to express itself in a non-violent spirit expressed by the spinning wheel and Khadi, the removal of untouchability and solidarity of the different sects and creeds. It is clear, however, that Khadi is the only thing in which the whole nation can take part. If we want to act non-violently, we must act constructively, patiently and with quiet and quenchless confidence in ourselves and in our method. We must evolve unity, strength and iron discipline. We must learn to give effect to our views in spite of the vast odds against us. Let us realise that the British rule is imposed upon us because British commerce is forced upon us. If we could but purify British commerce, we would purify the British connection. Our commercial transactions with the British as with the world should be on our terms and should therefore be mutually beneficial and absolutely voluntary. But Lancashire cloth is a symbol of our helpless exploitation, whereas Khadi is the symbol of self-help, self-reliance and freedom, not merely of individuals or groups, sects or clans, but of the whole nation. It is a movement in which the prince and the pauper, men and women, boys and girls, Hindus and Musalmans, Christians, Parsis and Jews, Englishmen, Americans and Japanese, if they wish well to India and get rid of the spirit of exploitation, can also take part. Thus it is a unique movement. It is good not merely for some, not merely for a vast majority, but it is good for all. We may do many other and many more things during the forthcoming National Week. But let us at least organise Khadi. Here are the ways:

1. We can every one of us buy as much Khadi as we can.
2. We can sell as much Khadi as we can.
3. We can spin as much yarn as we can.
4. We can give as much as we can to the All-India Spinners' Association and collect from others.
5. Lastly, if we have the will and the opportunity, we can dedicate ourselves wholly to Khadi work.

As I write this, the question arises in my own mind: 'But what about the immediate present, what about the Bengal detenues who are pining away in their prison-cells without any knowledge of charges against them, without any trial and without knowing how long they are to be detained?' My answer however is quite clear. If I could think of any other more expeditious method of setting them free, I would adopt it and suggest it today; but there is not. Slow, as this may seem, it is, in my humble opinion, the surest and the quickest method Let those therefore who have belief in Khadi or who have no belief in anything else, do their best bit during the National Week. A true soldier does not argue, as he marches, how success is going to be ultimately achieved. But he is confident that if he only plays his humble part well, somehow or other the battle will be won. It is in that spirit that every one of us should act. It is not given to us to know the future. But it is given to every one of us to know how to do our own part well. Let us then do that which we know is possible for us if we only will.

10th February, 1927

NATIONAL LANGUAGE

BY M. K. GANDHI

In reply to my innocent paragraph about the evil habit of using English at our public meetings, a habit happily growing less day by day, a correspondent writes:

"........With very great respect for you may I ask in all humility, whether in the suggestion which you have made, you have given your considered thought? I might just refer you to the life of the man of the moment in China—Dr. Eugene Chen, a character sketch of whom has been reprinted in the *National Herald* of 31st January. I make no apology for quoting the following sentence: 'And this is a curious point; Sir Robert Bredon added that though Chen is one of the most ardent Nationalists in China, he can hardly speak a word of Chinese; English is the only language he knows properly.' Speaking for myself, I may say that I hail from a place where we are supposed to speak a sort of Tamil in our daily life and we are taught altogether a different vernacular in schools—Malayalam. The result naturally is that such people do not know written Tamil at all and are not very proficient in Malayalam either. If any of them were asked to address a meeting in any of these languages he will be able to satisfy neither the Tamilians nor the Malayalees.

"Rightly or wrongly, too much attention has been and will be given to English and this is as it should be. Because, if there is one common language in India which brings people even in different districts (let alone the provinces) together, and can make them understand each other, it is the English language. Although the Congress has been in existence for 41 years, no one has suggested seriously with any degree of success that India should have a common language other than English. Indeed, it would be impossible to effect this innovation in an already illiterate population. More so, when it is remembered that we cannot claim to have a Government national in character.

"Just as you say it would be an insult to inflict English on an audience composed of colliery workmen, I contend that to inflict any other language but English on an audience composed of people collected from various parts of India will be an affront to the latter. You will remember that the President of this year's Congress was in the first instance called upon to speak in Hindi. It was only his rare courage and his rarer wit that saved him from what looked to be a very embarrassing situation. Supposing the President addressed that body in his own vernacular, how many in the audience would have understood him? Or for the matter of that, how many of the delegates assembled would have sat through the whole speech? I have no doubt in my own mind what would have been the result. And yet, many speakers have made it a habit even on the Congress platform to resort to their own vernaculars without showing any respect for the susceptibilities of the audience not acquainted with the language So long therefore as a common Indian language suitable to India and Burma is not agreed upon, English is bound to be and will be the only medium of communication among the Indian people. Instead of therefore setting your face against the use of the English language, and until such time as a common language is evolved for India, a man situated in your position should not add to the existing difficulties of the people by calling upon them to learn altogether a different language.

"The question as to what language should be used in public meetings (as distinct from sectional meetings), must be settled once and for all. To-day we have the miserable spectacle of public meetings held in cosmopolitan cities like Bombay, Calcutta and Madras being addressed in more languages than one. My humble and considered opinion is that in all public meetings, the proceedings should be

> wholly in the English language. Much more so, in assemblies like the National Congress and other political and industrial conferences where delegates from various parts of the country assemble, it would be a gross insult if any language but English were used. . ...

I publish the letter because it reflects an attitude with which one has to reckon. The correspondent in his eagerness to defend his own laziness, for it is difficult otherwise to characterise his mentality, has missed the following fundamental facts: English is known hardly to one per cent. of the population. It will never be learnt by the masses and we have to reckon daily more and more with the masses in all our political transactions. The Congress every year has delegates and visitors the majority of whom do not know and understand English, and when it becomes a thoroughly democratic body, whose delegates are scavengers, cobblers, farmers, washermen, tailors and such others, there will be very few to know English. As against hardly one per cent. of the total population knowing English, over 60 per cent. of the total population of India at the present moment understand the ordinary rustic Hindustani. For an Indian it is any day infinitely easier to learn Hindustani than English. These are the facts, but the correspondent has overlooked them.

Moreover, in his zeal to make English the official language of the Congress, the correspondent has forgotten the agitation that has been going on in the Congress ever since its inception for a wider recognition of Hindustani as the common medium and that there is now already a resolution of the Congress making Hindustani the common medium. The correspondent seems to think that I decry the use of even learning English, which I have never done. That the English-speaking Indians have rendered immense service to the country nobody can deny, but unfortunately it is equally undeniable that further progress is being blocked by us English-speaking Indians refusing to learn the language of the masses and to work amongst them in accordance with methods best suited to them.

The instance given by the correspondent of Mr. Chen is beside the point. I do not know what he is doing, but I do know that he is not speaking to the Chinese masses through English. And all I have claimed is that at our mixed mass meetings where the language of the province will not be understood by all, if any other language is to be adopted, it must be Hindustani. Surely it is a proposition which does not admit of any challenge.

17th February, 1927

OUT OF NOTHING

BY M K. GANDHI

When one thinks of the immense possibility of the Charkha, it is surprising that its simple message is taking so long to become universal. 'Nothing comes out of nothing,' says a Latin proverb. But the Charkha would seem to falsify at least the letter of the proverb. For without destroying or replacing anything useful, it seeks to utilise the waste and idle hours of the nation.

This idleness, whether it be regarded as enforced or voluntary, is killing the very soul of the nation. The more I penetrate the villages, the greater is the shock delivered as I perceive the blank stare in the eyes of the villagers I meet. Having nothing else to do but to work as labourers side by side with their bullocks, they have become almost like them. It is a tragedy of the first magnitude that millions have ceased to use their hands as hands. Nature is revenging herself upon us with terrible effect for this criminal waste of the gift she has bestowed upon us human beings. We refuse to make full use of the gift. And it is the exquisite mechanism of the hands that among a few other things separates us from the beast. Millions of us use them merely as feet. The result is that she starves both the body and the mind.

The spinning wheel alone can stop this reckless waste. It

can do that now and without any extraordinary outlay of money or intelligence. Owing to this waste, we are living in a state almost of suspended animation. It can be revived if only every home is again turned into a spinning-mill and every village into a weaving mill. With it will at once revive the ancient rustic art and the rustic song. A semi-starved nation can have neither religion nor art nor organisation.

The only objection that has been urged by its critics is that the wheel does not pay. But even if it pays only one pice per day, it does pay when we remember that our average income is six pice per day against the fourteen rupees and six rupees per day respectively of the average American and the average Englishman. The spinning wheel is an attempt to produce something out of nothing. If we save sixty crores of rupees to the nation through the spinning wheel, as we certainly can, we add that vast amount to the national income. In the process we automatically organise our villages. And as almost the whole of the amount must be distributed amongst the poorest of the land, it becomes a scheme of just and nearly equal distribution of so much wealth. Add to this the immense moral value of such distribution and the case for the Charkha becomes irresistible.

17th February, 1927

A GREAT SPINNER

BY M. K. GANDHI

When at the end of the Bihar tour and on my way to the Central Provinces, I heard at Calcutta of the death of Babu Jogeshwar Chatterjee whom I had the privilege of knowing as a spinner who gave promise of being able to revive the old Dacca *shubnum*,— the night-dew muslin,—I at once sent a message to Kshitish Babu of Khadi Pratishthan to supply me with details of the deceased's life. These have been now received and I share them with the reader.

"Jogeshwar Chatterjee, son of Sjt. Jatileshwar Chatterjee of village Panpur in the district of 24—Parganas, was attacked with Cholera on Thursday, the 27th January and died on Sunday, the 30th January morning. He left behind him his wife, a daughter aged one year, a younger brother and aged father. His younger brother is employed in the E. B. Railway.

"Jogeshwar Babu read up to B. A., and was a teacher for some time. He then took service in the E. B. R., and served it for seven years at Kanchrapara Executive Engineer's office. He was aged 35 at the time of death.

"He took to spinning during the Non-co-operation days, and was an ardent spinner. He came in close touch with the Pratishthan when he handed over his 60 count yarn to the Pratishthan for weaving in 1924. The cotton of this yarn was grown in his garden. The cloth woven out of this yarn was presented by him to Gandhiji, and Gandhiji handed over same to the Pratishthan for show. He showed his speed and high count spinning (100 count) at the Cawnpore Exhibition in 1925, and 200 count spinning at the last Gauhati Exhibition in December 1926 The Khadi Pratishthan arranged both these spinning demonstrations. During Pratishthan's annual Puja Exhibition at the Mirzapur Park he used to show his skill. At the Gauhati Exhibition a muslin of 200 counts was exhibited by the Pratishthan the yarn of which was spun by Jogeswar Babu, During one year—Cawnpore Exhibition to Gauhati Exhibition—he spun 200 count yarn for the above muslin, and sufficient yarn of 100 count, out of which 2 dhoties are made Of the last 2 dhoties, one was for Acharyya P. C. Ray and the other for his father.

"On his return from Gauhati and at the request of Satish Babu he was spinning 300 counts yarn. He was all along spinning on the Pratishthan's Box Charkha. He was out and out a Khadi-man, who used to spin during leisure hours, and made such a rapid progress in spinning,"

I tender my condolences to the family of the deceased and hope that the attempt to reproduce the ancient art will not die with Jogesh Babu's death. Let it be remembered that Jogesh Babu's was a labour of patriotic love. And it is only voluntary spinners who can follow up Jogesh Babu's grand effort.

24th February, 1927

HONOURABLE COMPROMISE

BY M. K. GANDHI

Sir Mahomed Habibullah and his colleagues are to be congratulated upon having secured a settlement that is honourable to both parties. It is not the best that could be conceived, but it is the best that was possible. I doubt if any other deputation could have done more. The Class Areas Bill, which brought about the Conference and round which the battle raged, is dead and gone. The Right Hon. Srinivasa Sastri, who when the deputation sailed for South Africa was of all members the most communicative, and had warned us not to expect much, did not conceal at the end of the labours of the Conference his satisfaction at the result. A perusal of the settlement warrants the satisfaction.

But like all compromises this one is not without its danger points. The dropping of the Class Areas Bill is balanced by repatriation, re-emerging as re-emigration. If the name is more dignified, it is also more dangerous. Repatriation could only be to India. Re-emigration can be to any country. The following sentence in the settlement clearly points to that interpretation :—'The Union Government therefore will organise a scheme of assisted emigration to India or other countries where Western standards are not required.' This assisted emigration to other countries I hold to be dangerous, for there is no knowing what may happen to the poor ignorant men going to an unknown land, where they would be utter strangers. Such countries as would take them would only be either Fiji or British Guiana. Neither has a good name in India. It is decidedly a disadvantage to have been party to assisted emigration to any other part of the world.

The good point about this assisted emigration is that whereas before the settlement the repatriates lost their domicile, the re-emigrants now retain it and lose it only if they absent themselves so long as to warrant the inference that there is no intention on their part to return to South Africa. How many assisted emigrants can hope to refund the assistance in money they might have received or how many can hope to return with their families is a different question. The non-forfeiture clause is clearly designed not so much to guarantee a substantial right as not to hurt national self-respect.

The annexure, containing a summary of 'conclusions reached by the Round Table Conference on the Indian question in South Africa', is a remarkable document betraying in every paragraph a heroic attempt to reconcile conflicting interests and sentiments. The industrious reader will have no difficulty in discovering hopeful paragraphs. I shall therefore content myself with drawing attention to a paragraph that is fraught with grave danger. The Union Government is 'to take special steps under the Public Health Act for an investigation into the sanitary and housing conditions in and around Durban, which will include the question of the limitation of sale of municipal lands subject to restrictive conditions.' I do not know what is aimed at in this paragraph, but my suspecting mind—and my suspicion is based upon previous bitter experience of interpretations, warranted and unwarranted, that a strong party places upon agreements with a weak party to the latter's disadvantage —conjures up all kinds of frightful consequences arising from this proposed committee and limitation. Already the Durban Corporation has been invested with powers which it has utilised for the suppression of its Indian citizens. So far as I know a committee can bring to light nothing that is not known to the Corporation or the Government. The appointment of an advisory committee of Indians may be simple padding. The Health Committee may bring in a hysterical report, as a previous committee to my knowledge has done, and limitations may be put upon the purchase of municipal lands by Indians which may cramp the Indian community residing in Durban. Nor do I like the paragraph which seems to imply that provincial Governments are at liberty to take any action they might against the Indian settlers without reference to the Central Government.

But the compromise is acceptable in spite of the dangers referred to by me, not so much for what has been actually achieved as for the almost sudden transformation of the atmosphere in South Africa from one of remorseless hostility towards Indians to that of a generous toleration and from complete social ostracism to that of admission of Indians to social functions. Mr. Andrews sends me a glowing account of the utmost cordiality with which the Indian members of the Deputation were received alike by the Government and the people, how local Indians were able to gain entry to the most fashionable hotel in Cape Town without any let or hindrance and how the Europeans in South Africa were flocking to him to know all about the Indian deputation and the Indian question. If this atmosphere of good-will and sociability is kept up and encouraged, the settlement can be used as a solid foundation for erecting a beautiful temple of freedom for the Indian settlers in South Africa. But the success of the settlement very largely depends upon the selection of the Consul or the Commissioner who will be selected to represent the Government of India. He must be a person of eminence, great ability and great strength of character, and in my opinion, he must be an Indian. The very fact of his being an Indian will strike the imagination of the European population and raise the Indian settlers in European estimation. He will reach the heart of Indians in a way no Englishman, not even perhaps Mr. Andrews, can, and if a man can be selected who will command the equal esteem of the Union Government we need not fear the future. Such a man in my humble opinion is Mr. Srinivasa Sastri. I cannot conclude this hasty survey of the settlement without placing on record my deepest conviction that the happy result is predominantly due to the ceaseless and prayerful labours of that godly self-effacing Englishman, Charlie Andrews.

24th February, 1927

NOTES

A Simple Suggestion

During my tour I observe that at some of the meetings volunteers thoughtlessly begin distribution of papers, such as copies of addresses etc, just after the guest has arrived and the address has begun to be read They do not realise that this creates a fresh disturbance in already noisy and restless meetings. If papers are to be distributed, they should always be distributed before the proceedings commence. It is not even realised that if papers are distributed, they should be distributed to all who want them. In mass meetings such distribution is impossible unless thousands of copies are available. In my opinion this would mean an utterly useless waste of public money Whatever is absolutely necessary will surely be printed by local papers and the public should be satisfied with what the papers give. If they are unable to follow the proceedings without the papers it would not be a bad plan to sell such papers when there would be no question of favouritism All those who wish to possess copies can have them for a trifling charge to cover printing expenses and a small addition so as to form a contribution, however small, to the expense of organising meetings.

Stewards of the Nation

Much trouble, time and money can be saved by a little forethought. As it is, I often notice a reckless waste of public funds in connection with these meetings. Let organisers of all meetings, but especially of Khadi meetings, realise that we are the poorest country in the world, millions of whom are semi-starved, if only because their earnings are less even than three pice per day. Let organisers, therefore, understand as stewards for the nation it is their duty to spend public funds like misers and never to spend a pie without thought and without necessity. Organisers of Khadi meetings should further realise that every pice collected is a pice meant for the starving millions and so one pice means often a day's earning for a widow. They must not therefore spend where they need not. For instance, they spend money in paper decorations. This is no time for decorations. Let them save as much as they can by avoiding all decorations save only those which may be required to attract people's attention. In that case they can think of several artistic things which cost nothing or very little. Thus they can have flags and buntings out of waste Khaddar. We are now going in for extensive tailoring in connection with Khaddar sales. There is always much waste material in a tailor's shop which he throws away. Now every part of this waste can be used for buntings which unlike paper buntings can be preserved for further use.

Write your Addresses

Flowers may be avoided altogether and yarn garlands may be presented. Yarn must not be damaged by being tied into knots. It can be presented in its natural condition so that it can be subsequently used for weaving or any similar purpose. Money can also be saved by avoiding the printing of addresses. The best calligraphist among the organisers can write out the address on simple hand-made paper and the paper can be nicely sewn on to a piece of Khaddar, or if a little volunteer boy or girl would embroider the letters on a piece of Khaddar it would be still better, the thread for embroidery too being hand-spun. Such work will be at once artistic and even valuable. I have stolen the idea from the remarkable way in which Babu Mahendra Prasad's daughter Rama had embroidered for her father the

7

address presented by the Chapra municipality of which he is chairman. It costs the municipality nothing and I have become possessor of a work of art which will adorn the museum which Adhyapak Malkani has brought into being in the Gujarat National College.

Avoid Silver Caskets

Expensive caskets are not required, for I have no use for them, nor have I any room to keep them in. Latterly I have been putting to auction every expensive casket received by me and handing the proceeds to the All-India Deshabandhu Memorial Fund. Although these auctions have invariably proved profitable in that they have fetched much more than their intrinsic value it will not be proper to present caskets for the purpose of securing fancy prices. It will be a good exercise for organisers if they must give their Khaddar addresses in caskets to find out something cheap, local and artistic.

Not a Pleasure Trip

Well has Gangadharrao said that mine is not a pleasure trip, but a business tour during which I expect to do substantial business for my principal *Daridranarayan.* Every function therefore should be in fitting with that setting. I have observed that often more local men travel with me than are necessary for the purpose of the mission and that motor cars are hired without due regard to economy. Every item of expenditure should be previously and carefully thought out. Unless we do so we shall not raise into being an efficient economical organisation calculated to serve the starving millions and we shall be guilty of the same charge, no matter on however small a scale, of extravagance that we legitimately bring against the Government. Kitson burners should be avoided whenever possible. I notice, too, a lavish expenditure on feeding. Those who travel with me do not do so to be entertained. It is enough to provide clean lodging and clean food. Indeed I often feel like copying for the whole of my company the excellent example of Mr. Bharucha who always insists on carrying his own food with him. We spend much, too much, money and time upon food. It grieves me to see people sending for parcels of fruit from Bombay or Calcutta. Much of this expense is wholly unnecessary. Some fruit is no doubt an essential part of my dietary and unless obtainable locally, something has no doubt to be imported. But I am sure that the expense incurred in bringing fruit can at least be reduced by 75 per cent. 'But', argue over-zealous friends, 'why should not people who love you express their regard in some such loving acts of service? They will not spend money otherwise, nor will they give you all the money that they spend for your personal comfort. Let them therefore have the joy of spending some little money for you.' The argument is no doubt flattering but wholly unconvincing.

Transmutation into Service

If those who love cannot transfer this love to the thing for which I stand, their love is blind and of little value. I do not know if one should live to provide mere enjoyment for friends. Friendship means loving mutual service, and sometimes it is a positive disservice to indulge one's friends and to expose them to temptations. And if there are friends who would spend lavishly for providing luxuries for me, but would not spend for the cause I espouse, it is my clear duty to resist such luxuries. Friends to be friends must first provide me with necessaries of life before they think of indulging me with luxuries, and Khaddar work is a vital necessary of life for me, more vital than food. Reception Committees please note.

Auction of Garlands

The foregoing paragraphs were written, or rather dictated at the halts before we reached Ahmednagar at which latter place, there was an imposing meeting, where there were several addresses presented, the Municipal address being in a beautiful silver cylinder. The representatives of each body brought also expensive flower garlands. Mr. Firodia who presented the inevitable purse excused himself for its smallness by saying that Ahmednagar was a famine-ridden tract. When therefore

I began my reply, I could not help noticing the contrast between the palatial surroundings, the expensive ceremonial, and the statement of famine conditions. I told the audience that what was true of Ahmednagar was true of the whole of India. Was not India a famine-ridden land? But the fact did not prevent accumulation of wealth on the part of a few. We, the city-dwellers, lived upon the exploitation of the famine-stricken villagers and the Khaddar movement was intended somewhat to redress the wrong and to make some slight return to the millions whom we were exploiting. I therefore suggested that the acknowledgment of the fact that Ahmednagar was a famine area made it doubly the duty of its well-to-do citizens to give more rather than less. I told them also that it would ill-become me to accept for myself such caskets and rich floral tributes. I told them further that believing as I did that plants were as much endowed with life as we were ourselves I did not like the unnecessary plucking of a single flower. But in a place like Ahmednagar my dislike was heightened by the reminder that I was self-chosen representative of the very famine-stricken millions whom Mr. Firodia had mentioned. Every rupee spent upon unnecessary things meant a deprivation of the livelihood of 16 famishing women and I therefore suggested that they should auction the silver casket as also the flowers and if my remarks went home they would pay not the market value of the casket and the flowers but they would pay for the sentiment that the things would carry with them. The auctioning was entrusted naturally to the Chairman of the Municipality, Khan Bahadur Dorabseth. The casket was knocked down to Seth Magniramji the local philanthropist for Rs. 1,001 and the garlands and the bouquets were auctioned separately under the same able management and they fetched in all Rs. 502. The result of my appeal went beyond the meeting and the citizens seemed to catch the spirit of my address to them, and the purse of Rs. 1,700 for which Mr. Firodia had apologised went to nearly Rs. 6000 apart from a brisk sale of Khadi at the meeting. Future organisers beware!

I warn them that they need not present me with flowers and rich caskets, but if they do I shall assume that they are presented for the purpose of being auctioned and in order that their contribution to the poor people's fund may be substantially increased.

Tilak Swaraj Fund

During the Maharashtra tour at one or two meetings I was asked what had become of the crore collected for Tilak Swaraj Fund. The questioners had every right to put this question even though they might not have contributed a pie to the fund. A public fund becomes public property and therefore every member of the public is entitled to know in detail the administration of such funds. I therefore answered the question fairly exhaustively. The gist of my answer will bear repetition although the question has been answered in these pages already.

The accounts have been published regularly by the All-India Congress Committee. Copies of the audited account can be had at any time from the Congress Secretaries or the Treasurers. Every pie has been accounted for. There is no doubt that in some instances those to whom funds were entrusted were not faithful to the trust, but that is as much as to say that the Congress like all human institutions is an imperfect body having in its fold all sorts of men. I know of no institution in the world which does not have dishonest agents The Congress is no exception. But I can say this that no loss has been sustained beyond what a most careful merchant suffers. The little loss that had been sustained is due not to negligence, but has occurred in spite of vigilant inspection and auditing. It should be further borne in mind that the Congress has had in Pandit Jawaharlal Nehru and in Seth Jamnalal Bajaj an incorruptible working Secretary and an incorruptible working Treasurer respectively. Moreover 75 per cent. of the funds were administered locally by local representatives who had assisted in raising the funds and who were trusted by the people. Lastly, the largest amounts were mostly earmarked and controlled by the donors, subject no doubt to the conditions that they were to be used only for purposes coming within the programme of Non-co-operation and the accounts were to be open to inspection by Congress agents. Personally, I have absolutely no regret about having raised the Fund and my conscience is clear as to its administration. Everything that was humanly possible to guard against fraud, maladministration or misappropriation was done. The Fund has served an immense national purpose. The tremendous organisation that came into being all of a sudden could not have been created without this great national fund to which both rich and poor contributed so handsomely.

3rd March, 1927

IS INDIA PROHIBITIONIST?

BY M. K. GANDHI

An English friend who is anxious to undertake prohibition work for India writes:

> "I know that what every one will say to me is that the Indians themselves have shown no overpowering desire for Prohibition and that as *they* have not organised any movement for this, it is interference on our part to move in the matter. Moreover of all the Councils only one or two have declared for Prohibition. Already people are saying this to me. I always point them to the Non-co-operation move ment when the volunteers picketed the liquor shops. But when they say that was five years ago and they have shown no great enthusiasm lately, what is the answer?"

The puzzle the friend asks me to solve is not new. The question is bound to occur to one who does not know the history of the total prohibition movement in India. And a stranger coming in our midst is bound to ask himself, 'If India wants total prohibition, why does she not agitate or it as she does for many other things ? One observes that people do not agitate when they feel absolutely helpless. It is our helplessness which prevents us from agitating beyond having resolutions by temperance societies and sometimes petitions to the Legislative bodies. The cry for Swaraj came out of a realisation of growing helplessness in matters of paramount importance to our well-being. Take the military expenditure. Every one recognises that much of it is a criminal waste of money collected from the starving millions. Instead of agitating for reduction in military expenditure, we agitate for Swaraj, the argument being that nothing is possible without Swaraj. Who can say that there is no great deal of truth in the argument? When in 1920 we felt that we were getting Swaraj, we took the law into our own hands, we successfully picketed the liquor shop and the Government was frightened to notice an immediate fall in the liquor revenue. Liquor dealers trembled in their shoes and for a moment it appeared as if the drink evil had gone. Unfortunately the party of non-violence had not attained sufficient control over the people. Violence broke out. It was discovered that pickets did not everywhere carry out the instructions to create a blockade without resort to violence or threats to use it. The picketing had therefore to be suspended.

But the history of 1920-21 shows in unmistakable terms what India would do if she had the power and what she did do when she thought that she had it. Let it be further borne in mind that millions of Indians are tee-totallers by religion and by habit. Millions therefore cannot possibly be interested in keeping up the nefarious liquor traffic. Thus in so far as it can be said that there is no agitation in India in favour of total prohibition, absence of agitation is due not to want of desire on the part of the people to secure total prohibition, but it is due to a consciousness of helplessness and to the certain knowledge that it is an integral part of the struggle for Swaraj.

The very fact that it is necessary for any Englishman to defend liquor revenue on the ground that there is no agitation among us for total prohibition, makes out an irresistible case for Swaraj. For, it shows utter ignorance of Indian condition where the opinion is honestly held. There is no agitation on the part of the people against malaria and scores of other diseases. Is that any reason for taking no measures for eradicating malaria and other diseases? In order to deal with a known evil, no agitation should be necessary for taking prompt measures. The drink and the drug evil is in many respects infinitely worse than the evil caused by malaria and the like; for, whilst the latter only injures the body, the former saps both body and soul. The drink revenue, military expenditure, and the Lancashire exploitation of India through its calico, constitute the threefold wrong done by British rule to India. When Englishmen realise that it is sinful to trade upon the drink habit of the poor labourers of India, that it is sinful to dump down English and other foreign calico on the Indian soil when India's starving millions can easily produce during their spare hours all the cloth needed for her requirements, and when they realise that it is sinful to impose a terrific military burden upon India under the ostensible purpose of defending her borders but in reality for the sake of holding her people under subjection against their will, it would be a complete demonstration of change of heart, and co-operation on a basis of absolute equality will become a real possiblity. The only agitation therefore that India can carry on is to end the system which makes these wrongs possible, which is the same thing as saying that the agitation for Swaraj is the agitation for the removal of these wrongs. This removal is the acid test, in my opinion, of English sincerity.

3rd March, 1927

THE ARGUMENT OF INDIVIDUAL LIBERTY

BY C. RAJAGOPALACHAR

The cry of the richer classes in Europe and America for freedom to get exhilaration and "happiness" from liquor is not a plea for freedom of the individual, but is a cruel exhibition of selfish indifference to the welfare of the poor. "We can afford to pay and get intoxicated. Why should we give up this privilege? Let there be liquor in the land," say the opulent few. But the poor cannot afford to be tempted. To them it does not merely mean a little expense or drowning one's cares in the evening at the club; it means ruin and desolation of home and hearth. The rich man can choose when to drink and when not, and even if he is gone complete, it does not much matter to his wife and children. The estate keeps them and the servants look after them. But miserable wretches in the lower strata of society cannot stop when once they begin drowning their cares in strong drink. More and more, and every day, the devil takes them along, for their cares cannot be drowned easily; they are too, too many for moderate doses to drown. Liquor means destruction to the poor. Can the rich few claim that for the sake of their occasional indulgence in artificial "happiness," the poor must have always a deadly temptation wherever they go? Prohibition in America is yet struggling to get full enforcement. But even if the rich can pay fancy prices for smuggled liquor, the poor who cannot indulge in such a game are saved.

Then there is the argument of medical opinion in favour of Alcohol. A large and eminent body of medical experts have pronounced against the use of Alcohol. But no Prohibitionist need deny that Alcohol like other poisons may sometimes be used by the medical man with good effect. That is why every possible exception is made in Prohibition laws for the use of Alcohol upon medical men's prescriptions. This has no bearing on the argument for or against Prohibition.

There cannot be a more disingenuous argument than the oft-repeated plea of the liquor interests that Prohibition has bred contempt for law in America and that consequently the interests of the constitution demand a repeal of Prohibition. Those very people who want to nullify Prohibition and force a repeal of it, organise and encourage disobedience and evasion of the law and shed crocodile tears, about the spirit of lawlessness, that has been engendered by the new law. They seek to get reversal of the law by making it impossible to enforce it. Every minority in a democracy can, if they like, put forth such efforts as the defeated *wets* have done in America, and try to make government impossible. In the beginning a mere spirit of adventure may induce some men to disobey, and place themselves in the service of the scheming interests that seek to carry their point by sheer lawlessness. But after a time, when vigorous enforcement has proved the futility of such efforts, the misguided victims will realise the error of their allying themselves with interests obviously selfish.

The whole of the Anti-Prohibition talk of respect for law is a ridiculous plea of lawless people that to save the laws from being broken by themselves and to make them law-abiding the laws should be repealed. Their concern for the decreasing respect for law among citizens as a result of their being deprived of liquor is as ridiculous as disingenuous.

10th March, 1927

UNTOUCHABILITY, WOMEN AND SWARAJ

By M. K. Gandhi

I gladly publish Suhasini Devi's letter* which the reader will find in another column. Whilst the versatile President of the Congress is well able to defend himself, I am inclined to think that my fair correspondent has over-generalised from her own very brief experience. No statistics are needed to demonstrate the vast strides that the movement for the removal of untouchability has made. The barrier is breaking down everywhere. The higher classes are to be met with in every province ministering to the wants of the suppressed classes in the shape of conducting schools and boarding houses for their children. It was this phenomenon that the President evidently had in mind when he made the reference in his address.

* Omitted in this collection

There is however infinitely more yet to be done than has been already accomplished.

The question of breaking down the feminine prejudice is most difficult. It is in reality a question of female education. And in this it is a question not merely of education of girls but it is one of the education of married women. I have therefore repeatedly suggested that every patriotic husband should become the wife's own teacher and prepare her for work among her less fortunate sisters, I have also drawn attention to the implications of the suggestion. One of them is for husbands to cease to treat their wives as objects of their enjoyment but to regard them as co-partners in their work of nation-building. We cannot have Rama without Sita. And Sita got her real schooling under the gentle care of her partner during those terrible years of exile and probation. Well, we are all exiles in our own land and need to imitate Rama and Sita to the best of our abilities and opportunity. And in this connection, I cannot help drawing Suhasini Devi's attention to the fact that Sjt. Iyengar has not only broken down the barrier of untouchability for himself but has carried his wife and family too with him in the reform which perhaps he himself would have thought impossible only ten years ago.

The question of inter-dining must be kept distinct from that of untouchability. Exclusion in culinary matters permeates the whole of Hindu society. To confuse it with untouchability is to retard the progress of the latter movement which is aimed at removing the ban on the social service to which the so called untouchable has as much right as any other human being and on the same terms as the others receive it.

There is, too, confusion regarding Swaraj. The term Swaraj has many meanings. When Sjt. Iyengar says that removal of untouchability has nothing to do with Swaraj, I presume he means that its existence can be no hindrance to constitutional advance. It can surely have nothing to do with dyarchy or greater and effective powers being given the legislatures. Removal of untouchability is a social question to be handled by Hindus. Why should it prevent the Musalman and the Parsi in common with the Hindu from having the power to regulate the military expenditure, to determine the ratio or to achieve total prohibition or to impose a prohibitive tariff on foreign cloth and protecting the indigenous industries? Real organic Swaraj is a different question. That freedom which is associated with the term Swaraj in the popular mind is no doubt unattainable without not only the removal of untouchability and the promotion of heart unity between the different sections but also without removing many other social evils that can be easily named. That inward growth which must never stop we have come to understand by the comprehensive term Swaraj. And that Swaraj cannot be had so long as walls of prejudice, passion and superstition continue to stifle the growth of that stately oak.

10th March, 1927

WANTED WORKERS

By M. K. Gandhi

One hears loose talk about village organisation, about work in the villages. Paper schemes also for village organisation are now and again presented to the country and sometimes elegantly printed and often indifferently written. When questioned the authors tell us frankly that they have not tried their schemes, they have not got the resources, or the time or the inclination; but they think, that any idea that occurs to them they are in duty bound to put before the country, however ill-digested or impracticable it might be. Some of the authors get angry when they find that their schemes do not even get a start. But there is one scheme which has been now before the country for some years and which its authors have tried to work first individually, then collectively and which is now being worked through an ever growing organisation called the All-India Spinners' Association. The Spinning programme which has been demonstrated to be comparatively a success can be indefinitely extended if workers of the right type can be had.

During the Maharashtra tour, I have been taken to villages where there is almost continuous famine and where people are supposed to be without enough work and without enough to eat. Some of the villages are deserted for six or eight months during the year. The villagers go to Bombay, work under unhealthy and often immoral conditions, then return to their villages during the rainy season bringing with them corruption, drunkenness and disease. If the right type of workers go to these villages with the message of the wheel and with a patience that will not be exhausted and a faith that will not be moved, not one of the villagers need leave their homes. For it is not merely the wages earned by the spinners that are to be counted but it is the whole reconstruction that follows in the wake of the spinning wheel. The village weaver, the village dyer, the village washerman, the village blacksmith, the village carpenter, all and many others will then find themselves reinstated in their ancient dignity, as is already happening wherever the spinning wheel has gained a footing.

Who then can become a village worker? For the work that is required of him each worker should have a thorough knowledge both theoretical and practical of the science of spinning; he should therefore know the different varieties of cotton; he should know the method of picking cotton suitable for handspinning. For mill-spinning cotton is picked anyhow. For hand-spinning if cotton is properly picked it will save an immense amount of labour and yarn also will be stronger. He should know how to gin and should know the varieties of hand-gins used in Indian villages. He should know carding bows in use. He should be able to tell the different staples of cotton and should be able to spin a given number of counts. He should be able to test the strength and evenness and counts of yarn. He should know a good Charkha from a bad one and should be able to put dilapidated Charkhas under repair. He should be able to straighten an incorrect spindle.

If the worker is to live a model life in his village, he must know also the laws of civic sanitation and provide an object lesson in sanitation to the villagers. He should know the domestic treatment of diseases of daily occurrence. He should know simple accountancy Above all he must lead a pure and chaste life, if he is to make his mark amongst the villagers and gain their confidence. Naturally, a village worker must find happiness in a simple and frugal life. Let no one think that I have sketched what is an impossible requirement. I have not. The technique though it reads formidable is by no means so for a patient student. Purity of character must be a foregone conclusion in any of this work. And no village worker can help falling a prey to some disease or other if he does not know and observe in his own person the laws of sanitation and does not know domestic treatment of simple diseases. The spinning organisation is capable of accommodating any number of workers who can satisfy the simple test laid down above.

10th March, 1927

BURMA AND CEYLON

By M K. Gandhi

In reply to a correspondent, Gandhiji writes:

I have been to Burma and know that part of the world sufficiently to enable me to answer with confidence the question put by the correspondent. I cannot say the same thing of Ceylon, which, in spite of my desire, I have not yet been able to visit. I have no doubt in my mind that Burma cannot form part of India under Swaraj. British India is an artificial description reminding us of foreign, that is, British domination and therefore its boundary is contracted or expanded at the will of those who hold us in bondage. Free India will be an organic whole and will include those only who desire to remain as its free citizens. Therefore free India will have its geographical, ethnic and cultural limits. A free India will, therefore, recognise the differences in race and culture of the Burmese, and while it will extend the hand of fellowship and help to the Burmese nation, it will recognise its right to complete independence and help it to regain and retain it in so far as it lies in India's power. Needless to say that therefore in my scheme there is no demand upon the Burmese to learn Hindi or Hindustani. I expect those who are within the real Indian border to learn Hindustani* because they are the children of a common land and heirs to a common culture and are bound together by various other considerations and their provincial dialects contain so many common words.

About Ceylon I cannot speak with equal confidence. Although we have a common culture with Ceylon and although it is predominantly inhabited by Indians from the South, it is a separate entity. And as I have no imperial aspirations for India of my imagination, I should be content to regard Ceylon as an absolutely independent state; but I should not hesitate to accept Ceylon as part of free India if the Islanders express their wish to be so in an unmistakable language.

10th March, 1927

TWO SPEECHES

I summarise the speeches at Sholapur and Gulburga. As at Nasik the speech at Sholapur was a reply to questions and criticisms made in an open letter addressed to Gandhiji by some people from the town. Their first criticism was that those who appeared in Khadi on the occasion of Gandhiji's visit were hypocrites inasmuch as they would shelve it the day he left. Did that indicate the progress of Khadi?

"Well," said Gandhiji with gusto, "I do not know. I know that I am selling Khadi wherever I go, and there ends my work. Supposing you purchase from me millions of rupees worth of Khadi and sink it into the sea, the sale is not vitiated. But the criticism is unfair. I know that some wear Khadi for the occasion, but they do not disguise the fact. They appreciate the message of Khadi, but they say they cannot exclusively wear it for a number of reasons. Am I to tell them 'You are no good. I can do without your Khadi?' No, no. My duty is to define our *dharma* in its fulness. Their duty is to follow it as much as they can. People deceive me, you say: I do not understand how they can harm me even if they do. I am but a self-appointed agent of *Daridranarayan* and I shall take from you only what you can give me."

The other question was practically the same as was put at Nasik. "'You are good enough,' they say, 'but your work has ruined the country." I am but an erring mortal and like any one of you I am full of short-comings; therefore, I beseech you to reject them and simply make the best of my capacity for service. Turn my good points to account and reject the bad ones. If you do not pick and choose and simply reject me wholesale, what will the world say to you? Will you regret the service of a man as a carrier because he is blind?

"As I said at Nasik I fail to understand the *shuddhi, tabligh* and proselytisation as they are carried on today. I cannot understand a man changing the religion of his forefathers at the instance of another. But that is my personal conviction. No one need stop *shuddhi, tabligh* or proselytisation at my instance. My own duty is clear. I must go on purifying myself and hoping that only thereby would I react on my surroundings. It is my unshakable conviction that penance and self-purification are the only means for the protection of Hinduism. Do any amount of *Sangathan*, only let not that Sangathan be of the evil forces, let it be only of the forces of good."

Again in this speech he referred to the usual charge made against him of partiality for the Musalmans, and gave, if possible, a more vigorous answer: "You say I am partial to the Musalmans. So be it, though the Musalmans do not admit it. But my religion will not suffer by even an iota by reason of my partiality. I shall have to answer my God and my Maker if I give any one less than his due, but I am sure that He will bless me if He knows that I gave some one more than his due. I ask you to understand me. If my hand or heart has done anything more than was anyone's due, you should be proud of it, rather than deplore it. It should be a matter of pride to you as Hindus to think that there was amongst you at least one mad Gandhi who was not only just to the Musalmans, but even went out of his way in giving them more than their due. Hinduism is replete with instances of tolerance, sacrifice and forgiveness. Think of the sacrifice of the Pandavas, think of the forgiveness of Yudhishthira. Should it be a matter for sorrow for you, that there is at least one man who has tried to carry out the precept of Hinduism to the letter?"

But these to him were nothing before the charge of hypocrisy of the so-called followers which was more serious, and he concluded the speech with a fervent appeal to them: "If there is anything in the charge that you are wearing Khadi just to please me, and for show, I say for God's sake do not do so. I am not a Mahatma. If I am one, the Mahatmaship is but the expression of some Shakti. Pray do nothing for my sake. I shuddered when some one proposed that though I was silent I should exhibit myself for *darshan*. I assure you the words *darshan* and *Mahatma* stink in my nostrils. I am unworthy of giving *darshan*. Even like you I am a vessel of clay, liable to all the affections and passions that flesh is heir to. How can I be fit to give you *darshan*? One and only one *darshan* is necessary, *viz*., that of the Nameless, formless, indefinable, absolute. Try if you can to see Him everywhere, in a poor man's hut as in a palace, in a latrine as well as in a temple. Have if you will the *darshan* of Khadi and visualise its immense potentialities. Dismiss the mortal frame called Gandhi from your mind. Its *darshan* will be of no avail."

The Gulburga speech was a more passionate outpouring

of the heart agony. Though no reference was made, either in the addresses given or the speeches made at the meeting, to the 'Gulburga gone mad' of 1924, the memory of it was not absent from any one's mind, not at any rate from Gandhiji's mind. In the course of a speech which must have thrilled both the Hindus and Musalmans gathered in the vast courtyard of the famous Sharana Basappa Temple which still bore the marks of the mob-fury of 1924, Gandhiji said:

"My heart burns with agony when I see young men dressed in foreign caps and clothes. It is surprising that they do not see that whilst the rupees that they spend on foreign caps are wasted, the annas that they need spend on Khadi caps all go to the pockets of the poor. The man who shuts his eyes to the poor of his land and seeks to befriend the poor of the world must be mad indeed. God will find him guilty of arrogating to himself His function. The Hindu who recites his *Gayatri* regularly and the Musalman who says his *namaaz* five times a day are doing so in vain, if they have no corner in their hearts for the poor of their land. This is the message I would leave with the Hindus and Musalmans of this place."

Turning to the Hindu-Muslim question he said: "Much as I would like to pour out my agony before you I know that it will be a cry in the wilderness. I, therefore daily, send out my prayer to God: 'Lord, do somehow deliver us from this conflagration.' But I should be untrue to my creed if as a believing and Satyagrahi Hindu I disguised from you the feelings within me. When I went into the temple I was shown the spot where the idol was removed and the *Nandi* was desecrated. I tell you the sight pained me. You may call me an idolator if you will. I see God everywhere and in everything. I tell you God would never approve of those acts of desecration. Whilst in Yerawada jail, I read Maulana Shibli's life of the Prophet, I also read *Usva-e-Sahaba* and can say that those who did the acts were wrong, that Islam never sanctions such things and they were guilty before God and man. When I heard of these things I was convinced that the matter had passed out of human hands. If there were men who devoted all their time and energy to the cause of Hindu-Muslim unity I at least was one of them, but when my efforts did not seem to bear any fruit I threw myself on God. When the saints and God-fearing people of Islam saw that there was discord and strife after the passing away of the Prophet, they dissociated themselves from them, migrated to Egypt, Persia and other lands and there retired into seclusion and sent up their prayers to God. It is these saints that have kept Islam alive. How often have I wished to retire thus into seclusion! And though I know that history will take note of my efforts as those of one who was a servant of God, who committed Himalayan blunders but who had also the courage to confess them and repent for them, I know that today I can do no better than be silent on this question.

"But if you will not listen to me in that matter, you certainly will not disdain to think of the millions of the poor amongst you. Do you know that many of the spinners in Bihar, Bengal and the Punjab out of the 50,000 spinners in India for whom the A. I. S. A. finds employment, are Musalmans? Have you read the heart-rending tales of woe of some of them? One of the workers in Gujarat asked a Musalman woman aged 65 as to why she bothered to spin when spinning brought her only an anna per day. She said the fact that there was some one to give her an anna in return for the yarn she spun convinced her that there surely must be God somewhere. Fight, therefore, as much as you wish, but when a man like me appeals for help, pray forget your quarrels and your hostilities and do something for the cause he pleads."

M. D.

17th March, 1927

MR. SPEAKER'S DONATION

It was not without regret that I had to withhold the pleasure from the readers of sharing the news contained in the following correspondence between Sjt. Vithalbhai Patel and myself,

I

Arya Bhawan, Sandhurst Road,
Bombay, 10th May, 1926.

Dear Mahatmaji,

When I accepted the office of President of the Legislative Assembly I had made a resolve within myself that I would devote the savings from my salary towards the furtherance of some object calculated to promote the national welfare. It was not possible for me, for various reasons, to save anything worth the name within the first six months, however I am glad to say that I am quite out of the wood, and can and do save a substantial amount. I find, that on an average, I require Rs. 2,000 per month for my expenses. The amount of my net salary excluding income tax is Rs. 3,625. I propose, therefore, to set apart Rs. 1,625 per month, beginning from the last month, to be utlised hereafter in such manner and for such purpose as you may approve. I have, of course, some ideas in the matter, and I will in due course discuss them with you. But whether you agree with me in those ideas or not, the amount is at your disposal. I enclose herewith a cheque for Rs. 1,625 from my salary for the month of April.

I trust you will not decline to take this responsibility.

I am,
Yours sincerely,
(Sd) V. J. Patel

II

"Sukhdale" Simla;
31st May, 1926.

My dear Mahatmaji,

I enclose herewith a cheque for Rs 4,325, Rs. 1,625 being my contribution from my salary for the month of May, and

Rs. 2,700 representing the balance I had in hand out of the amount of Rs. 3,200 actually collected for the purse of Rs. 5,000 which my colleagues of the Bombay Corporation had subscribed on the expiry of my term of office as President of the Corporation. I had already explained to you personally when I last met you at Sabarmati, why this balance, which in normal circumstances I had intended and announced to spend for such purposes of the Swaraj Party and the Bombay Municipal Nationalist Party, as I considered proper, I now propose to remit to you to be added to the fund to be started from my monthly contribution out of my salary.

Yours sincerely,
(Sd.) V. J. Patel

III

The Ashram,
Sabarmati, 25-7-26

Dear Vithalbhai,

I have your letters with cheques in all amounting to Rs. 7,575 being a portion of your three months' salary as the Speaker of the Assembly together with the balance of the purse of Rs. 5,000 presented to you. You have asked me to spend the amount for 'an object calculated to promote the national welfare in such manner as I may approve.' Since writing that letter, you have discussed with me personally your views about the use of your handsome donation. I have been taking myself as to what I should really do and I have finally come to the decision to let the amount accumulate for the present. And I am therefore depositing the money in the Agency account of the Ashram for six months certain so as to get a fair interest. And, as soon as party feeling has ceased, I propose to invite the co-operation of a few mutual friends and then in consultation with you and them to use the money for some commendable national purpose.

Meanwhile, I tender my congratulations for the generous spirit which has actuated you in parting with a large portion of your salary for a public object. Let me hope that your example will prove infectious.

Yours sincerely,
(Sd) M. K. Gandhi

IV

20 Akbar Road,
New Delhi 9th March, 1927.

My dear Mahatmaji,

I have decided, as you are already aware, to remit to you as before such amount as I think I can reasonably save every month from my salary for the purpose mentioned in my letter to you on the subject in the month of April last. I propose to continue this arrangement as far as possible during the whole period of my office as President of the Assembly.

I enclose herewith a cheque for Rs. 2,000 representing such savings till the end of February.

Yours sincerely,
(Sd.) V. J. Patel

The news was withheld at the express wish of Sjt. Vithalbhai Patel. He felt a delicacy about the announcement whilst the elections were pending. After the elections too I was unable to obtain his consent till last week. I would myself have encouraged the hesitancy, if public good had not demanded publicity. I know that Vithalbai desires his example to be copied. If for some reason or other salaries out of all proportion to Indian environment must be drawn, an adequate proportion of them may be set aside for some public good. I am aware that there are several highly salaried men who devote their income not for personal enjoyment but for public good. But they direct their use in any manner they choose. Vithalbhai desires to constitute of such donations a special fund and leave its administration in the hands of men of known standing. If the object is to be attained, the board of trustees should, whilst it ought to be completely national, be representative of as many parties as it is possible to bring at a common board. I, therefore, invite criticism and suggestion from those who approve of the plan. I have no desire to take sole charge of the funds or to use them only for the purposes to which my life is devoted. I know that I shall be best fulfilling the purpose of Vithalbhai's great gift by seeking the co-operation of as many as would help.

M. K. G.

17th March, 1927

NO AND YES

BY M. K. GANDHI

'Comrade' Saklatwala is dreadfully in earnest. His sincerity is transparent. His sacrifices are great. His passion for the poor is unquestioned. I have therefore given his fervent open appeal to me that close attention which that of a sincere patriot and humanitarian must command. But in spite of all my desire to say 'yes' to his appeal, I must say 'no' if I am to return sincerity for sincerity or if I am to act according to my faith. But I can say 'yes' to his appeal after my own fashion. For underneath his intense desire that I should co-operate with him on his terms, there is the emphatic implied condition that I must say 'yes' only if his argument satisfies my head and heart. A 'no' uttered from deepest conviction is better and greater than a 'yes' merely uttered to please, or what is worse, to avoid trouble.

In spite of all the desire to offer hearty co-operation, I find myself against a blind wall. His facts are fiction and his deductions based upon fiction are necessarily baseless. And where these facts are true, my whole energy is concentrated upon nullifying their (to me) poisonous results. I am sorry, but we do stand at opposite poles. There is however one great thing in common between us. Both claim to have the good of the country and humanity as our only goal. Though therefore we may for the moment seem to be going in opposite directions, I expect we shall meet some day. I promise to make ample amends when I discover my error. Meanwhile, however, my error, since I do not recognise it as such, must be my shield and my solace.

For unlike 'Comrade' Saklatwala, I do not believe that multiplication of wants and machinery contrived to supply them is taking the world a single step nearer its goal. 'Comrade' Saklatwala swears by the modern rush. I whole-heartedly detest this mad desire to destroy distance and time, to increase animal appetites and go to the ends of the earth in search of their satisfaction. If modern civilisation stands for all this, and I have understood it to do so, I call it satanic and with it the present system of Government, its best exponent. I distrust its schemes of amelioration of the lot of the poor, I distrust its currency reform, I distrust its army and navy. In the name of civilisation and its own safety this Government has continuously bled the masses, it has enslaved the people, it has bribed the powerful with distinctions and riches and it has sought to crush under the weight of its despotic regulations the liberty-loving patriots who would not be won over either by flattery or riches. I would destroy that system today, if I had the power. I would use the most deadly weapons, if I believed that they would destroy it. I refrain only because the use of such weapons would only perpetuate the system though it may destroy its present administrators. Those, who seek to destroy men rather than their manners, adopt the latter and become worse than those whom they destroy under the mistaken belief that the manners will die with the men. They do not know the root of the evil.

The movement of 1920 was designed to show that we could not reform the soul-less system by violent means, thus becoming soul-less ourselves, but we could do so only by not becoming victims of the system, *i.e.* by non-co-operation, by saying an emphatic 'no' to every advance made to entrap us into the nets spread by Satan.

That movement suffered a check but is not dead. My promise was conditional. The conditions were simple and easy. But they proved too difficult for those who took a leading part in the movement.

What 'Comrade' Saklatwala believes to be my error and failure I regard to be the expression of my strength and deep conviction. It may be an error but so long as my conviction that it is truth that abides, my very error must, as it does, sustain me. My retracing my steps at Bardoli, I hold, to be an act of wisdom and supreme service to the country. The Government is the weaker for that decision. It would have regained all lost position if I had persisted after Chauri Chaura in carrying out the terms of what was regarded as an ultimatum to the Vicerory.

My 'comrade' is wrong in saying that the South African movement was a failure. If it was, my whole life must be written down as a failure. And his invitation to me to enlist under his colours must be held to be meaningless. South Africa gave the start to my life's mission. Nor do I consider it to be wrong to have offered, during the late war, the services of my companions and myself, under my then convictions, as ambulance men.

This great M. P. is in a hurry. He disdains to study facts. Let me inform him that the Khadi movement is not on the wane. It did last year at least twenty times as much work as during 1920. It is now serving not less than 50,000 spinners in 1,500 villages besides weavers, washermen, printers, dyers and tailors.

Mr. Saklatwala asks what Khaddar stands for. Well, it stands for simplicity not shoddiness. It sits well on the shoulders of the poor and it can be made, as it was made in the days of yore, to adorn the bodies of the richest and the most artistic men and women. It is reviving ancient art and crafts. It does not seek to destroy all machinery but it does regulate its use and check its weedy growth. It uses machinery for the service of the poorest in their own cottages. The wheel is itself an exquisite piece of machinery.

Khaddar delivers the poor from the bonds of the rich and creates a moral and spiritual bond between the classes and the masses. It restores to the poor somewhat of what the rich have taken from them.

Khaddar does not displace a single cottage industry. On the contrary it is being daily recognised that it is becoming the centre of other village industries. Khaddar brings a ray of hope to the widow's broken up home.

But it does not prevent her from earning more if she can. It prevents no one from seeking a better occupation. Khaddar offers honourable employment to those in need of some. It utilises the idle hours of the nation. The esteemed comrade quotes with pride the work of those who offer more lucrative employment. Let him know that Khaddar does that automatically, It cannot put annas into the pockets of the poor without putting rupees into the pockets of some. Whereas those who begin their work in the cities, though they are no doubt doing good work, touch but the fringe of the question. Khaddar touches the very centre and therefore necessarily includes the rest.

But the whole of the impatient communist's letter concentrates itself upon the cities and thus ignores India and Indian conditions which are to be found only in her 700,000 villages. The half a dozen modern cities are an excrescence and serve at the present moment the evil purpose of draining the life-blood of the villages. Khaddar is an attempt to revise and reverse the process and establish a better relationship between the cities and the villages The cities with their insolent torts are a constant menace to the life and liberty of the villagers.

Khaddar has the greatest organising power in it because it has itself to be organised and because it affects all India. If Khaddar rained from heaven it would be a calamity. But as it can only be manufactured by the willing co-operation of starving millions and thousands of middle class men and women, its success means the best organisation conceivable along peaceful lines. If cooking had to be revived and required the same organisation, I should claim for it the same merit that I claim for Khaddar.

My communist comrade finds fault with my work among the labourers in Jamshedpur because I accepted an address in Jamshedpur not from the Tatas but from the employees. His disapprobation is due, I expect, to the fact that the late Mr. Ratan Tata was in the chair. Well, I am not ashamed of the honour. Mr. Tata appeared to me to be a humane and considerate employer. He readily granted, I think, all the prayers of the employees and I heard later that the agreement was being honourably kept. I do ask and receive donations for my work from the rich as well as the poor. The former gladly give me their donations. This is no personal triumph. It is the triumph of non-violence which I endeavour to represent, be it ever so inadequately. It is to me a matter of perennial satisfaction that I retain generally the affection and the trust of those whose principles and policies I oppose. The South Africans gave me personally their confidence and extended their friendship. In spite of my denunciation of British policy and system I enjoy the affection of thousands of Englishmen and women, and in spite of unqualified condemnation of modern materialistic civilisation, the circle of European and American friends is ever widening. It is again a triumph of non-violence.

Lastly about labour in the cities. Let there be no misunderstanding. I am not opposed to organisation of labour, but, as in everything else, I want its organisation along Indian lines, or if you will, my lines. I am doing it. The Indian labourer knows it instinctively. I do not regard capital to be the enemy of labour. I hold their co-ordination to be perfectly possible. The organisation of labour that I undertook in South Africa, Champaran or Ahmedabad was in no spirit of hostility to the capitalists. The resistance in each case and to the extent it was thought necessary was wholly successful. My ideal is equal distribution, but so far as I can see, it is not to be realised. I therefore work for equitable distribution. This I seek to attain through Khaddar. And since its attainment must sterilise British exploitation at its centre, it is calculated to purify the British connection. Hence in that sense Khaddar leads to Swaraj.

The Mahatma I must leave to his fate. Though a non-co-operator I shall gladly subscribe to a bill to make it criminal for anybody to call me Mahatma and to touch my feet. Where I can impose the law myself, *i.e.*, at the Ashram, the practice is criminal.

17th March, 1927

THE RATNAGIRI SPEECH

After describing Ratnagiri as a place of pilgrimage for the whole of India, as it was Lokamanya's birth place, and after a feeling reference to Sjt. V. D. Savarkar, Gandhiji said:

"You know Lokamanya's Swaraj *Mantra*. I do not think there has been any follower of Lokamanya who has tried to carry out the *Mantra* more than I. There may be many whose efforts are equal to mine, but no one can claim to have put forth greater effort. For I know that not only is Swaraj our birthright, but that it is our sacred duty to win it. For in so far as we are removed from Swaraj we are removed from manhood. A proper manifestation of all our powers is impossible without Swaraj. And the Swaraj that Lokamanya had in view was not the Swaraj for Ratnagiri people or for Maharashtris, but for the whole of India, poor as well as rich, and Swaraj has no meaning for the poor unless they have enough to eat. Why should we not serve our mills, you ask. Seth Narottam Morarji, the owner of the Sholapur mills is a friend of mine, and I was the guest of his son who showered his affection on me. But does that mean that I must use cloth from the Sholapur mills and serve that 'poor' Seth Narottam and his son? Even they will not say that I would be serving the poor by using their cloth.

"I have been told everywhere Konkan is poor. If you are poor, the situation must be unbearable for you. You say that poor people from your parts go to Bombay and earn a living there. Do you know the price that they have to pay for that living? They live in hovels without light and air, a few feet by a few feet, where several men and women are huddled together without regard for their bodily cleanliness or decency. Are you ready to send your mothers and sisters to live under such conditions? Do you not agree that the women that go to the Bombay mills are your mothers and sisters and the men your brothers? Are you prepared to see your brothers and sisters take to a life of drunkenness and shame and return home and spread the infection of their vices? Is it worth while paying this terrible price for the eight annas they manage to earn there?

"Our cattle are destroyed because we do not know true cow protection and our villages are ruined because we do not know true economics and sociology. The Charkha can stop that ruinous process. Do you know the daily income per head of our country? Our economists say that it is one anna and six pies, though even that is misleading. If some one were to work out the average depth of a river as four feet from the fact that the river was six feet deep in certain places and two feet in others, and proceeded to ford it, would he not be drowned? That is how statistics mislead. The average income is worked out from the figures of the income of the poor man as also of the Viceroy and the millionaires. The actual income will therefore be hardly three pice per head. Now, if I supplement that income by even three pice with the help of the Charkha, am I not right in calling the Charkha my cow of plenty? Some people attribute superhuman powers to me, some say I have an extraordinary character. God alone knows what I am. It is also possible to disagree about the efficacy of Satyagraha, but I do not think there is any reason for disagreement on these obvious facts about the

Charkha. If some one convinces me today that there is no poverty in India, that there are few in India who starve for want of even a few pice a day, I shall own myself to have been mistaken and shall destroy the spinning wheel.

"I ask you therefore to bear in mind what you mean when you say that Konkan is poor. If you are really poor there is nothing like the wheel which can cure your impoverishment and which is a safeguard for the honour of your women. Seek ye first the Charkha and its concomitants and everything else will be added unto you. How can you disregard a thing which is of such a national and universal character? Does it behove the followers of Lokamanya to deride or reject the wheel?

"But you will ask, as a youth who sought to heckle me asked, 'If Lokamanya liked this thing, why did he not ask the country to take it up?' Well, I cannot be taken in by your question. Whether or not Lokamanya had Khadi in mind when he defined Swadeshi, surely his Swadeshi cannot but include Khadi. I am but the heir of Lokamanya, and if I do not add to the patrimony he has left me, I would not be a worthy son of a worthy father. I pondered well over Lokamanya's message, applied my many years' experience to it and came to the conclusion that Lokamanya's message must mean Khadi. Do you know what he used to do? I am telling you of an incident that happened a short time before his death. When Maulana Shaukatali approached him as regards the Khilafat question, Lokamanya said to him: 'I shall put my signature to whatever Gandhi signs, for I trust to his better knowledge in this matter.' Supposing therefore Lokamanya had not Khadi in mind when he advised Swadeshi, what does it matter? Supposing we were manufacturing spectacles here and some one were to say, 'We cannot use them, Lokamanya did not advise the use thereof,' would it be proper? We would dismiss him as a literalist, *Vedavadarata* as Gita would describe him. As the literalist interpreter of the Vedas, does not grasp the infinite meaning of the Vedas even so these literalist interpreters of Lokamanya's message miss its infinite power.

"But some one comes and says 'When Musalmans are converting us who is going to listen to your Khadi?' Have you, I ask, become so impotent that you will be Musalmans because some one compels you to embrace Islam? If you have true *Dharma* in you, no one dare violate it. But I want to protect even our *Dharma* by means of Khadi. For Khadi means the service not only of Hindu but of Musalman women. A Maulvi in Bengal went and asked some of those women not to spin on the ground that the Khadi movement was a Hindu movement. They listened to him for a couple of days, but the third day they came asking for cotton. For what could they do? They could not go on starving and the Maulvi had no food to offer them. The learned author of the Mahabharata has described Vishvamitra the sage as ready to eat what was forbidden to him and even to steal, when he was oppressed by the pangs of hunger. One cannot say what a hungry man or woman would not stoop to. I therefore tell you that you must take to Khadi if only to alleviate the poverty and safeguard the honour of your women.

"I am asked to take part in the *Shuddhi* movement. How can I, when I wish that its Muslim and Christian counterparts should also cease? It is unthinkable that a man will become good or attain salvation only if he embraces a particular religion,—Hinduism, Cristianity or Islam. Purity of character and salvation depend on the purity of heart. I therefore say to the Hindus, 'Do whatever you like, but don't ask a man like me, who has come to his conclusions after the maturest thinking, to take up what he cannot.' Man's capacity is after all limited. I can do what is within my power, not what is beyond it. I cannot do a hundred or even half a dozen things at a time. I would think myself blessed even if I can do one thing well at a time. If you agree with me that the Charkha is the best *Sangathan* that is possible, give me as much help as you can render."

24th March, 1927

KANGRI GURUKULA

By M. K. Gandhi

Kangri Gurukula was the body in which the soul of Shraddhanandji resided, no matter where its temporary earthly tabernacle wandered from time to time, and Shraddhanandji lives so long as the Gurukula lives. The best memorial therefore that can be erected to the memory of the deceased martyr is to perpetuate the Gurukula. No doubt the really permanent memorial will have to come through the character of the professor and the scholars of the Gurukula and through their determination to retain in it the predominance of ancient teaching and conduct based on it. Shraddhanandji used with ample justification to plead that his Gurukula was a national institution in the non-co-operation sense long before the birth of non-co-operation. He believed that to belong to a Government educational institution was to subscribe to the predominance of western influence whether we willed or no. He did not object to assimilate what was useful of the West on his own terms and in his own time. To be a fitting memorial of the Swami the Gurukula must, therefore, keep its complete independence of the Government. And it is a matter of no small satisfaction that the Gurukula in spite of its independence of Government aid or influence continues to grow in numbers as I hope too it does in character, in the spirit of its revered founder.

But if the memorial depends for its real existence ultimately on the character of the scholars and the professors it has to depend presently upon financial support from the public. Acharya Ramadeva has issued an appeal for three lacs of rupees. I understand that nearly two lacs are already subscribed. The scene I witnessed when the appeal was made in that huge pandal on the Gurukula ground on the 19th instant was a never-to-be-forgotten sight. People—men and women—vied with one another in pouring their rupees and notes into the buckets with which volunteers moved about among the visitors. There were hardly any coppers to be seen. I heartily commend this appeal to the attention of the public. I have stated my differences with the Arya Samaj and its doctrines. They abide. I have my differences about the conduct of Gurukulas. But I am not blind to the services of the Arya Samaj and the necessity of Gurukulas. They have revivified religion, if they have also limited its growth. Every reform has that tendency in it. The wise sift the good from the bad and conserve what is good. The Gurukula has much in it to conserve and those who would want it to be better than it is have but to prove their friendliness before they seek to introduce changes for its betterment. I have therefore no hesitation in identifying myself with the appeal for funds. There should be no delay or difficulty in making up the modest sum required.

24th March, 1927

SELF-CONTROL *

BY M. K. GANDHI

That the first edition was sold out practically within a week of its publication is a matter of joy to me. The correspondence that the series of articles collected in this volume has given rise to shows the need of such a publication. May those who have not made self-indulgence a religion, but who are struggling to regain lost self-control, which should under normal conditions be our natural state, find some help from a perusal of these pages. For their guidance the following instructions may prove useful:

1. Remember if you are married that your wife is your friend, companion and co-worker, not an instrument of sexual enjoyment.

* Foreword to the second edition of *Self-Restraint v. Self-Indulgence.* Price Re. 1.

2. Self-control is the law of your being. Therefore the sexual act can be performed only when both desire it and that too subject to rules which in their lucidity both may have agreed upon.

3. If you are unmarried you owe it to yourself, to society and to your future partner to keep yourself pure. If you cultivate this sense of loyalty, you will find it as an infallible protection against all temptation.

4. Think always of that unseen Power which though we may never see we all feel within us as watching and noting every impure thought and you will find that Power ever helping you.

5. Laws governing a life of self-restraint must be necessarily different from a life of self-indulgence. Therefore, you will regulate your society, your reading, your haunts of recreation and your food.

You will seek the society of the good and the pure.

You will resolutely refrain from reading passion-breeding novels and magazines and read the works that sustain humanity. You will make one book your constant companion for reference and guidance.

You will avoid theatres and cinemas. Recreation is where you may not dissipate yourself. You will, therefore, attend *Bhajan Mandalis* where the word and the tune uplift the soul.

You will eat not to satisfy your palate but your hunger. A self-indulgent man lives to eat; a self-restrained man eats to live. Therefore you will abstain from all irritating condiments, alcohol which excites the nerves, and narcotics which deaden the sense of right and wrong. You will regulate the quantity and times of your meals.

6. When your passions threaten to get the better of you go down on your knees and cry out to God for help. *Ramanama* is my infallible Help. As extraneous aid take a hip-bath *i. e.,* sit in a tub full of cold water with your legs out of it, and you will find your passions have immediately cooled. Sit in it for a few minutes unless you are weak and there is danger of a chill.

7. Take brisk walking exercise in the open air early in the morning and at night before going to bed.

8. 'Early to bed and early to rise, makes a man healthy, wealthy and wise,' is a sound proverb. 9 o'clock to bed and 4 o'clock to rise is a good rule. Go to bed on an empty stomach. Therefore your last meal must not be after 6 p. m.

9. Remember that man is a representative of God to serve all that lives and thus to express God's dignity and love. Let service be your sole joy and you will need no other enjoyment in life.

31st March, 1927

CONDITIONS OF COW-PROTECTION

By M. K. Gandhi

It has been a matter of sorrow for me to have taken up the burden of cow-protection during the ending years of my life. But there need be no sorrow when burdens come not of one's seeking but when they seek one irresistibly. And so has been for me the case with cow-protection.

Recently at Ghatkopar, Bombay, I had the occasion to visit the institution of the humanitarian society ably managed by its secretary, Sjt. Nagindas. It is now conducting an experiment in dairying with the laudable object ultimately of replacing the ill-managed and disease-breeding private dairies of Bombay which are situated in the heart of the city and where there is no exercise ground for the cattle, and where the best cattle are prematurely given to the butcher's knife.

But though the institution is ably managed, it has some inherent defects to which upon its invitation I had to draw the Society's attention. Incidentally, I ventured to lay down the conditions of cow-protection which are well-worth repeating:

1. Every such institution should be situated out in the open, where it is possible to have plenty, *i.e.*, thousands of

acres, of open ground capable of growing fodder and giving exercise to the cattle. If I had the management of all the *goshalas*, I should sell the majority of the present ones at handsome profits and buy suitable plots in the vicinity except where the existing places may be needed for mere receiving depots.

2. Every *goshala* should be turned into a model dairy and a model tannery. Every single head of dead cattle should be retained and scientifically treated and the hide, bones, entrails etc. should be used to the best advantage. I should regard the hide of dead cattle to be sacred and usable as distinguished from the hide and other parts of slaughtered cattle, which should be deemed to be unfit for human use or at least for Hindu use.

3. Urine and dung in many *goshalas* are thrown away. This I regard as criminal waste.

4. All *goshalas* should be managed under scientific supervision and guidance.

5. Properly managed, every *goshala* should be and can be made self-supporting, donations being used for its extension. The idea is never to make these institutions profit-making concerns, all profits being utilised towards buying maimed and disabled cattle and buying in the open market *all* cattle destined for the slaughter-house.

6 This consummation is impossible if the *goshalas* take in buffaloes, goats etc. So far as I can see, much as I would like it to be otherwise, not until the whole of India becomes vegetarian, can goats and sheep be saved from the butcher's knife. Buffaloes can be saved if we will not insist upon buffalo's milk and religiously avoid it in preference to cow's milk. In Bombay on the other hand, the practice is to take buffalo's milk *instead* of cow's milk. Physicians unanimously declare that cow's milk is medically superior to buffalo's milk and it is the opinion of dairy experts that cow's milk can by judicious management be made much richer than it is at present found to be. I hold that it is possible to save both the buffalo and the cow. The cow can be saved only if buffalo-

breeding is given up. The buffalo cannot be used for agricultural purposes on a wide scale. It is just possible to save the existing stock, if we will cease to breed it any further. It is no part of religion to breed buffaloes or for that matter cows. We breed for our own uses. It is cruelty to the cow as well as to the buffalo to breed the latter. Humanitarians should know that Hindu shepherds even at the present moment mercilessly kill young male buffaloes as they cannot profitably feed them. To save the cow and her progeny—and that only is a feasible proposition—the Hindus will forego profits from the trade concerning the cow and her products, but never otherwise. Religion to be true must satisfy what may be termed humanitarian economics, *i.e.*, where the income and the expenditure balance each other. The attainment of such economics is just possible with the cow and the cow only with the assistance of donations for some years from pious Hindus. It should be remembered that this great humanitarian attempt is being made in the face of a beef-eating world. Not till the whole world turns predominantly vegetarian is it possible to make any advance upon the limitations I have sought to describe. To succeed to that extent is to open the way, for future generations, to further effort. To overstep the limitation is to consign the cow for ever to the slaughter-house in addition to the buffalo and the other animals.

Hindus and the humanitarian societies in charge of *goshalas* and *pinjarapoles*, if they are wisely religious, will bear the foregoing conditions of cow-protection in mind and proceed immediately to give effect to them.

31st March, 1927

MACAULAY ON SWADESHI

At a time when 'Comrade' Sak is insisting upon Indians beginning their charity in Lancashire and not at home, giving the *ato* (flour) to the *Upadhyaya* leaving their own children to lick and lap the grinding mill, condemning their own selves to idleness and starvation in order to provide work and food to the British workman, the following from Macaulay's speech on the sugar duties delivered in 1845, which makes an admirable commentary on the Gita doctrine in

Sve Sve Karmanyabhirathah Samsiddhim Labhate Narah

will be read with interest:

'I say then, Sir, that I fully admit the paramount authority of moral obligations. But it is important that we should accurately understand the nature and extent of these obligations. We are clearly bound to wrong no man. Nay more, we are bound to regard all men with benevolence. But to every individual, and to every society, Providence hath assigned a sphere within which benevolence ought to be peculiarly active; and if an individual or a society neglects what lies within that sphere in order to attend to what lies without, the result is likely to be harm, and not good.

'It is thus in private life. We should not be justified in injuring a stranger in order to benefit ourselves or those who are dearest to us. Every stranger is entitled, by the laws of humanity, to claim from us certain reasonable good offices. Bu it is not true that we are bound to exert ourselves to serve a mere stranger as we are bound to exert ourselves to serve our own relations. A man would not be justified in subjecting his wife and children to disagreeble privations, in order to save even from utter ruin some foreigner whom he never saw. And if a man were so absurd and perverse as to starve his own family in order to relieve people with whom he had no acquaintance, there can be no doubt that his crazy charity would produce much more misery than happiness.

'It is the same with nations. No statesman ought to injure other countries in order to benefit his own country. No statesman ought to lose any fair opportunity of rendering to foreign nations such good offices as he can render without a breach of the duty which he owes to the society of which he is a member. But, after all, our country is our country, and has the first claim on our attention. There is nothing, I conceive, of narrow mindedness in this patriotism. I do not say that we ought to prefer the happiness of one particular society to the happiness of mankind; but I say, that by exerting oursevles to promote the happiness of the society with which we are most nearly connected, and with which we are best acquainted, we shall do more to promote the happiness of mankind, than by busying ourselves about matters which we do not fully understand and cannot efficiently control.' V. G. D.

31st March, 1927

THE BUGBEAR OF POLITICS

A friend writes to Gandhiji;

"In reply to a letter from me asking definitely if there is anything preventing Government servants from contributing to the Khaddar movement (Khadi fund) I am informed by the Chief Secretary to the Government of Madras in Memorandum No. 465-I of 17-2-1927, "that a Government servant may not subscribe in aid of any political movement in India or relating to Indian affairs." The balance of opinion, however, seems distinctly to be in favour of the view that the Khadi movement and the Khadi fund have nothing whatever to do with 'any political movement in India or relating to Indian affairs.' Still the matter being one of considerable public interest and considering also the fact that rightly or wrongly there lurks in the minds of many Government servants the suspicion whether after all there is not some thing political behind the Khadi movement, despite the assurances of Messrs. C. Rajagopalachari and Shankarlal Banker to the contrary, may I request you to take up the matter and demonstrate that, first and last, the Khadi movement is one of economics alone, in which both the Government and its servants are at liberty, or I may even say bound, to participate."

A similar question was asked the other day in the Assembly and elicited the same evasive reply as our friend got from the Chief Secretary There are some who are really in doubt whether Khadi partakes of a political character, whereas there are not wanting people who have made up their minds that it has ultimately a political bearing and therefore they should have none of it. Several missionary friends also asked Gandhiji the same question about Khadi and some of them promised their sympathy provided Gandhiji emphasised its humanitarian aspect. And at Kolhapur the Diwan also whilst expressing his sympathy added the condition that political use should not be made of it.

Let us briefly examine the question. What is political? Is compulsory primary education political? If not, why not? By sending the children compulsorily to school you reduce the illiteracy of the country, and pave the way for national or political consciousness. They will not read their *Navajivan* and *Young India*, not to talk of Burke and Mill and Tom Paine, unless they are educated. And the poison should be removed in the beginning if it is not to be allowed to spread further. But we know the Government is not opposed to primary education, and whenever there is compulsory primary education the law applies to the children of Government servants as much as to others. In spite therefore of its ultimately political bearing, there is no ban on primary education even in respect of Government servants.

Let us now take social reform, e g. prohibition of infant marriages, promotion of widow remarriages, removal of untouchability. Is there any doubt about the fact that the measures are calculated to weld each community, and through them the nation, together? And what is the end and aim of politics but the welding of a nation? And yet we have not heard any one say that Government is opposed to any one of these measures. In fact they have given their passive, and in some cases even active, sympathy in the mattter of the reforms.

Let us take Hindu Muslim unity. Is there any greater essential for the attainment of Swaraj than the complete realisation of Hindu Muslim unity? And yet in profession at least there is no greater advocate of Hindu Muslim unity than Government.

Then take temperance. The political effect of temperance is very well-known and though the Government are opposed to prohibition on the score of revenue there is no regulation prohibiting Government servants from refraining from drink.

Why then this evasive attitude about Khadi? Is it because apart from the ultimate result of the attainment of Swaraj, there is the immediate effect of every yard of Khadi hitting Lancashire to that extent? Then the fact of the whole matter is that Government object to Khadi not because it has a political bearing—for all other things in our programme have no less a political bearing—but because they have full concious-ness of the power of every yard of Khadi that is manufactured in India. In the matter of social reform, Hindu Muslim unity, and temperance, they can still rely on our indolence and vice, on our petty jealousies and narrow interests, and there is no immediate effect to fear from. In the matter of Khadi they cannot any longer rely on our indolence, if only because there are crores of hungry people who have to go without food for want of employment. So the politics, that is, the remote effect, of our social and economic reform does not matter to Government, it is the immediate effect that matters. How can we help it? Let not Government servants hesitate in such an obvious matter as this. Let them take courage in both their hands and challenge Government to do what they like. Spinning and wearing Khadi and contributing for it is as much their religious duty as social and sanitary reform, and no Government can be suffered to interfere with the performance of a religious duty.

M. D.

7th April, 1927

FULFIL THE WHOLE

Beginning with less than a lakh of rupees worth of Khaddar produced and sold in the year 1921, we have by now come to an annual production and sale of over 20 lakhs. And all the while there has been a very false impression among some people that Khaddar has been steadily losing ground. This is perhaps typical of the fate of all work of an intensive and quiet nature. More people use Khadi to day than its adversaries or even its votaries are aware of. The growing brotherhood and sisterhood linked by a frail handspun, if for the time being ill-spun, thread in the service of the poor millions is spread far and wide.

We have thoroughly succeeded in resuscitating in a measure the old spinning wheel. But what about the new? Go to the various villages in any province mentioned in the Khadi Guide and in the latest report of the All-India Spinners' Association and you will find that almost all the yarn that goes to make the Khaddar you wear is spun on ancient wheels dug out, so to say, from their very graves. A fifty-year-old wheel, at one time the Annapurna of the family, actively plying again after a long lapse with a repair or two by the rustic carpenter is a frequent sight good enough to cheer the optimistic and the pessimistic alike. Within a few months, for aught one knows, many of those wheels might have been broken up for fuel but for the timely heartening message which reached the sluggish ears of the peasant folk. It took painful years to organise. First the Khadi Board and then the centralised All-India Spinners' Association went through the heavy spadework of systematising the movement. But what about the new Charkhas, *i e.* what about raising new spinners and therefore what about self-spinners? This part of our undertaking seems to have flagged for the time being.

Much of the time of the limited number of workers at the disposal of the All-India Spinners' Association is absorbed in the villages where the resuscitated wheels have resumed work under already trained hands. There are of course notable instances of work in the new direction as in the case of Bardoli. But these are few and far between. Self-spinning or voluntary spinning connotes the ethical and sacramental side of spinning. It is essential to the abiding grace and moral effect of the movement. Have we slackened our efforts in that direction? It looks as though we have. Once the main object of helping to keep the wolf from the doors of the starving poor began in some small measure to be realised we naturally felt rewarded and pleased. Nothing, of course, has been lost thereby while everything has been gained. Let it just be recognised, if it is true, that voluntary or self-spinning has not received that attention of late which it did at one time. It is no easy thing to train bodies of peasant men and women who have never had anything to do with handicraft in systematic spinning. Yet it is these who must spin in their larger numbers before misery could be allayed and an appreciable degree of exclusion of foreign cloth brought about. That it is no impossible feat to introduce new wheels in homes where spinning has been traditionally unknown is proved by the few examples we have in many provinces of successful work of this character. With money forthcoming and honest workers giving themselves up for some time to the business, there is no doubt that wonderful strides could be made.

But nothing great may be expected so long as we the so-called higher classes neglect to set an example to the others by taking to voluntary spinning. The causes of the lack of proper effort are few and definite. The existing arrangements for teaching the art in different areas to those desirous of adopting it whether for the purpose of sacrificial spinning or self-spinning *i. e.* spinning for personal use, are inadequate. For the first two months or so the beginner meets with a variety of difficulties with his wheel which he need not be left unaided to solve. A good spinning teacher, who could teach carding as well, to be had within easy reach in as many centres as possible is a crying need. The fact that the Satyagrahashram, Sabarmati, is still approached for the supply of trifling Charkha accessories and even Charkhas from all parts of the country points to the necessity for better equipment in the various centres of the Spinners' Association. While carding should always go hand in hand with self-spinning, if the latter is to be given a fair trial good slivers should always be made easily available to voluntary spinners It lies mainly in the hands of individual initiative among Khadi workers to remedy these and other defects.

To look at the other side of the picture, there has been found very often a tendency among self-spinners to lose courage and ultimately abandon spinning because they find it difficult in the beginning Given a little more perseverance and proper instruments this trouble should not generally arise. Many continue spinning without attempting to improve their yarn. Still others spin perfunctorily. Spun yarn is often allowed to lie about and ultimately to get lost. In many cases the difficulty arises from an ignorance of certain elementary details in regard to yarn and its conversion into cloth. Very few have any idea, for instance, of the quantities of yarn of different counts required to make a substantial piece of cloth. The table on the next page may perhaps be useful in the matter. Many put their yarn away and do not attempt to get it woven because they think the quantity is too small or the quality too bad. By far the easiest solution of these difficulties is for every experienced voluntary spinner who has tided over the initial stages himself to make himself available by means of publicity if necessary to others in his neighbourhood for guidance and help.

It is by co-ordination and co-operation, a spirit of imparting as soon as possible to our neighbour every little bit of useful knowledge we possess that we shall be able to make an advance on the present position.

D. M. G.

7th April, 1927

WHAT SHALL I DO?

BY M. K. GANDHI

The Satyagraha Week is on us. By the time this appears in print one day of the precious week will have gone. I would urge the reader not to fritter away the week by asking the question, 'What shall *we* do?,' but to make the best possible use of it by asking, 'What shall *I* do?' There was a time when we could usefully ask and did ask the other question. And if each one will do his or her duty to the fullest measure possible, we shall soon be able to ask, What shall *we* do next?

The foundation of Satyagraha as of nation-building is undoubtedly self-purification, self-dedication, selflessness. Let each one ask oneself, How then can I purify myself in terms of the nation? Rectitude of private character is surely the beginning of the structure. If my private character is foul, I am like 'a sounding brass and tinkling cymbal.' If then I am not right inside, I must this very instant purge myself and be a fit vessel for dedication. Government cannot help me or interfere with me here. I must be the sole author of my making or undoing.

Having ensured a pure personal character I must ask the next question, What shall I do as a national servant? If a Hindu, if I hate the Musalman or a person of another faith, I must at once make an honourable peace with him. If I regard any single person as an untouchable, I must blot the sin from my heart and hug the one whom I have hitherto in my arrogance or ignorance regarded as untouchable and as a token I must render him some personal service, if it is only going to his quarters and collecting the children and playing with them. In these things again, I need no support from the Government and yet in doing these things wholeheartedly I have surely brought Swaraj nearer for the effort and rendered myself fitter for joint service whenever the occasion arises.

Is there a drink-shop near me? I must try to wean an erring brother from going to the house of his own destruction.

We began this work gloriously in 1921. Our violence brought it to an inglorious end. Individual effort in this matter is still possible even though the atmosphere for wholesale action is for the moment wanting.

And last but not least, I must do my share of spinning, if I have but faith in its capacity to serve the poorest, so graphically described in Markham's words reproduced in last week's *Young India*. I must hawk Khadi. If I have the power, I must induce my neighbour to spin for the sake of Daridra Narayan and if he or she wears foreign cloth, I must induce him or her to discard it.

This is by no means an exhaustive list. I have simply given an indication of the enormous possibilities of individual effort. Let each one find out for him or herself the best way of service during this week of privilege. The seeker will be amazed to discover in the search after individual action, the immense possibilities of silent, sustained and fruitful common action. Let not the immensity of a common programme daze or paralyse us. What is true of the individual will be to-morrow true of the whole nation if individuals will but refuse to lose heart and hope

---

14th April, 1927

FAITH *v* REASON

BY M. K. GANDHI

An M. B. B. S. from Mandalay sends a string of questions of which the first is:

> "You once expressed your opinion in the pages of *Young India* that faith begins where reason ends. Then I expect you will call it faith, if a person believes in a thing for which he can give no reasons. Is it not then clear that faith is believing unreasonably? Do you think it truth or justice if anybody believed in anything unreasonable? I think it is folly to believe in that way. I do not know

what your barrister mind will call it. If you think like me I hope you will call faith as nothing but folly."

If the worthy doctor will excuse my saying so, there is in his question a clear failure to understand my meaning. That which is beyond reason is surely not unreasonable. Unreasonable belief is blind faith and is often superstition. To ask anybody to believe without proof what is capable of proof would be unreasonable as for instance asking an intelligent person to believe without the proof that the sum of the angles of a triangle is equal to two right angles. But, for an experienced person to ask another to believe without being able to prove that there is God is humbly to confess his limitations and to ask another to accept in faith the statement of his experience. It is merely a question of that person's credibility. In ordinary matters of life we accept in faith the word of persons on whom we choose to rely although we are often cheated. Why may we not then in matters of life and death accept the testimony of sages all the world over that there is God and that He is to be seen by following Truth and Innocence (non-violence)? It is at least as reasonable for me to ask my correspondent to have that faith in this universal testimony as it would be for him to ask me to take his medicine in faith even though many a medicine-man might have failed me. I make bold to say that without faith this world would come to naught in a moment. True faith is appropriation of the reasoned experience of people whom we believe to have lived a life purified by prayer and penance. Belief, therefore, in prophets or incarnations who have lived in remote ages is not an idle superstition but a satisfaction of an inmost spiritual want. The formula, therefore, I have humbly suggested for guidance is rejection of every demand for faith where a matter is capable of present proof and unquestioned acceptance on faith of that which is itself incapable of proof except through personal experience.

The correspondent's next question is:

"In *Young India* for December 9, 1926, there appeared a press-cutting that one doctor Harold Blazer, who chloroformed his daughter because he felt that his own end was near and there was no one to care for her when he was gone, was fully acquitted. Dr. Blazer's counsel, Mr. Howry declared: 'Blazer did a right and moral thing by keeping the poor girl from becoming a charge on others.' To this you expressed your opinion that Dr. Blazer was wrong in taking the life of his daughter because it betrayed want of faith in the humanity of those round him and that there was no warrant for him to suppose that the daughter would not have been cared for by others. I would say that in expressing your opinion you have not pleaded like a pleader. I would request you to think over it again, for I think this is not an ordinary matter. For it is evident that you have got no scruples to put a useless burden on society simply because you have got enough faith in the society to shoulder the burden. For God's sake please excuse us from believing in that useless, nay, extremely harmful faith. Such a faith of yours, I sincerely believe, is very harmful to the best interests of India. Please see what did Dr. Blazer's counsel plead. He declared that Dr. Blazer did a right and moral thing by preventing the poor useless girl from becoming a burden on the society. The question whether the society would have cared for the child or not is beside the point. I would ask you one question: If after many more years of faithful service of India, you become blind, dumb and deaf, etc., or in other words become absolutely useless to society, will you like the society to feed you because you have got still life left in you or because you served so well? I do not know what curious ideas you have got about Ahimsa but my answer is quite clear. If I were quite useless for society even after many years of service, I should like to be killed rather than become a burden on society; for I reasonably believe that I shall be benefiting the society by being killed, thus removing the burden upon the society which I love. That it is the duty of society to care for all useful human beings and animals is quite a different thing."

I do believe that whilst the jury was right in acquitting, Dr. Blazer, considered from the strictly moral point of view, Dr. Blazer was wrong. My correspondent in his utilitarian zeal has overlooked the frightful consequences and implications of the doctrine he lays down. Indeed, his doctrine would belie his own profession. What would he say if a young practitioner chloroformed to death a patient, whom he, the junior practitioner, considered to be incurable and therefore a useless burden to society and whom another, as a senior, subsequently found to be a case quite capable of cure. Is it not the boast of medical science to treat no case as finally incurable? As for myself, well, I do expect my countrymen to support me when I become a useless and burdensome article, assuming, of course, that I shall still want to live. What is more, I have full faith in my countrymen supporting me if that event comes to pass. I wonder whether my correspondent will have all the lepers, the blind, the deaf, one fine night to be chloroformed to sweet everlasting sleep. And yet Damien was a leper and Milton was a blind poet. Man is not all body but he is something infinitely higher.

The correspondent's third question is:

"In the same article, *i.e.*, 'The greatest good of all,' you wrote, that a votary of Ahimsa cannot subscribe to the utilitarian formula. He will strive for the greatest good of all and die in the attempt to realise the ideal. He will therefore be willing to die so that the others may live. May I conclude then that you will prefer to be bitten by a poisonous snake and die rather than kill the same in trying to save yourself? If I am right in my conclusion, I think that in allowing yourself to be bitten by the snake rather than kill it, you will be committing the greatest sin I can ever think of. In that way you will be doing the greatest possible harm to India by trying to save a harmful living creature and by dying willingly in trying

10

to realise the ideal of your so-called greatest good of all. Is it not clear to you now? Will you not change your opinion now about benefiting all? I fear you will harm India in trying to benefit the whole world. You admit that you are an imperfect mortal. So it is impossible for you to benefit the whole of the world. It is even impossible for you to benefit the whole of India in all possible ways. Therefore it is quite reasonable to be contented with the greatest good of the greatest number, rather than pretend to do the greatest good to all without exception,——the good and the wicked, the useful and the useless, man, animal, etc. etc.".

This is a question I would fain avoid answering, not because of want of faith but because of want of courage. But I must not conceal my faith even though I may not have the courage to act up to it when it is put on its trial. Here then is my answer. I do not want to live at the cost of the life even of a snake, I should let him bite me to death rather than kill him. But it is likely that, if God puts me to that cruel test and permits a snake to assault me, I may not have the courage to die, but that the beast in me may assert itself and I may seek to kill the snake in defending this perishable body. I admit that my belief has not yet become so incarnate in me as to warrant my stating emphatically that I have shed all fear of snakes so as to befriend them as I would like to be able to. It is my implicit belief that snakes, tigers etc. are God's answer to the poisonous, wicked, evil thoughts that we harbour. Anna Kingsford saw in the streets of Paris tigers in men already taking shape. I believe that all life is one. Thoughts take definite forms. Tigers and snakes have kinship with us. They are a warning to us to avoid harbouring evil, wicked, lustful thoughts. If I want to rid the earth of venomous beasts and reptiles, I must rid myself of all venomous thoughts, I shall not do so if in my impatient ignorance and in my desire to prolong the existence of the body I seek to kill the so-called venomous beasts and reptiles. If in not seeking to defend myself against such noxious animals I die, I should die to rise again a better and a fuller man. With that faith in me how should I seek to kill a fellow-being in a snake? Bu this is philosophy. Let me pray and let my readers join in the prayer to God that He may give me the strength to live up to that philosophy. For philosophy without life corresponding is like a body without life.

I know that in this land of ours we have enough philosophy and but little life. But I know also that the laws governing the conduct of man have still to be explored and the condition of exploration is imperative and unalterable, We shall explore them only by dying, never by killing. We must become living embodiments of Truth and Love, for God is Truth and Love.

14th April, 1927

VOLUNTARY SPINNING

That spinning is an art, and no less useful an art than cooking, and even one of the fine arts, is known to those who have seen good spinners spin on good wheels. The ancients knew well its value and its utility. Even as the rice and cereals they grew in their fields were cooked in the homes, so also let the cotton similarly grown be spun in the homes, they had decided. The plan worked well. Every woman held spinning to be as essential a part of her daily work as cooking, and one came as naturally to her as the other. The mother who fed us also made clothes for us in the natural course of things, so long as matters of greater moment than the mode of dress and food absorbed the major portion of the time of our ancestors, and one individual had not begun as now to burden his body with cloth enough to cover five persons. When our requirements of cloth began to be measured by the size of our wardrobes the spinning wheel was thrown on the scrapheap. Spinning survived merely as a profession. As an occupation and recreation for leisure hours it has left its traces in Assam where a father cannot give away his daughter in marriage unless she knows spinning and weaving. It may be now a mere relic of the old tradition but none the less it exists. All, including many who demur to the idea generally, would like the women of India to know spinning if it were possible by a miracle. Spinning by itself is nice as an accomplishment, apart from anything else.

The lead has to come from men. Now that women have lost or are fast losing the art which came naturally to them at one time, men must help them to acquire it again. It is the men who took the initiative wherever voluntary spinning or self-spinning has made any headway. Here is a lesson for all those who would like their mothers and wives and sisters to spin. Spinning is an art and for the uninitiated it is no joke mastering it. In no household have women been known to have taken to it entirely independently of assistance. It is a superstition to suppose that spinning being traditionally a concern of the gentler sex, they are better able to pick it up. No, the inspiration and encouragement have to come from the other side. Therefore, to be helpful to the women we, the men, must acquire the art ourselves. With our help the women will learn and do it readily. Without it, what with the hundred little ailments the Charkha suffers from under inexperienced hands, they are apt to give it up as a bother, as indeed they have done in many cases. On the other hand there are cases of the type of Srimati Kamalamma of Andhradesha which forcibly illustrate the advantage of such help and encouragement. Her husband was a law student when she first attracted public attention three years ago by spinning the record count of 600. Without vigilant care and attention which he bestowed on the work she would have been handicapped. The cotton was carefully selected by him. The condition of the wheel was under his constant observation. In fact he all but spun for his wife. And last, yet not the least, it was the active personal interest he took that did it. So may it be with all young men who would have their wives spin. D. M. G.

14th April, 1927

THE SELF-SPINNER'S TABLE

One frequently meets such queries as "How much cloth would I get if I spun such and such a quantity of yarn?" "How much should I spin to make me a dhoti?" The table published in the last issue furnishes a reply in detail. The figures, based on the personal experience of experts, are representative of the conditions obtaining more or less in all the provinces. The reader will kindly read the following brief explanations along with the table:

1. These are the various counts or numbers representing the different thickness of yarn that are used all over the country. The higher the count the finer the yarn. Average Khaddar is not above 16 counts at present. It used to be 8 to 10 counts a few years ago. Khadi made out of yarn of 20 counts and above is used at present for *saris* and *dhotis* of superior quality.

2. If you know the number of threads that are placed side by side in an inch of width you are able to make your own calculation for any width you choose. As the present practice goes, these figures meet the requirements of close weaving and are supposed to be above the average in common Khaddar. Remember that the warp runs lengthwise and the weft crossways.

3. This gives you the number of warp threads to be used in a width of 50 inches. It has no reference to length which may be anything from zero upwards.

4. Column 3 multiplied by the number of yards wanted and then doubled so as to include the cross threads or the weft which, filling as it does the same amount of space as the warp in all fabrics, is the same quantity as the warp, gives the full length of yarn required. The present lengths indicate the quantity of yarn of the respective counts to make 50 yards of cloth of 50 inches width.

5. 21 yards of yarn of one count make a tola in weight.

Thus, any length divided by the count of the yarn multiplied by 21 gives the weight in tolas, or rupees. Observe that the weight drops as the count rises. Also that the cloth can be lighter or heavier as the threads per inch are less or more.

6. The price of cotton is never steady. But the figures given are by no means liberal.

7. This column exists in the table on sufferance. No self-spinning, *i.e.* spinning for one's personal or family requirements, is complete without carding being made part of it. To get slivers made by others is to get bad ones. If possible, carding is easier than spinning. With good practice you can in an hour card and roll into slivers enough cotton to last you on the Charkha for six hours. Home-made slivers are always better because you make them for yourself, while those which you buy you get after worry and delay and they can never approach home-made ones because somebody else made them for money.

8. This is according to the system in vogue in Gujarat. The weaver is paid 3 pies for every unit of 160 warp threads per yard. The system is scientific as the weaver is automatically the loser or gainer as the case may be according to the number of the threads he has to manipulate.

9. The table errs, if at all, on the side of overstatement. The total cost as given includes carding charges which the spinner will save by doing that part himself. But on the whole, taking into consideration a few incidental small recurring expenses the selfspinner is bound to incur for the present in the purchase of spindles and in repairs, very little reduction in the total cost may be expected. But in some provinces such as Bihar the cost may come to much less.

10. This is more for the daily spinner's ready reference. Remember that it is not one person who spins for the time stipulated but it is the Charkha that has to be kept busy for that period everyday on an average, no matter how many lend their hands.

11. Let every reader who is a self-spinner or wishes to be

one see if he can be tempted to try to turn out one *dhoti* or *sari* a month. Better still give it a fair trial without delay.

Many middle class families of two adults and two children do not require more than 50 yards of cloth per year for personal wear. Among others it is a single member who may require the whole quantity. The table is presented to both. If those who have the necessary plot of land will grow their own cotton, they will find that it is on the whole much easier than to have to buy any kind of cotton that is available in the bazaar. So much depends on the way the cotton is picked from the plants, that to do it oneself is to ensure the maximum good results all round, *i.e.* in carding, spinning and weaving and in enhancing the durability of the cloth, and the cost in the long run is reduced by half. The villagers in Bardoli and many other places do it today with absolute success.

But the self-spinner has no class high or low. He spins because he takes a pleasure in spinning and because he sees its importance, if not to himself so much, to the vast masses of the country. He spins in sympathy for the poor and takes pride in adding a yard of his own to the growing production of hand-spun cloth which is to be the serious rival of all foreign imported cloth in time to come. If he has a sister or a wife he will make her spin too. And ultimately the womanhood of India if they choose would be able to clothe the whole population as they did before without anybody else including Lancashire having to bother about it.

Figures after all are figures and the table can help no one to get the yarn if he does not exert himself. But it should be of value to the spinner who means business with his wheel and no camouflage.

Let the spinner keep in mind a few cardinal principles. Spinning to be easy must be learnt with diligence and perseverance. After a few days of regular struggle the hands and fingers get accustomed to the art and it is well for every beginner to give two to three hours daily until tolerable perfection is reached. Do not cast aside the wheel because you think it is out of order.

More often than not it is the spinner who has wearied and not the wheel that is out of order. When it does give trouble perhaps it wants oiling or ordinary adjusting. Don't send your yarn to the weaver bit by bit, because he always likes to have enough to make about ten yards or so and wastes less in bigger pieces. If you do not know how to get your yarn woven write to the All-India Spinners' Association or to any other Khadi concern.

Difficulties may also be referred to the writer care of *Young India.*

D. M. G.

21st April, 1927

TRUTH IS ONE

By M. K. Gandhi

A Polish professor writes:

"I am reading with intense joy your fascinating articles in *Young India* and wish to impress upon you the truth that they are the source of power not only for your own country but for the world. And as you have such a wide spiritual experience, may I ask you one question to be answered if possible in *Young India*? It is a very important fundamental question to which an answer from you would have a great value. Do you admit that there is in human thought some absolute certainty, as for instance as to God and prayer, where we might be said to have reached perfect unchangeable truth? Do you also confess that some particular experience led you to change your first opinion, for instance as to the right of killing certain dangerous animals? Now my fundamental question is, on what particular points do you change your opinion? And what guarantee can these changes leave as to the unshaken truth of what remains certain? How can we distingnish opportunistic change of opinion from the permanence of an absolute certainty in essentials? Can you define in what things we may change and what kind of things remain unchangeable? Is independence of each country or people one of those absolute truths, or is there some innate incapacity in some nations for self-government and in others an innate capacity for governing such incapable nations, as the Germans profess to have a capacity for governing other nations and thus justify their ruling ambition?"

I have taken the liberty of altering a word here and there in this letter for the purpose of making the writer's meaning clearer than it appears to be to me in the original. Without in any shape or form endorsing the claim to the powers that the writer ascribes to me, I would in all humility endeavour to answer his questions. My own conscious claim is very simple and emphatic. I am a humble but very earnest seeker after truth. And in my search, I take all fellow-seekers in uttermost confidence so that I may know my mistakes and correct them. I confess that I have often erred in my estimates and judgments. As for instance, whereas I thought from insufficient data that the people of Kheda were ready for civil disobedience, I suddenly discovered that I had committed a Himalayan miscalculation and saw that they could not offer civil disobedience inasmuch as they had not known what it was to tender willing obedience to laws which might be even considered irksome but not immoral. Immediately I made the discovery, I retraced my steps. A similar error of judgment was committed by me when I presented what has been described as the Bardoli ultimatum. I had then believed that the country, that is the people, had been awakened and touched by the movement, had understood the utility of non-violence. I discovered my error within twenty four hours of the delivery of the ultimatum and retraced my steps. And inasmuch as in every case I retraced my steps, no permanent harm was done. On the contrary, the fundamental truth of non-violence has been made infinitely more manifest than it ever has been, and the country has in no way been permanently injured.

But I am not aware of having changed my opinion about the necessity of killing certain dangerous animals in certain circumstances specifically mentioned in my articles. So far as I am aware of my own opinions, I have ever held the opinion expressed by me in those articles. That however does not mean that the opinion is unchangeable. I claim to have no infallible guidance or inspiration. So far as my experience goes, the claim to infallibility on the part of a human being would be untenable, seeing that inspiration too can come only to one who is free from the action of pairs of opposites, and it will be difficult to judge on a given occasion whether the claim to freedom from pairs of opposites is justified, The claim to infallibility would thus always be a most dangerous claim to make. This however does not leave us without any guidance whatsoever. The sum-total of the experience of the sages of the world is available to us and would be for all time to come. Moreover there are not many fundamental truths, but there is only one fundamental truth which is Truth itself, otherwise known as Non-violence. Finite human being shall never know in its fulness Truth and Love which is in itself infinite. But we do know enough for our guidance. We shall err, and sometimes grievously, in our application. But man is a self-governing being, and self-government necessarily includes the power as much to commit errors as to set them right as often as they are made. I do not know whether this will satisty my correspondent. But whether it does or not, I have no power in me to give him a more satisfactory answer. After all each one must be a law unto himself, the invariable condition being that he must then walk in the fear of God and therefore continually keep on purifying his heart. A man to be man must be twice-born as Hindus would say, reborn as Christians would say.

The concluding questions of the correspondent are easily answered. In fact, the answers can be inferred from the foregoing remarks. I do think that independence of each country is a truth in the same sense and to the same extent that independence of each man is. There is therefore no inherent incapacity for self-government in any country or nation and therefore no inherent capacity for governing other nations. No doubt my correspondent honestly thinks that Germans profess to have a god-given capacity for ruling over other nations. But if there are German imperialists, there are also humble German democrats, who are content if they can quietly govern themselves.

28th April, 1927

UNTOUCHABILITY AND UNREASON

By M. K. Gandhi

A correspondent from Mahad writes :

" It gives me much sorrow to let you know that there was a riot on the 20th of March last between touchables and untouchables at Mahad. There was held a conference of the Colaba District depressed classes on the 19th and 20th ultimo. The meeting was quite successful. But whilst the crowd was dispersing, Mr. A. V. Chitre of the Social Service League of Bombay told the people as they were thirsty and as the sun was very hot that they could go to the public tank and drink water. There were some who tried to dissuade the men from going to the tank. But Dr. Ambedkar, the president, decided to march the men to the tank. Even the police inspector could not feel the gravity of the situation, and instead of stopping the crowd from proceeding to the tank, went with them. The tank is situated in the midst of the Brahmin locality. As however no one was aware that the untouchables were going to the tank there was no disturbance, and hundreds of them quenched their thirst at the tank with cries of Hara Hara Mahadev. Meanwhile the touchables came to the scene and they watched the incident with rage. The crowd of untouchables then went back to the pandal for their meals. Within an hour of this the Mahad public was suddenly awakened by the wild cry *Gurava* and they were told that the untouchables were thinking of entering the temple of Vireshwar.

"It was a false cry: but in no time the temple was filled by an infuriated mob of touchables who had sticks in their hands. The poor untouchables had no intention whatsoever of going to the temple. But the touchables finding no untouchables attempting to enter the temple practically ran amuck, went to the bazar and began to beat any untouchable they came across in the street. All the while this beating was going on on the part of the touchables, not one untouchable offered any resistance. A few touchables, who sympathised with the untouchables, tried to protect them; but the furious mob would not be checked. They even rushed into the huts of shoe-makers and such others and beat them severely. The helpless untouchables ran wildly for help; but none was offered by the shopkeepers. The untouchables who were in the pandal were derided by the touchables for not coming out in the open to fight. There were nearly 1,500 of the former in the pandal and if they had offered to fight there would have been a great calamity and Hinduism would have been disgraced. Dr Ambedkar justified the advice that he had given on the strength of the resolution that was passed in the Bombay Legislative Council and on the opinion expressed by the Mahad Municipality that the untouchables were lawfully entitled to take water from public tanks and wells."

I have omitted from the correspondent's letter several passages giving further details. But the letter appears to me to be genuine and does not in any way appear to be an overestimate. Assuming then that the incident is correctly reported there can be no question about the unprovoked lawlessness on the part of the so-called higher classes. For, it should be remembered that it was not the drinking of water at the tank, which had brought together the 'touchables' to the temple, but the false report that the untouchables were wanting to enter the temple. But one can hardly expect sanity to exist side by side with unreason. Untouchability itself has no reason behind it. It is an inhuman institution. It is tottering and it is sought to be supported by the so-called orthodox party by sheer brute force.

The so-called untouchables have brought the question a step nearer solution by their exemplary self-restraint under most provoking circumstances. Had they retaliated, it would have been perhaps difficult to distribute the blame. As it is, the blame is all on the side of the 'touchables.' Brute force will not sustain untouchability. It will bring about a revulsion of feeling in favour of the suppressed classes. It is a sign of the times that there were at least some 'touchables' who tried to defend the poor untouchables. One could wish that there were many more in Mahad. Silent sympathy on such occasions is not of much use. Every Hindu, who considers the removal of untouchability to be of paramount importance, should on such occasions prove his sympathy by publicly defending the suppressed classes and having his own head broken in defending the helpless and the down-trodden.

I cannot help thinking that Dr. Ambedkar was fully justified in putting to test the resolutions of the Bombay Legislative Council and the Mahad Municipality by advising the so-called untouchables to go to the tank to quench their thirst. No incident of this character should pass by unnoticed on the part of associations like the Hindu Mahasabha interested in this reform. Let them investigate the statements made by my correspondent and if they can be substantiated, let them condemn the action of the 'touchables.' There is nothing like the growth of enlightened public opinion for eradicating everything evil, which untouchability undoubtedly is.

28th April, 1927

SASTRI AS FIRST AMBASSADOR

BY M. K. GANDHI

Very considerable relief will be felt by the Indian settlers in South Africa over the announcement that the Right Hon. V. S. Srinivasa Sastri has consented to become India's first Agent-general in that sub-continent, if the post is finally offered to him by the Government of India. It is a great sacrifice that Sastri and the Servants of India Society have made. It is an open secret that, left to himself, he was not inclined to undertake the responsibility and to leave his work in India. But he has yielded to the pressure of friends, especially when it was urged upon him that he alone could successfully inaugurate the working of the Agreement, in bringing about which, he played not an inconsiderable part. We know from the cables that were sent from time to time from South Africa that the Europeans were anxious that he should accept the honour. Sjt. Srinivasa Sastri had by his eloquence, transparent sincerity, sweet reasonableness, and extreme earnestness won the esteem and respect of the Union Government and the Europeans in South Africa during the short time that he was there as a member of the Habibullah deputation. I know how nervously anxious our countrymen in South Africa were that he should become the first Agent. It was impossible for Sjt. Srinivasa Sastri whom God has endowed with a generous nature not to respond to such a unanimous call from South Africa. It is almost a foregone conclusion that the appointment will be duly made and very shortly announced.

The first Agent-general will have his work cut out for him. Both the Union Government and our countrymen have no doubt high expectations of India's first ambassador. The Union Government no doubt think, that, being an Indian and a person of great distinction, he will make their path smooth with the Indian community in connection with any measures that they may take. In other words, they will expect him to be their sympathetic interpreter both to the Indian community and to the Government of India. Our countrymen equally surely expect him to insist upon an honourable and even a liberal interpretation and fulfilment of the Agreement. It is any time a delicate task to please rival claimants, more so now in south Africa where the clash of conflicting interests is simply bewildering. But I know that if anybody can hold the scales absolutely even and thus give satisfaction to all parties concerned, Sjt. Srinivasa Sastri is certainly the one to be able to do so. I feel certain that the Union Ministers do not expect the new Agent to surrender an inch of what is justly due to the Indian Community. All he can be expected to do is to persuade the Indian settlers not to go behind and travel beyond the settlement of 1914, for some time to come at any rate, until they have proved themselves entitled, by exemplary self-restraint and behaviour, to an enlargement of the position attained by the agreement of 1914.

Our countrymen in South Africa, if they intend to make the Agent's position fairly easy and their own position secure, will not expect him to work wonders. It will be wrong to look forward to a complete transformation of the old position, because an honourable agreement has been arrived at and because a great countryman is going to South Africa to see to the fulfilment of that agreement. They must remember that the Rt. Hon. Srinivasa Sastri is not going there as their counsel briefed to attend to every individual grievance. To smother him with detailed individual grievances would be to kill the goose that lays the golden eggs. He goes there as a trustee for India's honour. He goes there to safeguard the rights and liberty of the general body of Indian settlers. He will be there to see that no fresh restrictive legislation is embarked upon by the Union Government and that the existing restrictive laws are administered liberally and with due regard to the vested rights. Any individual grievance therefore that he might be called upon to tackle will have to be in terms of the position I have set forth, that is to say, it will have to be illustrative of some general principle of wide application. Unless therefore the Indian community exercises prudential restraint upon themselves in approaching him for redress of their individual grievances, they will make the Agent's position intolerable and even useless for the high purpose for which it is intended. Indeed such an ambassador's usefulness lies not so much in work appertaining to his official capacity as to the indirect service he can render by his sociableness, and by his character, which leaves its impress upon anything and anybody that it comes in contact with officially or otherwise. And if our countrymen desire to make use of the great qualities of head and heart that Sjt. Sastri possesses, they will bear in mind the limitations I have endeavoured to set forth.

I understand that if Sjt. Sastri goes, Mrs. Sastri too will accompany him. This will be a great gain to the settlers. Let the Indian sisters in South Africa gather round Mrs. Sastri and surround her with every affection. They will find in her an invaluable instrument of social service. She will act as a leaven in their midst to raise the general tone among the many thousand Indian sisters who are scattered throughout South Africa.

28th April, 1927

A TERRIBLE CONTRAST

BY M. K. GANDHI

A friend having for the first time seen New Delhi and the Assembly Hall in March last writes:

"I would like to draw your attention to a very important matter. It is this. I was the other day for the first time in the Assembly Hall and it was for the first time then that I saw New Delhi also. I could see how millions must have been poured into the construction of New Delhi to make it so imposing. The Assembly Hall too presents an equally imposing appearance. But as I came out of the

Assembly Hall, I saw dilapidated huts which turned out to be the labour camp where I thought must be living the coolies working at the construction of New Delhi. I went in and the sight of it caused me deep distress. I saw that the huts given to the poor labourers were practically unfit for human habitation. And these dilapidated structures were the place where, after a day's strenuous labours, these poor people were expected to retire for well-deserved rest. In some places the walls were made without any mortar, without any mud; simply bricks seemed to have been piled one upon another.

"The contrast between the palaces built in New Delhi for wealthy people and the miserable huts allotted to the people whose labour was responsible for the palaces was too terrible for contemplation. The cooly women seemed to be unconcerned. It was in the evening that I saw this labour camp and the women were returning from work. And as they went, they were singing. But my heart was weeping. How could the Government spend millions after the comforts of high-placed officials and monied men when the labourers themselves were so wretchedly housed? How, I thought to myself, could the members of the Assembly day after day miss the horrible contrast which I could see even during the few moments that I was in New Delhi? They talked of many big things; they brought forward many resolutions; could they not put in one word on behalf of the poor, dumb and ignorant labourers? Could they not imagine how the labourers could have passed terribly cold winter nights in New Delhi in their miserable huts? I have said nothing to any of the members: But could you not do anything in this matter? I have said nothing because I could influence no one; but you may think it worth while doing something. You are a friend of the poor and might be able to secure some relief. Any way I could not help disburdening myself to you."

I have summarised the main contents of the letter which my

fair correspondent has written in Hindi. The criminal disparity that exists between the condition of labour and that of capital is no new thing in modern times. The discovery made by the friend reminds one of the discovery said to have been made centuries ago by Gautama Buddha. It was no new thing he saw. But the shock received by the sight of old age, disease and other miseries of life transformed his life and materially affected the fortunes of the world. It is well that this lady has received her first shock. If she and the other cultured women of India, who have received their education at the expense of the very poor people of whom the correspondent writes so pathetically, will dive deeper and make some slight return to these poor people by making common cause with them, some alleviation in their distressful condition will not be long in coming. Every palace that one sees in India is a demonstration not of her riches but of the insolence of power that riches give to the few, who owe them to the miserably requited labours of the millions of the paupers of India. We have a Government which is based upon and which only exists by the exploitation of the toiling millions.

A friend sent me the other day a cutting from an English newspaper, which considered Rs. 1,500 for an Englishman to be not enough for his wants in India, and it warned Englishmen from venturing out to India if they could get not more than Rs. 1,500 per month. There is no need to quarrel with that standard. From the writer's own standpoint, Rs. 1,500 per month is demonstrably inadequate because he regards club life, a motor car, migration to a hill-station during the hot months, education of children in England to be the necessary minimum. All one can say and one must say about this standard is, that if it is the indispensable minimum, it is a standard too expensive for India to afford; and however beneficial in the abstract may the services of English officials be demonstrated to be, if the toiling millions are to live, they must get along without these beneficial services for the simple reason that the benefit is beyond the reach of their pockets. I suppose it is possible to demonstrate that if the millions of India could be translated to some bracing Himalayan plateau, they would be able to double the length of their days on earth. But it is a proposition which they will laugh out of court as beyond their reach.

What the lady observed in New Delhi is but a tiny symptom of an ever-growing and deep-seated disease which is daily destroying the lives of thousands of people. It is quite possible to imagine that, if an energetic member of the Assembly moved a resolution calling upon the Government to provide better housing accommodation for the labourers, the resolution would be carried, that it would not be vetoed and that the Government would gladly give effect to it at the expense of millions poorer still than these labourers. I am sure that this is not what the fair friend really desires. What she desires in common with every Indian, who knows anything of the country, is a radical change in the system of government, which is top-heavy and which under its intolerable weight is crushing day after day the poor inhabitants of this country who are groaning at the bottom. I have pointed the way out of this difficult situation times without number. I do not know another.

5th May, 1927

MAN'S INHUMANITY TO MAN

BY M. K. GANDHI

In another column* will be seen an extract from *Navajivan* of a most disgraceful case of calculated inhumanity of a medical man towards the dying wife of a member of the suppressed class in a Kathiawad village. Sjt. Amritlal Thakkar who is responsible for giving the details of the case has withheld the names of the place and the parties for fear of the poor suppressed class school-master being further molested by the medical man. I wish, however, that the names will be disclosed. Time must come when the suppressed class people will have to be encouraged by us to dare to suffer further hardships and

* See Page 64.

tyranny. Their sufferings are already too great for any further sufferings to be really felt. Public opinion cannot be roused over grievances that cannot be verified and traced to their sources. I do not know the rules of the Medical Council in Bombay. I know that in other places a medical practitioner, who refused to attend before his fees were paid, would be answerable to the Council and would be liable to have his name removed from the Council's list and be otherwise subject to disciplinary action. Fees are no doubt exactable; but proper attendance upon patients is the first duty of a medical practitioner. The real inhumanity, however, if the facts stated are true, consists in the practitioner refusing to enter the untouchable's quarters, refusing himself to see the patient, and refusing himself to apply the thermometer. And if the doctrine of untouchability can ever be applied in any circumstances, it is certainly applicable to this member of the profession which he has disgraced. But I am hoping that there is some exaggeration in the statement made by Sjt. Thakkar's correspondent and, if there is none, that the medical practioner will himself come forth and make ample amends to the society which he has so outraged by his inhuman conduct.

5th May, 1927

READ, REFLECT AND WEEP

There is a school for children of the suppressed classes in a village in Kathiawad. The teacher is a cultured, patriotic man belonging to the *Dhedh* or Weaver (untouchable) class. He owes his education to the compulsory education policy of His Highness the Gayakwad and has been doing his little bit for the amelioration of the community. He is a man of cleanly habits and refined manners, so that no one can recognise him as belonging to the untouchable class. But because he has had the fortune or misfortune of teaching the children of his own community in a conservative village in Kathiawad, every one regards him as an untouchable. But unmindful of that he has been silently working away. There are some moments, however, when the most patient man living under intolerable conditions may give vent to his agony and indignation, which are evident in the following letters from the school-master. Every little sentence in it is surcharged with pathos. I have purposely omitted the names of the village and all the people mentioned in the letter, lest the school-master should come into further trouble.

I Dated 9-4-'27

Namaskar. My wife was delivered of a child on the 5th instant. On the 7th she was taken ill, had motions, lost her speech, had hard breathing and swelling on the chest, and her ribs were aching painfully. I went to call in Dr.—, but he said: 'I will not come to the untouchables quarters. I will not examine her either.' Then I approached the Nagarsheth—and the Garasia Darbar—, and requested them to use their good offices for me. They came and on the Nagarsheth standing surety for me for the payment of Rs. 2 as the doctor's fee, and on condition that the patient would be brought outside the untouchables' quarters, he consented to come. He came, we took out the woman who had a baby only two days ago. Then the doctor gave his thermometer to a Musalman who gave it to me. I applied the thermometer and then returned it to the Musalman who gave it to the doctor. It was about eight o'clock, and having inspected the thermometer in the light of a lamp, he said: 'She has pneumonia and suffocation.' After this the doctor left and sent medicine. I got linseed from the market and we are applying linseed poultice and giving her the medicine. The doctor would not condescend to examine her, simply looked at her from a distance. Of course I gave Rs. 2 for his fee. It is a serious illness. Everything is in His hands.'

II

The light in my life has gone out. She passed away at 2 o'clock this afternoon.

Comment is needless. What shall one say about the inhumanity of the doctor who, being an educated man, refused to apply the thermometer except through the medium of a Musalman to purify it, and who treated an ailing woman lying in for two days worse than a dog or a cat? What shall one say of the society that tolerates this inhumanity? One can but reflect and weep.

(*Navajivan*) A. V. THAKKAR.

5th May, 1927

NATIONAL WEEK AT SABARMATI

There have been some striking achievements in spinning during National Week celebrations at Satyagrahashram which are worth recording. A band of young spinners at the Ashram makes it a point of honour to demonstrate on every possible occasion the fullest possibilities of the spinning wheel. In speed and efficiency, it is no exaggeration to say that they have led the way not only in the Ashram but perhaps in the whole country. Year after year these lads beat their own previous records. One among them stands head and shoulders above the rest. His achievements have all along perhaps been a wonderful testimony as much of his superior skill and courage as of the capacity of the wheel itself.

On the last day of the National Week many persons worked continuously at their wheels for a number of hours. Two spun full twenty four hours, not permitting themselves any stoppage whatever during the time. The amount of endurance this means may be seen from what one of them writes in a letter: "I began to lose courage in the eighth hour. The hands refused to work, my head reeled. Much against my will I left the wheel and lay down on my back; but I could get no peace. Suddenly the thought of the Jallianwalla Bagh, the anniversary of which we were celebrating, came to me and with it the picture of those that lay bleeding in the Bagh for over twelve hours untended. Then my fatigue left me and with a bound I was at the wheel again."

Here are the figures of the work of the best four of these young men:

Name	Total yards	Average per hour	Hours spun
1. Keshubhai	14,784	641	23
2. Kanti Parekh	12,880	536	24
3. Krishnadas	10,933	475	23
4. Kanti	5,761	523	11

In fairness to the other two, it must be said that Nos. 1 and 3 took assistance in reeling the yarn off their spindles which does mean a substantial advantage. All the four are good spinners, Keshubhai being the undisputed leader. It may be remembered that at the Cawnpore Congress competition he held his own against a formidable rival from Bengal in speed and won ultimately in points. The present is his own highest record which it is difficult to beat. For the first twelve hours, he maintained an average speed of over 665 yards per hour. And it is claimed, that had the quality of the slivers not deteriorated towards the end, he would easily have done much better. His rate began to fall after the twelfth hour. But later he was able to recover a great deal of lost ground by raising his speed up to 700 yards. It was a deep disappointment to him not to have finished 16,000 yards in 24 hours.

It is interesting to note that the quality of the yarn in all the four cases was found to be quite satisfactory, the counts ranging from 13 to 15, the strength from 67 to 70 per cent. and evenness from 79 to 93 per cent.

The Gurkha lady Shrimati Krishnamaiya Devi, who has been in the Ashram ever since her husband Dal Bahadur Giri s death, did 5,333 yards on the last day in 13 hours, at 408 yards per hour, the yarn being of 26 counts, 85 per cent. strength and 84 per cent. evenness, beating the above four in quality.

The spinning results for the whole week in the Ashram have also been remarkable. About 110 members in all participated in the spinning. Below are the figures for April 1926 and April 1927 for comparison:

	1927		1926	
	Total Yards	Daily Average per spinner	Total Yards	Daily Average per spinner
Adult men	2,54,630	589	2,49,943	640
" women	1,58,272	658	2,02,685	846
Youngsters	4,07,289	1,696	3,16,013	1,449
Children	5,59,945	624	47,032	465
	8,80,136	869	8,15,673	858

The youngsters easily take the palm with their daily average of 1696 yards per spinner. Most remarkable of all, however, is the achievement of Mani, a little girl of nine, who did 3,000 yards every day during the week.

The average speed in the Ashram is easily about 350 yards per hour. The average quantity spun by each spinner during the National Week was 869 yards per day. This means that 2½ hours were given to spinning each day on an average by those who were able to partake in the programme. The cloth value of the total quantity spun in the week is 342 yards of 36 inches width.

The Sabarmati Ashram has no monopoly of high speed or efficiency. Wherever any serious efforts have been made equally good results have been obtained. And this only points to the immense possibilities of the Charkha. In many places professional speed almost reaches the speed of the champion spinners of the Ashram. In Tiruchengodu, for instance, it has been calculated that the peasant-women spin at the rate of 500 yards per hour. A woman taking two pounds of cotton lint on a Saturday comes back with the yarn spun out of it on the following Saturday to receive her wages and to take the next week's supply of cotton. During the week she has spun not more than 40 hours, a good part of the rest of the time being devoted to household work besides cleaning and carding the

12th May, 1927

EVILS OF MACHINE MILLING

M. K. GANDHI

Mr. Andrews, who is working himself almost to death in the interest of the Indian settlers of South Africa, cannot forget things that he has at heart in India itself. Having read Mahadev Desai's account of the Bihar tour, he cabled sometime ago; "Tell Mahadev delighted accounts Bihar tour, give love Rajendraprasad, suggest your emphasising hand-milling. Have witnessed evils rice mills, including destruction of vitamins. Warn public against unauthorised cables from South Africa." The reader can see, that the foregoing cablegram was sent, in order that I may warn the public against accepting everything that comes from South Africa, unless it bears Andrews' own hallmark. But I hardly think that the caution is required. Naturally the public here will discount anything sensational that may come from South Africa, unless it is duly countersigned. But let us hope, that the Rt. Hon'ble Srinivasa Sastri will soon be on his way to South Africa, when all cause for alarm or anxiety will be set at rest. Without, therefore, dilating upon the South African part of the cable, I return to the rice mills, whose evils have distressed him so much as to prompt the cabling of his opinion. The reader will appreciate Andrews' anxiety when I inform him that he has to live whilst in India in the midst of rice mills. For whereas when he first went to Shantiniketan near Bolepur, there was no rice mill in Bolepur, at the present moment several such mills are working in that once quiet place. He often spoke to me about the din, the dust and the smoke and the fraudulent trafficking that has been going on in Bolepur since the advent of rice mills, and spoke also of the deprivation of a useful cottage industry by reason of the installation of these mills. There can be no doubt that hand-husked rice is infinitely superior to mill-husked rice. Medical men can, however, speak on the evil with greater authority than I can. The moral evil of those mills stares one in the face, as soon as one goes to places where these mills have found a place. In spite, however, of my knowledge of the evil of this growing destruction of cottage industries, had I not been bed-ridden, I should not have undertaken the task that Andrews out of his good nature and out of the abundance of love that he has for India suggests that I should do. For I regard myself as an economical worker fully cognisant of my own limitations. In trying to revive handspinning I feel that I am touching the root of the evil, that it is enough to occupy all my energy, and that if that movement becomes successful, as I am daily becoming more and more convinced that it will, the undoubted evils of rice mills, to which Andrews draws attention, and others which can be named will automatically disappear. Let us not make the mistake of thinking that what has happened in India about the spinning wheel, and what is now happenning about other cottage industries, such as hand-milling of rice, need cause no harm to national life, because such things have happened in the West without the West having come to grief. In the first place it is yet too early to say positively that the destruction of village life in the West has been either a benefit to it, or to mankind in general. In the second place, and this is more pertinent, assuming that the new life that has come into being in the West is calculated to benefit mankind, let us understand that whereas in the West the villagers whose industry was destroyed readily found another occupation, and were, therefore, somehow provided, with us only an infinitesimal portion of those whom the erection of these mills deprives of their occupation is otherwise provided, and that the vast majority are left idle and penniless. Let not the reader also rush to the conclusion that the handspinning movement is an indiscriminate onslaught upon machinery. This movement is intended to displace only such machinery worked by power as is harmful to the moral and material welfare of the starving millions. The fact is that we are too much obsessed by the glamour of the West, and the ready-made literature that is poured down upon us from week to week. We forget that what may be perfectly good for certain conditions in the West is not necessarily good for certain other, and often diametrically opposite, conditions in the East. Free Trade which may have been good enough for England would certainly have ruined Germany. Germany prospered, only because her thinkers, instead of slavishly following England, took note of the special conditions of their own land, and devised economics suited to them. And both England and Germany will have to revise their policy in economics immediately the nations that are now being exploited by them come to their own, and refuse to be exploited. The civilisation of both is based upon the exploitation of other lands. Let us remember that even if we have desire, we have not the power to exploit any single nation on earth. Hence if we are to live as an independent nation, we must evolve economics and conditions suited to our growth.

Most Economical

A friend, who fell ill about the same time as I became incapacitated, writing out of sympathy, and herself in search of it, says in her letter:—"I had time to philosophise and there was one thought I was working at ever since I lost my voice. And I have discovered that there is no necessity for living, and that Fate in giving us death early, is most economical. For thereby she economises the power that abides in us whereas we waste it by living when living becomes manifestly unnecessary. I spun the thought out until I felt exhausted, and I said to myself—'After all what is the good? The call somehow or other has not come. And so I must be wasted till there is nothing more left to be wasted." What a comforting thought it is to think of death, whenever it comes, as a wise plan in the economy of Nature? If we could realise this law of our being and be prepared for death as a welcome friend and deliverer, we should cease to engage in the frantic struggle for life. We shall cease to want to live at the cost of other lives and in contempt of all considerations of humanity. But to philosophise, as this friend has done, is one thing; to realise at the required moment the truth of the philosophy is totally another. Such realisation is impossible without a due conception of the definite and grave limitations of the body and an abiding faith in God and His unchangeable Law of Karma.

12th May, 1927

YOUNG AT 75

By M. K. Gandhi

An English friend writes:

"I want just to tell you of a letter and photographs I have had from a dear old Swiss peasant woman of over 70, who spins and weaves away up in the mountains above Villeneuve. She writes in answer to letters that she has had of mine, and then she says (in French dialect), 'We are commencing the winter and the snows are coming down to keep us company for many months. I shall have plenty of time to occupy myself with my loom. And I have now got an order for 2 pieces at 59 metres, so I shall need the time, as I get tired easily in these days' (at 75 years old!). Her life is a perfect example of the full, yet peaceful and contented existence, which should be the lot of all peasantry. In the summer she works in the fields, with just a few odd hours of spinning and weaving put in here and there when the days are wet, and in the winter when the land is under snow, she works away at her wheel and her loom all day. Take this hand-industry away from her, and she would be lost in complete misery. As it is, she is the happiest and sweetest-natured person on the mountain side. Why? Because she alone, of all the peasants in that place, has retained the old industry, and she alone has a full and true life. I enclose you one of the little photographs which shows her sitting on a log of wood caressing one of her goats, which may give you some slight idea of her dear old face. The younger woman is her daughter-in-law."

I have the beautiful photograph which I am unable to reproduce in *Young India*, but the imaginative reader will have no difficulty in filling in the picture. The point of the letter however is that even in that machine-ridden country, there are people who find their true peace in this at one time universal home-industry of the wheel and the loom. And if this old woman, who for her industry is young at 75, finds her solace, not her livelihood, in the wheel and the loom, how much greater is their need in this land where very few women reach the age of 75, where the majority needlessly *are* old at 50, and where millions of women need not merely the solace of an innocent cottage industry to occupy their idle hours but who need it even more to keep the wolf from the door?

'If that is so, why do not the millions take to the home industry, even as the dear old Swiss sister does, and find from it their solace and their food? What is there to prevent them from doing so?' asks the ignorant scoffer. But somewhat similar was the question put by a burly rough looking Englishman to Surendranath Bannerjea in 1889 or 1890 when he was haranguing an English audience. This worthy member of the firm of John Bull and Company asked the then uncrowned king of Bengal, if what the latter said was true that India desired freedom, what prevented her from taking it, how was it that they, members of this numerous and powerful firm, never heard of breaking of window-panes, let alone heads, as they the members were wont to do when they could not get what they wanted? So far as my memory serves me right, the papers recorded no answer from the orator. There was only a 'hear, hear' from the audience. But what the honest Englishman said to Surendranath may be safely repeated even today, and we know that such a question will be no answer to the cry for freedom. We may not know how to win it. Knowing the way, we may not have the power or the will to adopt it. Nevertheless the cry for freedom is both just and natural. Be it ever so ineffective, it is the first step to freedom.

In the instance of the starving millions the scoffers forget in their ignorance that the millions have not even the wish to cry out for work or bread. Hence we join the English historian in calling them 'dumb millions.' *We* (including the scoffers) have to be their voice. *We* have to teach the dumb millions the first lesson. *We*, not *they*, are responsible for their awful poverty and ignorance. They don't know what they want or need. They are living corpses.

Who shall dare say to the untouchable that if they want their freedom, who prevents them from taking it? God is long-suffering and patient. He lets the tyrant dig his own grave, only issuing grave warnings at stated intervals.

We would say, and justly, that though the taunt of the Englishman could be theoretically justified, it would ill become Englishmen to beg the question in that manner, when any one of us, though feeling helpless, is yet expressing the natural desire for feedom. So will it ill become us, middle class men and women, to hurl the taunt put by me in the mouth of the imaginary scoffer in answer to the crying need of the millions —a need which they may not even feel but which a few of us feel for them. The way to answer the need is to multiply the number of such representatives who would not only be the mouth-piece of the dumb millions but would adopt corresponding measures by themselves taking up the wheel, by throwing away foreign fineries, by wearing Khadi and by not resting till every idle hour of the nation is usefully occupied. Then, but not till then, shall India's women be young, happy and God-fearing at 75, even as the Swiss sister of 75 is represented to be.

12th May, 1927

THE SKELETONS OF ORISSA

[According to my theory, if Khadi work cannot be made a success in Utkal, it cannot be made a success anywhere. Yet, strange though it may appear, nowhere have the Khadi workers experienced a greater difficulty in organising hand-spinning than there. The eyes of the living skeletons of Utkal are unlit by a single ray of hope. What interest can the means of livelihood have for one who has despaired of life itself? Those who have taken to spinning in Utkal are men who still retain some hope of life. The Khadi worker there has not yet been able to touch the vast majority who have lost all hope. The people are dying under our very eyes. We could see it clearly if only we had the eyes to see. We would then take up spinning for sacrifice and give away all our hoarded money for Khadi work, or in case we had none, we would cut down our luxuries and superfluous expense and devote the savings to the same end.

It is only if we ourselves spin that we will be able to create the spinning atmosphere necessary to quicken these skeletons to life. But a spinning atmosphere by itself cannot do more than merely touch the fringe of the problem. Progress depends upon funds. No *yajna* can be complete without *dakshina*. And it is clear to me as daylight that spinning is the one true *yajna* today and to contribute funds for its advancement is the only *dakshina*. For those who have not yet realised this simple truth the following letter will serve as an eye-opener. M. K. G.

The Utkal Khadi organisation runs two weaving centres, two spinning centres and four sale depots, besides a printing and dyeing department at Berhampore which is the headquarters. In all forty workers are employed. The average salary per worker is Rs. 22 per mensem. The annual out-turn per worker comes to Rs. 1,000. Thanks to the efforts of Sjt.

Satish Chandra Das Gupta the work in Orissa is now fairly well organised compared with the conditions that prevailed in the early stages. It is noteworthy that all the Khadi produced in Utkal is consumed locally. There is very little cotton cultivation in the province and almost all the cotton needed for the Khadi work has to be imported from other provinces. This makes Khadi in Orissa costlier than it would otherwise have been. Formerly Khadi was imported from other provinces into Utkal, and both indigenous and outside Khadi was sold at the price of the latter. Outside Khadi being cheaper, this meant some loss. This system has now been discarded, and only locally produced Khadi is stocked in the sale depots. With the growing production the workers hope to place the whole organisation on a self-supporting basis though for capital and the disposal of stock when production is increased they may have to depend on outside assistance.

Sjt. Shankarlal and I reached Berhampore on *Sankranti* which is a great Hindu festival common all over the country. We were told that according to custom nobody would spin or card on that day. This was very disappointing news for us as we had to get away the same day. But we were determined to do our best. I went to one of the centres called Kodala, Sjt. Shankarlal staying away to attend to other work. I was told that at Kodala the peasant women did not card their own cotton but were only spinners. Spinning is looked upon here as an occupation superior to weaving and carding. Carding is done by weaver-women who charge an anna and a half to card one pound. In many cases the spinner does slivering herself. When we explained the purpose of our visit they agreed to give us a demonstration of their spinning and carding. The objection to working on *Sankranti* was only if it was to be done for wage-earning. One of them brought a little cotton and began to card. The bow was a small instrument made of solid bamboo and had two gut strings, each consisting of four strands. We were told that two strings helped to remove the cotton fibres that got twisted round the strings in the process of carding. The woman who gave the demonstration used a dumbbell-beater. The carding was good though I noticed that it was slighly overdone resulting in the characteristic specks. I then took my bow out and gave a demonstration of hand-bow-carding. The twang of the bow soon brought around me a crowd of women and children watching the process with eager interest. Using a local friend as interpreter I explained to them the difference between good and bad carding. The professional carders immediately began to take a keen interest. They appreciated the beauty of good carding. One after another they tried my bow. "We can certainly card as well as you but who would pay us extra for the additional labour?" they remonstrated. I know that some of these carders were weavers. Addressing my remarks to them, I said, "If you card cotton like this, and spin and weave it yourselves, I can assure you, you will find your labour amply rewarded."

We now proceeded to examine weaving. Khadi of various designs and patterns was to be seen on the looms. We were told that all these weavers had confined themselves for the last four years exclusively to Khadi weaving. They are now able to weave six or seven yards a day which is double the quantity of what they wove four years ago. The weaving charges are generally two and a half annas per yard. Considering the poor quality of the yarn, the texture of the cloth was good.

A good feature noticed in this village was that the weavers wore Khadi themselves.

The spinners too readily departed from their rule of observing a holiday and spun at our request. The wheel seen by us was twenty seven inches diameter and the *mal* ran over a bare spindle instead of on a pulley. The spinner spun in our presence at the rate of about 150 yards per hour. She used slivers made by the woman who had just given us the carding demonstration. As she spun, she was busy saying things of which I understood nothing. I was told that it was all a bitter lecture addressed to the carding woman who made bad slivers and charged too much for making them. The thread was coarse and broke very often owing to the poor quality of the slivers. I sat down and spun a little myself, The thread came even and fine and did not break. 'Hullo, he manages it well?" they exclaimed. I told them that if they carded their own cotton they would be able to do quite as well as I did and could save the carding charges in the bargain. There was a chorus of protest. 'We to card!" they said, "No, that is the weaver-woman's work and if we took to it, we should be excommunicated at once." There are ever so many difficulties in the way of the Khadi workers. They have not merely to reform the wheels and the carding bows which is comparatively easy but have to reform customs and remove prejudices which is decidedly tough work. I contributed my share by pleading the case for carding. I saw that they felt convinced in their minds, but they could not summon enough courage there and then to promise to do it.

Spinning wages at these centres is annas 4 a pound, but at Bolgadh, which happened to be an exception in the matter of the common prejudice against carding, a different and more efficient practice is followed. In place of money payment the spinners get cotton one and half times the quantity in return for yarn. The extra cotton thus obtained by the spinner is spun for cloth for personal wear. The system works well and the organisers have decided to adopt it at the new centres they contemplate opening.

Under the guidance of Sjt. Gopabandhu Das famine relief work through spinning is carried on at Puri; but for want of time, we were not able to see anything of it.

There is no province so poverty-stricken as Orissa. Draught and excessive rainfall have both contributed to this. The people are everywhere mere skeletons. Thousands carry on a lingering existence because death is not merciful enough to relieve their agony quickly. To induce these people who have lost all interest in life to take to even such a light occupation as spinning will mean time. The faithful and earnest band of workers now ready for extensive work in Orissa affords the most hopeful sign. Given initial capital outlay and the assurance that every yard of Khadi produced in Orissa would be bought up, they may be expected to do a great deal to alleviate the present dire distress.

(*Navajivan*) LAKSHMIDAS PURUSHOTTAM

19th May, 1927

COW v. BUFFALO OR COW *cum* BUFFALO

BY. M. K. GANDHI

A worker in the cause of cow protection writes from Konkan:

> "In your recent article giving the conditions of cow protection you said that the question of the protection of the cow should not be mixed up with that of the protection of the buffalo. At the back of this suggestion seems to be the fact that the buffalo bull is not useful for agricultural purposes. But in Konkan he is fairly useful. It is the buffalo bull which draws the municipal refuse carts, which works waterpumps, and even draws the plough, especially when there is a heavy downpour disabling the bullock, and most of the agriculture in Konkan is being done under monsoon conditions. The buffalo bull has therefore his place in Konkan.
>
> "The Konkan cow does not yield more than one pound of milk, whereas the buffalo yields 5 to 10 lbs. It may be possible, after systematic breeding, to make the cow yield more and richer milk, but the buffalo needs no special culture at all. Does not therefore the buffalo in Konkan at any rate need as much protection as cow? Please correct me if I am wrong.
>
> "The buffalo, I admit, has no place on the *ghauts* where the temperature is higher, fields are bigger and water scarce. He needs much water both to drink and bathe in. Konkan is the place for him.

> "Your tannery and dairy are for cities. For the villages you must suggest some more practical ways and means. Let every village possess a stud-bull, maintain him partly from the common fund and partly from contributions from those who make use of it. This can be done everywhere and it will improve the stock. Could you not suggest similar other remedies?"

These are appropriate questions. My article was not intended to throw the buffalo by the board, it suggested the stopping of buffalo-breeding in her own interest. In other words it meant freedom of the buffalo from its bondage. We have domesticated the cow for our own uses and therefore it has become part of our religion to protect her. It was my object to show that in trying to breed the buffalo, as we do the cow, we might lose both.

The Konkan example does not affect my proposition. We must, of course, make use of the existing stock of buffaloes, and let it be done in parts like Konkan. But our duty is clear. We must not increase our responsibility by breeding the buffalo where we can do with the cow alone. We must therefore content ourselves with the use of cow's milk only. It should not be necessary in a city like Bombay to use buffalo's milk in preference to cow's milk. An endeavour should be organised on a large scale to cheapen the supply of pure cow's milk, and to improve the milk yield of the cow. It is possible too to make cow's milk richer. All these things have been developed into a science in Europe, especially in Denmark. Cows in those countries yield richer and more milk than our buffaloes. I have heard from Vaidyas that buffalo's milk lacks and can never be made to have the hygienic and health-giving properties that cow's milk possesses. Pious people have told me, that cow's milk is *Sattwik* (possessing finer qualities) whereas buffalo's milk is *tamasik* (gross). I do not know how far this is true. I am trying to ascertain the truth through the proper channel. But it does seem to me, that all that the buffalo can give and even more, the cow also can or can be made to give. If this is true, why should man, having regard to his own needs, make himself responsible for breeding the buffalo? And having regard to the need of the buffalo, why should we needlessly keep her in bondage? Or to put it more simply, why should we press her into our service?

The fact that some people make a pecuniary gain out of buffalo breeding can have no place in this religious discussion in which we have in view the good of all. In thinking solely of the narrow interest of the self or of the moment, we have ruined ourselves, *i.e.*, our country and our religion. We can be a nation, only when we try to think in terms of the wider interests of the country. If we cannot even think in those terms, it is no use talking of religion. From the national point of view the good of the country is the supreme consideration. From the religious point of view the good of all living beings from the cow down to the ant is the supreme consideration.

Let the reader now turn to the table given elsewhere in this issue. The table relates to the income from and expenditure on the cattle maintained at the Satyagrahashram. The names are those of different cows. The manager in his covering letter says:

> "It is by no means the rule that the buffalo yields more than the cow. Some of the cows in the table yield a net profit, some just pay their way and some are boarders. These last we shall prevent from breeding and propose to take light work from them. A sterile cow has already been trained to do some work. The buffalo calves sell cheap, whereas some calves of the cow are worth Rs. 100 each. Two or three have taken the place of the horse with the result that we have dispensed with our horse-carriage."

The Ashram has decided to have no more buffaloes. We may not draw large deductions from the table, but it is certainly obvious that if the cow is spread properly, she compares favourably with the buffalo in her yield, she does not cost more, and her calves are much more useful.

I propose to publish in *Navajivan* the results of the further experiments that are being conducted in the Ashram.

The Konkan friend is not right when he says that the dairy and the tannery are useful only in and for the city, and have no place in the villages. The cow has become a costly proposition even in the villages. It is as essential to keep proper accounts of her yield and to improve her stock and her milk in villages as in cities. And the skinning of dead cattle and the prompt and skilled treatment of the hides is more essential in villages than in cities and that is the work to be done in tanneries.

It is a painful fact that in our present condition we have to cultivate the science of tanning in the cities and then take it to the villages. For one thing it is impossible to conduct big experiments in the villages, and cattle that are slaughtered in the cities come from the villages. If we can therefore conduct experiments in dairying and tanning from the religious and national point of view in the cities, we can easily give the benefit of them to the villages, and the cattle wealth of India which is at the present day being destroyed because of our ignorance, will be saved, and man and animal will both be less unhappy than now.

(Translated from *Navajivan* by M. D.)

19th May, 1927

NAGPUR SATYAGRAHA

BY M. K. GANDHI

I see an Associated Press telegram in the papers, in which Mr. Manchershah Awari is reported to have said, that he had my consent and full sympathy for his movement of civil disobedience with regard to the Arms Act and the Explosive Substances Act, designed for the release of the Bengal detenues.

If my recollection is correct, either the A. P. representative has misunderstood Mr. Awari, or the latter has misunderstood me. I have no recollection of having given my consent in advance to Mr. Awari's proposed launching out on civil disobedience in any connection whatsover. It is really contrary to my practice to give such consent in advance. I did discuss the theory of civil disobedience with Mr. Awari, for whose patriotic spirit and self-sacrifice I have great regard. I drew his attention to the grave limitations of civil disobedience. He spoke, and rightly, with great warmth and concern about the Bengal detenues, and I remember having said, that if some movement in the shape of civil disobedience could be conceived and successfully launched, it would be a great thing. I hold that view even at the present moment. For I regard the indefinite detention of the Bengal patriots without any trial of any sort as a grave injustice. And if I have remained dumb, it is not because I do not feel the wrong as keenly as the closest friends of the detenues, but because I do not desire to make a fruitless exhibition of my powerlessness. A public worker has to learn to endure with fortitude what he cannot cure. And bed-ridden though I am, if I could think of any feasible civil plan for securing the release of these prisoners, I should embark upon it without the slightest hesitation. But I confess that I have none in view. My own personal opinion is that there is no atmosphere in the country for civil disobedience. We have fallen upon evil times. The atmosphere today is one not of non-violent disobedience but of very violent and suicidal disobedience.

I have no knowledge whatsoever of what is being done in Nagpur. I can pronounce no judgment upon Mr. Awari's movement. I have given no consent for the movement. I had intended to say not one word about the movement, and it would have been well if Mr. Awari had not dragged in my name. If he thought that his movement had my consent, he should have laid the whole of his plan in a concrete form before me and secured it in writing. If I had approved of it and if I could not have taken an active part myself, I would at least have backed it with all the force at my command through these columns. He must now thank himself if my disclaimer harms his movement in any way.

And let it be a warning in future to every one concerned against using my name in connection with any movement without my previous consent in writing. Indeed it is necessary for workers to become self-reliant and dare to prosecute their plans if they so desire without hankering after the backing of names of persons supposed to be great and influential. Let them rely upon the strength of their own conviction and the cause they seek to espouse. Mistakes there will be. Suffering even avoidable there must be. But nations are not easily made. There will have to be rigid and iron discipline before we achieve anything great and enduring, and that discipline will not come by mere academic argument and appeal to reason and logic. Discipline is learnt in the school of adversity. And when zealous young men will train themselves to responsible work without any shield, they will learn what responsibility and discipline are. And out of this army of candidate leaders, will arise one real leader, who will not have to plead for obedience and discipline but who will command it as a matter of course, because he will have been tried in many a skirmish and will have proved his right to undisputed leadership.

19th May, 1927

APPEAL TO SOUTH AFRICAN INDIANS

The following appeal addressed to the Indians in South Africa by Gandhiji is translated from *Navajivan* :-

The Rt. Hon. Srinivas Sastri has yielded to the pressure of friends in accepting the office of the first Ambassador for India in South Africa, at the sacrifice of his cherished wishes, solely with the object of serving you. It rests with you to make the best use of his services and his presence amongst you. You cannot do so unless you fulfil the following conditions:—

1. You will not expect too much.
2. You will not try to seek relief in purely individual cases through him.

3. You will not swerve from truth in your dealings with him. To be false to him would be to be false to yourselves.
4. You will remain completely united.
5. You will put your own house in order and purify yourselves.

You will not assume that all your grievances will disappear with the coming of the Rt. Hon. Sastri as first Agent. He will have done enough if he succeeds in seeing that no new restrictive legislation is passed against you, that the operation of the old restrictive enactments is not made unnecessarily harsh and that the spirit of the new Agreement is carried out by the Union Government.

The Rt. Hon. Sastri is going there as the representative, not of individuals, but of India as a whole. He is going there to uphold the prestige of India. Therefore you will not run to him for relief in every individual case. If you do, you will make the mistake of expending a pound for the matter of a penny.

Our strength depends solely on truth. No matter how you behave in your business dealings, you will never in the interests of the community think of swerving from the path of truth in your dealings with the Rt. Hon. Sastri. In attempting to deceive him you will be working your own ruin.

19th May, 1927

HORRIBLE PRACTICES

BY M. K. GANDHI

Mr. Andrews in the course of a letter from Durban says:

"I am sorely troubled about one thing that is going on among the Indians here. There is a great deal of self-torture being practised in evil forms at Umbilo Temple and it is likely to spread elsewhere. There was a whole page of horrible pictures in the *Natal Advertiser* showing Indians with skewers stuck through cheeks and other forms of torture, and there have been what they call 'fire walking' festivals and also the slaughter of goats etc. The newspapers are taking this up in a sensational manner just when the attitude of Europeans is becoming more friendly. It is doing infinite harm.

"Little by little we must win through; but I cannot possibly express to you how tired I have become. The truth is I have hardly had a chance of recovery and the strain has never for a moment been relaxed. But I know that by God's grace all will be well. It is there that all our strength lies."

I know the temple at Umbilo, which may really be called a suburb of Durban. Even years ago, when the temple was erected, I had my misgivings. Bitter experience has taught me that all temples are not houses of God. They can be habitations of the devil. These places of worship have no value unless the keeper is a good man of God. Temples, mosques, churches are what man makes them to be. I am therefore not surprised at the painful and horribly superstitious practices going on in this so-called temple. The origin of these practices is easy enough to trace. There are three classes of Indians in South Africa. The free Indian trader has nothing to do with these practices. Nor have the large number of Colonial-born Indians who have received in the face of terrible odds a tolerably liberal education. The third class is the indentured Indian, now become free. He is drawn naturally from the poorest class here. Nothing has ever been done by the Government or the employers or by the free Indian community to help these unfortunate men and women out of their ignorance and superstition. The result is that they are preyed upon by superstitious and even evil-minded men who pose as priests and holy men. They mutter a few Sanskrit verses whose meaning they do not know and which they horribly mispronounce, and resort to all kinds of awe-inspiring practices. And what can be better than a temple, where simple people congregate and where every kind of superstition derives a halo from associations attributed to temples? I think that the common law of South Africa is wide enough to deal with these practices if the Government desires to put them down.

The fact is, unfortunately, that the prejudice against Indians in South Africa is not ascribable to these practices, nor is it directed against the men who are victims of this barbarism. It is directed chiefly against the free trading class who have nothing to do with these practices. And therefore these practices have gone without any notice or comment. And if they are now being noticed, it is in order to prejudice the European mind against the Habibullah Agreement and against what little relief is sought to be given by it to the Indian settlers. It should also be borne in mind that these practices are by no means common amongst Indians throughout South Africa. They are confined only to the part of the coast of Natal where indentured Indians are to be found in their largest numbers. If therefore the Government intend to put these practices down, they can do so under the common law with ease, and they can be dealt with also through municipal bye-laws. I am sure, that if action is taken, not a voice will be raised against it in the name of religion falsely so-called for sheltering these practices. No cultured Indian will have any thing to do with them, and the ignorant people who witness these tortures with awe will not dare to defend them in a court of law. What we can do here is to encourage cultured Indians in South Africa to fight the superstition. They should, without seeking Government intervention, work in the midst of the poor people, and wean them from these barbarisms, and advise them to help the Government, if they choose to prosecute those who take part in those practices, thus showing their desire not to reproduce in South Africa all that is bad in our life, but to reproduce only that which is good in our civilisation. It is our duty to advise and encourage our countrymen in South Africa to do nothing that will give a handle to the agitation against them.

26th May, 1927

AMONG RANIPARAJ PEOPLE

[Readers of *Young India* and *Navajivan* are now familiar with the Raniparaj people (forest-dwellers) in Surat District. An account of their Conference was given in these pages over a month ago. The Conference appointed a Committee to inquire into their economic condition and their agrarian difficulties and suggest methods of reform. Sjt. Kishorlal Mashruwala who accompanied the Committee as an independent observer has given two pictures, one dark and the other bright, of conditions observed by him in an article in *Navajivan* which is summarised below.

M. D.]

THE FIRST PICTURE

The first of the two pictures that have come under my observation is painful. It is disgraceful. It relates to Parsi canteen-keepers. I write this not having in view the liquor traffic which is mainly in the hands of the Parsis in those parts. It is a matter in which Government also is involved. I have quite another thing in mind.

They have penetrated to the remotest village in the jungle. I had an impression that this lone adventure had nothing worse than love of lucre to disgrace it. But I got a rude shock when I came to know that many of these men were living immoral lives with women of the Raniparaj tribe. One of the liquor-sellers seemed to admit the fact with some amount of pride. Another has seven children by a woman of the community. In a number of places I happened to be told of illegitimate children by Parsi fathers. In some places they are living a life of promiscuous immorality, and in others, each has a woman for himself. From a superficial view one is apt to think that these foresters must have very low morals and that they do not mind their women being dishonoured. But one of them who gave me a most pathetic account of this convinced me that they put up with the humiliation not because they do not mind it, but because they are perfectly helpless.

Why they are helpless and why they are drawn into this immorality I shall leave the Raniparaj Committee to report. I simply want to invite the attention of my Parsi brethren to this sore spot which affects the moral being of their community. There should be no indifference to the debauchery that is being indulged in by some of its members in these forest tracts. I do not lay the blame at the door of the community as a whole. But I invite its attention to this deplorable state of things. This sort of relationship, if tolerated, will put a premium on vice and ruin the morals of the race.

THE OTHER PICTURE

But there is a picture to redeem the gloom. There is a little village in Mahuva Taluka under the Baroda State where a Nayak family (belonging to the Raniparaj tribe) is making an honest living. It is a big joint family, full not only of sons and sons' sons, but daughters and daughters' children, 80 all told, 48 looking after the agriculture in one village and 32 in another. They do not mess together, but they work together and pool their earnings. Kalyan a circumspect and fairly literate man is the head of the family. It has in all 270 bighas of land, for which they pay an annual rental of Rs. 1,800.

Kalyan expended Rs. 500 annually on liquor before the wave of moral reform that came over the community in 1921-22. This was exclusive of the Rs. 150 on tobacco which with these people is a matter of course. With the reform came an awakening in this family which has been permanent. Liquor and *toddy* became taboo, and close on their abolition came the Charkha which now received a warm welcome. Twenty wheels were introduced in the section with 48 members, all excepting five or seven children turning them. Home-made Khadi took the place of mill-made cloth. But Kalyan was not the man to rest satisfied with this. He sent two young men from the family to learn weaving and as soon as they returned thoroughly qualified, two looms were introduced in the house. One of the young men learnt tailoring and then the family invested in a Singer's sewing machine. The weavers and the tailor add to the agricultural income of the family. The weavers not only weave the yarn of the family, but they get yarn from the neighbourhood too, and one of them makes 20 to 22 rupees a month. The other is yet a novice, but soon he will also earn the same amount. The tailor does not get much work from outside, but he has not to give his whole time either; and earns Rs. 7 to 8 a month. It must be remembered that in these parts the wage of a day labourer in the off-season is two to three annas, and in some villages it is not possible to earn even an anna a day. With the coming of the Charkha, tobacco, the only luxury, has also gone, except in the case of three or four old members, and that means a saving of Rs. 100.

The family is no doubt in debt like all other families of this community. But it has established a unique credit now, and can easily get money at the rate of 9 per cent.

One more thing may be mentioned. Kalyan has also been alive to the educational needs of the children. He started a school at his own expense, and now the state has taken charge of it.

To summarise the savings and additional income of the family as a result of the disappearance of drink and introduction of the Charkha:

SAVINGS

Expenses on liquor and *toddy*	Rs.	500
„ „ tobacco	Rs.	100
„ „ cloth (Rs. 25 per head)	Rs.	1,200
Saving of 4 p. c. interest on a debt of Rs. 1,300	Rs.	52
	Rs.	1,852

ADDITIONAL INCOME

Weaving Rs. 30 p. m.	Rs.	360
Tailoring Rs. 7 p. m.	Rs.	84
	Rs.	444

I have not been able to get figures of the addition in agricultural income following in the wake of reform in the habits of the family.

26th May, 1927

HIGHLY UNSATISFACTORY

BY M. K. GANDHI

I wish it was possible for me to tender the Government of Bengal congratulations upon the release of Sjt. Subash Chandra Bose. The release has been granted, not because public opinion demanded it, not because Government consider the Chief Officer of the Calcutta Corporation to be guiltless, nor because they considered that he had been sufficiently punished for a crime of which neither he nor the public has any knowledge, but because their own medical officers considered the distinguished prisoner to be seriously ill, so seriously ill as to cause fear about his life. If Sjt. Subash Chandra Bose is a danger to society or to the life of anybody, and if he is a man of determination as he is reputed to be and even believed by the Government to be, he is no less dangerous because he is seriously ill. Why should the Government be afraid of his dying in their prison? Surely it is not customary with them to release every prisoner who becomes dangerously ill. And if it was right to discharge him for his illness, why was he not discharged when he first showed signs of tuberculosis? Papers have been for a long time full of information about the alarming character of his disease. His brother repeatedly warned the Government about the prisoner's illness.

It is, I venture to suggest, cowardly to fling a dying man in the face of his relatives and wash oneself of the guilt of his death. This release brings us no nearer to the solution of the question of imprisonment or indefinite detention, without trial, of prisoners whom the Government choose to suspect. The Bengal Regulation remains where it was. More or less healthy detenus must continue to rot, and are now deprived of the support of an agitation which was kept at a fairly high pitch because a powerful man was under detention. No doubt some sort of agitation will still continue for the release of the other detenus. But there is every fear of its lacking strength. Indian nature is grateful for the smallest mercies. It is easily satisfied. And the public will condone the detention of the other prisoners for the release of Sjt. Subash Chandra Bose, forgetting that the release is due not to any relenting on the part of the Government, but due to nature's supreme intervention.

It may seem cruel, but I must confess that I would far rather not have any release at all than have a release on false issues, which merely complicate the main issue and make it more difficult to deal with than before; for behind the agitation for the release of the detenus is the great question of the liberty of the citizens and the question of extraordinary powers exercised over the lives of people by an utterly irresponsible Government. The one consolation that the public can derive from this painful affair is, that Sjt. Subash Chandra Bose up to the very last moment manfully declined to accept the humiliating conditions from time to time proposed by the Government for his discharge. Let us hope and pray that he will be soon restored to health and that a long life of service will be vouchsafed to him.

26th May, 1927

AN APPEAL TO INDIAN HUMANITY

BY M. K. GANDHI

In another place will be found a substance of the observations made in the columns of *Navajivan* by Sjt. Kishorlal Mashruwala. He is a worker of long standing and was up to recently Registrar of the Gujarat Vidyapith, and it was only due to illness that he was obliged to relinquish the post. He is one of the most thoughtful among the silent workers we have in India. He weighs every word he writes or utters. I mention these qualifications of his; for I am anxious that his reflections should not be dismissed out of consideration as so many writings now-a-days have to be.

The story of the abuse of the helpless women of the Raniparaj community is a blot upon the nation. Sjt. Kishorlal Mashruwala has made his appeal to the Parsis, and from his standpoint, rightly too. For it is the Parsis who will be better able, if any one is, to influence the Parsi men who are said to be corrupting innocent womanhood. But I am painfully aware of the fact, that it is not the Parsis alone who hold so cheap the honour of poor sisters. Indians belonging to the other faiths, placed in similar circumstances, have been known to behave exactly as the Parsi canteen-keepers are reported to be doing. But that is no justification whatsoever for the inhuman crimes of the latter. The lust for money, which drives these adventurers to a trade which they know saps the manhood of the otherwise fine forest-dwellers miscalled Kaliparaj *i.e.* black people, tempts them to the worse crime of defilement.

The British Government or rather the Government of India and the Baroda State must be held primarily responsible for the tragedy described by Sjt. Mashruwala; for it is they, who for their wretched revenue allow liquor shops to be opened or to exist in the midst of these simple people. These people have never asked for these shops, and even if they had, it would be still criminal to open liquor shops for them, even as it would be to allow a little child to play with fire because he desires it. But a reformer does not *stop* before commencing action to philosophise or to distribute blame through golden scales. He begins his reform wherever the opportunity offers itself. And now that the corruption has been brought to light, it behoves Parsi reformers to go to the delinquents and appeal to their sense of honour and try to wean them from the crime of violating the womanhood of the simple innocent and guileless Raniparaj, even if they cannot also be weaned from trafficking in liquor.

Unfortunately, there is much truth in the taunt levelled at us as a nation, that we have not sufficient regard for the honour of our women. It is no use false patriotism seeking cover under *tu quoque* argument; nor must we mix up sexual immorality in which depraved men and women of equal status indulge of their own free but unbridled will with the instances of crime quoted by Sjt. Kishorlal Mashruwala.

Immoralities of the first kind are bad enough and do incredible harm to mankind; but the crimes like those of the Parsi canteen-keepers are infinitely worse and have not yet, thank God, received the tacit endorsement of fashionable society. In the instances quoted by Sjt. Kishorelal Mashruwala, the canteen keepers are in the position of trustees, and it is insufferable that they should induce ignorant women in whose midst they are living to become instruments of their criminal lust. It is this kind of indifference to the honour of ignorant sisters who come under the influence or protection of the so-called better class men, which has been justifiably criticised, and which we must, if we want to become a self-respecting and independent nation, outgrow at any cost. The honour of the least among our sisters must be as dear to us as that of our blood-sisters.

26th May, 1927

VIVEKANANDA AND SPINNING

A correspondent sends me interesting extracts from Vivekananda's answers to his American questioners. I take the following from them on spinning :—

> Speaking of Indian village life he says: "In some places the common village girl with her spinning wheel says: 'Do not talk to me of dualism, my spinning wheel says, So'ham, So'ham, I am He, I am He.' What is the value of all these machines and sciences? They have only one result; they spread knowledge. You have not solved the problem of want, but only made it keener. Machines do not solve the poverty problem; they simply make men struggle the more. Competition gets keener. . . . . . The value of everything is to be decided by how far it is a manifestation of God." M. K. G.

2nd June, 1927

THE WHEEL OF LIFE AND THE VEDAS

By M. K. Gandhi

Pandit Satavalekar of Aundh wrote in 1922 a booklet in Hindi called *Vedmem charkha i.e. Charkha in the Vedas*, and favoured me with a copy whilst I was resting in the Yeravada jail. I glanced then thrugh its pages and with interest, but asked myself what good would it be to us in this age of so called advancement to know that the Charkha was to be found in the Vedas. Everybody knows that our remote ancestors spun and wove in their cottages even as they did so many other things. But we no longer do them. So I said to myself. The booklet, I hastily concluded, was not of much practical value and I laid it aside. On the sickbed I have again an opportunity of turning, so far as my strength permits, to quiet studies. Another book of Pandit Satavalekar (of which more hereafter) has attracted me to his writings, and he has now favoured me with another copy of the booklet in question. I observe that it has undergone a second edition. I have read it this time more carefully, and I find that the *mantras* cited by the author from the Vedas demonstrate not merely the fact that our ancestors in those times were spinning and weaving, but they present, perhaps, for us, a novel way of looking at the wheel. Here is what may be called the key *mantra* for spinners and weavers from Rig-Veda X, 53-6 quoted by the author:

Tantum Tanvan Rajaso Bhanumanvihi Jyotishmataha Patho Rakshadhiya Kritan | *Anulbanam Vayata Joguvamapo Manurbhava Janaya Daivyam Janam* ||

I give a free rendering as follows:

"Having spun the thread and given it a shining colour weave it without knots, and so guard the pathways which the enlightened have chalked out, and thinking well, lead posterity unto the divine light, or (according to the author's rendering) bring forth divine progeny. This truly is the work of poets."

If the translation is at all correct,—and the author has not merely given his own rendering but has reproduced Griffith's translation also in his booklet,—the mantra proves not merely the existence of spinning and weaving in the Vedic times, but that it was the calling of the noblest men and women as well of the humblest. It was one of the pathways which wisdom hath prepared and to guard which was the work of poets. Little did I know, when I humbly presented the Charkha to our Poet as a sacrificial rite, that I had behind me the authority of what is understood to be the oldest Veda. I commend the *mantra* to all those who are engaged in reviving this ancient and sacred industry and art. Let them thoughtfully recite this *mantra* whilst doing their sacrificial spinning. Let them treasure it in their hearts and keep their faith unshaken even in the face of disappointments and reverses in their forward march.

I cannot resist quoting another beautiful *mantra* from the booklet:

Yo Yajna Visvatastantubhistata Ekasatam Devakarmebhi-rayataha | Ime Vayanti Pitaro Cha Ayayuyuh Pra Vayapa Vayetyasate Tate ||

This is again from the Rig-Veda (X, 130-1). It means:

"Hundred and one artists are working at the sacrifice, which through the myriad threads overspreads the earth. Here are the elderly guardians. They watch the processes saying 'Weave on here, do this right there.'"

Thus we see that spinning and weaving was regarded as a sacrifice even in those ancient days and commanded the protecting care of the elders The author shows by abundant evidence that both spinning and weaving were done by men as well as women. In fact the industry was as universal as farming. He shows too that the sartorial art was well advanced in those times. There were different dresses prescribed for different occasions as also for different states. If the farmer had his *langoti*, royalty had its robes. There is mention of colours, fringes and gold borders. The author has also shown that some of the most beautiful metaphors have been taken from the language of spinners and weavers.

I must resist the temptation to quote more extracts from this thoughtfully written booklet. There is a *mantra* which proves that the soldiers of those days were not above doing these processes; that the bridegroom's garment was always made by the bride as is still the custom in Assam.

There is one thing, however, the author leaves to other research scholars in the Vedic lore to discover. So far as he has been able to study the Vedas, he has not found a single equivalent for cotton as he has for wool and silk. He is, therefore, unable to say whether in those days our ancestors had only woollen and silken garments or whether they had already discovered the cotton fibre.

2nd June, 1927

CHOICE BEFORE US

BY M. K. GANDHI

A correspondent sends me a cutting from the press giving most gruesome facts about the growing infantile crimes and illicit gratification among girls in the New World.

A boy of 4 years is reported to have shot his mother, because she forbade him to play with matches. When the police confronted him, he was in no way taken aback. He threatened to shoot them too, and when questioned by the coroner, he grew so impatient with him, that he picked up a knife from among the exhibits lying in front of him and rushed to strike him. It is said, that hardly a day passes in America without some crime being committed by a boy or a girl, and in most American colleges there are said to be suicide clubs or crime societies, and the more horrible part of the account shows, that many girls, even of exclusive colleges, have become so lawless as to run away in pursuit of illicit adventures.

It is difficult, in an age in which newspapers, in order to provide sensational food for their readers, invent stories when they have no facts to weave narratives from, to believe without reservation reports such as I have condensed. But whilst one may make ample allowance for exaggeration, there is no doubt that infantile crime and lawlessness among boys and girls are sufficiently extensive in the New World to make us beware of a civilisation which must be held responsible for these crimes and lawlessness. That life in the West goes on,—and it may be said progressively after a fashion,—in spite of these infantile crimes, may be granted. And it may also be granted that the wise people of the West are not only not unaware of the evil, but that they are manfully struggling to overtake it. Nevertheless we have to decide whether we shall indiscriminately copy this civilisation. We may well pause in the face of the awful revelations that come to us from the West from time to time, and ask ourselves, whether after all it is not better to hold by our own civilisation and seek, in the light of the comparative knowledge that is available to us, to re-form it by removing its known excrescences. For there is no doubt, that if the West has its terrific problem arising out of its own civilisation, we have no less grave problems of our own to deal with.

It is perhaps unnecessary, if not useless, in this connection to weigh the merits of the two civilisations. It is likely that the West has evolved a civilisation suited to *its* climate and surroundings, and similarly, we have a civilisation suited to *our* conditions, and both are good in their own respective spheres. This may be safely said, that the crimes and the lawlessness described by me are almost impossible with us, and I hold that this is due to our pacific training and the restraining influence in the midst of which we are brought up. Cowardliness which often springs from pacific training, and obsequiousness which comes from the restraint that is handed down from generation to generation, have somehow to be avoided, if the ancient civilisation is not to perish before the mad modern rush. The distinguishing characteristic of modern civilisation is an indefinite multiplicity of human wants. The characteristic of ancient civilisation is an imperative restriction upon and a strict regulating of these wants. The modern or Western insatiableness arises really from want of a living faith in a future state and therefore also in Divinity. The restraint of ancient or Eastern civilisation arises from a belief, often in spite of ourselves, in a future state and the existence of a Divine Power. The record condensed above is a warning, if we will take it, against a blind imitation of the West, which one sees so often in the city life of India and especially among the educated classes. Some of the immediate and brilliant results of modern inventions are too maddening to resist. But I have no manner of doubt that the victory of man lies in that resistance. We are in danger of bartering away the permanent good for a momentary pleasure.

2nd June, 1927

HOW TO PROTECT THE COW

BY M. K. GANDHI

[I gladly publish these notes from Sjt. C. V. Vaidya. Those, who believe in the methods advocated in these columns for cow protection, will be glad to find, that a scholar of Sjt. C. V. Vaidya's repute is in substantial agreement with those methods. The distinction that the learned writer draws between *panjrapole* and *goshala* need not cause any anxiety or difficulty. My own opinion is, that either may be also the other, so long as separate accounts are kept and separate methods of feeding and housing the disabled and the working animals are adopted. Legislation and the state aid advocated by Sjt. Vaidya need not at present distract our attention. For there is immense scope for private effort building public opinion in favour of the proposed methods and showing their workability in practice. We are so far behind, indeed, that we have not even enough trained workers to conduct dairies and tanneries along the lines suggested by Sjt. Vaidya. There are at least 1,500 *Panjrapoles* and *Ghoshalas* according to the figures in my possession, which can, without much further donation, but by efficient management, test the usefulness of the methods. Their adoption will simply revolutionise the management of these institutions and put life into these, today for the most part, lifeless bodies. These *panjrapoles* and *goshalas*, as they are at present being conducted, are more a salve to our conscience than a protection to the cow. The learned writer's categorical statement, that during the Vedic and the Brahmana period cow slaughter was countenanced and beef was eaten, will be hotly contested by Pandit Saravalekar, who has been a close student of Vedic lore for the past 35 years, and by Acharya Ramadeva who claims to be a historian and to have critically studied the ancient history of Bharatavarsha. But with the historical portion practical men and women will not concern themselves. They will perhaps be content like me to hope that our ancestors in the Vedic times knew better than to seek to gain merit by sacrificing innocent animals or to satisfy their palate by eating beef.]

1. True *Goraksha* will not be undertaken by the Hindus unless and until they and also others take to the use of cow's milk, curds, whey, butter and ghee instead of buffalo's milk etc. The medical properties of the former are superior and they prevent disease as also give mental vigour. Because the buffalo gives more milk and ghee, most Hindus prefer to keep her, but they not only forget the sacredness of the cow and of cow's milk etc. but they also forget the superior medical properties of cow's milk, and other products. Propaganda, therefore, must first be made for inducing people to use cow's milk etc., Buffalo's milk etc, may be used by *Halwais* or on marriage and other occasions only to prepare sweetmeat. It is the buffalo which has really killed the cow, or rather the blind human tendency to prefer cheapness to merit. Cow's milk is greatly strengthening, especially to children, and every child taking exercise should drink cow's milk.

2. The difference between *Panjarapole* and *Goshala* should be clearly seen and maintained. *Panjarapoles* owe their origin to the sentiment of *Ahimsa* which is entertained both by Hindus and Jains, while *Goshalas* owe their origin to the feeling of reverence for the sacredness of cow and bull alone. *Panjarapoles*, therefore, must be confined to maintaining sick and old animals of all kinds. But *Ghoshalas* should be started and maintained for *Dharma* alone, meaning thereby the saving of bovine cattle from slaughter as also their good rearing and maintenance in strength and vigour for milk and draught. *Panjarapoles*, therefore, can never be worked economically and ought never to be so maintained. But *Goshalas* should be economically managed, in fact on dairy lines, for cows and bulls alone and should supply pure cow's milk to the people. *Panjraapoles* and *Goshalas* should, however, work conjointly, as far as possible, so that manure and dead cattle may be utilised. But they may even be worked separately, *Goshalas* confining

their activity to cows and bulls which are considered sacred by the Hindus. The latter may even feed cows and bulls sick temporarily, but should transfer the useless cows to *Panjarapoles*. Definite rules can easily be laid down when the difference in the two is clearly grasped.

3. Why does Burma, a Buddhist country, import dried beef in such quantities? It is a mystery to me.

4. The most vital questions regarding cow protection are:

(1) How to prevent slaughter of *cows* and *bulls* for beef?

(2) How to bring together Hindus and Mahomedans?

(3) How to induce Hindus to rear good cows instead of merely reverencing them?

(4) How to secure greater fodder for the cattle? My answers in brief are:

(1) Put a tax on the slaughter of bulls and cows (including heifers) of thirty rupees per head and prohibit all slaughter before the age of 10 of such cattle.

Also stop all export of milch cows and stud bulls and impose a heavy duty on the export of raw hides, prohibiting altogether export of hides of cows and bulls slaughtered or killed.

(2) Mahomedans should stop cow sacrifice altogether and Hindus should stop music before mosques. Thus they will respect each other's religion.

(3) Hindus should be induced to use cow's milk etc. and cease using buffalo's milk etc. except for *Halwai* purposes.

(4) Government should at once declare certain parts of protected forest as pastures for cows without fees for grazing, and fodder crop raising should be encouraged to the public by lowering taxation on such lands.

5. The ancient history of India *re* cow protection is as follows, keeping in mind that *Ahimsa* is distinct from reverence for the cow:

	Period	Dates	Sacredness	Slaughter
1.	Vedic period	ending 3000 B. C.	maintained	allowed for sacrifice and then for food
2.	Brahmana period	3000–2000 B. C.	"	"
3.	Epic period	2000–600 B. C.	"	only for higher sacrifice
4.	Buddhist period	600 B. C.–650 A. C.	"	by some Hindus for sacrifice only
5.	Hindu "	650–1250 A. C.	"	stopped altogether
6.	Mahomedan "	1250–1650 " "	"	by Mahomedans for food and sacrifice
7.	Maratha "	1650–1850 " "	"	stopped again altogether
8.	British "	from 1850	"	resumed by Mahomedans for sacrifice and food, by Christians for food.

Suggestions for the Future

1. *Vrishothsarga* and *Gopradhana* should be made by Hindus in money. If rich men wish to make it in kind, stud bulls and milch cows of *Goshalas* should be shown, and their value fixed at Rs. 100 and 25 which amount as well as the bulls and cows, should be paid and returned to the *Goshalas*, the donee Brahmins getting Rs. 50 and Rs. 12-8-0 respectively for the bull and the cow.

2. *Goshalas* should be started in every district in suitable places, preferably in every tahasil or taluka. They should secure good grazing plots. Dry cows and bulls brought by people should be sent to these grazing plots by the *Goshalas* and returned to owners when in good condition after paymant of certain fees.

3. *Goshalas* should purchase at market price all such cows and bulls as cultivators and even other owners wish to sell, so that they may not fall into the hands of butchers. Cultivators, therefore, in need of money, should be requested not to take their cows and bulls to the bazar but to the *Goshala*.

4. *Goshalas* should lend milch cows to such house-holders as wish to keep them in their houses for milch. When dry they should be taken back after charging such fees as may be fixed.

5. *Goshalas* should keep stud-bulls, improve the breed and the milk-producing capacity of cows, and they should undertake to supply milk to towns and cities.

6. Tanneries and bone-crushing mills should be started by *Goshalas*. Heavy export duty should be imposed on raw hides and skins. Forward contracts for the delivery of raw hides and skins should be declared illegal as they tend to increase illicit slaughter.

7. It is the duty of Vaishyas or rich merchants to make cow protection (*Goraksha*) real. They should come forward with money contributions, and Brahmins should come forward with personal labour, and both should combine to see that the price of milk is reduced. Prices have gone high all round, but milk has specially become very dear in India compared with other countries.

8. After settling the Hindu-Muslim differences as above, both should combine to bring a cow protection bill in the Legislative Assembly, embodying provision for a tax of thirty rupees on cow slaughter, prohibiting slaughter of milch cows and of cows and bulls before the 10th year, etc. If Government refuses or vetoes it, obstruction should be resorted to.

It must be remembered that Mahomedan emperors even before Babar and Akbar levied a tax on cow slaughter both from the economic and the religious points of view. The British Government should rely on foreign beef for the food of British soldiers.

The bill should also prohibit the export of bones. Exporting bones is exporting the very bones of Indian people, as it removes every year the best manure from the country.

9. There should be a cow protection *sabha* in every district with *Goshalas*, tanneries, bone-crushing mills and godowns, and manure should be sold at cheap rates, *e. g.* cow dung and bone dust.

10. It does not follow from cow-slaughter sacrifices in Vedic times, that the Aryans did not then reverence the cow. The old world religion was everywhere sacrifice and it was often thought meritorious to sacrifice one's own son as the dearest offering that could be made to God. We have such stories in the Vedas as also in the Old Testament.

11. With regard to the feed of cows, special care should be taken for preventing them from eating human excreta. Also very little corn should be given them, as it makes their milk less pure, and cooked cakes etc. should never be given them. In short, care should be taken to see that milch cows and cows generally should be as described in our ancient books (*Agramagram charantheenamoshadheenam vane vane*).

Khaddar work in Nellore District

Deshabhakta Konda Venkatappayya sends the following remarkable notes about the progress of Khadi in the Nellore District of Andhra. There is much in the notes which can be copied by every municipality and other Khadi associations.

Besides the sale depot in the town of Nellore and the production centre Kanupur, a village in the interior of the district, both of which are in the direct management of the A. I. S. A. (Andhra Branch), there are two independent co-operative societies doing Khaddar work, one in Nellore and the other at Kavali, the second important town in the district. The latter owns a capital of Rs. 1,000, sells cotton to the spinners, purchases yarn from them and gets it woven into cloth which it also sells. The co-operative society at Nellore has a capital of Rs. 500 and conducts merely a sale depot. The Allur Co-operative Union has recently subscribed a capital of Rs. 2,000 to be invested in the production and sale of Khaddar and have applied to the Registrar of Co-operative Societies for necessary sanction.

The Municipality of Nellore has evinced considerable zeal for the development of Khaddar. Spinning is made compulsory in the 15 elementary girls' schools under its management. The lady teachers, who have been trained in spinning, are themselves giving instruction in spinning to the girls in their charge. Last year the Municipality spent Rs. 500 for spinning charges in the schools. This year it has sanctioned Rs. 1,000 for instruction in spinning both for boys and girls in all the elementary schools which are 30 in number.

The Mahomedan Middle School for girls which is under the management of the Municipality has adopted Khaddar weaving for vocational training. The same Municipality has sanctioned recently a sum of Rs. 1,000 for the introduction of Khaddar weaving in the three middle schools under its management. In the Municipal Gosha Hospital, Nellore, the in-patients are clad in Khaddar, the same being supplied by the Municipality. The disabled poor living in the *Langarkhana* under the charge of the Municipality are supplied Khaddar for their wearing free of charge.

A sum of Rs. 1,500 has been sanctioned for the purchase of Khaddar to be utilised for the uniforms of the municipal scavengers. These scavengers have themselves purchased Khaddar worth Rs. 400 for their personal use, having raised the amount by way of loan, which they have undertaken to pay in three monthly instalments out of their salaries.

The municipal teachers also have purchased Khaddar for their wearing, having received a loan of Rs. 500 free of interest from a gentleman who is a great lover of Khadi. The teachers have stipulated the payment of the loan in four equal instalments out of their salaries. The District Board of Nellore also has realised the necessity and importance of instruction in spinning and weaving Khaddar. For the last four years instruction in both spinning and weaving has been arranged for in the three high schools and two middle schools under the management of the Board.

This Board has also sanctioned a grant of Rs. 20 per month for similar instruction to the girls in the Kasturi Bai Pathashala, a national school in the town of Nellore.

Ashram Tannery

It is possible for me now to inform readers that they can get from the Sabarmati Satyagrahashram*, Tannery Department, well prepared dead-cattle hide. Sandals, belts and such other things are already being made but not yet in quantities large enough for executing all the orders that may be received. But it is possible now to meet a fair demand for prepared dead-cattle hide in three colours, black, dark-brown and yellow, and two qualities at Rs. 1-8-0 and Rs. 1-4-0 per pound. Those who are interested in making this experiment a success and who desire to use only dead-cattle hide should correspond with the Manager, Satyagrahashram, Tannery Department for all further information. Till the Ashram is ready to execute orders for boots, shoes and other prepared leather articles, I suggest the purchase of dead-cattle hide which is now available at the Ashram, and getting what they want prepared through their own shoe-makers. It is easier, cheaper and more expeditious for people to get used to buying hide as they buy Khadi, and to get articles prepared for themselves as they get their clothes prepared from the Khadi they purchase. It is not easy to open many tanneries. It would be a proper division of labour to take the work of manufacture off the hands of tanneries, if the work of taking possession of all the raw hide of dead cattle with a view to replacing the hide of slaughtered cattle is to be done with expedition.

9th June, 1927

KHADI FRANCHISE

By M. K. Gandhi

Sjt. Srinivasa Iyengar, who is endeavouring with might and main to signalise his year of office as President of the Congress by achieving, if human effort can, Hindu-Muslim Unity and by doing many other things, asked me when he kindly visited me at Nandi, whether I would relent in the matter of the obligation

* Since called Harijan Ashram.

on every member of a Congress organisation habitually to wear Khadi. I told him that there was nothing for me to relent about. At Gauhati I was not insistent on the present clause. When asked, I merely gave my opinion, that experience had shown that either the Khadi clause should go altogether, or it should be stiffened to mean habitual as distinguished from ceremonial wear. I have seen nothing since to alter that opinion.

But if the members do not desire any discipline, or desiring discipline, they do not want the clause about habitual Khadi wear, and if they would laugh the Khadi clause to scorn and break the rule on every occasion that offered itself to them, the clause should be undoubtedly removed. In a popular institution, it must be the opinion of the majority that must count. But I have always held that when a respectable minority objects to any rule of conduct, it would be dignified for the majority, and would conduce to the good of the Congress, for the majority to yield to the minority. Numerical strength savours of violence when it acts in total disregard of any strongly felt opinion of a minority. The rule of majority is perfectly sound, only where there is no rigid insistence on the part of the dissenters upon their dissent, and where there is on their behalf a sportsmanlike obedience to the opinion of the majority. No organisation can run smoothly when it is divided into camps, each growling at the other and each determined to have its own way by hook or by crook. I had therefore no hesitation in telling the President, that he should assist the removal of the clause about Khadi if that clause could not gain willing submission from the minority.

This, however, is totally different from the question of my opinion. Any appeal to me to change my opinion, as has been done so often before, would be, to say the least, unfair to me. I must be allowed to retain my opinion as to the Khadi clause or as to the method of running the Congress organisation. All I can say is, that my opinion should have no greater weight than the opinion of any other member of the Congress. My own opinion is emphatically, that it will be wrong for the Congress, if it is to have an organic connection with the starving millions, to break this one and only bond between the classes and the masses. But I know that there is another school of thought in our country, which rejects Khadi as any token of a bond between the classes and the masses, and regards it as a mere *mahatmaic* freak or fad. That school is entitled to the same respect for its opinion as I venture to claim for my own. The President and the other members of the Congress have really to decide the question upon its merits, and ask themselves what is good for the Congress and fearlessly decide accordingly.

After all Khadi is a force to be reckoned with, if it has come to stay. If it has staunch, true and self-sacrificing workers to back it, and if it has intrinsic value, it will prosper even though the Congress should in its wisdom give it up as part of the franchise, or even give it up altogether. The Congress will be the first to recognise anything that becomes a living force in the country. It may legitimately ignore it till it has proved its vitality. There may be and there are no doubt many things which are good in themselves. But a vast popular organisation like the Congress cannot possibly take up things merely because they are good. It can only take up things that are good, provided they have popular backing. Without such backing the Congress would cease to be representative of the people and would merely represent a body of reformers or faddists.

Let the members of the Congress therefore come to a decision untrammelled by my opinion or anybody else's. If their experience tells them that Khadi has no backing in the country, if they think that it has nothing to do with the masses, they should unhesitatingly repeal the offending clause.

I have repeatedly held, that in every matter of urgency the All-India Congress Committee has not only the power but is bound to deal with the urgency as if it was itself the Congress, and run the risk of its decision being overturned at the next ordinary session of the Congress. A special session becomes necessary only when on any matter of urgency opinion is sharply divided, or when on any such matter public opinion requires to be educated, or lastly, when a popular demonstration on an intensive scale on any given question is required. In every other circumstance, and in every other matter of urgency, I venture to think that the All-India Congress Committee will be abdicating its function if it does not give its decisive opinion and act upon it.

9th June, 1927

STUDENTS IN CONFERENCE

By M. K. Gandhi

The Secretary of the sixth Sindh Students' Conference sent me a printed circular asking for a message. I received a wire also asking for the same thing But being in a somewhat inaccessible place, both circular letter and telegram were received too late for me to send a message. Nor am I in a position to comply with numerous requests for messages, articles and what not. But as I profess to be interested in everything connected with students as I am somewhat in touch with the student world all over India, I could not help criticising within myself the programme sketched in the circular letter. Thinking that it might be helpful, I reduce some of it to writing and present it to the student world. I take the following from the circular letter which by the way is badly printed and contains mistakes which are hardly pardonable for a students' society:

> "The organisers of this Conference are endeavouring their utmost to make this Conference as interesting and instructive as possible.........We intend organising a series of educational discourses and we request you to give us the benefit.........The problem of female education here in Sind deserves a special consideration...........We are not

blind to the other necessities of students. Sports competitions are being organised and along with elocution competitions they will, it is hoped, make the Conference more interesting. Nor have we eliminated drama and music from our programme.... .....Pieces in Urdu and English will also be staged."

I have not omitted a single operative sentence that would give one an idea of what the Conference was expected to do, and yet one fails to find a single reference to things of permanent interest to the student world. I have no doubt that the dramatic and musical and gymnastic performances were all provided on a "grand scale." I take the phrase in inverted commas from the circular. I have no doubt also that the Conference had attractive papers on female education. But so far as the circular is concerned, there is no mention of the disgraceful *deti leti* (dowry) practices, from which the students have not freed themselves and which in many respects makes the lives of Sindhi girls a hell upon earth and of parents of daughters a torture. There is nothing in the circular to show that the Conference intended to tackle the question of the morals of the students. Nor is there anything to show that the Conference was to do anything to show the students the way to become fearless nation-builders. It is a matter of no small credit to Sindh that it is supplying so many institutions with brilliant professors, but more is always expected from those who give much. And I, who have every reason to be grateful to Sindhi friends for giving me fine co-workers for the Gujarat Vidyapith, am not going to be satisfied with getting professors and Khadi workers. Sindh has got its Sadhu Vasvani. It can boast of a number of great reformers. But the students will put themselves in the wrong, if they will be contented with appropriation of the merit gained by the sadhus and reformers of Sindh. They have got to become nation-builders. The base imitation of the West, the ability to speak and write correct and polished English, will not add one brick to the temple of freedom. The student world, which is receiving an education far too expensive for starving India and an education which only a microscopic minority can ever hope to receive, is expected to qualify itself for it by giving its life-blood to the nation. Students must become pioneers in conservative reform, conserving all that is good in the nation and fearlessly ridding society of the innumerable abuses that have crept into it.

These conferences should open the eyes of students to the realities before them. They should result in making them think of things which, in the class room adapted to its foreign setting, they do not get an opportunity of learning. They may not be able in these conferences to discuss questions regarded as purely political. But they can and they must study and discuss social and economic questions which are as important to our generation as the highest political question. A nation-building programme can leave no part of the nation untouched. Students have to react upon the dumb millions. They have to learn to think not in terms of a province, or a town, or a class, or a caste, but in terms of a continent and of the millions who include untouchables, drunkards, hooligans and even prostitutes, for whose existence in our midst every one of us is responsible. Students in olden times were called *brahmacharis*, that is those who walked with and in the fear of God. They were honoured by kings and elders. They were a voluntary charge on the nation, and in return they gave to the nation a hundredfold strong souls, strong brains, strong arms. Students in the modern world, wherever they are to be found among fallen nations, are considered to be their hope, and have become the self-sacrificing leaders of reforms in every department. Not that we have no such examples in India; but they are far too few. What I plead for is that students' conferences should stand for this kind of organised work befitting the status of *brahmacharis*.

9th June, 1927

WHAT WE ARE LOSING

BY M. K. GANDHI

The readers of *Young India* are familiar with Mr. Gregg's name. He is studying in a very concrete manner and with a passion worthy of a patriotic son of the soil the many questions affecting this land. His studies and experiments in hand-spinning continue unabated. He is experimenting in education of the children of backward classes. He is interested in the welfare of these classes. And in that connection, he is studying the question of agriculture. Having watched the economic and highly hygienic disposal of night-soil at the Satyagrahashram, Sabarmati, he is now studying that question in a methodical manner. In the course of a letter suggesting the establishment of an experimental farm he says:

"The special feature of the farm would be its use of night-soil as fertilizer, burying it as is done at the Satyagrahashram, or treating it as do the farmers of China and Japan. The whole body of sweepers in the entire area from which the collections would be made would need to be carefully organised and gradually trained into the best ways of handling the stuff.

"In a very short time such a farm would become wonderfully productive in either grain, cattle-fodder, fruit or certain kinds of vegetables, all of which could be sold in the same locality, thus avoiding transportation charges in the marketing and yielding a fair profit for the further development of the scheme or the education and betterment of the whole sweeper community of the city or district. Such use of the night-soil would be an enormous saving of very valuable manurial material which is now not only almost entirely wasted, I believe, but is a source of much illness and consequent economic loss to the entire community, through the breeding of flies and the carrying of all sorts of germs and filth."

Mr. Gregg then continues:

"As instances of the wealth latent in night-soil let me quote from a book which I got from Maganlal. It is by an American Professor of soil-chemistry and soil-physics in Wisconsin State College of Agriculture, and contains the results of his study of Chinese and Japanese agriculture. His name was F. H. King, and the book is called *Farmers of Forty Centuries*. On page 193 ff. he says:

"'From the analyses of mixed human excreta made by Wolff in Europe and by Kellner in Japan, it appears that, as an average, these carry in every 2,000 pounds 12 7 pounds of nitrogen, 4 pounds of potassium, and 1.7 pounds of phosphorus. On this basis and that of Carpenter, who estimates the average amount of excreta per day for the adult at 40 ounces, the average annual production per million of adult population is 5,794,300 pounds of nitrogen, 1,825,000 pounds of potassium, and 775,000 pounds of phosphorus carried in 456,250 tons of excreta. . . .

"'In 1908 the International Concessions of the city of Shanghai sold to one Chinese contractor for $31,000 gold, [about Rs. 83,784], the privilege of collecting 78,000 tons of human waste, under stipulated regulations, and of removing it to the country for sale to farmers. . . .

"'In the Far East, for more than thirty centuries, these enormous wastes have been religiously saved and today the four hundred million of adult population send back to their fields annually 150,000 tons of phosphorus, 376,000 tons of potassium, and 1,158,000 tons of nitrogen comprised in a gross weight exceeding 182 million tons, gathered from every home, from the country villages and from the great cities like Hankow-Wuchang-Hanyang with its 1,770,000 people swarming on a land area delimited by a radius of four miles. . . ,

"'The rivers of North America are estimated to carry to the sea more than 500 tons of phosphorus with each cubic mile of water. To such loss modern civilisation is adding that of hydraulic sewage disposal through which the waste of five hundred million people might be more than 194,300 tons of phosphorus annually, which could not be replaced by 1,295,000 tons of rock phosphate, 75 per cent. pure. The Mongolian races, with a population now approaching the figure named, occupying an area little more than one half that of the United States, tilling less than 8,00,000 square miles of land, and much of this during twenty, thirty or perhaps forty centuries, unable to avail themselves of mineral fertilisers, could not survive and tolerate such waste.'

"'Dr. Arthur Stanley, health officer of the city of Shanghai in his annual report for 1889, considering this subject as a municipal problem, wrote:

"'Regarding the bearing on the sanitation of Shanghai of the relationship between Eastern and Western hygiene, it may be said, that if prolonged national life is indicative of sound sanitation, the Chinese are a race worthy of study by all who concern themselves with Public Health. Even without the returns of the Registrar General it is evident that in China the birth rate must very considerably exceed the death rate, and have done so in an average way during the three or four thousand years that the Chinese nation has existed. Chinese hygiene, when compared with mediaeval English, appears to advantage. The main problem of sanitation is to cleanse the dwelling day by day, and if this can be done at a profit, so much the better. While the ultra-civilised Westerner elaborates destructors for burning garbage at a financial loss and turns sewage into the sea, the Chinaman uses both for manure. He wastes nothing, while the sacred duty of agriculture is uppermost in his mind. . . .

"'During our ride to Akashi on the early morning train, we passed long processions of carts drawn by cattle, horses or by men, moving along the country road, which paralleled the railway, all loaded with the waste of the city of Kobe, going to its destination in the fields, some of it a distance of twelve miles, where it was sold at from 44 cents to $ 1.63 per ton.'

"May be I misinterpret *Ahimsa*, but it seems to me to lie within the spirit of *Ahimsa* to so guide matter, that it shall not allow flies and disease bacteria which prey upon human life to come into being, but instead use it to create fine food for cows and men. The communities of flies and bacteria in this country do not seem to me to be having nearly so wretched a time as the people.

"I realise the aversion which people have toward night-soil, but it is based on a fallacy and seems to me to be utterly inconsistent with the Hindu belief in the Immanence of God in all things. It is certain that life comes everywhere, and we can in part determine whether it will take the form of flies, mosquitoes, etc. or cabbages and wheat, for instance.

"To me, as an outsider, the scheme offers a chance of using a vast source of wealth now being wasted,—not only wasted but a source of physical and moral enfeeblement of the entire population. It may be noticed, in passing, that in Bengal it is found that malaria is always worse in the district where the soil is poorest. So such a scheme as this might tend to decrease that malady too. It seems so silly for us to be so fussy about washing our hands before meals and at the same time to let excrement lie around the ground anywhere within a couple of hundred yards, so that the flies come gaily in after tramping around on that stuff and eating it and then walk on our fingers and food, and, according to their habit, vomit on our food the other stuff they have just been eating. I would much prefer to have *bhangis* in my kitchen and dining room than flies. Travellers in China remark on the scarcity of flies, I have heard."

16th June, 1927

HINDU-MUSLIM UNITY

By M. K. Gandhi

When the President of the Congress wired that a unanimous resolution on the Hindu-Muslim question was reached by the All-India Congress Committee, I could not enthuse over the information. The wire told me enough about the contents of the resolution. When the President paid me a visit at Nandi, he asked me whether I would write on it. I told him I did not think I could write anything helpful. A few days after the visit I got a message from a friend. Its purport was; 'You are responsible for the mischief that is going on in our midst. If you had not dragged the Hindus into the Khilafat agitation, the recent tragic events would not have happened. But you alone can now save us.'

In translating the message I have softened the bitterness of the language of the original. It seems to me to call for a reiteration of my belief about Hindu-Muslim Unity.

I do not repent of my part in the Khilafat agitation. It was a duty I discharged towards my Musalman countrymen. The Hindus would have been wrong, if they had not helped their brethern in their distress. However ugly the present look of things may be, future generations of Musalmans will recall with gratitude this great act of friendship on the part of Hindus. But the future apart, as I believe in the proverb that virtue is its own reward, I should always defend my action on the Khilafat question. I therefore received the friend's message of rebuke with perfect calmness.

But I wish I could fulfil his expectations and assist immediately and materially in bringing about peace. For I am just as strong a believer as ever in unity and the necessity for it. If it could be achieved by giving my life, I have the will to give it and I hope I have the strength for it. I should with the greatest joy undertake an indefinite fast, as I very nearly did at Delhi, in 1924, if it would melt and change the stony hearts of Hindus and Musalmans. But I have no sign from God within to undertake the penance. If a penance is itself an act of purification, it has also to be preceded by an equal measure of initial purification. I am obviously not pure enough for that supreme penance.

If the reader does not see me now often refer to the question in these pages, it is because the sense of humiliation has gone too deep for words. It matters little to me whether the perpetrators of shameful deeds are Hindus or Musalmans. It is enough to know that some of us are blaspheming a patient God and doing inhuman deeds in the sacred name of religion. I know too that neither assassination, nor fratricidal acts can possibly save religion. Religion worth the name can only be saved by purity, humility and fearlessness of the uttermost type among its professors. It is the only *shuddhi* and only propaganda.

Hence has the resolution of the All-India Congress Committee left me unmoved. For I know that we have not yet changed our hearts. We have not shed fear of one another. Any compromise that is unaccompanied by these two conditions must be a mere make-shift.

Moreover, I feel that any agreement between the component parts of the nation must be voluntary and must remain so for all time. It must not, if it is conceived in terms of Swaraj, depend for its final ratification or enforcement upon a legal enactment. Ratification by our respective organisations must be held to be final and binding. Enforcement must depend upon the honour of the leaders of respective parties and ultimately, in the absence of reliance on non-violence, on the arbitrament of civil war fought decently or indecently as the case may be. It is a sign of weakness, not of fitness for Swaraj to go to the foreign ruling power to arbitrate between us or to enforce the peace between us at the point of the bayonet.

If we the so-called leaders have no control over our fighting elements, our agreement must be held to be unreal and useless. Before we think of real Swaraj, we must learn to behave ourselves. The agreement had no effect on Delhi, and to our eternal shame the Government has been the keeper of the peace on Bakr-Id.

My creed of non-violence is an extremely active force. It has no room for cowardice or even weakness. There is hope for a violent man to be some day non-violent, but there is none for a coward. I have therefore said more than once in these pages that if we do not know how to defend ourselves, our women and our places of worship by the force of suffering, i.e., non-violence, we must, if we are men, be at least able to defend all these by fighting. It is unmanly to ask or expect the Government to ensure the peace between rival parties or to defend our women against ourselves. And while we remain so unmanly it is hopeless to expect Swaraj. In well-ordered societies, Governments merely undertake the police work. But the recent elaborate preparations at Delhi or Lahore were no part of police work. Differences we shall always have. But we must learn to settle them all, whether religious or other, by arbitration. Before the rulers we must be able to present a united front and demonstrate to the world our capacity for regulating our own manners if we would have Swaraj.

If, however, we have no leaders whom we can elect as arbitrators who would give wise and impartial decisions, or, if we are too unruly and barbarous to wait for and abide by decisions of arbitrators of our choice, we must fight till we are exhausted and come to our senses. The Government will no doubt always intervene, whether we will or no, either to keep the public peace or to preserve its own safety. But it will weaken us the least, if the rival factions will courageously and straightforwardly refrain from courting the protection or assistance of Government. Why should a murderer in such warfare be defended? Let him seek the gallows. Let breakers of places of worship come forth boldly and say, we have done this for the sake of religion, punish us if you like! Let those who kill innocent passers-by deliver themselves to the police and say, we have done it all for God's sake! All this may read heartless. But I have merely endeavoured to suggest a way that is straighter and less weak than the one we have hitherto adopted.

And if you cannot, after the manner of civilised men, resort to voluntary arbitration or, after the manner of brave barbarous races, fight out differences without seeking the intervention of British justice or bayonets, all we may expect to get in the shape of reforms is an increased agent's share in the bureaucratic Government; in other words, an increasing share in the exploitation of dumb millions. Let us take care that any agreement we may come to does not reduce us to that unenviable condition.

16th June, 1927

HAVE I BOYCOTTED ANDHRA?

BY M. K. GANDHI

When Deshabhakta Konda Venkatappa saw me at Nandi and again at Bangalore, he told me that as Andhra was not on the tour list for the year, many Andhra friends had enquired of him whether I had boycotted Andhra. My old love of the Andhra people and the happy memories of my connection with them will not let me boycott Andhra, even if I wish to, though some of the Andhra workers do some times vex one into wishing to boycott the province till they set themselves right. They are fine men. They have got the patriotic spirit. But some of them are workers only so called. They are all leaders and when everybody wants to lead there is nobody to serve, no one to obey and in the exercise of that false independence the people are neglected. I hope the workers to whom these remarks may apply will not say to themselves or to me that they are no worse than other provinces. It would be a wrong way of looking at the right thing. After all Andhra men and women who at one time gave promise of being the first in the field for real civil disobedience must not be satisfied with being as bad as the rest. Those who seek to compete for civil disobedience have to prove their capacity for exemplary obedience, restraint and discipline. Andhra, which might have easily been first in Khadi and every one of its departments, has yet to come up to the mark. But I must not exhaust the whole of my battery of criticism. I must reserve it for my forthcoming visit, as I had never given up the idea of visiting Andhradesh. As a suitable month could not be set apart this year, the idea was to reserve Andhra for next year unless I could give it, as it was then thought, the first fortnight of December. God has, however, upset all my plan and the whole of the programme for the second half of this year has been dislocated. And if I am at all fit and well and there is no accident, I would like to be in Andhradesh not for a few days but for a month or two next year. I have therefore told Konda Venkatappayya that if the people will still have me, I would like to visit Andhra early next year and combine rest with work. I must not be expected to rush through space and programmes as before. Let the workers also realise that I shall be devoting the stay in Andhra to Khadi work alone.

Untouchability work is no doubt part of my being. But that work is largely included in Khadi work. For, it is designed to level up those who occupy the lowest rung of the ladder with those who are at the top. It is the cotton thread which beginning in the humblest cottage of India and reaching the highest in the land can alone indissolubly bind the two and make them feel akin. I know that the Andhra workers are ambitious. Let their ambition percolate down to the lowest stratum of society and all will be well.

16th June, 1927

A WELCOME STEP

By M. K. Gandhi

A correspondent from Holalkere in Mysore writes:

"I am highly glad to inform you that the people belonging to Lambani community of my taluk have completely abstained from drinking toddy and other liquors since a month and a half. It was in the Lambani Conference held in this town at the end of last April that they had taken an oath not to touch any liquor, prostrating themselves before the evening sun. Since then, they have not swerved from their oath. If anyone of that community is seen near toddy shop, he is strictly dealt with by the Naik, Yajaman and and Karabhan of that hamlet. Their women carry to us every day the glad news, there are no broils at their hovel and that they lead a very peaceful life. This is instance to show that your movement of purification had entered our State even before your entering it."

I congratulate the Lambani community upon the great step they have taken, and hope that they will not slide back like many who did so after the exultation of 1921 had subsided. Let me invite the attention of the leaders of the community to the case recorded in these pages of the Raniparaj people of whom those abstainers who took to the Charkha as a means of occupying their time and attention, not only had no hankering after liquor but were able to double their savings. For they not only saved what was spent upon the drink but they also added to their income by saving in the cost of clothing. It is the universal experience of temperance reformers that if the people who take pledges do not usefully occupy their time, the hankering returns and it becomes too strong to resist temptation. I hope too that other villages will follow the example of Holalkere and that when I am enabled to begin my tour in Mysore, I shall receive side by side with glowing accounts which I have been promised of the progress of Khadi accounts also of eradication of the drink habit.

16th June, 1927

RANIPARAJ INQUIRY COMMITTEE

BY M. K. GANDHI

Sjt. Vallabhbhai Patel has lost no time in embarking upon the work of the committee that was only recently appointed at the Raniparaj Conference. The following extracts from the interim report of the second tour of the committee will be read with interest:

"Interesting information was elicited from these

forest-dwellers regarding their social and economic condition. The Committee had the honour of having a personal interview with the Maharaja Saheb of Bansda on the 12th instant. His Highness received the members very courteously and evinced a keen interest in the welfare of his Raniparaj subjects. He considered our suggestions in their practical bearing and said that he will be only too glad if his people took the subsidiary industry of hand spinning. His Highness has already instructed the Diwan Saheb to supply the Committee with the necessary statistics from State records.

"The question of prohibition was a delicate affair. His Highness on principle is for total prohibition, but he has his practical difficulties. Out of his annual income of seven lakhs and seventy thousand about four lakhs are realised from the excise. Not that he would not forego a substantial part of this income of questionable morality, but he sees that he is helpless. His little territory is surrounded on all sides by British, Gaekwadi and Dharampur territories. So long as they have not inaugurated a policy of prohibition his own people can very easily have access to the accursed drink. It is the old argument of let others do their bit, then only can I find my own way to do mine. We could see that the Maharaja sincerely wishes that his people lead a sober life. Is it too much for the Indian princes to combine in a war against drink, the greatest foe of the half-starved masses? Solitary sacrifices may not show tangible results immediately but a moral step acts as a great leaven, and greater the sacrifice the more far reaching is its moral effect.

"An instance of the sincerity of His Highness may be noted here. At the end of our interview he sent for the labourers working about his palace and allowed them to vent their grievances in our presence. The thing was not a mere show. One of the labourers, a tee-totaller could summon up courage and submit before His Highness the hardships of forced labour for the State during their busiest seasons The Maharaja promised to inquire into the matter.

"During this tour the witnesses mainly came from the Dhodia community. A few amongst them have courageously given up drink. City people can have no idea of what this means Those who give up drink amongst these backward people have to suffer an amount of social ostracism. Superstition runs rampant amongst them. Drink is often regarded as a semi-religious ceremony. Those who give up drink are regarded as so many rebels against the communal law It requires more than ordinary moral courage to stand for purity in the teeth of communal persecution. The so-called superior classes may well take a lesson from these humble and silent reformers.

"In every meeting that we held, there was a great demand for the spinning wheel. It was gratifying to see that the people are fast realising the necessity of the uplift movement and especially the vast potentiality of organised spinning. Already a ray of hope has penetrated the utter darkness of despair in their hearts and they are looking up for a brotherly hand to lift them up. It is a call for self-sacrificing youths with robust health and equally robust faith and optimism. Will our young men respond?

"The Christian missionaries are already on the field. Their wonderful devotion and tenacity ought to fill us with shame and set us thinking. There is a regular network of mission schools and boardings not only for boys but also for girls, in the forest area of Bulsar and Chikhli Talukas. Indian work of a similar type is conspicuous by its absence. There is no hope for this land so long as the upper and well-to-do classes do not realise their duty by their unfortunate and ignorant brothers who after all are the backbone of the country.

"A remarkable thing has come to our notice during this tour. Mostly those who have taken to spinning find it possible to stick to their vow of giving up drink. Many who had given up drink relapsed into their old habit in the absence in their house of the silent social reformer *viz.* the spinning wheel. In some cases individuals come forward and candidly say that they cannot give up drink but they would welcome the spinning wheel, little knowing that the wheel was ultimately to save them against drink in spite of themselves.

"Lastly, we congratulate the Chikhli Taluka Local Board for the very useful work done by them by sinking wells for the 'untouchables' wherever it was necessary."

The Committee visited eighteen villages recording statements of witnesses from 47 villages in the Chikhli and Bulsar Talukas and in the state of Bansda. It reflects credit upon the Bansda State that the Committee is able to give a glowing account of the interest that the Maharaja Saheb of Bansda is taking in his people. But all the good that is undoubtedly being done by His Highness to his people, is really undone so long as he considers it necessary to derive an income from the drink traffic. No doubt the fact that the three neighbours adjacent to the Bansda territory, that is the British, the Gaekwad and Dharampur have no prohibition, makes it difficult for Bansda to carry out the policy of successful prohibition. But great things cannot be done without great sacrifice and great measures. Bansda cannot only lead the way by declaring out and out prohibition, but can then agitate for prohibition in the neighbouring states. The chief thing is to be prepared to sacrifice the drink revenue. An immediate beginning can be made by deciding not to use that revenue for any purpose however laudable it may be, save for that of carrying on an intensive anti-drink propaganda amongst the tribes given to drink. For, there is no doubt that any state that seriously wants its people to give up the evil habit cannot be satisfied merely with making it legally impossible to indulge in the evil habit, but to find out the cause of the habit and to educate the people to give it up. In the end, no state need suffer by depriving itself of the drink revenue. The inevitable outcome of any policy of prohibition carried out side by side with constructive work of the nature suggested by me must result in an ever increasing prosperity of the people and therefore of the state. India is the most promising country in the world for carrying out total prohibition for the simple reason that addiction to drink is not considered respectable or fashionable and is confined only to a certain class of people.

23rd June, 1927

LANCASHIRE BLOCK

By M. K. Gandhi

The long delay which took place in the publication of the Tariff Board report was almost a certain indication of the rejection of any recommendation for granting further protection to the great mill industry. The Government will not offend Japan by discriminating against it and favouring Lancashire. And it dare not displease Lancashire by applying it any protective duty. For Lancashire is the Government in substance; and to grant India effective protection against Lancashire would be almost like committing suicide.

This question of protection for the mill industry against Lancashire and other foreign competition is a question of life and death for India as it is supposedly one of life and death also for Lancashire. To realise the truth of this statement, one has merely to look at the table of imports. Imports from Lancashire are by far the largest of all the other imports, nearly half of all British imports. Lancashire has risen on the ashes of India's greatest cottage industry and it is sustained by the exploitation of the helpless millions of this land. The indigenous mill industry is really regarded as an interloper, and if it could be decently squashed in the interest of Lancashire, it would be suppressed without ceremony. The stupendous interest of Lancashire is allowed to over-ride every moral consideration. The existence of that industry harms both Lancashire and India. It has reduced India to pauperism, and India's pauperism reduces Lancashire to moral bankruptcy.

The mill-owners of India will never be able to vindicate their position in the face of this almost insurmountable obstacle, unless they courageously make common cause with the people and force protection from the Government. It is the country's right. If a country has the right to determine the composition of its inhabitants, and to exclude those whom it considers to be detrimental to its existence, it has a greater right to determine the composition of the goods that it would permit to be imported within its borders and to exclude those that it may consider to be harmful to its population.

There can be no doubt that foreign cloth is the most harmful among all our imports. The mill industry may for a time flourish somehow, it may also show a temporary prosperity by various manipulations or by favourable accidents; but unless it secures effective protection against all foreign cloth, it is bound to go under sooner or later, and certainly much sooner than one expects. Some day or other there is bound to be a real sustained mass awakening, whether mad and undisciplined but organised in its own madness, or (as I hope), disciplined and organised non-violently. And when it comes the indigenous mill industry, unless it is recognised as their own by the masses, will perish in the flames that must overtake foreign cloth. It is time for the mill-owners to make common cause with Khadi and wrest protection from an unwilling Government. There is room enough for years to come for both, if the province of each is now marked out and rigidly respected. It is then possible for them to prosper in spite of Government aloofness and even insidious opposition. But this pre-supposes intelligent sacrifice on the part of the mill-owners, a vital combination amongst them and an iron determination to carry through their programme.

I was glad to notice an authoritative repudiation of the rumour that a cut in the wages of the mill-hands was contemplated as a reply to the Government's decision It would have been suicidal. What is wanted at this time is not antagonising labour, but making common cause with labour and regarding mill-hands as much proprietors of the mills as the share-holders and agents. If the share-holders supply the capital, the labourers supply the muscle for the conversion of capital into cloth. A combination, therefore, between the mill-owners, the mill-hands and the masses would be an irresistible combination which the Government dare not ignore. Will the mill-owners have enough foresight, courage and patriotism for the task? The Is. 6d. ratio, it was contended (with a great degree of force in the contention), was a hit against that great industry and a gift to Lancashire. I wonder whether this last hit will stir the mill-owners to right action. No petition, no resolution in the Legislative Assembly will be of any use unless it is backed by effective mass action, and, in my humble opinion, it is not possible to conceive of any milder mass action than I have ventured to suggest.

23rd June, 1927

THE FORTHCOMING TOUR

BY M. K. GANDHI

If the progress I am supposed to be making continues to the end of the month, Drs. Subbarao and Krishnaswami Rao who have been kindly attending on me tell me that I should be able to resume a moderate amount of touring taken in easy stages. In view, therefore, of the possible resumption, I would like the workers and all concerned to bear in mind that I shall not be able to sustain the strain to which I seemed to be equal up to the end of March. Processions and noises must be abandoned and people should be repeatedly warned against crowding round me shouting and touching my feet; nor may I be expected to visit institutions in the places to which I may be taken. One meet ng and informal discussion with workers is about all I shall be able to manage per day. It is, I know, ungracious to use Chikballapur as my illustration to show how not to do it. The people of Chikballapur have been extraordinarily kind to me personally. A friend who noticed the exquisite attention paid to me at Nandi Hill by the representatives who used to come from Chikballapur from time to time to see that everything was supplied and in order, and who noticed the loving attention of the volunteers all drawn from representative families of Mysore, could not help remarking that it was a wonderful manifestation of selfless love that the people of Mysore exhibited, in that I had done nothing, specially for the people of Mysore. I had hardly even seen the country except for the flying visits to Bangalore. I could not help endorsing the spontaneous remark made by this friend. It was so true. The reception committee of Chikballapur left no stone unturned to anticipate my wants and supply them at considerable sacrifice of time and money. I would therefore gladly have avoided using Chikballapur for an unfavourable illustration.

But what happened there was so typical that I must not omit to mention it. Although there was to be no procession, and I was to be taken quickly and quietly to the place of the meeting which was to be perfectly noiseless, the leaders and the people lost their heads when they saw my car, and though the sun was beating hot, Mr. Hamza Husain Saheb, who is the chairman of the general reception committee and who was escorting me, had to submit to the pain of seeing the hood taken off and the motor carried in procession at a snail's pace. Officiating Dewan and ex-Police Commissioner though he was, he knew that at this moment he was connected with a representative of India's paupers, and as such had meekly to submit to the risk of all the good that Nandi had done to his charge being undone. I pleaded with the leaders whom I had seen in Nandi and who were near the car to restrain the enthusiasm and quickly take the motor to the meeting place. "We shall soon reach it,' was the only reply I could get. The meeting, too, was none too orderly, and on the top of that, though the majority of the audience did not understand English, the address was read to me in that language in spite of my repeated warning in these pages, that it would be more in keeping with the surroundings, at least at meetings where poor people gather in thousands, to conduct proceedings in their mother tongue supplying me when necessary with a translation in Hindi. But this much must be said for Chikballapur. Its mistakes too were due to affection. I was told that they never had a popular meeting of this character before. They naturally did not wish to damp the enthusiasm of the people. They lost their heads themselves for the moment, being caught in the wave of enthusiasm, and for the Hindi translation possibly they had not a single person in Chikballapur knowing Hindi. But let the other local reception committees profit by the unavoidable mistakes of Chikballapur. Let them have previous rehearsals in checking their enthusiasm. Let them translate it into Khadi purchases and hard work at the spinning wheel That would be an intelligent, profitable and national application of the energy created by the enthusiasm, and it would not only gladden their guest but will also strengthen him body, mind and soul.

Indecent Advertisements.

Lying on my back and trying at times, in obedience to medical instructions, to take my mind off serious reading, I chance upon advertisement sheets of news-papers. They are sometimes painfully instructive. I see often in respectable papers advertisements of a lewd nature. The headings are deceptive. In one case, the heading was 'books relating to *Yoga*.' On looking at the contents of the advertisement, I discovered hardly one book out of ten having any reference to *Yoga*; all the rest had reference to sex, suggesting that young men and women may indulge in sexual pleasures without coming to grief, promising to divulge secret remedies. I came upon worse things which I do not propose to copy in these pages. Hardly a newspaper is free from liquor advertisements, and advertisements regarding medicines designed to debase and corrupt youthful minds. The editors and the proprietors who are themselves known to be pure and opposed to drink, to smoking and such other evils, are at times found not to be averse to deriving an income from advertisements which are obviously intended to spread the evils which they shun. The argument sometimes advanced is that it is not possible to conduct a newspaper on any other condition. But is it necessary to conduct newspapers at any cost? Is the good that they do so great as to outweigh the evil that mischievous advertisements cause? We have a journalists' association. Is it not possible through it to cultivate a uniform code of morals among them and to create a public opinion that would make it impossible for a respectable journal to violate the prescribed code?

30th June, 1927

OUR SHAME

BY M. K. GANDHI

Sjt. S. D. Nadkarni is a clear writer, and has a very large heart for the so-called untouchables. I publish in another column, without any alteration, a letter* from him, in which he has poured out his feeling for the suppressed classes. And he has rightly used me as a peg, on which to hang his indictment of the touchables. Leaving aside, however, myself out of account, it seems to me, that his deep feeling has overpowered the sense of logic which as a rule does not fail him. I venture to think, that terrible as the case for untouchables is, it had no place either in the discussions of the All-India Congress Committee at Bombay, or at the Unity Conference at Delhi, when the question of Hindu-Muslim unity alone was on the anvil. It would have been just as logical to discuss at these meetings the question, say, of the woes of child widows, terrible as these are, as it would have been to handle the question of

* Omitted in this collection.

untouchability. But the slight illogicality of the letter must not be allowed to blur the very important question so forcibly presented by Sjt. Nadkarni. I entirely agree with him, that if there is no Swaraj without Hindu-Muslim unity, much less is there Swaraj without the removal of the shame of Hinduism, which untouchability certainly is. I am unconcerned with the question, what place untouchables will have in any political constitution that may be drawn up. Every one of the artificial props, that may be set up in the constitution, will be broken to bits, if we Hindus do not wish to play the game. The reasoning I have given against separate electorates and against separate treatment in the constitution is equally applicable in the case of untouchables. This removal of untouchability is not to be brought about by any legal enactment. It will only be brought about, when the Hindu conscience is roused to action, and of its own accord *removes* the shame. It is a duty the touchables owe to the untouchables.

"Let them not wait till the Suppressed Class Leagues and Touchable-Untouchable riots open their eyes to the needs of the most needy among us Indians." This is a terrible sentence occurring in the concluding portion of the letter. It is impossible to deny the force behind it. It reminds me of the conversation, that took place between the late Hari Narayan Apte and myself just before Gokhale died. It was at the Servants of India Society's quarters in Poona, that I was pleading for work amongst the so-called higher classes, rather than agitating amongst the suppressed classes after the fashion of some missionaries, and creating unrest among them. I was new to the work. I had not drunk deep of the ocean of miseries, in which the suppressed classes were being drowned, as the late Hari Narayan Apte had. In my philosophical prudence I asked this reformer, burning with the shame of the wrongs heaped upon the suppressed classes by the suppressing classes, whether he would incite suppressed classes against us. Instantly and indignantly came the reply: "Certainly, if I could, I would make them rebel against us today, and wrest from us by force what we will not give them voluntarily and as a matter of duty."

Much progress has been achieved in the matter of this reform. But infinitely more remains to be done. Most reforms have been preceded by bloodshed There seems to arrive a point, at which patience of the downtrodden is exhausted, and taking the law into their own hands and maddened with grief and rage, they make short work of the tyrant, and in their turn repeat, on an opportunity occurring, all the mistakes of the tyrant. Though, therefore, I share now to the fullest extent, I hope, the indignation that filled Hari Narayan Apte, I must work in the hope, that the so-called higher class Hindus will, whilst there is yet time, retrace their steps, and render to the suppressed classes the justice, which has become long overdue, and, in the further hope, that should the former not repent, the suppressed classes will know better than to rise in revolt against the wrong-doers. I must continue to work in the hope, that they will vindicate themselves and their Hinduism by going through a process of conscious suffering and self-purification, and thus proving themselves superior Hindus to those who are today disgracing themselves and Hinduism before man and God Every individual Hindu, who feels as Sjt. Nadkarni does for the untouchables, can meanwhile make common cause with them by himself or herself becoming untouchable by sharing their sorrows and their trials.

7th July, 1927

DESHABANDHU DAY AT DARJEELING

BY M. K. GANDHI

The reader will be glad to share the following with me from Mrs. Blair from Darjeeling:

"It may perhaps interest you to know, that the Darjeeling Mahila Samiti held a meeting on June 15th in memory of the great patriot, the late Mr. C. R. Das, at which

Shrimati Urmila Devi spoke. Her subject was the wearing of Khadi and the obligation on those who wished to help the poor of their country, to spin at least half an hour a day. On the following Wednesday, 22nd inst., nine of the members in the presence of Shrimati Urmila Devi promised to spin at least half an hour a day. Later on they may feel worthy to become members of the A. I. S. A. At present they are going to spin in order to be able to give warm clothes in the winter to the Baby Clinic and the Hospital."

It is a good thing, that the ladies of Darjeeling observed the anniversary of Deshabandhu in the manner described by Mrs. Blair. I hope, that the nine ladies who have given their names will persist in their effort. We have in this country a habit of making promises in a fit of enthusiasm, keeping them for a time, and then forgetting them altogether. I hope that these members will be steadfast enough to continue their sacrificial spinning, so long as a single Indian has to starve for want of work in his or her own home. One knows the fashion of saying, 'If they have no work, why do they not emigrate, why do they not go to the tea plantations, why do they not go to the cities where labour is in demand, and earn as much as 8 annas?' I have in these pages often demonstrated the falsity of this argument. Millions cannot leave their home, even if they wish to. And it would be a calamity if they all did. Coal at the pit's mouth in Newcastle is probably to be had for nothing, or very little. But such cannot be the case in Bombay. If Bombay must use Newcastle coal, it has to pay for transport. Similarly work to be had in Bombay will be of no use to the millions, who cannot, will not and must not leave their cottages and fields. Work has got therefore to be transported to their cottages, and inversely as in the case of coal at Newcastle, the work transported to cottages is less paying than work in Bombay in terms of coin. But in terms of mental satisfaction, and grain or vegetable, the work obtained in the cottages is far more profitable than that obtainable in Bombay.

7th July, 1927

ADI KARNATAKAS

By M. K. Gandhi

All the readers of *Young India* may not know who Adi-Karnatakas are. They are the suppressed classes of Karnatak. Just as at the Raniparaj Conference, friends of the Raniparaj altered the name Kaliparaj to the more appropriate name Raniparaj, so the suppressed classes all over India have been not unnaturally taking for themselves names which have no bad odour about them. In this spirit the suppressed classes in Karnatak describe themselves as Adi Karnatakas. And so I notice under that heading two paragraphs in the address of the Diwan of Mysore to its Representative Assembly. One observes from these paragraphs, that 'exceptional facilities have been created for the education of the members of these classes, and methods have been adopted to suit their special circumstances.' 'Among these methods are scholarships, exemptions from school fees, a free supply of clothes and school requisites, free hostels; and over and above the right of admission to all schools, 605 special schools have been provided for them. There are altogether 16,575 students of this class receiving tuition in Mysore.' An attempt is being made to organise a co-operative agricultural scheme with due provision of land, live-stock and direction.'

The paragraphs end with the following suggestion:

> "These people ought to be the strength of our strength. Shall we let them become our weakness? They have a rankling sense of wrong which only kindness can heal. The aim should be to 'Hinduise' them more and more, for they belong to the Hindu community, and to offer them every facility to remain within the fold. They will be a mighty accession to the strength of our body politic; if not, they will be an equally heavy subtraction from it. Alienated, they will introduce an additional element of heterogeneity which will further complicate the already

difficult problems of administration. No possible means of amelioration should be neglected, and every friend of Hindu society, every lover of Mysore, should supplement the efforts of Government with all his strength."

This suggestion is a gentle warning both to the Christian missionary and the Musalman missionary not to try to wean these suppressed classes from Hinduism, but if they at all wish to interfere, to act so that they may become better Hindus. If the suggestion is acted upon by the parties concerned, it will be a substantial contribution towards the attainment of real peace in the land

---

7th July, 1927

THE COW IN MYSORE

By M. K. Gandhi

I have received letters from Cow Protection Societies in Mysore, protesting against my letter to the Mysore Cow Protection Committee appointed by the State. My letter was in answer to a questionaire issued by that Committee. Extracts from that letter published in the Madras press led the Cow Protection Societies in question to think, that I was totally against legal prohibition of cow slaughter under any circumstances whatsoever. I was surprised to receive these letters, and I wondered whether, in a moment of forgetfulness or inadvertence, I had ever said that there should never be any legislation against cow slaughter. I therefore asked for a copy of my letter from the Cow Protection Committee, which they have kindly sent me. As the letter represents my considered opinion, and as it has been given some importance by the Committee and has caused misunderstanding among the public of Mysore interested in this very important question, I reproduce the whole of it below:

"I must apologise to you for the very long delay in acknowledging your letter of 27th November 1926. I duly received your first intimation, which I thought was purely formal, and as I had nothing effective to say, I did not send you a reply. From your second letter, however, I observe that you were anxious to have my opinion. But when I received it, I was so overwhelmed with work, that I had no time to collect my thoughts and give you a considered reply. Even as it is, I am sending you this reply in the midst of my Bihar tour. I hope you will accept these facts as sufficient excuse for the delay that has been caused in sending you my reply. Probably now it is of no use. Even so I give myself the satisfaction of telling you, that there was no discourtesy intended by me in the first instance in not replying, and now in replying at a time when my reply may prove too late.

"In matters of religion I am against any state interference, and the cow question is in India a mixed matter of religion and economy. So far as economy is concerned, I have no doubt that it is the concern of every state, whether Hindu or Musalman, to conserve the cattle supply. But, if I have understood your questionaire rightly, the underlying note is whether the State would be justified in interposing itself between Hindus and Musalmans and regulate cow slaughter even for purposes which Musalmans considered to be religious. In India which I consider to be as much the land of Hindus born in it as of Musalmans, Christians and others born in it, even a Hindu State may not prohibit cow slaughter for purposes considered to be religious by any of its subjects, without the consent of the intelligent majority of such subjects, so long as such slaughter is conducted in private and without any intention of provoking or giving offence to Hindus. That the very knowledge of any such slaughter would give offence to Hindus is inevitable. But unfortunately we know, that in India cow slaughter is often resorted to to defy and wound Hindu sentiment. This should be put down by every state that has the slightest regard for its subjects. But in my opinion the economic side of the cow question, if it is properly handled, automatically provides for the delicate religious side. Cow slaughter should be and can be made economically impossible, whereas unfortunately of all the places in the world it is the sacred animal of the Hindus which has become the cheapest for slaughter. To this end I suggest the following:

1. The State should in the open market buy out every cattle offered for sale by out-bidding every other buyer.

2. The State should run dairies in all principal towns ensuring a cheap supply of milk.

3. The State should run tanneries where the hides, bones, etc., of all dead cattle in its possession should be utilised, and should offer to buy again in the open market all private-owned dead cattle.

4. The State should keep model cattle-farms, and instruct the people in the art of breeding and keeping cattle.

5. The State should make liberal provision for pasture land and import the best experts in the world for imparting a knowledge of the science of cattle to the people.

6. There should be a separate department created for the purpose, and no profit should be made in the department, so that the people may receive the full benefit of every improvement, that might be made in the different breeds of cattle, and other matters pertaining to them.

"The foregoing scheme presupposes the State up-keep of all old, maimed and diseased cattle. This no doubt constitutes a heavy burden, but it is a burden which all states, but above all a Hindu state, should gladly bear. My own study of the question leads me to think that running of scientific dairies and tanneries would enable the State to cover the expenses of the upkeep of cattle that have become economically useless, apart from the manure they yield, and to sell at market rates leather, leather-goods, milk and milk products, besides manure and many other things that can be manufactured from dead cattle, and which today, owing to want of scientific knowledge or false sentiment, are practically going to waste, or from which the greatest advantage is not received. If you desire any further information on the scheme submitted, by way of elaboration of any parts of it, you will please let me know."

Neither the discussion with the members of the several Cow Protection Societies, nor the correspondence before me warrants any alteration of the opinion expressed in this letter. The reader will observe that I have nowhere said, that there should never be any legislation against cow slaughter. But what I have said is, that there should be no prohibition of cow slaughter by legislation *without the consent of the intelligent majority of the subjects* adversely affected by it. Therefore, the Mysore State will be perfectly justified, and indeed, bound to undertake legislation prohibiting cow slaughter, if it has the consent of the intelligent majority of its Musalman population. The members of the Cow Protection Societies that met me assured me that the relations between Hindus and Musalmans in Mysore were cordial, and that a majority of Musalmans in Mysore were as much in favour of legislative prohibition as Hindus, and I was glad to be assured by them, that many Europeans, especially missionaries, were in favour of such prohibition. So far, therefore, as the question of legislation in Mysore is concerned, if the statements made to me are correct the way is clear for legislative prohibition. But let me reiterate what I have pointed out in my letter, and what I have emphasised so often in these columns, namely, that legislative prohibition is the smallest part of any programme of cow protection. The trend of the letters received by me, and the activity of most Cow Protection Societies, however, show, that they would be satisfied with mere legal prohibition. I wish to warn all such societies against staking their all on legislation. We have already too much of it in this law-ridden country. People seem to think, that when a law is passed against any evil, it will die without any further effort. There never was a grosser self-deception. Legislation is intended and is effective against an ignorant or a small evil-minded minority; but no legislation which is opposed by an intelligent and organised public opinion, or under cover of religion by a fanatical minority, can ever succeed. The more I study the question of cow protection, the stronger the conviction grows upon me, that protection of the cow and her progeny can be attained, only if there is continuous and sustained constructive effort along the lines suggested by me. There may be, probably there is, room for supplementing or amending the constructive programme sketched by me. But there is no room for doubting the absolute necessity of a vast constructive programme, if India's cattle are to be saved from destruction. And the preservation of cattle really means also a step towards the preservation of the starving millions of India's men and women, who have also been reduced to the condition of her cattle. The Indian states undoubtedly can in this as in many such matters give the lead to the rest of India. And among the states, probably, there is none better fitted, or better able, to make the right beginning than Mysore. It has, from all accounts received by me, a popular prince, an enlightened public opinion, no Hindu-Musalman question, and a sympathetic Diwan. Mysore had also the Imperial Institute of Dairying and Animal Husbandry, and Mr. William Smith, the Imperial Dairy Expert, is himself stationed at Bangalore. The State has, therefore, all the materials necessary for evolving a constructive policy. Add to this the fact, that Nature has endowed Mysore with a glorious climate. The title a Hindu king dearly cherishes is that of defender of the cow and the *brahman*. The cow means not merely the animal, the giver of milk and innumerable other things to India, but it means also the helpless, the downtrodden and the poor. Brahman means the representative of divine knowledge and experience. But today, alas! Hindu princes are powerless, and in many cases even indifferent, if not unwilling, to ensure this full protection. Unless the States and the people co-operate with one another to control and regulate the breeding of cattle, the production of milk supply, and the disposal of dead cattle, for the benefit of the people as a whole, the cattle of India will be bred but to die an unnatural death at the hands of the butcher, notwithstanding all the legislation that may be passed against cow slaughter. The ignorance of Nature's Law will be accepted as no excuse when men and women of India appear before the Throne of Judgment.

I was shocked to learn from the members of the Cow Protection Society, that beef slaughtered in Bangalore and in Mysore was given to the animals in the State gardens, that beef was much cheaper than any other meat, and that the Adi Karnatakas, who claimed to be and were recognised as Hindus, and who knew the *Ramayana* and the *Mahabharata* as well as any other Hindu, were addicted to beef-eating. If all this is true, the better-placed Hindus are clearly to blame for such a state of things. If the Adi Karnatakas do not respect the sanctity of the cow, it is because they know no better. But what is to be said of the Hindus, who have so criminally neglected their brethren as to omit to acquaint them with a fundamental truth of Hinduism?

7th July, 1927

WHAT IS A POLITICAL ASSOCIATION?

BY M. K. GANDHI

I read the following in the *Hindu* of the 25th June last:

> "Under rule 23 (1) of Government Servants' Conduct Rules, Government have, I understand, prohibited Government servants from subscribing to the Khadi fund, which is in aid of the All-India Spinners' Association. The reasons for this prohibition are stated to be, (1) that it is an association, established with the consent of the All-India Congress Committee, as an integral part of the Congress organisation, (2) that it declares itself prepared to receive and acknowledge yarn subscriptions for membership of the Congress and (3) that therefore it must be regarded as a political association."

If the information supplied by the special correspondent of

the *Hindu* is correct, the ruling of the Madras Government appears to me to be a case of perverted judgment, and a gross interference with the private liberty of its servants. If it is intended merely as an attack upon Khadi or the All-India Spinners' Association, I have no doubt that both will survive the shock. And if it is an invitation to the All-India Spinners' Association to sever its connection with the Congress, I should be extremely sorry if I discovered that the Association had done anything to deserve such an invitation. The Association is proud of its being an integral part of the Congress organisation, and it will deem it an honour and a privilege to work under the Congress banner, so long as that venerable national institution regards it as worthy of its patronage. But if merely owning the parentage and patronage of the Congress, an institution becomes a political association, the interpretation would involve most awkward consequences, which I hope no self-respecting Government servant will tolerate.

There are many schools for suppressed class children run in several provinces under the Congress aegis, and with Congress funds, to which Government servants also have been known to contribute without any secrecy. Was it wrong for them to do so? And are schools for 'untouchables' political bodies, because they are run with Congress funds and by Congressmen? Provincial Congress Committees have been known to open famine relief funds, and invite subscriptions to which Government servants have subscribed. Was it a breach of Government Servants' Conduct Rules? These relief committees were and the suppressed class committees are integral parts of the Congress organisation. Are they, therefore, political associations? The Congress may open hospitals as an integral part of the Congress organisation and its activity. Will the hospitals therefore become political associations? Khadi is at the present moment an integral part of the Congress franchise. Is it a crime therefore for Government servants to wear it? Is it not possible for the Congress to have its political, its social, its moral, its economic, medical, sociological and such other departments, all integral parts of that organisation, and yet wholly self-governing and wholly independent each of the others? Every Congressman regrets that the Congress, although among all the national bodies it is the most influential and the most important, is not yet able to command men and money enough to organise every department of national life. But as time goes on, and as it is able to draw to it men of the right stamp, as well as money, it will certainly touch every part of our national life. It would be ridiculous then to say, that all its non-political activities became tainted with politics, and were therefore taboo to the Government servants. And if the Government dared to issue such a boycott, it would prove to be its own death warrant.

I am painfully conscious of the fact that the Congress is a long way off from attaining that height. But when it does, the Government will be absorbed by it, and there will be nobody to resent, resist, or interfere with the Congress influence. That the Government has been able,—assuming that the information given in the *Hindu* is correct,—to regard the All-India Spinners' Association as a political association, shows, that the Congress influence is at a discount at the present moment, that the public voice is ineffective, and that therefore, it is open for the Government to issue any ruling, no matter how insulting, or how ridiculous, it may be. I can only hope, that there will be Government servants courageous enough to disregard this monstrous ruling, and openly help the Spinners' Association, which in spite of the Government order, I submit, is entirely a non-political body, and was in so many words intended by the Congress to be and to remain, for the reasons stated in the resolution, which brought the Association into being. Here are the words of the resolution, which is part of the constitution of the All-India Spinners' Association:

" Whereas the time has arrived for the establishment of an expert organisation for the development of handspinning and Khaddar, and whereas experience has shown; that such development is not possible without a permanent organisation, *unaffected and uncontrolled by politics, by political changes or political bodies,* an organisation called the All-India Spinners' Association is hereby established with the consent of the All-India Congress Committee, as an integral part of the Congress organisation, but *with independent existence and powers.*"

Two things stand out unequivocal and emphatic in this preamble, namely, that it is unaffected and uncontrolled by politics, political changes, or political bodies, and that it has an independent existence and powers. How such an association could be called a political association, simply because it is an integral part of the Congress, and also because like a bank it has accepted the agency of the Congress for the collection of yarn subscription, passes comprehension. But acts of governments are often incomprehensible. It would have been more honest, if the reported action of the Madras Government had taken the form of a straight order to its servants to have nothing to do with the All-India Spinners' Association on the simple and intelligible ground, that it does not like the penetration of the Charkha into the villages and the consequent progress of Khadi and all that it means.

7th July, 1927

AGES-OLD PROBLEM

BY M. K. GANDHI

A Sannyasi from Almoda writes as follows:

"In replying to a correspondent, you have said in *Young India* of 15th April last, that even if you were attacked by a snake, you would not wish to kill it. In my opinion, this would be improper; for in the first place, you would be thereby killing yourself, and secondly, by letting such a venomous reptile free, you would be instrumental in causing injury to others. Take another instance. If the owner of a house, in which a snake has entered, removed the snake without killing it from his house, it is sure to enter some other house and injure its inmates. Surely the responsibility for the injury, it may be fatal, to the inmates of the other house, done by the snake that was let off, will be on the head of him, who has under a false notion of pity let the snake off. There are many other reptiles, beasts and insects which injure human beings or spread disease. Surely if the destruction of this life be considered *himsa,* then it is infinitely less than the destruction wrought by these creatures. Let it be granted that when a man kills for his own sake, it is *himsa*; but it cannot be when destruction is resorted to for the sake of saving many other precious lives. After all, the quality of an act is determined by the motive prompting it, and when the motive for destruction is the higher good, such destruction becomes a duty and ceases to be *himsa.* I would like you to answer this argument in the pages of *Young India.*"

The Sannyasi's argument is ages old. There is no doubt that there is very considerable force in it. Had it not been so, destruction would not have gone on as it has from ancient times. Few men are wantonly wicked. The most heinous and the most cruel crimes of which history has record have been committed under cover of religion or equally other noble motive. But in my opinion, we are no better off for the destruction that has gone on even under the highest sanction, that is, of religion. No doubt destruction in some form or other of some life is inevitable. Life lives upon life. Hence only is the highest bliss attainable ascribed by seers to a state, in which life is possible without the necessity of a perishable case, for whose sustenance destruction becomes at all necessary. And it is possible for man whilst in the body to hope to attain that state, only if he confines himself to the least possible destruction such as is caused in his taking of vegetable life. The freer he is, consciously and deliberately, from the necessity of living upon the destruction of other life, the nearer he is to Truth and God. That all mankind is not likely to accept what may appear to be an unattractive existence does not affect the validity of my argument. Men, who lead this life of utter selflessness and of pity for the meanest creature that lives, enable us to understand the power of God, and serve as leaven to lift up humanity, and light its path towards its goal. We have no right to destroy life that we cannot create. It seems to me to be atheistical to think, that God has created some life only to be destroyed by man, either for his pleasure or for sustaining a body, which, he knows, is after all doomed to death any moment. We do not know what part the many so-called noxious creatures play in the economy of nature. We shall never know the laws of Nature by destruction. We have records of men, whose love has travelled beyond their kind, living in perfect safety even in the midst of ferocious beasts. There seems to be so much affinity between all life, that tigers, lions and snakes have refrained from harming men, who have shed all fear of them and will approach them as friends.

The argument, that if I do not destroy a snake known to be venomous, he will cause death of many men and women, is deceptive. It is no part of my duty to set about seeking out all the venomous creatures and destroying them. Nor need I take it for granted, that if I do not destroy a snake I encounter it is bound to bite the next passer-by. I must not be the judge between the snake and my neighbours. I have sufficiently discharged my duty to my neighbours if I do unto them as I would that they should do unto me, and if I do not expose them to any greater risk than I do myself, and if I do not better my own condition in any way whatsoever at their expense. I may not therefore leave the snake in my neighbour's compound as is very often done. The utmost I can do is to leave the reptile as much out of harm's way as possible, and warn my neighbours about its appearance in the neighbourhood and its disposal by me. I am aware, that this is no comfort for my neighbours, nor any protection; but we are living in the midst of death trying to grope our way to Truth. Perhaps it is as well, that we are beset with danger at every point in our life; for, in spite of our knowledge of the danger and of our precarious existence, our indifference to the Source of all life is excelled only by our amazing arrogance.

I am not satisfied with the answer given to the Sannyasi. His letter, which is written in Hindi, shows that my correspondent is himself a fellow seeker after Truth. Hence only have I felt the call to answer his query in public. My own position is pitiable. My intellect rebels against the destruction of any life in any shape whatsoever. But my heart is not strong enough to befriend those creatures, which, experience has shown, are destructive. The language convincing confidence, which comes from actual experience, fails me and it will continue to be so, so long as I am cowardly enough to fear snakes, tigers and the like. I have entered upon the reply with the greatest diffidence. But I felt, that it would be wrong not to declare my belief for fear of losing caste and being regarded as a dangerous animal myself. I was once so regarded by friends in South Africa. We were all sitting at a table, and discussion turned upon the very topic I have here discussed, They were English missionery friends. They did not mind my views about transmigration, cow protection, vegetarianism, though they all appeared to be very crude to them. But they could not help betraying their disgust, which was written in their faces, when I said, that I would not, if God gave me the courage, kill a snake even if I knew, that not to kill would be certain death for me. Disgust was hidden by the suppressed laughter which accompanied 'Oh! you are a dangerous man then!'

14th July, 1927

REFORM OF PANJRAPOLE

BY M. K. GANDHI

It has been my privilege during my convalescence at Bangalore to pay regular visits to the Imperial Animal Husbandry and Dairy Institute, and to take there, what may be called, regular lessons. Mr. William Smith, is the Imperial

Dairy Expert and Head of this Institute, and his assistants, have most carefully shown me the working of the Institute and the different departments into which it is divided. I trust I shall make use of the knowledge thus gained in conducting the dairying experiment at the Satyagraha Ashram on behalf of the All-India Cow Protection Association. As a result of several discussions with Mr. Smith I asked him kindly to prepare for me notes on the working of *panjrapoles* and on methods of cattle-improvement in our villages, which he very kindly and promptly undertook to do I am already in possession of two valuable notes. I give below his note on *Panjrapoles*.

"Some of the existing *panjrapoles* with more or less permanent and assured incomes are fairly well managed, and do provide a comfortable refuge for a certain number of cattle which have ceased to be economically useful in their old age. In many of these institutions it is however not an uncommon thing, when trade is bad and subscriptions are slow in coming in, to find cattle being kept in these places in a state of starvation which must mean great suffering to the animals and which eventually kills them. In cases like this instead of being a refuge for the animals the *Goshala* becomes a cow killing institution, the method of killing being a cruel death by starvation. In at least six cases have I seen the cattle in *Goshalas* being starved to death. The first thing then to be done with the existing *panjrapoles* is to see that they do not under any circumstances whatever admit to their shelters a larger number of animals than they can feed properly, house comfortably and take care of until they die a really natural death.

All the larger *panjrapoles* with an assured income, and which can command capital, should in my opinion be divided into three departments, the whole being managed by a trained dairy farm-manager.

1. The refuge department where old and economically useless cattle excluding buffaloes should be comfortably fed and cared for until they die naturally.

2. A dairy department where all cows sent to the *panjrapole* to escape slaughter and capable of breeding and all other cows capable of bearing calves and yielding milk should be fed, housed and milked as a commercial dairy herd with careful milk recording, and the milk sold to the best advantage. The very best class of stud bulls should be used in this herd and all calves carefully reared, males not good enough for issue as stud bulls to be castrated and those considered good enough for breeding either transferred to the stud department or issued to villages as breeding bulls. All female stock to be reared as milkers and breeders. When the home-bred progeny of this department gets too numerous for the *panjrapole* to deal with, they could be sold to reputable Hindu owners on the distinct understanding that they are to be returned to the refuge department of the *panjrapole* when too old to work or milk.

3. A stud department where the very best of the right class of breeding bulls should be kept at stud for the use of the breeders in the district. The service of these animals could be given free for all cows passed by the expert manager as suitable for breeding with the *panjrapole* stud animals and careful records of all servings kept. This department might also undertake the castration of all unsuitable animals in the district free of charge.

It is not necessary to take any specific steps to improve the quality of buffaloes. India cannot afford to keep any class of bovin which does not possess dual purpose qualities *i.e.*, milk in the case of the female and draught in the case of the male. Generally speaking the male buffalo is unsuitable for field or cart work, and consequently unless the males except those required for stud purposes are slaughtered at birth, they remain an incubus in the country. The majority of the people in India do not approve of the killing of any kind of animals, and in any case it is not an economic proposition to rear and kill these animals for beef, as the value of this class of meat in India is far below cost of production.

The buffalo exists and increases in India owing to the poor milking quality of the cows, and the aim of all cattle breeding propaganda ought to be to so increase the milk yielding capacity of all classes of cows, that they will not only provide sufficient milk to rear a strong, healthy calf, but in addition to this give as much milk as pay the cost of their feed. If and when we attain to this standard there will be no need for the buffalo which will be automatically eliminated by economic forces. The existing conditions prevailing in many parts of India today where a cultivator keeps two or three cows to rear bullocks from and one or two buffaloes to provide milk and *ghi* for his household, cannot continue. It is too costly and there is no reason whatever why the cows now kept for breeding should not in the future rear their calves and provide in addition all the milk and *ghi* required by the household. Our cattle have little or no beef value and we cannot afford to keep cows for draught cattle production and buffaloes for milk. The cow alone can and must do both duties. For these reasons the *panjrapole* societies should confine themselves to caring for and improving the cow. Agriculture in India depends upon the efficiency of the cow as a bullock producer not the buffalo; and the health of the people can be maintained and improved by the milk of the cow. In a sense the buffalo is an interloper introduced because of the poor milking qualities of the cow.

If all *panjrapoles* employed really qualified men capable of managing the *panjrapoles* on the foregoing lines, they could undoubtedly do a great work for India."

The reader will observe from the foregoing that Mr. Smith has written with a knowledge of the existing *panjrapoles*. He told me that he had visited many of them. In his opinion the *panjrapoles* should serve the purpose not merely of being a home for aged and otherwise disabled cattle, but also for protecting the cow, and educating the people in the art of such protection. To that end they must have a properly equipped model dairy and a stud department. I add to these conditions a tannery department. I discussed with Mr. Smith the question of adding tanneries. The idea appeared attractive to him, but being a specialist he naturally did not want to travel beyond his province. Mr. Smith's cautious remarks about the buffalo are worthy of attention. He has not, and he cannot be expected to have, the same feeling about animal slaughter, but he recognises that in India any proposition suggesting slaughter of useless animals would be just as much out of place as a proposition for the destruction of aged and disabled parents would be anywhere. He has, therefore, endeavoured to enter into the Hindu feeling as much as possible, and suggested means of protection and conservation of cattle consistently with Indian traditions. I hope that managers of *panjrapoles* will study the suggestions made in Mr. Smith's important note and make the necessary alterations in their management, which, I am certain, can be made with very little extra cost in the beginning, and with much profit in the end. I must deal in a future issue with the other material Mr. Smith has kindly placed at my disposal.

14th July, 1927

AN ALL-INDIA SCRIPT

BY M. K. GANDHI

A Gujarati correspondent wrote some time ago to *Navajivan* a letter advising that I should print *Navajivan* in Devanagari script, so as to give a practical demonstration of my belief in the necessity of there being one script for all India. Although it is my firm conviction that there should be one script for all the Indian languages, and that that script can only be Devanagri, I could not follow the correspondent's advice for the reasons stated in my note in *Navajivan*, and which I need not reiterate here. But there is no doubt that we ought to seize the opportunity that the great national awakening gives us, o not merely popularising the idea but of doing something concrete in that direction. The Hindu-Muslim madness no doubt stands in the way of a thorough reform. But before the acceptance of Devanagari script becomes a universal fact in India, Hindu India has got to be converted to the idea of one script for all the languages derived from Sanskrit and the Dravidian stock. At the present moment we have Bengali script in Bengal, Gurmukhi in the Punjab, Sindhi in Sindh, Orriya in Utkal, Gujarati in Gujarat, Telugu in Andhradesha, Tamil in Tamilnad, Malayali in Kerala, Kanarese in Karnatak, not to speak of Kaithi in Behar and Modi in the Deccan. If all these scripts could be replaced by Devanagari for all practical and national purposes, it would mean a tremendous step forward. It will help to solidify Hindu India and bring the different provinces in closer touch. Any one who has any knowledge of the different Indian languages and scripts knows to his cost what time it takes to master a new script. For the love of his country, no doubt, nothing is difficult, and time spent in mastering the different scripts, some of which are are very beautiful, is in no way idly spent. But this spirit of abandon is not to be expected of millions. National leaders have to make things easy for them. Therefore, we must have an easily adaptable universal script for all India, and there is nothing so adaptable and readymade as Devanagari script. There is, or there used to be, an All-India organisation for this very purpose. I do not know what its activities are at present. But if the work has to be done, either the original association should be strengthened, or a new one formed for this purpose. The movement should in no way be confused with the spread of Hindi or Hindustani as the *lingua franca*. The latter work is going on very slowly, but steadily. Use of one script will facilitate the spread of one language. But the functions of the two run parallel only up to a point. Hindi or Hindustani is not designed to replace the provincial languages, but is intended to supplement them, and to be used for inter-provincial contact. And till the Hindu-Muslim tension lasts it takes the form either of Urdu written in the Persian script and containing a preponderance of Persian or Arabic words, or Hindi written in Devanagari, and containing a preponderance of Sanskrit words. When the hearts of the two meet, the two forms of the same language will be fused together, and we shall have a resultant of the two, containing as many Sanskrit, Persian, Arabic or other words as may be necessary for its full growth and full expression.

But one script is undoubtedly designed to displace all the different scripts so as to render it easy for people belonging to different provinces to learn provincial languages. The best way of achieving the purpose is first to make the learning of Devanagari script compulsory at least for Hindus in all the schools, as it is in Gujarat, and secondly to print the important literature in different Indian languages in Devanagari script. Such effort has already been made to a certain extent. I have seen Gitanjali printed in Devanagari script. But the effort requires to be made on a large scale, and there should be propaganda carried on for the spread of such books. Though I know that it is out of fashion just now to suggest anything along constructive lines that may bring Hindus and Musalmans together, I cannot help repeating what I have said in these columns and elsewhere, that Hindus must learn Urdu if they will come nearer their Musalman brethern, and Musalmans must learn Hindi if they will come nearer their Hindu brethern. Those who have faith in real unity between Hindus and Musalmans need not be disconcerted by the present terrible expression of mutual hatred. Their faith, if it is of any value, must make them actively but unobtrusively perform whenever possible, all acts of mutual toleration, affection and courtsey, and learning of one another's language is the least that one can do in that direction. Is it not better for Hindus to learn through the many ably-written Urdu books by devout Musalmans what Musalmans think of the Koran and the Prophet, and for Musalmans to learn through equally well-written Hindi books by devout Hindus what Hindus think of the Gita and Krishna than that the respective parties should learn all the bad things that might have been said about their respective religious books and their inspirers through their ignorant or fanatical detractors?

14th July, 192

LIMITATIONS OF SATYAGRAHA

BY M. K. GANDHI

An innocent paragraph, occurring in a letter in reply to one covering other subjects, has led to what I venture to call a thoughtless misrepresentation of Satyagraha and its author. The paragraph is part of a private letter written in Gujarati to Mr. Bharucha. It is no thesis on Satyagraha, and like every letter it contains many things understood between the writer of the original letter and that of the reply. It was not meant for publication. But when Mr. Bharucha telegraphed asking for permission to publish the paragraph, I had no hesitation in wiring permission. It appears from the newspaper report before me that the speakers at the Nagpur meeting suggested that I should have explained at the time the Nagpur Satyagraha was launched out what I have explained in my letter to Mr. Bharucha. I must dissent from the view. Had Mr. Avari not ascribed to me endorsement of his campaign, I should not even have written the article I did in repudiation. Where I cannot help, it is my rule not to hinder by any unnecessary or uncalled-for interference on my part. Instead, therefore, of giving an exhaustive opinion on what I then knew of Nagpur Satyagraha, I confined myself to a repudiation and an opinion on the general atmosphere of violence prevalent in the country. And I cannot help saying that it was an unlawful use to make of my private letter for suspending Nagpur Satyagraha, if those who were permitted to see the letter did not accept the reasoning contained in it. Moreover when they decided to make public use of the letter, they owed it to me to have made clear to them the points which they could not understand, or which appeared to them to be inconsistent with my previous writings. They owed it to the enthusiastic young men in Nagpur neither to damp their zeal nor to disconcert them by hurling in their midst an opinion which the receivers did not understand and did not accept. For myself I do not consider it to be any part of my duty to express an opinion upon the many insane things that are going on in this country, for I am humble enough to recognise that what may appear to me to be insane need not appear so to those who are doing those acts, and may even be in reality an epitome of wisdom. Though, therefore, things are being done in the name of Satyagraha in several places, I have not felt called upon to say one word about them. And I do suggest to the young men in Nagpur and to all concerned that they are not in any way bound to receive the permission of the Congress to offer Satyagraha or any other resistance to any unjust act so long as they do not use the Congress name. And if they are really of opinion that the Nagpur Satyagraha was justified, that it was really Satyagraha, it would amount to a desertion on their part of their commander and other comrades in gaol not to immediately re-embark upon their campaign, unless they think with me that what they thought was Satyagraha was not so in fact.

Having cleared the ground so far, let me now try to remove the confusion, that the well-meaning friends, who have undertaken to criticise the letter in question, have created about Satyagraha. I do maintain that the Arms Act could not be broken in terms of Satyagraha in the way it was in Nagpur. Let it be remembered that the bone of contention between the 'Republican Army' of Nagpur and the Government was not the Arms Act but the unjust and lawless detention of many patriotic young Bengalis. It was in every way wrong, therefore, to select the Arms Act for Civil Disobedience. Several speakers have read into my letter a meaning which I hold it does not bear and was never intended to bear. As long ago as

1917 or '18, I said that amongst the many black deeds of the Government, disarmament was the blackest. An out and out believer in non-violence, though I am, I hold that it is the right of any Indian who wishes to bear arms to do so under lawful permission. I do submit that an Arms Act is now and will ever be a necessity of good Government. I do not believe in the inherent right of every citizen to possess as many arms as he chooses without a licence. On the contrary, I hold it to be absolutely necessary for good government that the State should have the authority to prohibit the holding of arms except under prescribed conditions. I can also conceive the possibility of Satyagraha being offered against an unjust Arms Act or its unjust administration, as I can justify Satyagraha against an unjust Act for preventing thefts or other crimes. But I do maintain that just as Satyagraha cannot be offered against an unjust Crimes Act by committing the specific crimes, so can Satyagraha not be offered against an unjust Arms Act by carrying arms.

Let us also appreciate the distinction between Satyagraha and Civil Disobedience. All Civil Disobedience is a part or branch of Satyagraha, but all Satyagraha is not Civil Disobedience. And seeing that the Nagpur friends have suspended what they were pleased to call Satyagraha or Civil Disobedience, let me suggest for their information, and that of others how Satyagraha can be legitimately offered with reference to the Bengal detenues. If they will not be angry with me or laugh at me, let me commence by saying that they can offer Satyagraha by developing the power of the people through Khadi, and through Khadi achieving boycott of foreign cloth. They can offer Satyagraha by becoming precursors of Hindu-Muslim unity, by allowing their heads to be broken whenever there is a quarrel between the two, and whilst there is no active quarrel in their parts by performing silent acts of service to those of the opposite faith to theirs. If such constructive methods are too flat for them, and if they will be satisfied by nothing less than Civil Disobedience in spite of the violence of thought, word and deed raging round us, I suggest the following prescription of individual Civil Disobedience, which even one man can offer, not indeed in the hope of securing immediate release of detenues, but certainly in the hope of the individual sacrifice ultimately eventuating in such release. Let a batch, or only one person, say from Nagpur, march on foot to the Government House in Calcutta, and if a march is irksome or impossible then let him, her, or them beg enough money for train fare from friends, and having reached Calcutta let only one Satyagrahi march to the Government House and walk on to the point where he or she is stopped. There let him or her stop and demand the release of detenues or his or her own arrest. To preserve intact the civil nature of this disobedience the Satyagrahi must be wholly unarmed, and in spite of insults, kicks or worse must meekly stand the ground and be arrested without the slightest opposition. He may carry his own food in his pocket, a bottle-ful of water, take his Gita, the Koran, the Bible, the Zend Avesta or the Granth Sahib, as the case may be, and his *takli*. If there are many such real Satyagrahis, they will certainly transform the atmosphere in an immensely short time, even as one gentle shower transforms the plains of India into a beautiful green carpet in one single day.

The question will legitimately be asked, 'If you really mean what you say, why don't you take the lead, never mind whether any one follows you or not?' My answer is: I do not regard myself as pure enough to undertake such a heroic mission. I am trying every moment of my life to attain the requisite purity of thought, word and deed. As it is, I confess that I am swayed by many passions. Anger wells up in my breast when I see or hear about what I consider to be misdeeds. All I can humbly claim for myself is that I can keep these passions and moods under fair subjection, and prevent them from gaining mastery over me. But the standard of purity that I want, for any such heroic measure is not to have such passions at all and yet to hate the wrong.

When I feel that I have become incapable even of thinking evil, and I hold it to be possible for every God-fearing man to attain that state, I shall wait for no man's advice, and even at the risk of being called the maddest of men, I shall not hesitate to knock at the Viceregal gate or go wherever God leads me, and demand what is due to this country which is being ground to dust today.

Meanwhile let no man mock at Satyagraha. Let no man parody it. If it is at all possible, leave Satyagraha alone, and the whole field is open for unchecked action. On a chartless sea in which there is no light-house a captain dares whither he wills. But a captain who, knowing the existence of a light-house and its position, sails anyhow, or takes no precaution for knowing the light-house from deceiving stars, will be considered unfit for his post. If the reader can bear with me, let him understand that I claim to be the keeper of the light-house called Satyagraha in the otherwise chartless sea of Indian politics. And therefore, it is that I have suggested, that those who make for Satyagraha will do well to go to its keeper. But I know that I have no patent rights in Satyagraha. I can, therefore, merely rely upon the indulgence of fellow-workers for recognition of my office.

HINDU-MUSLIM UNITY

I entirely agree with my correspondent that if there is a special provision in any future Swaraj constitution in one case, there will have to be in every other similar case, whether there is clamour in connection with it or not. I have in my recent article on Hindu-Muslim unity given my deliberate opinion against any legal enactment with reference to any understanding that might be arrived at between Hindus and Mussalmans. No special legislation without a change of heart can possibly bring about organic unity. And when there is a change of heart no such legislation can possibly be necessary. My effort which takes the form of prayer in our present helpless condition is mainly devoted to procuring that change of heart. And what is true of Hindu-Muslim unity is more true of the suppressed class. No protective legislation will help them unless the so-called higher class Hindus cleanse themselves, and are eager to do justice to the suppressed class. And when they have cleansed themselves no such legislation is necessary. At the present moment law enables them to use public schools and public wells, but the so-called high class Hindus successfully prevent their use by them. What, therefore, I would advise all fellow-reformers in this direction is to concentrate attention upon bettering in a concrete condition the lot of the suppressed class by providing schools, wells, and temples for them and reformers themselves using all these in preference to those from which the suppressed classes may be excluded.

M. K. G.

21st july, 1927

THE LATE SIR GANGA RAM

BY M. K. GANDHI

The death of Sir Ganga Ram removes from our midst an able and practical agriculturist, a great philanthropist and a friend of the widow. Though advanced in years, Sir Ganga Ram had the energy of youth. His optimism was equal to the obstinacy with which he held on to his views. I had the privilege of coming in fair contact with him recently. And though we could not agree on several matters, I recognised in him a sincere reformer and a great worker. And although, with all the respect due to his age and experience, I expressed my dissent from many of his views with energy and insistence, his affection for me, whom he regarded comparatively to him as a young man of but yesterday, grew with my opposition to some of his extraordinary views on Indian poverty. He was so eager for long discussions with me, and so hopeful of weaning me from the error of my ways, that he offered to take me to England at his own expense, and promised to drive all the nonsense out of my head. Though I could not accept the offer which he had seriously meant, I wrote to him on the eve of his departure, promising to see him and undertaking to convert him to the creed of the spinning wheel, which he thought was fit only to be burnt as firewood. The reader may well imagine my grief therefore over the news of his sudden death. But it is a death which we could all wish to have. For he went to England not on a pleasure trip, but on what he considered to be a peremptory duty. He has therefore died in harness. India has every reason to be proud of having a man like Sir Ganga Ram as one of her distinguished sons. I tender both my congratulations and condolences to the family of the deceased reformer.

CONGRESS PRESIDENT FOR '28

The election of Dr. Ansari as President of the National Assembly for the coming year is a foregone conclusion. There is no one on the national horizon to challenge the election. Dr Ansari is as good an Indian as he is a Musalman. He has been never suspected of fanaticism. He has been continuously Joint Secretary of the Congress for years. His recent efforts to promote union are well-known. And as a matter of fact, had I not stood in the way at Belgaum, Shrimati Sarojini Devi at Cawnpore and Sjt. Srinivas Iyengar at Gauhati, Dr. Ansari would have been elected on any of these occasions. For his name was on every-body's lips when these elections took place. But special reasons postponed Dr. Ansari's claim, and it now seems, that fates had conspired to postpone the election so that he might come in when he was most wanted. If any possible scheme of Hindu-Muslim unity is to be found acceptable to both the parties, Dr. Ansari undoubtedly is the man to pilot such a scheme through the Congress. I respectfully dissent from the view, that in a Congress which is predominantly Hindu, a Hindu should be the President, so that such a scheme might be claimed to have whole-hearted acceptance by the Hindus. On the contrary, nothing can be more auspicious for the inauguration of such a scheme than that, in spite of the poisonous atmosphere prevailing in the country, a national association containing a preponderating majority of Hindus should unanimously and whole-heartedly elect a Musalman as its President. That fact by itself would be an earnest of the Hindu desire for such unity. And of all the Musalman nationalists there is no Musalman more respected than Dr. Ansari by the Musalmans in general. It is therefore, in my opinion, in every way desirable, that Dr. Ansari should guide the National Congress during the coming year. For it is not merely the passing of a scheme that is wanted, but a proper working of it is, perhaps, more necessary than its acceptance by the two parties. And assuming that a scheme acceptable to both is passed, ceaseless watch will be required during the coming year as to its operation. Dr. Ansari is the most fitted for this work. I hope therefore that all the provinces will unanimously recommend Dr. Ansari's name for the highest honour that is in the gift of of the National Assembly.

M. K. G.

21st July, 1927

STARVING MUNICIPAL BOARDS

BY M. K. GANDHI

The brief address, that Sjt. Vallabhbhai Patel delivered before the First Conference held in Gujarat of its Municipalities and Local Boards, is worthy of study by every one interested in the efficient working of Municipalities, Local Boards and District Boards. It is packed with facts as startling as they are disturbing. On the one hand, he says, the responsibilities of these bodies have been increased by conferring on them larger rights, and on the other, the means of discharging those responsibilities have been somehow or other curtailed. Himself being President of one of the first class Municipalities of India, he has a long record of municipal service behind him. Even the Government have been obliged to give his administration of Ahmedabad Municipality unstinted and unmixed praise. He has slaved for his Municipality as few persons have done. Like Phirozeshah Mehta, having accepted the chair, he has held the work of his office to be far more important for him than any other national work, no matter how urgent or greater in extent it might be. Having made the choice of his *dharma*, he has preferred it, even though a superior has often called for the exercise of his singular abilities and powers of application. His address, therefore, needs to be studied carefully by every one concerned. He backs his assertions with concrete facts which anybody may challenge. He thinks that the 157 Municipalities of the Bombay Presidency are economically in straitened circumstances. In some cases, he says, the salaries of municipal teachers are in arrears. Their incomes are really inadequate for the work before them. Their sanitary measures have to be held in abeyance for want of funds. Compulsory education schemes are shelved for similar reasons. He adduces in support of many of his statements his own painful experience, and he severely criticises the Government's niggardly policy in connection with Municipalities.

The President is as unsparing of the citizens as he is of the Government. He exclaims: 'Citizens of our cities regulate their lives as if they were living not in cities but in villages, and therefore, many houses have no sanitary accommodation or receptacle reserved for collection of rubbish. They do not hesitate to keep their cattle anyhow, though living in crowded quarters. Shepherds bring their droves of cattle and plant them in the midst of cities with the greatest unconcern. Generally speaking, people are indifferent about observing simple rules of health and sanitation. They neither know how to observe them for themselves or for the sake of their neighbours. It is common experience to see them shoving rubbish on to their neighbour's yards. They do not hesitate to throw from their heights rubbish or water on to the streets heedless of the passers-by. They would spit any where, they would perform their natural functions anywhere. The condition of villages is no better. Rubbish-heaps meet your gaze on approaching them. Village ponds become stinking cess-pools, and soaking dirt near village wells is a common feature.' Sjt. Vallabhbhai Patel says, and most people would agree with him, 'that it would be criminal to look to the Government for help in such matters.'

I suppose, that he has purposely refrained from touching in his address upon the petty intrigues that go on in Municipalities, and make the work of the real worker and reformer almost an impossibility. Some of the foremost workers tried, but to meet severe disappointment. Pandit Jawaharlal Nehru in Allahabad, Babu Rajendraprasad in Patna found intrigues to be too trying for them. Deshabandhu Chittaranjan Das strove manfully against heavy odds, and the responsibility nearly crushed him. The fact is, that the municipal voter has not yet become alive to a sense of his civic responsibility. He does not regard himself as in any way responsible for the well-being of all the citizens. Our educational system is not designed to give an object-lesson in corporate responsibility. Municipal councillors therefore need feel responsible to no one.

In the heyday of non-co-operation, I ventured to suggest that if the people had really developed a sense of civic responsibility, three-fourths of the municipal work could be done without Government's assistance or patronage. I showed by taking facts and figures of municipal work in Mehmadabad, that the citizens could manage their municipal work with half the cost without having a statutory Municipality. And I showed too that a statutory Municipality became a necessity only when the councillors had no co-operation from the people, or when they wished to force their reform schemes down the throats of unwilling citizens. They needed in a small place like Mehmadabad no elaborate machinery to light their streets, to clean their latrines and their roads, and to manage their schools, and there could be no question of police, if the citizens were all good and pure, or if they had a citizen guard for guarding peaceful citizens against thieves, loafers or hooligans. Those men, who are real servants of the people, would become municipal councillors for the sake of service and not for the sake of gaining fame or engaging in intrigues and finding employment for their needy friends or relatives. What is wanted, therefore, is zealous education of the people on the part of workers, not merely by means of speeches, but through silent social service rendered without the slightest expectation of reward, even in the shape of thanks, but on the contrary, with every expectation of receiving the execration and worse of a public enraged over any attempt to make it give up its superstitious or insanitary habits. I know of a poor sanitary inspector, who was very nearly lynched for his zeal in impartially getting hold of all the culprits, who with criminal indifference dirtied the streets of the town, whose sanitation the poor man was paid to guard.

4th August, 1927

GUJARAT IN DISTRESS

Gujarat—the garden of India—is desolated. Fifty to eighty inches of torrential rains within four or five days have wrought unprecedented havoc in most parts of Gujarat and east Kathiawad. These parts were completely isolated from the rest of India for a full week and the whole area was engulfed in one vast deluge. In Ahmedabad city alone nearly six thousand houses have collapsed, and no one can possibly tell the number of the huts of the poorer and less fortunate classes which have been destroyed.

The plight of the villages it is not possible for me to describe. Whole villages have been completely swept away. Houses and huts, crops, cattle, fodder and all belongings large and small, have been swept away denuding the whole countryside.

Thank God, the loss of life, except in Baroda, has been small everywhere. The people, whom adversity made all akin, have rescued their compatriots at all costs. All differences of caste, creed and community and even the curse of untouchability, have been completely forgotten in the face of common danger. In Baroda and its villages the loss of life has been terrible.

Reports of the rarest heroism and self-help are being daily received. People everywhere rose equal to the occasion and acquitted themselves like men.

Now that the reports of all the area affected have arrived and the extent of the distress can be fairly estimated, I venture to make this appeal to India. Gujarat has always done her bit whenever the opportunity to contribute her mite to alleviate distress in other provinces of India has presented itself to her, and by God's infinite mercy has never had to call to the other provinces for help. But this time the disaster is so vast, that I cannot help making this appeal on behalf of unhappy Gujarat to all India for help.

Relief centres have been already at work for the last six days under the Gujarat Provincial Congress Committee. I have received telegrams of sympathy and offers of volunteer batches for help from Nasik, Karnatak, Andheri and other places for which I am grateful. The local workers and volunteer groups with intimate knowledge of the affected areas have already offered themselves for the work of relief in sufficient numbers and we expect we will not need more men. Money contributions, big and small, will be gratefully received by the Committee and acknowledged in *Young India.*

VALLABHBHAI PATEL

President, Gujarat Provincial Congress Committee

4th August, 1927

INDIAN SHIPPING

BY M. K. GANDHI

The ceremony performed by Sjt. Vithalbhai Patel at the launching of *Jalabala*, the Scindia Steam Navigation Company's new ship, does not evoke any feeling of national pride or rejoicing. It only serves as a reminder of our fallen state. What is the addition of one little ship to our microscopic fleet? The sadness of the reminder is heightened by the fact, that our mercantile fleet may at any moment be turned into a fleet warring against our own liberty or against that of nations with which India has no quarrel and with whose aspirations India may even have every sympathy, as for instance, China. There is nothing to prevent the Government from commandeering any one of the ships belonging to the Swadeshi companies for carrying soldiers to punish China for daring to fight for liberty. There is no wonder, therefore, that Vithalbhai Patel, who in spite of his being the Speaker of the Legislative Assembly cannot cease to be an ardent nationalist, recalled the history of the calculated destruction of India's mercantile marine. He pointed out to his audience that "there was a time when first-rate vessels built, owned, manned and managed by Indians used to carry the rich products of India to distant lands. A combination of circumstances," which the Speaker did not think it worth while to mention, "made it extremely difficult for Indians to pursue it, killed that industry outright, and subsequently made it extremely difficult for Indians to revive their past glory." Sjt. Vithalbhai went on: "It is again interesting to note that shipping companies were started during the last 50 years in India, but they were all wiped out of existence by the rate war and other methods, about which the less said the better."

But even as a patient derives comfort, if anything gives him a little hope and a little energy, and the whole family joins him in rejoicing over the acquisition of slight unexpected strength, so did Vithalbhai Patel derive joy and hope from the launching of this new enterprise of the Scindia Steam Navigation Company. Let us hope, that *Jalabala* will be a precursor of many other steamers and that in the near future it would be possible to revive the old ship-building trade of India, and for some patriot to perform the ceremony of launching an Indian-built ship on Indian waters free of the fear of its being used for warring against ourselves or any other nation and free also from the greed of exploitation of any other country.

4th August, 1927

CULTURAL SPINNING

M. K. GANDHI

An English friend sends me a cutting from the *Scotsman* of 21st April. It is entitled "Value of Rhythm." It is an account of a spinning demonstration at the Easter Conference held at Edinburgh under the auspices of the Institute of Handicraft Teachers. Dr. John Gunn presided at the meeting. The lecture demonstration was given by Mr. William Kirkness F. S. A. (Scot.) I quote below *verbatim* the interesting report from the *Scotsman*:

"Spinning and weaving, said Mr. Kirkness, had from earliest times been one of the most important domestic occupations. Penelope and the maid Arachne he cited as classical instances of early spinners, and he traced the history of the craft from prehistoric times, when man, imitating the action of the wind, had learnt to make thread. He showed how the distaff and the spinning wheel were gradually evolved, and demonstrated the various processes of teasing and carding and preparing the wool for weaving. Skeins of knitting wool were next produced and the stages of handweaving shown, the lecturer demonstrating personally the working of the different handlooms, which he had assembled on the platform.

"Weaving, said Mr. Kirkness, had long been established in schools, but spinning, to the best of his knowledge, had never been properly explored. He spoke of his own experiments in this direction, carried on over a period of years. His first class had consisted of three girls of thirteen, and they had found spinning difficult. A simpler system had been worked out by which girls of seven could be taught. *He spoke highly of the value of spinning in the education of temperamental children. Invariably he had found that spinning settled them, and he quoted the opinion of a doctor that in the case of nervous children it was curative.*

"At this point Mr. Kirkness's class came on to the platform, and seated each at the spinning wheel which she herself had chosen to work within school, commenced *the rhythmic movements which, so far from being fatiguing, are rather recreative in effect.* Two of the girls had suffered from sleeping sickness, and they were all children who, for temperamental or other reasons, had been unable to profit fully by the normal school curriculum. With regard to the choice of spinning wheels it was observed, that the one with the slowest motion was selected by the least energetic of the girls, while the one with the quickest tread had been chosen by the child who had the most difficulty in sitting still.

"In a plea for the inclusion of spinning among handicrafts taught in all schools, Mr. Kirkness said that spinning had been part of every woman's domestic equipment until within a hundred years ago. Its rhythm was a highly desirable and satisfactory feature of muscular movement, and very fragile people could work hours longer when their movements were rhythmic.

"Dr. Drever, who took part in the discussion which followed said, that there was no doubt that Mr. Kirkness had put his finger on the value of a first rate occupation for the education of a certain type of child. He was also right in his contentions as to the general educational value of the work."

4th August, 1927

VILLAGE CATTLE IMPROVEMENT

[This week I give Mr. Wm. Smith's note on a co-operative scheme for the improvement of village cattle. The *Panjrapole* scheme published in the issue of July 7th is capable of being enforced almost immediately, because the machinery is ready and only requires supplementary improvement, whereas the proposed scheme for the villages outside the *ghi* producing tract and remote from cities is comparatively difficult of operation. But real improvement has to begin from these numerous villages, which, on account of economic pressure and the ignorance of people in cattle-breeding, helplessly become centres for slaughter-houses to draw upon. If a careful student were to study the movement of cattle that find themselves in the numerous slaughter-houses of India, he will find, that agents who know no principle save that of making money as fast as possible and anyhow, purchase cattle from these remote villages for the slaughter-houses. A *gosevak* is not easily made, certainly never for the wishing. He has to study his art as much as an engineer or a lawyer or a doctor, and has to take more pains than any of them. Mr. Smith's scheme should, therefore, be studied by those who desire the welfare of cattle and of Indian villages, with a view to putting it into operation in select villages. There is nothing sacrosanct about the scheme. It serves as a model for one who knows nothing about cattle-breeding or co-operative schemes. Nor need a non-co-operator be frightened of it, because of the mention of Government co-operative department. There is no such thing as national non-co-operation at the present moment. When it was in vogue, it did not touch all Government departments. There were non-co-operators who did not taboo co-operative societies, and I know several today who call themselves non-co-operators although they belong to active co-operative organisations. But a *gosevak* who does not wish to take advantage of a statutory co-operative society may still utilise the scheme. Indeed I do not know, that on the whole it would not be better to do without seeking the shelter of a statutory society. He may take the advice of the co-operative department if it will whole-heartedly give it to him, and may also make use of studs if any are available. The chief thing is to make a beginning in the matter of the education of villagers in cattle improvement. The proposed scheme is a help in that direction. Mr Smith promises a double increase in the value of cattle and the yield of milk if the scheme is properly worked. M. K. G.]

A note on the improvement of the cattle in a typical Indian village remote from a railway station with say 500 inhabitants and 50 to 100 adult cows and female buffaloes.

In a village of this class and size the total milk available after feeding calves would and should for some time to come be consumed in one form or another by the inhabitants of the village.

The whole of the cattle owners of the village should be formed into a co-operative cattle improvement society under the aegis of the Provincial Government Co-operative Department, each cattle-owner taking shares in this society to the extent of say as. 4 per head of bovine stock of all ages belonging to him or her. This co-operative society should be controlled by a small executive committee of say 6 or 8 men elected by the share-holders on the principle of one member one vote. This executive committee should elect a chairman, an honorary secretary and an honorary treasurer, the chairman being of course a member of the executive committee, but the honorary secretary and treasurer need not necessarily be members of the committee.

Such a society would be of little use, unless at the commencement of its career especially, it could obtain and be guided by expert advice in regard to finance, records, and technical cattle breeding, feeding and management, including cattle diseases. It should therefore be under the supervision of the local co-operative department as regards its organisation, finance, accounts, and audit, and it should be advised and assisted by the local agricultural and veterinary departments. All its records and accounts would be kept in the vernacular of the district. The work which this society would set out to do in the order of urgency would be:

1. Make a survey with record and all particulars of all the cattle in the village of all ages.

2. Arrange to have each bovine animal tattooed in the ear or branded with a number indicating the ownership of the animal.

3. Arrange with the assistance of the local agricultural department for the housing, feeding and supervision of one suitable stud bull for every fifty adult cows belonging to its members and further arrange to keep a careful record of the servings of each of these bulls.

4. Procure through the agency or with the approval of local agricultural department suitable stud bulls as above, and issue public notice that they were available for service to members of the society free, and if considered desirable, to a limited number of non-members from outside areas at a fee.

5. Arrange with the local veterinary department for the castration of all male stock in the village with the exception of say one specially selected bull per 50 cows or buffaloes as a reserve for stud purposes. These reserve bulls to be purchased by the society from their owners, and housed and fed along with their stud bulls referred to in 4 above.

6. In consultation with the local agricultural department draw up a scheme for the growing, conserving and storing on a co-operative basis of fodder sufficient for the cattle of all members including fodder reserves.

7. Inaugurate a milk recording scheme, whereby the milk yield of the best cows and buffaloes belonging to members of the society could be recorded and authenticated. To do this, the society could select the best milkers up to say half the total in milk, and by means of honorary workers of repute, have each cow so selected milked in their presence one day each week

during the lactation period of the animal. The quantities so recorded would be taken as the average daily yield for that week, and by multiplying each figure by seven, the total lactation yield ascertained with fair accuracy.

In calculating the amount of capital required, it has been assumed that the local Government would supply suitable stud bulls for half cost as is done by the Punjab and other Governments. The society with the assistance of the local agricultural and veterinary departments and with its milk records as a guide decide as time went on, which males born to cattle owned by its members were to be castrated and which retained as stud bulls.

It is not necessary to take any specific steps to improve the quality of village buffaloes. India cannot afford to keep any class of bovine which does not possess dual purpose qualities, *i.e.*, milk in the case of the female and draught in the case of the male. Generally speaking the male buffalo is unsuitable for field or cart work and consequently unless the males, except those required for stud purposes, are slaughtered at birth, they remain an incubus in the country. The majority of the people in India do not approve of the killing of any kind of animals, and in any case it is not an economic proposition to rear and kill these animals for beef, as the value of this class of meat in India is far below cost of production.

The buffalo exists and increases in India owing to the poor milking quality of the cows, and the aim of all cattle breeding propaganda ought to be to so increase the milk yielding capacity of all classes of cows, that they will not only provide sufficient milk to rear a strong, healthy calf, but in addition to this give as much milk as would pay the cost of their feed. If and when we attain to this standard, there will be no need for the buffalo, which will be automatically eliminated by economic forces. The existing conditions prevailing in many parts of India today, where a cultivator keeps two or three cows to rear bullocks from, and one or two buffaloes to provide milk and *ghi* for his household, continue, it is too costly and there is no reason-whatever why the cows now kept for breeding should not in the future rear their calves and provide in addition all the milk and *ghi* required by the household. Our cattle have little or no beef value, and we cannot afford to keep cows for draught cattle production and buffaloes for milk. The cows alone can and must do both duties. Buffalo owners in villages should be encouraged to join the co-operative cattle improvement society and to gradually substitute cows for buffaloes, as the milk yield of the former improved through careful breeding. Later on, when the society has to tackle the question of the disposal of the surplus milk of its members, it should of course deal with the milk of both cows and buffaloes.

There are a hundred and one other directions in which this society could and would extend its activities, but as it would have little or no income and merely exist for the benefit of the cattle owners of the village, it would require to raise capital on which it would pay no interest. No money need be spent on interest to share-holders, and the following is an estimate of the initial and recurring expenditure which such a society would be called upon to incur:

Initial (capital) expenditure

Say 2 stud bulls at Rs. 175/- each (half cost)		Rs. 350
1 set tattoing instruments	... ...	90
1 reserve bull local	... ...	60
1 milk weighing machine for recording	...	150
Office furniture etc.	... ...	50
Total	..	Rs. 700

Recurring expenditure per annum

Keep of three bulls for one year	... ...	Rs. 370
Pay of one attendant „ „ „	... ...	150
Rent of bull yard, say ...	... ..	60
„ „ room for office & committee	...	50
Contingencies & miscellaneous	... ...	50

Casualties & condemnations in live stock (replacement of bulls)	..	100
Medicines etc.	... ...	20
Interest on capital, say (to Bank)	... ...	50
Total	...	Rs. 850

Estimated income per annum

By sale of manure	... ...	Rs. 40
By service fees from outsiders	... ...	10
Total	...	Rs. 50

Deduct income Rs. 50.

Total yearly cost of working, Rs. 800.

The raising of the necessary capital should not be a difficult matter, as the central co-operative bank would probably advance the moderate sum indicated on the personal security of the members of the executive committee jointly and collectively.

To meet the yearly recurring expenditure, the society might ask the Agricultural or Co-operative Department of the local Government for a yearly grant equal to the amount which it would itself collect. This means that the society would require to raise Rs. 400 per annum. This would be done partly by asking for subscriptions from public-spirited citizens, and by collecting from its members a cess of say as. 2 per bovine head per month. If there were 300 head of cattle all told in the village, this smallness would meet half the cost of running the society.

If a co-operative society were honestly worked on these lines the value of the cattle and the yield of milk could, I think, be doubled in three generations, say ten years.

11th August, 1927

HELP GUJARAT

BY M. K. GANDHI

Proud Gujarat is laid low and she who has hitherto filled the beggars' bowl is now obliged to take the bowl herself. I have had up to now nothing to go by except the newspaper reports. Though Sjt. Vallabhbhai Patel was preparing me for worst through his private wires he was unable to give details. I give below his telegram just received on my return from Hassan:

"Most part of Gujarat North of Narmada and Kathiawad devastated. People rendered homeless. Cattle and belongings washed away. Total damage in crores. Loss of life small except in Baroda. Kheda district is worst with 100 inches of rain. Borsad still isolated. Piteous appeals for help coming from all parts of Gujarat and Kathiawad. Public meeting was held on August 2nd, Relief Committee formed. Three lakhs for food relief Ahmedabad district and ten lakhs for advancing loans reconstruction of houses to be raised. Provincial relief to be separately conducted under Prantik Samiti. Relief centres have been opened under Amritlal Thakkar, Lakshmidas Purushottam and Narahari Parikh respectively at Anand, Nadiad and Mehmedabad. Maganlal Gandhi will reach Borsad and establish communications. Other centres are also being reached and relief operations started. Amritlal Sheth is trying to reach areas of Kathiawad and is organising relief. The immediate problem is one of saving life by the timely supply of foodstuffs. Local resources are inadequate. Pray issue a general appeal to all India for succour without delay."

Sjt. Fulchand Shah sends a detailed wire from Nadiad about Kheda. Dr. Chandulal of Broach sends an angry wire asking me what I intend doing towards the relief of the distress in Gujarat. I have been dumbstruck by the newspaper reports. Those who know anything of the devastating floods in the South can somewhat realise what a howling wilderness parts of

Gujarat must have become. Kheda owes its fertility to the industry of its resourceful farmers. It is no joke for them to find the whole of their crops washed away and their fields stinking with the stench of the carcasses of their valuable and splendid cattle.

I know that no human effort can possibly make up for the loss of crores' worth of crops, cattle and belonging, together with rich manure washed away into the ocean, but human sympathy can do much to relieve the mental agony of the people who have lost their all. I do hope that all who see this appeal and who can will send their mite towards relief.

Sjt. Patel is a seasoned soldier and has no other occupation than that of service. He has got an efficient agency of workers under him. Donors need, therefore, have no fear of wasteful expense or misappropriation. Properly audited accounts will be published, and all sums received will be acknowledged in the columns of *Young India* and if necessary *Navajivan*. Relief work will be done by him in collaboration with other agencies that may be brought in to being. The chief thing is to send help. Let the donor choose his favourite and most trusted agency, but let him make sure that he sends not the least but the most he can.

11th August, 1927

INDIAN SETTLERS IN SOUTH AFRICA

BY M. K. GANDHI

India's first Ambassador has not allowed the grass to grow under his feet. He is busily sowing seeds of true union by a seasonable word now addressed to the Europeans and now to the Indian settlers, and he seems to be having fair success with both. Europeans gracefully acknowledge his splendid worth and exquisite impartiality. Indians gratefully recognise the immense strength of character which backs every word that this great son of India utters.

He has now appealed to them to produce an army of social workers in the cause of public health and sanitation. Let us hope that his appeal will not fall upon deaf ears, and that well-to-do and educated Indians will respond as zealousy as they did when C. F. Andrews appealed to them for assistance for the scavenging work he did during the outbreak of small-pox in Durban some months ago. Agent though he is of the Government, if Reuter's report is correct, Sjt. Sastri did not spare it over its criminal indifference about the sanitary and social welfare of the indentured Indians. For the neglect of sanitation amongst the indentured Indians, three parties are really responsible,—the Government of India, the employers, and the Local Government. If the Government of India had insisted upon a minimum standard, and if the employers had taken a a human interest in the employees and the Local Government had considered the indentured Indians as future citizens of South Africa they would have learnt, during their five year's indenture, habits of modern sanitation. For during the five years of indenture they had to live like soldiers in barracks and they would have been made to conform to any reasonable sanitary regulations that might have been framed, even as they were made to conform to labour regulations which were often even harsh and severe. But this is past history. There is no more indentured emigration now.

The question is how to make of the existing Indian population model citizens, and if the Government and the Indian settlers co-operate, it is not at all impossible to set a better tone and create a healthy Indian public opinion that would not tolerate any insanitation or ugliness. Let the Indian settlers do their part by forming sanitation brigades, cleaning up latrines and streets and instructing ignorant people in the elementary laws of sanitation, even as they did in 1897 in Durban. Sjt. Sastri's work will be fruitless unless he is willingly, intelligently and whole-heartedly helped by the Indian settlers. They must conform to the wholesome maxim of law that those who seek justice or equity must come with clean hands. Let the settlers be clean in body, mind and soul, and thus make the best use of the golden opportunity they have of having an Ambassador who has got the ability to serve them and who has in a remarkable measure the ear of the European inhabitants of South Africa.

THE HAVOC IN GUJARAT

The destruction wrought by the heavy floods in Gujarat appears to be of an unprecedented character. The meagre accounts I have seen in the press supplemented by two telegrams from Vallabhbhai Patel and one from the Ashram gave me but a faint idea of the enormous damage done by the flood. I am handicapped, too, as I am writing this in an out of the way place in Mysore where newspapers reach very late. When communications are thoroughly established, the total extent of the damage done will probably be found to be much eavier than the estimates made by responsible workers. Benevolent and wealthy gentlemen of Bombay and Gujarat have been as prompt in their work of mercy as Nature has been furious in her work of destruction. Sjt. Vallabhbhai Patel has already issued an appeal. I hope that there will be a liberal response to the appeal. A private telegram tells me that Sir Purushottamdas Thakordas has also, as is his wont on such occasions, started relief work. On occasions of such calamities when deepest emotions are stirred, many relief agencies are brought into being to render help. They must be all welcome. Not one agency can hope to overtake the whole work of relief over such a vast area. However, it will be the duty of several agencies to co-operate with one another, so as to avoid overlapping and so as to make every rupee go the longest length and every grain of wheat find its way to the neediest hands. Let those whom God has blessed with ability to give remember the proverb, 'He gives twice who gives the quickest.' M. K. G.

WELCOME GOOD SAMARITAN

Some one gave C. F. Andrews the affectionate title of Dinabandhu. It certainly fits him. His overpowering ambition in life is to be friend of those in need, and the way he helps is by utter self-effacement. It is fitting therefore that the first city in India should have voted an address to be presented on his return which takes place on the 20th instant. I have no doubt that the address will be worthy of the occasion. But in the abundance of their affection let the members of the Corporation not forget, that Dinabandhu Andrews is not a monied man. He has almost literally nowhere to lay his head on. He has no cupboard, no treasure chest, no house of his own. For his very few belongings he needs a caretaker. He never keeps anything for himself. Anybody may take away his box with its contents. When in South Africa, Pearson and I used to despair of him ever taking care of himself or things which could be called his own. To present him with a rich casket or any casket at all would be a cruelty to him.

But if the Corporation would spend any money it would be proper to vote a purse for him to be used for his life mission. He appreciates affection. But he is never so awkward as when he receives thanks and honours and wonders why he should be thanked or honoured at all. But however awkward he may feel, let the honour to be done to him be not a hole and corner affair. For whilst it is undoubtedly due to him for his magnificent work in South Africa, it will also serve the purpose of reciprocating the goodwill that has been created in South Africa, and would be a demonstration of the fact, that in his work he carried with him the weight of opinion of all India, and that he was no less an ambassador for India, than Sjt. Sastri.

M. K. G.

11th August, 1927

UNITY IN VARIETY

By M. K. Gandhi

The Polish professor whose earnest questions I endeavoured to answer a few months back, having read my answer, sends me the following further questions:

1 "Men are not equal. Do you also admit that there is a vast inequality between nations?

2. "If this is true, do you think that representative elective bodies, called parliaments, which have brought Europe to the Great War, are really suitable for India?

3. "Do you think that India may become one nation in a similar sense as Italy or France?

4 "Is it right to suppose that the future of Asia depends on this unification of India, which alone could overrule the materialistic tendencies of Japan and China?

5. "Is this not the real alternative for Asia, either superficial Europeanisation as in Japan, or going back to ancient Aryan tradition which seems to be the rule for great Indian masters?

6. "Has this recalling of original Aryan tradition also an importance for Europe?

7. "Do you not see in European civilisation, with all its faults, a new power which goes beyond all Hindu experience?

8. "Is there, in all India, a single little town, like many French little towns, in which everybody is really free to follow his aspirations, all people are well-to-do, all have a very high level of education and sociability, and representatives of opposite tendencies meet in friendly intercourse? I know such towns in France and also in England. I wonder whether such a thing exists in India."

My correspondent has stated only a half-truth when he says, 'Men are not equal.' The other half is that they are equal. For, though they are not all of the same age, the same height, the same skin, and the same intellect, these inequalities are temporary and superficial, the soul that is hidden beneath this earthy crust is one and the same for all men and women belonging to all climes. It would therefore be, perhaps, more accurate to say, that there is a real and substantial unity in all the variety that we see around us. The word 'inequality' has a bad odour about it, and it has led to arrogance and inhumanities, both in the East and the West. What is true about men is also true about nations, which are but groups of men. The false and rigid doctrine of inequality has led to the insolent exploitation of the nations of Asia and Africa. Who knows that the present ability of the West to prey upon the East is a sign of Western superiority and Eastern inferiority? I know that the East meekly, and all too hastily, submits to this pernicious doctrine, and then makes an ineffectual attempt to imitate the West. There is, after all, a world of truth in the poetic statement, 'Things are not what they seem.'

The second question does not seem to follow from the first. And seeing that I reject the doctrine of inequality in the sense used by the writer, I am unable to admit that the representative elective bodies are really unsuitable for India. But for the reasons, which I have stated in the *Indian Home Rule* and which in the main I have found no occasion during the past 20 years to revise, I should be extremely sorry, if India entirely copies the Western model. Representative elective bodies were not unknown to India before the European advent. But the contents of the words 'representation' and 'election' were, so far as I can see, far different from the European.

In my opinion, India is today one nation, even as Italy or France is; and this I maintain in spite of a vivid and painful knowledge of the fact, that Hindus and Musalmans are murdering one another, that Brahmans and Non-brahmans are preparing for a similar battle, and that both Brahmans and Non-Brahmans exclude from their purview the classes which both have left no stone unturned to suppress. But I have known similar quarrels in families and in other nations. It has often seemed to me, that a family connection is necessary to establish a good ground for a quarrel. But it flatters me to be able heartily to endorse the proposition, that the future of Asia depends upon a proper and demonstrable unification of India.

I do not, however, think that the alternative to superficial Europeanisation consists in a complete reversion to the ancient Aryan tradition. I hold with that great thinker, the late Justice Ranade, that there is no such thing as a literal complete revival of ancient tradition possible, even if it were desirable. In the first place, no one knows authoritatively what the ancient Aryan tradition was or is. It is difficult to state unerringly the period which can be described as the 'golden age' and then to give a categorical description of that age. And I am humble enough to admit, that there is much that we can profitably assimilate from the West. Wisdom is no monopoly of one continent or one race. My resistance to Western civilisation is really a resistance to its indiscriminate and thoughtless imitation based on the assumption that Asiatics are fit only to copy everything that comes from the West. I do believe, that if India has patience enough to go through the fire of suffering and to resist any unlawful encroachment upon its own civilisation which, imperfect though it undoubtedly is, has hitherto stood the ravages of time, she can make a lasting contribution to the peace and solid progress of the world.

I gladly admit that a new power for good is slowly but surely arising in the West. Whether it will transcend all Hindu experience or not, I do not know. But I should welcome every fresh contribution to the enrichment of humanity, no matter where it comes from.

Lastly, I am unable to say anything about the glowing tribute that the learned professor pays to the self-contained French and English little towns. I know so little about English towns, and still less about the French. I own I have my doubts. But I know that if the professor could stand the almost forbidden exterior of Indian villages, I would undertake to take him to some of them where he would see a culture of a high order, and though he will miss the literary polish he will not miss the human heart and the human touch, and where, if he can accommodate himself to the strange Indian ways about exclusive eating and drinking, he will see amazing tolerance of opposite ideas and friendliest intercourse of the mind and the soul. Let me also remind the professor that the English and the French prosperity and amenities which such prosperity brings depend upon, what I must again repeat and what I would gladly avoid if I could, namely, exploitation.

11th August, 1927.

'HUMANISING WAR'

BY M. K. GANDHI

I extract the following interesting paragraphs from an article headed 'War' in the March number of the *Brotherhood*:

"Last time the women and children were only starved,—it was done by a process cunningly disguised as "economic pressure,"—but next time they are to be gassed to death. Aeroplanes will drop penetrating poisons which will exterminate civil populations,—Edison says that it should not be difficult to dispose of London's millions in three hours. In every civilised country the chemists are at work searching for some particularly deadly poisons. In England, says *Truth*, our Government is busy experimenting with improvements in poison gas and killing animals at the rate of two a day in the process. It obtained in one year 689 cats, guinea pigs, goats, mice, monkeys, rabbits and rats, and killed 618 of them with poison gas in search of improvements.

"Some idea of the horrors of the next war may be gathered from the fact that the range of guns has been doubled since the Armistice, and that machine guns are now available which fire 1500 shots a minute. An automatic cannon will fire one and a quarter pound shells at the rate of 120 a minute, and there is a sixteen-inch gun which hurls a missile weighing more than a ton for a distance of twenty-seven miles. The Chemical Warfare Service in America has discovered a liquid three drops of which when applied to any part of the skin will cause a man's death. One aeroplane, carrying two tons of this liquid, could kill the whole population over miles of territory. General Swinton, of the British Army says: 'The great future weapon of war will be deadly germs. We have since the war discovered and developed germs which, dropped down upon cities and armies, will slaughter a nation in a day.'

"If anyone is ever in danger of becoming unduly optimistic, let him remember that we spent in 1924 forty millions in education, a hundred and twenty one millions on armaments, and three hundred and sixteen millions on drink. The business of scientific killing is very expensive, and I am told that enough nitrogen was thrown away in one small and indecisive battle in France to save India from a famine. The great world powers are still pouring out an incredible amount of their treasure upon armaments, although history so plainly teaches that increasing armaments do nothing but increase the likelihood of wars. Peace-loving America voted eighty-five million dollars for aviation expansion in a few minutes, and no one took the slightest notice of this forward movement in the race for armaments. The irony of the situation is, that while Great Britain is spending nearly twice as much money on armaments today as she spent in 1913, the victorious nations have relieved Germany of the burden of such expenditure, so that, in competing with her in industry and commerce they work under a severe handicap of their own creation"

I add to this the following from the *Lancet* (June 18, 1927):

"Since the arrival of the British troops, there have been many cases of influenza and pneumonia, but the question of venereal disease has been the most clamant one, and in spite of every possible precaution the number of those affected has steadily increased. . . . Numbers of prostitutes from North and South have flocked to Shanghai, most of them being Chinese (60 per cent.), Russians (30 per cent.), and Japanese (5 per cent.). The majority of the brothels are in the French Concession and in Chinese districts bordering on municipal roads. The high venereal rate has given the Command much concern, and no stone is left unturned in the effort to lower it."

And yet there are intelligent men who talk, and gullible men who subscribe to the talk, of the 'humanising influence' of war!

11th August, 1927

WHEN SCIENCE AND ART ARE REAL

BY M. K. GANDHI

A friend sends me an extract from Anton Tchehov's stories which is worth reproducing. The Extract runs as follows:

"I have a very definite opinion on this subject, I assure you. To my mind, all these schools, dispensaries, libraries, medical relief societies, under present conditions, only serve to aggravate the bondage of the people. The peasants are fettered by a great chain, and you do not break the chain, but only add fresh links to it.

"What matters is, not that Anna died in childbirth, but that all these Annas, Mavras, Pelageas toil from early morning till dark, fall ill from working beyond their strength, all their lives tremble for their sick and hungry children, all their lives are being doctored, and in dread of death and disease, fade and grow old early and die in filth and stench.

"Their children begin the same story over again as soon as they grow up, and so it goes on for hundreds of years, and millions of men live worse than beasts,—in continual terror, for a mere crust of bread. The whole horror of their position lies in their never having time to think of their souls, of their image and semblance. Cold, hunger, animal terror, a burden of toil, like avalanches of snow, block for them every way to spiritual activity,—that is, to what distinguishes a man from the brutes and what is the only thing which makes life worth living.

"You go to their help with hospitals and schools, but you do not free them from their fetters by that. On the contrary, you bind them in closer bonds, as by introducing new prejudices, you increase the number of their wants, to say nothing of the fact that they have got to pay the Zemstvo for blisters and books and so toil harder than ever.

"Yes, I am against medicine. It would be necessary only for the study of disease as natural phenomena, and not for the cure of them. If one must cure, it should not be diseases, but the cause of them. Remove the principal cause,—physical labour,—and then there will be no disease.

"I do not believe in a science that cures disease. When science and art are real, they aim not at temporary and private ends, but at eternal and universal,—they seek for truth and the meaning of life, they seek for God, for the Soul, and when they are tied down to the needs and evils of the day, to dispensaries and libraries, they only complicate and hamper life.

"Scientific men, writers, artists are hard at work. Thanks to them, the conveniences of life are multiplied from day to day. Our physical demands increase, yet truth is still a long way off, and man still remains the most rapacious and dirty animal; everything is tending to the degeneration of the majority of mankind and the loss for ever of fitness for life."

I have not read the original story, but I suppose physical labour which the author refers to as the principal cause of diseases is not wholesome farm labour or any such labour, but the grinding toil which for the sake of eking a miserable livelihood the peasants of his experience must have been obliged to undergo. It would be interesting to know the original Russian word which has been rendered by the translator as 'physical labour.'

The most telling passage in the extract is perhaps that

which distinguishes real science and art from the ephemeral. Who can deny that much that passes for science and art today destroys the soul instead of uplifting it and instead of evoking the best in us panders to our basest passions?

11th August, 1927

TEST OF FIDELITY

BY M. K. GANDHI

A study of the chart of membership of the All-India Spinners' Association discloses a painful fact. Out of 1,980 members of the A Class, 1,255 have been found to be unsteady in their fidelity to their promise regularly to send their yarn quota. Let no one think, that if it was an insignificant monetary contribution rather than that of self-spun yarn, the result would have been very different. Somehow or other people are neglectful in the performance of self-imposed duties, whose breach does not carry with it an immediate punitive consequence. But unless a nation contains a large enough number of men and women who would carry out their voluntary obligations, although their breach may not entail any felt punishment, it can make slow progress. Forfeiture of rights of membership of an organisation which carries with it no pecuniary or other earthly loss is lightly regarded by the members, and some even consider that by belonging to such an institution they confer on it a patronage which should be treasured by the institution in question. But I warn the members, if there are any, against harbouring such notions about the All-India Spinners' Association. To belong to the Association should be considered a rare privilege, because by contributing half an hour's free and intelligent labour capable of being easily performed by any ordinary man, woman or child, a member becomes a partaker in the tremendous aggregate effect of the contributions. I would therefore urge the defaulting members to be as punctual in sending their quota as they would be in keeping the time for catching their train or attending their offices. Let them remember, that apart from the intrinsic value of spinning, there is no less value in cultivating regularly a daily remembrance of the condition of the dumb millions and a daily concentration over drawing an even strong thread as much for themselves as for the rest of the 300 millions of India. I understand that each one of the members has been sent a reminder. Let the defaulters please realise, that each reminder costs at least half an anna over and above the salaries of men employed in attending to the writing and despatch of reminder cards. It has been suggested, that some postpone sending their quota till several months' contributions are collected, so as to save postage. The saving of postage is a proper consideration. But those who would save postage should send their contributions in advance. To spin 12,000 yards in a month's time is not a very great strain as must be abundantly clear to every reader of these pages. And if after having sent one lot in advance, the spinners continue to give 30 minutes regularly to the wheel, they will never be in arrears, and they will never feel the strain of the work, no matter how busy they may be otherwise. And if punishment has any appeal to them, let them remember, that at the end of the first five years of the existence of the All-India Spinners' Association, it will descend surely and swiftly upon them, when the time comes for revising the constitution and conferring further privileges upon members.

11th August, 1927

TRUE SACRIFICE

BY M. K. GANDHI

Two young men only the other day presented themselves before me and placed into my hands Rs. 10 being the commission they had earned in terms of the rules of the All-India Spinners' Association for hawking Khadi. They were entitled to keep this money themselves. But they did not wish to retain this commission; for they felt the force of the argument that there were millions who were much worse off than themselves. The young men went away promising to bring me more such refunds.

Whilst I mention this instance in appreciation of the self-sacrifice of these young men, no Khadi hawker is to infer from it that he is also expected to refund his commission, in other words, that every Khadi hawker is expected to hawk without any charge. I know that is not possible for every one to do so, and Khadi work requires as many honest, industrious and intelligent hawkers as can be had. To recommend for all the standard that the two young men have chosen for themselves would be to restrict the number of Khadi hawkers, whereas the object is to attract as many young men for the work as possible.

After all the commission to be had out of Khadi sales is not much and is not easily earned because it is not possible to command sales of Khadi simply for exhibiting it for sale. I know that hawkers have to go from door to door often even without any response whatsoever, and seeing that the commission is given only on actual sales, Khadi hawking means earning one's bread by the sweat of one's brow. Let the example of these young men, therefore, spur those who are doing nothing for Khadi to some effort, and let the example result in adding to the number of hawkers without their being expected to refund their hard-earned commission. There are no doubt many young men and young women who have plenty of leisure and do not need any pecuniary reward. They may follow the example of these young men and offer their services for hawking. Let would-be Khadi hawkers, however, understand that they cannot get Khadi to hawk unless they are able to produce certificates of character and are able to furnish security for the amount of Khadi they may receive for sale.

MILL 'KHADDAR'

A Friend writes:

"I know you have several times alluded to what is mistakenly called 'mill Khaddar', but apparently the mill-owners are still unable to resist the temptation of the name. The worst offender in this respect is . . . . who openly quotes and advertises mill Khaddar. This is for your information, and what action you may like to take in preserving the purity attached to the name Khaddar."

What the correspondent says is unfortunately but too true. And I have been painfully aware of it. I had hoped that the mill-owners would give up the undesirable practice. But it was hoping against hope. Wherever I have gone people have drawn my attention to this unpatriotic conduct on the part of some mill-owners. The only comfort I have derived from the usurpation by the mill-owners of the name 'Khaddar' is, that it is proof of the popularity of Khaddar among the masses upon whose ignorance the mill-owners are playing. For I know that wherever the buyers have discovered the deception, they have cursed themselves and the mill-owners. The only remedy against this deception is for the buyers to beware, and for Khadi lovers to educate the people so as to enable them to distinguish between real Khaddar and its imitation.

M. K. G.

11th August, 1927

HANDSPINNING IN ALMORA

BY M. K. GANDHI

A correspondent sends me an interesting report of the progress that handspinning of wool has made in the schools conducted by the District Board of Almora. The following should prove both interesting and instructive to those who believe in the introduction of *takli* spinning in municipal schools:

"The elections of 1925 to the Almora District Board returned the Swarajists in a majority. Since then the Swarajist members have in various ways tried to give a national stamp to the institution, particularly its educational side. The most important work in that direction has been the introduction of national songs, national sentiments, Khadi uniform and wool spinning into the village schools.

"The village teachers of a number of District Board schools purchased wool at their own cost and thus spinning came into being. The Board, seeing the popularity of these voluntary and spontaneous efforts, constituted a spinning and weaving sub-committee and granted Rs. 3,000 at the beginning of 1926 for purchasing wool to be spun at District Board schools in the district. Some nineteen maunds of wool was purchased and distributed throughout the district in village schools. This happened about eight months ago. The boys everywhere welcomed the *takli* or *katua*, and the village schoolmasters did their best to make wool-spinning successful. The 19 maunds of wool has already been spun and another instalment despatched to the schools. Spinning is going on and a third instalment will have to be sent soon. The Board has sanctioned another sum of Rs. 5,000; thus the total sum granted comes to Rs. 8,000 in all. The Board deserves congratulations for giving this support, in spite of the opposition of conservatives.

"Up to this time only about 175 village schools have benefited by the scheme and the scope of the scheme has to be limited for lack of funds. The Board has ordered spinning classes to be held after school hours as the curriculam has no provision for this type of education. In order to enthuse the masses and to encourage the village students, several *katua dangals* (spinning matches) have been arranged at different centres of the district during fairs. Prizes (including Khadi, Khadi caps, national flags and national books) have been awarded to the best spinners. This feature has been very much appreciated by the people and has been of great educative and demonstrative value. Seeing the spinning of young schoolboys, the villages have been conscience-striken and at many places the long-forgotton art of spinning is undergoing a revival. The villagers at several places have established their own looms to weave their hand-spun wool-yarn. So the spinning in schools is touching the masses as well.

"*Katua* or *takli* has been in use in these Himalayan frontiers from ages. Our experiments, in wool spinning convinced us that there was nothing better than *katua* or *takli* for wool spinning,—simple, light, inexpensive and practical. So *katua* or *takli*, is reigning supreme in the Board's schools as well. A small boy can make his own *katua* without any trouble or expense and play with it at any time or any place whenever or wherever he likes.

"The boys are still novices in the art and their first attempts have not been ideal. There remains much to be done in the direction of teaching them better spinning. But the little that they have done is sufficiently promising. Some middle-school boys and teachers have sent in fine wool yarn and medals have been awarded to the best spinners. *Sut sammelan* or Yarn Conference was held at Almora in March 1927, where yarn spun by village schools was displayed. The show proved a great success, so much so that the great co-operators of the town blessed the spinning movement in village schools and promised their full support."

If this experiment is continued and spinning is properly supervised, it can not only become self-supporting but be even profitable. For if handweaving is not also done by the boys, spun wool should find a ready market; or it can be woven on behalf of the Board or the school concerned, and the woven stuff either used by the boys themselves or sold in the open market.

18th August, 1927

RELIEF AND RECONSTRUCTION

Gujarat has recovered from the first shock of the terrible wound inflicted by the recent floods. Relief operations on an extensive scale were promptly organised from one end of the province to the other and responsible and tried workers were placed at various centres throughout the affected area. Large numbers of volunteers have been placed under them and they have penetrated the whole area. There is hardly a village left which has not been now approached. Several bands of volunteers have come from Bombay and spread themselves over the affected regions. They have brought with them food-stuffs, clothing and money and are distributing relief either in co-operation with the local relief centres or independently of them. Thus the question of immediate relief by way of food and clothing is being effectively dealt with by non-official agency, thanks to the quick response and generous sympathy all round.

From the reports received it appears that this kind of relief will not be needed for more than a fortnight except in certain areas where it is feared such relief will have to be continued much longer. My Committee is grateful to the Bombay public for the generous and ready response they accorded to our secretary Sjt Manilal Kothari, who by chance happened to be in Bombay at the time, when we were absolutely cut off from the outside world, and enabled him to collect Rs. 32,000 in a day, thus assisting us materially to start relief operations in the nick of time. Similarly timely assistance was rendered by Bombay to Broach and Kathiawad too, which were not then accessible from the centre. About two lacs of rupess more will still be required for relief to the areas specially hard hit and the distribution of seeds on an extensive scale at reduced rates, and we are confident that the flow of charity will continue till our requirements are met with.

Side by side with the distribution of immediate relief, we were faced with the problem of resowing as the crops had been completely washed away in most parts. And as in tackling this problem, there was a desperate race with time, it was not possible to wait till the Government machinery, which, even, when there is no lack of will, is slow to move, could undertake the distribution of seeds. Thus we had covered nearly half the ground before the Agricultural Department arrived on the scene. In the Conference at Nadiad on the 14th presided over by the Finance Member, it was admitted on behalf of the Government that the Agricultural Department had stocked only a thousand maunds of seeds which they proposed to sell to the cultivators at cost price, but as their rates were higher and as the estimated requirement of Kheda District alone was 70,000 maunds, it was mutually agreed to that the distribution of seeds be left to the Gujarât Provincial Congress Committee which was already dealing with the question successfully.

The greatest question, however, still remains to be solved. That is the question of reconstruction, and here the Government alone can cope with the situation. The magnitude of this task can be gauged from the fact, that in Kheda District alone 72,000 out of 1,83,450 houses have been partially or wholly damaged and the estimated loss is about a crore and five lacs. Ahmedabad District has suffered equally heavily. In reply to the resolution passed by the public meeting in Ahmedabad in which this issue was clearly stated, and which was communicated by wire to the Government, His Excellency the Governor has expressed the Government's determination to do all they can and the Conference was then held at Nadiad where almost all the departments of the Government were represented. Suggestions have been made in various quarters that the reconstruction of villages should now be undertaken on model lines, and that Government should shoulder the responsibility however difficult the task may be. But in view of the studied silence of the Government experts at the Conference on the question of replanning the villages, there is not much hope for such rebuilding of villages on model lines by Government. However, Sir Purshottamdas in consultation with us placed before the Conference a very modest scheme of housing those who have been rendered homeless and who are not in a position to repair or rebuild their houses. According to very rough estimate such a scheme would require financing to the tune of at least Rs. 1,30,000,00. Thus there is not much difference between the people's demand as voiced by the Ahmedabad public meeting, where the idea was first mooted, and the demand formulated with the help of official figures of damage placed before the Nadiad Conference. It now rests with Government finally to decide their policy on this most important question. It has been conceded by all that the need of the hour is the announcement of a definite policy so as to enable the unhappy people of Gujarat to know where they stand. It is hoped that the scheme will be considered in a generous spirit and no time will be lost by the Government in making a definite declaration so as to hearten the afflicted peasantry of Gujarat.

VALLABHBHAI PATEL

President, Gujarat Provincial Congress Committee.

18th August, 1937

THE HEROES OF THE FLOOD

As Bhagavan, a ninety-five years old Rajput villager in Kathiawad, is reported to have stated, nothing like the terrible disaster which has overtaken Gujarat and Kathiawad has been seen or heard of in these parts for at least a century. Large tracts of land in Kheda, Bharuch, Baroda and the narrow neck which constitutes the 'land debatable' between Gujarat and Kathiawad were literally converted into a sea for a number of days Hardly was a house left standing in these parts; the crops, the household belongings and the cattle were swept away, and human beings barely escaped with their lives by starving for about a week on the tops of trees, sometimes in the company of reptiles which shed their ferocity in the face of the catastrophe which overwhelmed all living beings alike.

Crores worth of property was destroyed and thousands of men became homeless and penniless, who must now recommence their life as on a clean state. But there have been redeeming features in this unprecedented havoc, with which we propose here to deal.

We know of quite a number of cases in which brave men tried to rescue or succour their compatriots even at the risk of their own lives. And among these perhaps the palm must be awarded to Mr. Morley, District Traffic Superintendent, Ahmedabad. When this gentleman was told that the station staff of Gothaj was in danger, he hurried to the place but had to halt at the Shedhi bridge as the train could not proceed further. From here he saw some villagers shouting for help, and he beckoned to them all to join him in his train. At great personal risk he plunged into the flooded river and brought these villagers, about two hundred all told, safe to Nadiad. He again went to the bridge from Nadiad and made swimming arrangements, which however failed as the ropes got entangled in bushes. Mr. Morley and his companions could not be seen for a while. But they reached Gothaj station, swimming the flooded river. From there Mr. Morley sent word that early next morning he would come to the bridge to take food for the Gothaj people. He thus supplied the starving staff with food, and in doing so received serious injuries caused by the bushes and his legs were swollen.

A second incident illustrating Mr. Morley's humanity and courage also deserves to be placed on record. The Station Master Sayma was drowned with his brother and son. When Mr. Morley received this information by wire, he at once went to Sayma, though the line was washed out and no trains were running, to console the widow of the Station Master. When he learned that the corpse of her deceased son had not yet been found, he went to the culvert, searched for the corpse and found it out. Then he went to the widow, consoled her and told her that every assistance whether by way of cash or in any other way, would be rendered to her.

The accounts of heroism in Baroda are no less thrilling. As the city became a sheet of water with islands in the shape of lofty buildings, the people went up to their house tops but were hardly safe as the houses might collapse any moment. From this unenviable position they were extricated by the District Magistrate, the Khangi Karbhari and police officers with the help of the state elephants and improvised rafts and boats. Not all the unfortunates thus marooned could be rescued, and many persons remained on house tops for days, thoroughly exposed to the fury of the storm and without food or water, until the arrival of boats from Godhra. The patients and staff of the hospital had to starve for two days and only on the third day could food be sent to them on rafts. The college students mounted the terrace and lived there for three days on four *puris* each. They improvised rafts with empty casks, kerosine tins and wooden boards, and made ropes out of the wire fence. Thus equipped they saved about fifty men from the building opposite to the college.

A buiding collapsed and about 200 persons who lived in it knew not what to do. One of them with great presence of mind broke a window in the building opposite, and placed in position a plank of wood which served as a bridge for the people to get over there with the help of ropes. Even so about a dozen persons could not get out of the devoted building and were crushed under its weight.

Some prisoners had been taken out for extramural work on the model farm, where they were surrounded by the oncoming waters. Twenty of them who were great swimmers saved many lives with rafts. In course of one of their relief expeditions, the wire fastened to the raft was snapped and the lives of the ten persons upon the raft were in danger. But they were saved by the bravery of a prisoner named Gaurishanker, who plunged into the water and with his hands steered the raft clear of all obtacles including a live electric wire till it was safe. One Chhotukan also saved 18 lives at great risk to himself.

In Broach district a fisherman of the name of Haidar Gulab is reported to have made sevaral trips in a rudderless and sailless boat and several villagers who were marooned without food or water for five days.

Two women and a child were stranded on a tree with eight feet of water below. Five members of their family had been drowned, and when two brave volunteers made up to them, they refused to be rescued and in sheer desperation said, 'Let us die here.' Eventually they were brought to think better of it, and the volunteers took them on their backs and swam to land.

Three villagers were carried away by the flood but managed to save themselves by catching hold of a tree near Modasar and getting up to its branches. From here they were rescued by Sr. Karunashankar, the Head Master and a companion of his, who made up to them by swimming against the current for a mile and brought them away.

The inhabitants of Hadala rescued their Station Master as well as the cultivators of Jasapur, a neighbouring village by means of rafts.

The authorities and Sadhus of the Swami Narayan temple in Vadtal also saved many lives with the help of boats and fed two to three thousand men for a number of days.

We have not the space here to consider subsequent measures of relief. If we had, we would refer to the big donations of the well-to-do in Bambay and Ahmedabad, to that of Sr. Vithalbhai Patel, as well as to the 'widow's mite' contributed by the textile workers of Bombay and by schoolboys and others who forego several meals or work as labourers in order to win the joy of giving, to the indefatigable labours of Sr. Vallabhbhai Patel who hardly sleeps three hours a day, of Lady Vidyagauri Nilkanth under whose guidence 2,500 school children of Ahmedabad collected 1,25,000 clothes old and new, and of many others who cannot be named and whose merit is therefore all the greater. Last but not the least, we would refer to the relief expedition of

Killick, Nixon and Company's s.s. *Bahaduri* organised in Bombay by Sr. Amritlal Sheth of the *Saurashtra* with the help of Sir Purushottamdas Thakurdas and the European directors of the Company, who carried the volunteers with bags of food-stuffs and bales of clothing to Bhavnagar free of charge and Mr. Sultan Chinai of the Indian Radio Telegraph Company who fitted up the steamer with wireless at their own cost.

V. G. D.

18th August, 1927

BACKWARD CLASSES

By M. K. Gandhi

Our woes are numerous. We have suppressed classes and we have also backward classes. The distinction between the two is, that the suppressed classes as a rule include only the so-called 'untouchables', whereas, the backward classes refer to those who are mentally and morally behind the other classes. I have made the acquaintance of one such class in Mysore. They are the Lambanis. Since the Belgaum Congress one of them who has received a fair education has been exerting himself for their uplift. They had even a Conference last year and the state contributed a small sum towards its expenses. These appear originally to have come from Gujarat. They are otherwise recognised as gypsies. Their dialect corresponds to Gujarati. The address which they gave me whilst I was passing Arsikere on my way to Hassan was written in Devanagari. The majority of the words in it were Gujarati. The curious student will see the specimens from the address reproduced in *Navajavan*. He will not fail to notice even the Gujarati grammar in the language of the address. The customs of these people I find described as follows in the address of the President of the Conference:

"I am told that the Lambanis are otherwise known as Vanjaris; and that they were the grain-carriers of India when it had no good roads and railways; they worship to this day their queen Durga, a wealthy Lambani lady of the 13th century, who brought grain from Nepal, China and Burma, and saved many lives in a continuous famine that raged for twelve years in India; their chief God is Balaji and Goddess Tulaja Bhavani, and their principal feast is Gokulashtami, the day of the birth of Shri Krishna. They long respected cows and Brahmans, and to this day they abjure animal food and liquor at death dinners; they cremate the married dead and bury the unmarried. They were as a rule a robust and well-built class, and peaceful and well-behaved.

"But, alas! their carrying trade has practically ceased since the opening of roads and railways. Some of them now deal in cattle; some have settled as husbandmen, a few live by driving carts, a few others spin coarse hemp '*tag*' and sell grass and fuel and work as labourers; some are under police surveillance, some are reputed to be robbers, cattle-lifters, kidnappers of women and children, manufacturers of false coin and distillers of illicit liquor. But these sinners can be reclaimed and should be reclaimed."

I understand that workers in their midst are now carrying on propaganda to combat the evil customs Like all backward classes the Lambani womenfolk are heavily laden with cheap and tawdry ornaments devoid of all art. Like the Raniparaj, the reform amongst these people has gone side by side with the introduction of the spinning wheel. The yarn which they presented to me of their own spinning was fairly good and fine. These Lambanis number roughly 45,740 in Mysore state alone, and there are many also in British Karnatak. There is work here for many a reformer.

18th August, 1927

THE GUJARAT FLOODS

BY M. K. GANDHI

On reading the reports of flood relief operations as well as Swami Anand's article in *Navajivan* I hesitated, and still hesitate, to believe in the examples there given of the people's heroism, solidarity and humanity, as false praise, exaggeration and self-deception are the order of the day in the country. But I have no reason to disbelieve these reports. Exaggeration, untruth and the like are studiously eschewed in *Navajivan*. The Swami knows this ever since the paper was started, and indeed it is this policy of the paper which induces him to interest himself in and work for it.

Therefore so long as I have not any reason to consider the *Navajivan* reports as erroneous, I must take them to be true. And I tender my congratulations to Gujarat and the Gujaratis. For a moment one is almost tempted to welcome a disaster which has been the occasion for the people to display such virtues.

Catastrophes and calamities will now and then overtake the country. Wealth may be in our possession today and be lost tomorrow. We construct houses and make farms and gardens, and when these are destroyed, we can remake them. The distress will soon be forgotten.

But what if Gujarat along with the distress also forgets the virtues which she has realised in herself on the present occasion? We are everywhere familiar with momentary fits of heroism and renunciation. If Gujarat's present heroism proves to be only a temporary fit, the lesson of the floods will have been lost upon her. Let the Gujaratis, men as well as women, beware.

Let us convert the virtues of courage, patience, and humanity in us, of which we have had a sudden glimpse, into a possession for ever. Hindus and Musalmans embraced one another as brothers. The higher classes sheltered and succoured the suppressed like blood-brothers. If we now give up these relations as only suited for the days of adversity, our last state will be worse than the first, and we will have passed in vain through this calamity, which is really the throes of a new birth. And such calamities there will be. so long as we have not experienced a true rebirth.

Gujarat's doings on this occasion amount in my view to pure Swaraj. If the virtues now manifested by the people become a permanent feature of their daily life, Gujarat may be said to have acquired the fitness for, as well the power to win, Swaraj.

The havoc worked by the floods was of a most unprecedented character, before which even Dyerism pales into insignificance. Dyer killed or wounded a thousand or twelve hundred men. No one can tell the heavy toll of life exacted, of the immense property, destroyed by the floods. But we did not abuse the floods. We practised Satyagraha against them. We purified ourselves. We did constructive work. We achieved Hindu-Muslim unity. We removed untouchability. We became self-reliant. We placed our all at the disposal of our brothers and sisters. We did not wait for a leader. Instead of falling back before the enemy, we bravely faced him, and set to work as if nothing had happened. If we had feared the floods, if we had wasted precious time in abusing them, if we had engaged in violent struggle with them, we would only have multiplied our troubles.

All honour to Gujarat for the proof she has given of her greatness.

But has a Gujarati, who is away from the scene of danger and of achievement, the right thus to bestow praise and tender congratulations?

I received three wires and a letter asking me to come and lead the relief operations in Gujarat. The letter was Swami Anand's and the wires were from Sarojini Devi, Chandulal whom I mistook for Dr. Chandulal and Devchand Parekh.

But I did not give myself to anxiety. I was fully confident

of Gujarat's self-reliance, I had not the shadow of a doubt that monetary help would be forthcoming in an adequate measure. I whole-heartedly trusted to Vallabhbhai to do the needful. I was in touch with him by wire. I wired to him, informing him of the insistent calls I had received and asking him to let me know if he thought my presence necessary. Vallabhbhai at once wired me in reply, that though the distress of the people was beyond words, it was not advisable for me to come over to Gujarat in the present state of my health; that my effort to make Gujarat self-reliant and the organisation I had helped to set up therein had achieved more for her than my presence would have done; that people there would be, who would misinterpret my absence but it could not be helped; and that I must continue to rest without worrying over my absence from Gujarat.

I have not related this history in defence of myself. A servant of the people never needs to offer defence. Again I do not think my health is so delicate, that I could not come over. My health is certainly delicate. Physically I am not today equal to even a tithe of the strain which I successfully stood during the days of the Kheda Satyagraha. The brain is nearly useless and is easily fagged. I have still to keep to my bed. But when there breaks out a fire, even a person who is ill must at risk to himself take a bucket of water and do his bit if he can. Even if he can only sit himself and issue orders to others, he must attend the place in a stretcher and help to extinguish the conflagration.

But I propose to point a moral from these events and to put co-workers on their guard. In Gujarat we have obeyed an unwritten law that when once a task has been entrusted to a worker, others should not seek to have a hand in it unless the worker in charge wishes or permits it; that the workers in charge of various branches of activity should be trusted but fearlessly removed in case they betray their trust. Our leader in Gujarat is Vallabhbhai. I may pass as an elder, but so far as work in Gujarat is concerned, I must bow to Vallabhbhai's rulings. It is only by a strict observance of this rule, that we have been enabled to do whatever stands to our credit in Gujarat. We have thus subjected ourselves to discipline, conserved our energies and carried out an efficient division of labour.

But even independently of Vallabhbhai's instructions, I was of opinion that my presence was not needed in Gujarat. I have implicit confidence in Vallabhbhai's ability to serve the country. He has been my co-worker ever since the Kheda struggle. The self-sacrifice of none of us is greater than his. He has often placed before Gujarat the ripe fruits of his intelligence. He has previous experience of such relief work. In view of all this I fail to see what I myself could possibly have done more than he has.

Again if I came over to Gujarat specifically for this, Vallabhbhai according to his temperament would expect a lead from me, and would resign his liberty of action in my presence On occasions like the present I should consider this to be nothing short of misfortune. If I ran up there and began to meddle with this, that and the other thing, new as I would be to the work, I should only make an exhibition of ignorant vanity.

And I am not here enjoying a holiday. According to my lights I am pretty fully occupied in grappling with the fatal disease which is eating into the vitals not only of Gujarat but of India as a whole, a disease which is beyond all comparison very much more powerful and insidious than a week's deluge. It would not only be not meritorious but on the other hand a clear breach of duty on my part to give up this work for something else that is more tempting. We have the charge often levelled against us that we are apt to lose our heads in times of danger. To the extent that this is true, we must get rid of this shortcoming.

None of us, especially no leader should allow himself to disobey the inner voice in the face of pressure from outside. Any leader who succumbs in this way forfeits his right of leadership. There is much truth in the homely Gujarati proverb that 'the person concerned can see things in the earthen pot and his neighbour cannot see them even in a mirror.' I have not been able to see that it was my duty on the present occasion to run up to Gujarat.

The insistent calls I have received are evidence of a wrong attachment which we must surmount at all costs. I am nothing but a mere lump of earth in the hands of the Potter. Truth and Love—*Ahimsa*—is the only thing that counts. Where this is present, everything rights itself in the end. This is a law to which there is no exception. It would be very bad indeed that Gujarat or India should look up to me and sit with folded hands. Let her worship Truth and Love, look up to that divine couple, employ servants like myself so long as they tread the strait and narrow path and check them when they swerve from it.

If I had come over to Gujarat, perhaps she would not have done what she has done and is still doing.

Invalided leaders or public servants should give up the hankering after active leadership or service. There is no place for a sick man in these operations for relief, which require only such persons as are able-bodied, can run up from place to place, and have the power of enduring hunger and thirst, heat and cold. Those who do not reach this standard would only act as a drag on a quickly marching army.

Finally, a servant of the people should never fear or give way to bitterness if he finds himself a victim of misunderstanding, whether unintentional or wilful. The acts of men who have come out to serve or lead have always been misunderstood since the beginning of the world and none can help it. To put up with these misrepresentations and to stick to one's guns come what might,—this is the essence of the gift of leadership. Misunderstandings have been my lot ever since I entered public life, and I have got inured to them.

In short let Gujarat ever be, as it has been on the present occasion, self-reliant and self-helpful and proceed from achievement to achievement. Men like myself will come and go, but let Gujarat go on for ever.

A few words more to co-workers.

1. I take it that none of the workers will allow their pride to come in the way of their heartily cooperating with their compatriots.

2. Any one who works for name and fame on an occasion like this incurs sin.

3. There should be the fullest co-operation between the various agencies at work.

4. Where Government offers help on our own terms we should freely accept it, as it does not involve any breach of the principle of non-co-operation. But all hair-splitting is out of place where the question is one of serving the people and serving them in time and to the fullest extent possible. If the money in the hand of the Government is available for *good use*, we should unhesitatingly ask for it and accept it.

5. Let us not forget that organisations are meant for the service of the people, and not the people for the service of the organisations.

6. I see that there are three agencies at work, the Provincial Congress Committee under Vallabhbhai, the Saurashtra Sevasamiti under Amritlal Sheth and the Servants of India Society under Sjt. Deodhar. Possibly there are others. But in any case we must prevent any overlapping and insure the closest cooperation among the agencies. Workers who have not still reported themselves should join the centre of work which is nearest to them or which they like best. Any one who remains aloof either from angularity or from pride will dig his own grave. The people will fail to benefit by his services and will think lightly of him.

7. It would be really terrible if any one in disregard of existing organisations tries to start a fresh one. Seeing that time lost can never be regained, every one should take his place at the point which he can reach the soonest.

(Translated from Gujarati by V. G. D.)

25th August, 1927

STUDENTS AND THE GITA

By M. K. Gandhi

The other day, in the course of a conversation, a missionary friend asked me, if India was really a spiritually advanced country, why it was that he found only a few students having any knowledge of their own religion, even of the Bhagavad Gita. In support of the statement, the friend who is himself an educationist told me, that he had made it a point to ask the students he met whether they had any knowledge of their religion or of the Bhagavad Gita. A vast majority of them were found to be innocent of any such knowledge.

I do not propose to take up at the present moment the inference, that because certain students had no knowledge of their own religion, India was not a spiritually advanced country, beyond saying that the ignorance on the part of the students of religious books did not necessarily mean absence of all religious life or want of spirituality among the people to which the students belonged. But there is no doubt, that the vast majority of students who pass through the Government educational institutions are devoid of any religious instruction. The remark of the missionary had reference to the Mysore students, and I was somewhat pained to observe that even the students of Mysore had no religious instruction in the State schools. I know that there is a school of thought which believes in only secular instruction being given in public schools. I know also that in a country like India, where there are most religions of the world represented and where there are so many denominations in the same religion, there must be a difficulty about making provision for religious instruction. But if India is not to declare spiritual bankruptcy, religious instruction of its youth must be held to be at least as necessary as secular instruction. It is true, that knowledge of religious books is no equivalent of that of religion. But if we cannot have religion we must be satisfied with providing our boys and girls with what is next best. And whether there is such instruction given in the schools or not, grown up students must cultivate the art of self-help about matters religious as about others. They may start their own class just as they have their debating and now spinners' clubs.

Addressing the Collegiate High School students at Shimoga, I found upon enquiry at the meeting that out of a hundred or more Hindu boys, there were hardly eight who had read the Bhagavad Gita. None raised his hand in answer to the question, whether of the few who had read the Gita there was any who understood it. Out of five or six Musalman boys all raised their hands as having read the Koran. But only one could say that he knew its meaning. The Gita is, in my opinion, a very easy book to understand. It does present some fundamental problems which are no doubt difficult of solution. But the general trend of the Gita is in my opinion unmistakable. It is accepted by all Hindu sects as authoritative. It is free from any form of dogma. In a short compass it gives a complete reasoned moral code. It satisfies both the intellect and the heart. It is thus both philosophical and devotional. Its appeal is universal. The language is incredibly simple. But I nevertheless think that there should be an authoritative version in each vernacular, and the translations should be so prepared as to avoid technicalities and in a manner that would make the teaching of the Gita intelligible to the average man. The suggestion is not intended in any way to supplement the original. For I reiterate my opinion that every Hindu boy and girl should know Sanskrit. But for a long time to come, there will be millions without any knowledge of Sanskrit. It would be suicidal to keep them deprived of the teachings of the Bhagavad Gita because they do not know Sanskrit.

25th August, 1927

INSOLENT REMINDERS

By M. K. Gandhi

The trial of two young men in Madras, one a Hindu aged about 30 and the other a Musalman aged 25, on a charge of having attempted to disfigure a statue in Mount Road, Madras, of General Neil of the Mutiny fame, has a deep significance. Their attempt reminds one of the abortive effort made in Lahore during the hey-day of Non-co-operation to have the Lawrence statue, or at least the highly offensive inscription 'the pen or the sword,' removed. The Lahore attempt was on the part of the general populace. The Madras attempt was confined to two young men who went about their work with quiet determination and without any fuss. The following statement made by the accused according to the *Hindu* report will be read with great interest:

> "The first accused stated that he was born in Tinnevelly but lived in Madura. He knew what kind of punishment he would get before doing this act. They were prepared to undergo anything for this. From his study of history he knew that Neil had done much harm to the country, and thought that his statue should not be there, and he (the accused) determined to destroy it. They had brought the hammer and the axe as they came from their place. They did not bring the hammer and axe for this particular purpose. After coming to Madras they went round the city for sight-seeing in the course of which they saw the statue. They remembered his history and so attempted to destroy it this morning. But the statue was neither bronze nor marble as they thought. As it was copper only some parts broke. After that the sergeant took them to the police station. For that offence they were prepared to take any punishment His Worship might think fit to impose."

Asked as to whether they pleaded guilty, they said that

they were guilty "if they were bound by the law of the Government," but in their own opinion they "do not feel guilty,"

It is impossible to withhold sympathy from these brave young men, alike for the motive which prompted the act and for the dignity with which they approached their trial. The report before me adds, that the accused were unrepresented and did not even cross-examine the prosecution witnesses. There seems to be no doubt that as national consciousness grows, the resentment over the insolent reminders, which such statues are, of abused British prowess and British barbarity will grow in strength. A wise Government, however powerful it may be, will remove every such offensive reminder, and not goad infuriated public opinion into acts, which, however regrettable and reprehensible as they may be in themselves, will be held justifiable as a fitting answer to the criminal indifference to legitimate national sentiment. And every abortion of attempts to remove these running sores only adds to the bitterness, and widens the gulf that separates us and the British. Surely the Municipality of Madras which owns the statue should remove it.

25th August, 1927

TOO GOOD TO BE TRUE

By M. K. Gandhi

Swami Anand has collected, in the issue of *Navajivan* of 7th August 1927, information about the heroic deeds of people all over Gujarat. In the sketches are given instances of Hindus and Musalmans helping one another as if they had never quarrelled, also of the suppressed and the suppressors living together under the same roof and sharing the same food, people saving one another at great personal risk. Whilst I was reading the sketches I was wondering if they could be all true. Then I remembered, that it was *Navajivan* I was reading, and that unauthenticated stories were inadmissible in its columns, and that Swami himself was, if it was possible, more careful than I about admitting anything doubtful. The sketches show from Bhavnagar to Broach—a wide enough area of distress—stories of unexampled self-help, self-reliance and mutual help. As Swami well remarks, for the moment the 'people exhibited every quality that makes a nation great and self-governing.' There was no fear, no panic, but grim determination to battle with death. If the account is true,—I must still be cautious,—it reflects the highest credit on all concerned. All were leaders and all were led. It was a spontaneous organisation that came into being on the advent of distress.

The thing for the leaders to see to is, whether the lessons of the mighty deluge can be made permanent. Will the Hindu-Muslim friendship outlast the immediate need, will the yoke of the suppressed be lifted for ever, will the self be used to subserve the benefit of all in everyday transactions? Will the pre-deluge avarice remain under check in the face of the charity that is freely flowing Gujaratward? Will the stewards in charge of relief funds resist the temptation to steal or misappropriate trust funds, will there be no feigning of distress and no needless applications for relief?

The answers to these and many such questions can only be satisfactorily given, if the many leaders who are now operating will be good as gold. That would mean real change of heart and real penitence and purification. It is said that there is always, after a deluge of any magnitude, a reformation of life among the survivors. It may be, that extensive as the calamity was, it may not be classed as a real deluge warranting a sweeping reformation. Mankind is notoriously too dense to read the signs that God sends from time to time. We require drums to be beaten into our ears, before we would wake from our trance and hear the warning and *see* that to lose oneself in all is the only way to find oneself. Will Gujarat show enough advance to regard the recent floods as an all-sufficing warning to us to write a new and brilliant chapter in the history of this afflicted land of ours? Posterity will have every reason to distrust the contemporary accounts of heroism, self-reliance and mutual help, if the people of Gujarat are unable to show any lasting and demonstrable reformation.

---

25 August, 1927

THE LAW OF CONTINENCE

By M. K. Gandhi

[A friend sends me relevant extracts from *The Science of a New Life* by Dr. Cowen. I have not read the book. But the advice contained in the extracts is certainly sound. I have omitted from the extracts certain paragraphs about food which are not of much value to the Indian reader. Let no one desirous of leading a pure and chaste life think that the practice of it is not worth pursuing because the expected result is not attained in a moment. And let no one expect perfection of body after successful practice of continence even for a long time. The majority of us who endeavour to follow the rules laid down for observing continence labour under three handicaps. We have inherited imperfect bodies and weak wills from our parents, and by an incorrect life we find ourselves to have further debilitated both our bodies and wills. When a writing advocating purity of life attracts us, we begin the reformation. Such reformation is never too late. But we must not expect the results described in such writings; for those results are to be expected only from a strictly regulated life from early youth. And the third handicap we labour under is, that in spite of the exercise of all the artificial and outward restraint we find ourselves unable to restrain and regularise our thoughts. And let every aspirant after a pure life take from me, that an impure thought is often as powerful in undermining the body as an impure act. Control over thought is a long, painful and laborious process. But I am convinced that no time, no labour and no pain is too much for the glorious result to be reached. The purity of thought is possible only with a faith in God bordering on definite experience. M. K. G.]

"So dear to Heaven is saintly Chastity
That, when a soul is found sincerely so
A thousand liveried angels lackey her"– Milton.

"By the use of the term continence is meant the voluntary and entire abstinence from sexual indulgence in any form and the having complete control over the passions by one who knows their power, and who, but for his pure life and steady will, not only could but would indulge in them.

* * *

"The advantages of a strictly continent life are; The nervous system is invigorated and strengthened. The special senses—the sight, hearing etc.—are strong, delicate and acute. The digestive system is kept normal and the man knows not what a sick day is. The growth of body is filled up and rounded out, and a full measure of years may come but old age never; for the last days in their pleasurable enjoyment of good health and a sound mind are as were the days of his childhood. The brain is enlarged and perfect, memory grows strong, the perceptive and reflective faculties increase in power as shown in the ability to originate and execute, the calm, self-possessed strength to endure, and gentleness, courage, generosity and nobleness of character. The normal sentiments are elevated, love grows and ripens, and the soul, in its exercise, reaches up and commingles with the Spirit of God. The reproductive element is preserved in all its life-renewing and life-giving power until full ripeness of years.

* * *

"The Plan of Life;—It is required in the individuals whose desire it is to join the noble army of the Continent of mankind, that they relinquish many of their souls' idols. The object aimed at is a high one and they will have many sore and bitter trials; but the exercise of a firm will, the strength of a new manhood, and the courage of a positive soul will conquer, and so enable them to enjoy the glorious attribute of continence.

"By the individual whose earnest desire is for a pure and

healthy life, no suggestion or hint should be overlooked, that will, in the remotest way, help to the desired end. An individual, be he never so incontinent or licentious, will, if he adopts this Plan of Life, very speedily recover though it may cause him much mental and bodily misery. A sound faith, coupled with determined perseverance, will accomplish the desirable and happy end.

"The following are to be strictly avoided by those whose desire it is to lead a pure, chaste, and continent life: Tobacco in all its forms. All manner of alcoholic liquors. Tea, coffee and chocolate. Late suppers and over-eating. Sweetmeats, candies etc. White bread when it is possible to get the graham. Pork and all fat and salt meats, sausages, pickles etc. Salt except in moderate quantities, pepper, mustard, spices, vinegar and other condiments. Mince and other pies and all manner of pastry.

"All constriction of dress about the body.

"Feather beds and pillows and heavy bed coverings. Unventilated and unlighted bedrooms. Remaining in bed in the morning after awaking. Uncleanliness of the body, Turkish and Russian baths.

"Idleness and inaction of body and mind Companions of doubtful or bad natures. Irresolute will.

"Drugs and patent medicines. Quack doctors.

"In the foregoing list there are many things that the majority of mankind will think twice about before relinquishing their use. Yet to the individual whose desire is for a true life, all and each item of the list must be discarded. There is not an article of food, condiment or so-called luxury mentioned above, that is in the remotest way necessary to the growth and nourishment of a healthy body and soul. I assert, without the fear of successful contradiction, that any person, disregarding in whole or in part the foregoing Plan of Life, cannot be healthy, chaste, continent or even a Christian.

"The things above enumerated you are commanded to discard. If you would avoid a sickly, irritable, fretful, licentious and curtailed life. The things below enumerated you are requested to observe, use and enjoy, if you would live a healthy life, a continent life, a happy and a long life:

"The cultivation of a firm and determined will. The active morning and evening exercise of the religious sentiments.

"In the right and faithful observance of these laws, man will find all the requirements necessary to the growth of perfect health, purity of body, nobleness of soul, and, above and over all *Continence.* By the just observance of these laws, woman will acquire and retain beauty,—beauty of face, form and character, and she will retain and gain strength,—strength of body, mind and soul; but above and over all, will she be pure, lovable and chaste."

25th August, 1927

SPINNING WHEEL IN POETRY

It is a happy augury that prejudice against the spinning wheel among the intelligentsia is beginning to wear off at least so far as the South is concerned. The South Indian mind has always been noted for its keenness and was not likely to remain long insensible to the poetry and pathos of the spinning wheel that had inspired poet after poet into song among all people and in all ages. Catullus immortalised the "loaded distaff" in his inimitable nature lyrics as early as 90 B. C. A celebrated English writer summed up the entire romance of a happy, by-gone age in the words, "When the spinning wheels hummed busily in the farm-houses,—and even great ladies, clothed in silk and thread-lace, had their toy spinning-wheels of polished oak." The use made by Goethe of the spinning wheel in his world drama of *Faust* to soothe and restore peace to the agonised soul of his heroine after she has unsuccessfully tried to compose her mind by turning over the pages of the Holy Bible is too well known to need recapitulation here. But while George Eliot's interest in the spinning wheel was inspired by her woman's aesthetic instinct, and Goethe's was the interest of a master-psychologist in a scientific discovery, it was reserved for that seer among the English poets—Wordsworth—to sing of the wheel as a friend of the poor and a prop to piety and domestic virtue. Not that he was insensible of that other aspect of it celebrated by the German poet. For he has devoted an entire sonnet to it, depicting with a rare insight and skill, its power to allay by its gentle motion the tumult of an excessive grief or joy:

"Grief, thou hast lost an ever-ready friend,
Now that the cottage spinning wheel is mute,
And care—a comforter that best could suit
Her forward mood, and softliest reprehend;
And love—a champion's voice, that used to lend,
More efficaciously than aught that flows
From harp or lute, kind influence to compose
The throbbing pulse—else troubled without end,
Even joy could tell, joy craving truce and rest
From her own overflow, what power sedate
On those revolving motions did await
Assiduously to soothe her aching breast
And—to a point of just relief abate
The mantling joys of a day too blest."

But what appealed to him most in it was its humanitarian aspect. For he was over and above all the poet of the lowly and the poor, 'who in lone valleys dwell.' He had come in close contact with the silent drama of their everyday existence, their patient struggle against their 'little ironies' of life, and had discovered in them, behind an unpretentious exterior, a creature 'almost as spiritual as that of books.' The onset of the Industrial Revolution filled him with alarm and dismay. He beheld its baneful effects all around him—the depopulation and decay of the countryside, the disintegration of home life, the seething vice and corruption in the factories. In the days gone by, before

"The arts abused inventions were unknown
And benefits were weighed in reason's scale,"

the virtuous housewife would ply her wheel beside an evening fire to prepare fresh raiment for her family for the coming Christmas. Her occupation not only added to her material comforts but morally uplifted her also. But what a sad change, what a picture of desolation it presented, now that the spinning wheel was silenced!

"domestic bliss
How art thou blighted from the poor man's hearth!
Lo! in such neighbourhood from morn to eve
The habitations empty! or perchance
The mother left alone,—no helping hand
To rock the cradle of the peevish babe
No daughters round her busy at the wheel
Or in dispatch of each day's little growth
Of household occupation."

Here was a sickly little child issuing out of a factory, his clothes whitened over with cotton wool, his gait creeping, his look covering, his lips pale, his respirations "quick and audible" —what hope for the future was there for this poor creature, shut off from all healthy influences at such a tender age and forced to live amid scenes of squalor and vice, which reduced him to a complete physical and moral wreck at the very threshold of his life? None whatever; "He is a slave to whom release comes not, and cannot come." Nor was his a solitary example; There were besides him tens of thousands who "suffered wrongs as deep." And yet there were not wanting philosophers who held that all this insensate sacrifice was necessary for the prosperity of the state! What a lie? "Unfeeling thought and heartless! Can a mother thrive by the destruction of her innocent sons?" he exclaimed, and he raised his voice in indignant protest against this new dispensation that set up Gain as the "master-idol of the realm" to the exclusion of all human and humane sentiment. But it remained a mere cry in the wilderness. The wheels of industrialism rolled on in their ruthless career. In the desolation of his grief he instinctively turned to the spinning wheel "as a lover or a child," And it gave him

21

comfort and relief. For at its every turn it hummed to his poetic ear the "still sad music of humanity," the dirge of the poor. Would God in his heaven allow this noble art, "once so dear to household virtues," to succumb before the "proud discoveries of the intellect" and the short-sighted cupidity of those in power? he asked himself. And the answer came an emphatic 'No,' from the depth of his prophetic soul, as he saw Sarah Hutchinson take out her wheel, that "slept with dust overspread" from its corner and ply it, not for the sake of show or fashion, but from a sincere love of the occupation itself.

"Even she who toils to spin our vital thread
Might smile on work, O Lady, once so dear
To household virtues. Venerable art,
Torn from the poor, yet shall kind Heaven protect
Its own, though rulers, with undue respect
Trusting to crowded factory and mart
And proud discoveries of the intellect,
Heed not the pillage of man's ancient heart."

He would have laughed to scorn the idea, that the occupations of spinning or weaving were tedious or boring, or that they had a cramping effect upon the intellect. From his own experience he had come to the conclusion, that self-imposed restrictions for the sake of discipline are not a hindrance but a help to a healthy development of the intellect inasmuch as they gave to it the necessary poise and balance. Far from discovering in it any suggestion of confinement, the only thing with which he could compare the occupation of the 'maids at their wheels, the weavers at their loom,' was the *sanctum sanctorum* of a convent where those who like him had felt the "weight of too much liberty" could find an hour's peace and rest for their weary spirit.

Although he saw almost all of his cherished dreams one after another laid low, he never to the very end lost faith in the ultimate victory of the people's cause. The forces of reaction, he argued, had triumphed for the time, because they had on their side "superior energies more strict affiance in each other, a faith more firm in their "unhallowed principle," while those who represented the people had shown themselves to be weak-willed and fickle and unsteady. That was not the spirit that could redeem mankind: it must be made of sterner stuff:

"Short-lived likings may be bred
By a glance of fickle eyes,
But true love is like the thread
Which the kindly wool supplies."

He prophesied that a time would come when the good would shed their weakness and the righteous cause gain defenders as zealous and devout as they who had opposed her.

"Then shall our triumph be as complete as theirs."

To us, who are living in an age so strikingly like that in which this great poet lived, his words cannot but convey a special significance. To serve the people's cause is no joke. It requires an iron will, no end of patience and perseverance, a steady unquenchable faith that never flags or wavers even in the face of the heaviest odds and disappointments and above all a continuous, silent and unostentatious love of service for service' sake. And who can deny that the spinning wheel is the best school for the cultivation of all these qualities?

THE BLIND SPINNERS

On reading an account of the blind spinner at the recently held Khadi Exhibition in Bangalore, a correspondent has sent me the following beautiful lines by Helen Hunt Jackson:

"Like a blind spinner in the sun
　I tread my day;
I know that all the threads will run
　Appointed way;
I know each day will bring its task,
　And, being blind, no more I ask.
I do not know the use or name
　Of what I spin;

I only know that some one came
  And laid within
My hand the thread and said, 'Sir, you
  Are blind, but one thing you can do.'
Sometimes the threads so rough and fast
  And tangled fly,
I know wild storms are sweeping past,
  And fear that I
Shall fall, but dare not fly to find
  A safer place, since I am blind.
I know not why, but I am sure
  That time and place,
In some great fabric to endure
  Past time and race,
My threads will have; so from the first,
  Though blind, I never felt accurst."

What a transformation there would be in our country, if all who can—who cannot?—will spin with the faith of the blind spinner. Can we not feel that every thread we spin will have place 'in some great fabric to endure'?

M. K. G.

1st September, 1927

RELIEF FROM DAY TO DAY

In the first stage of distress people have acquitted themselves nobly. Although the Government was slow to realise the enormity of the distress and damage they have been fairly active of late. Responsible Ministers and Members of Government have personally visited some of the flooded areas and His Excellency the Governor's programme for a week's tour has been announced. A Press Note has also been issued announcing that the Government have decided to make free use of the Famine Insurance Fund for helping the people in re-housing them by advances on easy terms. Both non-official as well as official agencies are busy collecting figures in order to ascertain the amount of help required so as to enable Government to come to a final official decision. As this official inquiry can only be made through the village *Talatis* there is bound to be difference of opinion on these estimates. The non-official agencies must therefore complete their task as early as possible.

We have now entered the second stage in the relief operations. In this stage our task is delicate and difficult. Able-bodied people must be dissuaded from relying on charity and and should be induced to turn to honest labour. There is sufficient demand for agricultural labour and hence the problem of providing for this class is being automatically solved. We have only to supplement the earnings of labour wherever they are not adequate for maintenance.

But the question of relieving the distress of a fairly large class of peasants and other middle class people is not so easy to solve. Ordinarily they are unwilling to accept any charity. Yet their need is urgent and quite a number of them are on the verge of starvation. In some of the Dholka villages it was found that a good number of people refused to accept free relief although they had come to the end of their tether. These people must have to be provided for for three months more till the next crop season by some device compatible with their sentiment and sense of self-respect. The Ahmedabad District Relief Committee therefore sanctioned after close investigation Rs. 50,000 to be advanced to these people as loans without interest. This amount is estimated to meet their requirements for a month at the end of which further sanctions will be considered. In addition to this Rs. 25,000 have been sanctioned to meet the deficit in providing them with seeds at cheap rates. This may be taken as a typical instance of the enormity of the task before us. Numerous applications for private help are being received and the condition of this class of people in the afflicted areas has to be closely watched for several months.

About two hundred principal workers from various relief

centres in Gujarat including most of the centres in Baroda State, Cambay and Kathiawad met on Sunday last at Anand and after discussing the whole situation decided on concerted action and laid down general lines for future work. It has been agreed that no independent appeals for funds should be made and a consolidated statement of work as also their needs should be submitted to the Gujarat Provincial Congress Committee from time to time; that free relief should henceforward be confined generally to the washed-off areas only; that cheap grain shops should be opened at all centres and arrangements should be made for supply of seeds for Rabi crops; that quinine and other medicines should be supplied to all centres for free distribution. The whole area has been divided into two divisions, and Sjt. Amritlal Thakkar and Keshavbhai Ganeshji Patel have been appointed inspectors. The former has also been entrusted with the work of reporting on the question of opening depots of building materials. Arrangements have also been made for inquiry in the Agency areas and Sjt. Maganlal Gandhi has already visited Sadra and is now in Katosan. Workers have also been instructed to inquire into cases of villages requiring a change of site and possibilities for doing so

All workers have agreed to continue at their posts for at least three months more, and they resolved to meet again after a month.

According to reports from centres hitherto received Rs. 1,85,851 have been spent on distribution of relief. The Committee has till now received Rs. 2,44,047-6-3. All contributions big and small will be gratefully accepted by the committee and acknowledged in these columns.

VALLABHBHAI PATEL

President, Gujarat Provincial Congress Committee

1st September, 1927

IS IT MARRIAGE?

BY M. K. GANDHI

I give the following from a letter received by me while I was hardly able to attend to any correspondence, that is during the first days of my recent illness. I have omitted the names of parties though the correspondent gives every detail.

> "During this marriage season there has been a heart-breaking marriage ceremony at Sadashivgad, Karwar. The bride is about 12 years and comes from a very poor family from Goa. The bridegroom—is 60 years old. His first wife died about three years ago, leaving two children behind her out of eight or nine. The bridegroom is the founder of an English School. Last year he tried to secure a bride of tender age, but owing to the agitation in his community, the transaction was abandoned. This year he succeeded by offering rupees two hundred to the parents of the bride. What is to be done in the matter? Men like......who are social reformers of the place do not raise their little finger against this inhuman act."

There seems to me to be no reason to doubt the accuracy of the statement made in the letter from which I have given the foregoing condensation. I wish it were possible to say that this is only a rare instance. Instances of this character occur often enough to call for a drastic remedy. One remedy is undoubtedly to publish every such case and expose it and create a healthy strong public opinion against repetition of such crimes against womanhood. But local agitation whenever such immoral alliances are impending is no doubt the most effective. According to this correspondent, the first attempt on the part of this old progenitor of eight children was frustrated because of timely agitation. I wonder why such an agitation did not take place in the present instance. Surely many people in the locality must have known about the attempt to secure possession of a girl of tender age for the old widower. I wonder why agitation was not set on foot immediately to save the girl from a life of torture and misery. But in my opinion, if local public opinion can be mobilised it is not too late even now to help the girl-wife. I gather from the correspondent's letter that the widower seems to have been a kind of a philanthropist at one time. May he not be persuaded to put the girl away from him at the Seva Sadan or some such institution for education, and then, when she is of full age, be given the choice either of living with him or regarding the marriage bond as a nullity? But whether in the present moribund condition of society such a step is possible or not, there is no reason why young men of undoubted character should not form themselves into bands of mercy pledged by all just and legitimate means to prevent child marriages and to promote wherever possible remarriage of child widows. The two things appear to me to go hand in hand. These bands of mercy to be able to do effective work must localise their activity. They will find then that in the course of a few years, they would become an irresistible force. The majority of our towns have after all a very small population each, and it is not impossible to know when immoral bargains such as the correspondent has drawn attention to are contemplated, or to know the child widows of their respective towns. There is no doubt however that a great deal of tact and exemplary self-restraint will have to be exercised by these bands of mercy. The slightest impatience or violence on their part will cause revulsion against them and frustrate the very object they have in view.

1st September, 1927

LEST WE FORGET

There is some danger of the calamities of Orissa and Sindh being forgotton in the midst of the universal attention that the Gujarat floods have attracted. Probably the distress is more felt in Sindh than in Gujarat and the most felt in Orissa, for it is the least organised and the poorest of our provinces. Gujarat has produced an army of workers whose numbers are already proving embarrassing to Sjt. Vallabhbhai. After all everywhere it is the merchant class that is the freest with its purse and most able to organise relief in times of distress. Let those Gujaratis, who are not wanted for work in Gujarat, or who can be spared turn their attention to the places where help may be most needed. The distress of Gujarat must not blind the Gujaratis to the need of the other provinces. The present distress must be utilised to make us less provincial and more national. We must feel one with the least and the remotest of the thirty crores of God's creatures who inhabit this land.

M. K. G.

1st September, 1927

TRUE SHRADDHA

By M. K. Gandhi

A friend sends from Rangoon rupees twenty-five as donation for the propaganda of the spinning wheel and writes:

> "My father died on the 18th April 1927 at Tanjore (S. India) while I was there on a short leave. When I was confronted with the question of 'Sixteenth Day Ceremony,' a slavish, meaningless imitation of *Shraddha*, I resolutely refused to abide by the desire of my relatives simply because I have no belief in it *as it prevails today*. I do not believe in a departed soul waiting in *Pitriloka* or some such other unseen places for water or riceballs. Nor can I see any reason to attach any importance to the rite

performed by a mercenary priest and in a language which is Greek both to me and the officiating priest. In short the whole affair seems to be a hoax designed to be practised on the religious susceptibilities of the people. But I can believe in *Shraddha* as a thing offered in piety and devotion with a charitable intention. From a commonsense point of view the main principle and the original purpose of this ceremony ought to be charity. As you say in *Young India* dated 24-2-'27, 'only two classes of people are entitled to charity and none else—the Brahman who possesses nothing and whose business it is to spread holy learning, and the cripple and the blind.' Our great immortal sage, Thiruvalluvar has said: 'A Brahman is that Sannyasi who has an overflowing love towards all living creatures.' Because I could not conceive of a man who has a better claim than you and a more charitable purpose than that of the spinning wheel, I have sent you this amount. There is also another way of commemorating the memory of one's own parents. The same sage Thiruvalluvar has again said: 'The gratitude of a son to his father must consist in the son conducting himself in the world in such a way as to *excite* from the world the approbation that his father must have performed a great *tapasya* to beget this son' I may add that I have this ideal at my heart."

I have omitted from the letter several personal references.

Though I have performed *Shraddha* ceremonies myself in my youth, I have not been able to understand their religious usefulness. This letter is not the first of its kind I have received. But not being able to understand the hidden meaning, if any, of the practices which are almost universal in Hinduism, I have hitherto refrained from dealing with them in these pages. The rule that the correspondent has chosen has however appealed to me. We do very often meekly submit to many conventional ceremonies although we may have no faith in them, and although they may have no meaning for us.

Submission to convention in trivial matters in which there is no danger of deceiving others or oneself is often desirable and even necessary. But submission in matters of religion, especially where there is a positive repugnance from within and a danger of deceiving our neighbours and ourselves, cannot but be debasing. There are today many religious ceremonies, which, whatever meaning and importance they might have had in ages gone by, have neither importance nor meaning for the rising generation. There can be no doubt that it is necessary for this generation to strike out an original path by giving a new form and even meaning to many old ceremonies. The idea of keeping green and of respecting the memory of one's parents is not to be given up. But it is hardly necessary on that account to retain the old conventions and forms, which have lost their reality and therefore ceased so have any influence on us. I therefore commend the example of the correspondent to those who are anxious to do only that which is right, and free themselves from self-deception.

1st September, 1927

HOW TO KEEP HEALTH

BY M. K. GANDHI

The Polish professor with whom the reader is now familiar writing on my illness says:

> "As I have been reading in *Young India* about your illness and discussion with 'jailors', let me tell you of my own experience how to prevent such breakdowns. Within the last 9 months—September to May—I have visited 40 towns all over Poland, and lectured for 100 days at the rate of 3-7 hours a day. At the age of 64, I feel as young as 40 years ago whenever I stand before the public. My rules are:
>
> "1. No *worry* whatever. There is an Almighty God who takes care of all, and nothing happens without His

permission. I am not His chief steward, only a very humble servant with a clearly defined task, and have to look at that task, that small part of universal becoming. If there is somewhere on earth an earthquake or a flood or a famine, no real harm can happen to immortal souls, nobody can suffer without some advantage to him designed by God, and everywhere God has His servants who help so far as He permits them. Therefore worry is weakness of faith, and my faith being infinite I cannot worry.

2. *Much sleep* in every moment when I am not at work, even for a few minutes many times a day. Before falling into sleep always praying: Lord Jesus enlighten me, give me strength and joy With this prayer a clear image of joy, light, strength flowing into me. Such a sleep is prayer, is intercourse with the Highest and refreshing. When I wake up from such a sleep, I know exactly what I have to do, and I do it gladly."

The professor adds a third rule which is about fasting and diet. As it is incomplete, I have asked for further information before sharing it with the reader. But there is no douht that the two rules above mentioned about absence of worry and necessity for sleep are golden rules. There is nothing that wastes the body like worry, and one who has any faith in God should be ashamed to worry about anything whatsoever It is a difficult rule no doubt for the simple reason, that faith in God with the majority of mankind is either an intellectual belief or a blind belief, a kind of superstitious fear of something indefinable. But to ensure absolute freedom from worry requires a living utter faith which is a plant of slow, almost unperceived, growth and requires to be constantly watered by tears that accompany genuine prayer. They are the tears of a lover who cannot brook a moment's separation from the loved one, or of the penitent who knows that it is some trace of impurity in him that keeps him away from the loved one.

The ability to sleep during odd moments seems to be a necessity in old age. Whilst the first rule is applicable to all young and old, the rule about sleep is not to be copied by youngsters. It is the privilege only of babies and old people. And to induce such sweet innocent sleep, it is surely necessary to put oneself in tune with the Infinite at every step. This sleep is not to be mistaken for the sleep of the sluggard or the opium-eater. But it is 'Nature's sweet restorer,' a tonic for a brain that gets easily fagged in old age.

8th September, 1927

TOTAL PROHIBITION

By M. K. Gandhi

"I ask you to realise the fact that the alteration of the present Abkari Act with regard to making, manufacture and possession of liquor etc. must necessarily, to a large extent, lead to harassing of the people. You must be prepared for such a harassment which is an inevitable concomitant of the policy of prohibition. I must count then upon your unstinted support. I do not want your support for picketing shops, to preach about the evils of drink and other kindred work. But I want your help in the matter of putting down illicit manufacture of liquor and kindred crimes."

This is an extract from the speech of the Madras Minister for Public Health and Excise reported in the *Hindu*. There is one more assistance the Minister has asked the people to render, *i.e.* submit to increased taxation. Of this I do not propose at present to say anything except that where the people are able, they should submit to further taxation on proof of necessity. No monetary cost is too great to pay for achieving total prohibition.

But at the present moment, I would confine myself to the extract quoted by me. I fear that the Minister has taken a wrong view of prohibition. In my opinion, it has not to be taken piece-meal. To be successful it should be taken as a whole. It is not a one-district question but it is an all-India question. I have not hesitated to give my opinion, that it was a wicked thing for the Imperial Government to have transferred this the most immoral source of revenue to the provinces and to have thus made this tainted revenue the one source for defraying the cost of the education of Indian youth.

But what pains me about the Minister's speech is his superficial treatment of a question which affects the well-being of the masses. Surely he is not serious about his scheme if he expects the people to do his police work. And why does he frighten the people by saying that *there must be harassment* if prohibition is tried? Is there harassment of the people because theft or manufacture of gunpowder are classed as crimes? Is not unlicensed distillation even now a crime? What the minister implies therefore is, that the men who to-day hold licences to manufacture or sell liquor will after the prohibition distil surreptitiously and that therefore they will be harassed. There need be, in this, no harassment of the people.

But it betrays want of imagination and lack of sympathy with the people, if the Minister believes that as a prohibitionist he has nothing more to do but to declare prohibition and prosecute those who will break his laws. I venture to submit that prosecutions are the smallest and the destructive part of prohibition. I suggest that there is a larger and constructive side to prohibition. People drink because of the conditions to which they are reduced. It is the factory labourers and others that drink. They are forlorn, uncared for, and they take to drink. They are no more vicious by nature than tee-totallers are saints by nature. The majority of people are controlled by their environment. Any minister who is sincerely anxious to make prohibition a success will have to develop the zeal and qualities of a reformer. He will then require precisely the help that the Madras Minister is reported to have scorned. In my humble opinion, he does need pickets and men and women who would 'preach about the evils of the drink' and do 'other kindred work.' It is just in these very things that he will want an army of volunteers who will be associated with him in reforming the life of the drunkard. He will have to convert every drink shop into a refreshment shop and concert room combined. Poor labourers will want some place where they can congregate and get wholesome, cheap, refreshing, non-intoxicating drinks, and if they can have some good music at the same time, it would prove as a tonic to them and draw them. These can by judicious management and association of the people become paying concerns for the state. He who will handle the problem of temperance will have to give a more serious study to it than the Minister seems to have done. Let him study the methods adopted in America and tried by the great temperance organisations of the world. This study will give but limited help. For the Western conditions are widely different from the Indian. Our methods too, will have, therefore, to be largely different. Whereas total prohibition in the West is most difficult of accomplishment, I hold that it is the easiest of accomplishment in this country. When an evil like drink in the West attains the status of respectability, it is the most difficult to deal with. With us drink is still, thank God, sufficiently disrespectable and confined not to the general body of the people but to a minority of the poor classes.

8th September, 1927

WHAT STUDENTS CAN DO

The following is a verbatim report of Gandhiji's address to the students of Vellore:

At the outset I would like to express my very deep sorrow over the domestic affliction that has befallen your Principal. I heard of it as soon as I reached here. I appreciate, Mr. Principal, the very courteous consideration that you have shown by not merely allowing this function to take place under your roof but also, in spite of your overwhelming grief, gracing this function by your presence and presiding at it. I ask you to regard me as a partner in your grief.

I thank all the students and others for the address that has been presented to me this afternoon and the purse for the Khadi fund. This demonstration of your personal affection for me and your identification with the poorest of the land does not surprise me now, because it has become a common feature wherever I go, throughout the length and breadth of our beautiful country. It has been a matter of the greatest joy to me and consolation, in the face of many difficulties, to find that the student world throughout India has a warm corner for me in their heart. The students have lightened my burden to a very great extent. But I cannot suppress from me the feeling that in spite of this personal affection that the students have shown to me everywhere and even identification with the poorest of the land, the students have yet to cover a vast amount of ground For you are the hope of the future. You will be called upon, when you are discharged from your colleges and schools, to enter upon public life to lead the poor people of this country. I would therefore like you, students, to have a sense of responsibility and show it in a much more tangible manner. It is a remarkable fact and a regrettable fact that in the case of the vast majority of students, whilst they entertain noble impulses during their student days, these disappear when they finish their studies. The vast majority of them look out for loaves and fishes. Surely, there is something wrong in this. There is one reason which is obvious. Every educationist, every one who has had anything to do with the students, has realised that our educational system is faulty. It does not correspond to the requirements of the country, certainly not to the requirements of pauper India. There is no correspondence between the education that is given and the home life and the village life. But that is, I fear, a larger question than you and I can deal with in a meeting of this character.

Taking things as they are, we have to consider what is possible for the students to do and what more we can do in order to serve the country. The answer that has come to me and to many, who are eager to see that the student world gives a good account of itself, is that the students have to search within and look after their personal character. Purity of personal life is the one indispensable condition for building a sound education. And my meetings with thousands of students and the correspondence which I continuously have with the students in which they pour out their innermost feelings and take me into their confidence show me quite clearly that there is much left to be desired. I am sure that all of you understand thoroughly what I mean. In our languages there is a beautiful word equivalent for the word student, that is, Brahmachari. Vidyarthi is a coined word and a poor equivalent for Brahmachari. And I hope you know what the word Brahmachari means. It means searcher after God, one who conducts himself so as to bring himself nearest to God in the least possible time. And all the great religions of the world, however much they may differ, are absolutely one on this fundamental thing that no man or woman with an impure heart can possibly appear before the Great White Throne. All our learning or recitation of the Vedas, correct knowledge of Sanskrit, Latin, Greek and what not will avail us nothing if they do not enable us to cultivate absolute purity of heart. The end of all knowledge must be building up of character.

An English friend in Shimoga, whom I did not know before came up to me and asked me, why it was, if India was really a spiritually advanced country, he did not observe in the students a real yearning after knowledge of God, why was it that the students, many of them, did not even know what the Bhagavad Gita was. I gave what appeared to me an honest explanation and excuse for this discovery of his. But I do not propose to give that explanation to you nor seek to excuse this very great and grave defect. The very first and earnest request that I would make to the students before me here is that each one of you should search within, and wherever you find that my remarks are justified, you will begin to reform and rebuild yourself, and those of you who are Hindus, and the vast majority are Hindus I know, will endeavour to understand the very simple, beautiful, and to me soulful message of the Gita. The experience, and I think I can say the experience without a single exception, of those who have really carried on this search after truth to render their hearts pure is that it is an utterly impossible effort, unless it is accompanied by a hearty prayer to the Almighty. Whatever, therefore, you do, do not lose faith in God. I cannot reason out the thing for you, because really speaking, it is a fact which transcends reason. But I want you to cultivate a spirit of real humility and not summarily reject the experiences of so many teachers, Rishis and others of the world and not regard them as so many superstitious men. And if you will but do this,—all the rest that I want to say will be as clear as crystal to you. This will be to me the test of your sincerity of profession. If you have real faith in God, you cannot but feel for the humblest of his creation. And whether it is the spinning-wheel and Khadi, or untouchability, or total prohibition, or social reform in connection with child-widows and child-wives and many other similar things, you will find that all these activities are derived from the same source. I was therefore glad to find that you sympathise with and approve of the spinning movement, the struggle against untouchability and other things with which I am identified. I accept your assurance that henceforth you will do better in regard to Khadi.

It is really the easiest thing in the world for you to make your choice once for all and say to yourself that you shall use henceforth nothing but Khadi since it puts a few coppers into the pockets of those who need them most. In this one institution alone, I understand, you are more than 1,400. Just think what the 1,400 by giving only half an hour to spinning can add materially to the wealth of the country. Think also what 1,400 can do on behalf of the so-called untouchables, and if all the 1,400 young men were to make a solemn resolve, and they can do so, that they are not going to have anything whatsoever to do with child-wives, imagine what a great reform you will make in society around you. If the 1,400 amongst you, or a respectable number even devote your leisure hours or part of your Sundays to going amidst those who are given to drink and in the kindliest manner possible steal into their hearts, imagine what service you will render to them and to the country. All these things you can do in spite of the existing faulty education. Nor do you require much effort for doing these things except that you have got to change your heart, and to use a current expression in the political world, alter the 'angle of vision.'

And I want you to turn this occasion to advantage, and you will do so, if only you will consider the solemn circumstance under which we have met this evening and by reference to which I started my address. A mere man of the world would be justified, and he will be held justified by the world, if he excused himself from attending a function of this character on account of domestic affliction. Surely there is something noble and majestic when a man, instead of brooding over such sorrows, transmutes them into service for God and humanity. Every such act enables us to understand the essential oneness of humanity. May God enable you to understand the words that I have spoken to you. I thank you once more for your address and the purse and all that you have said.

15th September, 1927

DRAIN INSPECTOR'S REPORT

BY M. K. GANDHI

" *On the lips of the good vice becomes virtue,*

" *And even virtue appears as vice in the mouth of the evil-minded: this need not surprise us.*

" *For, do not the mighty clouds drink the salt waters of the ocean and return it as sweet refreshing rain,*

" *And does not the cobra, drinking sweet milk, belch it forth as the deadliest poison?*"

" *Rivers drink not of their own waters, the trees do not themselves eat the fruit which they bear,*

"Nor do the clouds partake of the grains they grow; even so the good devote their powers to the good of others."

Several correspondents have sent me cuttings containing reviews of, or protests against, Miss Mayo's *Mother India*. A few have in addition asked me to give my own opinion on it. An enraged correspondent from London asks me to give him answers to several questions that he has framed upon the authoress's references to me. Miss Mayo has herself favoured me with a copy of her book.

I would certainly not have made time, especially when I have only limited energy, and caution has been enjoined upon me by medical friends against overwork, to read the book during my tour. But these letters made it obligatory on me to read the book at once.

The book is cleverly and powerfully written. The carefully chosen quotations give it the appearance of a truthful book. But the impression it leaves on my mind is, that it is the report of a drain inspector sent out with the one purpose of opening and examining the drains of the country to be reported upon, or to give a graphic description of the stench exuded by the opened drains. If Miss Mayo had confessed that she had gone to India merely to open out and examine the drains of India, there would perhaps be little to complain about her compilation. But she says in effect with a certain amount of triumph, 'The drains are India.' True, in the concluding chapter there is a caution. But her caution is cleverly made to enforce her sweeping condemnation. I feel that no one who has any knowledge of India can possibly accept her terrible accusations against the thought and the life of the people of this unhappy country

The book is without doubt untruthful, be the facts stated ever so truthful. If I open out and describe with punctilious care all the stench exuded from the drains of London and say "Behold London," my facts will be incapable of challenge, but my judgment will be rightly condemned as a travesty of truth. Miss Mayo's book is nothing better, nothing else.

The authoress says she was dissatisfied with the literature she read about India, and so she came to India "to see what a volunteer unsubsidised, uncommitted and unattached, could observe of common things in daily human life."

After having read the book with great attention, I regret to say that I find it difficult to accept this claim. Unsubsidised she may be. Uncommitted and unattached she certainly fails to show herself in any page. We in India are accustomed to interested publications patronised,—'patronised' is accepted as an elegant synonym for 'subsidised,'—by the Government. We have become used to understanding from pre-British days, that the art (perfected by the British) of government includes the harnessing of the secret services of men learned, and reported to be honest and honourable for shadowing suspects and for writing up the virtues of the Government of the day as if the certificate had come from disinterested quarters. I hope that Miss Mayo will not take offence if she comes under the shadow of such suspicion. It may be some consolation to her to know that even some of the best English friends of India have been so suspected.

But ruling out of consideration the suspicion, it remains to be seen why she has written this untruthful book. It is doubly untruthful. It is untruthful in that she condemns a whole nation or in her words 'the peoples of India' (she will not have us as one nation) practically without any reservation as to their sanitation, morals, religion etc. It is also untruthful because she claims for the British Government merits which cannot be sustained and which many an honest British officer would blush to see the Government credited with.

If she is not subsidised, Miss Mayo is an avowed Indophobe and Anglophil refusing to see anything good about Indians and anything bad about the British and their rule.

She does not give one an elevated idea of Western standard of judgment. Though she represents a class of sensational writers in the West, it is a class that, I flatter myself with the belief, is on the wane. There is a growing body of Americans who hate anything sensational, smart or crooked. But the pity of it is that there are still thousands in the West who delight in 'shilling shockers.' Nor are all the authoress's quotations or isolated facts truthfully stated. I propose to pick up those I have personal knowledge of. The book bristles with quotations torn from their contexts and with extracts which have been authoritatively challenged.

The authoress has violated all sense of propriety by associating the Poet's name with child-marriage. The Poet has indeed referred to early marriages as not an undesirable institution. But there is a world of difference between child-marriage and early marriage. If she had taken the trouble of making the acquaintance of the free and freedom-loving girls and women of Shantiniketan, she would have known the Poet's meaning of early marriage.

She has done me the honour of quoting me frequently in support of her argument. Any person who collects extracts from a reformer's diary, tears them from their context and proceeds to condemn, on the strength of these, the people in whose midst the reformer has worked, would get no hearing from sane and unbiassed readers or hearers. But in her hurry to see everything Indian in a bad light, she has not only taken liberty with my writings, but she has not thought it necessary even to verify through me certain things ascribed by her or others to me. In fact she has combined in her own person what we understand in India the judicial and the executive officer. She is both the prosecutor and the judge. She has described the visit to me, and informed her readers that there are always with me two "secretaries" who write down every word I say. I know that this is not a wilful perversion of facts. Nevertheless the statement is not true. I beg to inform her, that I have no one near me who has been appointed or is expected to write down every word that I say. I have by me a co-worker called Mahadev Desai who is striving to out-Boswell Boswell and does, whenever he is near me, take down whatever he considers to be wisdom dropping from my lips. I can't repel his advances, even if I would, for the relationship between us is, like the Hindu marriage, indissoluble. But the real crime committed against me is described by her at pages 387-88. She ascribes to the Poet 'a fervent declaration that Ayurvedic science surpasses anything that the West can offer.' (She has this time no quotation to back her statement). Then she quotes my opinion that hospitals are institutions for propagating sin, and then distorts out of all recognition a sacred incident, honourable to the British surgeons and, I hope, to myself. I must ask the reader to excuse me for giving the full quotation from the book:

> "As he happened to be in the prison at the time, a British surgeon of the Indian Medical Service came straightaway to see him. 'Mr. Gandhi,' said the surgeon, as the incident was then reported, 'I am sorry to tell you that you have appendicitis. If you were my patient, I should operate at once. But you will probably prefer to call in your Ayurvedic physician."
>
> "Mr. Gandhi proved otherwise minded.
>
> "'I should prefer not to operate,' pursued the surgeon, 'because in case the outcome should be unfortunate, all your friends will lay it as a charge of malicious intent against us whose duty is to care for you.'
>
> "'If you will only consent to operate,' pleaded Mr. Gandhi, 'I will call in my friends, now, and explain to them that you do so at my request.'
>
> "So Mr. Gandhi wilfully went to an 'institution for propagating sin,' was operated upon by one of the 'worst of all,' an officer of the Indian Medical Service and was attentively nursed through convalescence by an English Sister whom he is understood to have thought after all rather a 'useful sort of person."

This is a travesty of truth. I shall confine myself to correcting only what is libellous and not the other inaccuracies. There was no question here of calling in any Ayurvedic physician. Col. Maddock who performed the operation had the right, if he had so chosen, to perform the operation without a reference to me, and even in spite of me. But he and Surgeon-General Hooton showed a delicate consideration to me, and asked me whether I would wait for my own doctors who were known to them and who were also trained in the Western medical and surgical science. I would not be behind-hand in returning their courtesy and consideration, and I immediately told them that they could perform the operation without waiting for my doctors to whom they had telegraphed, and that I would gladly give them a note for their protection in the event of the operation miscarrying. I endeavoured to show that I had no distrust either in their ability or their good faith. It was to me a happy opportunity of demonstrating my personal goodwill.

So far as my opinion about hospitals and the like is concerned, it stands, in spite of my having subjected myself and my wards to treatment more than once by physicians and surgeons, Indian and European, trained in the Western school of medicine. Similarly I use motor cars and railways, whilst holding to my condemnation of them as strongly as ever. I hold the body itself to be an evil and an impediment in my progress. But I see no inconsistency in my making use of it while it lasts, and trying in the best manner I know to use it for its own destruction. This is a sample of distortion of which I have a personal knowledge.

But the book is brimful of descriptions of incidents of which an average Indian, at any rate, has no knowledge. Thus she describes an ovation said to have been given to the Prince of Wales, of which Indian India has no knowledge, but which could not possibly escape it if it had happened. A crowd is reported to have fought its way to the Prince's car somewhere in Bombay. "The Police," Miss Mayo says, "tried vainly to form a hedge round the car moving at a crawl unprotected now through a solid mass of shouting humanity which won through to the railway station at last." Then at the railway station while there were three minutes for the train to steam out, the

Prince is reported by Miss Mayo to have ordered the barriers to be dropped and the "mobs" to be let in. The authoress then proceeds, "Like the sweep of a river in floods, interminable multitude rolled in, and shouted and laughed and wept, and when the train started, ran alongside the Royal carriage till they could run no more." All this is supposed to have happened in 1921 on the evening of November 22nd, whilst the dying embers of the riots were still hot. There is much of this kind of stuff in this romantic chapter, which is headed "Behold a light."

The nineteenth chapter is a collection of authorities in praise of the achievements of the British Government, almost every one of which has been repeatedly challenged both by English and Indian writers of unimpeachable integrity. The seventeenth chapter is written to show that we are a 'world-menace.' If as a result of Miss Mayo's effort the League of Nations is moved to declare India a segregated country unfit for exploitation I have no doubt both the West and the East would be the gainers. We may then have our internecine wars. Hindus may be eaten up, as she threatens, by the hordes from the North-West and Central Asia,—that were a position infinitely superior to one of ever-growing emasculation. Even as electrocution is a humaner method of killing than the torturous method of roasting alive, so would a sudden overwhelming sweep from Central Asia upon the unresisting, insanitary, superstitious and sexuality-ridden Hindus, as Miss Mayo describes us to be, be a humane deliverance from the living and ignominious death which we are going through at the present moment. Unfortunately however, such is not Miss Mayo's goal. Her case is to perpetuate white domination in India on the plea of India's unfitness to rule herself.

The picturesque statements that this clever authoress puts into the mouths of the various characters read like so many pages from a sensational novel in which no regard has to be paid to truth. Many of her statements seem to me to be utterly unworthy of belief and do not put the men and women to whom they are ascribed in a favourable light. Take for instance this statement put in the mouth of a prince:

> "'Our treaties are with the Crown of England,' one of them said to me, with incisive calm. 'The princes of India made no treaty with a Government that included Bengali *babus.* We shall never deal with this new lot of Jacks-in-office. While Britain stays, Britain will send us English gentlemen to speak for the King Emperor, and all will be as it should be between friends. If Britain leaves, we, the princes will know how to straighten out India, even as princes should.'" Page 316.

However fallen Indian princes may be, I should want unimpeachable evidence before I could believe that there can be in India a prince so degraded as to make such a statement. Needless to say the authoress does not give the name of the prince.

A still more scandalous statement occurs on page 314 and reads as follows:

> "'His Highness does not believe,' said the Dewan, 'that Britain is going to leave India. But still, under this new regime in England, they may be so ill-advised. So His Highness is getting his troops in shape, accumulating munitions and coining silver. And if the English do go, three months afterward, not a rupee or a virgin will be left in all Bengal.'"

The reader is kept in darkness as to the name of His Highness or of the enlightened Dewan.

There are many statements which Miss Mayo puts into the mouths of Englishmen and Englishwomen living in India. All I can say with reference to these statements is that if some of them were really made by the authors, they are unworthy of the trust reposed in them and they have done an injustice to their wards or patients as well as the race to which they belong. I should be sorry indeed to think that there are many Englishmen and Englishwomen who say one thing to their Indian friends and another to their Western confidants. Those

Englishmen and English-women who may chance to read the sweepings gathered together by Miss Mayo with her muck-rake will recognise the statements I have in mind. In seeking to see an India degraded Miss Mayo has unconsciously degraded the characters whom she has used as her instruments for proving her facts which she boasts cannot be 'disproved or shaken.' I hope I have given sufficient *prima facie* proof in this article to show that many of her facts stand disproved even in isolation. Put together they give a wholly false picture.

But why am I writing this article? Not for the Indian readers but for the many American and English readers who read these pages from week to week with sympathy and attention. I warn them against believing this book. I do not remember having given the message Miss Mayo imputes to me. The only one present who took any notes at all has no recollection of the message imputed to me. But I do know what message I give every American who comes to see me: "Do not believe newspapers and the catchy literature you get in America. But if you want to know anything about India, go to India as students, study India for yourself. If you cannot go, make a study of all that is written about India for her and against her and then form your own conclusions. The ordinary literature you get is either exaggerated vilification of India or exaggerated praise." I warn Americans and Englishmen against copying Miss Mayo. She came not with an open mind as she claims, but with her preconceived notions and prejudices which she betrays on every page, not excluding even the introductory chapter in which she recites the claim. She came to India not to see things with her own eyes, but to gather material three fourths of which she could as well have gathered in America

That a book like Miss Mayo's can command a large circulation furnishes a sad commentary on Western literature and culture.

I am writing this article also in the hope, be it ever so

distant, that Miss Mayo herself may relent and repent of having done, I hope unconsciously, atrocious injustice to an ancient people and equally atrocious injustice to the Americans by having exploited her undoubted ability to prejudice without warrant their minds against India.

The irony of it all is that she has inscribed this book' 'To the peoples of India.' She has certainly not written it as a reformer, and out of love. If I am mistaken in my estimate let her come back to India. Let her subject herself to cross-examination, and if her statements escape unhurt through the fire of cross-examination, let her live in our midst and reform our lives. So much for Miss Mayo and her readers.

I must now come to the other side of the picture. Whilst I consider the book to be unfit to be placed before Americans and Englishmen (for it can do no good to them), it is a book that every Indian can read with some degree of profit. We may repudiate the charge as it has been framed by her, but we may not repudiate the substance underlying the many allegations she has made. It is a good thing to see ourselves as others see us. We need not even examine the motive with which the book is written. A cautious reformer may make some use of it.

There are statements in it which demand investigation. For instance she says that the Vaishnava mark has an obscene meaning. I am a born Vaishnavite. I have perfect recollection of my visits to Vaishnava temples. Mine were orthodox people. I used to have the mark myself as a child, but neither I nor any one else in our family ever knew that this harmless and rather elegant-looking mark had any obscene significance at all. I asked a party of Vaishnavites in Madras where this article is being written. They knew nothing about the alleged obscene significance. I do not therefore suggest that it never had such significance. But I do suggest that millions are unaware of the obscenity alleged to be behind it. It has remained for our Western visitors to acquaint us with the obscenity of many practices which we have hitherto innocently indulged in. It was in a missionary book that I first learnt that Shivalingam had any obscene significance at all, and even now when I see a Shivalingam neither the shape nor the association in which I see it suggests any obscenity. It was again in a missionary book that I learnt that the temples in Orissa were disfigured with obscene statues. When I went to Puri it was not without an effort that I was able to see those things. But I do know that the thousands who flock to the temple know nothing about the obscenity surrounding these figures. The people are unprepared and the figures do not obtrude themselves upon your gaze.

But let us not resent being made aware of the dark side of the picture wherever it exhists. Overdrawn her pictures of our insanitation, child-marriages etc. undoubtedly are. But let them serve as a spur to much greater effort than we have hitherto put forth in order to rid society of all cause of reproach. Whilst we may be thankful for anything good that foreign visitors may be able honestly to say of us, if we curb our anger, we shall learn, as I have certainly learnt, more from our critics than from our patrons. Our indignation which we are bound to express against the slanderous book must not blind us to our obvious imperfections and our great limitations. Our anger will leave Miss Mayo absolutely unhurt and it will only recoil upon ourselves. We too have our due share of thoughtless readers as the West has, and in seeking to disprove everything Miss Mayo has written, we shall make the reading public believe that we are a race of perfect human beings against whom nothing can be said, no one can dare say one word. The agitation that has been set up against the book is in danger of being overdone. There is no cause for fury. I would here close this review which I have undertaken with the greatest reluctance and under great pressure of work with a paraphrase of a beautiful couplet from Tulasidas:

"Everything created by God, animate or inanimate, has its good and bad side. The wise man, like the fabled bird which separating the cream of milk from its water helps himself to the cream leaving the water alone, will take the good from everything leaving the bad alone."

15th September, 1927

TWO SPEECHES

By M. K. Gandhi

[With the number of speeches that Gandhiji has been addressing these days, the readers of *Young India*, will, I hope, not expect him to write much. Some of the speeches are as good as articles and more, and I am selecting two for this week. M. D.]

A RELIGIOUS DISCOURSE

(At the Young Men's Christian Association.)

The Chairman has asked me to give you a religious discourse. I do not know that I have ever given a religious discourse, or to put it the other way, I do not know a single speech of mine or a talk of mine, within my own recollection, which has not been a religious discourse. I think, if I am not deceived, that at the back of every word that I have uttered since I have known what public life is, and of every act that I have done, there has been a religious consciousness and a downright religious motive. My acts may have appeared to my audiences or to the readers of the word that I have written, political, economical and many other things. But I ask you to accept my word that the motive behind every one of them has been essentially and predominantly religious. And so is it to be this morning.

When I asked what I was expected to speak about, I was told that I was to speak what I liked. Well, the message came to me this morning as I was on my way to this meeting and I propose now to think before you aloud.

I had very precious moments with a missionary friend in Vellore. I had a heart-to-heart talk with the students of that place, and the next morning I was told something like this: "Your speech was very nice. You talked of the things of the spirit. But how is it that in the middle of the speech like King Charles' head with the renowned Mr. Dick, Khadi came up?

Can you explain what connection Khadi can possibly have with spirituality?" Then he went on, "You spoke about temperance; that delighted us and it was certainly spiritual. You spoke about untouchability, a very fine subject for an audience spiritually inclined or for a spiritually inclined man to speak about. But both these came in your speech after your message of Khadi It seemed to jar on some of us." I have given you the substance of the conversation in my own words but faithfully. I gave the answer that came to me at the time and this morning I want to amplify that answer.

It is quite true that I place Khadder first and then only untouchabilty and temperance. All these came at the end of the speech I gave to the students of Vellore, in which I made a fervent appeal for purity of life and told them that without purity of life all their learning would be as dust and probably a hindrance to the true progress of the world. Then I took up these three things and a few more by way of illustration. Throughout 35 years' unbroken experience of public service in several parts of the world, I have not yet understood that there is anything like spiritual or moral value apart from work and action. I have often repeated to audiences like this that great verse which has always remained with me ever since I read it: "Not every one that says unto me Lord, Lord, shall enter the Kingdom of Heaven but he who doeth the will of my Father who is in Heaven." I have not reproduced that verse correctly but you know what that verse is and it is so true. I recall to my mind two brilliant instances of men in English public life who, in their own times, were regarded as very great reformers, and as pillars of spirituality. I am now talking to you of about 1889 and 1890 when many of you were not born. I used to attend temperance meetings in those days. I was interested in that reform. These two pillars of spirituality were supposed to be great temperance workers, but they were workers with their speeches. They were always in demand when a harangue was required on temperance. I am sorry to have to inform you that I was a witness to their fall.

Both of them were found out. They were no workers. The words God, Lord, Jehovah were on their lips always, but they simply adorned their lips, they were not in their hearts. They used the temperance platform for their own base ends. One of them was a speculator and the other was a moral leper. Perhaps you now understand what I want to say. In India also, I am not able to say that the temperance platform is always a spiritual platform or that the platform of untouchability must necessarily be a spiritual platform. I have known, I know now as I am talking to you, that both these platforms are being abused to-day in this very land by several people. Others are using them aright. The moral I want to submit to you is that every act may be done, conceived and presented from a spiritual standpoint or it may have none of it at all. I want to claim before you to-day that the message of the spinning wheel and Khadi is supremely a spiritual message; and it is because it is supremely a spiritual message for this land that it has got tremendous economic consequences as also political consequences.

Only the other day, an American friend, Prof. Sam Higginbottom, writing to me upon a subject in which both he and I are deeply interested, said,—I give you the substance of the letter—"I don't believe in a religion bereft of economics. Religion to be worth anything must be capable of being reduced when neccessary to terms of economics." I entirely endorse that remark with a big mental reservation. Not that Mr. Higginbottom also had not that reservation. But I must not claim to speak for him. The mental reservation is this, that whereas religion to be worth anything must be capable of being reduced to terms of economics, economics, to be worth anything, must also be capable of being reduced to terms of religion or spirituality. Therefore in this scheme of religion *cum* economics there is no room for exploitation and for Americanisation as the technical term is known. As a distinguished son of India put it,—he is no other than Sir. M. Vishveshvarayya,—whereas an Englishman owns 30 slaves, or is it

36,—I speak subject to correction,—an American owns 33 slaves. Personally, I think their is no room in true economics which is convertible with religion for the owning of slaves whether they are human beings, cattle or machinery. There is no room for slavery in economics. Then I suggest to you that you cannot escape Khadi and it has the largest limit. Temperance takes in its orbit a certain number of people. It blesses the man who converts the drunkard to teetotalism, and it undoubtedly blesses the drunkard who is so converted by the word of the reformer. Untouchability takes in its orbit at the most seven crores of people of this unhappy land, and not everyone of us can do untouchability work. You may certainly give the untouchable education; you may dig wells for him and build temples. But these would not make him touchable unless the so-called touchables will come down from their insolent heights and brother the untouchable. So you will see it is a somewhat complex problem for the man and woman in the street to handle. And as a man whose sole occupation in life is, be it ever so humble, to find out truth, I was searching for something that every one can do without exception, everybody in this room,—that something which would also remedy the most deep-seated disease of India.

And the most deep-seated disease of India is undoubtedly not drunkenness, undoubtedly not untouchability, great as those diseases are and greater perhaps for those who are suffering from them; but when you examine the numerical content of this disease, you will find with me, if you take any census returns, or any authentic book on history, such for instance as Sir William Hunter's history, or take the evidence of Mr. Higginbottom given before a Commission only two years ago, —he said that the largest number of people in India were poverty-stricken, and Sir William Hunter says that one-tenth of the population in India is living barely on one meal a day consisting of a stale *roti* and a pinch of dirty salt which perhaps you and I will not touch,—that state of things persists in

India to-day. If you were to go into the interior, outside the railway track, you will find as I have found that the villages are being reduced to dung-heaps, the villagers are not there, vultures are to be seen because they could not support themselves, and were reduced to carcasses.

India is suffering from menengitis, and if you will perform the necessary operation and make some return to those starving millions to-day, I say there is nothing but Khadi for you. And if as men spiritually inclined, you will think of those less fortunate than you are and who have not even enough to support themselves or clothe themselves, if you will have an indissoluble bond between them and yourselves, I say once more there is nothing for you but Khadi. But it jars, and the reason why it jars is that this is a new thing and is a visionary thing, a day-dream as it appears to many. The missionary friend of Vellore, of whom I spoke about, told me at the end of our conversation, "Yes, but can you stem the march of modern progress? Can you put back the hands of the clock, and induce people to take to your Khadi and make them work on a mere pittance?" All I could say is that this friend did not know his India. From the Vellore meeting I went to two places, Arcot and Arni. I did not see much of the people there, I assure you, but saw the villagers less well clad than I am. I saw them not in their tens but in their tens of thousands. They were in their rags and their wages were practically nil for four months in the year. They gave me of their substance; I was hungrily looking at the thing they gave me. They gave me not pices; they gave pies.

Come with me to Orissa, in November, to Puri, a holy place, and a sanatorium, where you will find soldiers and the Governor's residence during summer months. Within ten miles' radius of Puri you will see skin and bone. With this very hand I have collected soiled pies from them tied tightly in their rags, and their hands were more paralysed than mine were at Kolhapur. Talk to them of modern progress. Insult them by taking the name of God before them in vain. They will call you and me fiends if we talk about God to them. They know, if they know any God at all, a God of terror, vengeance, a pitiless tyrant. They do not know what love is. What can you do for them? You will find it difficult to change these delightful sisters (pointing to the ladies present) from their silk *sadis* to coarse Khadi woven by those paralytic and crude hands. Khadi is rough! It is too heavy! Silk is soft to be touched and they can wear 9 yards of silk, but they cannot wear 9 yards of Khadi. The poor sisters of Orissa have no *sadis*; they are in rags. But they have not lost all sense of decency, but I assure you we have. We are naked in spite of our clothing, and they are clothed in spite of their nakedness. It is because of these that I wandar about from place to place, I humour my people, I humour my American friends. I humoured two stripling youths from Harvard. When they wanted my autograph, I said, 'No autograph for Americans.' We struck a bargain. 'I give you my autograph; and you take to Khadi.' They have promised and I rely on the word of an American gentleman. Many of them are doing this work,—make no mistake about it,—and they like it also.

But I cannot be satisfied, not till every man and woman in India is working at his or at her wheel. Burn that wheel if you find a better substitute. This is the one and only work which can supply the needs of the millions without disturbing them from their homes. It is a mighty task and I know that I cannot do it. I know also that God can do it. The mightiest and strongest matter is but a tiny affair for Him, when it pleases Him. He can destroy them all in the twinkling of an eye, as He has destroyed now thousands of homes in Gujarat and as He had destroyed thousands of homes a few years ago in South India. I carry this message of Khadi and the spinning wheel with the fullest faith in God, and therefore in His creation, man. You may laugh at me to-day. You may call this a sordid thing. If you like you may distrust me and say this is some political schemer who has come to place his Khaddar before us, but he has got many things up his sleeve.

You may misinterpret me and my message. You may say: "We are too weak to do these things and too poor." I know it is possible for you to repel me by your arguments and make me speechless. But I shall not lose faith in you so long as I cannot lose faith in God. It is impossible for me to lose that faith, and therefore I cannot lose faith in the message of Khadi and the spinning wheel.'

If I have not succeded in opening out my heart to you, and if I have not succeeded in showing to you the rock-bottom spirituality of the message of Khaddar, I don't think I shall ever succeed in doing so. All I can say is I mean to succeed. My lips may not deliver the true message. God will do it all, in whose name I have delivered this message to you. God bless you.

15th September, 1927

THE STUDENTS' SHARE

By M. K. Gandhi

Speaking at Pachiappa's College, Gandhiji said:

I thank you sincerely for all the gifts you have given me for *Daridranarayan*. This is not the first time I enter this Hall. It was in 1896 that I entered this Hall in connection with the struggle in South Africa. Dr. Subramania Aiyar of revered memory presided at the function. The reason why I recall this meeting is that I made the acquaintance of the students of India then for the first time. As you may know I am a matriculate, and therefore never had any college education worth the name in India. But when after the address was finished and the thanksgiving completed I went out to students who were lying in wait for me and took away from me all the copies of the green pamphlet that I was then circulating throughout India, and it was for the sake of those students that I asked the late Mr. G. Parameshwaran Pillai, who befriended the cause and me as no one else did, to print copies and circul-

-ate them. With supreme pleasure he printed 10,000 copies of the pamphlet. Such was the demand on the part of the students for understanding the situation in South Africa and it pleased me immensely, and I said to myself, "Yes, India may be proud of her children and may baseall her hopes upon them." Since that time my acquaintance with students has been growing in volume and intensity. As I said in Bangalore, more is expected from those who give much, and since you have given me so much you have also given me the right to expect much more. I shall never be satisfied with all that you could give me. You have endorsed some of the work that it has been my privilege to do. You have mentioned with affection and reverence in your address the name of *Daridranarayan* and you, Sir (Principal), have—and I have no doubt with utmost sincerity—endorsed the claim that I have made on behalf of the spinning wheel. Many of my distinguished and learned countrymen, I know, have rejected that claim, saying that little bit of a wheel which was happily put away by our sisters and our mothers could never lead to the attainment of Swaraj. And yet you have endorsed that claim and pleased me immensely. Though you, students, have not said as much in your address, yet you have said sufficient in it to warrant the belief that you have in your hearts a real corner for the spinning wheel. Let not therfore this purse be the first and last demonstration of you, affection for the spinning wheel. I tell you it would be an embarrassment for me if it is the last demonstration of your affection; for I shall have no use for the money if the Khadi that may be produced through the distribution of that money amongst the starving millions is not used by you. After all a lip profession of faith in the charkha and the throwing of a few rupees at me in a patronising manner won't bring Swaraj and won't solve the problem of the ever-deepening poverty of the toiling and starving millions. I want to correct myself. I have said toiling millions. I wish that it was a true description. Unfortunately, as we have not revised our tastes about clothing, we have made it impossible for these starving millions to toil throughout the year. We have imposed upon them a vacation, which they do not need, for at least four months in the year. This is not a figment of my imagination, but it is a truth repeated by many English administrators, if you reject the testimony of your own countrymen who have moved in the midst of these masses. So then if I take this purse away and distribute it amongst the starving sisters, it does not solve the question. On the contrary it will impoverish their soul. They will become beggars and get into the habit of living upon charity. Heaven help the man, the woman or the nation that learns to live on charity. What you and I want to do is to provide work for those sisters of ours living protected in their own homes, and this is the only work that you can provide them with. It is dignified and honest work, and it is good enough work. One anna may mean nothing to you. You will throw it away in getting into a tram car and lazily passing your time instead of taking exercise for 2, 3, 4 or 5 miles as the case may be. But when it finds its way into the pockets of one poor sister it fructifies. She labours for it and she gives me beautiful yarn spun by her sacred hands, a yarn that has a history behind it. It is a thread worth weaving a garment out of for princes and potentates. A piece of calico from a mill has no such history behind it. I must not detain you over this one theme, great as it is for me, and though it engrosses practically the whole of my time. *This purse of yours will not be a help but a hindrance to me if it is not an earnest of your determination henceforth, if you have not it already that you are not going to wear anything else but Khadi.*

Let me not be deluded into the belief that you believe in this gospel of Khadi, because you give me the purse and because you applaud me. I want you to act up to your profession. I do not want it to be said of you,—the salt of India, —that yon gave this money merely to bamboozle me, that you do not want to wear Khadi and that you have no belief in it. Do not fulfil the prophecy that had been made by a distinguished son of Tamil Nadu and a friend of mine. He has said that when I die I will not need any other firewood to reduce my corpse to ashes but the wood that will be collected out of the spinning wheels that I am now distributing. He has no faith in the charkha and he thinks that those who utter the name of the charkha do so merely out of respect for me. It is an honest opinion. It will be a great national tragedy if the Khadi movement turns out to be that and you will have been direct contributors to the tragedy and participators in that crime. It will be a national suicide. If you have no living faith in the charkha reject it. It would be a truer demonstration of your love, you will open my eyes and I shall go about my way crying hoarse in the wilderness: "You have rejected the charkha and thereby you have rejected *Daridranarayan*." But save me and save yourselves the pain, the degradation and the humiliation that await us if there is any delusion or camouflage about this. This is one thing. But there are many things more in your address.

You have mentioned there child-marriage and child-widows. A learned Tamilian has written to me to address students on child-widows. He has said that the hardships of child-widows in this presidency are far greater than those of child-widows in other parts of India. I have not been able to test the truth of this statement. You should know that better than I do. But what I would like you, young men around me to do is that you should have a touch of chivalry about you. If you have that, I have a great suggestion to offer. I hope the majority of you are unmarried, and a fair number of you are also Brahmacharis. I have to say 'a fair number' because I know students; a student who casts his lustful eyes upon his sister is not a Brahmachari. I want you to make this sacred resolve that you are not going to marry a girl who is not a widow, you will seek out a widow-girl and if you cannot get a widow girl you are not going to marry at all. Make that determination, announce it to the world, announce it to your parents if you have them or to your sisters. I call them widow-girls by way of correction because I believe that a child ten or fifteen years old, who was no consenting party to the so-called marriage, who having married, having never lived with the so-called husband, is suddenly declared to be a widow, is not a widow. It is an abuse of the term, abuse of language and a sacrilege. The word "widow" in Hinduism has a sacred odour about it. I am a worshipper of a true widow like the late Mrs Ramabai Ranade who knew what it was to be a widow. But a child 9 years old knows nothing of what a husband should be. If it is not true that there are such child-widows in the presidency, then my case falls to the ground. But if there are such child-widows, it becomes your sacred duty to make the determination to marry a girl widow if you want to rid ourselves of this curse. I am superstitious enough to believe that all such sins that a nation commits react upon it physically. I believe that all these sins of ours have accumulated together to reduce us to a state of slavery. You may get the finest constitution that is conceivable dropping upon you from the House of Commons. It will be worthless if there are not men and women fit enough to work that constitution. Do you suppose that we can possibly call ourselves men worthy of ruling ourselves or others or shaping the destiny of a nation containing 30 crores so long as there is one single widow who wishes to fulfil her fundamental wants but is violently prevented from doing so? It is not religion, but irreligion. I say that, saturated as I am with the spirit of Hinduism. Do not make the mistake that it is the Western spirit in me that is speaking. I claim to be full to overflowing with the spirit of India undefiled. I have assimilated many things from the West but not this. There is no warrant for this kind of widowhood in Hinduism.

All I have said about child-widows necessarily applies to child-wives. You must be able surely to control your lust to this extent, that you are not going to marry a girl that is under 16 years of age. If I could do so I would lay down 20 as minimum. Twenty years is early enough even in India. It is we who are responsible for the precocity of girls, not even the Indian climate, because I know girls of the age of 20 who are pure and undefiled and able to stand the storm that may rage round. Let us not hug that precocity to ourselves. Some Brahman students tell me that they cannot follow this principle, that they cannot get Brahman girls sixteen years old, very few Brahmans keep their daughters unmarried till that age, the Brahman girls are married mostly before 10, 12 and 13 years. Then I say to the Brahman youth, "Cease to be a Brahman, if you cannot possibly control yourself. Choose a grown up girl of 16 who became a widow when she was a child. If you cannot get a Brahman widow who has reached that age, then go and take any girl you like. And I tell you that the God of the Hindus will pardon that boy who has preferred to marry out of his caste rather than ravish a girl of twelve. When your heart is not pure and you cannot master your passions, you cease to be an educated man. You have called your institution a premier institution. I want you to live up to the name of the premier institution which must produce boys who will occupy the front rank in character. And what is education without character and what is character without elementary personal purity? Brahmanism I adore. I have defended *Varnashrama Dharma.* But Brahmanism that can tolerate untouchability, virgin widowhood, spoliation of virgins, stinks in my nostrils. It is a parody of Brahmanism. There is no knowledge of Brahman therein. There is no true interpretation of the scriptures. It is undiluted animalism. Brahmanism is made of sterner stuff. I want these few remarks of mine to go deep down into your hearts. I am watching the boys whilst I am speaking, and it hurts me to hear a single giggle whilst I am pouring out my heart. I have not come to appeal to your intellects but to your hearts. You are the hope of the country and what I have said is of primary importance for you.

In response to the request of a Calicut professor I shall now proceed to say something about cigarette smoking and coffee and tea drinking. These are not necessities of life. There are some who manage to take ten cups of coffee a day. Is it necessary for their healty development and for keeping them awake for the performance of their duties? If it is necesary to take coffee or tea to keep them awake, let them not drink coffee or tea but go to sleep. We must not become slaves to these things. But the majority of the people who drink coffee or tea are slaves to them. Cigars and cigarettes, whether foreign or indigenous, must be avoided. Cigarette smoking is like an opiate and the cigars that you smoke have a touch of opium about them. They get to your nerves and you cannot leave them afterwards. How can a single student foul his mouth by converting it into a chimney? If you give up these habits of smoking cigars and cigarettes and drinking coffee and tea you will find out for yourselves how much you are able to save. A drunkard in Tolstoy's story is hesitating to execute his design of murder so long as he has not smoked his cigar But he puffs it, and then gets up smiling and saying, "What a coward am I," takes the dagger and does the deed. Tolstoy spoke from experience. He has written nothing without having had personal experience of it. And he is much more against cigars and cigarettes than against drink. But do not make the mistake that between drink and tobacco, drink is a lesser evil. No. If cigarette is Beelzebub, then drink is Satan.

Speaking next about Hindi, he said: There is the Hindi Prachar office supported by people in the North. They have spent nearly a lakh of rupees and the Hindi teachers have been doing their work regularly. Some progress has been made but we have yet to make substantial progress. You can all learn Hindi in one year provided you give one hour a day. You can understand simple Hindi in six months. I can't speak to you in Hindi because most of you do not know it. Hindi should be made the universal tongue in India. You should know also Sanskrit, for then you will be able to read Bhagavad Gita. As students of a premier Hindu institution, you ought to be taught Bhagavad Gita. I would expect Musalman boys also to read in this institution. (A voice: No Panchama is admitted) This is a discovery to me. This institution should be flung open to Panchamas and Musalmans. I would de-Hinduise this institution if a Panchama has no entry here. (Hear, hear). The fact that this is a Hindu institution is no reason why a Musalman or a Panchama could not receive education here. I think it is high time that the trustees revise their constitution, This is a petition from me, an earnest and a very God-fearing Hindu, saturated with the spirit of Hinduism, not from a petty-fogging reformer, but from one who is trying to live the best in Hinduism. Mr. Principal, you will please convey this petition to the proper quarters, and it will be a great joy to me to hear during my sojourn in this presidency that my petition has been heard. I thank you for listening to this message.

15th September, 1927

THE 'KHADDAR' IDEAL

BY C. F. ANDREWS

During the present year, when I was in South Africa, I found a remarkable interest taken in the National Movement in India by the Dutch people. These now outnumber the English, and are in power as a Nationalist Government. Twice over, I was asked by the students of Stellenbosch University near Capetown to lecture; and they gave me, of their own choice, the subject of 'Mahatma Gandhi's ideals.' The following is the substance of one of these lectures. The second was called *Ahimsa.* It will be understood, that I was obliged to present each subject in a very simple form, such as would arrest the imagination of those who had thought very little about it beforehand and belonged to another country.

The lecture on 'Khaddar' might be abbreviated as follows:

The word 'Khaddar' means home-spun and home woven cotton cloth, in which mrchinery has played no part at all from start to finish. The Khaddar ideal thus represents a very daring declaration that the Machine Age has carried in a wrong direction bringing along with it the disintegration of earlier moral values. It is leading directly to disaster, The simpler rural civilisation, so it is positively asserted, is the best. Mahatma Gandhi regards the ideal of simplicity and closeness to Nature as higher than the ideal of the civilisation of our modern towns together with the factory life which is bound up with them.

There is a famous story, told in China, about a disciple of the great sage, Confucius. This disciple, though poor was a scholar and a gentleman. He occupied the humble position of a gardener. One day a Mandarin, who was being carried past in a sedan chair, alighted to enjoy the cool shade of the garden. The Mandarin was also a scholar and a gentleman, profoundly versed in the venerable Confucian Classics. He sat down in the garden and fanned himself. While he was resting under the shade of some bamboo trees, he saw the gardener patiently toiling with a bucket in order to fetch water from a well in order to water the flowers in the midst of the garden.

The Mandarin said: "Let me show you a mechanical structure, whereby the water may be drawn up from the well without such a vast amount of human labour."

But the gardener, who was also a scholar and a gentleman, said: "Sir, I have read in the Ancient Classics that the man who perpetually employs mechanism comes at last to possess a mechanical mind. Now a mechanical mind is not in harmony with Nature. In my work as a gardener, I desire always to keep my mind in unison with Nature. Therefore, I prefer drawing water slowly in a bucket, while I enjoy quietly the beauties of this garden; and I have avoided bringing into the garden machinery, which might produce in me a mechanical mind."

The Mandarin was so pleased with the gardener's answer, that he reported it,—through the proper court authorities,— to the Emperor of China. This Emperor was himself a profound scholar and also a lover of Nature. So he sent for the gardener and placed him in charge of one of his summer palace gardens.

I have ventured to put forward that story, not merely as containing a charming idyll of ancient China, with its courtiers and emperors, its scholars and its summer palace gardens, but also as embodying the inner truth contained in what has been called in India the Khaddar ideal. It would symbolise the unique value of home-spinning and home-weaving undertaken in the country, as compared with the harmful employment of modern machinery in large towns.

Let me approach the same subject from another angle, as I came up against it in India at a sudden human crisis.

There had been one of those disasters that sometimes happen in the East and are beyond all ordinary human control. After a rainfall on the Himalayan slopes, which had reached the total of forty-eight inches in two days, the Bengal rivers were in flood. An area of 1,500 square miles, which had in early days been a shallow lake, became inundated so deep with water that all the rice harvest perished, and many cattle were also destroyed.

Then the flood subsided, and the hot sun began to dry up the caking mud. There were no cattle remaining to plough the fields and there was no money left to buy more cattle. In the area of the flooded district, where we were working at relief work, it seemed as though another harvest would inevitably be lost for want of proper ploughing. For the land had been broken up and sown some time before the next monsoon rains. With great difficulty we managed to get in a 'Ford' tractor and soon broke up the soil. It was a powerful machine and easily did the work that fifty men would do with their ox ploughing. The harvest that followed was a good one, and the land-owners came to us later asking for the use of this tractor for the coming year.

Then we sat down together and debated it all out. In the

end, we decided that we would not have the 'Ford' tractor.

What settled the matter was this. If we had brought in several 'Ford' tractors, the greater number of our villagers would immediately have been thrown out of all employment. Their life in the country was natural, simple, pure, and in a kindly way happily domestic. But if they were driven into the factories, to compete against other labourers under intolerable conditions, then what would become of them and their homes?

On the whole, the choice came back to the same point as that reached by the Confucian gardener in China. To live in accord with Nature, and to enjoy God's own pure air and country life,—this was surely better than to fill the ranks of the miserably housed and casually employed labourers in the factory towns.

Mahātma Gandhi, on his return to India from South Africa, after twenty years' absence, was overwhelmed with pity for the poor Indian villagers, who were being gradually driven from the land by the flood of manufactured goods. This was in reality a more desolating inundation than that caused by the heavy rainfall in the Himalayas.

He found the villagers literally inundated by these cheap foreign manufactures, and economically deprived of their own ancient industries of spinning and weaving on account of the insidious cheapness of the imported articles. Village after village had succumbed, until the amount of homespun and home-woven cloth, which used to be nearly cent. per cent., had fallen down to 20 per cent., and was still falling. In a very short time, there would have been no village cloth industries left. Instead of remaining in the villages and using their spare time in such industries, the younger members of the family were being forced by stress of poverty to go into the towns in order to work at the mills.

Mahatma Gandhi sought at once to reverse the whole process. He found that the villagers, who remained in the villages of India with its burning heat, used to spend five months of the year, when agriculture was at a stand-still, in doing almost nothing. They remained idle and listless. They possessed neither the energy nor the technical skill to spin and weave their own clothes. Thus there was in every home a terrible economic waste both of time and labour.

So Mahatma Gandhi went up and down India preaching his Khaddar ideal. Since everything in India turns sooner or later to religion, he preached the wearing of "Khaddar" as a religious duty among the rich and educated as well as among the poor. Beautiful white home-spun began slowly to take the place of the aniline-dyed cotton prints from Europe. Wherever the spinning wheel went the money that had been spent on artificial fabrics became carefully saved. Habits of home industry and thrift kept the villagers clear from the temptations and vices of the towns.

It remains yet to be seen whether the same Khaddar ideal has any message for the indigenous dwellers on the soil of Africa, whose gradual impoverishment is one of the saddest features of the present modern age.

22nd September, 1927

THREE SPEECHES

By M. K. Gandhi

A GREAT SATYAGRAHI

In his speech at Chidambaram, Gandhiji paid this tribute to the great 'untouchable' saint Nandanar:

'I knew that Chidambaram must be a place of pilgrimage for me. I have never claimed to be the one original Satyagrahi. What I have claimed is the application of that doctrine on an almost universal scale, and it yet remains to be seen and demonstrated that it is a doctrine which it capable of assimilation by thousands upon thousands of peoples in all ages and climes. I know, therefore, that mine is an experiment still in the making and it therefore always keeps me humble and rooted to the soil, and in that state of humility I always cling to every true example of Satyagraha that comes under my notice as a child clings to its mother's breast, and so when I heard and read the story of Nandanar and his lofty Satyagraha, and his great success, my head bowed before his spirit, and all the day long I have felt elevated to be able to be in a place hallowed by the holy feet of Nanda, and it will not be without a wrench that I shall be leaving this place in a few minutes' time.

"But it gave me great joy, and I considered it a great honour, that the very first act I was called upon to perform was to open the gateway of the temple that has been erected in memory of that great saint. How I wish that it could be said of the people of Chidambaram that at least they knew no distinction between the Brahman and the Panchama, and if the people of Chidambaram would rise to that lofty height, they would have done nothing more than what the Gita expects of every Hindu to do. In the eye of God there are no touchables and untouchables. Brahmans are called Brahmans not for their superiority, not for their ability to lord it over, but because of their ability to serve mankind by their knowledge and by their ability to efface themselves in the act of serving. Theirs is the privilege and theirs the duty, of serving their fellow men and they cannot do so to the full, unless they renounce every earthly reward. By his indomitable spirit, and by his overwhelming faith in God, Nanda was able to bear down the haughty spirit of the haughty Brahmans and to show that in his spirit he was infinitely superior to his persecutors, who considered themselves first among mankind. But let the Panchama Adi-Dravida brothers and sisters, profiting by the example of Nanda, live up to the spirit which they have inherited.

"Nanda broke down every barrier and won his way to freedom not by brag, not by bluster, but by the purest form of self-suffering. He did not swear against his persecutors, he would not even condescend to ask his persecutors for what was his due. But he shamed them into doing justice by his lofty prayer, by the purity of his character, and if one may put it in human language he compelled God Himself to descend and made Him open the eyes of the persecutors. And what Nanda did in his time and in his own person, it is open to every one of us to do to-day in our own person. And I wish that you, my hearers, will catch something of the spirit of Nanda, and if so many of us could possibly imitate Nanda and assimilate a spark of his spirit we can make this land a land again of holy people. I hope and pray that the temple with which the trustees have identified me to-day will keep green the memory of that great saint by keeping the atmosphere about the temple always pure. I would very much like to leave the atmosphere about this place at this stage filled with the spirit of Nanda.'

He went on in the same strain to describe what he called the Khadi spirit, and the inwardness of the Khadi movement:

'But it would be wrong perhaps on my part, if I did not say a few words showing how we can illustrate the spirit of Nandan in our daily life. In my humble opinion, we cannot better illustrate that spirit than by clothing ourselves with the "Khadi spirit." Please note the distinction I am making. I am not saying that we can illustrate the spirit of Nanda by wearing Khadi merely, but I say that we must have the "Khadi spirit." Even a blackguard, even a prostitute, should be expected to wear Khadi, since she or he, the blackguard, must wear something even as they eat the wheat and the rice in this country, in common with us, but the "Khadi spirit" means that we must know the meaning that the wearing of Khadi carries with it. Every time that we take our Khadi garment early in the morning to wear for going out we should remember that we are doing so in the name of *Daridranarayan* and for the sake of the starving millions of India. If we have the "Khadi spirit" in us we would surround ourselves with simplicity in every walk of life. The "Khadi spirit" means illimitable patience. For those who know anything about the production of Khadi know how patiently the spinners and the weavers have to toil at their trade, and even so must we have patience, whilst we are spinning "the thread of Swaraj." The "Khadi spirit" means also an equally illimitable faith. Even as the spinner toiling away at the spinning wheel has illimitable faith that the yarn he spins, by itself small enough, put in the aggregate would be enough to clothe every human being in India, so must we have illimitable faith in Truth and Non-violence ultimately conquering every obstacle in our way.

'The Khadi spirit means fellow-feeling with every human being on earth. It means a complete renunciation of everything that is likely to harm our fellow creatures, and if we but cultivate that spirit amongst the millions of our countrymen, what a land this India of ours would be! And the more I move about the country and the more I see the things for myself, the richer, the stronger is my faith growing in the capacity of the spinning wheel. If we try to reason out with our intellect the capacity of repeating of the mere name "Rama," our intellect will fail to satisfy our heart, and yet I hope that there is not one single person in this audience who would consider that those *rishis*, who gave us the heritage of repeating those names, were either fools or idiots. Even so I suggest to you that the Khadi spirit has all the capacity that I have just now described to you. But there is one condition behind it, I admit, one condition alone that attaches to the expression of that spirit. It is this,—that even as *Ramanama* became in our minds a living force, because it had behind it the unrivalled *tapashcharya* of those who gave it to us, so it is with the Khadi movement. It ought to have the *tapashcharya* of those who are behind it. Every minute of my time I am fully conscious of the fact, that if those who have consecrated their lives to Khadi will not incessantly insist on purity of life, Khadi is bound to stink in the nostrils of our countrymen. I am well aware that Khadi cannot compete with other articles of commerce on their own platform, on their own terms. Even as Satyagraha is a weapon unique of its kind and not one of the ordinary weapons used by people, so is Khadi a unique article of commerce which will not, cannot, succeed on terms common to other articles. But I know this also as certainly as I know that I am sitting here, that Khadi is unique and it would out-distance every article in India to-day. You will, therefore, perhaps understand why I do not enthuse over all these Khadi purses you have given me. I know that if you had even a tenth of the faith that I have in Khadi, you would not give your two hundreds and your two thousands out of your plenty, but you would satisfy me till there is no money required for Khadi.'

22nd September, 1927

BRAHMAN-NON-BRAHMAN

In his speech at Cuddalore, Gandhiji spoke at length on the Brahman Non-Brahman problem:

'But I must hasten to the important part of the Municipal address. You have drawn my attention to the existence of the dissensions between the Brahmans and the Non-Brahmans, and asked me to find out a solution. As a Non-Brahman myself, if I could remove the dissensions by forfeiting my life, I should do so this very moment. But God is a very hard taskmaster. He is never satisfied with fire-works display. His mills, although they grind surely and incessantly, grind excruciatingly slow, and He is never satisfied with hasty forfeitures of life. It is a sacrifice of the purest that He demands, and so you and I have prayerfully to plod on, live out the life so long as it is vouchsafed to us to live it. I have said, only very recently in Madras, that whenever you want me to take part in your deliberations, or want me to advise you, you will find me at your disposal. I have no clear-cut solution for this difficult question. I confess to you, that I do not even now know the points of differences between the two. I tried to draw out some Non-Brahmans, who came to me on Nandi Hill, and they promised to see me in my tour and place all the points of difference before me. I must confess to you that I am no wiser about the Brahman side of the question. And wily as the Brahmans are, I admit they have not told me wha the differences are, fully well knowing what my opinion would be about all these questions. As you are aware, though a Non-Brahman myself, I have lived more with them and amongst them than amongst Non-Brahmans, and on that account pardonably some of my Non-Brahman friends suspect me of having taken all my colouring from Brahman friends. I have a shrewd suspicion, that the Non-Brahman friends consider that I am not to be accepted as a hope for a proper solution, and so I find myself in the happy position of being isolated by both the parties, a position which in the present state of my health suits me admirably. But all the same I give you my assurance that I for my part hold myself in readiness to be wooed by either party. And I assure you too that I shall not plead physical unfitness.

'But I have for both the parties two counsels of perfection which I can lay before you. To the Brahman I will say: "Seeing that you are repositories of all knowledge and embodiments of sacrifice and that you have chosen the life of mendicancy, give up all that the Non-Brahman wants and be satisfied with that they may leave for you." But the modern Brahman would, I know, summarily reject my Non-Brahman interpretation of his *dharma*. To the Non-Brahman I say: "Seeing that you have got numbers on your side, seeing that you have got wealth on your side, what is it that you are worrying about? Resisting as you are, and as you must, untouchability, do not be guilty of creating a new untouchability in your midst. In your haste, in your blindness, in your anger against the Brahmans, you are trying to trample under foot the whole of the culture which you have inherited from ages past. With a stroke of the pen, may be at the point of the sword, you are impatient to rid Hinduism of its bed-rock. Being dissatisfied and properly dissatisfied with the husk of Hinduism, you are in danger of losing even the kernel, life itself. You in your impatience seem to think that there is abolutely nothing to be said about *Varnashrama*. Some of you are ready even to think that in defending *Varnashrama* I am also labouring under a delusion. Make no mistake about it. They who say this have not even taken the trouble of understanding what I mean by *Varnashrama*"

'It is a universal law, stated in so many words by Hinduism. It is a law of spiritual economics. Nations of the West and Islam itself unwittingly are obliged to follow that law. It has nothing to do with superiority or inferiority. The customs about eating, drinking and marriage are no integral part of *Varnashrama Dharma.* It was a law discovered by your ancestors and my ancestors, the *rishis* who saw that if they were to give the best part of their lives to God and to the world, and not to themselves, they must recognise that it is the law of heredity. It is a law designed to set free man's energy for higher pursuits in life What true Non-Brahmans should therefore set about doing is not to undermine the very foundations on which they are sitting, but to clean all the sweepings they have gathered on the foundation and make it perfectly clean. Fight by all means the monster that passes for *Varnashrama* to-day, and you will find me working side by side with you. My *Varnashrama* enables me to dine with anybody who will give me clean food, be he Hindu, Muslim, Christian, Parsi, whatever he is. My *Varnashrama* accommodates a pariah girl under my own roof as my own daughter. My *Varnashrama* accommodates many Panchama families with whom I dine with the greatest pleasure,—to dine with whom is a privilege. My *Varnashrama* refuses to bow the head before the greatest potentate on earth, but my *Varnashrama* compels me to bow down my head in all humility before knowledge, before purity, before every person, where I see God face to face. Do not therefore swear by words that have, at the present moment become absolutely meaningless and obsolete. Swear all you are worth, if you like, against Brahmans but never against Brahmanism, and even at the risk of being understood or being mistaken by you to be a pro-Brahman, I make bold to declare to you that whilst Brahmans have many sins to atone for, and many for which they will receive exemplary punishments, there are to-day Brahmans living in India who are watching the progress of Hinduism and who are trying to protect it with all the piety and all the austerity of which they are capable. Them you perhaps do not even know. They do not care to be known. They expect no reward, they ask for none. Their work is its own reward. They work in this fashion because they must. It is their nature. You and I may swear against them for all we are worth, but they are untouched. Do not run away with the belief that I am putting in a plea for Brahmans, Vakils and Ministers and even Justices of the High Courts in India. I have not thought of them in my mind at all. What, therefore, both Brahmans and Non-Brahmans and for that matter everybody who wants India to progress has to do, is to sweep his own house clean. I therefore suggest to Non-Brahmans, who have not yet lost their heads, to think out clearly what it is that they are grieved over, and make up your minds and fight for all they are worth to remove those grievances. I recognise however that I have this evening entered upon an academic discussion. Not knowing the merits of their quarrels, I do nothing else. But in my own humble opinion, I have indicated the lines of action for both and within the limits of your capacity, it is open to you to make use of it in any manner you like.

But in trying to grapple with this great problem do not forget little things for which I am touring in Tamil Nadu. Little they may appear to you but I assure you, that they are great enough to engage the attention of every one of you. I simply summarise them for you without entering into the discussion.

22nd September, 1927

HINDU STUDENTS AND THE GITA

(*From the address to the Mannargudi Students*)

You state in your address that you read the Gospels daily even as I do. I cannot say that I read the Gospels daily, but I can say that I have read the Gospels in a humble and prayerful spirit, and it is well with you if you are also reading the Gospels in that spirit. But I expect that the vast majority of you are Hindu boys. I wish that you could have said to me that at least your Hindu boys were reading the Bhagavad Gita daily to derive inspiration. For I believe that all the great religions of the world are true more or less. I say 'more or less' because I believe that everything that the human hand touches, by reason of the very fact that human beings are imperfect, becomes imperfect. Perfection is the exclusive attribute of God and it is indescribable, untranslatable. I do believe that it is possible for every human being to become perfect even as God is perfect. It is necessary for us all to aspire after perfection, but when that blessed state is attained, it becomes indescribable, indefinable. And I therefore admit, in all humility, that even the Vedas, the Koran and the Bible are the imperfect word of God, and imperfect beings that we are, swayed to and fro by a multitude of passions, it is impossible for us even to understand this word of God in its fullness, and so I say to a Hindu boy, that he must not uproot the traditions in which he has been brought up, as I say to a Musalman or a Christian boy that he must not uproot his traditions. And so whilst I would welcome your learning the Gospel and your learning the Koran, I would certainly insist on all of you Hindu boys, if I had the power of insistence, learning the Gita. It is my belief that the impurity that we see about boys in schools, the carelessness about things that matter in life, the levity with which the student world deals with the greatest and most fundamental questions of life is due to this uprooting of tradition from which boys have hitherto derived their sustenance.

'But I must not be misunderstood. I do not hold that everything ancient is good because it is ancient. I do not advocate surrender of God-given reasoning faculty in the face of ancient tradition. Any tradition, however ancient, if inconsistent with morality, is fit to be banished from the land.

Untouchability may be considered to be an ancient tradition, the institution of child widowhood and child marriage may be considered to be ancient tradition, and even so many an ancient horrible belief and superstitious practice. I would sweep them out of existence if I had the power. When, therefore, I talk of respecting the ancient tradition, you now understand what I mean, and it is because I see the same God in the Bhagavad Gita as I see in the Bible and the Koran that I say to the Hindu boys that they will derive greater inspiration from the Bhagavad Gita because they will be tuned to the Gita more than to any other book.'

22nd September, 1927

'RANGILA RASUL'

BY M. K. GANDHI

In spite of the goading of correspondents, wise and otherwise, I have hitherto resisted the temptation to be drawn into the controversy that has arisen over this pamphlet. I have endeavoured patiently to deal with these correspondents by private correspondence. But of late the correspondence has increased beyond my capacity to deal with it privately. The last letter is from a Muslim professor in Bihar. He sends me a newspaper cutting containing a letter rebuking me in that even I had chosen to join in the conspiracy of silence observed by the leading Hindus in general. The professor wants me to 'reply sharp.' I gladly do so in the hope that my correspondents will be satisfied with my good faith and understand the reason for my silence. As I do not read newspapers, save a local one, I know nothing about the 'conspiracy of silence' by Hindu leaders. The newspaper I read most frequently just now is the *Hindu* and I do remember having seen in it a strong article against the *Rangila Rasul.* So far as I am concerned, long before many Musalmans knew even of the existence of the pamphlet, it came into my possession. In order to test the veracity of my informant, I read it and wrote the following note in *Young India*, dated 19th June, 1924:

> A friend has sent me a pamphlet called *Rangila Rasul*, written in Urdu. The author's name is not given. It is published by the Manager, Arya Pustakalaya, Lahore. The very title is highly offensive. The contents are in keeping with the title. I cannot, without giving offence to the reader's sense of the fine, give the translation of some of the extracts. I have asked myself what the motive possibly could be in writing or printing such a book except to inflame passions. Abuse and caricature of the Prophet cannot wean a Musalman from his faith, and it can do no good to a Hindu who may have doubts about his own belief. As a contribution therefore to the religious propaganda work, it has no value whatsoever. The harm it can do is obvious.
>
> Another friend sends me a sheet called *Shaitan* printed at Public Printing Press, Lahore. It contains untranslatable abuse of Musalmans. I am aware of similar abuse by Musalman sheets. But that is no answer to or justification for the Hindu or the Arya Samaj abuse. I would not have even noticed these prints but for the information given to me that such writings command a fair patronage. The local leaders must find a way of stopping these publications or at least discrediting them and distributing clean literature instead, showing tolerance for each other's faiths.

Then followed protests from Arya Samajists enclosing viler writing against Arya Samajists and the great founder Rishi Dayanand, telling me that *Rangila Rasul* and such writings were in answer to the Muslim writings referred to above. I thereupon wrote the following second note (Y. I. 10th July, 1924).

> My remarks on the unreadable pamphlet on the Prophet and on the scurrilous sheet *Shaitan* have brought me a sheaf-ful of letters from Arya Samajists, who, whilst admitting the force and truth of my remarks, say that some

Musalman sheets are no better, and that they began the abuse and the Arya Samajists followed by way of retaliation. The writers have sent me some of these sheets. I have suffered the pain of going through a few of the extracts. The language in some parts is simply revolting. I cannot disfigure these pages by reproducing it. I have also been favoured with a life by a Musalman of Swami Dayanand. I am sorry to say it is largely a distortion of the great reformer. Nothing that he did has escaped the author's venom. One of my correspondents complains bitterly that my remarks have emboldened the Musalman speakers and writers to become more abusive than before towards the Arya Samaj and the Samajists. One of them sends me an account of a recently held Lahore meeting where unmentionable abuse was heaped upon the Samaj. Needless to say such writings and speeches can have no sympathy from me. In spite of the opinion I have expressed, I claim to be one of the many humble admirers of the founder of the Samaj. He pointed out the many abuses that were corrupting Hindu society. He inculcated a taste for Sanskrit learning. He challenged superstitious beliefs. By the chastity of his own life he raised the tone of the society in which he lived. He taught fearlessness, and he gave a new hope to many a despairing youth. Nor am I oblivious of his many services to the national cause. The Samaj has supplied it with many true and self-sacrificing workers. It has encouraged education among Hindu girls as perhaps no other Hindu institution save the Brahma Samaj has done. Ignorant critics have not hesitated to insinuate that my remarks about Shraddhanandji were due to his criticism of me. But the insinuation does not prevent me from re-acknowledging the pioneer work done by him in Gurukul. Whilst therefore I am unable to withdraw a single word of my criticism of the Samaj, the Satyartha Prakash, Rishi Dayanand and Swami Shraddhanandji, I repeat that my criticism was that of a friend with the desire that the Samaj may render greater service by ridding itself of the short-comings to which I drew attention. I want it to march with the times, give up the polemical spirit, and whilst adhering to its own opinions, extend that toleration to other faiths which it claims for itself. I want it to keep a watch on its workers and stop all discreditable writings. It is no answer in justification that Muslamans commenced the campaign of calumny. I do not know whether they did or not. But I do know that they would have been tired of repetition if there had been no retaliation. I have not even urged the Samajists to give up their Shuddhi. But I do urge them as I would urge Musalmans to revise the present idea of Shuddhi.

To the Musalman writers and speakers of whose conduct I have received the letters referred to, I venture to point out, that they neither enhance their own reputation nor that of the religion they profess by unrestrained abuse of the opponent. They can gain nothing, they cannot serve Islam, by swearing at the Samaj and the Samajists.

Thus I had anticipated the Musalman wrath. But in the present agitation the meeting-point ends there. I could not approve of the turn the agitation took. I regarded it as excessive and inflammatory. The attack against Justice Duleepsingh was uncalled for, undeserved and hysterical. The judiciary is by no means above being influenced by the Government, but it would be wholly unfit to render justice if it was open to popular attacks, threats and insults. So far as the Judges's integrity was concerned, it should have satisfied any Musalman that he condemned the pamphlet, as he did, in unmeasured terms. His reading of the section ought not to have been made a cause for virulent attack against him. That other judges have taken a different view from Justice Duleepsingh is irrelevant to the issue. Judges have been often known before now to have given honest and opposite interpretations of the same law. The agitation for strengthening the penal section may be wise. Personally I question the wisdom. Any stiffening of the section will react against ourselves, and will be utilised, as such sections have been utilised before, for strengthening the hold of British authority over our necks. But if Musalmans or Hindus want to agitate for unequivocally bringing such writings under the criminal law, they have a right to do so.

I hold strong views about Government protection. Time was when we knew better and disdained the protection of law courts in such matters. To stop anti-Muslim writings like the *Rangila Rasul* is the work of Hindus as to stop anti-Hindu writings is the work of Musalmans. The leaders have either lost control over mud-flingers or are in sympathy with them. In any case Government protection will not make us tolerant of one another. Each hater of the other's religion will under a stiffer law seek secret channels of making vicious attacks on his opponent's religion, or writing vilely enough to provoke anger but veiled enough to avoid the penal clauses of the law. But then I recognise that at the present moment we are not acting as sane nationalists or as men of religion. We are seeking under cover of religion to wreak mad vengeance upon one another.

My correspondents, both Hindu and Musalman, should understand that I am just now out of tune with the prevailing atmosphere. I recognise fully that I have no power over the fighters whether Hindu or Muslim. My solution for removing the tension is, I admit, not suited to the times. I therefore best serve the nation by holding my peace. But my faith in my solution is as immovable as my faith in the necessity and the possibility of real Hindu Muslim unity. Though therefore my helplessness is patent, there is no hopelessness in me. And as I believe that silent prayer is often mightier than any overt act, in my helplessness I continuously pray in the faith that the prayer of a pure heart never goes unanswered. And with all the strength at my command, I try to become a pure instrument for acceptable prayer.

29th September, 1927

THE NEILL STATUE AND NON-VIOLENCE

BY M. K. GANDHI

A Gujarati friend thus remonstrates in a letter to a common friend: "Sometimes Bapu's non-violence baffles one. He encourages the agitation for the removal of the Neill statue as he encouraged the one for the removal of the Lawrence statue. To me it looks very like violence; for the agitation must beget hatred against Englishmen—the very thing Bapu wants to avoid. And where I can see no violence he sees it, as in carrying arms for removing the Arms Act. It appears to me that in the first case there is every risk of violent temper being begotten by apparently non-violent means. And this according to Bapu should be avoided. In the second case only a slight risk of possibility of violence is incurred in order to achieve a worthy end—just the thing I should have imagined Bapu would brave."

In order to do justice to the argument and make it easily intelligible to the reader, I have somewhat extended the argument put cryptically in the original Gujarati.

Non-violence is made of sterner stuff. There is no doubt that the agitation for removing the Neill statue and the like is likely to increase the feeling of hatred against the English. A reformer seeking to spread non-violence must take note of the fact and guard against hatred, but dare not on any account hush causes of hatred. Non-violence in the form of love is the activest force in the world. As the Gujarati poet Shamal says 'There is no merit in returning good for good; most men do this. Merit lies in returning good for evil.' Merit here stands obviously for non-violence. Causes of hatred everywhere obtrude themselves on one's gaze. The seers of old saw that the only way of dealing with the situation was to neutralise hatred by love. This force of love therefore truly comes into play only when it meets with causes of hatred. True non-violence does not ignore or blind itself to causes of hatred, but in spite of the knowledge of their existence operates upon the person setting those causes in motion. Were it otherwise, the fight for Swaraj by non-violent means would be an impossibility. For at every step the Swarajist is bound to expose to view the blemishes of foreign rule and the foreign rulers. The law of non-violence,—returning good for evil, loving one's enemy,—involves a knowledge of the blemishes of the 'enemy.' Hence do the scriptures say,—*Kshama Virasya Bhushanam* 'Forgiveness is an attribute of the brave.'

It is perhaps now clear why a believer in non-violence must endorse any non-violent agitation for the removal of the Neill statue and the like. But the carrying of arms is not permissible for a non-violent man; for he is expected not to use them. And the total removal of the Arms Act in my opinion will never be held to be a just cause. Hence carrying arms for the removal of the Arms Act can never fall under any scheme of non-violence.

It is now perhaps necessary to look a little closer into the Neill statue agitation. Here is the inscription on the frontside of the pedestal of the statue :

"James George Smith Neill
A. D. C. to the Queen.
Lieut.-Colonel of the Madras Fusiliers
Brigadier-General in India
A brave, resolute, self-reliant soldier.
Universally acknowledged as the first
Who stemmed the torrent of rebellion in Bengal,
He fell gloriously
At the relief of Lucknow
25th September 1857.
Aged 47."

The inscription at the back reads :

"Erected by public subscription, 1860."

I venture to suggest that these are untruthful statements. The inscription is false history. At the time of writing this article I have not by me Kaye and Malleson's volumes, but a friend has obliged me by procuring for me Thompson's illuminating monograph *The Other side of the Medal*. It shows how false history is taught us in schools and colleges. I take the following extracts from that book:

> "These were General Neill's instructions to Major Renaud when he was hurrying with an advance guard to the relief of Cawnpore:
>
> 'Certain guilty villages were marked out for destruction, and all the men inhabiting them were to be slaughtered. All sepoys of mutinous regiments not giving a good account of themselves were to be hanged. The town of Futtehpore, which had revolted, had to be attacked, and the Pathan quarters destroyed with all their inhabitants. All heads of insurgents, particularly at Futtehpore, to be hanged. If the Deputy Collector is taken, hang him, and have his head cut off and stuck up on one of the principal (Mahomedan) buildings of the town.'"

According to Kaye:

> "Again, apart from Neill's doings, and certainly when a Major was sent on by Neill towards Cawnpore, there is no doubt that people were put to death in the most reckless manner. And afterwards Neill did things almost more than the massacre, putting to death with deliberate torture, in a way that has never been proved against the natives."
>
> "Sir George Campbell says: 'Neill is one of those people who have been elevated into a hero on the strength of a feminine sort of violence, and whose death much disarmed criticism at the time; but now that has passed into old history, I may say that, so far as I could learn from the most impartial sources, there was not much more in him. . . , I can never forgive Neill for his very bloody work and especially for his share in the mismanagement which caused the loss of the regiment of Loodiana. At Allahabad, by violence and mistrustful usage, he all but turned against us the Ferozepore regiment (only

second to the men of Loodiana in my affection) which afterwards did such splendid service.'"

There is much more that can be quoted to show the true character of the 'hero' in whose honour the statue was erected by 'public subscription.' Statues like these are a portent. They are an eloquent proof of what the British Government finally stands for,—terrorism and falsehood. These are strong expressions, but they are as true as they are strong. Hence is it the duty of every Indian, every true Englishman, to oppose this terrorism and falsehood with all his might. But the way to oppose these with all one's might lies not through retaliation, responsive terrorism and falsehood, but by the exact opposite of the twins, that is to say, by meeting terrorism with non-violence and falsehood with truth. It may be a difficult way, but it is the only way if India and the world are to live. If therefore the young men who have launched upon the battle will follow it up honestly and non-violently, they deserve all sympathy, and it is well that the local Congress Committee has taken up the matter in earnest.

29th September, 1927

BRAHMAN-NON-BRAHMAN

BY M. K. GANDHI

[*The following portion of Gandhiji's speech at Tanjore deals with the Brahman-Non-Brahman question. M. D*]

I had hoped on coming to Tanjore to-day to discuss the Brahman-Non-Brahman question here and I had the pleasure of having a brief discussion with some of the friends this afternoon. I am not free nor is it necessary for me to discuss and place before you the contents of our discussion. But I was exceedingly glad of this discussion. I now understand the movement perhaps a little better than I did before the discussion. I have placed my humble view before those friends, of which they are at liberty to make what use they like. But throughout the discussion I saw a note of one thing which seemed to oppress these friends. They seemed to think that I had identified myself with the notion of inherited superiority and inferiority. I assured them that nothing was farther from my thought and told them that I would gladly explain my meaning of *Varnashrama* more fully than I have done in order to remove the slightest misunderstanding as to this question of superiority. In my opinion there is no such thing as inherited or acquired superiority. I believe in the rock-bottom doctrine of Advaita and my interpretation of Advaita excludes totally any idea of superiority at any stage whatsoever. I believe implicitly that all men are born equal. All—whether born in India or in England or America or in any circumstances whatsoever—have the same soul as any other. And it is because I believe in this inherent equality of all men that I fight the doctrine of superiority which many of our rulers arrogate to themselves. I have fought this doctrine of superiority in South Africa inch by inch, and it is because of that inherent belief, that I delight in calling myself a scavenger, a spinner, a weaver, a farmer and a labourer. And I have fought against the Brahmans themselves wherever they have claimed any superiority for themselves either by reason of their birth or by reason of their subsequently acquired knowledge. *I consider that it is unmanly for any person to claim superiority over a fellow-being.* And there is the amplest warrant for the belief that I am enunciating in the Bhagavadgita, and I am therefore through and through with every Non-Brahman when he fights this monster of superiority, whether it is claimed by a Brahman or by anybody else. He who claims superiority at once forfeits his claim to be called a man. That is my opinion.

But in spite of all my beliefs, that I have explained to you, I still believe in *Varnashrama Dharma*. *Varnashrama Dharma* to my mind is a law which, however much you and I may deny, cannot be abrogated. To admit the working of that law is to free ourselves for the only pursuit in life for which we are born. *Varnashrama Dharma* is humility. Whilst I have said that all men and women are born equal, I do not wish therefore to suggest that qualities are not inherited, but on the contrary I believe that just as every one inherits a particular form so does he inherit the particular characteristics and qualities of his progenitors, and to make this admission is to conserve one's energy. That frank admission, if he will act up to it, would put a legitimate curb upon our material ambitions, and thereby our energy is set free for extending the field of spiritual research and spiritual evolution. It is this doctrine of *Varnashrama Dharma* which I have always accepted. You would be entitled to say that this is not how *Varnashrama* is understood in these days. I have myself said times without number that *Varnashrama* as it is at present understood and practised is a monstrous parody of the original, but in order to demolish this distortion let us not seek to demolish the original And if you say that the idealistic *Varnashrama* which I have placed before you is quite all right you have admitted all that I like you to admit. I would also urge on you to believe with me that no nation, no individual, can possibly live without proper ideals. And if you believe with me in the idealistic *Varnashrama*, you will also strive with me to reach that ideal so far as may be. As a matter of fact the world has not anywhere been able to fight against this law. What has happened and what must happen in fighting against the law is to hurt ourselves and to engage in a vain effort; and I suggest to you that your fight will be all the more successful if you understand all that our forefathers have bequeathed to us and engage in fighting all the evil excrescences that have grown round this great bequest. And if you accept what I have ventured to suggest to you, you will find that the solution of the Brahman and Non-Brahman question also, in so far as it is concerned with the religious aspect, becomes very easy. As a Non-Brahman I would seek to purify Brahmanism in so far as a Non-Brahman can, but not to destroy it. I would dislodge the Brahman from the arrogation of superiority or from places of profit. Immediately a Brahman becomes a profiteering agency he ceases to be a Brahman. But I would not touch his great learning wherever I see it. And whilst he may not claim superiority by reason of his learning I myself must not withhold that meed of homage that learning, wherever it resides, always commands. But I must not go deeper into the subject before a large audience of this kind.

After all I must fall upon one sovereign remedy which I think is applicable for all the ills of life. And that is, in whatever fight we engage, the fight should be clean and straight, and there should not be the slightest departure from truth and *ahimsa*. And if we will keep our carriage safely on these two rails you will find that our fight even though we may commit a thousand blunders will always smell clean and will be easier fought. And even as a train that is derailed comes to a disastrous end, so shall we, if we be derailed off these two rails, come to a disaster. A man who is truthful and does not mean ill even to his adversary will be slow to believe charges even against his foes. He will however try to understand the viewpoints of his opponents and will always keep an open mind and seek every opportunity of serving his opponents. I have endeavoured to apply this law in my relations with Englishmen and Europeans in general in South Africa as well as here and not without some success. How much more then should we apply this law in our homes, in our relations, in our domestic affairs, in connection with our own kith and kin?

6th October, 1927

MESSAGE TO CHETTINAD

By M. K. GANDHI

(I string together a few extracts from Gandhiji's many speeches in Chettinad which contain in a nut-shell his message to the Chettiars. Not only they but all wealthy communities in the country are likely to profit by it. *M. D)*

"Let me urge you to make Khadi your own much more

fully than you seem to have done. If you wish to, you have the power, even individual Chettiars have the power, of financing the whole of the Khadi movement in Tamilnad and even the whole of India. I said to my Marwadi friends, the Chettiars of the North, and I say to you that if you wish it you can organise the Khadi movement purely out of your superfluities. With your marvellous shrewdness you can even organise production, and so you will forgive me if I tell you that all the purses that I have been receiving since this morning have not in any shape or form given me satisfaction. Though the amount may be a few thousands it is merely a drop in the ocean of your wealth. . . . The greatest charity at the present moment that I can conceive for any Indian to do is to promote this Khadi work. Our rich friends are fond of giving free dinners to so-called poor people. I have often questioned the virtue of giving these dinners. The Bhagavad Gita says, that that gift only is a good gift which is given to a worthy man. It would be right to feed the blind and the maimed and those who somehow or other cannot work for a living. But I make bold to say that if all of you conspiring together make a fund for feeding 50,000 villages in India it would be a great thing"

"I venture to suggest to you that you are not using your riches wisely though you seem to be using them profusely. You have erected huge palaces, but you have not given any attention to your surroundings. I would like you therefore to ensure the supply of the purest water not only for yourselves but all those who are living in your midst. Your roads must be perfectly good. And all your tanks should look and actually be sweet-smelling, containing nothing but good, clear, sparkling, pure water. Your drainage must be in a perfect state. All these things are really incredibly simple, and if you will set your heart upon it you will find that it won't cost you anything that you will feel. If you will do all these things well you must get expert advice for all these things. But this requires a little sacrifice of personal inclinations and personal ease. It requires also a desire to live a corporate life—a life not merely for self, but for one's own country. It requires also a fellow-feeling for all your neighbours including the poorest. And immediately you have given that bent to your inclination you will find that it will cost little effort and still less money, and I assure you that you will be amply repaid for your pains."

"I have been watching during my stay in Chettinad that so far as outward corporate cleanliness is concerned, it is really lacking. If you all adopt concerted measures you can make your streets, yours tanks and your surroundings spotlessly clean. And I have letters from friends in Chettinad which have told me that the inside also is not particularly clean. That uncleanliness is worse than the one that I see in the streets and ponds here. The outward uncleanliness and insanitation you can really set right in a few days' time if you organise yourselves, have a body of volunteers and workers and put your streets and tanks in a wonderful sanitary condition. The first essential condition of corporate life, that is city life, is that an absolutely clean supply of water is guaranteed to the dwellers of the city and its accommodation made perfectly clean and sweet. When I was on the Nandi Hills I saw that the tank from which drinking water was drawn by the dwellers on those Hills was all day long well-guarded against pollution. Bathing tanks must be separate from the tanks that supply drinking water. I know that the inward cleanliness of which I have talked is a more difficult and very intricate proposition than the sanitation that I have just talked to you about. But having been in my own days in possession of some amount of money, I want to present you with my own recipe of how you can attain comparative personal cleanliness although you may possess riches. That recipe is nothing original that I am going to give you. It is really a part of our religion, and it is this that no matter how much money we have earned, we should regard ourselves as trustees holding these moneys for the welfare of all our neighbours. There is a verse which says that he, who eats without sacrifice, that is without giving, is a thief. If God gives us power and wealth He gives us the same so that we may use them for the benefit of mankind and not for our selfish carnal purpose."

"I do urge you to look after your sanitation and your water supply. Your palaces do not look to advantage at all in the midst of insanitary streets and tanks full of not pure sparkling water but foul water. I can show you how you can do these things at an incredibly small expense, not out of your capital but out of your savings. I understand that some of your marriage customs are very bad. There is very often a price put upon the head of a bride as much as Rs. 30,000. I understand that you do not hesitate to spend as much as Rs. 50,000 per marriage; but the custom I consider to be immoral. There can be no price put either way in the matter of such sacred contract as marriage. It must be as easy for a poor man to get a virtuous bride as for a rich man. Merit and mutual love are the sole tests for marriage contracts. The expenses for marriage ceremonies, though I do not consider them to be immoral, I do regard as a criminal waste. It is not becoming a rich man to dangle his wealth before the multitude in the fashion in which he very often does. *The art of amassing riches becomes a degrading and despicable art if it is not accompanied by the nobler art of how to spend wealth usefully.* So, out of this marriage reform alone and putting a wise restraint upon your extravagance on these ceremonies, you can turn this Chettinad into a fairy land. You can have if you will without much effort public parks, recreation grounds, water works and profitable dairies that will give a supply of cheap and pure milk to the poor people living in your midst. And I tell you as a man of experience and as a fellow Chetti that you treble your earning resources if you conserve your health by wise sanitation, by an absolutely pure supply of water and by ensuring pure milk for the rich and the poor."

"A lady doctor writing to me tells me that I should remind you about the immoral custom that is prevalent in Chettinad and that prevents you from thinking of these things of public usefulness. She tells me that the rich people of Chettinad have a due share in perpetuating the hideous immoral custom of assigning girls of tender age to a life of shame under the name of religion. She tells me that there are many *devadasis* in your midst. If this is true it is really a matter for hanging our heads in shame. *Let not possession of wealth be synonymous with degradation, vice, and profligacy.* And is it not a tragic irony that in spite of these vices, you are also spending money lavishly in erecting what you flatter yourself to believe as temples for gods to reside? Not every structure made by brick and mortar labelled temple is necessarily a temple. There are, I am sorry to say, many temples in our midst in this country which are no better than brothels. Do you know that in our religion it is not possible to call any single place a temple unless an elaborate ceremonial of purification has been made inside that building and unless the spirit of God has been invoked by men full of piety, so that God may reside in it? And so I would urge you to restrain yourselves and not lavishly spend in building temples, but in the first place dedicate your own bodies to the service of God, and for that reason first of all purify by ridding yourselves of the evils to which I have drawn attention. But I am glad to be able to inform you that I received only to-day a gratifying letter in which whilst the writer admits most of the evils to which I have referred just now tells me that there are in your midst several noble-minded 'Chetties rich enough not only in gold but in treasure of virtue also. He tells me that there are in your midst several *brahmacharis* going on with their godly life in a silent manner. He also tells with hope and pride that several young men are conducting against heavy odds a reform movement and I assure the young men that whilst the path of reforms is not all roses and whilst it is bestrewn with countless thorns, success is theirs if they will persevere prayerfully and with a pure heart. I understood that they are gradually trying to solve one very difficult question that faces every one of you. I understood that a rigid custom has grown up in your midst whereby no Chettiar going either to Burma, Singapore or Ceylon takes his wife with him. I regard this bar sinister against your womanhood as a double drawback and a great sin. It exposes you when you leave homes to avoidable temptations, and it deprives your life partners for a number of years of the privilege of your companionship, and the opportunity of broadening their outlook by travelling to distant lands with yourselves. I wish these young men therefore all deserved success in their chivalrous fight, and I urge the elders whom my voice may reach to give every assistance to the young men in their endeavour to carry on the necessary reforms in your midst."

"I was astonished to learn that you will not even give a proper and decent education to your own children. Your one ambition in life is, I was told, to make them even at a tender age money-making machines. It cannot be right. By all means make them your worthy successors in office, but before they embark upon stormy life, let them have an idea of our own knowledge in the shape of our own culture, let their character be formed and let them know something of the history of this country of ours. As it is, I am told, that you are tossed to and fro by all kinds of texts that are put before you by people parading to know the Shastras in the sacred name of Shastras. But let me tell you that every incantation whether it is in Sanskrit or whether it is in Tamil is not necessarily Shastra. *My definition of true Shastra is the chosen word that giveth us life.* Therefore any text, however ancient it may be described to be, which takes us along the path of perdition, which is therefore inconsistent with truth or the universal law of life, is not Shastra. And hence have we been taught that Shastras come really out of the mouth of people of character whom we describe as holy men, and not every man, who wears red coloured robe and smears his forehead and the whole of his body with all kinds of marks and rolls out verses after verses from things which he called scriptures, is a holy man. *A holy man is one who never considers himself superior to any single creature on earth and who has renounced all the pleasures of life.* But really in this *Kaliyuga* we do not easily come across a holy man. Therefore it becomes doubly our duty to give proper education to our children, so that they may be able to discriminate between good and evil. And you, who are rich and past the years of the stage of education, to you I would like to say what I have been saying elsewhere also during these three days; whatever you do, don't spoil your purity of life. I hear all sorts of stories which I hope are largely exaggerated. But I know that generally speaking it is the experience of the world that possession of gold is inconsistent with the possession of virtue; but though such is the unfortunate experience in the world it is by no means an inexorable law. We have the celebrated instance of Janaka, who, although he was rolling in riches and had a limitless power, being a great prince, was still one of the purest men of his age. And even in our own age I can cite from my own personal experience and tell you that I have the good fortune of knowing several moneyed men who do not find it impossible to lead a straight, pure life. What is possible for these few men is surely possible for every one of you. And I wish that my word can find an abiding place in your heart and I know how much good it will do you and the society in which you are living."

6th October, 1927

"AN INDIGNANT PROTEST"

By M. K. Gandhi

The Headmaster of a Bengali school writes:

"Your advice and utterances to students at Madras, asking them to marry widowed girls only, have horrified us and I send forth my humble but indignant protest.

"This kind of advice will tend to destroy the tendency of the widows to observe lifelong *brahmacharya* which has given Indian womanhood the greatest or rather the highest place in the world and destroy their chances of attaining salvation through *brahmacharya* in a single birth, throwing them on the filthy path of worldly happiness. Thus this kind of keen sympathy for widows will do a great disservice to them and an injustice to the maidens whose marriage problem has become at present one of complexity and difficulty. Your theory of marriage will over-turn the Hindu theory of transmigration, rebirth and even *mukti*, and will bring down Hindu society on the same level with other societies which we do not like. Our society has been demoralised no doubt, but we must have our eyes open to Hindu ideals and try to go up as far as we can and not be influenced by the examples of other societies and ideals Examples of Ahalyabai, Rani Bhavani, Behula, Sita, Savitri, Damayanti will guide the Hindu society and we must direct it according to their ideals. I beg most humbly, therefore, that you will refrain from giving your opinions on these knotty questions and allow the society to do what it thinks best."

The indignant protest leaves me unconverted and unrepentant. My advice will not wean from her purpose a single widow who has a will of her own and who knows *brahmacharya* and is bent upon observing it. But if the advice is followed, it will certainly bring great relief to those girls of tender age who knew not the meaning of marriage when they were put through the ceremony. The use of the term 'widow' in their connection is a violent abuse of a name with sacred associations. It is precisely for the very object that my correspondent has in view that I advice the youth of the country to marry these so-called widows or not at all. The sacredness of the institution can be preserved only when it is purged of the curse of child widowhood.

The statement that the widows attain *moksha* if they observe *brahmacharya* has no foundation whatsoever in experience. More things are necessary than mere *brahmacharya* for the attainment of the final bliss. And *brahmacharya* that is superimposed carries no merit with it, and often gives rise to secret vice that saps the morals of the society in which that vice exists. Let the correspondent know that I am writing from personal observation.

I should be glad indeed if my advice results in elementary justice being done to the maiden widows, and if for that reason the other maidens instead of being prematurely sold to man's lust are given an opportunity of waiting for maturity in age and wisdom.

I have no theory of marriage that is inconsistent with a belief in transmigration, rebirth or *mukti*. The reader should know that millions of Hindus whom he arrogantly describes as belonging to the lower order have no ban on widow remarriage. And I do not see how if re-marriage of old widowers does not interfere with that belief, real marriage of girls wrongly described as widows can interfere with that grand belief. I may mention for the edification of the correspondent that transmigration and rebirth are not mere theories with me but facts as patent as the daily rise of the sun. *Mukti* is a fact to realise which I am striving with all my might. And it is the contemplation of *mukti* which has given me a vivid consciousness of the wrong that is being done to these maiden widows. Let us not in our emasculation mention in the same breath as these modern injured maiden widows the immortal names of Sita and others referred to by the correspondent.

Lastly, whilst there is, and very properly, glorification of real widowhood in Hinduism, there is, so far as I am aware, no warrant for the belief that in the Vedic times there was any absolute ban upon re-marriage of widows. But my crusade is not against real widowhood. It is against its atrocious caricature. The better way is not to regard as widows at all the girls I have in view and whom every Hindu who has a spark of chivalry in him is bound to relieve from their intolerable yoke. I therefore humbly but emphatically repeat the advice to every young Hindu to refuse to marry any but these maidens miscalled widows.

6th October, 1927

A KHADI LOVER

By M. K. Gandhi

Dr. Kailas Nath Katju, a distinguished advocate of Allahabad, sent me a letter some time ago referring to several matters, and in that letter avowed his love of Khadi and enclosed the first instalment of his contribution to the A. I. S. A I felt that the part of the letter that concerned Khadi should be published by way of encouragement to other monied men, especially lawyers. I therefore wrote asking for his permission to publish his letter and incidentally expostulated with him about the foreign black *alpaca* and endeavoured to explain the value of sacrificial spinning. I am now able to publish below his two letters so far as they relate to Khadi.

"As a regular reader of *Young India* I follow with the deepest interest your travels in Mysore. I am a firm believer in Khadi and all that it implies. I have habitually worn Khadi since 1st August 1921, excepting my foreign black *alpaca* Chapkan in Court. My belief in Khadi is growing stronger and stronger and I think that I may now as well aid (in a very humble way indeed) the central organisation controlled by you. I have therefore decided to make a monthly contribution of Rs. 100 to Khadi fund, and am enclosing a cheque for Rs. 100 for September. I shall send the cheque to you so that you may allocate it to any fund you like; varying the allocation as you like.

"I may inform you that though I habitually wear hand-woven and hand-spun Khadi, I don't know how to spin and I am not a member of the A. I. S. A. I have a charkha at home, but—no doubt as a result of my irresolution—couldn't make much use of it. Further, I think that spinning, though very desirable as an example to others, is not an essential qualification for a lover of Khadi. . . . Amidst all the confusion and clamour, reigning just now in our land, I hold fast to Khadi as a bond between the masses and the classes and every word that you say on the subject appeals to my head and to my heart. May God give you strength to succeed in this noble endeavour."

"My first letter conveyed but imperfectly the strength of my belief in the Khadi movement. I was writing to you, and it would have been an impertinence on my part to dwell upon the beauty, simplicity, and the life-giving nourishment of which Khadi is to me a symbol. You may, if you think it is worth while, publish that part of the letter which relates to Khadi. Khadi can unite all classes and creeds because wretched poverty does not make any distinction between Hindus and Muslims. I am as certain as of anything that the message of Khadi will be received by the people of this country.

"It was not lack of time but irresolution, that was responsible for my not spinning. The busiest man can find—and does find—time to do all things. I am guilty of wasting many half-hours every day, and I can survive ridicule too. I don't know whether I shall be able to secure a *takli* in Allahabad. I will begin using it as soon as I get one. If you will kindly have one sent to me, I shall treasure it as a priceless possession.

"You kindly remark that you can secure fine black Khadi for a Court Chapkan. It is indeed kind of you to bestow such thought upon me. I kept on wearing foreign *alpaca* as a necessary evil. But now I will give up even that. I think I will be able to secure a 10 yards piece of fine black Khadi. I shall write to the manager of the Ashram at Sabarmati and probably he will supply it to me."

The lawyers and other professional men may not be able to do much in other respects, but they can all follow Dr. Katju's worthy example by adopting Khadi and contributing to the All India Spinners' Association which is always in want because of the growing demand for organising more villages than the Association has on hand. It is not possible to produce an increasing amount of Khadi without increasing the capital, and till Khadi has become universal in India the expenses of the organisation must remain a recurring item.

6th October, 1927

A DOUBLE SIN

BY M. K. GANDHI

A correspondent, who sends his name for my information but adopts the pseudonym of 'A Bachelor,' writes with reference to my article *Is it a marriage* published* some time ago a long letter which I abridge as follows:

> "I have read with interest the article in your paper of the 1st instant under the heading *Is it a Marriage*? Though the names of the parties are omitted it is an open secret to the Gaud Sarasvat Brahmans from Karwar. As a member of the community in which the marriage in question took place I wish to place before the public and the Gaud Sarasvat Brahmans throughout India in particular the following few lines for their careful consideration.
>
> "It is no doubt a disgrace for a man to buy a girl. But there is another custom among us which is equally bad, for a father among us is obliged to buy a husband for his daughter and the amount received by the husband is called dowry. It is not settled to suit the purse of the parents of girls but it would be according to the hereditary income of the would-be husband or it sometimes depends upon the education he has received. The more a man is educated, the higher the degrees he has received, the more is he worth in the matrimonial market.
>
> "A few months back the marriage took place in Bombay of a well-educated gentleman who is a high Government Official and it is said that a dowry of nearly Rs. 20,000 was presented to him. It is really a pity that the people who receive higher education are going lower and

* See page 327.

lower by resorting to the very practices they are expected to put down."

I have before me another letter on the subject from a member of the same community. It appears that those who wish to buy wives go to Goa in search, for it is there that poor Sarasvat Brahmans are to be found who are not ashamed to enrich themselves by selling their daughters to persons old enough to be their fathers or grand-fathers. Thus the community commits a double sin. An educated young man is open to the highest bidder for his hand, and needy parents are open to negotiate the sale of their daughters, hardly out of their teens, to the oldest men (sometimes educated) who are prepared tc pay the highest price. The only consolation that the Sarasvat community may derive, if it wishes to, and if it would postpone a dealing with the reform under some excuse or other, is that there are other 'castes' too that are not free from the same evil. The difference, if any, would be that of degree. But if the Sarasvat community would lead the reform, it will disdain to seek the doubtful refuge of the *to quoque* and will, now that the evil has been exposed, set about ridding itself of the double sin.

13th October, 1927

THE FALLACY OF HANDLOOM WEAVING

By M. K. Gandhi

Replying to the Saurashtras' address at Madura Gandhiji said:

"I am much touched by your reference to your connection with Rajkot, the home of my youth. But please remember that it is a difficult thing to claim such close kinship with me. Because you have thereby created for yourself a greater responsibility in connection with every activity of mine in so far as it commends itself to your attention. What can be the use of a man having such a large number of kinsmen if he may not fall back upon them in the hour of peril? But it is possible for you, if you will, to claim a still closer kinship with me. For though I am proud of being the son of a father who was the minister of a State, I am, if it was at all possible, prouder still on having become a fellow-weaver with you. For whilst my father was weaving the destiny of a little State that was placed under his charge for the time being; you and I, if we wish to, can weave the destiny of this great land by a profession which with you is hereditary, but which I have adopted by choice. And in taking that greater pride in reminding you of this kinship I am doing no violence to the memory, the sacred memory of my father because I am following in his footsteps in ministering to the needs of larger classes of people. And this claim of closer kinship with you brings me to an important paragraph in your address.

"You ask me to encourage hand-weaving even through foreign yarn or mill-made yarn inasmuch as, so you say in your address, it is not possible to-day to find hand-spun yarn of the fineness you require and in the quantity you require. Now I shall tell you as a fellow-weaver why I cannot possibly endorse your recommendation. If I endorse your recommendation, I hope to be able to show you that it would be bad for you and bad for the class which I have in view and which you also should have in view You should, as keen and shrewd business-men as some of you are, understand that every weaver who weaves yarn which is supplied by foreign mills or even by mills of India places himself at the disposal of and at the tender mercy of the mills. You as weavers should realise that this hand-weaving which you are to-day controlling to a certain extent will in time to come slip away from your hands as soon as the mills of the world or the mills of India are ready to weave the pattern that you are to-day exclusively weaving. Let me inform you, if you do not know the fact already, that various able mill-owners of the world are making experiments in order to weave the patterns which are to-day your monopoly. It is no fault of the mill-owners or the mill industry that that mill industry is endeavouring day after day to take away the monopolies and take this trade in its own hands. To make continuous improvements in its machinery and to make continuous encroachments upon the handicrafts of the world is really the objective and the ideal of these great industrialists. Indeed, it is the condition of their very existence that they should try to take this trade also from off your hands. What has befallen the industry of spinning will most decidedly befall the industry of hand-weaving also if the weaver will not take a leaf out of my book. Let me inform you and you don't know this—very few people in India know this fact—that I began as you are now doing. I first became a weaver in 1915. I told you that I became first a weaver and then a spinner. I have woven with these very hands both foreign yarns and our mill yarns. But you will excuse me for claiming to know more than you do the secret of this business. As I was sitting—I can point out the spot where I was sitting—as I was sitting at my hand-loom weaving cloth, certainly not half as fine as any of you perhaps weave, but as I was sitting at my loom, I was considering for myself where I should be and where thousands and ten thousands of weavers should be when mills were organised enough to weave that kind of cloth themselves. And as I was thinking of this thing my heart went out to the millions of starving sisters in our villages and I began, as I was weaving, to think of the lot of these sisters. I became sad and disconcerted, and together with my companions I began a diligent search for some spinner who would teach us hand-spinning and I began also to find whether there was a single village where I could find hand-spinning still going on. I knew nothing then of the fact that there were some sisters spinning in the Punjab. But as despair was creeping over me, I took shelter under a brave widow of Gujarat. She was working in the cause of untouchables. I shared this deep sorrow of mine with this great sister, and I charged her to wander from place to place in Gujarat and not rest content till she had found those sisters, who still had the art of hand-spinning in their possession. And it was she who discovered at Vijapur in Gujarat a few Musalman sisters who were prepared to spin if she would take their yarn from their hands. From that moment began the great revival which is now covering over fifteen hundred villages in India. And it was after this discovery that I decided not to weave a single thread of foreign yarn or mill-spun yarn in the Ashram of which I happened to be in charge.

"I place for your consideration yet another important fact. If you will study the history of the hand-weaving movement in India you will discover that at the present moment several thousands of weavers have simply been obliged to abandon their trade. Weavers, all of your own trade, Saurashtras, are to-day working in Bombay as scavengers. Weavers, in the Punjab are some of them hired soldiery and some of them have taken to the butcher's trade. And so you will understand why I cannot possibly endorse your recommendation. That does not mean that you may leave off weaving mill yarn from to-day. You do not need encouragement from me. But I venture to suggest to you that it is to your interest not to ask me to mix up this mill-spun yarn weaving together with this movement which I am leading in all humility. And it is equally to your interest to support this movement so that if it becomes stable, prosperous and immovable, every one of you would find a respectable living. I therefore suggest to you that if this hand-spinning movement grows apace it is likely that it may be of help to you."

13th October, 1927

HINDU LAW AND MYSORE

By M. K. Gandhi

Sjt. Bhashyam Aiyengar of Bangalore writes:

"The principles of Hindu Law as at present administered are antiquated and, opposed to our sense of equity and justice. I shall give a few instances:

1. Near and dear relations like the sister's daughter,

the daughter-in-law, the brother's widow and the step-mother are altogether denied the right of inheritance. If a man were to leave a widowed daughter-in-law as his only surviving relation, his properties escheat to the Government, and the poor girl who staked all her life and fortune on the family of her husband gets out into the street.

2. Even such near relations as are included in the list of heirs do not get a chance because of the priorities of distant agnates. The sister is an heir; but if only the deceased has left a fifth descendant of a great-great-grand-father of his, the latter takes the property and the sister gets nothing. So too the son's daughter, the sister's son and the brother's daughter.

3. Women are not allowed to exercise full rights of ownership in properties inherited by or gifted to them. A widow should carefully handle her husband's property and if only she spends more or incurs a debt on the security of the property, may be for her own livelihood, a distant *dayada* can drag her to the court and coerce her into giving up her rights. Mitakshara which is the prevailing authority here clearly and definitely says that all properties which a woman may get in any manner whatsoever are her *stri-dhana* and she can dispose of them at her will. The Privy Council refused to follow it stating that Indians always treated women as incapables and the author of Mitakshara is a fire-eater.

4. The deaf and the dumb are excluded from inheritance. In this we are beating the lame man with his own crutches.

5. The legality of widow-remarriage is not recognised in Mysore, as in British India.

6. It is doubtful whether post-puberty marriage is legal. The age of consent should be raised to 14 in the case of girls.

7. Divorce may be provided for if people agree. We had it in India formerly. We find Parashara mentioning

the circumstances under which a wife may marry a second husband during the lifetime of the first.

8. Inter-caste marriages are not allowed under the present law. They must be legalised. It was an institution freely recognised by our ancients. Many of our sages, such as Vasishtha, Vyasa, Narada and Parashara were the offspring of inter-caste marriages. If I may marry a Christian wife lawfully why may not I be permitted to marry a Hindu wife though of another caste?

9. An orphan is declared ineligible for adoption. If ever a boy be fit for adoption it is the orphan, and yet we have the prohibition.

10. Widows are not allowed to adopt unless they have been authorised by the husband or the consent of *sapindas* is taken. Authority should be presumed and the widow allowed to adopt unless directed by the husband not to do so. This is the law in Bombay.

There are many more such instances. I have chosen only a few.

Thinking people feel the oppressiveness and desire reform. The only way of changing the law is by legislation. The legislature is unable to pass any law without consulting public opinion. And public opinion can only be consulted by a committee appointed for the purpose. Hence I moved a resolution in the last Budget session of our Assembly asking for the appointment of a committee to go into the question, take evidence and report thereon formulating suggestions for legislative action. It was unanimously passed by the House.

The committee has not yet been appointed though people all over the State desire it. The fear seems to be that British India not having moved in the matter yet, it may be that any attempt by Mysore might be laughed at. This is absurd as you said. Mysore is peculiarly fitted to undertake the work, whereas there are real difficulties with British India. Mysore has peculiar advantages which it would be unwise on our part to ignore. We have now a most enlightened ruler and an equally earnest and progressive Dewan. If we cannot effect the desired reforms now we never can hope to do it.

Can you not take up this matter in *Young India*?"

The prominence I have given to the foregoing need not imply that I endorse every one of the reforms suggested by the writer. That some of them require immediate attention I have no doubt. Nor have I any doubt that all of them demand serious consideration from those who would rid Hindu society of its anachronisms.

In pre-British days there was no such thing as rigid Hindu Law governing the lives of millions. The body of regulations known as Smritis were indicative rather than inflexible codes of conduct. They never had the validity of law such as is known to modern lawyers. The observance of the restraints of the Smritis was enforced more by social than legal sanctions. The Smritis were, as is evident from the self-contradictory verses to be found in them, continually passing, like ourselves, through evolutionary changes, and were adapted to the new discoveries that were being made in social science. Wise kings were free to procure new interpretations to suit new conditions. Hindu religion or Hindu Shastras never had the changeless and unchanging character that is now being sought to be given to them. No doubt in those days there were kings and their councillors who had the wisdom and the authority required to command the respect and allegiance of society. But now the custom has grown up of thinking that Smritis and everything that goes by the name of Shastras is absolutely unchangeable. The verses which we find to be un-workable or altogether repugnant to our moral sense we conveniently ignore. This very unsatisfactory state of things has to be, some day or other and somehow changed if Hindu society is to become a progressive unit in human evolution. The British rulers cannot make these changes because of their different religion and their different ideal. Their ideal is to sustain their commercial supremacy and to sacrifice every other interest, moral or otherwise, for the attainment of that ideal. Unless therefore Hindu public opinion clearly demands it, and it can be made without any injury to their ideal, no drastic change in our customs or so-called laws will be attempted or countenanced by them. And it is difficult to focus Hindu public opinion on identical points in a vast territory like British India covering many schools of thought and law. And such public opinion as there is is naturally and necessarily pre-occupied with the struggle for political freedom. A state like Mysore however has no such limitations or pre-occupations. In my humble opinion, it is its duty to anticipate British India in the matter of removing the anachronisms in the Hindu Law and the like. Mysore state is large and important enough to attempt such changes. It has become a progressively constitutional monarchy. It has a Legislative Assembly representative enough to initiate social changes. It seems already to have passed a resolution asking for the appointment of a committee to consider what changes, if any, are necessary in the Hindu Law. And if a strong committee representing orthodox as well as progressive Hindu opinion is appointed, its recommendations must prove useful and pave the way towards making the necessary changes. I do not know the rules of the Mysore Assembly governing the constitution of such committees, but there is little doubt that they are elastic enough to admit of appointing or co-opting members from outside the Mysore State. Anyway Sjt. Bhashyam Aiyengar has shown that a revision of the Hindu Law is absolutely necessary in several cases. No State is better fitted than Mysore for initiating the belated reform.

13th October, 1927

NEILL STATUE SATYAGRAHA

BY M. K. GANDHI

In accordance with the promise made by the volunteers connected with this movement, they have sent me papers giving the particulars I had asked for. From them it appears that during the six weeks that the struggle had been on when the papers were sent to me thirty volunteers had courted imprisonment. Of these 29 are Hindus and one Musalman, one lady aged 35 and one girl aged 9, her daughter. Of these thirty, two apologised and got themselves released. The apology of a few, if it does not become infectious, does not matter. 'Blacklegs' will be found in every struggle. The men who have gone to gaol are not noted men. This is no loss, rather it is a gain in a Satyagraha struggle which requires no prestige save that of truth, and no strength save that of self-suffering which comes only from an immovable faith in one's cause and from a completely non-violent spirit.

The volunteers must not be impatient. Impatience is a phase of violence. A Satyagrahi has nothing to do with victory. He is sure of it, but he has also to know that it comes from God. His is but to suffer.

The papers give me an account of income and expenditure. The income is given in detail and amounts to Rs. 228-2-6. The expenditure amounting to Rs. 228-2-6 is made up as follows: Meals etc. Rs. 71-7-9, conveyance Rs. 53-2-6, notices for meetings etc. Rs. 39-4-0, establishment and postal charges Rs. 21-8-9, lights at meetings Rs. 22-8-0. I am not satisfied with these expenses. I have asked for more details. But subject to correction, I would warn the Satyagrahis against spending much on meals, conveyances and lights. I know that my own meetings are not free from extravagance in these items. The Congress work too is not unopen to the charge of over-expenditure. But it is better to illustrate what I mean by what happens to me the self-styled representative of *Daridranarayan*. Where six oranges will do, sixty are brought; where one car will do six are ready, and where a hurricane lantern will serve the purpose incandescent burners are produced. Let the Satyagrahis understand that they have to use every pice they get as a miser uses his hoards. I suggest their getting a local man of note to take charge of their monies and a philanthropic auditor auditing their accounts free of charge. Strictest honesty and care are necessary in the handling of public funds. This is an indispensable condition of growth of a healthy public life.

The third paper I have before me is their appeal to the public. A Satyagrahi's appeal must contain moderate language. The appeal before me though unexceptionable admits of improvement. 'Not only Neill but all of his nefarious breed must go,' is a sentence that mars the appeal. General Neill is no more. What we have to deal with is the statue and not even the statue as such. We seek to destroy the principle for which the statue stands. We wish to injure no man. And we wish to gain our object by enlisting public opinion not excluding English opinion in our favour by self-suffering. Here there is no room for the language of anger and hate.

So much for the volunteers.

The public owe a duty to them. They may not go to gaol but they can supervise, control and guide and help the movement in many ways. Agitation for the removal of the statue is agitation for the removal of but a symptom of a grave disease. And while the removal of the statue will not cure the disease it will alleviate the agony and point the way to reaching the disease itself. It is also often possible to reach a deep-seated disease by dealing with some of its symptoms. So long therefore as the Satyagrahi volunteers fight the battle in a clean manner and strictly in accordance with the conditions applicable to Satyagraha they deserve public support and sympathy.

20th October, 1927

WHY I AM A HINDU

By M. K. Gandhi

An American friend who subscribes herself as a lifelong friend of India writes:

> "As Hinduism is one of the prominent religions of the East, and as you have made a study of Christianity and Hinduism, and on the basis of that study have announced that you are a Hindu, I beg leave to ask of you if you will do me the favour to give me your reasons for that choice. Hindus and Christians alike realize that man's chief need is to know God and to worship Him in spirit and in truth. Believing that Christ was a revelation of God, Christians of America have sent to India thousands of their sons and daughters to tell the people of India about Christ. Will you in return kindly give us your interpretation of Hinduism and make a comparison of Hinduism with the teachings of Christ? I will be deeply grateful for this favour."

I have ventured at several missionary meetings to tell English and American missionaries that if they could have refrained from 'telling' India about Christ and had merely lived the life enjoined upon them by the Sermon on the Mount, India instead of suspecting them would have appreciated their living in the midst of her children and directly profited by their presence. Holding this view, I can 'tell' American friends nothing about Hinduism by way of 'return.' I do not believe in people telling others of their faith, especially with a view to conversion. Faith does not admit of telling. It has to be lived and then it becomes self-propagating.

Nor do I consider myself fit to interpret Hinduism except through my own life. And if I may not interpret Hinduism through my written word, I may not compare it with Christianity. The only thing it is possible for me therefore to do is to say as briefly as I can, why I am a Hindu.

Believing as I do in the influence of heredity, being born in a Hindu family, I have remained a Hindu. I should reject it, if I found it inconsistent with my moral sense or my spiritual growth. On examination I have found it to be the most tolerant of all religions known to me. Its freedom from dogma makes a forcible appeal to me in as much it gives the votary the largest scope for self-expression. Not being an exclusive religion, it enables the followers of that faith not merely to respect all the other religions, but it also enables them to admire and assimilate whatever may be good in the other faiths. Non-violence is common to all religions, but it has found the highest expression and application in Hinduism. (I do not regard Jainism or Buddhism as separate from Hinduism.) Hinduism believes in the oneness not of merely all human life but in the oneness of all that lives. Its worship of the cow is, in my opinion, its unique contribution to the evolution of humanitarianism. It is a practical application of the belief in the oneness and, therefore, sacredness, of all life. The great belief in transmigration is a direct consequence of that belief. Finally the discovery of the law of *Varnashrama* is a magnificent result of the ceaseless search for truth. I must not burden this article with definitions of the essentials sketched here, except to say that the present ideas of cow worship and *Varnashrama* are a caricature of what in my opinion the originals are. The curious may see the definitions of cow worship and *Varnashrama* in the previous numbers of *Young India*. I hope to have to say on *Varnashrama* in the near future. In this all too brief a sketch I have mentioned what occur to me to be the outstanding features of Hinduism that keep me in its fold.

20th October, 1927

MESSAGE TO TRAVANCORE

By M. K. Gandhi

"Whilst it gives me great plessure to pay a second visit to this most beautiful part of India, I cannot conceal from you the deep grief I feel for the fact that in this fair land untouchability has a sway which it does not exercise in any other part of India. I feel deeply humiliated as a Hindu to find that it is in this enlightened Hindu State that untouchability appears in its most hideous form of unseeability and unapproachability. I speak with a due sense of my responsibility that this untouchability is a curse that is eating into the vitals of Hinduism, and I often feel that unless we take due precautions and remove this curse from our midst, Hinduism itself is in danger of destruction. That in this age of reason, in this age of wide travel, in this age of a comparative study of religions, there should be found people, some of whom are educated, to uphold the hideous doctrine of treating a single human being as an untouchable, or unapproachable, or unseeable because of his birth, passes my comprehension. As a lay humble student of Hinduism and claiming to be one desirous of practising Hinduism in the spirit and to the letter let me tell you that I have found no warrant or support for this terrible doctrine. Let us not deceive ourselves into the belief that everything that is written in Sanskrit and printed is Shastra and has any binding effect upon us. That which is opposed to the fundamental maxims of morality, that which is opposed to trained reason, cannot be claimed as Shastra no matter how ancient it may be. There is enough warrant for the proposition that I have just stated in the Vedas, in the Mahabharata and in the Bhagvad Gita. I therefore hope that it will be possible for the enlightened ruler of Travancore to blot the curse out of the land during her reign. And what can be nobler than that a woman should be able to say to herself and her people that during her rule it has been possible for these people who have been suffering from age-long slavery to receive their full freedom?

"But I know also her difficulties and those of her councillors. A Government, be it ever so autocratic, is always timid and cautious in moving in such reforms. A wise Government will welcome an agitation in connection with such reforms. An unwise Government impatient of public opinion will use violence in putting down such agitations. But from my personal experience of Vykom Satyagraha I know that you have a Government which will not only tolerate but welcome agitation in order to strengthen its hands to achieve this reform. The real initiative therefore must lie with the people of Travancore, and that too not with the so-called untouchables miscalled also 'Avarna' Hindus. To me the very word 'Avarna' Hindu is a misnomer and a reproach to Hinduism. In many cases the remedy or the initiative lies not with them but with the so-called Savarna Hindus who have to rid themselves of the sin of untouchability. Let me tell you that it is not enough for you to hold the belief passively that untouchability is a crime. He who is a passive spectator of crime is really, and in law, an active participator in it. You must therefore begin and continue your agitation along all lawful and legitimate lines. Let me, if my voice will reach them, carry my voice to the Brahman priests who are opposing this belated reform. It is a painful fact, but it is a historical truth, that priests who should have been the real custodians of religion have been instrumental in destroying the religion of which they have been custodians. I see before my eyes the Brahman priests in Tranvancore and also elsewhere destroying the very religion of which they are supposed to be custodians, from their ignorance or worse. All their learning, when it is utilised in order to sustain a hideous superstition, a terrible wrong, turns to dust. I wish therefore that they will recognise before it is too late the signs of the times and march with the events which are taking them and us voluntarily or involuntarily along the path of truth. All the religions of the world, while they may differ in other respects unitedly proclaim that nothing lives in this world but truth.

"Let me also warn the impatient reformer that unless he keeps himself on the right, straight and narrow path, he will hurt himself and hinder the reform about which he is rightly impatient. I venture to claim that I have placed in the hands of the reformer a matchless and priceless weapon in the form of Satyagraha. But then the conditions of successful Satyagraha are fairly hard. If he has faith in God, faith in himself, faith in his cause, he will never be violent, not even against his most fierce opponent whom he would accuse rightly of injustice, ignorance and even violence. I state without fear of contradiction that truth has never been vindicated by violence. A Satyagrahi therefore expects to conquer his opponents or his so-called enemies not by violent force but by force of love, by process of conversion. His methods will be always gentle and gentlemanly. He will never exaggerate. And since non-violence is otherwise known as love it has no weapon but that of self-suffering. And above all in a movement like that of the removal of untouchability which in my opinion is essentially religious and one of self-purification there is no room for hate, no room for haste, no room for thoughtlessness and no room for exaggeration. Since Satyagraha is one of the most powerful methods of direct action, a Satyagrahi exhausts all other means before he resorts to Satyagraha. He will therefore constantly and continually approach the constituted authority, he will appeal to public opinion, educate public opinion, state his case calmly and coolly before everybody who wants to listen to him, and only after he has exhausted all these avenues will he resort to Satyagraha. But when he has found the impelling call of the inner voice within him and launches out upon Satyagraha he has burnt his boats and there is no receding. Let me however hope that it will not be necessary in this land for people to undergo all the suffering for removing a wrong which is so patent.

"You will be glad to learn that immediately I entered this place the Commissioner of Police was good enough to call on me and we discussed this great question. There are at the present moment two questions pending so far as I am aware: one in connection with the roads about Thiruvarppu and the other in connection with Suchindram. So far as I am aware in both these places the reformers have the right on their side. I understand that at the first place Satyagrahis have already commenced their battle. I think it is a hasty step. I have therefore sent them a telegram asking them to desist for the time being and to see me to-morrow at Trivandrum. And I propose, if I am given the opportunity, as I hope I shall be, to discuss both these questions with the authorities. Though this visit of mine to Travancore was intended to be confined principally to Khadi or Khadi collections, fate threw me into the untouchability fray immediately on my arrival. I shall not spare myself during the brief time that is at my disposal in endeavouring humbly to assist both the State and the people in arriving at an honourable settlement."

20th, October, 1927

THE SPIRIT OF HINDUISM

BY M. K. GANDHI

From the Trivandrum Speech

"As at Nagarcoil, here too the best part of the day has been devoted to discussing this problem. Though it was partly a social call that I paid to the Diwan, we naturally began to discuss this thorny question. And if you found me coming to the meeting a few minutes late it was because I had gone to pay my respects to Her Highness the Maharani Regent, and I found myself again discussing this very question with her. I have always, after having paid the first visit to Travancore, looked forward to a series of visits to this enchanting land. Its most beautiful scenery, the location of Kanyakumari in Travancore, and the simplicity and freedom of the women of Travancore captivated me when I first came here. But the pleasure that all these thoughts and associations always gave me has been seriously marred by the thought that untouchability had assumed its most terrible shape in Travancore, and it has pained me to think that this evil has existed in that terrible form in a most ancient Hindu State, which has the privilege of occupying the first place in all India in educational progress. And this existence of untouchability in its extreme form has always caused me so much pain, because I consider myself to be a Hindu of Hindus saturated with the spirit of Hinduism. I have failed to find a single warrant for the existence of untouchability as we believe and practice it today in all those books which we call as Hindu Shastras. But as I have repeatedly said in other places if I found that Hinduism really countenanced untouchability I should have no hesitation in renouncing Hinduism itself. For I hold that religion, to be worthy of the name, must not be inconsistent with the fundamental truths of ethics and morality. But as I believe that untouchability is no part of Hinduism, I cling to Hinduism but daily become more and more impatient of this hideous wrong. So, when I found that this question was agitating Travancore I had no hesitation in plunging myself into it. If I have taken up this question, I have done so not in any way to embarrass the State. For I believe that Her Highness the Maharani Regent is solicitous about the welfare of her people. She also claims to be a reformer along these lines, and I fancy that I commit no breach of confidence when I tell you that she is eager to see that this wrong is removed at the earliest possible moment.

"But then Governments cannot afford to lead in matters of reform. By their very nature Governments are but interpreters and executors of the expressed will of the people whom they govern, and even a most autocratic Government will find itself unable to impose a reform which its people cannot assimilate. So, if I was a subject of Travancore State I should be entirely satisfied to know that my Government was willing to carry forward this reform as speedily as the people were willing to assimilate it. But having satisfied myself of that one thing, I should not rest content for one single moment till I had carried the message of reform from mouth to mouth and village to village. Well-ordered, persistent agitation is the soul of healthy progress, and so if I were you, I would not let the Government rest till this reform was carried through. Not allowing the Government to rest does not by any means mean embarrassing the Government. A wise Government welcomes and needs the support and warmth and encouragement of such an agitation in order to achieve a reform which the Government itself wants. I know that when I was here last, I was told that the Savarna (caste) Hindus were all most anxious for this reform of the abolition of untouchability in every shape and form. But I am afraid that the Savarna Hindus have slept over their wish. They have not given a concrete form to their wish, and I believe that it is the bounden duty of every Hindu in the state to wake up to a sense of his duty and to wake up his lethargic brethren also to a sense of their duty. And I have no shadow of a doubt that if the Savarna Hindus could with one voice express their wish, this monster of untouchability would go. It would be wrong therefore to ascribe our own lethargy and slothfulness to the Government.

"But reformers in every community and every country are to be counted on one's finger tips; and I know that the brunt of all such reform falls upon the devoted heads of that small band of reformers. What are the reformers then to do in the face of this evil of such long standing,—is really the question one has to solve. The reformers all over the world have resorted to one or other of the two methods that I am about to mention. The vast majority of them have drawn attention to evils by creating wild agitation and resorting to violence. They have resorted to agitation that embarrasses the Government, that embarrasses the people and that disturbs the even tenor of the life of the citizens. The other school of reformers which I would call the non-violent school resorts to agitation of the gentle type. It disdains to draw attention by doing violence in thought, word or deed; but it draws attention by simple self-suffering. It never exaggerates. It never departs by a hair's breadth from truth, and whilst impatient of evil does not mean ill even to the evil-doer. I have given that a short name and I have placed it before this country as before South Africa in the name of Satyagraha. Do not for one moment mix up Satyagraha with civil disobedience, Civil disobedience is no doubt a branch of Satyagraha. It comes not, at the beginning but at the fag end. It presupposes immense discipline. It presupposes great self-restraint. It is based upon charity, and it never puts an unfavourable or unwarranted construction even upon the motives of its opponents. For it seeks not to coerce but to convert. You may therefore imagine my painful surprise when I found the whole of my doctrine and my remarks grossly misinterpreted by a friend who visited me in Virudhunagar. I saw in the *Trivandrum Express* a report given by him of what had occurred between him and myself. It is a distortion from start to finish of the conversation that I had with him (A voice; "Shame"). But there is no warrant for crying "shame". The gentleman who cried shame evidently does not know the virtue or meaning of charity. For I do not for one moment suggest that the friend who saw me has consciously or deliberately distorted my meaning. I am prepared to believe the explanation that he gave me this morning. But I have drawn your attention to this prominently in order to illustrate what I mean by Satyagraha and also to show you the danger of those who do not know this fine weapon dabbling in it. I am simply giving this example in order to warn the would-be reformer against undertaking this method unless he is absolutely sure of his ground and unless he has got more than the ordinary measure of self-control, and seeing that I am enamoured of this method of Satyagraha, which I consider to be a matchless weapon, I do not want it to be misused or abused, so long as I can prevent it. I therefore advised this friend to keep out of this problem until he had understood what Satyagraha really was, and unless he had assimilated the true spirit of it.

"But this again is not intended to damp the zeal of even a single reformer. I am going into the problem so much in detail, for the simple reason that I want you to work at it in order to get the quickest possible solution. I want therefore humbly to suggest that those of you who have had some experience of public life should take up this movement and make it their own and harness the energy and the will of the youths who are interested in this problem but do not know how to solve it. And I suggest also that you place yourselves in touch with the authorities and day after day worry the life out of them until this reform is achieved. For I am free to tell you that not only is Her Highness desirous of carrying out this reform but so is the Dewan himself. But belonging as he does to a different faith, you and I Hindus can appreciate his limitations. In my opinion, so far as the Government is concerned, it is on the side of reform; only the initiative will have to come from you and not from the Government. You will forgive me for having dealt with this very important question in a highly technical manner. I could not do otherwise as I have no other time at my disposal so that I could have convened a few of the leaders at a conference and discussed the pros and cons. I felt therefore that you would overlook the heaviness of my speech in connection with untouchability before a big audience as this.

"One question was put to me arising out of this question this morning, and that was what was the bearing of *Varnashrama Dharma* upon untouchability. That means that I should say a few words about my conception of *Varnashrama Dharma*. So far as I know anything at all of Hinduism, the meaning of *Varna* is incredibly simple. It simply means the following on the part of us all the hereditary and traditional calling of our forefathers, in so far as that traditional calling is not inconsistent with fundamental ethics, and this only for the purpose of earning one's livelihood. I regard this as the law of our being, if we would accept the definition of man given in all religions. Of all the animal creation of God, man is the only animal who has been created in order that he may know his Maker. Man's aim in life is not therefore to add from day to day to his material prospects and to his material possessions but his predominent calling is from day to day to come nearer his own Maker, and from this definition it was that the *Rishis* of old discovered this law of our being. You will realise that if all of us follow this law of *Varna* we would limit our material ambition, and our energy would be set free for exploring those vast fields whereby and wherethrough we can know God. You will at once then see that nine-tenths of the activities that are today going on throughout the world and which are engrossing our attention would fall into disuse. You will then be entitled to say that *Varna* as we observe it today is a travesty of the *Varna* that I have described to you. And so it undoubtedly is, but just as we do not hate truth because untruth parades itself as truth, but we sift untruth from truth and cling to the latter so also we can destroy the distortion that passes as *Varna*, and purify the state to which the Hindu society has been reduced today.

"*Ashrama* is a necessary corollary to what I have stated to you, and if *Varna* today has become distorted, *Ashrama* has altogether disappeared. *Ashrama* means the four stages in one's life, and I wish the students who have kindly presented their purses to me—the Arts and Science students and the Law College students—were able to assure me that they were living according to the laws of the first *Ashrama*, and that they were *brahmacharis* in thought, word and deed. The *Brahmacharya Ashrama* enjoins that only those who live the life of a *brahmachari*, at least up to 25 years, are entitled to enter upon the second *Ashrama*, *i.e.*, the *Grihasthashrama*. And because the whole conception of Hinduism is to make man better than he is and draw him nearer to his Maker, the *Rishis* set a limit even to the *Grihasthashrama* stage and imposed on us the obligation of *Vanaprastha* and *Sannyasa*. But today you will vainly search throughout the length and breadth of India for a true *brahmachari*, for a true *grihastha*, not to talk of a *vanaprastha* and *sannyasi*. We may, in our elongated wisdom, laugh at this scheme of life, if we wish to. But I have no doubt whatsoever that this is the secret of the great success of Hinduism. The Hindu civilization has survived the Egyptian, the Assyrian and the Babylonian. The Christian is but two thousand years old. The Islamic is but of yesterday. Great as both these are they are still in my humble opinion in the making. Christian Europe is not at all

Christian, but is groping, and so in my opinion is Islam still groping for its great secret, and there is today a competition, healthy as also extremely unhealthy and ugly, between these three great religions. As years go by, the conviction is daily growing upon me that *Varna* is the law of man's being and therefore as necessary for Christianity and Islam, as it has been necessary for Hinduism and has been its saving. I refuse, therefore, to believe that *Varnashrama* has been the curse of Hinduism, as it is the fashion nowadays in the south on the part of some Hindus to say. But that does not mean that you and I may tolerate for one moment or be gentle towards the hideous travesty of *Varnashrama* that we see about us today. There is nothing in common between *Varnashrama* and caste. Caste, if you will, is undoubtedly a drag upon Hindu progress, and untouchability is as I have already called it or described it an excrescence upon *Varnashrama.* It is a weedy growth fit only to be weeded out, as we weed out the weeds that we see growing in wheat fields or rice fields. In this conception of *Varna,* there is absolutely no idea of superiority and inferiority. If I again interpret the Hindu spirit rightly all life is absolutely equal and one. It is therefore an arrogant assumption on the part of the Brahman when he says, "I am superior to the other three *Varnas.*" That is not what the Brahmans of old said. They commanded homage not because they claimed superiority, but because they claimed the right of service through and through without the slightest expectation of a reward. The priests, who today arrogate to themselves the function of the Brahman and distort religion, are no custodians of Hinduism or Brahmanism. Consciously or unconsciously they are laying the axe at the root of the very tree on which they are sitting, and when they tell you that Shastras enjoin untouchability and when they talk of pollution distance, I have no hesitation in saying that they are belying their creed and that they are misinterpreting the spirit of Hinduism. You will now perhaps understand why it is absolutely necessary for you Hindus who are here and listening to me to energise yourselves and rid yourselves of this curse. You should take pride in leading the way of reform, belonging as you do to an ancient Hindu State. So far as I can read the atmosphere around you here, the moment is certainly propitious for you if you will sincerely and energetically undertake this reform."

20th October, 1927

APPEAL TO THE CASTE HINDUS

BY M. K. GANDHI

From the Quilon Speech

"Untouchability poisons Hinduism as a drop of arsenic poisons milk," said Gandhji at Quilon, and made an impassioned appeal to the caste Hindus to destroy the poison.

"Knowing the quality of milk, and the use of milk and knowing the quality of arsenic, we should be impatient with the man sitting near a pitcher of milk and trying to remove arsenic grain by grain, and we should throw the whole pitcher overboard. Even so do I as a Hindu feel that the curse of untouchability is rendering the milk of Hinduism altogether poisoned and impure. I feel therefore that patience in a matter of this character is not a virtue. It is impossible to restrain ourselves. Patience with evil is really trifling with evil and with ourselves. I have therefore not hesitated to say that the State of Travancore should lead in the matter of the reform and blot out the evil at a single stroke. But I know also that it was not possible even for a Hindu State to do away with this evil, unless it was backed and actively backed by its Hindu population. And so my appeal must be mostly to you rather than to the head of the State, and to every Hindu in this meeting I wish to make a definite personal appeal. You and I have long neglected our duty to the so-called untouchables and unapproachables, and to this extent you and I have been false representatives of Hinduism. I ask you without the slightest hesitation summarily to reject the advance of every person who comes to you in defence of untouchability. Remember that in this age whatever one man or group of men and women do does not remain secret for any length of time, and we are daily being weighed and found wanting so long as we nurse untouchability in our bosom. You must remember that all the great religions of the world are at the present time in the melting pot. Let us not ostrich-like hide our faces and ignore the danger that lies at the back of us. I have not a shadow of doubt that in the great turmoil now taking place either untouchability has to die or Hinduism has to disappear. But I do know that Hinduism is not dying, is not going to die, because I see untouchability is a corpse struggling with its last breath to hold on for a little while."

20th October, 1927

THE TRUCE

By M. K. Gandhi

(*From the Alleppey Speech*)

"I had a very long discussion with many of the Ezhuva leaders this afternoon, and I tell you that if I was not told that they were Ezhuvas I should not have known them to be such, nor could I see the slightest distinction between them and those who call themselves Savarnas (Caste-Hindus). Their pecuniary position is any day better than of many of the Savarnas. Their educational qualifications leave nothing to be desired, and their personal cleanliness appeared to be infinitely superior to that of many Brahmans and others whom I have seen during my travels from one end of the country to the other.. And so when I faced these friends and read their address, I hung my Hindu head in shame, that these friends were considered untouchable and unfit to walk along some of the public roads in Travancore, and that these were the friends whose presence in our temples would defile the temple ground, and that these were the men who could not send their sons and daughters to at least some of the Government schools although they were as much taxpayers as the tallest in this assembly. For let it be remembered that as against these inhuman disabilities, they are not excused from paying the tax in the same measure that Savarnas pay to the State. This then is in my opinion a cause to which it is the duty of many Hindus who feel for their religion to dedicate their lives, and I do hope that Her Highness the Maharani Regent enlightened, as she is, will not rest content until this disgrace is removed from Travancore, and from all the talks, I had with Her Highness, with the Dewan, and the Commissioner of Police, and last but not least the Devasvam Commissioner, I am leaving Travancore in the hope that at least the roads question will be solved to the satisfaction of all concerned, and it is in that fervent hope that I have not hesitated to advise the deputation today to suspend Satyagraha, and I am glad to be able to say to this meeting that this deputation were kind enough to listen to my advice and suspend Satyagraha whilst this question was being satisfactorily settled. God forbid that there should be any disappointment with reference to the hope that I carry with me. But I have told the friends that if the redress that is their due is not given in time, and if after they have exhausted all preliminary proposals they fail in getting relief it will not only be open to them, but it will be their bounden duty, to resort to Satyagraha in order to win what is their right. . . . .

"Let me reiterate to you the implications of the hope I am taking with me. Flimsy in one respect though I consider what is called the Vykom settlement to be, in other respects and from another point of view it is a settlement honourable alike to the State and the Avarna Hindus. It is a settlement which I consider to be the bedrock of freedom. I call it a bedrock of freedom because the settlement is a document between the people and the State constituting a big step in the direction of liberty in one respect at least. But so far as the Avarna Hindus are concerned it is in no sense a final settlement, it was the minimum that they permitted themselves to be satisfied with at the time and for the time being. It is necessarily a settlement for the Government never to recede from. Government by that settlement erected for themselves a platform to make further advances from. Its interpretation therefore must be always in favour of the Avarna Hindus. Nor can it ever be interpreted to curtail the liberties of non-Hindus. Applying this principle to the present trouble at Thiruvarappu it is not possible for Government to curtail any substantial right of Christians and other non-Hindus who have been using roads there. It is therefore their bounden duty to throw these roads open to Avarna Hindus, and any difficulty that there may be in the way of the roads being thrown open it is for the Government to get over, and not for the Avarna Hindus to accommodate the Government over. Similar though not precisely the same is the case now pending in connection with the roads round the Suchandram temple, and I am hoping that in the very near future the State will overcome all difficulties there may be in giving the relief I have suggested.

"Subject to this I have given my advice to the Ezhuva friends to suspend their activities, and I venture to hope that in the circumstances the order the Government have thought it necessary to serve on Sjt. Madhavan will be withdrawn without delay. I think the order at least now wholly unnecessary, as also is the general order prohibiting the holding of meetings within a certain radius of Thiruvarappu.

27th October, 1927

THE COIMBATORE SPEECH

By M. K. Gandhi

[I reproduce below important portions from Gandhiji's speech at Coimbatore. M. D.]

I will take up first of all the Municipal address. My sincere thanks are due to the Municipality for not only expressing their sentiments frankly, courteously and firmly but also for reminding me of the address which the Municipality gave me when I paid my last visit to Coimbatore. Throughout my life I have gained more from my critic friends than from my admirers, especially when the criticism was made in courteous and friendly language as the present one is. The first address I had the honour of receiving from this Municipality questioned the utility of non-co-operation especially regarding schools and public services. Many important and some of them painful events have happened since the birth of non-co-operation. I had two years of prayerful contemplation over the advice that I tendered the country for the first time in 1921. I have read and read with careful attention and open mind almost everything that has been written against non-co-operation, and as a result of my observation I am able to inform you, that not only have I not changed the views that I held in 1921 and that I expressed when I had the honour of meeting you last, but have been confirmed more and more in those views. It is my humble opinion, that within the last two generations our country has not gained as much as it has gained since the advent of non-violent non-co-operation. I entertain no doubt whatever as to the verdict of history upon non-violent non-co-operation. It is also my certain belief, that every student who left his school or college or every Government servant who left what passes as public services has gained immeasurably and lost nothing by having done so. That public services in spite of non-co-operation have not been abandoned, that Government schools have not been abandoned by our boys is no demonstration whatsoever of the failure of my doctrine, even as because men and women are not all votaries of truth, truth cannot be challenged as to its efficacy or soundness. But I want to go a step further and tell you, that he who wishes to study carefully and impartially current events will find ample testimony, that several Government servants who left their jobs and several students who left their schools are giving a good account of themselves. Is it a small thing that millions of people rose to a man as if by magic one fine morning under the spell of non-co-operation? If co-operation is a duty, I hold that non-co-operation also under certain conditions is equally a duty. I go further and contend, that if this country of ours is to gain its freedom by non-violent means, there is no other means open but for us some day to take up non-co-operation. Believe me, that if to-day I do not talk of non-violent non-co-operation, it is not because my faith is not burning as brightly as ever, but because as a practical man I do not find the atmosphere for working out that creed. I must not weary you with my arguments about my belief.

The present address of the Municipality in courteous but firm language enters a protest against the views that I have been expressing about *Varnashrama Dharma.* The signatories or framers of the address seem to me to regard *Varnashrama Dharma* as an unmitigated evil. I venture to re-affirm my belief, that *Varnashrama Dharma* is not only not an unmitigated evil, but it is one of the foundations on which Hinduism is built. In my humble opinion the framers of the address have mistaken the shadow for the substance. Instead of making, in my humble opinion, this serious blunder, if they invited me to join them in a crusade against the travesty that passes for *Varnashrama Dharma,* they would have found me enrolling myself as a volunteer under their banner. I hold it as a law of our being and whether we know such laws of our being or whether we do not, we have to obey them even as our forefathers obeyed the law of gravitation before it was discovered by a master mind. Nature's laws are inexorable. We may not disobey them and escape punishment. The conviction is daily forcing itself upon me that this India of ours and the rest of the world are suffering because of our breach of the law of *Varnashrama Dharma.* If Hinduism today seems to me to be in a fallen state, it is not because of *Varnashrama Dharma,* but because of its wilful disobedience of that *Dharma. Varnashrama Dharma* defines man's mission on this earth. He is not born day after day to explore avenues for amassing riches and to explore different means of livelihood; on the contrary man is born in order that he may utilise every atom of his energy for the purpose of knowing his Maker. It restricts him, therefore, for the purpose of holding body and soul together, to the occupation of his forefathers. That and nothing more or nothing less is *Varnashrama Dharma*, and it is not possible nor desirable nor necessary, that I should ignore *Varna Dharma* because the majority of Hindus seem to deny it in their lives. Thus conceived *Varnashrama Dharma* has nothing in common with castes as we know them to-day. *Varna Dharma* therefore can never mean and has never tolerated untouchability. *Varna Dharma* therefore has no idea of superiority or inferiority. Because many people or millions of people take the name of God in vain and even insult God and man in the name of God Himself, shall we disown our God and find another name for Him? I therefore invite respectfully the framers of the address and the audience to join me in a crusade against the spectre of caste and the curse of untouchability, and I promise that if you join me in this crusade, you will find at the end of it that there is nothing to fight against in Hinduism. I have been prayerfully studying the great Non-Brahman and Brahman question which has been agitating so many able men in the South and I am daily driven to the conclusion that the question, in so far as it is a Non-Brahman question, is a phase of the battle against untouchability. . . .

I now take up the Congress address. The Congress address invites me to take the lead again. Evidently they still have a lingering faith in the programme of 1920. Let them understand that I have never given up the lead. I am still leading, still wooing, but what shall I do if I do not find followers? But there is a better answer than I have given you. Let me tell you what I mean by leading. I made statements even before I went to jail, that the only lead that could be given to the country by a man with non-violence as his creed is to finish the constructive programme of the Congress. The most effective programme of the Congress is the message of the spinning wheel, and with the consent and permission of the

Congress duly given to me I am leading in that constructive programme as President of the All-India Spinners' Association. And the Spinners' Association is the creature of the Congress, a creature that works by dint of perseverance and systematic efforts ultimately to absorb the creator itself. Those who have real belief in the efficacy of non-violence for obtaining the freedom of their country cannot but believe in Khadi and put their shoulder to the wheel so that it may become universal in this country. They would talk of no other lead before this becomes an accomplished fact. If any one asks me for a lead and ignores the lead I am really giving, I really wonder whether the questioner has understood the implications of the struggle or of non-violence. Remember that the Spinners' Association which is designed to serve 300 millions of people including the poorest invokes and requires the greatest administrative skill and the widest possible platform. Remember that it requires for its success on the part of the workers ceaseless watch, ceaseless perseverance, indomitable faith in the face of sneers, in the face of opposition, in the face of malicious misrepresentations. It requires on the part of the workers an amount of sacrifice unexciting and sustained beyond compare, and if God helps India to run an organisation of this character and carry its work to the remotest village, we can imagine that with that one thing accomplished very little will remain to be done to make this land free. I have a growing faith in the capacity of India to respond to this effort, and whether you share my views about non-co-operation, *Varnashrama Dharma* and many other things in which I dabble, I ask you all to work for *Daridranarayan.*

27th October, 1927.

A GOOD SERVANT GONE

BY M. K. GANDHI

It was in 1921 at Bezwada, that at a great ladies' meeting I saw the only Khaddar-clad girl present there taking charge of the meeting, keeping order, and moving about with energy and decision. She was the first to give up, so far as I can remember, all her rich ornaments, bangles and a heavy gold chain. "Have you got the permission of your parents?" I asked her, as she was delivering all the ornaments to me. "My parents do not interfere with me and they let me do as I like," she replied. Annapurna Devi spoke English fluently. She had received her education at Bethune College in Calcutta. She went out amongst the huge mass of ladies for collections and brought ornaments and money. Ever since then she kept herself in touch with the movement—in fact dedicated herself to it. She was captain of lady volunteers at Coconada, and many have described in glowing terms her wonderful work at the time Unfortunately even at this time she was not in robust health. She was married to Sjt. Magunti Bapi Needu B. Sc. Whilst at Coimbatore I suddenly received a telegram several days after her death that she was no more. And now I have a letter from Sjt. Needu from which I take the following extracts:

> "At last the expected blow has fallen. It is my misfortune, that my first letter should carry the shocking news of the premature death of your favourite worker and my partner, Annapurna. When we both paid our respectful visit to you at Shrinivasa Iyengar's house, during your last Madras tour, I distinctly remember you asked me to keep you in touch about her health and advised me to send her to Ahmedabad for treatment. But I did not like to worry you about her health. Your instructions to us, to me to be her best nurse, to her to keep her courage and take particular care of her health, we implicitly followed. What was humanly possible I did but in vain.
>
> "In her you find one of the typical wrecks of your non-co-operation movement. She gave her all to the country —her jewels, even her wedding ring which I presented after my return—marriage property, best clothes, fine fashions, literary pursuits, her health and now her life.
>
> "It was her implicit faith in you that made her blindly

follow your *Health Guide.* Under your unbalanced fruit diet which she religiously followed for six months, her healthy constitution began to break down never to recover.

"Mahatmaji, I cannot be so cruel as to accuse you, but I am merely stating the fact. She much neglected her health during her propaganda work in the N-C-O. movement. It was too late when she realised her sin which cost her her life. You wrote in one letter to her: 'I knew always that you would most zealously work for Khaddar.' Yes, she did most zealously work for Khaddar. After my return from the United States, the first request she made to me, falling at my feet, was to promise to wear Khaddar. My suits, shirts, shorts and other foreign clothes no more I could claim as my own. I was not even allowed to find place for them in her home at Ellore. In one of her American letters she mentioned her vow to boycott foreign cloth and her resolve to stick to Khaddar for life. She did succeed. It is now left for me to respect the other half of the vow. She did not leave Khaddar even when she was literally reduced to mere skin and bone with bed sores caused by thick Khaddar *saris.* She was fortunate to be cremated with Khaddar on (as is the custom in my community). Perhaps she was anxious to introduce it in the other world too!

"Her message on the eve of my departure to U. S. A. was, 'You may even forget me; but never forget your mother country.' Once she was remarking to me, that if at all she had any desire to get rid of her chronic illness, it was for the country's cause, not for her husband's service. It is this ambition that gave her will to live for months when we all gave up hope. To the end she was hopeful; even at the last moment, on getting consciousness after injections, she was challenging the doctor that she would live, never die. She did live to die and died to live for the country.

"Her unpublished works on women, translations of

Ramakrishna's teachings from Bengali and some of her letters we mean giving due publicity to.

"Our little Jhansi, pet name after Jhansi 'Lakshmibai,' is our only comfort and hope. She expected that her arrival would bring a radical change in her health. It did bring a permanent change resulting in her departure.

"23rd October, the coming Sunday, is her Shraddha day, when a memorial service will be held, readings from her books and letters will be presented to her friends. An up-to-date national institution for women was her ideal. To fulfil it, a memorial committee consisting of men of light and leading will be formed. Can we include your name in the above committee? Pray send your blessings and consent by the 20th instant at least.

"Such a faithful follower you will miss. Such an ideal partner I have lost. My better half has left her other half dejected, depressed, detached, never adequately to fill the gap left by her."

It is true, indeed, that I have lost more than a devoted follower. I feel like having lost one of my many daughters whom I have the good fortune to own throughout India. And she was among the very best of these. She never wavered in her faith and worked without expectation of praise or reward. I wish that many wives will acquire, by their purity and single-minded devotion, the gentle but commanding influence Annapurna Devi acquired over her husband. I appreciate his mild rebuke to me for Annapurna Devi having worn her body out in pursuit of the service of the Motherland. I doubt not that many young men and young women will have to imitate this good woman and die martyrs to duty before India becomes once more holy and free as millions believe her to have been in ancient times.

I have not been able to respond to the request to serve on the committee referred to in the foregoing extracts. For I have many interests, and I could not cope with the burden of being a member of hundreds of committees. I have never believed in becoming merely an ornamental member of any committee or belonging to it for the sake of lending my name. That there should be a local memorial to perpetuate the memory of one so brave, pure and patriotic like Annapurna Devi I have no doubt. But the best memorial would be for her worthy husband to follow in the foot-steps of his wife, and perpetuate her memory by finding his lost partner in the country's cause. For according to his own testimony Annapurna Devi had already lost herself in that cause.

27th October, 1927

A WORTHY EXAMPLE

By M. K. Gandhi

The Vice-Chairman of the Municipality of Chanda (C. P.) writes as follows:

> "This is the first Municipality in Central Provinces and Berar to exempt Khadi from payment of octroi. Over and above this, from 1922 it has been regularly making an annual grant of Rs. 500 for Khadi work which is being utilised for maintaining a 'Shuddha Khadi Karyalaya' here. This Karyalaya has now been affiliated to the All-India Spinners' Association. The yarn produced in it has been found to be the best in Maharashtra, with regard to its count, evenness and strength. Since 1922 the Municipality has been employing, for all its purposes, exclusively Khadi manufactured in the 'Chanda Khadi Karyalaya.' It is now considering a scheme for introducing Khadi in its schools."

The resolution referred to reads:

> "Resolved that all the hand-spun and hand-woven Khadi certified for its genuineness, by the All-India Spinners' Association be exempted from payment of Octroi duty."

This is an example worthy of imitation by every Municipality. The Khadi work by this Municipality is no new love but it is well tried. It has survived the vicissitudes through which the other Municipalities, large and small, have passed, and it has grown from year to year. The Municipality has been able to achieve this success because many of its members not only believe in the message of the wheel but reduce their belief into practice in their own lives. The evolution of Khadi in this Municipality has been natural in its stages. It commenced with a monetary grant, then they introduced Khadi uniform for its servants. This has been followed up by the removal of octroi duty on Khadi, and it now proposes to introduce spinning in its schools. I hope that the introduction of spinning in the schools will be carried out in a scientific spirit, and that boys and girls will be induced to wear Khadi before they are called upon to spin, and will be told why they should spin rather than do any manual work. I suggest, too, that the spinning will be on the *takli* and not on the wheel. Those boys who show great aptitude and take a keen interest in spinning may be supplied with spinning wheels as loans to be worked not in the schools but in their homes, the wheels to be their property if they show continuous work for a period of one year. Both boys and girls should also be taught carding before they begin to spin, and their work should be tested daily and tabulated from time to time. M. K. G.

27th October, 1927

PROFITABLE COTTON CULTIVATION

BY M. K. GANDHI

A correspondent suggests that there should be a widespread movement to induce cotton cultivators to store a quantity of cotton for themselves to be converted into hand-spun yarn and finally into Khadi for their own use. He also suggests that in non-cotton areas individual peasants should be encouraged to grow enough cotton as they grow vegetables for their own requirements. The correspondent contends that if this becomes popular, it will cheapen Khadi for the peasantry. He says that in some parts of the South before the Khadi movement came there were cultivators who followed this method. The correspondent thinks that Indian States are best able to promote this kind of cultivation of cotton.

There is much force in the correspondent's suggestion. The experiment of inducing cotton cultivators to retain sufficient cotton for their own needs is being tried in Bijolia (Rajputana), Bardoli and Kathiawad. But it has been found difficult in Kathiawad for the cultivators to resist the temptation of selling stored cotton when prices ruled high. This is not possible, until the cultivators appreciate the economics of Khadi, and the fact that labour spent upon cotton during their leisure hours in subjecting it to the processes antecedent to weaving will bring about the same result that they achieve by selling cotton at a high price, and will in addition free themselves from the clutches of the speculator. This means that the All-India Spinners' Association will have to educate the cultivators in the economics of Khadi. There is no doubt that in order to overtake all the branches of Khadi work it is necessary for Khadi workers to come in close touch with the cotton growers, because even for buying cotton for the manufacture of Khadi for town consumption, it would be necessary to come in touch with the cotton-growers and buy from them direct instead of buying in the market as is being done at present. If we would be independent of the speculator and the fluctuations of the cotton market and stabilize the price of Khadi, we shall have to come in touch with the cultivator and induce him to deal with us directly. The greater the progress of Khadi, the more shall we find that our methods have to be far different from those hitherto adopted by the commercial world, which believes in selling at the highest price obtainable and buying at the cheapest rate possible. The world commerce at the present moment is not based upon equitable considerations. Its maxim is, 'Buyers beware.' The maxim of Khadi economics is, 'Equity for all.' It therefore rules out the present soul-killing competitive method. Khadi economics are designed in the interest of the poorest and the helpless, and Khadi will be successful only to the extent that the workers permeate the masses and command their confidence. And the only way of commanding their confidence is doing selfless work among them.

The correspondent's suggestion that the Indian States are more fortunately placed in the matter of storing cotton by cotton cultivators and growing enough for home consumption by other cultivators is no doubt true. The question however is, 'Who will bell the cat?' The majority of the States are little concerned with the welfare of the peasantry. Their aim in life for the present moment seems to be to increase their revenue as much as possible and at any cost, and to spend the largest part of it for their own pleasures. Moreover they like other capitalists have little faith in Khadi economics. A very cautious experiment is now being tried, in Mysore, of finding out the possibilities of the spinning wheel as a village industry. One may hope that if that experiment is tried scientifically and patiently and is found to succeed, it would prove infectious.

27th October, 1927

REMOVING UNTOUCHABILITY

By M. K. Gandhi

Sjt. S. D. Nadkarni in a letter from Karwar dated 10th September says:

> "Last week, my brother and I, helped by a band of young men, successfuly organised, against many and unexpected difficulties, a *Kara Sarvajanika Ganesothsava* (*i.e.* real all-inclusive Ganapati festival), so called because we included the 'untouchables' along with the other Hindus in our programme of processions, *puja*, *bhajan*, *arati*, *kirtan*, *purana* reading and lastly a drama specially got written and staged twice during

the festival. The drama is based on the real experience of the depressed-class member of our District School Board, who was refused admission into a school housed in a temple in a neighbouring village, while his Musalman fellow member and campanion was admitted to inspect the school! Could you believe it?—It was some of our own people (Hindu touch-me-nots) who tried to prevent the performance of the drama by setting up the local Muslims to petition to the authorities that the drama should be prohibited on the (totally false) ground that it was anti-Muslim. Could our people's opposition to a vital reform in our own community take a more suicidal course than this? But thank Reason and Justice, their attempts came to naught!

"With the help of Chitre Shastri of Poona (President of the Maharashtra Hindu Sabha) specially invited here for the purpose, we formed a local branch of the Hindu Sabha, with the object in particular of combating untouchability and securing admission to the 'untouchables' into our public temples."

The opposition, and the manner of it, from the 'touch-me-nots' as Sjt. Nadkarni calls the self-styled orthodox Hindus, to the presence of the so-called untouchables at the innocent performance organised by the reformers does not reflect any credit on them or their Hinduism, and it shows the lengths to which blind orthodoxy will go under the sacred name of religion. I congratulate Sjt. Nadkarni and his friends upon their having successfully taken the untouchable friends in their procession and admitted them to their theatrical performance. The only way to get rid of untouchability is for every reformer to do some such constructive work, be it ever so small, on behalf of the suppressed class and by gentleness combined with firmness break down the double wall of superstition and prejudice. I hope that the reformers of Karvar will succeed in their efforts to gain for the untouchables admission to the temples.

3rd November, 1927

INDIA 'SWALLOWING UP' GOLD?

Once more has the calumny been repeated that India is a sink for the absorption of precious metals, and this time by the now famous Miss Mayo in order to prove that India is not an 'essentially poor country.' This oft-repeated charge cannot be answered better than by extracting the following from Sir Stanley Reed's memorandum submitted to the Babington-Smith Committee (Appendix, p. 130):

"It is objected that India is a bottomless sink for the absorption of the precious metals, and that gold and silver once passed into general consumption in India is permanently lost to the rest of the world. This attempt to fasten upon India an exceptional and invidious responsibility for the consumption of bullion cannot be too vigorously combated. India is still an illiterate country, where the practice of holding small savings in gold and silver ornaments is centuries old. Yet its normal demand for the industrial arts and for the satisfaction of the social customs of three hundred and fifteen millions of people, was met before the war by about ten millions of gold annually. The United States of America was reported recently to be absorbing a million sterling in gold per month for industrial purposes. No one says that the United States is a bottomless sink in the matter of her gold absorption. It is stated that in England one of the most flourishing trades during the war was that in cheap jewellery, in which form the working classes invested a substantial proportion of their increased earnings. Every country in the world uses gold and silver for industrial and domestic purposes and it induces a sense of angry injustice to find that the Indian demand for precious metals, for precisely the same purposes, is perverted into senseless hoarding, especially when the history and conditions of India would justify larger gold absorption than the Western nations with their general literacy and easily organised credit system can claim." V. G D.

3rd November, 1927

COW PROTECTION

BY M. K. GANDHI

I have before me a press-cutting containing a long interrogatory addressed to me on the question of cow protection. The underlying suggestion obviously seems to be that the methods of cow protection advocated by me are not consistent with my profession of Hinduism. For in his introductory remarks to his questions the writer has tried to make light of the basic principle of cow protection that I have formulated, *viz.*, that what is economically wrong cannot be religiously right. In other words, if a religion cuts at the very fundamentals of economics it is not a true religion but only a delusion. My critic on the other hand believes that this view is opposed to the teachings of our ancient scriptures. I, at least, am not aware of a single text in opposition to this view nor do I know of any religious institution that is being maintained in any part of the world to-day in antagonism to the elementary principles of economics. As for nature, any one who has eyes can see, that it always observes the principle that I have stated. For instance, if it has implanted in its creation the instinct for food it also produces enough food to satisfy that instinct from day to day. But it does not produce a jot more. That is nature's way. But man, blinded by his selfish greed, grabs and consumes more than his requirements in defiance of nature's principle, in defiance of the elementary and immutable moralities of non-stealing and non-possession of other's property and thus brings down no end of misery upon himself and his fellow-creatures. To turn to another illustration, our Shastras have enjoined that the Brahman should give knowledge as charity without expecting any material reward for it for himself. But they have at the same time conferred upon him the privilege of asking for and receiving alms and have laid upon the other sections of the community the duty of giving alms, thus uniting religion and economics in a common bond of harmony. The reader will be able to find further instances of this kind for himself. The religious principle requires that the debit and credit sides of one's balance sheet should be perfectly square. That is also the truest economics and therefore true religion. Whenever there is any discrepancy between these two it spells bad economics and makes for unrighteousness. That is why the illustrious author of the Gita has defined *yoga* as "balance" or "evenness." But the majority of mankind do not understand this use of economics to subserve religion; they want it only for amassing "profits" for themselves. Humanitarian economics, on the other hand, for which I stand, rules out "profits" altogether. But it rules out 'deficit' no less for the simple reason that it is utterly impossible to safe-guard a religious institution by following a policy of dead loss. That is the reason why in spite of our 1,500 *goshalas* we have not only failed to protect the cow but its slaughter is day by day on the increase. If in spite of this we delude ourselves into the belief that we have done our duty by the cow by establishing these homes for cattle, and remain snugly self-satisfied there, whatever comfort it may give us, it won't bring us one whit nearer the goal of cow protection, whereas it can be demonstrably shown that by adopting the policy that I have suggested we can easily realise this goal. It does not require much effort to see that but for the fact that the cow yields us milk, the duty of cow protection would not have come into being at all. There are a host of other innocent animals besides the cow in the world but nobody has ever thought of setting up their protection as a religious obligation, and if somebody had attempted it, it would have simply remained a dead-letter. We have use for the cow. That is why it has become religiously incumbent on us to protect it.

To turn now to the questionaire drawn up by my critic, I will embody the questions in my answers without reproducing them separately.

1. Every *goshala* or *panjrapole* should have a tannery

adequate to its needs attached to it. In other words, the manager in charge of every such institution should have a thorough knowledge of the immediate steps necessary for utilising the remains of dead cattle. If this is done, the question, *viz.*, how many heads of cattle should a particular *goshala* contain, won't arise at all.

2. I do not know what the rate of mortality of cattle in a *goshala* is, nor is it relevant to my proposition. So long as there is a single head of cattle in a *goshala*, its manager ought to know how to dispose of its remains after it is dead, just as he is expected to know how to look after it while it is alive.

3. Such humanitarian institutions for the protection of cattle as I have described should normally take charge of the remains of the cattle that might die in the village. Therein lies the interest of the cattle, the depressed classes and the general public alike. In villages where there are no *goshalas* or the concomitant tanneries, some local person who believes in cow protection should take it upon himself to get the carcasses removed to the nearest tannery or get the preliminary processes performed upon it and send the useful parts there.

4. The establishment of such tanneries as I have described does not require much capital out-lay. Only some initial expenditure would be needed to train up workers for this work.

5. It is true that at present the leather prepared from slaughtered hides is superior in quality to that prepared from dead hides. But during the late war the Government of India spent enormous sums of money to improve the quality of leather from dead hides; and tannery experts have told me that dead hides can be tanned into as good leather as leather from slaughtered hides. I myself am conducting experiments in this direction. In Cuttack, Sjt. Madhusudan Das has been doing the same for a number of years and with success as he tells me. The Calcutta Government Research Tannery is also at present engaged in similar experiments.

But the tragedy of it today is that we annually export crores worth of hides to foreign countries, and by ignorantly using leather goods made from the hides of slaughtered cattle, become indirectly participators in the sin of their slaughter.

It rests in our hands entirely to prevent the export of hides of our dead cattle to foreign countries. And this we can easily do by bringing the export trade in hides under our control through the establishment of tanneries on altruistic lines. We can not only save nine crores of rupees annually to our country but by employing that sum properly save a countless number of cattle.

I need hardly say that the humanitarian tanneries that I have suggested would also be utilising the bones and other useful parts of the dead cattle. In fact it is more necessary than ever.

3rd November, 1927

NEED FOR SELF-CONVERSION

BY M. K. GANDHI

Lokamanya gave us his message in four simple words. But there are even now people who question the proposition that Swaraj is their birth-right even as there are some who question the existence of God. The Swaraj movement, therefore, is a movement to make us realise that Swaraj is our birth-right. In the midst of the many reminders that we already have of the existence of this need of self-conversion, the debate in the Madras Legislative Council on the Neill Statue Satyagraha came as an additional and emphatic reminder of that need. The innocent resolution asking for the removal of the offending statue was lost by an overwhelming majority. Almost all the Indian members, except the stalwarts, voted against the resolution. The motion showed the sharp difference between the Swarajist mentality and every other. This vote and the debate are a fresh demonstration of the fact that Swaraj is delayed not so much by the obstinacy of the English 'rulers' as by our own refusal to recognise and work for our status. This agitation for the removal of the Neill statue is, in my humble opinion, a step towards our goal. National self-respect demands the removal not only of the Neill statue but of every emblem of our slavery, as I regard this statue to be. The agitation gains force by reason of the fact that it has no material gain as its objective. Swaraj will be within easy reach when millions of Indians unite in sacrificing themselves for the vindication of mere self-respect. Why does an Englishman feel personally insulted by, and would die in the attempt to resent, an insult offered to the Union Jack? It is not a sentiment to be despised or curbed. The method he adopts to resent the wrong is no doubt often barbarous, but if he ceased to cherish the sentiment itself, he would lose national solidarity and the power of sacrificing himself for the nation to which he belongs Even so, if we were conscious of our birth-right, it should be a matter for pride for us to know that there are young men who resent the presence in our midst of a statue that is an insult to the nation. Many Indian members who took part in the debate betrayed no such consciousness or pride. To them the young men who were fighting the nation's battle were ignorant men whose conduct was worthy only of condemnation. They saw nothing wrong in the statue standing in a prominent public place where there should be statues only of national heroes whose lives would inspire and ennoble the nation.

It cannot be too clearly pointed out that this Satyagraha is not aimed at General Neill as man. It would be just as appropriate and necessary if instead of General Neill it was General Virsingh whose statue was erected in order to prepetuate a reign of 'frightfulness.'

There was in the debate a defence of the statue offered on behalf of the Europeans. It was cautiously, temperately and plausibly worded. Nevertheless it betrayed the European mentality. That for which General Neill stood was necessary for saving the Empire. And in order to cover the misdeeds of General Neill, it became necessary for the defender to vote down Mr. Thompson the author of *The Other Side of the Medal* as a neurotic, and to unearth a fulsome address presented to General Neill's regiment by 110 Hindus of Madras two years after the Mutiny. I have no means of ascertaining the circumstances in which the address was presented, but it does not appear to me to be at all strange that such an address was presented. For it is possible to quote such instances from contemporary events. Was not General Dyer presented with a similar address in Amritsar itself? And it would be strange if even now Sir Michael O'Dwyer, if he returned to India, did not find 110 Indians to present an address to him, if it was found necessary in the interest of good Government. Have not the most unpopular Viceroys received addresses and trophies in our own times?

It is a matter of great pity to find Englishmen applaud sentiments in us which they would be ashamed to see expressed by Englishmen. I remember the wife of a Governor leading loud applause at a conference at which in speaking to a resolution on loyalty a learned Indian permitted himself to say that he considered every Britisher to be his teacher and that he owed all he was to Britain. The Madras performance was somewhat after that style and it grieved me.

But let not the adverse vote of the Madras Council discourage the young men who are fighting the battle against symbols of terrorism They must not be angry against either Englighmen or the Indians who are now opposing the agitation. They must have faith in themselves and their cause, and they will convert the very men who are now opposing them. The agitation, of which they have laid the foundation, is bound to succeed, if they will keep it strictly non-violent and within the prescribed limits.

3rd November, 1927

THE THEORY AND PRACTICE OF SATYAGRAHA

By M. K. Gandhi.

[*The following is taken from an article by Gandhiji contributed to the Golden Number of Indian Opinion which was issued in 1914 as a souvenir of the eight years' Satyagraha in South Africa. V. G. D.*]

Carried out to its utmost limit, Satyagraha is independent of pecuniary or other material assistance; certainly, even in its elementary form, of physical force or violence. Indeed, violence is the negation of this great spiritual force, which can only be cultivated or wielded by those who will entirely eschew violence. It is a force that may be used by individuals as well as by communities. It may be used as well in political as in domestic affairs. Its universal applicability is a demonstration of its permanence and invincibility. It can be used alike by men, women and children. It is totally untrue to say that it is a force to be used only by the weak so long as they are not capable of meeting violence by violence. This superstition arises from the incompleteness of the English expression, 'passive resistance.' It is impossible for those who consider themselves to be weak to apply this force. Only those who realise that there is something in man which is superior to the brute nature in him and that the latter always yields to it, can effectively be Satyagrahis. This force is to violence, and therefore to all tyranny, all injustice, what light is to darkness. In politics, its use is based upon the immutable maxim, that government of the people is possible only so long as they consent either consciously or unconsciously to be governed We did not want to be governed by the Asiatic Act of 1907 of the Transvaal, and it had to go before this mighty force. Two courses were open to us—to use violence when we were called upon to submit to the Act, or to suffer the penalties prescribed under the Act, and thus to draw out and exhibit the force of the soul within us for a period long enough to appeal to the sympathetic chord in the governors or the law-makers. We have taken long to achieve what we set about striving for. That was because our Satyagraha was not of the most complete type. All Satyagrahis do not understand the full value of the force, nor have we men who always from conviction refrain from violence. The use of this force requires the adoption of poverty, in the sense that we must be indifferent whether we have the wherewithal to feed or clothe ourselves. During the past struggle, all Satyagrahis, if any at all, were not prepared to go that length. Some again were only Satyagrahis so-called. They came without any conviction, often with mixed motives, less often with impure motives. Some even, whilst engaged in the struggle, would gladly have resorted to violence but for most vigilant supervision. Thus it was that the struggle became prolonged; for the exercise of the purest soul-force, in its perfect form, brings about instantaneous relief. For this exercise, prolonged training of the individual soul is an absolute necessity, so that a perfect Satyagrahi has to be almost, if not entirely, a perfect man We cannot all suddenly become such men, but if my proposition is correct—as I know it to be correct—the greater the sprit of Satyagraha in us, the better men will we become. Its use, therefore, is, I think, indisputable, and it is a force which, if it become universal, would revolutionise social ideals and do away with despotisms and the ever-growing militarism under which the nations of the West are groaning and are being almost crushed to death, and which fairly promises to overwhelm even the nations of the East. If the past struggle has produced even a few Indians, who would dedicate themselves to the task of becoming Satyagrahis as nearly perfect as possible, they would not only have served themselves in the truest sense of the term, they would also have served humanity at large. Thus viewed, Satyagraha is the noblest and best education. It should come not after the ordinary education in letters of children, but it should precede it. It will not be denied, that a child before it begins to write its alphabet and to gain wordly knowledge, should know what the soul is, what truth is, what love is, what powers are latent in the soul. It should be an essential of real education that a child should learn, that in the struggle of life, it can easily conquer hate by love, untruth by truth, violence by self-suffering.

10th November, 1927

ESSENTIALS OF HINDU-MUSLIM UNITY

By M. K. Gandhi

(*Gandhiji's Speech at the Jamia Millia Islamia*)

The boys that were just introduced to you are grandsons of my friend and fellow worker who was like blood-brother to me, the late Ahmed Mahomed Kachhalia whom I naturally recall as I see the boys, and about whom I think I had better tell you something. Amongst the Hindus and Musalmans that lived in South Africa in the days of Satyagraha there was not a single Indian who could compare with Kachhalia in his bravery and his integrity. He sacrificed his all for the honour and prestige of his country. He cared not for his business nor for his wealth, nor for his friends, and plunged himself whole-heartedly into the struggle. Even in those days the cursed Hindu-Muslim differences now and then cropped up, but Kachalia held the scales even between the two. No one ever accused him of partiality for his community.

And he had learnt this great virtue of patriotism and tolerance not at any school nor in England, but in his own home, for he wrote even Gujarati with difficulty. Lawyers were amazed at the way in which he met their arguments and puzzled them, and his uncommon commonsense was often very helpful to them. It is he who led the Satyagrahis, and he died in harness. He had a son called Ali whom he had trusted to my care. A lad of 11 he was wonderfully restrained, and a devout Musalman. He never missed a day of fast during the sacred month of Ramzan. And yet he had no ill-will towards Hindu boys. To-day so-called religious devoutness in either is synonymous with a dislike, if not hatred, for other religions. Ali had no such dislike, no hatred. Well, both the father and son are to me names to conjure with, and may their example inspire you.

In those days when Hindus and Musalmans seemed to be one and ready to shed their blood for one another, and for their country, I appealed to the students to leave Government schools and colleges. The many years that have passed have left me utterly unrepentant for having asked those boys to come out of those institutions, and I am firmly of opinion that those who responded to the call served their land, and I am sure the future historian of India will record their sacrifice with approval.

I am glad to find here some of the traces of those proud days, and I am very happy that you are trying your utmost to keep the flag flying. Your number is small, but the world never overflowed with good and true men. I ask you not to worry yourselves about the smallness of the number, but to remember that however few you may be the freedom of the country depends on you. Freedom has very little to do with your learning the letters or even with mere mechanical plying of the *takli*. If you have not the things essential for the freedom of India, I do not know who else has them. Those things are fear of God and freedom from fear of any man or a combination of men called an Empire. If training in these two essentials cannot be had in your institutions, I do not know where else it can be had. But I know your professors, I know Hakim-saheb, and I am sure that these two essentials are being very carefully taught.

I do not mind the unsatisfactory state of your finances. In fact I am glad that we should be living from hand to mouth, so that we may all the better cherish our Maker and fear him.

Hakimji was quite right when he said that it was difficult for me to come to Delhi. But to come to you was a solace and a comfort. It is not to please you that I came here, but to please myself. I came with a selfish end in view, and that is to tell you that in spite of the storm of hatred and poison raging outside your Millia, in spite of the Muslim running at the Hindu's throat and *vice versa*, you boys here will keep your heads cool, will not deny your Maker, will give no room in your hearts to hatred, nor even in your mind gloat over the country and its religions going to wreck and ruin. That's the only hope that has drawn me to you.

You will have noticed that I have said nothing about Khadi or *takli*. That is because even Khadi and *takli* are nothing before the essentials I have talked to you about. You may ply your *taklis*, and wear Khadi, but if you do not do the things I have told you, your Khadi and *takli* will be of no account But you will, I am sure, not forget what Hakimsaheb has told you about the necessity of wearing Khaddar. You will bear in mind that it is by means of Khadi that we are supporting 50,000 spinners to-day besides hundreds of weavers, washermen, carpenters etc. Do not forget that many of these are Musalmans. Without the charkha; the Musalman women in many places would have been starving. There is no other way of identifying yourselves with the Hindu and Muslim poor than that of wearing Khadi.

Above all keep yourselves pure and clean, and learn to keep your promises even at the cost of life, and have the memory of examples I have cited to you ever green in your hearts.

10th November, 1927

WAS IT A FAILURE?

BY M. K. GANDHI

Repeatedly does one read in the papers that non-co-operation was a perfect failure. Several courteous critics often apologetically broach the question in conversations, and gently tell me that the country would have made great progress if I had not led it astray by my ill-conceived non-co-operation. I should not refer to this subject, which may be said to have no bearing in the politics of the day, but for my belief that non-co-operation has come to us as an active force that may assume a universal form any moment, and but for the purpose of re-assuring those who are bravely holding on in the face of criticism and skepticism. Let me, however, admit the dangerous half-truth that non-co-operation entirely failed the moment it became violent. Indeed, non-co-operation and violence are here contradictory terms. It is a living belief that violence lived on itself and it required counter-violence for its daily maintenance, that gave rise to non-violent non-co-operation. The fact, therefore, is that the moment non-co-operation became violent, it lost its vitality and nation-building character. But in so far as it was and remained non-violent, it was a demonstrably complete success. The mass awakening that took place in 1920 all of a sudden was perhaps the greatest demonstration of the efficacy of non-violence. The Government has lost prestige never to be regained. Titles, law-courts, educational institutions no longer inspire the awe they did in 1920. Some of the best lawyers in the country have given up law for ever as a profession and are happy for having accepted comparative poverty as their lot. The few national schools and colleges that remain are giving a good account of themselves as witness the great organisation that came into being in Gujarat when the floods turned into a waste what was once a rich garden. But for the students and teachers of national institutions and other non-co-operators the timely help that the afflicted peasantry of Gujarat received and so much needed would never have been at its disposal. It is possible to multiply illustrations of this character and prove that wherever there is real national life, a bond between the classes and masses in India, non-co-operation is the cause of it.

Take again the three constructive items of the programme. Khadi is a growing factor in national regeneration and is serving over 1,500 villages through an army of nearly two thousand workers and is giving tangible productive relief to over fifty thousand spinners and at least ten thousand weavers, printers, dyers, *dhobis* and other artisans. Untouchability is a waning thing just struggling for existence. Hindu-Muslim unity of 1920-21 showed its vast possibilities. The violence, deceit, falsehood and the like that mark the rupture between the two great communities to-day are no doubt ugly signs, but they are a demonstration of crude self-consciousness. The process of churning that the movement of non-co-operation was and is has brought the dirt to the surface. And if non-violent non-co-operation is a living and purifying force, it will presently bring to view the pure unity that is invisibly forming itself under the very visible dirt that obtrudes itself to our gaze to-day. It is therefore clear to me as daylight that real Swaraj, whenever it comes to us, will have to be not a donation rained on us from London, but a prize earned by hard and health-giving non-co-operation with organised forces of evil.

10th November, 1927

SACRED v. OBSCENE

Sjt. S. D. Nadkarni writes:

"With reference to Miss Mayo's remark about the Vaishnava mark having an obscene meaning (quoted by you in your article on her book), I am enclosing an extract from Vivekanand's writings which may interest you and readers of *Young India*:

'One sect has one particular form of ritual, and thinks that that is holy, while the rituals of another sect are simply arrant superstition. If one sect worships a peculiar sort of symbol, another sect says, Oh, it is horrible. Take for instance a general form of symbol. The phallus symbol is certainly a sexual symbol, but gradually that aspect of it has been forgotten, and it stands now as a symbol of the Creator. Those nations which have this as their symbol, never think of it as the phallus; it is just a symbol, and there it ends. But a man from another race or creed sees in it nothing but the phallus, and begins to condemn it; yet at the same time he may be doing something which to the so-called phallic worshippers appears most horrible. Let me take two points for illustration, the phallus symbol and the sacrament of the Christians. To the Christians the phallus is horrible, and to the Hindus the Christian sacrament is horrible. They say that the Christian sacrament, the killing of a man and the eating of his flesh and the drinking of his blood to get the good qualities of that man, is cannibalism. This is what some of the savage tribes do; if a man is brave, they kill him and eat his heart, because they think that it will give them the qualities of courage and bravery possessed by that man. Even such a devout Christian as Sir John Lubbock admits this, and says that the origin of this Christian symbol is in this savage idea. The Christians, of course, do not admit this view of its origin; and what it may imply never comes to their mind. It stands for a holy thing, and that is all they want to know.' So even in rituals there is no universal symbol, which can command general recognition and acceptance.' "

10th November, 1927

HEALTH HINTS

[*There is much that is full of wisdom and commonsense in that slender little volume by the Countess of Asquith—Lay Sermons. I cull a few acute observations on the preservation of health, based as they are on experience, and the experience of one who has suffered from most of the ailments of the rich.* *M. D.*]

" Most of the minor ailments—particularly among women—debility, anaemia, nerves, vapours and indigestion come from lack of occupation. This was noticeable during the War, when females who had never been tired of discussing their symptoms worked like beavers, and what with little sleep and less food added 50 per cent. to their general health.

"If doctors had the wits to suggest work instead of rest, their recommendations would have immediate results. Unfortunately, it is the fashion among medical men to-day to say we are all overworked, and their mistaken guidance finds many a fool to follow them. From my own observation I can truly say, few, if any, normal beings that I have ever known have been hurt by too much work."

"Most men and women eat, drink and sleep too much to keep their minds active or their bodies healthy. Children are seldom as greedy as grown-up people, and know with greater precision when they have eaten enough. I am amazed by observing how much time people spend of their lives in eating and drinking, and how careless they are as to what they swallow. They will pile their plates with bright green peas and India-rubber mushrooms out of tins with a courage that deserves the Victoria Cross, and are surprised when their stomachs or their complexions become like solitaire boards.

"It is an undisputed fact that the more you eat the more you want to eat, and starvation—though not recognised by doctors—is a safe cure for half the maladies that attack mankind. I do not think there are many societies to prevent people from over-eating, but it is high time that some of the enthusiastic fanaticism levelled against alcohol could be enlisted against meat.

"The rich and vain, finding themselves growing fat, empty their stomachs once a year in Germany, but having thus salved their conscience and diminished their weight, they return to the same way of living as they did before, and I have hardly a friend or a contemporary who has preserved an active and elastic figure.

"In this country you can write, talk and speak in public about birth-control, unnatural vices, and venereal diseases—almost any eschewed subject—but you may not mention constipation, and yet no one of my experience will deny that most of our bodily sufferings come from insufficient drainage, and poisoned intestines. You may evade, elude or fight shy of this proposition, but sooner or later you will have to face it. The average person in my class (whatever that may be) has three, if not four meals a day— breakfast, lunch, tea and dinner; some have no tea and some have late supper instead of dinner; be that as it may, they fill their stomachs three times a day, and think themselves injured if they do not spend at least eight hours in bed, whether asleep or awake. In spite of this, whether from lack of care or culpable ignorance, Nature is solicited capriciously, with the most disastrous consequences. Busy men and lazy women are unable to take enough exercise to open the pores of their skins, and an unobserved but steady process of poisoning sets in which is the starting point of many of the maladies which prove fatal in later life.

"When you hear of cancer-houses, you ask about the drains; but it would be more to the purpose to ask about the drainage of the victims than of the building. We may be on the eve of a great scientific discovery in connection with cancer, but in the meantime little is known about it. It is a step forward to learn in what part of the world certain intestinal afflictions seldom occur, and it is possible that, if people were more observant and at an early age of cancer could be influenced to tell men of science as much as they could of their diet and habits, it would be more valuable than all the experiments made upon rats and rabbits.

"After the age of forty no one needs as much food, drink or sleep as they did in their youth. It is a platitude to say they are exceptions; but when middle-aged people tell me they could not live without eight or nine hours' sleep, I answer they should be grateful if they can get six, and seven is enough for the majority of mankind. Bad nerves are not so much rejuvenated by sleep as by fresh air and a kind of repose that —though difficult—can be cultivated. Some of the strongest people I have known have been bad sleepers, and nothing conduces so much to healthy sleep as well-regulated bowels.

"The Lord Mayor of Cork lived from the 12th of August 1920 till the 25th of October of the same year without food, but he was kept warm in bed, and his doctors gave him mild aperients. Reading this made me realise for the first time that if eating nothing could accumulate poison, how much more danger there must be in overfeeding!

"Holy men in monasteries live to a ripe old age and spend most of their nights in prayer or meditation, and some of them are highly intelligent, whereas animals are asleep for longer hours than they are awake. Although sleeping too much cannot be said to be a danger, it is a disadvantage. . . . Sleep, like everything else, is a matter of habit, and although one can lay down no fixed rules, the more you accustom yourself to do without it the more alert you will be.

"Christian science has arrogated to itself powers of healing which are contradictory to commonsense.

"Ever since the world was inhabited men have interpreted God differently—one may say, without irreverence, that God has been made in the image of man—but the Christian scientists have made Him in the image of woman. You might have supposed that not being gifted with the highest kind of imagination, women could have armed themselves with penetrating logic, but Christian science undeceives you. Pushed to its logical conclusion, you can jump off a roof without being hurt. The practice of it never makes you sensible and seldom makes you kind. In my own experience I have seen it separate the dying from their parents, the loving from their loved; and by ignoring the discoveries that have inspired generations of scientific men for the alleviation of suffering, it has irritated the living, imposed upon the dying and shortened life. I hope I am tolerant of all creeds and faiths, and I do not suppose the Almighty cares by which road we come to Him as long as we come; nevertheless, there is a fine sound in the words: 'Thou shalt have none other gods but Me', and we need not presume that because God is good He is good-natured.

"But neither Faith-cures, Gold-cures, Rest-cures, cures in

Germany, sanatorium, suggestion, or doctors will ensure health. Nor can anything avail the nerves, the mind, or the body when tempers have been aroused. There is only one form of suggestion that never fails, and that is embodied in my text which forbids you to withhold forgiveness—'Let not the sun go down upon your wrath.'"

17th November, 1927

A COTTON QUOTATION

BY M. K. GANDHI

[*Mr. Richard Gregg, with whose name the reader of Young India is familiar as the joint author of the booklet on Takli Spinning, sends the following useful old quotation which he has unearthed in the course of his researches.* M. K. G.]

Quotation from *A Voyage to the East Indies* by Fra Paolino da San Bartolomeo, Member of the Academy of Velitti and formerly Professor of Oriental Languages in the Propaganda at Rome. From observations made during a residence of thirteen years, between 1776 and 1789 in Districts little frequented by Europeans. Printed in Rome originally in 1796. Translated into German in 1798. Translated from German into English by William Johnson, London, 1800.

Pages 396 to 400.

"Cotton, in Portuguese *Algodao* and in Latin *Gossipium*, is, in the Malabar language, called *Cerupagni*. A coarser sort, produced by the tree *Ilava*, is called, by the natives of Malabar, *Pagni*. The *Ilava* is a large lofty tree, and the cotton it yields is employed only for mattresses and bolsters. That which grows on the shrub *Parutti* is much finer. Both kinds are contained in an oval capsule divided into different small cells, and called by the French *La Coque*. The best cotton grows in Bengal and on the coast of Coromandel; and hence it happens that the cotton articles procured from these districts are the finest. The next in quality are those manufactured in the provinces of Madura, Marava, and on the coasts of

Pescaria and Malabar. The gradation proceeds thus to Canara, where the cotton is not spun so fine, and the articles consequently are much coarser.

"The shrub *Parutti*, which produces the finer kind of cotton, requires in India little cultivation or care; and the tree *Ilava* requires none at all. The former thrives best on the high mountainous districts, the latter in the flat open country. When the cotton has been gathered, it is thrown upon a floor and threshed, in order that it may be separated from the black seeds and the bushes which served it as a covering. It is then put into bags, or tied up in bales, containing from 300 to 320 *Aratel*, or pounds of fifteen ounces each. After it has been carded, it is spun out into such delicate threads that a piece of cotton cloth twenty yards in length may almost be concealed in the hollow of both hands. 'Most of these pieces of cloth are twice washed; others remain as they come from the loom, and are dipped in coco-nut oil, in order that they may be longer preserved. It is customary also to draw them through *Cangi*, or rice-water, that they may acquire more smoothness and body. The *Cangi* is sometimes applied to cotton articles in so ingenious a manner that purchasers are often deceived, and imagine the cloth to be much stronger than it really is; for, as soon as it is washed, the *Cangi* vanishes, and the cloth appears quite slight and thin.'

"There are reckoned to be no less than twenty-two different kinds of cotton articles manufactured in India, without including muslin or coloured stuffs. The latter are not, as in Europe, printed by means of wooden blocks, but painted with a brush made of the fibres of the rind of the coco-nut, which, when beat, approaches near to horse-hair; becomes very elastic, and can be formed into any shape the painter chooses. The colours employed are indigo, *Indaco*, *Anil*, or *Coachan*, all appellations borrowed from foreign languages; and which signify not a shrub as some have erroneously asserted, but a plant which grows in great abundance in the district of Agra, and in other places of India. The stem and leaves of this plant yield that beautiful dark blue with which the Indian chintzes, coverlets, *tappisendis* and other articles are painted, and which never loses the smallest shade of its beauty. Also *terra merita*, called *Curcuma* or Indian saffron, a plant which dyes yellow; and, in the last place, gumlac, together with some flowers, roots and fruits, which are used to dye red. With these few pigments, which are applied sometimes singly and sometimes mixed, the Indians produce on their cotton cloths that admirable and beautiful painting which exceeds everything of the kind exhibited in Europe.

"The French, English and Dutch have endeavoured to imitate these articles; but, notwithstanding all their labour and art, they have never yet been able either to produce these colours from the Vegetable Kingdom, or to attain to the same fineness in their cloth. No person in Turkey, Persia or Europe has yet imitated the Betille,* made at *Masulipatan* and known under the name of *Organdi* The manufacturing of this cloth, which was known in the time of Job, the painting of it, and the preparation of the colours, give employment in India to male and female, young and old.

"*It may with truth be asserted, that in spinning, weaving, and dyeing the Indians excel all other nations in the world.* A great deal of cotton is brought from Arabia and Persia, and mixed with that of India. The principal places where it is manufactured are: Bengal, Masulipatan, Paleacote, Madras, Sadras Pondicherri, Naur, Magapatnam, Paleamcotta, Tutticuri, Manapar, and Tiruvancoda. The Indians work slowly and unwillingly; a fault which is of great benefit to the Europeans. Were they more active and industrious, they would innundate our quarter of the world with their merchandize, and draw from us the little money still in circulation. We clothe ourselves in their stuffs, while our woollen cloths are to them unnecessary. On the contrary, we must pay money for all the goods which we procure from India and China; so that these two countries may be compared to two pits, in which

* A certain kind of white East Indian chintz.

we stand with both feet and still sink deeper. Pliny in ancient times complained of the luxury of his countrymen,† who procured similar articles from the island of *Taprobane*, now called Ceylon; but what would he say were he now alive and beheld our extravagance? *Woe to the people who are not contented with the productions of their native country!*"

In the preface to the German translation of this book, the translator wrote: "It is the more valuable, as the author understood the Tamulie or common Malabar language; and what is of more importance, was so well acquainted with the Samscred, (a language exceedingly difficult,) as to be able to write a grammar of it, which was published at Rome in 1790. It appears from some of his quotations, that he understood also English and French."

17th November, 1927

YOKE OF FOREIGN MEDIUM

By M. K. Gandhi

A friend sends me the following interesting extract from Mr. E. Sherman Oakley's 'Holy Himalaya', published in 1905:

"The Almora boys show great readiness in acquiring knowledge, and for several years have passed the examinations well and taken high places in the lists. The proficiency is no doubt due to the hill climate, which ought to give them superior energy. As an Indian educationist of some experience, I can testify that the Indian student is nowise lacking in mental powers. There are causes which go far to explain the somewhat unsatisfactory results of Anglo-Vernacular education in the country, and they are causes more clearly visible to the practical workers in the field than to the theorists whose opinions are mostly heard on the subject. The attempt to make the student do his thinking in a foreign language has naturally the effect of repressing originality and encouraging methods of cram which is still further fostered by the hard and

† Lib. VI, Cap. 17 et 22.

fast rules of the Education Department, which prescribes 'courses' and attempts to lay down the whole scheme of school teaching with the minutest particularity. This may be a help to indifferent or to incompetent teaching, but hampers the real teacher. . . . Great number of students are very poor. It is the poor, in fact, who seek knowledge in order to make a living. Insufficiently fed and clothed and lodged, the body languishes and the brain misses the nourishment that is essential to healthy and vigorous thinking. Yet, with all these adverse conditions, the achievements of Indian students often strike one with admiration. Scotland herself cannot show greater marvels of dogged persistence and patient heroism than the story of many an obscure Indian scholar. It is a common charge against Indian education that there is no 'pursuit of knowledge for its own sake'. This phrase has indeed become almost too familiar. It may be asked how many European students, who have a living to make, with perhaps several helpless beings dependent on them, and a difficult foreign language to master before they can even begin to see their goal in sight, would be found to cherish this wonderful but exceedingly rare 'love of knowledge for its own sake.' Education not being compulsory in India, most students are struggling youths who have to make their living. The rich either do not study, or pursue knowledge in their own way and in accordance with their native tastes, as might naturally be expected. The imposition of a foreign language as the medium of all higher education has cast somewhat of a blight on the national genius. Had the native languages been allowed a fair chance, they would in all likelihood by this time have developed some worthy literature and scientific phraseology of their own, instead of remaining in their undeveloped condition. A further result of 'English education in India is that it has led to an idea that the aim of school and college life is to get Government service—only that and nothing more. This notion has been fostered, indeed created, by Government itself making school and university examinations the test and qualification for its service. The result is that English education is regarded simply as a means of obtaining employment in some Government office, and there is almost a total absence of the much desiderated 'love of knowledge for its own sake' in connection with our schools and colleges. A still further result is the growth of a class of English-educated men whose numbers are vastly in excess of the requirements of Government, yet who have worked only with the object of winning a post under Government and consequently consider themselves ill-treated and deceived if they cannot succeed in their object, pursued often, as it has been, under such discouraging circumstances and with such amazing persistence. An official in Kumaon recently declared that he could not leave his house without finding an 'Entrance pass' standing under every tree along the road, with a petition in his hand for employment in a Government office.

"It is too late in the day now to attempt to reverse entirely the policy of English education adopted half a century ago under Macaulay's influence. For good and ill it must remain and the best must be made of it, as indeed Lord Curzon's Government is seeking to do by its careful inquiry into the conditions of secondary training, and by its recent University Act. But still the conviction remains with many of us that education conducted generally in a foreign tongue must fail to bring out the best that is in the scholars, and must remain more of a formula than a real eliciting of the natural powers of the mind. The difficulty in the way of employing the native languages for purposes of instruction is the very practical one that the Government and its Education Department is a foreign importation, and the impossibility of obtaining officers and teachers of the best Western training who are at the same time proficient in those languages. But it appears reasonable enough to hope that in course of time these conditions will remedy themselves, through the growth of a body of native savants of patriotic spirit who will make modern knowledge a common possession of the Indians, instead of a monopoly of the 'English-educated.'

When this knowledge is led to flow in its natural channels, as a part of the speech of the people, it will be much more widely diffused, and will become the source of a real national progress. Then, if ever, there will be the love of knowledge for its own sake, and the confusion which has led to education being regarded as merely a purveyor of bread will become a thing of the past. The love of knowledge was once strong enough in India, and may be so again. The anxiety to obtain Government service will no doubt be modified in time, as other openings for the employment of talent are found. It is a mistake, however, to suppose, as many Europeans do, that crowds of youths are being educated by the Government and the missionaries almost in spite of themselves and taken out of their natural hereditary rank and calling. The boys who attend high schools and secure English education are after all only a small percentage of the population, and are mostly the sons of Brahmins, Kayasths etc., who are really dependent on clerical and official work for a means of livelihood. The remedy for the surplusage of educated men in India is not to restrict education, which no civilised Government can do, but to develop and revive the trade, resources, and manufactures of the country so as to furnish other and varied avenues of employment for all the available ability in the land."

There is nothing new in the above extract for the readers of these pages. But it comes as a fresh reminder of how the foreign medium has stunted the growth of the youth of the country as the foreign rule has stunted the growth of the nation.

17th November, 1927

VARNASHRAMA AND ITS DISTORTION

By M. K. Gandhi

The reader will find in another column Sjt. Nadkarni's interesting letter on the Brahman non-Brahmin question. I gladly respond to his invitation to explain my views on *varnashrama* more fully than I have done in my speeches during the recent Tamil Nad tour, which have been more or less fully reproduced in these columns.

Let me clear the issue by dismissing from consideration the celebrated story of a Shudra said to have had his head cut off by Rama by reason of his having dared to become a Sannyasi. I do not read Shastras literally, certainly not as history. The story of the decapitation of Shambuka is not in keeping with the general character of Rama. And whatever may be said in the various Ramayanas, I hold my Rama to be incapable of having decapitated a Shudra or for that matter any one else. The story of Shambuka, if it proves anything, proves that in the days when the story arose it was held to be a capital crime for Shudras to perform certain rites. We are in the dark as to the meaning of the word Shudra here. I have heard even an allegorical meaning given to the whole version. But that would not alter the fact of certain unreasonable prohibitions operating against the Shudras at some stage in the evolution of Hinduism. Only I do not need to join Sjt. Nadkarni in doing penance for the alleged decapitation of Shambuka, for I do not believe in a historical person by that name having been decapitated by a historical person called Rama. For the general persecution of the so-called lower orders of Hinduism, especially the so-called untouchables, I am as a Hindu doing penance every moment of my life. In my opinion illustrations like that of Shambuka have no place in a religious consideration of the question of *varnashrama*. I propose therefore merely to say what I believe to be *varnashrama*, and I should not hesitate to reject the institution if it was proved to me that the interpretation put upon it by me has no warrant in Hinduism. *Varna* and *ashrama* are, as Sjt. Nadkarni says, two different words. The institution of four *ashramas* enables one the better to fulfil the purpose of life for which the law of *varna* is a necessity. The law of *varna* prescribes that a person should, for his living, follow the lawful occupation of his forefathers. I hold this to be a universal law governing the human family Its breach entails as it has entailed serious consequence for us. But the vast majority of men unwittingly follow the hereditary occupation of their fathers. Hinduism rendered a great service to mankind by the discovery of and conscious obedience to this law. If man's as distinguished from lower animals' function is to know God, it follows that he must not devote the chief part of his life to making experiments in finding out what occupation will best suit him for earning his livelihood On the contrary, he will recognise that it is best for him to follow his father's occupation, and devote his spare time and talent to qualifying himself for the task to which mankind is called.

Here then the difficulty suggested by my correspondent does not arise. For no one is precluded from rendering multitudinous acts of voluntary service and qualifying oneself for it. Thus Sjt. Nadkarni born of Brahman parents and I born of Vaishya parents may consistently with the law of *varna* certainly serve as honorary national volunteers or as honorary nurses or honorary scavengers in times of need, though in obedience to that law he as a Brahman would depend for his bread on the charity of his neighbours and I as a Vaishya would be earning my bread by selling drugs or groceries Every one is free to render any useful service so long as he does not claim reward for it

In this conception of the law of *varna* no one is superior to any other. All occupations are equal and honourable in so far as they are not in conflict with morals private or public. A scavenger has the same status as a Brahman Was it not Max Muller who said that it was in Hinduism more than in any other religion that life was no more and no less than Duty?

There is no doubt that at some stages of its evolution Hinduism suffered corruption, and the canker of superiority and inferiority entered and vitiated it But this notion of inequality seems to me to be wholly against the spirit of sacrifice which dominates every thing in Hinduism. There is no room for arrogation of superiority by one class over another in a scheme of life based on *ahimsa* whose active form is undefiled love for all life

Let it not be said against this law of *varna* that it makes life dull and robs it of all ambition. In my opinion the law of *varna* alone makes life livable by *all* and restores to ambition the only object worthy of it, namely self-realisation To-day we seem to think of and strive for material pursuits which are in their very nature transitory, and we do this almost to the exclusion of the one thing needful.

If I am told that the interpretation put by me upon *varna* is not supported by anything to be found in the Smritis which are codified Hindu conduct, my answer is that the codes of conduct based upon fundamental invariable maxims of life vary from time to time, as we gain fresh experience and make fresh observations. It is possible to show many rules of the Smritis which we no longer recognise as binding or even worthy of observance. Invariable maxims are few and common to all religions The latter vary in their application And no religion has exhausted the varieties of all possible applications. They must expand with the expansion of ideas and knowledge of new facts. Indeed I believe that the contents of words grow with the growth of human experience The connotation of the words sacrifice, truth, non-violence, *varnashrama* &c is infinitely richer to-day than it was during the known historic past. Applying this principle to the word *varna,* we need not be bound, it would be foolish and wrong to be bound, by the current interpretation, assuming that it is inconsistent with the requirements of the age or with our notions of morals To do otherwise will be suicide.

Varna considered in the manner above indicated has nothing in common with caste as we know it to-day, nor is prohibition as to interdining and intermarriage an essential part of the recognition of the law of *varna.* That these prohibitions were introduced for the conservation of *varnas* is possible Restrictions against promiscuous marriage are necessary in any scheme of of life based on self-restraint. Restraints on promiscuous dining arise either from sanitary considerations or differences in habits. But disregard of these restrictions formerly carried, or what is more, should now carry no social or legal punishment or forfeiture of one's *varna*.

Varnas were originally four. It was an intelligent and intelligible division. But the number is no part of the law of *varna*. A tailor for instance may not become a blacksmith although both may be and should be classed as *Vaishyas*.

The most forcible objection I heard raised in Tamil Nad was, that however good and innocuous *varnas* might appear under my interpretation, they must either be worked under a different name or destroyed altogether by reason of the evil odour that surrounded them. The objectors feared that my interpretation would be ignored and yet my authority would be freely quoted for supporting under cover of *varna* the hideous inequalities and tyrannies practised at the present day in Hinduism. They further observed that in the popular estimation caste and *varna* were mere synonymous terms and that the restraint of *varna* was nowhere practised, but the tyranny of caste was rampant everywhere. All these objections have no doubt much force in them. But they are objections such as can be advanced against many corrupted institutions that once were good. A reformer's business is to examine the institution itself and to set about reforming it, if its abuses can be separated from it. *Varna* is however not a mere institution made by man but it is a law discovered by him. It cannot therefore be set aside; its hidden meaning and potentialities should be explored and utilised for the good of society. We have seen that the evil is not in the law or the institution itself, but it lies in the doctrine of superiority and inferiority which are superadded to it.

The question too arises how the law is to be worked in these days when all the four *varnas* or *sub-varnas* break asunder all the restrictions, seeking by all means lawful and otherwise to advance their material welfare, and when some arrogate superiority over others who in their turn are rightly challenging the claim. The law will work itself out even if we ignore it. But that will be the way of punishment. If we will escape destruction, we will submit to it. And seeing that we are just now engaged in applying to ourselves the sub-human rule of survival of the fittest meaning the strongest (physically), it would be well to recognise ourselves as one *varna*, *viz.*, Shudras even though some may be teaching and some may be soldiering and some others may be engaged in commercial pursuits. I remember in 1915 the Chairman at the Social Conference in Nellore suggesting that formerly all were Brahmans, and that now too all should be recognised as such and that the other *varnas* should be abolished. It appeared to be then, as it appears to me now, as a weird suggestion. It is the so-called superior that has to descend from his heights, if the reform is to be peaceful. Those who for ages have been *trained* to consider themselves as the lowest in the social scale cannot suddenly have the equipment of the so-called higher classes. They can therefore rise to *power* only by bloodshed, in other words by destroying society itself. In the scheme of reconstruction I have in view, no mention has been made of the untouchables, for I find no place for untouchability in the law of *varna* or otherwise in Hinduism. They in common with the rest will be absorbed in the Shudras. Out of these the other three *varnas* will gradually emerge purified and equal in status though differing in occupations. The Brahmans will be very few. Fewer still will be the soldier class who will not be the hirelings of the unrestrained rulers of to-day, but real protectors and trustees of the nation laying down their lives for its service. The fewest will be the Shudras for in a well-ordered society a minimum amount of labour will be taken from fellowmen. The most numerous will be the Vaishyas—a *varna* that would include all professions—the agriculturists, the traders, the artisans &c. This scheme may sound utopian. I however prefer to live in this utopia of my imagination to trying to live up to the unbridled licence of a society that I see tottering to its disruption. It is surely given to individuals to live their own utopias even though they may not be able to see them accepted by society. Every reform has made its beginning with the individual, and that which had inherent vitality and the backing of a stout soul was accepted by the society in whose midst the reformer lived.

24th November, 1927

BRAHMAN NON-BRAHMAN QUESTION

(*A Catechism*)

During Gandhiji's tour in South India non-Brahman friends in various places sought interviews with him, and discussed the various aspects of the Brahman non-Brahman question. The same questions were often asked at various places, but the scope of the answers depended on the receptivity of the questioners at each place. I have brought all of them together, and arranged them in the form of a catechism. This covers all the talks in Tanjore, Chettinad, Virudhunagar and Tinnevelly. I was not present during the conversations at Madura, but I think the collected talks will cover the topics discussed there also. I omit, of course, the references to the question in public speeches at Cuddalore, Tanjore and Coimbatore which I have already given in these pages, and I omit also talks already summarised, as for instance the one at Tirupur on superiority and inferiority. M. D.

Gandhiji—I want you to make your position clear to me, as I do not want to be told that I refuse to try to understand or sympathise with your view-point. The impression left on my mind is that the real cause of the movement is political.

Non-Brahman friend—The movement is older than the exponents of its political aspect. There is the social and the religious aspect as well.

A Christian friend—The rise of the Justice party is due to

the feeling that the Brahmans have a monopolising tendency and hence cannot be trusted. I am speaking in reference only to the South Indian Brahmans of to-day.

At this stage there were swift questions and answers I summarise below Gandhiji's replies only. *M. D.*

Gandhiji—But should you not in considering the question consider the course that Brahmanism has taken in North India? In North India whatever status a Brahman enjoys has been given him by the non-Brahmans. He has no independent status. In fact the consideration in North and West India is not whether a particular leader is a Brahman or a non-Brahman but whether he can lead. In the Punjab Lalaji, a non-Brahman, is supreme as a leader. In the U. P. there is Malaviyaji, a Brahman. In Bengal Surendranath Banerji, a Brahman, was as much respected by the non-Brahmans as by Brahmans. In Gujarat the Patel Brothers, non-Brahmans, are as much respected by the Brahmans as by non-Brahmans.

In South India you seem to have divided Hinduism not only into two camps, but divided India into Brahmans and non-Brahmans, which term may include Musalmans and Christians as well. Now I want you to have a clear-cut crystallised notion of your own aims and ideals.

Supposing your aims to be merely political, and of destroying the alleged Brahman monopoly of places of power, I can perhaps understand your inclusive definition of the term non-Brahman, though even here I see many difficulties.

But if you aim also at reform, or the removal of religious and social disabilities, I should find it difficult to follow your definition of 'non-Brahman' so as to include non-Hindus. There is the question of untouchability or temple entry, for instance. With the best of motives in the world, how can a non-Hindu effectively interfere? May a non-Muslim dictate the reform of Islam? I fear that all non-Hindu interference in the matter of religion will be looked upon with the gravest suspicion.

I want you therefore to have the issue as clear-cut as possible. So far as your disabilities are concerned, there can be no question about them. They are there, and for their removal you have to offer stubborn battle. But have no illusions about the disabilities either. As to places of power, if I had any choice in the matter, I should strongly advise all Brahmans to leave them all for you, but when you raise the cry of Brahman monopoly in Khadi service I simply cannot understand it. The whole movement serves primarily the non-Brahman masses, practically all members of the executive committee of the A. I. S. A. are non-Brahmans. In South India can you in fairness contend that the Brahmans who are in Khadi service have joined it for material gain? And so far as voluntary service is concerned, is it at all proper to raise the cry of monopoly? But even there, give me non-Brahmans who will satisfy my requirements, and I promise that all Brahmans will vacate their places. So far as I know, the majority are there at considerable sacrifice.

Q. We do not understand your emphasis on *varnadharma*. Can you justify the present caste system? What is your definition of *varna*?

A. '*Varna*' means pre-determination of the choice of man's profession. The law of *varna* is that a man shall follow the profession of his ancestors for earning his livelihood. Every child naturally follows the 'colour' of his father, or chooses his father's profession. *Varna* therefore is in a way the law of heredity. *Varna* is not a thing that is superimposed on Hindus, but men who were trustees for their welfare discovered the law for them. It is not a human invention, but an immutable law of nature—the statement of a tendency that is ever present and at work like Newton's law of gravitation. Just as the law of gravitation existed even before it was discovered so did the law of *varna*. It was given to the Hindus to discover that law. By their discovery and application of certain laws of nature, the peoples of the West have easily increased their material possessions. Similarly, Hindus by their discovery of this irresistible social tendency have been able to achieve in the spiritual field what no other nation in the world has achieved.

Varna has nothing to do with caste. Caste is an excrescence, just like untouchability, upon Hinduism. All the excrescences that are emphasised to-day were never part of Hinduism. But don't you find similar ugly excrescences in Christianity and Islam also?

Fight them as much as you like. Down with the monster of the caste that masquerades in the guise of *varna*. It is this travesty of *varna* that has degraded Hinduism and India. Our failure to follow the law of *varna* is largely responsible both for our economic and spiritual ruin. It is one cause of unemployment and impoverishment, as it is responsible for untouchability and defections from our faith.

But in quarrelling with the present monstrous form, and monstrous practices to which the original law has been reduced, do not fight the law itself.

Q How many *varnas* are there?

A. Four *varnas*, though it is not a rigid division inherent in *varnas* itself. The Rishis after incessant experiment and research arrived at this fourfold division—the four ways of earning one's livelihood.

Q. Logically, therefore, there are as many *varnas* as there are professions?

A. Not necessarily. The different professions can easily be brought under the four main divisions—that of teaching, of defending, of wealth-producing, and of manual service. So far as the world is concerned, the dominant profession is the wealth producing, just as *grihastha ashrama* is the most dominant amongst all *ashramas*. Vaishya is the keynote among the *varnas*. The defender is not wanted if there is no wealth and property. The first two and the fourth are necessary because of the third. The first will always be very few because of the severe discipline required for it, the second must be few in a well-ordered society, and so the fourth.

Q. If a man practises a profession which does not belong to him by birth, what *varna* does he belong to?

A. According to the Hindu belief he belongs to the *varna*

in which he is born, but by not living up to it he will be doing violence to himself and becomes a degraded being—a *patita*.

Q. A *Shudra* does an act which belongs to a Brahman by birth. Does he become a *patita*?

A. A *Shudra* has as much right to knowledge as a Brahman, but he falls from his estate if he tries to gain his livelihood through teaching. In ancient times there were automatic trade guilds, and it was an unwritten law to support all the members of the profession. A hundred years ago a carpenter's son never wanted to become a lawyer. To-day he does, because he finds the profession the easiest way to steal money. The lawyer thinks that he must charge Rs. 15,000 as fees for the exercise of his brain, and a physician like Hakim Saheb thinks that he must charge Rs. 1,000 a day for his medical advice.

Q. But may not a man follow a profession after his heart?

A. But the only profession after his heart should be the profession of his fathers. There is nothing wrong in choosing that profession, on the contrary it is noble. What we find to-day are freaks, and that is why there is violence and disruption of society. Let us not confound ourselves by superficial illustrations. There are thousands of carpenters' sons following their fathers' calling, but not even a hundred carpenters' sons who are lawyers. In ages gone by there was not the ambition of encroaching on others' profession and amassing wealth. In Cicero's time, for instance, the lawyer's was an honorary profession. And it would be quite right for any brainy carpenter to become a lawyer for service, not for money. Later, ambition for fame and wealth crept in. Physicians served the society and rested content with what it gave them, but now they have become traders and even a danger to society. The medical and the legal professions were deservedly called liberal when the motive was purely philanthropic.

Q. All that is under ideal conditions. But what do you propose today when every one is hankering after paying professions?

A. It is a sweeping generalisation. Put together the number of boys studying in schools and colleges and determine the parentage of boys going in for the learned professions. Highway robbery is not open to every one. The present seems to be an agitation for highway robbery. How many can become lawyers and Government servants? Those who can be legitimately occupied in earning wealth are Vaishyas. Even there, when their profession becomes a highway robbery, it is hateful. There cannot be millions of millionaires.

Q. So far as Tamil Nad is concerned, all non-Brahmans want to take up professions to which they were not born.

A. I reject your claim to speak on behalf of the 22 million Tamilians. I give you a formula--*Let us not want to be what everyone else cannot be.* And you can work out this proposition only on the basis of *varna* as I have defined it.

Q. You have been saying that the law of *varna* curbs our worldly ambition. How?

A. When I follow my father's profession. I need not even go to a school to learn it, and my mental energy is set free for spiritual pursuits, because my money or rather livelihood is ensured. *Varna* is the best form of insurance for happiness and for real religious pursuit. When I concentrate my energy on other pursuits, I sell away my powers of self-realisation or sell my soul for a mess of pottage.

Q. You talk of releasing the energies for spiritual pursuits. To-day those who follow their father's professions have no spiritual culture at all—their very *varna* unfits them for it.

A. We are talking with crooked notions of *varna*. When *varna* was really practised, we had enough leisure for spiritual training. Even now, you go to distant villages and see what spiritual culture villagers have as compared to the town-dwellers. These know no self-control.

But you have spotted the mischief of the age. Let us not try to be what others cannot be. I would not even learn the *Gita* if every one who wished could not do it. That is why my whole soul rises against learning English for making money.

We have to re-arrange our lives so that we ensure to the millions the leisure that a fraction of us have to-day, and we cannot do it unless we follow the law of *varna*.

Q. You will excuse us, if we go back to the same question over and over again. We want to understand it properly. What is the *varna* of a man practising different professions at different times?

A. It may not make any difference in his *varna* so long as he gains his livelihood by following his father's profession. He may do anything he likes so long as he does it for love of service. But he who changes profession from time to time for the sake of gaining wealth degrades himself and falls from *varna*.

Q. A *Shudra* may have all the qualities of a Brahman and yet may not be called a Brahman?

A. He may not be called a Brahman in this birth. And it is a good thing for him not to arrogate a *varna* to which he is not born. It is a sign of true humility.

Q. Do you believe that qualities attaching to *varna* are inherited and not acquired?

A. They can be acquired. The inherited qualities can always be strengthened and new ones cultivated. But we need not, ought not, to seek new avenues for gaining wealth. We should be satisfied with those we have inherited from our forefathers so long as they are pure.

Q. Do you not find a man exhibiting qualities opposed to his family character?

A. That is a difficult question. We do not know all our antecedents. But you and I do not need to go deeper into this question for understanding the law of *varna* as I have endeavoured to explain to you. If my father is a trader and I exhibit the qualities of a soldier, I may without reward serve my country as a soldier, but must be content to earn my bread by trading.

Q. Caste, as we see it to-day, consists only in restrictions, about inter-dining and inter-marriage. Does preservation of *varna* then mean keeping these restrictions?

A. No, not at all. In its purest state, there can be no restrictions.

Q. Can they be omitted?

A. They can be, and *varna* is preserved even by marrying into other *varnas*.

Q. Then the mother's *varna* will be affected.

A. A wife follows the *varna* of her husband.

Q. Is the doctrine of *varnadharma*, as you have expounded it, to be found in our Shastras, or is it your own?

A. Not my own. I derive it from the Bhagavad Gita.

Q. Do you approve of the doctrine as given in *Manusmriti*?

A. The principle is there. But the applications do not appeal to me fully. There are parts of the book which are open to grave objections. I hope that they are later interpolations.

Q. Does not *Manusmriti* contain a lot of injustice?

A. Yes, a lot of injustice to women and the so-called lower 'castes.' All is not Shastra that goes by that name. The Shastras so called therefore need to be read with much caution.

Q. But you go by the Bhagavad Gita. It says *varna* is according to *guna* and *karma*. How did you bring in birth?

A. I swear by the Bhagavad Gita because it is the only book in which I find nothing to cavil at. It lays down principles and leaves you to find the application for yourself. The Gita does talk of *varna* being according to *guna* and *karma*; but *guna* and *karma* are inherited by birth. Lord Krishna says, all *varnas* have been *created* by me *chatur varnyam maya srushtam* i.e., I suppose by birth. The law of *varna* is nothing, if not by birth.

Q. But there is no superiority about *varna*?

A. No, not at all, though I do say Brahmanism is the culmination of other *varnas*, just as the head is the culmination of the body. It means capacity for superior service, but no superior status. The moment superior status is arrogated, it becomes worthy of being trampled under foot.

Q. *Kural* you know. Do you know that the author of

that Tamil classic says there is no caste by birth? At birth, he says, all life is equal.

A. He says it as an answer to the present-day exaggerations. When superiority was claimed by any *varna*, he had to raise his voice against it. But that does not cut at the root of *varna* by birth. It is only the reformer's attempt to cut at the root of inequality.

Q. The present practice is so distorted, that may it not be the best thing to give it up altogether and begin on a clean slate?

A. Only if were creators. We cannot by a stroke of the pen alter Hindu nature. We can find out a method of working the law, not destroying it.

Q. When authors of Shastras created new *smritis*, why not you?

A. If I could create a new creation! My state then would be far worse than Vishvamitra's and he was far greater than I.

Q. So long as you do not destroy *varna*, untouchability cannot be destroyed.

A. I do not think so. But if *varnashrama* goes to the dogs in the removal of untouchability, I shall not shed a tear. But what bearing has *varna* as defined by me on untouchability?

Q. But the opponents of reform quote you in support.

A. That is the lot of every reformer. He will be misquoted by interested parties, but you also know that some of them want me to relinquish Hinduism. Others would banish me if they could from the Hindu fold. I have gone nowhere to defend *varnadharma*, though for the removal of untouchability I went to Vykom. I am the author of a Congress resolution for propagation of Khadi, establishment of Hindu-Muslim unity, and removal of untouchability, the three pillars of Swaraj. But I have never placed establishment of *varnashramadharma* as the fourth pillar. You cannot therefore accuse me of placing a wrong emphasis on *varnashramadharma*.

Q. Do you know that many of your followers distort your teaching?

A. Do I not know it? I know that I have many followers only so called.

Q. Buddhism was driven out of India because Brahmans dominated the organisation. Similarly they will drive Hinduism out, if it does not serve their end.

A. Let them dare. But I am certain that Buddhism has not gone out of India. India is the country that imbibed most of the spirit of the Buddha as well as Christianity from the spirit of the Christ. They were successful in driving out Buddhism, because they had assimilated the central teaching of the Buddha.

Q. The same Brahman who assimilated the good things of Buddhism has committed the worst crimes, worse than the Amritsar wrong, by not allowing untouchables entry into temples and imposing on them cruel disabilities.

A. You are right to a certain extent. But you are wrong in fixing the guilt on Brahmans. It is the whole of Hinduism that is responsible. *Varnadharma* having become distorted gave rise to untouchability. There was no deliberate wickedness, but the result was a human tragedy.

Q. But so long as you use the word '*varnashramadharma*', it brings in with it the evil associations of to-day.

A. The moral is, destroy the evil association and restore *varnadharma* to its purity.

Q. There is an utter state of confusion. How shall we go back?

A. All I have to say to you is, do not destroy the foundation, let us try to purify. Instead you are trying to deliver a new religion to receive which no one is prepared. Brahmanism is synonymous with Hinduism. That is to say, the only term we had for Hinduism was Brahmanism, *i.e.*, Brahma Vidya, and in trying to destroy that you are to trying to destroy Hinduism. Fight the Brahman inch by inch, when he encroaches on your rights and try to reform him. But it is no use blackguarding every Brahman. There are Brahmans and Brahmans. One is an out-and-out reformer, the other is an opponent of reform. You must range the best of the reformer Brahmans on your side, and with their help carry out the constructive part of your programme, which can bring about the salvation both of Brahmans and non-Brahmans.

Fight the opponents of reform and tell them, 'We shall not call you Brahmans if you pursue wealth and power, and if you are not learned and are not able to teach us the true religion.' Then you will not evoke any opposition from them. You will carry on a fierce agitation to bring about reform, you will boycott the schools and temples which distinguish against any non-Brahmans. You will insist upon priests of pure character, of learning and without worldly ambition. You may build new temples if the old ones refuse to admit the so-called untouchables.

Then there is the question of inter-dining. I should not make that a ground for quarrel with any body. But I should boycott a function where there is a dividing line.

Then I would fraternise with untouchables and try to deal by them as I should with a blood brother, and break to pieces all little castes and sections. And therefore when I marry my boy I will go out of my way and seek a girl from other subsections We are really so hide-bound to-day by wretched custom that you will not give me a girl to domicile in Gujarat, and you will not take a girl from Gujarat to settle in Tamil Nad.

Then I would give the untouchables religious education, a grounding in the principles of Hinduism and morality. They are leading a purely animal life to-day. I would induce them to refrain from eating forbidden food and live a pure and clean life. You can easily expand these questions and work out a big constructive programme.

Q. We see you swear by Hinduism. May we know what Hinduism has done for us? Is it not a legacy of ugly superstitions and practices?

A. I thought I had made it clear already. *Varnashramadharma* itself is a unique contribution of Hinduism to the world. Hinduism has saved us from *bhaya*, *i.e.*, peril. If Hinduism had not come to my rescue the only course for me would have been suicide. I remain a Hindu because Hinduism is a leaven which makes the world worth living in. From Hinduism was born Buddhism. What we see to-day is not pure Hinduism, but often a parody of it. Otherwise it would require no pleading from me in its behalf, but would speak for itself, even as if I was absolutely pure I would not need to speak to you. God does not speak with His tongue, and man in the measure that he comes near God becomes like God. Hinduism teaches me that my body is a limitation of the power of the soul within.

Just as in the West they have made wonderful discoveries in things material, similarly Hinduism has made still more marvellous discoveries in things of religion, of the spirit, of the soul. But we have no eye for these great and fine discoveries. We are dazzled by the material progress that Western science has made. I am not enamoured of that progress. In fact, it almost seems as though God in His wisdom had prevented India from progressing along those lines so that it might fulfil its special mission of resisting the onrush of materialism. After all, there is something in Hinduism that has kept it alive up till now. It has witnessed the fall of Babylonian, Syrian Persian and Egyptian civilisation. Cast a look round you. Where is Rome and where is Greece? Can you find to-day anywhere the Italy of Gibbon, or rather the ancient Rome, for Rome was Italy? Go to Greece. Where is the world-famous Attic civilisation? Then come to India, let one go through the most ancient records and then look round you and you would be constrained to say, 'Yes, I see here ancient India still living.' True, there are dungheaps, too, here and there, but there are rich treasures buried under them. And the reason why it has survived is that the end which Hinduism set before it was not development along material but spiritual lines.

Among its many contributions the idea of man's identity with the dumb creation is a unique one. To me cow-worship is a great idea which is capable of expansion. Its freedom from the modern proselytisation is also to me a precious thing. It needs no preaching. It says, 'Live the life.' It is my business, it is your business to live the life, and then we will leave its influence on ages Then take its contribution in men; Ramanuja, Chaitanya, Ramakrishna, not to speak of the more modern names, have left their impress on Hinduism. Hinduism is by no means a spent force or a dead religion.

Then there is the contribution of the four *ashramas*, again a unique contribution. There is nothing like it in the whole world. The Catholics have the order of celibates corresponding to *brahmacharis*, but not as an institution, whereas in India every boy had to go through the first *ashrama*. What a grand conception it was! To-day our eyes are dirty, thoughts dirtier and bodies dirtiest of all, because we are denying Hinduism.

There is yet another thing I have not mentioned. Max Muller said forty years ago that it was dawning on Europe that transmigration is not a theory, but a fact. Well, it is entirely the contribution of Hinduism.

To-day *varnashramadharma* and Hinduism are misrepresented and denied by its votaries. The remedy is not destruction, but correction. Let us reproduce in ourselves the true Hindu spirit, and then ask whether it satisfies the soul or not.

24th November, 1927

MESSAGE TO BUDDHISTS

BY M. K. GANDHI

The following is the text of the speech delivered by Gandhiji at Vidyodaya College, Colombo, in reply to an address presented to him by the All-Ceylon Congress of Buddhist Associations:

"I thank you very sincerely for the address that you have given to me. I appreciate the courtesy, in that you have supplied me with a translation of your address in advance. I am equally grateful to His Holiness and the priests for the benediction that they have pronounced just now. I shall always esteem it as a great privilege that I have received this benediction this afternoon, and I can give His Holiness and the priests in the presence of this Assembly the assurance that I shall always strive to deserve that benediction. Your address mentions it and His Holiness also just now mentioned the fact about the Buddha Gaya temple which is situated in India. I have been interesting myself in this great institution for a long time, and when I presided over the deliberations of the Indian National Congress at Belgaum, I had the privilege of doing what was possible on behalf of the Congress in this connection. I had sent to me by some unknown friend in Ceylon the controversy that took place in connection with what I did at the Congress in this matter. I did not think it proper to take part in the controversy nor do I desire even now to go into it. I can only give you my assurance that everything that was humanly possible for me to do to advance your claim I did and I shall still do. I can only tell you, however, that the Congress does not possess the influence that I would like it to possess. There are several difficulties raised in connection with the proprietary rights. There are technical legal difficulties also in the way. The Congress appointed a Committee of the best men that were at its disposal to go into this matter and if possible even to come to terms with the Mahant who is at the present moment in possession of the temple. That Committee has already reported, and I take it that some of you have seen the report of that Committee. That Committee endeavoured to have an arbitration appointed, but it failed in its efforts to do so. But there is absolutely no reason to lose hope. However, I can tell you that all my personal spmpathies are absolutely with you, and if the rendering of its possession to you was in my giving you can have it to-day. In your address was mentioned another temple that is situated in Ceylon. I do not know anything about the controversy regarding this temple. I, therefore, like some of you to give me particulars about it, and tell me if there is anything that I can do in connection with it whilst I am in your midst. You may take it for granted that I should take a personal interest in it if I feel that there is anything that I can do, and I should do so not in order that I can oblige you, but in order to give myself satisfaction.

"For, you do not know perhaps that one of my sons, the eldest boy, accused me of being a follower of Buddha, and some of my Hindu countrymen also do not hesitate to accuse me of spreading Buddhistic teaching under the guise of Sanatana Hinduism. I sympathise with my son's accusations and the accusations of my Hindu friends. And sometimes I feel even proud of being accused of being a follower of the Buddha, and I have no hesitation in declaring in the presence of this audience that I owe a great deal to the inspiration that I have derived from the life of the Enlightened One. Indeed, at an anniversary celebration in the new Buddha Temple that has been erected in Calcutta I gave expression to this view. The leader in that meeting was Anagarika Dharmapala. He was weeping over the fact that he was not receiving the response that he desired for the cause which was close to his heart and I remember having rebuked him for shedding tears. I told the audience that though what passed under the name of Buddhism might have been driven out of India, the life of the Buddha and his teachings were by no means driven out of India. This incident happened I think now three years ago, and I have seen nothing since to alter the view which I pronounced at that meeting. It is my deliberate opinion that the essential part of the teachings of the Buddha now forms an integral part of Hinduism. It is impossible for Hindu India to-day to retrace her steps and go behind the great reformation that Gautama effected in Hinduism. By his immense sacrifice, by his great renunciation and by the immaculate purity of his life he left an indelible impress upon Hinduism and Hinduism owes an eternal debt of gratitude to that great teacher. And if you will forgive me for saying so, and if you will also give me the permission to say so, I would venture to tell you that what Hinduism did not assimilate of what passes as Buddhism to-day was not an essential part of Buddha's life and his teachings.

"It is my fixed opinion that Buddhism or rather the teaching of Buddha found its full fruition in India, and it could not be otherwise, for Gautama was himself a Hindu of Hindus. He was saturated with the best that was in Hinduism, and he gave life to some of the teachings that were buried in the Vedas and which were overgrown with weeds. His great Hindu spirit cut its way through the forest of words, meaningless words, which had overlaid the golden truth that was in the Vedas. He made some of the words in the Vedas yield a meaning to which the men of his generation were utter strangers, and he found in India the most congenial soil. And wherever the Buddha went, he was followed by and surrounded not by non-Hindus but Hindus, those who were themselves saturated with the Vedic law. But the Buddha's teaching like his heart was all-expanding and all-embracing and so it has survived his own body and swept across the face of the earth. And at the risk of being called a follower of Buddha I claim this achievement as a triumph of Hinduism. Buddha never rejected Hinduism, but he broadened its base. He gave it a new life and a new interpretation. But here comes the point where I shall need your forgiveness and your generosity, and I want to submit to you that the teaching of Buddha was not assimilated in its fulness whether it was in Ceylon, or in Burma, or in China or in Tibet. I know my own limitations. I lay no claim to scholarship in Buddhistic law. Probably, a Fifth Form boy from Nalanda Vidyalaya would plough me in a Buddhist catechism. I know that I speak in the presence of very learned priests and equally learned laymen, but I should be false to you and false to myself if I did not declare what my heart believes.

"You and those who call themselves Buddhists outside India have no doubt taken in a very large measure the teaching of the Buddha, but when I examine your life and when I cross-question the friends from Ceylon, Burma, China or Tibet, I feel confounded to find so many inconsistencies between what I have come to understand as the central fact of Buddha's life and your own practice, and if I am not tiring you out, I would like hurriedly to run through three prominent points that just now occurred to me. The first is the belief in an all-pervading Providence called God. I have heard it contended times without number and I have read in books also claiming to express the spirit of Buddhism that Buddha did not believe in God. In my humble opinion such a belief contradicts the very central fact of Buddha's teaching. In my humble opinion the confusion has arisen over his rejection and just rejection of all the base things that passed in his generation under the name of God. He undoubtedly rejected the notion that a being called God was actuated by malice, could repent of his actions, and like the kings of the earth could possibly be open to temptations and bribes and could possibly have favourites. His whole soul rose in mighty indignation against the belief that a being called God required for his satisfaction the living blood of animals in order that he might be pleased,—animals who were his own creation. He, therefore, reinstated God in the right place and dethroned the usurper who for the time being seemed to occupy that White Throne. He emphasised and re-declared the eternal and unalterable existence of the moral government of this universe. He unhesitatingly said that the law was God Himself.

"God's laws are eternal and unalterable and not separable from God Himself. It is an indispensable condition of His very perfection. And hence the great confusion that Buddha disbelieved in God and simply believed in the moral law, and because of this confusion about God Himself, arose the confusion about the proper understanding of the great word *nirvana*. *Nirvana* is undoubtedly not utter extinction. So far as I have been able to understand the central fact of Buddha's life, *nirvana* is utter extinction of all that is base in us, all that is vicious in us, all that is corrupt and corruptible in us. *Nirvana* is not like the black, dead peace of the grave, but the living peace, the living happiness of a soul which is conscious of itself, and conscious of having found its own abode in the heart of the Eternal.

"The third point is the low estimation in which the idea of sanctity of all life came to be held in its travels outside India. Great as Buddha's contribution to humanity was in restoring God to His eternal place, in my humble opinion greater still was his contribution to humanity in his exacting regard for all life, be it ever so low. I am aware that his own India did not rise to the height that he would fain have seen India occupy. But the teaching of Buddha, when it became Buddhism and travelled outside, came to mean that sacredness of animal life had not the sense that it had with an ordinary man. I am not aware of the exact practice and belief of Ceylonese Buddhism in this matter, but I am aware what shape it has taken in Burma and China. In Burma especially the Burmese Buddhists will not kill a single animal, but do not mind others killing the animals for them and dishing the carcases for them for their food. Now, if there was any teacher in the world who insisted upon the inexorable law of cause and effect, it was inevitably Gautama, and yet my friends, the Buddhists outside India, would, if they could, avoid the effects of their own acts. But I must not put an undue strain upon your patience. I have but lightly touched upon some of the points which I think it my duty to bring to your notice, and in all earnestness and equal humility I present them for your serious consideration.

"One thing more and I shall have done. Last night the members of the Reception Committee asked me to speak at one of these audiences of the connection Khadi had with Ceylon. I have not left much time for myself to expand this message before you, but I shall try to summarise it in two sentences. One thing is that you who regard Buddha as the ruler of your hearts owe something to the land of his birth, where millions of his descendants for whom he laboured and for whom he died are to-day living a life of misery, living in a state of perpetual semi-starvation. I venture, therefore, to suggest that Khadi enables you to establish a living bond between yourselves and the ruler of your hearts. If you will follow the central fact of his teaching and regard life as one of renunciation of all material things, all life being transitory, you will at once see the beauty of the message of Khadi which otherwise means simple living and high thinking. Taking these two thoughts with you, I suggest to every one of you to dot the i's and cross the t's and make out your own interpretation of the message of Khadi. I thank you again for the great kindness that you have shown, for the address and for the benediction, and I hope that you will receive the humble message that I have given to you in the same spirit in which it has been delivered. Regard it as a message not from a critic, but from a bosom friend."

1st December, 1927

HINDU MUSLIM UNITY

BY M. K. GANDHI

Dr. Ansari told me when I was recently in Delhi, that he heard in Calcutta from reliable men that I had lost faith and interest in Hindu Muslim unity, and that I was avoiding Musalman friends such as the Ali Brothers Dr. Ansari therefore proposed that in order to dispel any illusion and disarm suspicion, I should make a declaration of my faith before a public meeting in Delhi. I could not accept the proposal if only because the old Delhi of Hakim Saheb Ajmal Khan and Swami Shraddhanandji had become the new Delhi of hooligans where it was difficult for me to stay and much more so to address public meetings. I however promised Dr. Ansari that I would clear my position as early as I could through these pages. This I do now.

My interest and faith in Hindu Muslim unity and unity

among all the communities remain as strong as ever. My method of approach has changed. Whereas formerly I tried to achieve it by addressing meetings, joining in promoting and passing resolutions, now I have no faith in these devices. We have no atmosphere for them. In an atmosphere which is surcharged with distrust, fear and hopelessness, in my opinion these devices rather hinder than help heart-unity. I therefore rely upon prayer and such individual acts of friendship as are possible. Hence I have lost all desire to attend meetings held for achieving unity. This however does not mean that I disapprove of such attempts. On the contrary, those who have faith in such meetings must hold them. I should wish them all success.

I am out of tune with the present temper of both the communities. From their own standpoint they are perhaps entitled to say that my method has failed. I recognise that among those whose opinions count, I am in a hopeless minority. By my taking part in meetings and the like I could not render any useful service. And as I have no other interest but to see real unity established, where I cannot serve by my presence, I regard it as some service if I abstain

For me there is no hope save through truth and non-violence. I know that they will triumph when everything else has failed. Whether therefore I am in the minority of one or I have a majority, I must go along the course that God seems to have shown me. To-day non-violence as a mere policy is a broken reed. It answers well as a policy when there are no active forces working against it in your own camp. But when you have to reckon with those who believe in violence as a creed to be enforced under given circumstances the expedience of non-violence breaks down. Then is the time for the out and out believer in non-violence to test his creed. Both my creed and I are therefore on our trial. And if we do not seem to succeed, let the critic or the onlooker blame not the creed but me I know I am often obliged to struggle against myself. I have not become incapable as yet of violence in thought at least. But I am striving with all the might God has given me.

Now perhaps the reader understands why I am not found in the company of Ali brothers as often I was before. They still hold me in their pockets. They are still as dear to me as blood brothers. I am not sorry for having thrown in my lot with the Musalmans in the hour of their need. I should do so again if the occasion arose. But though we have a common cause we have not common methods to day. They would have had me at Simla and Calcutta. Since the Kohat riots we have not been able to agree as to the reading of facts. But friendship that insists upon agreement on all matters is not worth the name. Friendship to be real must ever sustain the weight of honest differences, however sharp they may be. I regard our differences, to be honest, and therefore let those who suspect a breach or even coolness between us know, that my friendship with the Ali brothers and other Musalman friends whom the reader can easily name remains as firm as ever.

1st December, 1927

MESSAGE TO CEYLON CONGRESS

(The Ceylon National Congress received Gandhiji at the Public Hall on November 22nd. Gandhiji in reply to the President's welcome delivered a speech which is given below. M. D.)

I thank you for the words that you have spoken about myself, and I thank you also for the pleasant reminder that you have given me of the ancient times when the connection between India and Ceylon was established. I do not purpose however to take up your time by giving my own views upon what that connection means to India, means to you, and shall I say to the world. But I will say this: that in my opinion the teaching of Gautama Buddha was not a new religion. In so far as I have been able to study those lofty teachings, I have come to the conclusion—and that conclusion I arrived long before now—that Gautama was one of the greatest of Hindu reformers, and that he left upon the people of his own time and upon the future generations an indelible impress of that reformation. But it would be wrong on my part to take up your time and my own, limited as it is, to consider that very fascinating subject. I therefore come to mundane matters relating to the Congress.

The Congress is a word in India to conjure with. It is an association with an unbroken record of over 40 years. And it enjoys to-day a reputation which no other political association in India enjoys, and that is in spite of the many ups and downs which the Congress in common with all worldly institutions and associations has gone through. I therefore take it for granted that in adopting this name you are also, as far as may be, and is necessary, following the traditions of the parent body, if I may call the National Congress of India by that name. And on that assumption I venture this afternoon to place before you my views of what a Congress should be, or how the National Congress in India has been able to build up its reputation. I know that after all my connection with the Congress in India does not stretch over a period longer than 10 years—or I may now say, more accurately speaking, 12 years. But as you are aware that 12 years' association is so close, and I have been so much identified with the Congress that probably what I may say might be taken with some degree of authority. But in one way my association with the parent body is nearly 30 years old now. It was in South Africa in the year 1893 when I went there that I dreamt about the Congress. I knew something about its activities, though I had never attended a single one of the annual sessions of that great institution. Just like you, as a youngster, I took my proper share in founding an association called the Natal Indian Congress, after the fashion of the Indian National Congress, making such changes as were necessary to suit the local conditions. I shall therefore be able to give you the results of my experience of public life in connection with such institutions dating back from 1893. And what I learnt even so early as 1894 was that any such association, to be really serviceable, to deserve the name of being called 'national,' requires a fair measure—I was going to say a great measure—of self-sacrifice on the part of the principal workers. I have no hesitation in confessing to you, that that ideal I found to be very difficult to put into practice even in that little community, because we were after all a very small body of men and women in Natal, which is the smallest province of South Africa, where we had a population of nearly 60 thousand Indians of whom the vast majority had no vote in the deliberations of the Congress. The Congress however was a representative institution and fully representative of things that interested the people, because it constituted itself the trustee of the welfare of those men. But I must not linger over the history of that institution. Even in that small body we found bickerings and a desire more for power than for service, a desire more for self-aggrandisement than for self effacement, and I have found during my 12 years' association with the parent body also, that there is a continuous desire for self-seeking and self-aggrandisement; and for you as for us who are still striving to find our feet, who have still to make good the claims for self-expression and self-government, self-sacrifice, self-effacement, and self-suppression are really absolutely necessary and indispensable for our existence and for our progress.

I do not profess to have studied your politics during the brief stay that I have made here, I do not know the internal working of this organisation, I do not know how strong it is, and how popular it is. I only hope it is strong and is popular. I hope you are free from the blemishes that I have just mentioned. It is, I know, a pleasurable pastime (and I have indulged in it sufficiently as you know), to strive against the powers that be, and to wrestle with the Government of the day, especially when that Government happens to be a foreign Government and a Government under which we rightly feel we have not that scope which we should have, and which we desire, for expansion and fullest self-expression. But I have also come to the conclusion that self-expression and self-government are not things which may be either taken from us by anybody or which can be given us by anybody. It is quite true that if those who happen to hold our destinies, or seem to hold our destinies in their hands, are favourably disposed, are sympathetic, understand our aspirations, no doubt it is then easier for us to expand. But after all self-government depends entirely upon our own internal strength, upon our ability to fight against the heaviest odds. Indeed, self-government which does not require that continuous striving to attain it and to sustain it is not worth the name. I have therefore endeavoured to show both in word and in deed, that political self-government—that is self-government for a large number of men and women,—is no better than individual self-government, and therefore it is to be attained by precisely the same means that are required for individual self-government or self-rule, and so as you know also, I have striven in India to place this ideal before the people in season and out of season, very often much to the disgust of those who are politically minded merely.

I belong to that body of political thought which was dominated by Gokhale. I have called him my political Guru: not that everything that he said or did I accepted or accept today, but just because the moving force of his life (as I who came in the closest touch with him came to understand) was his intense desire to 'spiritualise politics.' This was his own expression in the preamble to the prospectus of the Servants of India Society, of which he was the founder and the first president. He makes the deliberate statement that he founded that Society in order to introduce spirituality into politics. He had studied the politics not only around him in his own country but had been a close and careful student of history. He had studied the politics of all the countries of the world and having been keenly disappointed to see a complete divorce between politics and spirituality, he endeavoured to the best of his ability, and not without some success—I was almost going to say not without considerable success—to introduce that element into politics. And so it was that he adopted the name of the Servants of

India for his Society, which is now serving India in a variety of ways. I do not know whether what I am saying commends itself to you or not, but if I am to show my gratitude for all the kindness that you have lavishly showered upon me during my brief visit to this beautiful country, if I am to show it in truth, I can only tell you what I feel and not what will probably please you or tickle you. You know that this particular thing —truth—is an integral part of our Congress creed. And we have therefore in the creed the attainment of Swaraj by legitimate and non-violent means.

You will find that I have not been tired of insisting upon truth at any cost, and non-violence at any cost. Given these two conditions in my humble opinion, you can hurl defiance at the mightiest power on earth—and still come away not only yourselves unscathed but you will leave your so-called adversary also uninjured and unhurt. For the time being he may misunderstand the non-violent blows that you deal, he may misrepresent you also, but you don't need to consult his feelings or his opinions so long as you are fulfilling these two absolute conditions. Then it is well with you, and you can march forward with greater speed than otherwise. The way may appear to be long, but if you take my experience extending over a period of 30 years uninterruptedly, without exception, I give you my assurance that it is the shortest cut to success. I have known no shorter road. I know that it very often requires great faith and immense patience, but if this one thing is fixed on our minds, then there is no other way open to a politician, if he is to serve not himself, but the whole nation. If once that determination is made, then comes faith and with that faith comes also patience, because you know that there is no better or shorter road.

I am afraid as we are in India, so are you cut up into groups and communities. I read casually only to-day something in praise of communalism. In India also we have this blight—we call it a blight, we don't praise it. Even those who believe in communalism say frankly that it is a necessary evil to be got rid of at the earliest possible moment. In India we have to deal with 300 million people. But you have to deal with such a small mass of men and women that it is a matter for pain and surprise for me to find a defence—an energetic defence—of this communalism. But I know that it is totally opposed to nationalism. And you want, as you must want, Swaraj. It is not, the birthright of one country only; Swaraj is the birthright of all countries,—I feel constrained to say, the birthright even of the savage as of the most civilized man—how much more of people who have got a culture second to none in the world, a people who have got all that Nature can give you, have got resources in men and money and in natural gifts, who have everything that goes to make you a powerful nation on this globe of ours, yet at the present moment you seem to be far away from it. I don't suppose that any of you flatters himself or herself with the belief that you have at the present moment anything like what I should consider self-government. And that self-government you will not have—I was going to say you cannot have—unless you speak with the voice of one nation and not with the voice of Christians, Musalmans, Buddhists, Hindus, Europeans, Sinhalese, Tamils and Malays. I can't understand that.

As you, sir, said in your remarks that you represent all races and religions, I congratulate you upon that, and if you are really capable of vindicating that claim, all honour to you, and not only the Congress but you then deserve to be copied by us. We an older institution are not able to vindicate that claim. We are striving; we are groping in the dark; we are trying to suppress provincialism; we are trying to suppress racialism; we are trying to suppress religionism, if I may coin a word; we are trying to express nationalism in its fullest form but I am ashamed to confess to you that we are still far from it. But it is given to you to outstrip us and set us an example. It is easy for you, much easier for you than for us, but a condition indispensable for that is, that some of you at least will have to give your whole time to this and not only your whole time but your whole selves and you will have to suppress yourselves. As Gokhale said, politics had degenerated into a sort of game for leisure hours, whereas he desired that for some at least politics should be a wholetime occupation, it should engross the attention of some of the ablest men of the country. It is only when truth, fearlessness and non-violence are dominant factors that a person can devote himself unselfishly to the service of the nation.

I hope that in your Congress you have such a body of men and women, because woman must play her part side by side with man. As I said in India, our one limb is paralysed. Women have got to come up to the level of man. As I said to the ladies at a meeting to-day, they may not copy man in all the wildness of his nature, but they must come to the level of man in all that is best in him. Then in this Island you will have a beautiful blend, then you will be worthy of what Nature has so profusely showered on you.

As I travelled from Candy to Colombo his morning, I asked myself what was the Congress going to do in order to save Ceylon, whom God had blessed with enough natural intoxication, from the intoxication of that fiery liquid. I make a humble suggestion to you. If the Congress is to be fully national, it cannot leave this fundamental social question. In this temperate climate, where no artificial stimulant is necessary, it is a shame that a substantial part of your income should be derived from liquor. You may not know what is happening to the labourers whose trustees you are, whose will is only once expressed when they cast their votes in your favour. I saw thousands upon thousands of them at Hatton. I have lost all sense of smell, but a friend told me that some of them were stinking with liquor. They had gone mad over the fact that one of their own was going in their midst, and had broken the bounds of restraint. Well, I know what you will say. You will say it was the result of excess and that it is not bad to drink in moderation. Well, I tell you, I have found so many making that claim and ultimately proving dismal failures. I have come from cities of South Africa where I have seen Africans, Europeans, Indians, rolling in gutters under the influence of drink, I have seen proctors, advocates and barristers rolling in gutters and then the policemen taking them away in order to hide their shame. I have seen captains mad with drink leaving their cabin to the chief officer, or defiling the cabin where they were supposed to keep guard over the safety of their passengers. Claiming, as you do, allegiance to India, and endorsing, as you do, your connection with the story of Ramayana, you should be satisfied with nothing but Rama Raj which includes Swaraj. When the evil stalks from corner to corner of this enchanting fairy land, you must take up the question in right earnest and save the nation from ruin.

Then there is the other thing, untouchability. You consider the Rodiyas as untouchables and their women are not allowed to cover their upper parts. It is high time for the Congress to take up the question of the Rodiyas, make them their own and enrol them as volunteers in their work. Democracy is an impossible thing until the power is shared by all, but let not democracy degenerate into mobocracy. Even a pariah, a labourer, who makes it possible for you to earn your living, will have his share in self-government. But you will have to touch their lives, go to them, see their hovels where they live packed like sardines. It is up to you to look after this part of humanity. It is possible for you to make their lives or mar their lives. The Indian National Congress deals with both of these questions. They are living planks in our programme. I urge upon you, if you want to make your Congress truly national and truly representative of the poorest and meanest people of Ceylon, you will add these items to your programme, if you have not already added them, and introduce a full measure of spirituality into your politics and everything else will follow; self-government which is your birthright will drop in your hand like a fully ripe fruit from a laden tree. May this message produce its due effect and penetrate your hearts.

8th December, 1927

DISTORTION OF TRUTH

BY M. K. GANDHI.

A correspondent has been endeavouring with the help of the headmaster of a High School to introduce the teaching of the Gita among its boys. But at a recent meeting convened to organise Gita readings a Bank Manager got up and disturbed the even tenor of the proceedings by saying that students had not the *adhikara* 'qualification' for studying the Gita; it was not a plaything to be placed before students. The correspondent sends me a long and argued letter about the incident and sends in support of his contention some apt sayings from Ramakrishna Paramahamsa from which I cull the following:

> "Boys and youths should be encouraged to seek God. They are like unpecked fruits, being totally untainted by worldly desires. Once such desires have entered their minds, it is very difficult to make them tread the path to salvation.
>
> "Why do I love young men so much? Because they are masters of the whole (16 annas) of their minds, which get divided and sub-divided as they grow up. One half of the mind of a married man goes to his wife. When a child is born it takes away one-fourth (4 annas), and the remaining one-fourth (4 annas) is scattered over parents, worldly honours, dress etc. Therefore a young mind can easily know God. It is very difficult for old people to do so.
>
> "The parrot cannot be taught to sing if the membrane of its throat becomes hardened with age. It must be taught while it is young. Similarly, in old age it is difficult for the mind to be fixed on God. It can be easily done so in youth.
>
> "If a *seer* of adulterated milk contains a *chhatank* (sixteenth part of a *seer*) of water, it can be thickened into

kshira (condensed milk) with very little labour and consumption of fuel. But should there be three *paos* (¼ *seer*) of water in a *seer*, the milk cannot be easily thickened and a large consumption of fuel will be required. *A young mind, being but slightly adulterated with worldly desires can be easily turned towards God; this cannot be done with the minds of old people which are highly adulterated with such desires.*

"The tender bamboo can be easily bent, but the full-grown bamboo breaks when an attempt is made to bend it. It is easy to bend young hearts towards God, but the heart of the old escapes the hold when so drawn.

"The human mind is like a package of mustard seed. As it is very difficult to gather the seeds that escape out of a torn package and are scattered in all directions, so when the human mind runs in diverse directions and is occupied with many worldly things, it is not a very easy task to collect and concentrate it. The mind of a youth not running in diverse directions, can be easily fixed on anything; but the mind of an old man being totally occupied with worldly things, it is very hard for him to draw it away from them and fix it on God."

I had heard of *adhikara* in connection with the Vedas, but I never knew that the Gita required the qualifications that the Bank Manager had in mind. It would have been better if he had stated the nature of the qualifications he required. The Gita clearly states that it is meant for all but scoffers. If Hindu students may not read the Gita they may not read any religious works at all. Indeed the original conception in Hinduism is that the student life is the life of a *brahmachari* who should begin it with a knowledge of religion *coupled with practice* so that he may digest what he learns and weave religious conduct into his life. The student of old began to live his religion before he knew what it was, and this conduct was followed by due enlightenment, so that he might know the reason for the conduct prescribed for him.

Adhikara then there certainly was. But it was the *adhikara* of right conduct known as the five *yamas* or cardinal restraints, *ahimsa* (innocence), *satya* (truth), *asteya* (non-stealing), *aparigraha* (non-possession), and *brahmacharya* (celibacy). These were the rules that had to be observed by anybody who wished to study religion. He may not go to religious books for proving the necessity of these fundamentals of religion.

But today the word *adhikara* like many such potent words has suffered distortion, and a dissolute man, simply because he is called a *brahman*, has *adhikara* to read and expound Shastras to us, whereas a man, if he is labelled an untouchable because of his birth in a particular state, no matter how virtuous he may be, may not read them.

But the author of the Mahabharata of which the Gita is a part wrote his great work for the purpose of meeting this insane objection, and made it accessible to all irrespective of the so-called caste, provided, I presume, that he complied with the observances I have described. I add the qualifying expression 'I presume' for at the time of writing I do not recall the observance of the *yamas* as a condition precedent to a person studying the Mahabharata. Experience however shows that the purity of heart and the devotional frame of mind are necessary for a proper understanding of religious books.

The printing age has broken down all barriers and scoffers read religious books with the same freedom (if not greater) that the religiously minded have. But we are here discussing propriety of students reading the Gita as part of religious instruction and devotional exercise. Here I cannot imagine any class of persons more amenable to the restraints and thus more fitted than students for such instruction. Unfortunately it is to be admitted that neither the students nor the instructors in the majority of cases think anything of the real *adhikara* of the five restraints.

8th December, 1927

PLEA FOR BUDDHISTIC REVIVAL

BY M. K. GANDHI

Gandhiji addressed a large gathering of Buddhist young men on the premises of their association on the 25th November.

At the outset Gandhiji pleaded for toleration. He did not claim to be a scholar in any sense of the term. His first introduction to any religious study was through a single book, *viz.* Sir Edwin Arnold's *Light of Asia,* which fascinated and engrossed him. Ever since, the spirit of Buddha had haunted him, so much so that he had been accused of being a Buddhist in disguise. And as he had said on a previous occasion he accepted the accusation as a compliment though he knew that if he made any such claim it would be summarily rejected by orthodox Buddhists. As one, however, who had imbibed the spirit of Buddhism he would reassert in all humility, but unhesitatingly, if in a different language, what he said on the previous occasion.

"There are some conditions," he said, "laid down in Hinduism for a proper prayerful study of religions. They are of a universal character. Remember also that Gautama was a Hindu of Hindus. He was saturated with the spirit of Hinduism, with the Vedic spirit, he was born and bred up in those exhilarating surroundings,—exhilarating for the spirit,—and so far as I am aware, he never rejected Hinduism, or the message of the Vedas. What he did was therefore to introduce a living reformation in the petrified faith that surrounded him. I venture to suggest to you that *your study of Buddhism will be incomplete unless you study, the original sources from which the Master derived his inspiration,* that is, unless you study Sanskrit and the Sanskrit scriptures. But your duty, if you are to understand the spirit of the Buddha and not the letter of Buddhism, does not end there. That study has those conditions which I am about to describe to you. Those conditions are that a man or a woman who approaches a study of religion has first of all to observe what are called the five *yamas*. They are the five rules of self-restraint and I will repeat them before you. Firstly, *Brahmacharya*, celibacy; the second is *Satya*, truth; the third is *Ahimsa*, absolute innocence, not even hurting a fly; the next condition is *Asteya*, non-stealing, not merely, not stealing in the ordinary sense in which the word is understood, but if you appropriate or even cast your greedy eyes on anything that is not your own, it becomes stealing. Lastly, *Aparigraha*—a man, who wants to possess wordly riches or other things, won't be fit really to understand the spirit of the Buddha. These are the indispensable conditions. There are other conditions, but I am going into these, because these are the fundamental ones, and Gautama before he attained his knowledge had conformed to all these rules, and conformed, as few of his contemporaries had ever done, to the spirit of those rules. I suggest to you that you will not understand the spirit of the humble Buddha unless you have also yourselves conformed to these rules and then prayerfully tried to ascertain what the Master meant. It makes no difference that you know of him through all the books that have been written, but even these very books, I make bold to assure you, you will understand and you will interpret with a new light immediately you have gone, first of all, through these preliminary observances. Look what many critics of Islam have done—how they have torn the very book, that millions of Musalmans swear by, to pieces and held up the teachings of Islam to scorn. They were not dishonest men who wrote this criticism, they were honest men, they were not men who were not trying to search the truth, but they did not know the conditions that they had to fulfil before they could make any religious study. Again look at what the critics of Hinduism have done. I read many of those criticisms, trying to enter into the spirit of the critics but came to the conclusion that they did not know the A. B. C. of Hinduism and that they were grossly misinterpreting Hinduism. Take Christianity itself. Many Hindus have misinterpreted Christianity. They approach the Bible, the

Old Testament and the New Testament in a carping spirit, with preconceived notions. But why talk of the Hindus? Have I not read books written by Englishmen who, pretending to consider themselves atheists, have turned the Bible upside down and put all the fiery writings into the hands of innocent men and women and thereby done grave injury to the simple people who read them? I have laid these points before the young men of this association, because I am anxious that *you should be the pioneers of presenting Ceylon, and through Ceylon the world, with a real Buddhistic revival, that you should be the pioneers in presenting a living faith to the world, and not the dead bones of a traditional faith which the world will not grasp.*

"The priests," Gandhiji went on to say, "whom he had seen by deputy said they could not argue but that they could only say what the Master taught. It is all right, but to-day the spirit of enquiry is abroad. We have got to deal with that spirit. The world is trying to seek the truth, and thirsting for peace in the midst of this terrible strife. There is also the desire for knowing the truth, but as I have ventured to suggest to you, those, who made a scientific study of religion and those who gave their lives for arriving at the truth and those with whose bones the snows of the Himalayas are whitened, have left these treasures not merely for 300 millions of India, but they have left those treasures for everyone who cares to understand them, and they have said, 'We cannot deliver the truth to you.' It is incapable of being delivered through writings, it is incapable of being delivered with the lips, it is capable of being delivered only through life. It transcends reason. But it is not past experience. So they said, 'We tell you that such and such is the fact, but you will have to test it for yourselves. You will apply your reason, we do not want you to deaden your reason, but you yourselves, even as we, will come to the conclusion that reason which God has given is after all a limited thing, and that which is a limited thing will not be able to reach the limitless. Therefore, go through these preliminary conditions, even as when you want to study geometry or algebra, you have to go through preliminary process, however trying and tiresome. Observe them and then you will find that what we tell you with our own experience will be also yours.'

"I want to take you through only one illustration as to how the teaching of Buddha is now not being observed. I have retained this part of my talk upto almost the very last moment except that I hinted at it in my speech at the Vidyodaya College.

"You believe that Gautama taught the world to treat even the lowest creatures equal to himself. He held the life of even the crawling things of the earth as precious as his own. It is an arrogant assumption to say that human beings are lords and masters of the lower creation. On the contrary, being endowed with greater things in life, they are trustees of the lower animal kingdom. And the great sage lived that truth in his own life. I read as a mere youngster the passage in the *Light of Asia* describing how the Master took the lamb on his shoulders in face of the arrogant and ignorant Brahmans who thought that by offering the blood of these innocent lambs they were pleasing God, and he dared them to sacrifice a single one of them. His very presence softened the stony hearts of the Brahmans. They looked up to the Master, they threw away their deadly knives and every one of those animals was saved. Was this message given to the world in order to falsify it, as it is being falsified here? I feel that you who are the repositories of this great faith are not true to the spirit of the Master's teachings so long as you do not regard all animal creation as sacred, and you cannot do so, so long as you do not abstain from meat and delude yourselves into the belief that you are not guilty of the crime of that slaughter because some one else killed the animals for you. You entrench yourselves behind the wall of traditions. You say that the Master never prohibited meat-eating. I do not think so. If you would approach the teachings of the Master in the spirit indicated by me, and rub in the spirit of tradition, you will have a different vision and a different meaning. You will find that when the Master said, "I do not prohibit you from meat-eating," he was preaching to a people who were in Christian parlance hard of hearts. It was because he wanted to make allowance for their weakness that he allowed them to eat it, and not because he did not know the logic of his own teaching. If animals could not be sacrificed to the gods above, how could they be sacrificed to the epicure in us? When he prohibited sacrifice he knew what he was saying. Did he not know that the animals were sacrificed to be ultimately eaten? Why do they sacrifice thousands of sheep and goats to the Goddess Kali in Calcutta, be it said to their discredit and the discredit of Hinduism in spite of having received this message from the Hindu of Hindus—Gautama? Do they throw the carcasses away in the Hoogly? No, they eat every bit of the meat with the greatest delight, thinking that it has been sanctified because of the presentation to Kali. So the Buddha said, if you want to do any sacrifice, sacrifice yourself, your lust, all your material ambition, all worldly ambition. That will be an ennobling sacrifice. May the spirit of the Buddha brood over this meeting and enable you to measure and assimilate the meaning of the words that I have spoken to you."

8th December, 1927

GANDHIJI AT COLOMBO Y. M. C. A.

By M. K. Gandhi

Addressing a huge gathering in the hall of Y. M. C. A. Colombo, Gandhiji welcomed the occasion as one more instance of the close touch, he was daily finding himself in, of Christians throughout the world. 'There are some who will not even take my flat denial when I tell them that I am not a Christian,' said Gandhiji, and in trying to explain his own attitude to Christianity gave in his own humble way a message to the whole of the Christian world.

"The message of Jesus, as I understand it, is contained in his Sermon on the Mount unadulterated and taken as a whole, and even in connection with the Sermon on the Mount, my own humble interpretation of the message is in many respects different from the orthodox. The message, to my mind, has suffered distortion in the West. It may be presumptuous for me to say so, but as a devotee of truth, I should not hesitate to say what I feel. I know that the world is not waiting to know my opinion on Christianity.

"One's own religion is after all a matter between oneself and one's Maker and no one else's, but if I feel impelled to share my thoughts with you this evening, it is because I want to enlist your sympathy in my search for truth and because so many Christian friends are interested in my thoughts on the teachings of Jesus. If then I had to face only the Sermon on the Mount and my own interpretation of it, I should not hesittate to say, 'Oh yes, I am a Christian.' But I know that at the present moment if I said any such thing I would lay myself open to the gravest misinterpretation. I should lay myself open to fraudulent claims because I would have then to tell you what my own meaning of Christianity is, and I have no desire myself to give you my own view of Christianity. But negatively I can tell you that in my humble opinion, much of what passes as Christianity is a negation of the Sermon on the Mount. And please mark my words. I am not at the present moment speaking of Christian conduct. I am speaking of the Christian belief, of Christianity as it is understood in the West. I am painfully aware of the fact that conduct everywhere falls far short of belief. But I don't say this by way of criticism. I know from the treasures of my own experience that although I am every moment of my life trying to live up to my professions, my conduct falls short of these professions. Far therefore be it from me to say this is a spirit of criticism. But I am placing before you my fundamental difficulties. When I began as a prayerful student to study the Christian literature in South Africa in 1893, I asked myself 'Is this

Christianity?" and have always got the Vedic answer, 'Neti Neti' (not this, not this). And the deepest in me tells me that I am right.

"I claim to be a man of faith and prayer, and even if I was cut to pieces, God would give me the strength not to deny Him and to assert that He is. The Muslim says He is and there is no one else. The Christian says the same thing and so the Hindu, and if I may say so, even the Buddhist says the same thing, if in different words. We may each of us be putting our own interpretation on the word God,—God who embraces not only this tiny globe of ours, but millions and billions of such globes. How can we, little crawling creatures, so utterly helpless as He has made us, how could we possibly measure His greatness, His boundless love, His infinite compassion, such that He allows man insolently to deny Him, wrangle about Him, and cut the throat of his fellowman? How can we measure the greatness of God who is so forgiving, so divine? Thus though we may utter the same words they have not the same meaning for us all. And hence I say that we do not need to *proselytise* or do *shuddhi* or *tabligh* through our speech or writing. We can only do it really with our lives. Let them be open books for all to study. Would that I could persuade the missionary friends to take this view of their mission. Then there will be no distrust, no suspicion, no jealousy and no dissensions."

Gandhiji then took the case of modern China as a case in point. His heart, he said, went out to Young China in the throes of a great national upheaval, and he referred to the anti-Christian movement in China, about which he had occasion to read in a pamphlet received by him from the students' department of the Young Women's Christian Association and Young Men's Christian Association of China. The writers had put their own interpretation upon the anti-Christian movement, but there was no doubt that Young China regarded Christian movements as being opposed to Chinese self-expression. To Gandhiji the moral of the anti-Christian manifestation was clear. He said:

" Don't let your Christian propaganda be anti-national, say these young Chinese. And even their Christian friends have come to distrust the Christian endeavour that had come from the West. I present the thought to you that these essays written by young men have a deep meaning, a deep truth, because they were themselves trying to justify their Christian conduct in so far as they had been able to live up to the life it had taught them and at the same time find a basis for that opposition. The deduction I would like you all to draw from this manifestation is that you Ceylonese should not be torn from your moorings, and those from the West should not consciously or unconsciously lay violent hands upon the manners, customs and habits of the Ceylonese in so far as they are not repugnant to fundamental ethics and morality. Confuse not Jesus' teaching with what passes as modern civilisation, and pray do not do unconscious violence to the people among whom you cast your lot. It is no part of that call, I assure you, to tear the lives of the people of the East by its roots. Tolerate whatever is good in them and do not hastily, with your preconceived notions, judge them. Do not judge lest you be judged yourselves. In spite of your belief in the greatness of Western civilisation and in spite of your pride in all your achievements, I plead with you for humility, and ask you to leave some little room for doubt, in which as Tennyson sang, there was more truth, though by 'doubt' he no doubt meant a different thing. Let us each one live our life, and if ours is the right life, where is the cause for hurry? It will react of itself."

The Y. M. C. A. has among its members Buddhists also, and the president had specially asked Gandhiji to say a word of advice to the Christian and Buddhist youth. He gave them the following message:

" To you, young Ceylonese friends, I say: Don't be dazzled by the splendour that comes to you from the West. Do not be thrown off your feet by this passing show. The Enlightened One has told you in never-to-be forgotten words that this little span of life is but a passing shadow, a fleeting thing, and if you realise the nothingness of all that appears before your eyes, the nothingness of this material case that we see before us ever changing, then indeed there are treasures for you up above, and there is peace for you down here, peace which passeth all understanding, and happiness to which we are utter strangers. It requires an amazing faith, a divine faith and surrender of all that we see before us. What did Buddha do, and Christ do, and also Mahomed? Theirs were lives of self-sacrifice and renunciation. Buddha renounced every worldly happiness, because he wanted to share with the whole world his happiness which was to be had by men who sacrificed and suffered in search for truth. If it was a good thing to scale the heights of Mt. Everest, sacrificing precious lives in order to be able to go there and make some slight observations, if it was a glorious thing to give up life after life in planting a flag in the uttermost extremities of the earth, how much more glorious would it be to give not one life, surrender not a million lives but a billion lives in search of the potent and imperishable truth? So be not lifted off your feet, do not be drawn away from the simplicity of your ancestors. A time is coming when those, who are in the mad rush to-day of multiplying their wants, vainly thinking that they add to the real substance, real knowledge of the world, will retrace their steps and say: 'What have we done?' Civilisations have come and gone, and in spite of all our vaunted progress I am tempted to ask again and again 'To what purpose?' Wallace, a contemporary of Darwin, has said the same thing Fifty years of brilliant inventions and discoveries, he has said, has not added one inch to the moral height of mankind. So said a dreamer and visionary if you will,—Tolstoy. So said Jesus, and Buddha, and Mahomed, whose religion is being denied and falsified in my own country to-day.

"By all means drink deep of the fountains that are given to you in the Sermon on the Mount, but then you will have to take sackcloth and ashes. The teaching of the Sermon was meant for each and every one of us. You cannot serve both

God and Mammon. God the Compassionate and the Merciful, Tolerance incarnate, allows Mammon to have his nine days' wonder. But I say to you, youths of Ceylon, fly from that self-destroying but destructive show of Mammon."

Here in Ceylon where I am writing for *Young India* amid surroundings where nature has bountifully poured her richest treasures, I recall a letter written by a poetically inclined friend from similar scenes. I share with the reader a paragraph from that letter.

> "A lovely morning! Cool and cloudy, with a drowsy sun whose rays are as soft as velvet. It is a strangely quite morning—there is a hush upon it, as of prayer. And the mists are like incense, and the trees worshippers in a trance, and the birds and insects pilgrims come to chant *bhajans*. Oh! how I wish one could learn true abandonment from Nature! We seem to have forgotten our birthright to worship where and when and how we please. We build temples and mosques and churches to keep our worship safe from prying eyes and away from outside influences, but we forget that walls have eyes and ears, and the roofs might be swarming with ghosts—who knows!
>
> "Good Gracious, I shall find myself preaching next! How foolish, on a lovely morning like this? A little child in the garden adjoining is singing as unconsciously and joyously as a bird. I feel inclined to go and take the dust of its little feet. And since I cannot pour out my heart in sound as simply as that little one, my only refuge is in silence!"

Churches, mosques and temples, which cover so much hypocrisy and humbug and shut the poorest out of them, seem but a mockery of God and His worship, when one sees the eternally renewed temple of worship under the vast blue canopy inviting every one of us to real worship, instead of abusing His name by quarrelling in the name of religion.

8th December, 1927

THE TRIPLE MESSAGE

BY M. K. GANDHI

In the course of his speech at the public meeting, Badulla, Gandhiji said:

"A friend came to me and asked me what message had the spinning wheel for the people of Ceylon. He told me that there were men and women in this island who also needed work, and in answer to my cross-question he told me also that he wanted me to show a way whereby the people of this fair island could be weaned from hasty and indiscriminate imitation of the West. And another friend writes me a letter, which also came to my hands to-day, saying that all the beautiful garments that I see about some of the women of Ceylon and all the faultless European styles about so many young men must not be taken by me to be an indication of the possession of wealth by the wearers. My correspondent tells me that many of these slavishly dressed men often find themselves in the hands of Chetties and Pathan money-leaders. Well, the spinning wheel has a message for all this class of people. To the man or woman who has no other work possible for him or her to do, the spinning wheel says: 'Spin me, and you can find a crust of bread for yourself.'

"That is its economical message. But it has also a cultural message. What is the cultural message of the spinning wheel? It says to you and to me: 'There are millions on the face of this earth who are not sufficiently provided, and since I am the only instrument that can be placed in the hands of millions of people without taking work away from a single man, will you not spin me for the sake of these millions, and produce an atmosphere of honest industry, self-reliance and hope for all on God's earth?' That is the cultural message the spinning wheel addresses to all peoples of the earth, no matter to what country, religion or race they belong. And I beg to inform you that slowly but surely this cultural appeal of the spinning wheel is finding a lodgment in the remotest corners of the earth. I know Englishmen, Austrians, Germans, Poles, who have already accepted this appeal of the spinning wheel, and I assure the well-to-do men and women of Ceylon, that if they will accept this cultural message of the spinning wheel and try to make at least some part of their clothes for themselves, they will find themselves much taller than they are to-day.

"The spinning wheel has a third message which is metaphorical. It stands for simple life and high thinking. It is a standing rebuke against the modern mad rush for adding material comfort upon comfort and making life so complicated as to make one doubly unfit for knowing oneself or one's God. It says appealingly every minute of our lives to you and to me; 'Use me and if you unitedly make use of me, small and insignificant though I may appear, you will find in the end that I will become an irresistible force against the mad indiscriminate worship of the curse called machinery.' The spinning wheel is a standing rebuke to the men and women of Ceylon who go in for all kinds of fashions and styles, and it tells them: 'Don't for the sake of your country ape the manners and the customs of others which can only do harm to you, and for Heaven's sake do not wish to be what every one of the people of Ceylon cannot be.'"

15th December, 1927

DUTY OF CEYLON HINDUS

By M. K. Gandhi

Gandhiji's speech at a meeting of the Hindus of Jaffna.

This is the last of a series of many meetings, whose number even I cannot now remember, that I have been addressing today. Precious as all of them have been, this to me is the most precious, because you have convened a meeting of Hindus specially to be addressed by me. This I take to mean that I must speak to you Hindus as a Hindu. And it gives me the greatest pleasure to have been invited to do so. As you know, though my claim has not been accepted by those who call themselves orthodox Hindus I persist in calling myself an orthodox Hindu. But by making that claim I, a votary of Truth, must not mislead you in any way whatsoever. If orthodox Hinduism consists in dining or not dining with this man or that man, and touching this man and not touching that man, or in quarrelling with Musalmans and Christians, then I am certainly not an orthodox Hindu. But if orthodox Hinduism can mean an incessant search after what Hindusim possibly can be, if orthodox Hinduism can mean an incessant striving to live Hinduism to the best of one's lights, then I do claim to be an orthodox Hindu I am also an orthodox Hindu in the sense in which the author of the Mahabharata, the great Vyasa, would have it. He has said somewhere in the Mahabharata to this effect: Put Truth in one scale and all sacrifices whatever in the other; that scale which contains Truth will outweigh the one that contains all the sacrifices put together, not excluding *Rajasuya* and *Ashvamedha* Yajna. And if the Mahabharata may be accepted as the fifth Veda, then I can claim to be an orthodox Hindu, because every moment of the twenty four hours of my life I am endeavouring to follow truth counting no cost as too great.

Having thus registered my claim in the presence of this audience, I now wish to tell you as an orthodox Hindu what in my humble opinion your duty is in Jaffna, and in Ceylon. First of all I want to speak to you about your duty towards the predominant population in this Island. And I wish to suggest to you that they are your co-religionists. They will, if they choose to, repudiate the claim. For they will say that Buddhism is not Hinduism and they will be partly right. Many Hindus certainly repudiate the claim of Buddhism to be part and parcel of Hinduism. On the contrary they delight in saying that they successfully drove Buddhism out of India. But I tell you that they did nothing of the kind. Buddha himself was a Hindu. He endeavoured to reform Hinduism. And he succeeded in his attempt to a very great extent and what Hinduism did at that time was to assimilate and absorb all that was good and best in the teachings of the Buddha. And on that account I venture to say that Hinduism became broadened, and having assimilated the best of Buddhism, it is true that Hinduism drove out from India what might be termed the excrescences that had gathered round the teachings of Gautama. And the way in which you can demonstrate this to the Buddhists of Ceylon is by living the broadened Hinduism in their midst. The one thing that the Buddha showed India was that God was not a God who can be appeased by sacrificing innocent animals. On the contrary, he held that those who sacrificed animals in the hope of pleasing God were guilty of a double sin. So if you will be true to Hinduism, you will take care that you will not defile a single temple of yours by indulging in animal sacrifice. I am prepared to declare against the whole of Hindu India that it is wrong, sinful, and criminal to sacrifice a single animal for the purpose of gaining any end whatsoever, or for the purpose of propitiating God.

The second thing that Gautama taught was that all that caste means today—as it meant in his time also—was wholly wrong. That is to say, he abolished every distinction of superiority and inferiority that was even in his time eating into the vitals of Hinduism. But he did not abolish *varnashrama dharma*. *Varna dharma* is not caste. As I have said in so many speeches in South India, and as I have written fairly exhaustively on *varna dharma* in *Young India*, I hold that there is nothing in common between caste and *varna*. Whilst *varna* gives life, caste kills it, and untouchability is the hatefullest expression of caste. You will therefore banish untouchability from your midst. I make bold to say that there is no warrant whatsoever in Hinduism for untouchability as it is practised today. If therefore you want to live your Hinduism in its purity in the midst of Buddhist countrymen, you will take care that you will not consider a single human being as an untouchable. Unfortunately the Buddhists in Ceylon have themselves borrowed this curse from Hindus. They who should never have had this institution of caste have caste in their midst. For heaven's sake forget that some are high but others are low, remember that you are all Hindus—brothers in arms.

I have a letter from a Jaffna Hindu telling me that there are some temples in this place where you have dances by women of ill fame on certain occasions. If that information is correct, then let me tell you that you are converting temples of God into dens of prostitution. A temple, to be a house of worship, to be a temple of God, has got to conform to certain well-defined limitations. A prostitute has as much right to go to a house of worship as a saint. But she exercises that right when she enters the temple to purify herself. But when the trustees of a temple admit a prostitute under cover of religion or under cover of embellishing the worship of God, then they convert a house of God into one of prostitution. And if anybody no matter how high he may be comes to you and seeks to justify the admission of women of ill fame into your temples for dancing or any such purpose, reject him and agree to the proposal that I have made to you. If you want to be good Hindus, if you want to worship God, and if you are wise, you will fling the doors of all your temples open to the so-called untouchables. God makes no distinction between his worshippers. He accepts the worship of these untouchables just as well and as much as that of the so-called touchables, provided it comes from the bottom of the heart.

There are still certain things that demand your attention. You have to live at the present moment in a world which has Christians and Musalmans, great communities owning great faiths. In Jaffna you have a very small Musalman population hardly two or three per cent. The Christian population is 10 per cent. But you have to live your life in the midst of these whether they are two per cent, or twenty per cent. And if I know Hinduism aright, Hinduism is nothing if it is not tolerant and generous to every other faith. And since they are also as much inhabitants of this peninsula and this Island as you it is your duty to regard them as your brothers. Unless you do so, you will never evolve the truly national spirit that is necessary, and therefore you will not evolve the necessary Hindu and the humanitarian spirit. You have a right to control the education of your own children, and I am glad that you have got your own board of education. I would like you to strengthen that board in the right spirit as much as you can, but that should mean no jar whatsoever with the rival institutions of the Christian missionaries. If you have got an ably manned staff of educationists and provide the necessary facilities for the Hindu children, naturally all the Hindu children will come to your institutions. And I can see no reason whatsoever for mutual jealousies in the matter of education as I understand there is somewhat. I was delighted to find that only up to recent times, Hindus, Christians, and Musalmans were living in absolute friendship. A jar has been created only recently as between the Christians and yourselves. And seeing that you are in a vast majority, it is up to you to make advances and settle all your disputes. And if you will get rid of the wretched caste-spirit which has crept into Hinduism, you will find that all the difficulties will disappear.

And remember that since you are in a vast majority, the responsibility rests on your shoulders to make Jaffna, and through Jaffna, Ceylon also perfectly dry. Hinduism does not permit you drink. And if the board of education will do its duty, you will encourage Sanskrit study in your schools. I regard the education of any Hindu child as incomplete unless he has some knowledge of Sanskrit. And so far as I have been able to see we have in Hinduism no book so compact and so acceptable all round as the Bhagavad Gita. If you will therefore saturate your children and yourselves with the spirit of Hinduism, you will endeavour to understand the spirit of the teachings of the Gita. You should also cultivate a common knowledge of the Mahabharata and Ramayana.

Lastly I know no solution of the many difficulties that face the whole of the human family except the two things that I am saying everywhere. Speak the truth and remain non-violent also at any cost. I know as certainly as I know that I am sitting in front of you and speaking to you, that if I could but persuade you to understand the spirit of these two things and act up to them, every one of our difficulties will disappear like straws before wind, and God will descend from His Great White Throne and live in your midst and He will say 'You Hindus have done well.'

15th December, 1927

INDICTMENT

BY M. K. GANDHI

"Do you agree that it is the primary duty of an ideal Government and more so of a Great Soul to put down the wicked and to protect the righteous? If so, may we know how your political philosophy is consistent with this age-long dictum? Was not this the keynote of Shri Krishna's preaching to Arjuna on the battle-field of Kurukshetra?

"Was this not the shrewd policy of the Avataras, that brought about the dethronement of the renowned Bali, the destruction of Vali, and the annihilation of Jarasandha?

"How can you expect ordinary mortals, and that too large numbers at a time, to withstand the attacks of unscrupulous enemies without retaliation? In view of the above, are we not justified in considering your emotional preachings and teachings as impracticable and not within the realisation of ordinary persons? Your temporary and piecemeal success in South Africa had been exaggerated greatly by your admirers, and the Indians of average intelligence, innocently (sheep-like) following your lead, have been entangled in difficulties, not realising that the parallel of South Africa does not hold good in the case of a vast country of different languages and religious sections like

India. Have you not yourself realised, at the cost of the life-interests of a large number of young patriots, that all your talk of 'Swaraj within a year' has proved vain-glorious? Don't you admit that your somersault in the Bardoli affair caused much havoc to the people of Guntur who boldly and manfully withheld payment of taxes for a considerable period, in pursuance of your programme?

"May we know the net result of your participation in the Khilafat agitation and the consequent playing of the Congress into the hands of a few fanatical Musalmans? Has not the Hindu-Moslem unity of which you spoke and wrote so much, and in the name of which you appealed to all Hindus to join their Muhammadan brethren, in the hour of their trial, proved a veritable castle of cards, the moment the need of the Muhammadans was over? Can you ever expect by your pious teachings to bring about any real unity between the bigoted and brave Muhammadans and caste-ridden and timid Hindus? Have you ever realised the fact that the commun al feuds are increasing all the more, ever since you came into prominence in the Congress by virtue of your creed of Non-violence?

"Will you not admit that Pandit Malaviya, C. R. Das, Lala Lajpat Rai, Vijayaraghavachariar, Kelkar, Dr. Moonje and other All-India leaders were disgusted with your political philosophy, however much it might be garbed in the language of *Dharma*?

"Have you not recognised the leadership of that great soul Tilak at least at the beginning?

But how is it, you are today raking up intricate controversies of a social and religious character, to the detriment of the national cause? Do you not realise that these tend only to accentuate dissensions all the more among the docile Hindus? Are you not thereby indirectly playing into the hands of the enemies of, our cause, whose one argument against us is that we are socially unfit for political freedom?

"Is it worthy on your part to set up and encourage Panchamas to enter the holy temples of caste Hindus for whom and by whom they were built exclusively? Do you consider yourself to be a Trinetra (God Rudra) to set at naught these time-honoured customs at one stroke? Recently, we are surprised to note that you have taken up the cause of widows and boldly advised immature youths to marry widows. Don't you consider that Swami Vivekananda and others were prudent enough not to advocate widow marriage as they realised the difficulties which confront us even in the case of the marriages of maids, as they are taking place to-day? May we know how far it will help to create harmony by mixing up such highly controversial problems with the question of 'Swaraj' which is purely political and on which all of us are expected to make a united stand?

"Your charkha cannot be popularised in this advanced age of science. Don't you think that you will do well, in the light of practical experience, to confine your activities to the field of labour organisations?

"As a real believer in Ahimsa Dharma, is it not your clear duty to refuse addresses from municipalities, which are harbouring slaughter-houses?"

The foregoing is a condensation of a letter sent to me by a correspondent while I was in Berhampur. As I have reason to think that the correspondent has boldly voiced what many are harbouring in their breasts, I feel that the indictment deserves an answer.

It is hardly necessary to answer the questions in detail. Many of us make the very serious mistake of taking literally what is accepted as scriptures, forgetting that the letter killeth and the spirit giveth life. The Mahabharata and the Puranas are neither history nor simple religious maxims. They appear to me to be wonderfully designed to illustrate the religious history of man in a variety of ways. The heroes described therein are all imperfect mortals, even as we are—the difference being one of degree only. Their alleged actions are not infallible guides for us. The Mahabharata sums up its teachings by declaring emphatically that truth outweighs everything else on earth.

But I do not seek to justify everything written under the name of scriptures. I take, as all to be true must take, the sum total of the effect produced on me by a prayerful reading of such books Thus I hold that my belief in truth and non-violence is derived from and based on the scriptural teaching of the very books from which the correspondent presents me with conundrums Nay more, my belief today having become part of my fundamental being is capable of standing independent of these books or any other. Surely, there must come a time in the life of a very religiously minded man when his faith must be self-sustained. Whatever therefore the 'Avataras' may be proved to have done or not done is of little moment to me My experience daily growing stronger and richer tells me that there is no peace for individuals or for nations without practising truth and non-violence to the uttermost extent possible for man. The policy of retaliation has never succeeded. We must not be confounded by the isolated illustrations of retaliation, including frauds and force, having attained temporary and seeming success. The world lives because there is more love than hate, more truth than untruth in it. This is a proposition capable of being verified by every one who will take the trouble to think Fraud and force are diseases, truth and non-violence is health. The fact that the world has not perished is an ocular demonstration of the fact that there is more health than disease in it. Let us, then, who realise this, live up to the rules of health even in the midst of circumstances the most adverse.

My preaching and teaching are not emotional or unpractical, for I teach what is ancient and strive to practice what I preach. And I claim that what I practise is capable of being practised by all, because I am a very ordinary mortal open to the same temptations and liable to the same weaknesses as the least among us

The success in South Africa was complete according to the standard then aimed at. And what is true of small groups must be true of larger groups with correspondingly larger effort of the same type.

I have faith enough in my method to be able to prophesy, that posterity will consider the years 1920 and 1921 as among the most brilliant in the pages of India's history, and among them the Bardoli 'somersault' the most brilliant of all. The Bardoli decision has enabled India to look the world square in the face and to hold up her head. With her creed in the Congress constitution, it was the only correct, bold and honourable course for the nation to take. The battle for Swaraj was no camouflage. And if any suffered involuntarily, they suffered because they played with fire.

The participation in the Khilafat agitation has made both the parties strong and has resulted in a mass awakening which would have otherwise taken ages. If real unity is to come, it will come only by a due adherence to my teachings. The present Hindu-Muslim feuds and inter-Hindu feuds and even inter-Muslim feuds are a sign of the mass awakening. What we see happening today is nothing but the coming of dirt to the surface in the process of purification. Let the correspondent watch the process going on in a sugar refinery, and he will understand my meaning. This froth in the shape of feuds has come to the surface only to be thrown out in the end.

I am unaware of the fact that Pandit Madan Mohan Malaviyaji and the other leaders mentioned by the correspondent are disgusted with my political philosophy. Of some at least I know to the contrary. But even if they are disgusted I hope that my faith will stand the strain of the disgust of all the friends whose opinion I have learnt to value and cherish.

The correspondent betrays his ignorance of the Lokamanya when he imputes to him policies which I know he was never guilty of. I know that there were fundamental differences between us but not what the correspondent imagines. What we should learn from our heroes is not a slavish imitation of their actions which we may not know or understand. We need to assimilate their bravery, their great self-sacrifice, their equally great industry, their love of their country and a steady pursuit of their own ideals. We make fatal blunders when without relevance or without adequate knowledge we copy their isolated actions.

I hold that without the social reforms that I am advocating, thank God, in common with many of our distinguished countrymen, Hinduism is in danger of perishing.

The charkha is making steady progress in spite of the correspondent's unbelief. The charkha work is my contribution to the ocean of labour.

When I receive addresses from municipalities, I claim to remain untouched by the slaughter in the municipal slaughter-houses. On the contrary their addresses give me an opportunity of preaching my doctrines to them, and I am happy to say that they never resent them and some of them even adopt the suggestions I humbly place before them.

22nd December, 1927

OUR SHAME AND THEIR SHAME

By M. K. Gandhi

The long deferred Orissa visit has come to fill the bitter cup of sorrow and humiliation. It was at Bolgarh, thirty-one miles from the nearest railway station, that whilst I was sitting and talking with Dinabandu Andrews on the 11th instant, a man with a half-bent back wearing only a dirty loin cloth came crouching in front of us. He picked up a straw and put it in his mouth and then lay flat on his face with arms outstretched and then raised himself, folded his hands, bowed, took out the straw, arranged it in his hair and was about to leave. I was writhing in agony whilst I witnessed the scene. Immediately the performance was finished, I shouted for an interpreter, asked the friend to come near and began to talk to him. He was an 'untouchable' living in a village six miles away, and being in Bolgarh for the sale of his load of faggots and having heard of me had come to see me. Asked why he should have taken the straw in his mouth, he said that was to honour me. I hung my head in shame. The price of honour seemed to me to be too great to bear. My Hindu spirit was deeply wounded. I asked him for a gift. He searched a copper about his waist. 'I do not want your copper, but I want you to give me something better,' I said. 'I will give it,' he replied. I had ascertained from him that he drank and ate carrion because it was custom.

'The gift I want you to give me is a promise never again to take the straw in your mouth for any person on earth, it is beneath man's dignity to do so; never again to drink because it reduces man to the condition of a beast, and never again to eat carrion, for it is against Hinduism and no civilised person would ever eat carrion,

'But my people will excommunicate me, if I do not drink and eat carrion,' the poor man said.

'Then suffer excommunication and if need be leave the village.'

This down-trodden humble man made the promise. If he keeps it, his threefold gift is more precious than the rupees that generous countrymen entrust to my care.

This untouchability is our greatest shame. The humiliation of it is sinking deeper.

But this never-to-be-forgotten incident was only part of the shame and sorrow. Never since the days of Champaran (in 1916) have I witnessed such death-like quiet as I did on entering political Orissa through Banpur. And I fear that the quiet of Orissa is worse than that of Champaran. There was spirit in the ryots of Champaran after a few days' stay in their midst. I doubt if the Orissa ryot would respond so quickly. I was told that the Zamindars, the Rajas and the local police had conspired to frighten the ryots out of coming near me. I had began to flatter myself with the belief that the Rajas, the Zamindars and the pettiest police officials had ceased to distrust or fear me. The experiences of Orissa have chastened me. Being too weak to go about much, I sent my friends among the people and ascertained the cause. They brought the news that people were told, on pain of punishment, not to come near me or to take part in any demonstration in my honour. Such warnings have been issued before and in other provinces, but they have had little or no effect in normal times such as these. The ryots in Orisa, however, seemed to me to be living in a perpetual state of fear and liable to be acted upon by the slightest attempt.

This is a shame both we and the foreign rulers have to share. It is true that the Rajas and Zamindars and the petty officials are our own kith and kin. But the primary source of fright is in the rulers. Their system is based on 'frightfulness.' In the name of prestige they have compelled somehow or other the tallest amongst us to bend low. They have intensified, where they have not created, demoralisation. They have known the existence of abject fear among the ryots. But they have done nothing to remove it and the causes, where they have not hugged the condition of things in the alleged interest of their rule. Whilst therefore they may not be directly responsible for the pathetic scenes I witnessed, they cannot be acquitted of a considerable share of responsibility for them.

But our shame is greater. If we were strong, self-respecting and not susceptible to frightfulness, the foreign rulers would have been powerless for mischief. Those only who are susceptible to fear are frightened by others. And it has to be confessed that long before the British advent we were habituated to fear by our own Zamindars and Rajas. The present rulers have but reduced to a science what was in existence before in a more or less crude shape. The workers in Orissa have therefore to teach the ryot to shed the oppressive nervous timidity bordering on cowardice. And this they will not do by swearing at the Zamindar, the Raja or the police officials. These latter become docile and even friendly when they find that the ryot has unlearned the unmanly habit.

29th December, 1927

POLITICAL PRISONERS

BY M. K. GANDHI

Lala Dunichand of Ambala has sent me a copy of the statement published by him in England about political prisoners who are undergoing incarceration in the various jails of India. The statement contains nothing new for the Indian public and might easily have been fuller and more precise for the purpose intended by the author. In a covering note he administers to me a gentle rebuke for rarely mentioning these prisoners. If the absence of mention of these countrymen of ours means apathy or negligence on my part, the rebuke is well deserved. But I claim that I yield to no one in my desire to see these prisoners released. But the omission to mention these cases is deliberate. I hope that the pages of *Young India* do not contain many idle words. Whatever is written in these pages has a definite purpose. Time was when I used to analyse these cases and expose the injustice done in many of them. But that was when I had faith in the British system and when I used to take pride in its ultimate goodness. Having lost that faith, I have lost also the power of making an effective appeal to the administrators of that system. I can no longer write about British fairplay and the British sense of justice. On the contrary, I feel that the administrators are precluded by their system from dealing out fairplay or justice when their system is or seems to them to be in jeopardy. It is still possible, I admit, to secure justice from them when their system is not at stake in any shape or form. But when that system is or is felt by them to be in danger they lose not only their sense of justice and fair-play but they lose their balance and no means appear to them to be too dishonourable or despicable for adoption to sustain it. Dyerism and O'dwyerism were no isolated phenomena. Only I was blind to them before Jallianwala. As a matter of fact, they have been resorted to in all climes and at all times whenever they have felt the need of them.

I am satisfied that the political prisoners who are held under restraint with or without trial, decorous or farcical, are so held in the interest of that system. The administrators would far rather discharge a murderer caught red-handed and found guilty of murder committed for private ends than discharge a political prisoner suspected of designs on their system especially if he the suspect is believed to have violent means in view.

It seems to me therefore to be waste of time and inconsistent with self-respect to make any appeal to the administrators in behalf of the political prisoners Lala Dunichand has in view. And he has in mind the prisoners of the Gadr party, the Punjab Martial law prisoners and the Bengal detenus. Nor need we be led astray by solitary discharges like that of Sjt. Subhas Bose. In spite of the agitation that was set on foot he would in all probability not have been discharged if his precarious health had not come to the rescue. Indeed, have they not said in the plainest language possible that they were released purely on grounds of ill health? Has not Earl Winterton flatly declined to release the Bengal detenus in answer to the appeal to create a favourable atmosphere for their precious Statutory Commission?

Let those who still have faith in the system by all means make an appeal to the British sense of justice and fairplay.

My course is clear. We have not yet paid anything like adequate price for the freedom we would fain breathe. I therefore regard these imprisonments as only a small part of the price we have to pay if we would have the freedom which is the birthright of man. And we shall have to march as willing victims to the slaughter house and not helplessly like goats and sheep. We may do this violently or non-violently. The way of violence can only lead us to a blind alley and must cause endless suffering to unwilling ignorant men and women who do not know what freedom is and who have no desire to buy the valuable article. The way of non-violence is the surest and the quickest way to freedom and causes the least suffering and that only to those who are prepared for it, indeed would gladly court it. But suffering, intense, extensive and agonising there must be in every case. What we have gone through is but a sample of what is to come.

Therefore the task before those, who share my views about the inherent evil of the system, is to cease to appeal to the administrators, and ceaselessly and with unquenchable faith in our cause and the means to appeal to the nation. Not until the nation has developed enough strength to open the prison gates, can these prisoners be released with honour and dignity for it and them. Till then let us with becoming patience and courage submit to the imprisonments of the prisoners and ourselves prepare joyfully to share their fate. We shall certainly not hasten the advent of freedom by appealing to deaf ears for mercy and thus unconsciously inducing in the people a mentality that would dread prisons and the gallows. Lovers of freedom have to learn to regard these as welcome friends and deliverers.

YOUNG INDIA

1928

5th January, 1928

THE NATIONAL CONGRESS

By M. K. Gandhi

The special feature of Dr. Ansari's speech was its intense hunger for unity. He knew that he was expected to bring it about. And if any single person could do it, it was certainly Dr. Ansari. He accepted the highest honour in the gift of the nation because he had confidence in the nation, the cause and himself. He certainly left no stone unturned to achieve his ambition. Stars favoured him. Sjt. Srinivasa Aiyengar helped him by his very recklessness. No other president would perhaps have dared as he did after the partial failure at Simla. But Sjt. Aiyengar was not the man to shrink. He took Dr. Ansari, the Ali Brothers, Maulana Abul Kalam Azad and others with him and with his accustomed impetuosity carried his resolution. He was not committed to any formula. When the almost fatal flaw in the resolution about the cow and music was pointed out and a substitute submitted, he whole-heartedly frankly and generously admitted the flaw and accepted the substitute as a great improvement on the original. The Musalmans present rose to the occasion, and though not without some reluctance and hesitation at first, accepted the substitute without reserve. Pandit Malaviyaji had come with the full intention of accommodating himself to the general wish so far as it was possible for him. He knew and everybody realised that it was within his power to block the way. He did not. True, he had many amendments which he considered were necessary but he was not going to resist the resolution if his amendments could not be carried. Pandit Malaviyaji is probably the oldest Congressman. His loyalty to the Congress is beyond compare. His patriotism is of the highest order. But my Musalman friends have hitherto always belittled my faith in his *bona fides* and nationalism as against communalism. I have never been able to suspect either even where I have not been able to share his views on Hindu Muslim questions. It was therefore a great joy to me that the Ali Brothers warmly acclaimed his great speech on the unity resolution. So long as Hindu and Musalman leaders distrust one another's motives speeches and actions, there can be no real unity in spite of perfect resolutions. Let us hope that the trust generated at the meeting will continue and prove highly infectious. Maulana Mahomed Ali in his joy over Malaviyaji's speech said that the Musalmans no longer wanted protection of minorities from Earl Winterton for it could be better secured by Malaviyaji. If there be one Hindu who can guarantee such protection on behalf of Hindus it is Malaviyaji. But whether he can 'deliver goods' or not, I would like the Maulana and the other Musalmans and all minorities once for all to renounce the idea of expecting or getting protection from a third party. It were better, if such protection be not given voluntarily by the majority, to wrest it by force from unwilling hands than that a third party should be invited to intervene and should weaken and humiliate both and hold the nation under bondage. The greatest contribution of the Congress then to me was this apparent change of heart.

So far as the vast mass of Hindus are concerned they are interested only in the cow and music resolution. It was wholly bad in its original form. As it has finally emerged from the Subjects Committee and passed, all that can be said for it is that it is innocuous and that it is the best that could be had at this stage of the national evolution. But I for one cannot enthuse over it. I can only tolerate it as possible Nevertheless it has great possibilities. If the appeal of the Congress penetrates the hearts of Hindus and Musalmans and if each party spares the feelings of the other in terms of the claims advanced by each, peace is in sight and Swaraj within easy grasp. A definite realisation of the folly of fratricide and corresponding action will be the best and the most dignified answer to Lord Birkenhead's insolent flaunting of British might in the nation's face.

It is, therefore, profitable to examine the meaning of the

Congress appeal. I know what would spare the Hindus' feeling in the matter of the cow. It is nothing short of complete voluntary stoppage of cow-slaughter by Musalmans whether for sacrifice or for food. The Hindu *dharma* will not be satisfied if some tyrant secured by force of arms immunity of the cow from the slaughter. Islam in India cannot make a better gift to the Hindus than this voluntary self-denial. And I know enough of Islam to be able to assert that Islam does not compel cow-slaughter and it does compel its followers to spare and respect to the full the feelings of their neighbours whenever it is humanly possible. For me, music before mosques is not on a par with cow-slaughter. But it has assumed an importance which it would be folly to ignore. It is for the Musalmans to say what would spare Musalman feelings. And if complete stoppage of music before mosques will be the only thing that will spare the Musalman feelings, it is the duty of the Hindus to do so without a moment's thought. If we are to reach unity of hearts, we must each be prepared to perform an adequate measure of sacrifice.

If this much-to-be-desired consummation is to be reached Dr. Ansari will have to send out peace parties with definite instructions to preach the message and secure for it the approval of the masses. Have we sufficient energy for the mission, have we enough honest, industrious and willing missionaries? Let us hope.

Though I was not able to attend any of the Committee meetings, I could not fail to perceive that irresponsible talk and work were the order of the day. Indiscipline was not a rare feature. Resolutions involving great consequences were sprung upon the Subjects Committee and readily accepted by that august body without much thought or discussion. The independence resolution that was rejected last year was passed almost without opposition. I know that its wording was harmless but in my humble opinion it was hastily conceived and thoughtlessly passed. I hope to deal with this resolution separately. (*See page 545*)

The boycott of British goods resolution was passed with an equally light heart. The Congress stultifies itself by repeating year after year resolutions of this character when it knows that it is not capable of carrying them into effect. By passing such resolutions we make an exhibition of our impotence, become the laughing-stock of critics and invite the contempt of the adversary.

Let me not be misunderstood. The Congress has a perfect right to boycott British goods, if it so wishes. But as the most representative assembly in India, it has no right to expose itself to ridicule by using threats which it cannot carry into effect. I have singled out but two out of the several irresponsible resolutions passed by the Congress.

The conception behind the Congress constitution was to make it the most representative and authoritative body in all India, and by its commanding voluntary obedience on the part of millions, automatically, almost imperceptibly, to replace the sham enslaving assemblies and councils and the other foreign machinery masquerading under the name of representative bodies. But the Congress cannot become the irresistible force it was and is intended to be, if its resolutions are ill-conceived and are to remain merely paper resolutions having no response from the people or having no correspondence to the popular wants and aspirations and if the members are not to observe the rules of discipline, decorum and common honesty. If they only knew, if they would regard themselves as servants of the nation, the members of the All-India Congress Committee have the rights and opportunities of service equal to those of the members of any parliament in the world. But at the present moment we have almost sunk to the level of the 'schoolboys' debating society.'

The Working Committee is the national cabinet. It has to enforce the resolutions of the Congress and the All-India Congress Committee. It must therefore be the body responsible for bringing before the A.I.C.C. resolutions required for the attainment of the Congress goal. Any non-official resolution sprung upon the A. I. C. C. must be carefully scrutinised and should have but a remote chance of passing, if opposed by the Working Committee. Every resolution, official or unofficial, must have behind it a working plan. When therefore an unofficial resolution is brought forward, the sponsor must be prepared to disclose his plan of action if his proposal is to be accepted. A resolution proposing the establishment in every village of a free night school for its adult population has everything to commend itself to a body like the Congress. But if the proposer has no definite feasible plan of action behind it, the A. I. C. C. would be justified and bound to reject it summarily. If then the Congress is to retain its prestige and usefulness, the members of the A. I. C. C. will have to revise their attitude and realise their great responsibility.

In my humble opinion the Reception Committee of the Congress at Madras committed a grave blunder by permitting and countenancing the so-called All-India Exhibition under its *aegis*. That it received Government patronage and *imprimatur* adds nothing to its merits, if it does not rob it of what little merit it otherwise might have had. The Congress long ago outlived Government favours and frowns. The ideals, for which the Congress has been working since, say 1918 to go no further back, were almost all ignored in the plan of this Exhibition. Let me point out what the All-India Exhibition contained. Among the pavillions were several assigned to foreign firms for exhibiting their wares, one assigned to machinery and mechanical contrivances, some to textiles containing foreign yarn, others to foreign clocks and watches. There was little of Swadeshi, much of foreign and British goods about the Exhibition, and this in the name of and under the patronage of a Congress which promulgates the gospel of Swadeshi and which has on its programme a boycott of British goods. There was hardly anything to interest or instruct the villagers. The Exhibition represented not the rural civilisation of India but the exploiting civilisation of the West. It was a denial of the Congress spirit and was in marked contrast to the Khadi and

Swadeshi Exhibitions of the past six years. The textile Court seemed to have been designed to ridicule Khadi although the Congress still retains the Khadi franchise and lends its name to the activities of the All-India Spinners' Association. As if the visitors were to be all English all the notices were printed in English. Here is one designed to belittle Khadi:

"*Feed* the poor and *work* the able
Let the charkha spin the weft
And the mill the warp
In this combination lies the solution."

Unless the author of this notice has a deliberately mischievous intention, he has demonstrated his ignorance of the evolution of Khadi. The fallacy of charkha weft and mill warp has been often exposed and refuted in these columns. Suffice it here to say that the charkha would have died a well-deserved death if the policy of using charkha yarn for weft only had long continued. Experience has shown that the combination was bad in every respect.

Here is another equally, if not more mischievous, poster:

"To force a weaver to use handspun warp yarn
Is like forcing him to fight a battleship with a knife.
To cut a weaver off from the best methods of work
Is like cutting off his thumbs."

This poster betrays venomous prejudice against Khadi and ignorance of the art of weaving and the condition of weavers. The writer forgets that all the world over, a time was when weavers took delight in using handspun yarn both for weft and warp and that the art then exhibited by the weaver has never yet been excelled. The writer could easily have corrected himself by visiting the Khadi Court outside the precious All-India Exhibiton Court. He would there have seen weavers actually working fairy tales on handspun warp with the same ease and facility that they would have with mill-spun yarn. It is easy of proof that whereas mill-spun yarn must in time—not far off—kill out the weaver, handspun yarn must revive and is reviving the weaver and has already rescued some of them from the butcher's trade and closet-cleaning work. Every ten hand-spinners mean an addition of one whole-time weaver, one whole-time carder, not to mention more work for *dhobis*, tailors, carpenters, blacksmiths, dyers, printers etc.

The coming into being of this foreign and anti-India spirit Exhibition under the Congress *aegis* is an ocular and forcible demonstration, the irresponsibility to which I have already adverted. I do not think any Congressman deliberately countenanced this white elephant. Want of thought, want of care, want of responsibility are answerable for—I cannot help calling—this scandalous creation.

There was no doubt the ant of the Khadi Exhibition was happily thrown outside the elephant Court. Rumour has it that the Madras Government would not have a Khadi Exhibition inside the All-India Court. It certainly suited me. For, having gained a knowledge of what this All-India Exhibition was, I would have found it difficult if not impossible even for opening the Khadi Exhibition to enter what was chiefly a foreign Court—a reminder of national humiliation. The Khadi Exhibition on the other hand was, though like an ant, a work of indigenous art. It was a school for study and demonstration of the potency of Khadi. There was beside it an Indian Fine Arts Court, a result of the devoted labours of Dr. J. H. Cousins. No doubt there were a few other things purely Indian or a result of Indian enterprise in this so-called All-India Exhibition. But they only served to entrap the unwary and as a shield for the predominant foreign show.

Let future Reception Committees beware.

5th January, 1928

IN MEMORIAM

BY M. K. GANDHI

In the death of Hakim Saheb Ajmalkhan the country has lost one of its truest servants. Hakim Saheb's was a many-sided personality. He was not merely an able physician who practised his art as much for the rich as for the poor. But he was a courtier patriot. Though he passed his time among potentates, he was a thorough-going democrat. He was a great Musalman and equally a great Indian. He loved equally Hindus and Musalmans and was in turn equally respected and loved by both. Hindu Muslim unity was the breath of his nostrils. His later days were soured because of our dissensions. But he never lost faith in his country or his people. He felt that both the communities were bound in the end to unite. Having that unchangeable faith, he never ceased to work for unity. Though he took time, he finally threw in his lot with the non-co-operators and did not hesitate to put in peril his fondest and greatest creation, the Tibbia College. He loved this College with a passion which only those who knew him well could realise. In Hakimji I have lost not merely a wise and steadfast co-worker, I have lost a friend on whom I could rely in the hour of need. He was my constant guide in the matter of Hindu Muslim unity. His judgment, sobriety and knowledge of human nature enabled him for the most part to give correct decisions. Such a man never dies. Though he is no longer in the flesh with us, his spirit shall be ever with us and calls us even now to a faithful discharge of our duty. And no memorial that we can raise to perpetuate his memory can be complete until we have achieved real Hindu-Muslim unity. May God grant that we may learn to do through his death what we failed to do in his lifetime.

But Hakimji was no idle dreamer. He believed in realising his dream. As he realised his dream about medicine through the Tibbia College, so he sought partially to realise his political dream through the Jamia Milia. When this national university was almost on the point of dying, he, almost single-handed, carried out the plan of removing the institution from Aligadh to Delhi. But the removal meant more worry for him. He believed himself henceforward to be specially responsible for the financial stability of the College. He was the principal man to find support for it either from his own pocket or by way of contributions collected from personal friends. The immediate and indispensable memorial that the nation can raise is to put the financial condition of the Jamia on a stable basis. Both Hindus and Musalmans are and should be equally interested in it. It is one of the four national universities still struggling for existence, the other three being the Bihar, Kashi and Gujarat Vidyapiths. When the Jamia was brought into being, Hindus subscribed liberally to it. The national ideal has been kept intact in this Muslim institution. I commend to the attention of the reader the note prepared by Sjt. Ramachandran out of his own experience covering over twelve months. In Principal Zakir Husain it has a learned Principal of liberal views and undoubted nationalism. The principal is ably assisted by a chosen staff some of whom have travelled abroad and possess foreign degrees. The institution has grown since its transfer to Delhi and if it is well supported, it promises rich results. There can be no doubt that it is the duty of those Hindus and Musalmans who wish to honour the memory of Hakim Saheb, who believe in the constructive side of non-co-operation and who believe in Hindu Muslim unity, to give as much financial assistance as is possible for them to give. Dr. Ansari, Sjt. Shrinivas Aiyengar, Sheth Jamnalal Bajaj and Pandit Jawaharlal Nehru have already issued an appeal in this matter. I am now trying through Principal Zakir Husain to find out the exact condition and placing myself in correspondence with Dr. Ansari, and as soon as I have collected enough information, I hope to lay it before the readers. In the meantime I invite subscriptions so as not to lose time. The subscriptions received will not be handed to any one unless a proper committee is formed and an absolutely correct administration of funds is assured. I do hope that Hindus and Musalmans will vie with one another to swell the subscription list.

5th January, 1928

KHADI EXHIBITION, MADRAS

I remember having seen, when very young, Exhibitions which were held at Bombay and Allahabad in connection with the Congress which was held at those places in 1904 and 1910 respectively, and I also remember how I returned from the Exhibitions admiring the beautiful cycle and motor shows and the maze arranged for the fun of the visitors. The All-India industrial Exhibition held under the *ægis* of the Congress this year must, I am afraid, have left much the same impression on most of the people who visited it. There was very little in it that was indigenous, very little to represent the various cottage industries of India, the bulk of the space being taken up by stalls set up by foreign engineering firms. Gandhiji called this Exhibition an elephant as contrasted with the Khadi Exhibition which he called an ant. The elephant and the ant are in their respective places equally harmless and useful, but here the elephant seemed to be designed to crush the ant. As an American friend remarked, it was Mammon on one side and righteousness on the other. The one was intended to interest the well-to-do customer to go in for machinery and fill the pockets of rich foreign manufacturers, the other was intended to educate the poor in the one and only life-giving cottage industry of India, and to tempt the rich to help the poor in the only effective way. Apart from this obvious difference in the aim and object, the 'elephant' was poor even in point of arrangement and organisation and the little in it that was useful or of educative value was lost in the useless litter that encumbered the vast space.

The Khadi Exhibition was identical in conception with the Exhibition held at Bangalore some months ago and described in these columns, but it was on a larger scale. One missed in this Exhibition Shrimati Virumma, the queen of the Bangalore Exhibition, but the eye of the Exhibition, namely the blind old woman from Karnatak, was there spinning away the whole day indifferent to the admiring crowd around her. For educative propaganda there were more charts and photographs in this Exhibition, challenging the attention of the student and the critic, and the demonstration of all the processes from ginning to weaving and printing was more thorough than at Bangalore. Miss Mithuben Petit was there not only with her fine fabrics and beautiful little pincushions and other things of daily use, artistically done in fine Khadi, but she had two ladies from her school to demonstrate the delicate embroidery and needlework that makes her fabrics so attractive.

There were as usual competitions in high speed spinning, high count spinning, *takli* spinning and carding with the hand bow, and it is worthy of note that the results were even better than the fine ones achieved at Bangalore, and some of the recipients of prizes were new in the field. To a student interested in the various processes the following results will be very instructive:

Among high speed prize winners the first prize was won by young Keshu Gandhi who broke all his previous records and spun 1400 yards of 87 p. c. uniformity and 74 p. c. test of 21 counts in two hours. The second prize was won by Sjt. Deodhar who spun 1426 yards of the same quality but of 14½ counts.

Amongst the high count prize winners the first rank was taken by Sjt. Minakshisundaram who spun 319 yards of 150 counts in two hours, the second by Sjt. Chokhalingam (with whom the readers of my Chettinad letter are familiar) who spun 214 yards of 145 counts and the third by Keshu Gandhi the first prize winner in the first competition who spun 346 yards of 117 counts. These results are the highest yet achieved at the annual competitions.

Among the *takli* spinners Sjt. Rajgopala Ganapati Shastri still held the field with his 160 yards per hour of 45 counts. The other prize winners also scored as high as 140 yards of 38 counts and 123 yards of 40 counts.

Amongst the carders Sjt. Kanti Parekh broke his previous records by carding 26 tolas in one hour, and Sjts. G. K. Pandit and Govindbhai Patel ran a close race with him with 24 and 23 tolas per hour respectively.

The number of stalls was naturally much larger than at Bangalore, the highest sale at one single stall per day being over Rs. 1,500,—a testimony to the increasing popularity of Khadi, and increasing capacity of the producers to satisfy all tastes and fashions. The prettiest stall was Miss Petit's, but the most attractive was the Punjab stall with its beautifully patterned dyed carpets and tablecloth which attracted every visitor. Of no less interest was a stall where a cabinet-maker had exhibited very fine pieces of his furniture all upholstered in beautifully fine and artistic Khadi, the whole stall giving an idea of how a fashionable drawing room could be tastefully fitted up in Khadi.

It was a veritable sight to see how the different varieties of cloth exhibited attracted the attention of visitors not only from Burma and Ceylon, but of Europeans as well, and seemed to satisfy requirements of their purses as well as their aesthetic sense. Pandit Malaviyaji who in the midst of his numerous engagements found time to visit the Exhibition, and took particular care to visit every demonstration stall and every shop, could not contain himself with the admiration that he felt for the work that was being done. 'Let us stud our country with numerous such exhibitions,' he said. 'Let us spread broadcast all the literature about Khadi in thousands and hundreds of thousands of copies, and let us have a Khadi show in every educational centre in India.' Seeing the blind spinner busy at her wheel the Panditji was deeply moved and said, 'I wish I could carry about with me this old blind woman wherever I go, and appeal to our apathetic countrymen to open their eyes and see what the Khadi movement means.' That is what Gandhiji also said in effect when in his opening speech he appealed to all Congressmen to think of the skeletons of Orissa. Both were appeals full of sorrow and sadness, coming from the stricken hearts of Panditji and Gandhiji which seemed to exclaim to their countrymen, 'Behold and see if there be any sorrow like unto my sorrow.'

M. D.

12th January, 1928

'THE POOR IN SPIRIT

For over a year, practically, we have been like birds wandering from their nests, and it was with a positive feeling of relief that we returned to the Ashram. Thanks to the decision of the All-India Spinners' Association, the impending tours in February and March have been for the time being cancelled, so as to give Gandhiji an unbroken period of quiet time at the Ashram.

The quiet time, however, does not mean lack of work. It is a time of 'toil unsevered from tranquillity,' of communings with the inmates of the Ashram and of self-examination. Among the many problems that we have to face in the Ashram one is that of malaria which visits us regularly every year after the end of the monsoon. Doctors have been consulted as to the causes and the means of prevention, and one of the usual means suggested is protection from mosquitoes with the help of a mosquito-net. 'How can all afford a mosquito-net? Is there no means which the poorest can afford?' Gandhiji seems to have asked the doctors, who said there was one. That is keeping the body properly covered, and smearing the face with Kerosene oil. Gandhiji generally uses the mosquito-net, but as soon as he saw that there was a poor man's remedy, he asked the net to be removed and has been smearing his face with Kerosene oil before bed time. 'The poor in spirit' of the beatitudes are not the poor who cannot afford a thing, but those who, affording the thing, deny themselves its use because the poor cannot afford it.

Another and much more forcible illustration occurred during the same week. 'I have to give you this evening an instance of a folly of which three of us have an equal share,' said Gandhiji at one of our prayer meetings. 'Or rather my share is the biggest inasmuch as, I, as the head of the Ashram, am expected to be much more vigilant than any one of you' Many of us could not imagine what this would be. But he narrated it in vivid and, as he is wont to describe his mistakes, in exaggerated detail. Those who have seen Gandhiji's room in the Ashram will remember that between the wall which faces the river and the roof there is a piece of lattice work. It is meant for ventilation, but it also lets in the sun's rays straight on Gandhiji's face. So he asked one of us to put something there as a screen. This friend asked another who immediately brought in the carpenter with a board. He naturally thought a shutter would be better than a screen, and asked if Gandhiji would like it. Gandhiji agreed, but soon after the carpenter began his work, he seems to have perceived that he had not done the right thing. So he began to think aloud. He first told the friends who had been sharers in the mistake, then the ladies whom he meets every morning for half an hour, and finally the prayer meeting. 'Now this is not what we who are pledged to poverty may do It ought to have occurred to me that a piece of cardboard or a piece of cloth would serve as well as this shutter which costs a couple of rupees and three hours' labour for the carpenter. The cardboard or the piece of old cloth would have cost nothing and any one could have fixed it there with a couple of nails. It is in these simple little things that our creed is tested. The Kingdom of Heaven is for those who are poor in spirit Let us therefore learn at every step to reduce our needs and wants to the terms of the poor and try to be truly poor in spirit.'

We have hymns every morning and evening, and usually it is Khare Shastri, our music teacher who conducts the prayer and sings the hymns. During his absence in Madras, however, Pandit Totaramji, who has a store-house of Kabir's songs, had been conducting the prayers, and one morning he gave a very sweet song which none of us had heard before. After the evening prayers Gandhiji asked the children if any one could say what song they had heard in the morning. None of them could say, and that gave Gandhiji an opportunity of giving us a brief sermon on prayer and on the song itself. 'Well, I do not remember the exact words of the song,' he said. 'But no one can forget the substance of the song. It is not only the music but the substance that has been haunting me the whole day. You do not come to prayer to listen to music, or to admire this man's or that man's voice, but in order that you may carry with you for the day something from what you hear to guide and inspire you in all your actions. If we do not do so, all our prayer would be like sounding brass or a tinkling cymbal. What a great song was today's! Kabir in his homely telling way has described the treasures of the humble. It is not he that exalteth himself, but he that humbleth himself that shall see God, says Kabir. We have to be humble like the ant and not proud like the elephant.' But I give the song itself:

'Only he who humbleth himself will find the Lord.

'It is no use your going to the weaver with coarse yarn, and asking for fine cloth from him.

'Hard earth is no use to the potter, unless he beats it into very fine powder for clay. Then and then only can it be fit for the wheel.

'An elephant will try in vain to pick up the grains of sugar scattered in grains of sand. But an ant will easily pick them up. Humble thyself therefore.

'For he who exalteth himself shall be crushed. But says Kabir, he who humbleth himself shall find God.

The evening talk, whenever he gives one, is devoted to topics arising out of the everyday life of the members. The morning ones are almost always about some thought or other from the Gita. No elaborate comment. Just a few words or sentences on the chapter recited, to serve as a sort of approach to the chapter. For instance: "Chapter Nine contains what I would describe as the healing balm for us afflicted morals—afflicted not only with physical ills, but with ills of the spirit. The chapter contains the promise of God to all erring mortals, nay even to those who may be 'born from the very womb of Sin.' Those that turn to Him shall have no cause to grieve. The chapter also shows that the Gita was written when *varnashrama* had ceased to exist in its pristine purity and had come to mean, as it does today, a classification of high and low. Let us forget that, and remember that the promise is given to all *apicheth Sudurácharo* even if they be steeped in sin. And when we are all steeped in sin, more or less, who dare cast the stone at whom? 'Be thou certain, none can perish, trusting Me,' says the Lord, but let it not be understood to mean that our sins will be washed away by merely trusting Him without any striving Only he who struggles hard against the allurements of sense objects, and turns in tears and grief to the Lord, will be comforted."

Again, Chapter Eleven and Twelve: 'What can more forcefully turn one to God than this panoramic vision of His multitudinous manifestations, and having thus prepared us for *bhakti*, the Lord gives us the essence of *bhakti* in the twelfth chapter which is so brief that any one can commit it to memory to call it to his aid in moments of trial.'

Chapters Fourteen and Fifteen.

"Chapter fourteen and the threefold division of the qualities of nature remind me of Henry Drummond's book I read about 30 years ago—*The Natural Law in the Spiritual World*. The laws are numerous but they have been broadly classified under three heads. The fourteenth chapter describes the laws to which man is subject and the fifteenth describes Purushottama the Perfect Man. The 'ascent of man' is what we have to learn from these chapters. There is no man who is governed exclusively by one of the three *gunas—sattva, rajas* or *tamas*. We have each of us to rise to a state in which we are governed predominantly by the *sattva* principle, until at last we rise beyond the three and are 'Perfect Man.' I can think of an illustration from the physical world. Take water, which in its solid state remains on the earth; it cannot ascend until it is rarefied into steam. But once it is rarefied into steam it rises up in the sky where at last it is transformed into clouds which drop down in the form of rain and fructify and bless the earth. We are all like water, we have to strive so to rarefy ourselves that all the ego in us perishes and we merge in the infinite to the eternal good of all."

One of the candidates for the Khadi service went in one day with his own ailment. He said he was very much prone to anger and he wanted to cleanse himself with fasting. 'I warn you,' said Gandhiji, 'that fasting is not always a penance for sins. Humble surrender to God is the only escape from sin, and all fasting except when it is undertaken to help that surrender is useless. I would suggest a better remedy. Go and apologise to the man you were angry with, ask him to prescribe the penance for you and do that. That will be much better expiation than fasting.' The friend went and did likewise. But what should the man who has been wronged do in this case? Simply forgive? Forgiveness, we have been told, is the ornament of the brave, but what is that forgiveness? Passivity? Taking the blow lying down? Is that the meaning of resisting not evil?

This was the subject of a talk one evening and I summarise it briefly: "This talk of passive non-resistance has been the bane of our national life. Forgiveness is a quality of the soul, and therefore a positive quality. It is not negative. 'Conquer anger,' says Lord Buddha, 'by non-anger.' But what is that 'non-anger?' It is a positive quality and means the supreme virtue of charity or love. You must be roused to this supreme virtue which must express itself in your going to the angry man, ascertaining from him the cause of his anger, making amends if you have given any cause for offence and then bringing home to him the error of his way and convincing him that it is wrong to be provoked. This consciousness of the quality of the soul, and deliberate exercise of it, elevate not only the man but the surrounding atmosphere. Of course only he who has that love will exercise it. This love can certainly be cultivated by incessant striving." M. D.

12th January, 1928

MYSORE GOVERNMENT'S KHADI CENTRE

BY M. K. GANDHI

The Mysore Government have taken up an experiment in production and have started work in real earnest at a centre called Badanval, taking advantage of help from the A. I. S. A. in regard to workers and plan of work. Sjt. Rajagopalachari has received a letter from one of the workers from which the following interesting account of progress of work is extracted. It shows how easily Khadi spreads if the work is started on right lines in rural areas where the need for a supplementary occupation is keenly felt:

"300 spinners have received advances from us in the shape of cotton or cash to buy the same while 100 others have been supplying yarn without having received any advance. The average liability of each spinner is Re. 1. The spinning area has extended to the interior towards Gundlupet Taluk up to some fifteen miles south of Badanval. The Badanval spinning circle has now developed into an ellipse which necessitates the opening of a second spinning focus; else it is difficult to keep the balance. Two thirds of the quantity of yarn that is being collected now flows into Badanval from an area which had never been thought of by the founders of this circle. In fact, if anything like a survey had been effected before hitting upon Badanval as the centre, they should have fixed the centre somewhere between Badanval and Gundlupet. But all this rearrangement cannot be effected immediately.

"The following statement will explain the present condition of the work:

	As on Nov. 30th	As on Dec. 26th
No. of villages to which we have extended our operations	25	40
No. of spinners	230	400

Yarn produced	Rs. 160 (lbs. 212)	Rs. 502 (lbs. 715)
Cloth produced	Rs. 145 (380 yds.)	Rs. 445 (825 yds.)

Weekly earnings of spinner 0—9—0

Weekly earnings of weaver 3—6—0

"We have not yet made suitable arrangement for bleaching. This hinders the immediate disposal of our Khadi. We are trying to get over this difficulty.

"Cotton has never been and will never be a money crop in this area. There is no extensive cultivation. Next year every spinner is sure to stock her own cotton to feed her spindle and her buffalo with. While the lint converts itself into thick warm *dupatti*, the seed converts itself into nice butter which fattens the luxurious city folk. I do not know whether Nunjangad butter and Nunjangad Khadi will appeal to the taste of the Bangalore folk in the same degree.

"We are going to Gundlupet area in a couple of days and we shall return after a week."

12th January, 1928

INDEPENDENCE v. SWARAJ

BY M. K. GANDHI

It is said that the Independence resolution is a fitting answer to Lord Birkenhead. If this be a serious contention, we have little notion of the answer that we should make to the appointment of the Statutory Commission and the circumstances attending the announcement of the appointment. The act of appointment needs, for an answer, not speeches however heroic they may be, not declarations however brave they may be, but corresponding action adequate to the act of the British Minister, his colleagues and his followers. Supposing the Congress had passed no resolution whatsoever but had just made a bonfire of every yard of foreign cloth in its possession, and induced a like performance on the part of the whole nation, it would have been some answer, though hardly adequate, to what the act of appointment means. If the Congress could have brought about a strike of every Government employee beginning with the Chief Judges and ending with the petty peons, not excluding soldiers, that act would have been a fairly adequate answer. It would certainly have disturbed the comfortable equanimity with which the British ministers and those concerned are looking upon all our heroics.

It may be said this is merely a counsel of perfection which I should know is not capable of execution. I do not hold that view. Many Indians who are not speaking today are undoubtedly preparing in their own manner for the happy day when every Indian now sustaining the system of Government which holds the nation in bondage will leave the denationalising service. It is contended that it is courage, it is undoubtedly wisdom, to restrain the tongue whilst one is unprepared for action. Mere brave speech without action is letting off useless steam. And the strongest speech shed its bravery when in 1920 patriots learnt to court imprisonment for strong speeches. Speech is necessary for those who are dumbstruck. Restraint is necessary for the garrulous. The English administrators chaff us for our speech and occasionally betray by their acts their contempt of our speeches and thereby tell us more effectively than by words 'Act if you dare.' Till we can take up the challenge every single threatening speech or gesture of ours is in my opinion a humiliation, an admission of impotence. I have seen prisoners in chains spitting frothy oaths only to provide mirth for their gaolers.

Moreover, has independence suddenly become a goal in answer to something offensive that some Englishman has done? Do men conceive their goals in order to oblige people or to resent their action? I submit that if it is a goal, it must be declared and pursued irrespective of the acts or threats of others.

Let us, therefore, understand what we mean by independence. England, Russia, Spain, Italy, Turkey,

Chilli, Bhutan have all their independence. Which independence do we want? I must not be accused of begging the question. For if I were told that it is Indian independence that is desired, it is possible to show that no two persons will give the same definition. The fact of the matter is that we do not know our distant goal. It will be determined not by our definitions but by our acts, voluntary and involuntary. If we are wise, we will take care of the present and the future will take care of itself. God has given us only a limited sphere of action and a limited vision. Sufficient unto the day is the good thereof.

I submit that Swaraj is an all-satisfying goal for all time. We the English-educated Indians often unconsciously make the terrible mistake of thinking that the microscopic minority of English-speaking Indians is the whole of India. I defy any one to give for independence a common Indian word intelligible to the masses. Our goal at any rate may be known by an indigenous word understood by the three hundred millions. And we have such a word in Swaraj first used in the name of the Nation by Dadabhai Naoroji. It is infinitely greater than and includes independence. It is a vital word. It has been sanctified by the noble sacrifices of thousands of Indians. It is a word which, if it has not penetrated the remotest corner of India, has at least got the largest currency of any similar word. It is a sacrilege to displace that word by a foreign importation of doubtful value. This independence resolution is perhaps the final reason for conducting Congress proceedings in Hindustani and that alone. No tragedy like that of the independence resolution would then have been possible. The most valiant speakers would then have ornamented the native meaning of the word Swaraj and attempted all kinds of definitions, glorious and inglorious. Would that the independents would profit by their experience and resolve henceforth to work among the masses for whom they desire freedom and taboo English speech in its entirety in so far as mass meetings such as the Congress are concerned.

Personally I crave not for 'independence,' which I do not understand, but I long for freedom from the English yoke. I would pay any price for it. I would accept chaos in exchange for it. For the English peace is the peace of the grave. Anything would be better than this living death of a whole people. This satanic rule has well-nigh ruined this fair land materially, morally and spiritually. I daily see its law courts denying justice and murdering truth. I have just come from terrorised Orissa. This rule is using my own countrymen for its sinful sustenance. I have a number of affidavits swearing that in the district of Khurda acknowledgments of enhancement of revenue are being forced from the people practically at the point of the bayonet. The unparalleled extravagance of this rule has demented the Rajas and the Maharajas who, unmindful of consequences, ape it and grind their subjects to dust. In order to protect its immoral commerce this rule regards no means too mean, and in order to keep three hundred millions under the heels of a hundred thousand it carries a military expenditure which is keeping millions in a state of semi-starvation and polluting thousands of mouths with intoxicating liquor.

But my creed is *non-violence* under all circumstances. My method is conversion, not coercion; it is self-suffering, not the suffering of the tyrant. I know that method to be infallible. I know that a whole people can adopt it without accepting it as its creed and without understanding its philosophy. People generally do not understand the philosophy of all their acts. My ambition is much higher than independence. Through the deliverance of India, I seek to deliver the so-called weaker races of the earth from the crushing heels of Western exploitation in which England is the greatest partner. If India converts, as it can convert, Englishmen, it can become the predominant partner in a world commonwealth of which England can have the privilege of becoming a partner if she chooses. India has the right, if she only knew, of becoming the predominant partner by reason of her numbers, geographical position and culture inherited for ages. This is big talk I know. For a fallen India to aspire to move the world and protect weaker races is seemingly an impertinence. But in explaining my strong opposition to this cry for independence, I can no longer hide the light under a bushel. Mine is an ambition worth living for and worth dying for. In no case do I want to reconcile myself to a state lower than the best for fear of consequences. It is therefore not out of expedience that I oppose independence as my goal. I want India to come to her own and that state cannot be better defined by any single word than Swaraj. Its content will vary with the action that the nation is able to put forth at a given moment. India's coming to her own will mean every nation doing likewise.

TAKING UNLAWFUL LIBERTY

A Sindhi friend writes:

"I am enclosing herewith a cutting from the *Sind Observer* of Karachi wherein you will find your name among others used in support of medicines sought to be popularised and sold through the medium of such advertisement.

"I can hardly believe you could have spoken or written appreciatively of the medicines, mixtures, pills or potions of the pharmacy in question.

"I hope you would write in *Young India* about this matter."

I have seen the advertisement too. It is taking an unlawful liberty with my name and I doubt not the names of other leaders. It is remarkable the freedom these pharmacies take in order to find custom for their wretched traffic. In my opinion this use of names of persons without their permission is an illegality punishable in law. Since as a non-co-operator I may not seek the protection of the law, I must be satisfied with warning the public against being misled by the use of my name in connection with any drug whatsoever. My disbelief in drugs in general is as strong as ever notwithstanding the very limited use by me in recent times of one or two comparatively harmless and well-known opening drugs and quinine. I have no desire to see pharmacies multiplied in this country. I would rather see people freed from the slavery of drugs.

M. K. G.

12th January, 1928

MADRAS KHADI EXHIBITION

BY M. K. GANDHI

Mr. Polak being in Madras during the Congress week, I invited him to visit the Khadi Exhibition and give me his criticism. He has now sent me a letter from which I take the following extract:

"I find myself unable to give you any real summary of my views on the Exhibition, first, because I was there too short a time, secondly, because there was no adequate guide to the work, and thirdly, because of my defective knowledge of the subject. The following must therefore serve inadequately. The site was bad, owing to its being partly bounded by an open ditch in which either running or stagnant water stood. The inconvenience must have been considerable, Owing to the open nature of the Exhibition, dust must have frequently swept over both visitors and stalls. Because of the very nature of the Exhibition and the strong sunlight, there could be very little display of goods and therefore there was not much to catch the eye, unless one specially looked out for particular things. I think that this is a distinct defect, where so much in this country depends upon an appeal to the eye. The usual propaganda, through charts, diagrams and maps, was good, but might have been and might be considerably better. The simpler the appeal and the larger the scale, the more success with the multitude.

"Again I think it would have been better if products

had been arranged according to kind than according to district, if this had been possible. Thus, plain cloth all together; plain block-printed cloth ditto; coloured-printed cloth, ditto; dyed cloth, ditto; and so on. Then it would have been possible better to compare like things from different areas, and one could better have judged where one district excelled and another lagged behind.

"On the other hand, I found an immense advance in quantity and quality of production from what I had been led to expect. There was a remarkable variety of product both in quality and in kind, and this seems clearly to indicate that the demand is growing and is being supplied. By the way, I hope that indigenous vegetable dyes will be encouraged to the exclusion of imported artificial ones. I was told that Khadi did not take vegetable dyes as well as the latter.

"I am sure that Khadi has come to stay; but I believe that it is only by encouragement from the higher classes that the populace will take to it generously. The only way to get the higher classes genuinely to interest themselves in the matter—for patriotism and self-interest are not often bed fellows — is to give them beautiful and artistic things of good quality from *their* point of view. I don't believe they will adopt yours, except verbally and to please you. Unless Khadi can be as cheap, as good, as satisfying for all needs, as the machine product, you will have a losing fight except in so far as you are content to have a cottage industry for self-clothing adjunct to agriculture.

"These few thoughts—that you will probably and rightly discard as the superficial views of an egotistical and ill-informed amateur—occur to me but as I promised to send you them, there they are."

Though the criticism is not a considered opinion, it will be useful to the organisers of future exhibitions. I do not share the view that educated Indians will not patronise Khadi unless they have it supplied to them on the same terms as machine-made cloth as to price, quality, durability &c. Whilst they do expect a particular standard to satisfy their artistic taste they are gladly paying extra cost, and are by no means insistent on equality with machine-made cloth in point of quality.

The knowledge that Khadi supports the poorest of the land who would otherwise be without such support is a great determining factor with the educated and well-to-do classes in buying Khadi. But that of course is no reason for Khadi producers to be remiss in their attempt to improve the quality. Indeed the advance made in this direction is highly encouraging. The workers are not going to be contented with anything less than the excellence that Khadi had when there was no machine-made cloth and which no machine has been yet able even to equal.

19th January, 1928

GUJARAT VIDYAPITH CONVOCATION

By M. K. Gandhi

The Vidyapith continues to show a decline in point of numbers, 15 primary schools having been disaffiliated during the past year for their inability to comply with the spinning and Khadi conditions. The attendance at the Mahavidyalaya too shows a steady decline; from over 50 the number is now reduced to 37. It may be therefore impertinence to describe as a university an institution having but a few schools containing a few thousand boys affiliated to it and a college containing less than 50 boys. But 'university' like independence is an elastic term open to anybody to appropriate or mis-appropriate and we frankly confess that to call the Vidyapith a university is a misappropriation. Vidyapith therefore is the only correct term to use carrying with it no reproach. It merely means a seat of learning which may hold from one to one million pupils. The term 'university' immediately sets the mind thinking of the big foreign growth that has been super-imposed on India. If we speak of national institutions as universities, we are likely to forget the denationalising associations of these foreign universities and may use their hugeness as our measure and then be despondent to find ours to be small and uninspiring. But the report that the Registrar read, if it showed a decline in numbers, showed also with pride that it was the effort at national education that had enabled Vallabhbhai Patel to carry on the marvellous organisation of flood relief. No wonder therefore that the following address of Dinabandhu C. F. Andrews who was invited to deliver the Convocation address deeply touched the audience. The pathos and deliberation with which he read it lent an added force to it:

"When the call suddenly came to me, through your Chancellor and Vice-Chancellor, to deliver this year the Convocation address at the Gujarat Vidyapith, one subject was uppermost in my mind, namely the shock that came to us all in the unexpected death of Hakim Ajmal Khan.

"He was one of the truest friends I have ever had in my life. For nearly a quarter of a century we had been intimately associated together. Therefore, the thought suddenly flashed upon me, that I could not better bring home to my audience today the essential qualities of National Education than by making the personality of Hakim Ajmal Khan of Delhi the centre of my subject.'

"For it is almost a truism that education can never properly be studied in the abstract, as if it were merely a system. The best part of our education comes from the impact of personal character at the impressionable age of youth. I have long ago forgotten the classical lectures, that I attended at Cambridge; but I can most vividly remember, even today, the saintly presence and child-like faith of Sir George Gabriel Stokes, the profoundest physical scientist of his own generation and the humblest servant of God. He made me, when I was a mere boy, the friend of his old age. To sit silently in his presence was the most impressive university education I ever received.

"How, then, can I bring to you, quite simply, even in a reflected light, the personality of Hakim Ajmal Khan, which impressed me so much in what I might call the Indian side of my education? Let me try in a few words. He revealed to me the true type of a great soul. He gave to me, when I first came to India at the beginning of the present century, a very high ideal of what India stood for among the nations of mankind. He was the heir of a lofty tradition in Islam,—the Moghul tradition of old Delhi. Among the religious civilizations of the world, that have still within them, in our own times, the active living power to produce great personalities, Islam stands out in the vanguard of modern history. There are qualities in it, for character building, that are unique. They may be found, in different types, in different countries and cities.

"In Delhi, this Muslim tradition had come into intimate touch with Hindu ideals. A fruitful synthesis had resulted. The singular perfection of the poetic thought of Kabir, Dadu, Nanak is parallel to the beauty of the architecture of the Taj Mahal. They represent a unity of life, an excellence that has penetrated the thought of a whole people. The more I study the Moghul period, the deeper becomes the sense of this impression of unity between Hindu and Musalman, strengthening and purifying both religious faiths. Not only have I been able to trace this historically, but also I have had the good fortune to be able to see it exemplified among my own personal friends in Delhi, of whom Hakim Ajmal Khan was the oldest. The tradition has not yet passed away; and in Dr. Ansari, the President of the National Congress, the Indian Nation has rightly chosen, at this critical hour, the one man who could lead us forward into that haven of freedom about which the Poet prays that this country may awake.

"Hakim Ajmal Khan, from childhood onwards, moved about and had his being in this environment of old Delhi, with its courtesy and gentle kindness, its dignity and calm. It formed the all-sufficient foundation of his own early training. It fashioned, as nothing else could do, his character, giving him an innate nobility of spirit. It made him,—what we all felt in him,—the perfect gentleman, loved by the Hindu and Muslim poor of Delhi as a healer and a saviour. His father and grandfather had held the same position in the city. Often I have gone to see him and watched him hour after hour while he attended to the sick and dying. The poorest of the poor, Hindu, Musalman, Sikh, Christian, were alike regarded as his own children. There are some Indian Christians in Delhi, drawn from the depressed classes. I have seen them coming in their simple trust to Hakim Ajmal Khan with the certainty that he would give as much care and attention to their sufferings as he would to the royal patients who used to ask for his medical aid. As I have watched him, the picture has come to me, from the Gospels, of one about whom it was written: 'When eventide was come, they brought to Him out of the city the sick and infirm and diseased and He healed them all.' While I have seen Hakim Ajmal Khan in his court-yard near the Chandni Chowk, with the very poorest round him, I have had (let me say it with all reverence) the vision of the Christ.

"There was a dignity about everything he said and did. This was so natural to him, because his home, his religion, his social environment, were all of one piece. He was not jerked about, as he grew up, from one civilization to another, at one time half western, at another time almost violently eastern by reaction. He was never blown about by every passing fashion of the hour. His life grew silently upward, like a tree, that roots itself firm and strong in mother earth. He was very deeply grounded in the tradition and culture of his own country. He had access, at his very door, to the highest that Islam and India had to give him, and he made use of this to the full. It became, as it were, the very air he breathed; it was his life-force, drawn from without and also working from within.

"Here, I think, is the reason why Hakim Ajmal Khan became one of the strongest supporters of Indian National Education,—education, that is to say, rooted and grounded in the very soul of India herself. Indeed, it may be said, with strict adherence to the truth, that he actually sacrificed his own life in order to foster and promote this higher type of education. For not only was the Tibbia at Delhi his own creation, but the Jamia Milia also, when transferred to Delhi, became the object of his special devotion. He wore himself out in his efforts to help each institution and to keep things going. It has been a great joy to me to read that your Chancellor, with characteristic all-embracing love, in this time of national sorrow, has received the Jamia Milia into his own arms to bless it, making this a pious act of memory towards Hakim Ajmal Khan, whose death the whole Indian nation mourns.

"Let me tell a story of a visit that I recently paid to the Jamia Milia. One of my old pupils, Ramachandra, who is well known and loved both in Shantiniketan and Sabarmati, took me there to speak to the students. It was a privilege to share, even for a short time, their poverty and sacrifice in the cause of a great ideal. The teachers and students were of one heart and one soul, sharing their common life of poverty as brothers. The library, with its valuable books, was their one costly treasure; and their pride in it was delightful to witness. Shantiniketan came into my mind at once, where the library forms the centre of our own aspirations and is the pride and care of our Gurudev Rabindranath Tagore.

"Whenever I go from the Jamia Milia to Sabarmati, and from Sabarmati to Shantiniketan, I feel the same spirit of sacrifice abroad. We are living today in India in one of the great Ages of Faith,—such a period as that which saw the birth of Nalanda and Taxila of old. My own mind goes back for its parallel to that wonderful Thirteenth Century in Europe, when S. Francis of Assisi sang his songs of joy at the beauty of all creation; when Giotto painted his marvellous pictures; when

Dante wrote his immortal epic of the purification of the human soul till it attains the beatific vision.

"Let me describe to you the early beginnings of my own college at Cambridge, which was a Franciscan Foundation. Truly faith in those days wrought miracles, and removed mountains of difficulty. Lady Valence Mary of Pembroke, our pious foundress, was devoted to the Franciscan Order. Her husband was tragically killed during the tournament, held on her wedding day, and she built Pembroke College in his memory. She established it, at first, simply by erecting twelve huts, made of wattle and thatch, on the banks of the river Cam. There, in the beginning, she gave a yearly income to twelve Franciscan scholars with their pupils. All this happened six hundred years ago; and we rejoice that from our Alma Mater of Pembroke College have gone forth poets, such as Edmund Spenser and Thomas Gray; martyrs, like Ridley and Bradford; statesmen, like William Pitt; and scholars, like Edward Granville Browne, who died last year,—the one, perhaps, that did more to represent the truth and nobility of Islamic culture to the West than any other man of our own times.

"This period, in which we live, is, as I have said, another age of faith in India. The faith of Rabindranath Tagore, sacrificing all the riches of his genius to give life to his own Shantiniketan; the faith of Hakim Ajmal Khan, establishing at such a cost the Tibbia and Jamia Milia at Delhi; the faith of Mahatma Gandhi, building up his own Ashram at Sabarmati and also this Gujarat Vidyapith,—all this has its historic counterpart in what I have just related about the early beginnings of my own college; it has also its parallel in every page of Indian History. It corresponds to that grand definition of faith, which says, 'Now Faith is the substance of things hoped for, the evidence of things not seen.'

"Brothers and sisters, I cannot carry my great subject any further. I have given you a glimpse only into the heart of Hakim Ajmal Khan and what he stood for. 'He endured as seeing him who is Invisible,'— Invisible God, whom we call by many names, but who is ever the Shantam, Shivam, Advaitam. India, for countless ages, has set out as a pilgrim on her search for the One. She has laid aside the riches and the glory of the world and taken up the robe of Sannyasa, in her search for the One. Others who are satisfied with earthly riches may despise her; but we, who can be satisfied with nothing but the Truth itself, shall reverence even the tattered and the worn robe in which our own indigenous centres of learning veil themselves today. Their very poverty will be our joy, our pride. For in their hearts is ever echoing the music of the love-song of the Eternal."

He added a few words by way of a personal appeal to the graduates and laid stress on *brahmacharya.* Passions he said were to be conquered by a deeper passion, *i. e.,* passion for God.

At the end of the proceedings a portrait of Acharya Gidwani was unveiled by Gandhiji who alluded to the great sacrifice made by him when he first joined the Vidyapith and made its existence possible.

19th January, 1920

TO 'NO CHANGERS'

BY M. K. GANDHI

I see that the news that there was to be at Sabarmati a meeting of 'No Changers' some time this month has found its way to the press. Perhaps this was inevitable. But I am sorry to have to inform all concerned that the idea has been dropped for the time being at any rate. Many 'No Changers' have been long suggesting such a meeting with a view to the formation of a programme and a general interchange of views. The demand became insistent at Madras when the 'No Changers' who attended the Congress felt that on several resolutions they should have a definite joint policy and that they should be able to act as a distinct party within the Congress. Though I was not enamoured of the idea of forming a party, I was not averse to the calling of a meeting of 'No Changers' for the purpose of discussion. But as I came to the drafting of a circular letter, I saw that it was a difficult performance and it was an equally difficult thing to select the names of invitees. I found both to be hopeless tasks. On going into the thing deeper I found that the convening of such a meeting might embarrass Dr. Ansari and make the working of the national programme of boycott more difficult by drawing the attention of the country away from the boycott and distracting it by a discussion of matters that may well await a better opportunity. I discovered further that the formation of a 'No Change' party without me in it was not likely to function fully and vigorously so long as I was alive, available and retained a fairly healthy and active mind. And the idea behind the suggested meeting was to form a party in which I need not take any part. It may be theoretically possible, but in practice reference would always be made to me for opinion on many matters, which opinion would be more likely to be faulty than it would be, if I was present at the discussion from which the matters for opinion might have risen. These considerations made me incline to the view that the meeting might at least be postponed. Vallabhbhai with whom I first shared my revised opinion agreed with me. Other friends came to the same conclusion on other and independent grounds. The idea of the meeting therefore remains under suspension for the time being.

I hope that the suspension will not disappoint the 'No Changers.' I am not sure that it is not a better arrangement. Whilst non-co-operation as a national programme is partially suspended, individual non-co-operators have an opportunity of testing the strength of their faith. Their faith will be all the stronger standing alone without the warmth of a party. When anything assumes the strength of a creed which non-co-operation must be with those who still remain true to it, it becomes self-sustained and derives the needed support from within. Let us also have faith in the country that when a forward movement becomes possible, all those who left non-co-operation will rejoin it whole-heartedly. I have no forward step to suggest at the present moment. Anything intermediate I can suggest may disturb the joint programme that various parties in the country are trying to evolve. Meanwhile I can only invite the attention of 'No Changers' to the great constructive programme of Khadi. Those who do not appreciate it, do not understand the most potent and the most operative part of non-co-operation, viz., non-violence. Non-co-operation without non-violence can never rise to the dignity of a creed and becomes merely one among many strategies in a campaign. Non-violent non-co-operation has been conceived as an infallible remedy replacing all others. And Khadi is the corner stone of its positive side. Here is a reluctant testimony in favour of Khadi given by Mr. Harcourt Robertson in the *Daily Despatch*. The writer is claimed by the editor to be 'one who has spent many years in British India where he was engaged in occupations demanding an intimate knowledge of market conditions and the Indian psychology.' I am indebted to the *Leader* of the twelfth instant for the following:

"He (Mr. Robertson) ascribes the heavy drop in the amount of British cotton fabrics purchased by India not to post-war dislocation and economic stress, nor to the poverty of the masses; for 'the Indian peasant is always appallingly poor,' nor to famines, for 'famine in India is of almost yearly occurrence,' but to the competition of Indian and Japanese mills and most of all to Khaddar which, he writes, towers like a giant above all other causes. He regards Khaddar as the real enemy. His description of it and of its high priest, Mahatma Gandhi, will be read with interest. He says:

"'Khaddar is a native-made cloth woven on primitive looms from hand-spun yarn by unskilled, amateurish workers. It is coarse, stiff, full of knots and faults, and always looks dirty,—yet there is a positive vogue for it, even wealthy natives taking a pride in garments made from it. For Khaddar represents in concrete form the slogan of the rapidly growing Nationalist Party: 'India for the Indians.' Not a penny of the money spent on it leaves the country. He who wears it helps to feed India's starving millions, proclaims his country's independence and shows himself a patriot of the first water......Khaddar is one of the weapons used by—and indeed, invented by—Mahatma Gandhi in his fight against foreign rule in India. Half saint, half fanatic, and wholly patriot, Mahatma Gandhi now speaks, in his person and through the native press to the very hearts of India's educated classes. Non-co-operation is not dead in India because it is no longer talked. It has now reached the stage of silent and dangerous activity. . . . . Let Mr. Gandhi's missionaries once rope in the masses, and India will no longer be a poor buyer, she will be no buyer at all. . . . . The blow is aimed not only at cotton. It is a definite attempt to ruin the market for all British goods.'

"These remarks cannot but hearten those who have been working, under the inspiring leadership of Mahatma Gandhi, for the spread of Khaddar. That great apostle of non-violence believes that through the charkha India can win economic freedom, and that political freedom must follow in its wake. Mr. Robertson is alarmed and suggests a remedy and it is this: 'Restore confidence in the British Raj, inculcate the Empire idea, cause the masses of India to realise how much they owe to British rule, and Britain will recover her Indian market.' He urges that pro-British propaganda should be carried on through cinema films, which should be exhibited free of cost to the ignorant masses, other means of propaganda, such as the press, not being neglected. If his suggestion is given effect to, 'India may yet be saved to us, and our market there is by no means irretrievably lost yet.' No time is to be lost, for 'in a few short years the Nationalist leaven may well have worked so that any attempt to neutralise it would fail because of being made too late.' In the meantime he suggests that something should be done to give wide publicity in India to ideas such as 'Lancashire fabrics of Indian cotton.' 'India's best customer is Lancashire,' 'To buy Lancashire cloth is to help India's cultivators.' Unless these and similar remedies,' he concludes, 'are applied at once it seems certain that the Indian market for Lancashire cotton goods is not a sick but a dying one.' The writer is greately mistaken in thinking that the capitalistic propaganda of the nature he suggests will stem the tide of the national movement. India's masses and classes are not so un-sophisticated as not to see through the whole game. The only effect of propaganda organised for purposes of economic exploitation is likely to be to give a stimulus to the Khaddar movement and make even those among Indians who at present do not attach much importance to its economic potentiality look at the charkha from a different angle of vision. A propaganda of the nature suggested would be a clear admission that Khaddar is winning its way, and this will have the effect of inducing faith in it on the part of those who belong to the category of doubters. It is not by interested propaganda but by substantial concessions to the national demands of Indians that the relations of the two countries can be placed on a healthy footing and the causes which are operating to the detriment of Lancashire's trade with India removed."

Needless to say that Khadi is not a threat. It is the breath of national life like Swaraj. The Khadi movement like Swaraj cannot be given up against any concessions however generous. To give up Khadi would be to sell the masses, the soul of India.

19th January, 1928

FRIENDS OF A FEATHER

Two events of a far-reaching importance occurred last week—the visit to the Ashram of friends of the International Fellowship, and the convocation of the Vidyapith. And if I devote more space to the one than to the other, it is not because I attach more value to it, but because it is not so familiar as the other coming every year.

It was in the fitness of things that the members of the Council of the International Federation with their friends should have thought of having their meeting in the Ashram, itself an international fellowship in its own way. If the friendly company that visited us was as varied as it could be, no less varied were we their hosts—men and women drawn from different countries and bound together by a common ideal. It is possible that the friends came to Sabarmati attracted by the name of the Ashram and its founder, but I have no doubt that many of them left with the feeling that during the three days that they spent with us they were amidst another fellowship inspired as much as they by the ideal of peace on earth and good-will to men.

To take only a few names, among our guests were friends like Dinabandhu Andrews, the warmth of whose friendship and cooperation any association working for peace must prize; friends like Professor P A. Wadia, a Zoroastrian, loving 'to scorn delight and live laborious days,' like Mr. DeBoer from Vellore and Mr. Dewick from the other end of India, Calcutta, and Mr. and Mrs. Henriod from Switzerland, working for the welfare of the student world; ladies like Miss Varkey from Madras, loving to call herself 'a mother of three hundred children,' and Shrimati Janaki Ammal from Malabar and Mrs. Maclean and Miss Manibai from Bombay and Miss Van Doren from Poona, all fired with the same ideals of social service; men like Mr. Elwyn of the Society of Christ, just out of his teens and fresh from Oxford, come to India, as he said to do some atonement for the sin of his countrymen in keeping India in chains; Indian friends like Dr. Jesudasan and Sjt. Sankaran Nair and Mr. Hameed Khan from South India and Mr. Kumaraswamy from Ceylon—Christians, Hindus, a Parsi and a Moslem; Indians, Americans, English, Swiss, a Russian and a Swede—a fellowship of faiths and nationalities and aspirations for good-will and unity. They have an Indian secretary in Mr. A. A. Paul, loved by them all, and ever active and industrious.

They stayed with us for three days and came in fairly close contact with the members of our Ashram, rejoicing to conform to all our rules of daily life and contenting themselves with the meagre comforts that it was in our power to give them. Many of them took part in the morning prayer and all in the evening prayer, English translations of our verses and songs being specially supplied to them, and in addition to the Indian songs usually sung we had a hymn each day given us by the Christian congregation. We were thus a happy fraternity enjoying these days of privilege and grace.

Prof. Wadia opened the sessions with a devotional speech of which the keynote was love, not only between individuals and individuals, but nations and nations. The next day Mr. Andrews led with readings from the Bible and 'When I survey the wondrous Cross,' and invited Khare Shastri to give a song from the Ashram Bhajanavali and Imamsaheb to recite verses from the Holy Koran. After this Gandhiji was requested to open a discussion on what should be the fundamental objective of the fellowship. There was no doubt about their object, but they had yet to formulate a creed which whilst it was free from narrowness was also free from any trace of latitudinarianism. The discussion lasted for two days, and though they could not arrive at any definite result, it was far from fruitless. It led to a free and frank exchange of views ultimately bound to establish a better understanding. It also showed that however much we swear by the fundamentals, most of us labour under what Bacon classified as the idols of the tribe, the cave, the forum and the theatre. Thus there was no difference of opinion as to the object of all to work for the widest toleration, to combine and side with the forces of light against the forces of darkness, or as Dinabandhu Andrews said, with those who seek God, truth and divine light, against those who blankly leave God out and become materialists. Every one seemed to be agreed on this, but many seemed to run away from what would appear to be the necessary corollary of the proposition. This was defined by Gandhiji at some length at this and other meetings, and the discussion clearly showed the various points of contact and difference.

"In order to attain a perfect fellowship," said Gandhiji, "every act of its members must be a religious act and an act of sacrifice. I came to the conclusion long ago, after prayerful search and study and discussion with as many people as I could meet, that all religions were true and also that all had some error in them, and that whilst I hold by my own, I should hold others as dear as Hinduism, from which it logically follows that we should hold all as dear as our nearest kith and kin and that we should make no distinction between them. So we can only pray, if we are Hindus, not that a Christian should become a Hindu, or if we are Musalmans, not that a Hindu or a Christian should become a Musalman, nor should we even secretly pray that any one should be converted, but our inmost prayer should be that a Hindu should be a better Hindu, a Muslim a better Muslim and a Christian a better Christian. That is the fundamental truth of fellowship. That is the meaning of the wonderful passion, the story of which Andrews read out to you of the song and verses that Khare Shastri and Imamsaheb recited. If Andrews invited them to give their song and verses for mere courtesy or by way of patronising toleration, he was false to the fellowship. In that case he should not have done so, but I have known Charlie Andrews too well, and I know that he has given the same love to others as he has for his own, and thereby broadened his Christianity, as I broaden my Hinduism by loving other religions as my own.

If however there is any suspicion in your mind that only one religion can be true, and others false you must reject the doctrine of fellowship placed before you. Then we would have a continuous process of exclusion and found our fellowship on an exclusive basis. Above all I plead for utter truthfulness. If we do not feel for other religions as we feel for our own, we had better disband ourselves, for we do not want a wishy-washy toleration. My doctrine of toleration does not include toleration of evil, though it does the toleration of the evil-minded. It does not therefore mean that you have to invite each and every one who is evil-minded or tolerate a false faith. By a true faith I mean one the sum total of whose energy is for the good of its adherents, by a false I mean that which is predominantly false. If you therefore feel that the sum total of Hinduism has been bad for the Hindus and the world, you must reject it as a false faith."

Gandhiji's insistence on a member of the followship not even secretly wishing that a member of another faith should be converted to his own led to a general discussion on the question of conversion. Gandhiji again defined his position more clearly than before: 'I would not only not try to convert but would not even secretly pray that any one should embrace my faith. My prayer would always be that Imam-saheb should be a better Musalman, or become the best he can. Hinduism with its message of Ahimsa is to me the most glorious religion in the world,—as my wife to me is the most beautiful woman in the world,—but others may feel the same about their own religion. Cases of real honest conversion are quite possible. If some people for their inward satisfaction and growth change their religion let them do so. As regards taking our message to the aborigines. I do not think I should go and give my message out of my own wisdom. Do it in all humility, it is said. Well, I have been an unfortunate witness of arrogance often going in the garb of humility. If I am perfect I know that my thought will reach others. It taxes all my time to reach the goal I have set to myself. What have I to take to the aborigines, and the Assamese hillmen except to go in my nakedness to them? Rather than ask them to join my prayer, I would join their prayer. We were strangers to this sort of classification—'animists,' 'aborigines' etc., but we have learnt it from English rulers. I must have the desire to serve and it must put me right with people. Conversion and service go ill together."

The next day early morning the friends met for an informal conversation with Gandhiji when again the same question was asked by many of them.

'Would you have a ruling of such a character that those who had a desire to convert should not be eligible for membership?'

'Personally,' said Gandhiji, 'I think they should not be eligible. I should have framed a resolution to that effect as I regard it as the logical outcome of fellowship. It is essential for inter-religious relationship and contact.'

'Is not the impulse to proselytise God-given?' inquired another friend.

'I question it,' said Gandhiji. 'But if all impulses are God-given, as some of our Hindus believe, He has also given us discrimination. He will say, I have given you many impulses so that your capacity to face temptation may be tested.'

'But you do believe in preaching an economic order? inquired one of the fair sex.

'I do, as I believe in preaching laws of health.'

'Then why not apply the same rule in religious matters?'

'It is a relevant question. But you must not forget that we have started with the fundamental principle that all religions are true. If there were different but good and true health laws for different communities, I should hesitate to preach some as true and some as false. I am positive that with people not prepared to tolerate one another's religious belief there can be no international fellowship.

'Moreover physical analogies when applied to spiritual

matters are good only up to a certain point. When you take up an analogy from nature you can stretch it only to a certain point. But I would take an illustration from the physical world and explain what I mean. If I want to hand a rose to you, there is a definite movement. But if I want to transmit its scent I do so without any movement. The rose transmits its own scent without a movement. Let us rise a step higher, and we can understand that spiritual experiences are self-acting. Therefore the analogy of preaching sanitation etc. does not hold good. If we have spiritual truth it will transmit itself. You talk of the joy of a spiritual experience and say you cannot but share it. Well, if it is real joy, boundless joy, it will spread itself without a vehicle of speech. In spiritual matters we have merely to step out of the way. Let God work His way. If we interfere we may do harm. Good is a self-acting force. Evil is not, because it is a negative force. It requires the cloak of virtue before it can march forward.'

'Did not Jesus Himself teach and preach?'

'We are on dangerous ground here. You ask me to give my interpretation of the life of Christ. Well, I may say that I do not accept everything in the gospels as historical truth. And it must be remembered that he was working amongst his own people, and he said he had not come to destroy but to fulfil. I draw a great distinction between the Sermon on the Mount and the Letters of Paul. They are a graft on Christ's teaching, his own gloss apart from Christ's own experience.

When a German professor came the other day to visit Gandhiji after having visited the Mahavidyalaya, and expressed his satisfaction with it, Gandhiji said: 'Well, you may express your satisfaction. But there is not much to see in it today. It lies buried deep down in the earth. In the beginning it looked as though the seeds had sprouted, and the shoots would grow into a big tree, but they withered away. If the seeds are dead we shall have deserved it, but I am sure they are not dead. A day will come, when they will sprout again, and blossom into a tree.' In these words he put in a nutshell the present position of the national university and his view about its future. On the day of the Convocation Gandhiji took upon himself the task of interpreting Mr. Andrews' address, which he did in his own way, endorsed all the sentiments, above all the great message of faith,—" *Now faith is the substance of things hoped for, the evidence of things not seen,*"—and reiterated with, if possible, greater emphasis the sentiments he had expressed before the German professor. He commended the address of Mr. Andrews, as the production of a poet, artist and orator, and of a man of God and man of faith. "Fifteen primary schools had to be disaffiliated during the year, you have heard the Registrar say," said Gandhiji. "What if more have to be disaffiliated? They had to be disaffiliated because we would not relax our rigid programme, because we said that they must accept compulsory spinning, otherwise go. It may be that this may result ultimately in the whole Vidyapith being emptied, with its Chancellor as the sole occupant, his own teacher and his own pupil. What then? Well, I will continue sitting there working away at my wheel. If you have that faith, you may be sure that you will have not only one Pembroke but hundreds of Pembrokes springing up out of the huts of wattle and mud." Concluding he said: "You will know in a few days, what shape the Vidyapith is going to take. But I want you to wait in faith and patience, and the assurance that so long as any one of us is living, he will be ready to be buried here alive before he sees the Vidyapith closed down. Stay and go through the fire. If you cannot go through the fire, do not blame your fate. But if any of us fail you, I tell you, although I am a votary of non-violence, that we will deserve to be torn to pieces."

19th January, 1928

SICILIAN GIRLS AND SPINNING

C. K. G. sends the following interesting extracts from *National Geographic Magazine*:

"Nearly every Sicilian woman learns when she is quite young how to spin and weave cotton cloth. Many of the girls make cloth to sell, and weave special pieces at odd moments for their dowries. Until recent years, they wove all the clothes for the family and the bed linen as well. During the American Civil War, when the supply from the United States was cut off, cotton was grown abundantly in the southern districts of the island."

"Their melons spread on aprons at their feet, these women improve the time by spinning while awaiting a customer."

M. K. G.

26th January, 1928

DEVADASIS

By M. K. Gandhi

Dinabandhu Andrews writes in reference to the so-called devadasis:

> "Nothing in all my long experience of India ever touched me so deeply as the appeal of my sisters, the Kalavatis, or 'devadasis,' at Cocanada, that I should come to them and visit them in order to hear their pitiful story.
>
> "The one who brought me to the place was himself the son of a 'devadasi', and he was able to interpret for me the requests that were made for my help by my sisters, as they gathered to tell me their tale of misery and degradation.
>
> "It was as clear as possible to me, that those who spoke to me and pleaded with me for my support had kept a purity of heart still unsullied, and that they were far more sinned against than sinning. The hideous mockery

of justice was this, that the world's blame and shame fell upon *them*, while those men, who sinned far more deeply in dragging them down, were often honoured and respected members of society. As far as I could gather, on enquiry, no social ban reached these men at all, only these poor innocent women suffered. I have called them 'innocent' without in any sense condoning the evil, because the noxious evil did not lie with them, but with those who had brought such a system into being and had produced this abomination into which they had been born.

"In one thing I could feel at once that the consciences of those, who were gathered before me, had begun to make them suffer deeply. They had with them little daughters of their own, and these children were there before me, seated with their mothers. When I asked the question, would not the mothers wish their daughters to abandon their life of misery, they unanimously said 'yes.' Indeed, they told me that this was the very reason for which they had called me."

26th January, 1928

BOYCOTT OF BRITISH GOODS

BY M. K. GANDHI

It is not at all surprising that the nation should wish to show resentment of the studiously insulting and defiant acts of the British Government. Every new discovery in the direction adds fuel to the fire. The latest is the abhorrence the late King Edward VII and his son the present King are reported to have betrayed of 'natives' and that in connection with Lord Sinha. The representatives of the nation have for years past endeavoured to demonstrate their resentment by bringing about a partial or complete boycott of British goods. It is the nation's right to bring it about if it so wishes. There is no doubt that it will produce a great effect if it could succeed to the necessary extent.

But it has been my misfortune or good fortune consistently to oppose the cry for the boycott of British goods. Though I adhere to the fundamental ground that the proposed boycott is contrary to non-violence, I wish to confine myself at present to an examination of its possibility. The fact that we have hitherto made no headway whatsoever with it in spite of the agitation for so long a time is proof presumptive of its very great difficulty. If we were to take even such a simple instance as soap, we shall discover that we have made no progress even in the boycott of British-made soap. The Committee appointed by the Congress recommended certain articles for boycott. So far as I am aware no such effort has yet been made in the direction of excluding even one such article from the nation's use. The use of a punitive boycott lies in its effectiveness. Any one studying the articles of import will soon discover the utter futility of spending labour on achieving the boycott of most of these articles from the standpoint of creating an impression on the British Government. It should not be forgotten that for all these long long years, we have not been able to have a body of specialists devoted to this single task. It is the fashion in some quarters now-a-days to blame me for the failure of any and every resolution that the Congress passes. I am told that a particular resolution does not succeed because I oppose it or do not work at it. There can be nothing more humiliating for a nation than to be in such an impotent state. Surely boycott of British goods was conceived and vehemently advocated before I returned from South Africa. The real and the more natural reason for the failure of the British goods boycott resolution lies in the obvious fact that no committee of experts has yet been able to arrive at a satisfactory plan of working it out. It has been suggested that we can succeed if China has succeeded. Yes, we can if we have the will, the courage and the opportunity to regulate the boycott by armed force, by creating an army of open revolutionaries, by forcing for that specific purpose a strike of dock labourers and others connected with the handling of British goods. It seems to me that even if we have the will, we have neither the means nor yet the capacity for managing such an open armed revolution. And neither those who have advocated boycott of British goods nor the special committee appointed by the Civil Disobedience Inquiry Committee have ever contemplated armed force. I hold therefore that it will be more consistent with national dignity, prestige and welfare to give up the cry, proved to be useless, and almost impossible, of boycott of British goods. The permanent necessity of advocating true Swadeshi in all things capable of being produced at home is untouched by the argument against the punitive boycott.

But there is no cause whatsoever for despair. We have a means ready made and most effective of signifying our resentment over the series of wrongs being continuously heaped upon our devoted heads. If we have the will, I claim that we have the present capacity of achieving a complete boycott not merely of British cloth but of all foreign cloth. And if we do this, we not only successfully demonstrate our resentment but we serve the masses in a manner we have never done before and we secure their co-operation in a national effort. We have got an army of workers for doing this work. We have experts who have first-hand knowledge of the thing. There is no division of opinion on the propriety of the thing. The only thing that retards our progress towards the completion of boycott of foreign cloth is our own disbelief. It is strange but tragic that through our ignorance we believe more in the possibility of achieving a boycott of certain British goods than of foreign cloth.

But even this boycott of foreign cloth cannot be achieved without a well-thought out and prepared plan. If it is the mere boycott we want rather than the higher and the more permanent result in the shape of the economic well-being of the masses, we can do so quickly enough if we receive the co-operation of mills on our terms. Without honest and hearty co-operation of our weaving and spinning mills, to attempt to achieve the boycott with mill cloth would be to court suicide and to run into the arms of profiteering mill-owners. If indigenous mill cloth is to play a part in this great national effort, the mills must come to terms with the Congress as to the kind of production and the prices to be charged. The mill agents should with the consent and co-operation of their shareholders cease to be merely trustees for themselves and shareholders, but both should become trustees for the whole nation. Then with Khadi foreign cloth can be successfully and permanently banished from the land. But it is possible, even without the co-operation of mills, though less easy in point of time, to achieve the boycott of foreign cloth through Khadi alone. Mills will still play a part but that will be in spite of the owners. Khadi will put an effective check on their greed; it will prevent a famine of cloth and it will give life and hope and work to starving millions, re-instate weavers of plain cloth in their ancient calling and will eventually but within a short time lead to a replacing of foreign cloth and regularising of mill profits. Time limit can be determined by the strength of the nation's will and its capacity for sacrificing a little of its taste for fine cloth and a little money never beyond the capacity of individual users of cloth.

26th January, 1934

KATHIAWAD POLITICAL CONFERENCE

The Kathiawad Political Conference met last week under the presidentship of Sjt. Amritlal Thakkar, a true and tried servant of India, who is known all over Gujarat as the tribune of the Dhedhs and the Bhils—the two suppressed communities of Gujarat. Like Gandhiji, Sjt. Thakkar also hails from Kathiawad, and it was well that Thakkar Bapa, as he is affectionately called, should follow Gandhiji as the President.

Porbandar is a state where the relations between the rulers and the ruled are admittedly good. Both therefore contributed to the success of the Conference, the Maharana Saheb fully helping the Reception Committee by according the State's hospitality to the President and distinguished guests. Among these were Gandhiji, Messrs. Abbas Tyebji, Vallabhbhai Patel, Darbar Saheb Gopaldas and other leaders, and Mrs. Gandhi, Mrs. Perin Captain, Miraben, Shrimati Jamnaben, Mrs. Pyarali, Miss Mithubai Petit, and Mrs. Santanam of Lahore. His Highness also invited the members of the Subjects Committee to a garden party, and attended the Conference with his Dewan for a few minutes. This bodes well for the future relations between the rulers and the ruled, and may be followed as a welcome precedent by all the rulers who mean well by their subjects.

Another noticeable feature of the reception, worthy of being copied wherever possible, was the voluntary offer of hospitality, by each of the heads of the various communities of castes in Porbander, to all the members of their respective castes attending the Conference. The Reception Committee was thus saved both the bother and expenses of providing for and entertaining its delegates and members. The institution of caste, while it lasts, may thus, if it so chooses, exercise its influence for good, and by keeping abreast of the times become a powerful agent for reform. One would however like the responsibility shared by citizens without reference to caste.

The presidential address was a well-worded, reasoned, political utterance, which took one back to the times of Pherozeshah Mehta and Gokhale, whose traditions the President has inherited and followed in his life. From a social worker who lives and moves and has his being among the humblest of the people, sharing their joys and sorrows, one might have expected a sort of people's address, descriptive of their troubles and their travails, their needs and their aspirations, and a self-revealing narrative of his own experiences as an active social worker. But Sjt. Thakkar rarely likes to speak about himself, and preferred to play the modest role of a sober political thinker. The address urged the States to realise the spirit of the times, and to vouchsafe to their people real freedom of association, freedom of person and property, and of speech and the press—the elementary political rights of all people on earth. It animadverted on some of the glaring faults in the administration of the States, urged the adoption of an equitable revenue system, the abolition of all forced labour, and an amalgamation of the numerous little railway administrations which are a constant source of worry and discomfort, inconvenience and hardship to the passengers in Kathiawad. It concluded with an appeal to the people to prosecute the constructive part of the programme, and a peroration in which he adumbrated his dream of a federation of Kathiawad States all responsible to their people, and all administered under one system, towards which he appealed to the rulers and the ruled to work.

Most of the resolutions were on the lines indicated in the address, urging the removal of the odious customs line at Viramgam, and as between the different States, urging the people to refuse all forced labour, and the like. But the main resolution for which the Conference will for long remain memorable,—as having exerted its influence for good or bad, only the future can say,—was one which requires separate treatment.

For the first time in its history the Conference by a regular resolution imposed on itself a self-denying ordinance, considerably restricting its liberty of expression, and withal calculated to ensure its continuance and steady growth. Here is a translation of the resolution which was in Gujarati:

"With a view to avoiding the possibility of any misunderstanding between the rulers and the ruled, and with a view to a fuller recognition of its own limitations, as also in confirmation of the custom which has been for some time in operation, this Conference resolves that it shall not pass any resolution condemning or criticising an individual State."

At various formal and informal meetings, Gandhiji, the author of the resolution, explained to the friends assembled at Porbander the paramount importance of passing this resolution. His full speech was explanatory of the reasons which were embodied in the resolution itself. He said that even within the limits prescribed by the resolution it was open to the Conference to do much useful work if the delegates only worked during the time intervening between any two Conferences. He asked the audience to regard the resolution as a prudent and open confession of the helplessness of the Conference in many matters. The resolution did not preclude individuals who might have any forward and effective policy from enforcing it outside the Conference. It did not limit individual action. For its very existence the Conference publicly recognised its own limitations. It rendered easy the position of those States that permitted the holding of the Conference within their borders.

On his way back from Porbandar, Gandhiji was invited to lay the foundation of a temple for the 'untouchables' in connection with their Ashram at Vartej under Bhavnagar State. Mulchandbhai Parekh is the soul of the Ashram. The State contributed Rs. 7,500 out of the Rs. 13,000 budgeted for the building of the Ashram and the temple. Sir Prabhashankar Pattani made a point of being present at the ceremony.

Gandhiji in laying the foundation made an important speech on the duties of the Hindus and on the essentials of a true temple and its place in life. He welcomed the function as an opportunity of rendering some service to the suppressed classes. and of thus expiating somewhat for the great sin that Hinduism had committed against them. Let no one, he said, lay the flattering unction to his soul, that he need not do any atonement if he himself was rendering some service to the suppressed community. The wrong of one Hindu was the wrong of all, and so long as we labelled ourselves as Hindus and Musalmans, we were bound to share the crime of every member of the community to which we belonged. A beautifully built structure, with a beautiful image of stone or marble therein, could not by itself deserve the name of 'temple,' unless it was a living temple of God, unless the man who built it had a life of penance and sacrifice to sanctify it, unless the temple was filled with an atmosphere that inspires and touches one's soul the moment one enters it. Without these qualities, all the buildings that went by the name of temples were so many whited sepulchres encumbering the earth, serving no useful purpose, and even capable of mischief. He had a word for the untouchables too. After all one could uplift oneself only by one's own effort, and the suppressed classes were no exception to the rule. They must reform themselves, and make it a rule not to enter the temple, unless they were leading pure lives, free from vice and filthy habits. Let them not say that those who were keeping them down-trodden were no better than they. The world might excuse those favoured ones, but not them, and so they must purify themselves if they wanted to deserve what they claimed.

M. D.

2nd February, 1928

MISS MAYO AGAIN

By M. K. Gandhi

Miss Mayo is clearly trading upon her knowledge that what we in India write can at best reach but a few hundred Americans, and that what she writes reaches thousands. She therefore feels perfectly free, just as it suits her, to misquote, half-quote or distort other people's writings or speeches intended to contradict her. She has done me the honour again of referring to me in her article in *Liberty* and attempted to discredit my writing* about her compilation *Mother India*. This she has felt called upon to do, I suppose, because I enjoy a certain amount of credit among cultured Americans, and lest therefore their judgment may be affected by my article. But in her article in *Liberty* she has outdone herself. Her reference to my secretaries is a clever attempt to hoodwink the unwary reader. All that could be inferred from my repudiation of the statement that I had two secretaries (whether always or not is

* Vide *Young India* dated 15th September 1927. See page 340.

not the point) is that Miss Mayo was at least a careless writer if not a wilful perverter of truth. But the manner in which she described the secretaries leaves the reader under the belief that I have always two secretaries. Her adherence to the statement that I did give her the message she ascribes to me proves her to be guilty of a gross suppression of truth. She seems to have thought that I would not have a copy of the corrected interview between her and me. Unfortunately for her I happen to possess a copy of her notes.[1] Here is the full quotation referring to the hum of the wheel:

> "My message to America is simply the hum of this wheel.' Letters and newspaper cuttings I get from America show that one set of people over-rates the results of Non-violent Non-co-operation and the other not only underrates it but imputes all kinds of motives to those who are concerned with the movement. Don't exaggerate one way or the other. If therefore some earnest Americans will study the movement impartially and patiently, then it is likely that the United States may know something of the movement which I do consider to be unique although I am the author of it. What I mean is that our movement is summed up in the spinning wheel with all its implications. It is to me a substitute for gun-powder. For it brings the message of self-reliance and hope to the millions of India. And when they are really awakened they would not need to lift their little finger in order to regain their freedom. The message of the spinning wheel is, really, to replace the spirit of exploitation by the spirit of service. The dominant note in the West is the note of exploitation. I have no desire that my country should copy that spirit or that note."

The first sentence only of the foregoing extract, which Miss Mayo quotes without the most important commentary on it, is intended to ridicule me. But the whole paragraph, I hope, makes my meaning and message clear and intelligible. I wrote my article on her book whilst I was travelling. Had I had the notes before me I should have quoted from them, and thus added force to my article. I claim however that the message as it appears in the full paragraph quoted is not different from what I have stated in the article Miss Mayo attempts to shake.

Whilst therefore even in 'the trivial quibble' as she rightly calls the subject-matter of her contradiction, she is, I trust, proved wholly unsuccessful, I claim that even if my memory had betrayed me, my conclusive reply to her is left unanswered and untouched. Having no case, she has followed the method of the pettifogging lawyer who vainly tries to discredit a hostile but unshakable witness by making him state things from memory which might be found on verification to be not quite accurate. It gives me pain to have to say that her article in *Liberty* proves her to be not only an unreliable writer but an unscrupulous person devoid of a sense of right and wrong.

2nd February, 1928

A SOLEMN CEREMONY

Gandhiji returned to the Ashram from his Kathiawad tour to celebrate the wedding of his third son Ramdas Gandhi on the 27th January. A domestic event in the history of the Ashram may by itself have no importance for the public. But there were certain features of the wedding which make it worthy of note in *Young India*.

The engagement took place nearly two years ago, but Gandhiji would not consent to the marriage until the bride had finished her seventeenth year, So the people on the bride's side gladly waited for two years. Ramdas was 30 at the time of the marriage. In order to ensure the utmost simplicity and solemnity the bride's people agreed to bring her down to the Ashram for the ceremony. They came with about half a dozen people, stayed a few hours and left the Ashram on the same day. The ceremony began at 8 A. M. and lasted until 9-30 A. M., but before the actual ceremony began the bride and the groom had been asked to consecrate it by (1) fasting, (2) manual labour in the shape of spinning and cleaning the well basin, (3) cleaning the cowshed, (4) watering the trees so as to symbolise unity with the whole creation, and (5) reading a chapter from the Bhagavad Gita. The ceremony mainly consisted in the vow of faithfulness and dedication to service being taken by the bride and bridegroom before the sacrificial fire and in the presence of the elders. There was no music and nothing like a wedding party or dinner. A few friends from the city who had heard of the wedding came to give their blessings. There were practically no wedding gifts except the gift of a *mangala mala* of his own spinning, a copy of the Bhagavad Gita and Ashrama Bhajanavali from Gandhiji and that of a spinning wheel by the bride's mother and of a pair of *taklis* by Gandhiji. Both were dressed in spotlessly white Khadi, and neither had any gold or other ornament on his or her person.

Exactly at 9-30 A. M. all gathered together on the prayer ground and Gandhiji blessed the couple in a brief speech which was as solemn as the occasion itself. It was a most moving scene in Gandhiji's life. Those present could see that Gandhiji on such occasions could be as human as any of them. He was nearly moved to tears as he referred to Ramdas and Devdas as two of his sons who had been brought up exclusively by him and under his care. The consciousness that the son had never deceived him, and had hidden none of his faults and failings from him nearly choked him with a feeling of grateful pride. "You have confessed your faults to me, but they have never alarmed me, for your frank confession has exonerated you in my eyes. I am glad that you would rather be deceived by the whole world than deceive any one. May you live always in the same truthful way.

"You will guard your wife's honour and be not her master, but her true friend. You will hold her body and her soul as sacred as I trust she will hold your body and your soul. To that end you will have to live a life of prayerful toil, and simplicity and self-restraint. Let not either of you regard another as the object of his or her lust.

"You have both had part of your training here. Let your lives be consecrated to the service of the Motherland, and toil away until you wear out your bodies. We are pledged to poverty. You will therefore both earn your bread in the sweat of your brow as poor people do. You will help each other in daily toil and rejoice in it.

"I have given you no gifts. I can give none except a pair of *taklis* and copies of my dearly beloved Bhagavad Gita and Bhajanavali. Let the cotton garlands be a shield of protection for you. Could I have procured rich gifts for you from friends, the world would rightly have ridiculed my conceit, but today it will bear testimony that I have given you only such things as become one in my position.

"Let the Gita be to you a mine of diamonds, as it has been to me, let it be your constant guide and friend on life's way. Let it light your path and dignify your labour. May God give you a long life of service."

In the evening he referred to the public aspect of the question. He dilated on the pernicious system, which had divided the four original *varnas* into numerous castes and sub-castes and hoped that the wedding just celebrated would perhaps be for the Ashram the last as between parties belonging to the same caste. It behoved people in the Ashram to take the lead in this respect, because people outside might find it difficult to initiate the reform. The rule should be on the part of the Ashram to discountenance marriages between parties of the same caste and to encourage those between parties belonging to different sub-castes. He wished girls could be kept unmarried up to 20 and even 25. Towards the end he again came back to the solemn significance of the ceremony.

"Do not think that the Ashram has as its object the popularisation of marriage. It has and will have the promotion of lifelong *brahmacharya* as its object. It countenances marriage only to the extent that it serves as an instrument of restraint rather than of indulgence. And those who are for a life of restraint must order their lives differently from those who are for indulgence. Remember that there is always a limit to self-indulgence but none to self-restraint, and let us daily progress in that direction."

Another important incident of the week is Gandhiji's decision to live with the boys of the Mahavidyalaya for some time. Those who have followed Gandhiji's article on the changes in the Vidyapith will not need much by way of explanation for this step. If the resolution at the Kathiawad Political Conference was an instance of the fact that Gandhiji has his eye on the future and thinks of the present in the terms of the future, the resolution regarding the re-construction of the Vidyapith and his decision to spend some time with the Vidyalaya boys are another and equally forcible instance. The resolution seeks to inaugurate changes of a far-reaching character in the life and career of the boys, and Gandhiji feels that the boys should have the benefit of his constant contact to see that there is nothing alarming about the changes, but everything conducive to their growth and spiritual advance.

But the spirit in which he has gone there will be better understood if I give here a gist of his talk to the students of the Vidyalaya after the prayer in the early hours of the first morning there.

"I have not come to take you by storm, not in the Cæsarian spirit of *veni, vidi, vici.* But I have simply thrown myself in your midst, so that you can make whatever use you like of me on the eve of the changes that are impending. It would perhaps be better if I said that I have come to clear a long-standing debt I have long owed to you as your Chancellor to come and stay in your midst and identify myself with you as much as I could. But I have never been able to do so. I am thankful to the Giver of all good for having given me this opportunity of spending some time with you.

"I have not come to create any disturbance in the even tenor of your lives. I do not insist on your attending the four o'clock morning prayers. If you are convinced that prayer is an essential thing in one's life and that it is best to begin one's day with prayer in the early hours of the morning, you will attend it. If you do not, I shall certainly be sorry but will not resent your absence. In the same way I should like you to accompany me every evening to the Ashram to attend the evening prayer there. That also you will do if the spirit moves you, and if you feel that your work will permit you to do so. I want you to go there, not because I want you to join the Ashram though I would be glad if you did so, but because I want you to understand and identify yourselves somewhat with the Ashram. For I make no secret of it that the Ashram is the best of my creations. I can myself point out numerous defects in it, and can add many more from your own experience. But I assure you that I am more conscious of them than any one else and yet I hold that with all its short-comings it is the best of my creations. I would have me and my work judged by the Ashram more than by anything else. Hence I would love you to attend the evening prayer daily. But this is a mere suggestion to be rejected or adopted out of your own free will.

"Let me not live in your midst as a burden, but as a friend, and if possible a guide if you will.

"I am willing to give you a quarter of an hour every day or two periods every week just as you might desire. I am not sure what I shall read with you, but that also I shall leave to you to decide." M. D.

2nd February, 1928

GUJARAT VIDYAPITH

By M. K. Gandhi

This National University, the first of its kind, established when Non-co-operation was at its height has been struggling for existence for the past three or four years. The attendance of boys has gone down considerably. Several schools affiliated to it have closed or sought Government recognition. There would be nothing to worry over this decline, if there were no internal causes for it. But most of us including myself have felt that we have not done all we might have for this most useful work of national reconstruction. But whilst, if all had been vigilant, the defections might have been not so large as they have been, there are for the decline causes over which no one had any control. And though the quality of the work already done might have been easily better, what has been achieved is such as any institution would be proud of. I make bold to assert that but for the Vidyapith, Vallabhbhai Patel would not have been able to command the valuable assistance he did of so many workers during the late disastrous floods. Indeed the Vidyapith volunteers went even to Sindh in order to assist Professor Malkani who has been doing heroic work there in connection with the Sindh floods. I hope some day to deal with the Vidyapith graduates' work of which an accurate but brief analysis has been prepared by a graduate proud of being owned by it. Sufficient for the time being to make the confession of our neglect both avoidable and unavoidable and to state that we seem now to have been roused from our slumbers.

The preliminary cleansing step was taken on Sunday last when the Senate handed over charge of the valuable property and the still more valuable responsibility connected with the Vidyapith to a Board of Trustees by means of a resolution of which I give the translation below.

> "This meeting of the Senate of the Gujarat Vidyapith is of opinion that
>
> 1. By having established the Gujarat Vidyapith in connection with the Non-co-operation movement and by maintaining it in spite of a set-back in the movement, Gujarat has rendered essential service to the nation;
>
> 2. The Vidyapith has however continued year after year to suffer in point of numbers;
>
> 3. The Vidyapith could have achieved better results

in point of quality, had the internal conditions been favourable; and

4. The Vidyapith has now reached a stage in its evolution, when, in order to make it work more effectively and in order to ensure an unswerving observance of the principles, hereinafter enunciated, the administration of the Vidyapith should be entrusted to a Board of Trustees.

Therefore and in pursuance of the resolution for the reconstruction of the Vidyapith passed by this Senate on the 4th of December 1927, the Senate appoints a Board of Trustees called the Gujarat Vidyapith Mandal to be composed of those who from the list herein below pledge themselves to subscribe to and to observe the principles hereinafter enunciated; hands over charge of all the institutions connected with the Vidyapith, along with their property, moveable and immoveable, so also all the right and responsibilities pertaining thereto, to the said Vidyapith Mandal; and authorises the Mandal to add to its membership subject to the same qualifications so as not to exceed 25, and authorises it to exercise all other rights including that of filling vacancies caused by resignation, death, or dismissal of any member for breach of the pledge or similar other reason, the latter to take place by a vote of four-fifths of their number.

NAMES OF MEMBERS

1. Sjt. Vallabhbhai Patel
2. " Nrisimhaprasad Bhatt
3. " Kaka Kalelkar
4. " Shankarlal Banker
5. " Mahadev Desai
6. " Abdul Kadar Bavazir
7. " Manilal Kothari
8. " Kishorlal Mashruvala
9. " Narahari Parikh
10. " Valji Desai

11. „ Hariprasad Vrajrai Desai
12. „ Jugatram Dave
13. „ Gokulbhai Bhatt
14. „ Sukhlalji Pandit
15. „ Parikshitlal Mazumdar
16. „ Gopalrao Kulkarni
17. „ Mama Phadke
18. Shrimati Maniben V. Patel

PRINCIPLES

1. The principal object of the Vidyapith shall be to prepare workers of character, ability, education and conscientiousness, necessary for the conduct of the movements connected with the attainment of Swaraj.

2. All the institutions conducted by and affiliated to the Vidyapith shall be fully non-co-operating and shall therefore have nothing to do with any help from Government.

3. Whereas the Vidyapith has come into being in connection with Swaraj, and Non-violent Non-co-operation as a means thereof, its teachers and trustees shall restrict themselves to those means only which are not inconsistent with truth and non-violence and shall consciously strive to carry them out.

4. The teachers and the trustees of the Vidyapith, as also all the institutions affiliated to it, shall regard untouchability as a blot on Hinduism, shall strive to the best of their power for its removal and shall not exclude a boy or girl for reason of his or her untouchability nor shall give him or her differential treatment having once accorded admission to him or her.

5. The teachers and the trustees of and all the institutions affiliated to the Vidyapith shall regard handspinning as an essential part of the Swaraj movement and shall therefore spin regularly, except when disabled, and shall habitually wear Khadi

6. The language of the Province shall have the principal place in the Vidyapith and shall be the medium of instruction.

Explanation:—Languages other than Gujarati may be taught by direct method.

7. The teaching of Hindi—Hindustani shall be compulsory in the curricula of the Vidyapith.

8. Manual training shall receive the same importance as intellectual training and only such occupations as are useful for the life of the nation shall be taught.

9. Whereas the growth of the nation depends not on cities but its villages, the bulk of the funds of the Vidyapith and a majority of the teachers of the Vidyapith shall be employed in the propagation of education conducive to the welfare of the villagers.

10. In laying down the curricula, the needs of village dwellers shall have principal consideration.

11. There shall be complete toleration of all established religions in all institutions conducted by and affiliated to the Vidyapith, and for the spiritual development of the pupils, religious instruction shall be imparted in consonance with truth and non-violence.

12. For the physical development of the nation physical exercise and physical training shall be compulsory in all the institutions conducted by and affiliated to the Vidyapith.

Note. Hindi-Hindustani means the language commonly spoken by the masses of the North both Hindu and Mussalman written in the Devanagari or the Persian script."

But drastic as the step is, it may mean nothing if it is not to be followed up by quick persistent and vigilant effort. Such effort may for the time being even result in further defections. The Senate, now the Board of Trustees, have been quite aware of the possibility. They want quality and feel that if the quality is assured, quantity will come in its own time. They are prepared to sacrifice everything to quality. It would be wrong, to use donations of those who have given and will give in the belief that the principles for which the institution has professed to stand will be worked out in practice in so far as it is humanly possible. As reformers the trustees would belie their trust if they sacrifice principles for holding the institution together anyhow. Personally I have no fear as to the result if the trustees remain staunch as I have every reason to believe they will.

On the surface there would appear to be a descent from democracy to oligarchy. As a matter of fact it is not. The large elected body could not be sustained when the principles for which the elected Senate for the time being stood were in the melting pot. A democracy's ideals and principles vary with the times. A reformer's principles are rigid and fixed. When Non-co-operation ceased to be national, those who believed in it as a creed, the only final solution for the removal of India's fetters, were bound to save the creed by working it to its logical conclusion in their own lives. Hence did the Congress bring into being an independent self-governing body styled the All-India Spinners' Association composed of those who had a living faith in the message of the wheel. The unwritten understanding was that the Association would work out the programme of Khadi so as to become in process of time a tower of strength to the parent body. The permanent trust has been created in the hope of evolving a truly democratic institution, And there is a democracy such as the world has never seen if Khadi becomes a truly national institution. Even so has the Senate emerged as a Board of Trustees pledged to work out its present ideals so as to make national education a living force, so as, that is to say, to cover every village in Gujarat, to enable the students to realise the dignity of labour equal with the dignity of learning, to produce national servants who will serve the nation in her villages. The Senate, when after a full discussion it came to the resolution on Sunday, had no less a hope, the Trustees shouldered no less a responsibility. No oligarchy can arise from a voluntary surrender such as the Senate's was. It gave up its powers to a permanent body when it was in possession of the fullest powers and in a position to exercise them to the fullest extent. It was an act of self-denial whose virtue has to be proved by the Trustees. Theirs is an awful responsibility. But with proper consecration, it will sit lightly on their shoulders and Gujarat as well as India will be the gainer thereby. They will be judged not by the quantity of result turned out but by the quantity and the quality of self-service put in.

2nd February, 1928

KATHIAWAD POLITICAL CONFERENCE

(I referred in my Weekly Letter last week to a resolution of the Kathiawad Political Conference, which I described as a self-denying ordinance. Gandhiji devotes a long leading article to the resolution in the columns of the latest issue of *Navajivan* which I summarise below.)

M. D.

I shall refer here only to one resolution which I drafted and moved, and with which I think I have served the Conference and Kathiawad. Here is the resolution:

> "With a view to avoiding the possibility of any misunderstanding between the rulers and the ruled, and with a view to a fuller recognition of its own limitations, as also in confirmation of the custom which has been for some time in operation, this Conference resolves that it shall not pass any resolution condemning or criticising an individual State."

The resolution is a result of my devotion to truth. I said that the Conference could not have been held in Porbandar but for an implicit understanding with H. H. the Maharanasaheb of Porbandar, and that it must continue to be held only under such condition for some time longer. This was a measure of the helplessness of the Conference--a helplessness which could not be remedied except by a candid public confession thereof. A patient can ill afford to conceal his disease. If he does so he becomes his own enemy.

Two resolutions criticising individual States were brought up before the Subjects Committee. I cannot say there was no occasion for them, but I saw that they were beyond the understood limitations of the Conference. The Subjects Committee rejected them. The Conference could not live long if it were to entertain such resolutions. And so I advised the Conference to confess its helplessness. It was a bitter dose for the Subjects Committee. It was no pleasure to me to tender the advice, but my duty and the duty of the Conference, however painful, was clear to me. Some of the members disapproved of the resolution, but they accepted my advice out of their generosity and far-sightedness.

This added to my responsibility, for I know that I should hold myself principally to blame for any untoward result that may arise out of this. But I have no misgivings. Self-imposed restraint is always beneficial.

If the members of the Conference observe this resolution in thought, word and deed, it will enhance the capacity of the Conference to do the work within the scope defined by the resolution. Ruling princes have been until now loath to permit the holding of the Conference in their States, for fear of its entertaining resolutions condemning or criticising individual States. In the face of this difficulty it were waste of energy to engage in the alluring but futile attempt to criticise the drawbacks of individual States, and then to plead want of time for less alluring constructive work would be hypocritical. Now with the resolution members can either set about the unexciting but essential work of reconstruction, or close their shop, and as no one likes to go into bankruptcy, the executive body of the Conference, let us hope, will do the things needful.

Let not the resolution be taken to mean a declaration on the part of the Conference that the administration of these

States is beyond cavil, but it merely means that we have no power today to criticise a State in a Conference held in another State. Nor does it mean that the wrongs of an individual State may not be discussed before the Subjects Committee. Indeed a member may seek the advice of the Committee in all such cases. Only no such resolution can be passed by the Conference. The executive body of the Conference may open correspondence with the States concerned, may interview the Princes or their officials, and request them to redress the wrongs complained of, or in case the complaints in question are disproved, declare that they had no foundation. It is possible that responsible States will welcome this unobtrusive gentle procedure and may even use it as a shield, and correct themselves.

This intervention on the part of the Conference presupposes ability, perseverance and discretion on the part of its executive. Let them not proceed on assumptions or presumptions. They must have confidence to melt the heart of the Princes. This confidence arises out of a genuine desire to serve both the State and the subjects, and a recognition that the object of the Conference is not to end but mend these States. If the former is intended, the States are no place in which to hold the Conference.

Ahimsa is a constructive, not a destructive force; founder of democracies, not subversive of princes or States; achieves the assimilation of all that is best in the rulers and the ruled. In a word, it seeks to establish a bond between the two, sustained not by armed force but by affection. The modern tendencies are subversive, the ancient culture conserves all that is best. *Ahimsa* aims at the greatest good of all, *himsa* builds the prosperity of one on the destruction of another. Democracy is not always good, autocracy is not always bad. Both have their uses for a Conference that seeks to reach its goal through truth and non-violence.

The field of work, that is open to the Conference, is vast. There is Khadi, there is untouchability, there is temperance work, also social reform, water storage for years of drought, planting trees, and many other things.

These indeed need the co-operation of Princes, but more the co-operation of their servants. These are drawn from the articulate section of the people and unless they realise their duty, unless they make up their minds to interest themselves in public service fearlessly, no reform is possible. The effort of the Conference will therefore primarily be among the people themselves. For people are the roots, the state is the fruit. If the roots are sweet, the fruits are bound to be sweet.

The Subjects of each State can have their own Conferences in their respective States and they may certainly criticise their respective administrations with due restraint. But this also can be built on a foundation of constructive work.

This needs selfless, fearless workers. Have we got them? Let those that are available plod on ceaselessly and patiently.

So much for the people. If the princes will only understand, the resolution increases their responsibility. Many of them boycott the Conference for fear of criticism or condemnation. But now I submit, it behoves them to welcome this resolution, appreciate the wisdom and goodwill of the Conference, and satisfy it by using it as a bridge between themselves and the people. From the evidence before me I cannot say that all the administration of all the Kathiawad States is beyond cavil. Some of them, I hear, have grievously erred. Let them recognise the signs of the times. The cataclysm that is sweeping over the earth today and which threatens India too is a great sign. As a chaotic force it is pernicious, but it has at its back a noble object. The world, though not itself virtuous pays an unconscious homage to virtue. It is tired of autocratic tyrannies, it is impatient of them. In its impatience, it forgets that the remedy that it seeks to employ is worse than the disease, but it desires reform, it desires the reign of equity and justice. Votaries of truth and *ahimsa* like myself are convinced that that way equity and justice do not lie, but they are no less convinced that unless the men in power take the warning they are doomed. Let the ruling Princes beware. Let them not choose the way to moral bankruptcy. The unswerving faith that India will not go that way sustains me. May the ruling Princes not falsify that faith.

2nd February, 1928

A SISTER'S DIFFICULTY

By M. K. Gandhi

A sister writes:

> "A year ago I heard you speaking on the supreme necessity of every one of us wearing Khadi and thereupon decided to adopt it. But we are poor people. My husband says that Khadi is costly. Belonging as I do to Maharashtra, I wear a *sadi* 9 yards long. Now if I reduce the length of my *sadi* to 6 yards, there would be a great saving, but the elders will not hear of any such reduction. I reason with them that wearing Khadi is the more important thing and that the style and length of the *sadi* is absolutely immaterial, but in vain. They say that it is my youth that puts all these new-fangled notions into my head. But I expect they will agree to the proposed reduction in length if you are good enough to write to me, saying that Khadi ought to be used, even at the cost of the style of clothing."

I have sent the desired reply to the sister. But I take note of her difficulty here, as I know that the same difficulty is encountered by many other sisters as well.

The letter in question bears witness to the strong patriotic feeling of the writer, for there are not many sisters who, like her, are ready to give up old styles or old customs on their own initiative. The number of such sisters and brothers is legion, as would gladly have Swaraj if it could be attained without suffering any discomfort or incurring any expenditure and in spite of their sticking to old customs regardless of their propriety or the reverse. But Swaraj is not such a cheap commodity. To attain Swaraj implies the cultivation of a spirit of self-sacrifice, including the sacrifice of provincialism.

Provincialism is a bar not only to the realisation of national Swaraj, but also the achievement of provincial autonomy. Women perhaps are more responsible than men for keeping up this narrow spirit. Variety is worth cherishing up to a certain limit, but if the limit is exceeded, amenities and customs masquerading under the name of variety are subversive of nationalism. The Deccani *sadi* is a thing of beauty, but the beauty must be let go if it can be secured only by sacrificing the nation. We should consider the Kachchhi style of short *sadi* or the Punjabi *odhni* to be really artistic if the wearing of Khadi can be cheapened and facilitated by their means. The Deccani, Gujarati, Kachchhi and Bengali styles of wearing *sadi* are all of them various national styles, and each of them is as national as the rest. Such being the case, preference should be accorded to that style which requires the smallest amount of cloth consistently with the demands of decency. Such is the Kachchhi style, which takes up only 3 yards of cloth, that is, about half the length of the Gujarati *sadi*, not to mention the saving of trouble in having to carry a smaller weight. If the *pachhedo* and the petticoat are of the same colour, one cannot at once make out whether it is only a *pachhedo* or full *sadi*. The mutual exchange and imitation of such national styles is eminently desirable.

Well-to-do people might well keep in their wardrobes all possible provincial styles of clothing. It would be very courteous and patriotic on the part of a Gujarati host and hostess to put on the Bengali style of dress when they entertain Bengali guests, and *vice versa*. But such procedure is open only to the patriotic rich. Patriotic people of the middle and poorer classes should take pride in adopting that particular provincial style which cheapens as well as facilitates the wearing of Khadi. And even there they should fix their eye upon the clothing style of the poorest of the poor.

Swadeshi does not mean drowning oneself in one's own little puddle but making it tributary to the ocean that is the nation. And it can claim to contribute to the ocean only if it is and keeps itself pure. It is therefore clear that only such local or provincial customs should have a nation-wide vogue as are not impure or immoral. And when once this truth is grasped, nationalism is transmuted into the enthusiasm of humanity.

What is true of clothing is equally true of language, food, etc. As we might imitate the dress of other provinces on a suitable occasion, so might we utilise the language and other things. But at present all our energy is wasted in the useless, impossible and fatal attempt to give English the pride of place to the neglect, conscious or unconscious, of our mother tongue and all the more so, of the languages of other provinces.

9th February, 1928

DEFENDING NATIONAL EDUCATION

The following is a summary of the address delivered by Acharya Kripalani to the students of the Vidyapith after its Convocation:

" It is not unoften that people have talked to me about the large sums that we have spent and are still spending on national education in Gujarat. I have been told that compared to the money spent, the results have not been satisfactory. I am by nature a miser, but in spite of this I am of opinion that Gujarat has benefited ten times as much as the small amount of money spent on the Vidyapith. It has decidedly been a profitable investment. I have experience at least of four Indian universities. In one I was a student, in three others I served as professor. I can therefore say with confidence, that thanks to our cultural *samskaras*, during the short period the Vidyapith has been in existence, and with the modest amount of money at our disposal, we have achieved results that can compare favourably with those of the orthodox universities. The proof of what I say would be obvious if we critically examine this very meeting of the graduates of the Vidyapith. To whichever direction I turn my eyes I find that at least every second man amongst you is engaged in some form of national activity. I also know that wherever our graduates are working they hold positions of honour, trust, and responsibility.

"The Kulanayak just told us that we are groping in the dark about national education, that we have not yet seen the light. I agree with Nanabhai in what he has said, but at the same time I would add that either we shall never see the light, or we never were in real darkness. I believe that light only comes by churning the ocean of darkness. I would try to make my meaning clear. When a man has a small fund of virtue, he naturally feels that he is a sinner. But as his virtue increases, he finds the sense of sin increasing proportionately. The greater the saint, the greater the consciousness of his own shortcomings and weaknesses. Were it not so, we would not find men of the highest virtue deprecating themselves as great sinners. Are they falsely modest, or hypocritical? They could not be so. The explanation lies in the fact, that as the light of virtue illumines their path, they realise more and more the great distance that separates them from their objective. They might be infinitely better than the average man, but they know how far away they are from the perfection which is their only goal. As a man climbing the Himalayas surmounts range after range, and finds that what appeared to him to be the heights from a distance were nothing but the low ranges at the base and every height conquered becomes but the beginning of a new effort, similarly is the case with us. We are not therefore afraid if we are groping. All honour to those who have made up their minds to explore the heights. The progress may be slow, there may be even losing of the way, but if effort is not abandoned, through all darkness and failure, one day we will find ourselves in the midst of the glorious sunshine that eternally illumines the snowy peaks far above the clouds of this earth. But supposing we never reach the top, and perish on the way. What then? Even failure here is more glorious than success elsewhere. There can be no retrogression, no loss in this. It is even as Shri Krishna said: "Victorious thou shalt enjoy a prosperous kingdom, defeated thou shalt enjoy heaven, reserved for the brave who fall fighting in a righteous cause." So I am not afraid of groping in the dark. To me it is the sign of life, that we have at least begun groping about national education.

"You will naturally expect me to speak a few words of advice to you, now that some of you are just on the threshold of life for which the college career was but a preparation. I always feel diffident about giving advice. I can never play the role of a moral preacher. I know the responsibilities attaching to the position. I am conscious of my limitations, and I realise that mine is not the life that I could keep before my pupils. Also I can learn a good deal from the book of life possessed by several of you. To all such I have ever rendered my reverence in secret; and yet the position I unfortunately occupy, the position of the head of the institution, obliges me to do what I would refuse to do under ordinary circumstances. You will, therefore, please not look to my life, but take me even as a finger-post, a lamp-post on the road that indicates the way but cannot walk the way itself. I cannot present my life as an example. But there are other lives being lived in our midst today from which you may derive the necessary inspiration. I would however give you a word of warning. Whomsoever you follow, howsoever great he might be, see to it, that you follow the spirit of the master, and not imitate him mechanically. 'The word killeth, but the spirit giveth life.' Let there be no mechanical following of the outward action without any reference to the spirit which is behind that action. Let each follow according to his *svabhava* and *svadharma*, according to his individual development. 'Better one's *dharma* though destitute of merit than the *dharma* of another. Another's *dharma* is full of danger.'

"Let the following be not of the outward form; such following offends the master. The Jews crucified the Christ but once. How often since has he not been crucified by his followers? Let us therefore so act that when we are face to face with the master, we are not told, 'I know you not, ye workers of iniquity.' Let us work even in the spirit of the Gita, which lays down no mechanical rule of conduct, but calls upon the disciple to have the inner calm, the inner poise. It calls him to equality, to indifference to success or failure. When Arjuna asks the qualities of the stable-minded, the *Dhira*, "How does he walk, how does he sit, how talk?" Shri Krishna describes neither the talk nor the walk, but the psychological inner signs,—freedom from anxiety, indifference amidst pleasure and pain, freedom from passion, fear, anger and the rest. 'He, who performs such action as his duty independently of the fruits of the actions, is a Sannyasi, a Yogi, not he who is without fire and rites." Even in the matter of food it is not this or that particular food, that is prescribed or proscribed, but only psychological tests are given. Remember, 'God fulfils himself in many ways.' I emphasize this because you have passed through the portal of a university. You have received higher liberal education. Higher education stands for unity, for catholicity, for toleration and wide outlook. The culture that a university imparts should make you find the points of contact, and avoid those of conflict. If you could see the inner springs of actions, and not the outward manifestations thereof, you would find a wonderful unity. This is true even in the realm of religion. Leave the outward expression, the doctrine, the dogma and the form, and behold the unity and oneness of spirit. Ordering your lives thus, you will imbibe the true spirit of charity. Then there will be no need to divide this universe of ours between heaven and hell, no need to divide fellow-beings into virtuous and vicious, the eternally saved and the eternally damned. Love shall inform your actions and pervade your life.

"One thing more I would like to bring to your notice.

The study of Indian history and my own observations have shown me that we, Indians, are not inferior to other people in individual virtues. What we lack are social and collective virtues. Indian history is rich in exceptional individuals; in fact it is the history of individual geniuses. It lacks social and collective effort and interest. A Sikh, a Gurkha, or a Pathan individually would be more than a match for any English, German or French soldier. But a company of the former would be no match for a company of the latter. We as a rule keep our persons and houses clean; there is no lack of individual hygiene; but combine us and make us live as neighbours in some *pole* in Ahmedabad, and we will produce dirt and squalor unknown even among uncivilised people elsewhere. If we are to compete with other nations, and if we are to occupy a position of equality with them, we must draw out the social and collective virtues that lie dormant in us. The spirit to combine, to co-operate, to find out points of contact, to avoid points of conflict must be there. With us every opinion becomes a principle, which we defend with a vehemence worthy of a better cause. Let therefore the unalterable principles, wherein there can be no give and take, be as few as possible. Let us also make the wholesome division between public and private life. There may be people with whom we may have differences in private life, but in no case must these differences divide us in public. We may have private friends, but their influence shall in no way make us swerve from public duties, we shall reserve our hearts' affection, the hospitality of our homes for our friends, but in public life we recognise only one set of friends and one set of opponents. Those who are with us in our struggle and ideals are our friends; those who are opposed are opponents. You know the venerable lady Dr. Besant working in our midst, working for the uplift of our country. During her political career she has, at different periods of her life, stood opposed to some of our highly respected leaders and even denounced them. But as soon as her political ideas coincided with them, she forgot her former opposition, and not only fell in line with them, but even followed their lead. If you have the charity and love about which I talked to you in the beginning, you will not find it difficult to evolve the social and collective virtues which will make association possible. However, it may come to pass that an over-emphasis on collective action and public virtue may have an adverse effect on character. This is seen in the political life of the West. An honourable gentleman, who would be ashamed to break his word, or to tell a lie in private life, would not hesitate to do so in public life. He would not be ashamed, nor would his conscience bite him. From these doubtful and double values we shall be saved, if we follow the lead of Gandhiji. He has an indomitable faith in the moral law. He believes that in the long run, no good can be done to collective life at the sacrifice of individual virtues. He has also shown us how effective a man can be even in the political field without deviating from the path of truth. *Ahimsa* is another guarantee against the excesses of collective life. If we but follow in his footsteps, I have no doubt we shall be true, even as he is, both to this earth below and the heaven above. We shall function in this world with effect, and yet the next shall not be lost to us. In this spirit worked the old masters—Janaka and others."

9th February, 1928

AFTER HARTAL?

BY M. K. GANDHI

With great deliberation and not without the exercise of great self-restraint have I hitherto refrained practically from writing anything about the boycott of the Statutory Commission. I recognised the force of the appeal made to me by the *Leader* of Allahabad not to meddle with or influence the boycott movement but to let the various parties manage it themselves. I recognised that my interference was bound to bring in the masses more prominently into the movement and might possibly embarrass the promoters. Now that the great demonstration is over I feel free to say a word. I tender my congratulations to the organisers for the very great success they achieved on the *hartal* day. It did my soul good to see Liberals, Independents and Congressmen ranged together on the same platform. I could not but admire the courage of the students of Government Colleges in absenting themselves from their Colleges for the sake of the national cause. All the world over students are playing a most important and effective part in shaping and strengthening national movements. It would be monstrous if the students of India did less.

My object now is to draw attention to the fact that the very success of the *hartal* will be turned against us, if it is not followed up by sufficient and persistent action. We must belie the prophecy of Lord Sinha that the *hartal* was but a passing cloud. Let us bear in mind that notwithstanding our opposition, the Commission backed as it is by British bayonets will go its own way. Where it cannot get *bona fide* recognition, it will be manufactured for it. Did not a so-called deputation on behalf of 'untouchables' welcome the Commission as its true deliverers? Claiming to know the 'untouchables' more than the members of the deputation, I make bold to assert that they no more represented the 'untouchables' than would a party of Japs for instance.

If then we are to ensure a complete boycott, not only will there have to be a joint organisation by all the parties for carrying it out and possibly picketting, wherever the Commission goes, but there must be some further demonstration of the nation's strength. Even though mine may be a voice in the wilderness and even at the risk of repeating a thousandth time the same old story, I suggest that there is nothing before the nation other than boycott of foreign cloth which can be brought about effectively and quickly. But like all great undertakings, it requires planning and organising. It requires sustained and vigilant effort by a party of earnest, able and honest men and women exclusively devoted to the task. It is not an easy task. If it was, it would not produce the great results that are promised for it. It must evoke the best in the nation before it is accomplished. But let us also frankly recognise that if we cannot organise this one thing, we shall organise nothing else.

Let me make my own position clear. I have no desire even now to interfere with the present evolution of the national movement except through occasional writings. This is written therefore by way of a humble appeal to the different parties who are jointly acting in order to vindicate national honour.

9th February, 1928

UNION OF SOUTH AFRICA

Though through the heroic efforts of the Rt. Hon. Shrinivasa Shastri, the social status of our countrymen in South Africa has undoubtedly improved and life is becoming less unbearable for self-respecting Indians, reminders come now and then from that sub-continent that much yet remains to be done before the Indian settlers enjoy the ordinary civic rights and feel their position safe. The latest shock comes through a cable just received from Mr. Albert Christopher, the new Deputy President of the South African Indian Congress. Mr. Christopher was one of the volunteers who served as well during the Boer War as during the late War. He is South Africa born and has just returned after finishing his education in England. The cable runs as follows :—

> "Second reading Liquor Bill now going through Parliament notwithstanding strong protest. Bill seeks deprive three thousand Indians their families and dependents of livelihood ultimately drive them out of country. Bill direct conflict letter spirit Capetown Agreement. Clear racial legislation. Indians greatly alarmed Government's attitude. If Bill passes Capetown Agreement smashed. Earnestly appeal your immediate intervention."

Even the respectable South African press agrees with the opinion of the South African Congress that the Bill violates the Agreement which resulted from the Round Table Conference. That it is aimed even at those who are already earning an honest livelihood in hotels and bars is unquestioned. If the Union Parliament persists in the Bill, it simply means that being the stronger party to the contract, it can safely commit breach of contract whenever it wills. Our hope lies in Sjt. Sastri's gentle diplomacy, saving not only the situation, but the honour of the Union Government, the Union Parliament and the white people of South Africa in spite of themselves. He, however, needs energetic support from the Indian press and the Indian public.

M. K. G.

9th February, 1928

A PARALLEL FROM CHINA

BY M. K. GANDHI

A friend sends me a cutting from the *New York Times* containing the report of an interview with Mr. Ku Hung-Ming, one of the most prominent Chinese, referring to the cultural greatness of the Chinese people and its being belittled by foreigners. And referring to the inroads of foreign merchants upon China Mr. Ku says:

> "I was similarly blind when I first returned from my long years abroad," he admits with disarming frankness. "At first I was ashamed to admit I was Chinese; now I am so proud of my heritage that I am conceited enough to think the rest of you are all barbarians.
>
> "You see, our main trouble is economic. You Americans, for instance, thought a great influx of Chinese labourers would upset your industry and lower your standard of living. You acted promptly and shut your door against Chinese.

"But we in China have suffered an invasion of your foreign machines and of cheap machine-made goods, and those things have ruined us, just as an influx of several million Chinese coolie labourers would have ruined your industrial scheme.

"When I was a young man, for instance, even the women in our own families spun and wove. At that time fully 100,000,000 Chinese women spun and wove. Then came cheap foreign cotton goods and these 100,000,000 women have no productive life but must live on the labours of their menfolk. We are prevented from following your example of shutting the door by the fact that the treaties forbid our taking any action. We do not have even tariff autonomy.

"If I were an artist, I would draw you a cartoon which would show you what I think of the unequal treaties.

"Picture a Chinese prone upon the ground and a foreigner standing over him holding him down with his foot. 'Get up,' says the foreigner. 'Take your foot off first,' says the Chinese. 'No, you get up first,' says the foreigner, putting more weight upon the foot."

9th February, 1928

KHADI IN THE PUNJAB IN 1885

By M. K. Gandhi

I extract the following valuable information that Sjt. Balaji Rao of Coimbatore collects for me from time to time from several books. The extract is taken from a Monograph on the Cotton Manufacture in 1885 by E. B. Francis:

P. 2. "It thus appears that 8,57,000 mds. of raw cotton, or 84 p.c. of the whole yield of the province, are locally consumed."

P. 3. "Spinning is the domestic employment, during the greater part of their leisure time, of women of all classes, and like most of such employments is very ill-paid. A woman cannot spin more than one chitak or 2 ozs. daily unless the thread be coarse, when she may accomplish two chitaks, and her remuneration is only from 4 to 8 annas a seer, so that she earns but half an anna a day. The above is the highest rate quoted in any of the reports. That of the Rawalpindi district states that the pay is only 5 pice a seer and the Jullunder report estimates the earnings of a spinner at only Rs. 3-12-7 a year! The difference between the average value of cotton and of cotton thread is only about 3 as. a seer. In the census tables 1,99,164 women and 273 men are returned as cotton spinners. At the rate of 1½ chitaks a day each person would be able to produce less than one maund of thread in a year, so that if 8,00,000 mds. of cotton are annually converted into thread, ... a much larger number than the census shows must really employ themselves in spinning. That is to say, a great number of females who habitually spin failed to describe themselves as spinners by occupation. The bulk of the country yarn is very uneven in thickness and unfit for anything but the coarsest cloth. Comparatively few persons can produce fine and even thread, and many of these spin only for the use of their own households.

P. 2. "Census: Cotton ginners—3,257 men and 1,345 women—these figures do not represent the numbers really so employed. This operation is very frequently performed by members of the household of the person to whom the cotton belongs.

P. 3. "Census: 32,268 men and 4,395 women scutchers, or carders. Women who spin cotton sometimes scutch it for themselves. The wages are 3 pice or one anna for a seer. Average turn out 4 seers a day.

P. 9. "Country cloth was exported from the Punjab to the extent of 1,39,911 mds a year, 93,000 to other parts of India and 46,000 beyond Western and North Western Frontier.

P. 4. "The imported thread is fine, clean and even and can be had in a variety of attractive colours. It varied from Rs. 100 to Rs. 65 a maund, (while country yarn was valued at Rs. 22 a maund)."

That the remuneration earned by the spinners was low did not baffle the good workers, for as the author says, they worked during the leisure hours and whatever they earned was so much gained. If the things are different now, it is because the tastes have become vulgarised and foreign cloth under an insidious system of indirect protection has been dumped down on this unhappy land.

16th February, 1928

FAREWELL TO ACHARYA KRIPALANI

The large gathering of Ahmedabad citizens and students that met the other day in the quadrangle of the Vidyapith under the chairmanship of Sheth Ambalal Sarabhai to bid farewell to Acharya Kripalani who has returned to Benares to take charge of his Ashram there was an eloquent tribute to the Acharya's popularity. Originally a teacher and a professor, Acharya Kripalani threw himself into the fray, as soon as an opportunity offered itself in Bihar in 1917. The zeal with which he took the lead in giving Gandhiji the first welcome in Champaran cost him his comfortable job in the Government college at Muzaffarpur and ever since he has been in one or other national movement. After Champaran came a brief brilliant career at the Hindu University, Benares, which came to a glorious end in N.-C.-O. days, when he left the University with a large batch of students. He later helped in organising the Kashi Vidyapith, but gave his time and energy to building on the nucleus of a few of his students the Gandhi Ashram at Benares. Then came the great days of 1921 which saw every important man in the U. P. in jail and Kripalani had also his share of the glory. On release from jail he set out putting his Ashram on a firm and solid footing, but the Gujarat

Vidyapith needed him and he came away leaving his work in charge of his students who had now become his co-workers. Even from Gujarat he gave them his guidance and every vacation found him in Benares nursing his old love. After five and a half years of service as Acharya of the Mahavidyalaya he has gone again back into the arms of his old love. Benares' gain is Gujarat's loss, though he has promised not to sever his connection with the Vidyalaya and to come and spend time here occasionally. Even if he had not given the promise, the great farewell meeting could not but have been to him an eloquent reminder of what not only his students, but the students outside the Vidyalaya and the citizens of Ahmedabad will expect of him. The citizens have on many an occasion had experience of his independence and his uncanny criticism which endeared him all the more, and the students outside felt his moral force quite as much as those in the Vidyalaya.

Professor Pathak, his colleague, who has had many differences with him, paid him a tribute which he will not easily forget. He praised in a few well-chosen words not merely his great qualities as a teacher, but his manly courage, his patriotism, his austere simplicity, his burning passion for Hinduism, above all his sagacity and political sense which put the speaker in mind of independent America where teachers have risen from the professor's quarters to the White House. The speeches of the students were all tributes to one who had been their guide, philosopher, and friend, and where they were uncannily outspoken, showed in what furnace their brains had been forged. For there is an abandon in Kripalani of which his students are the least likely to escape the influence. That abandon showed itself even in his speech in reply to the address and the other speeches. The fine speech was, I am afraid, marred by generalisations which had their basis, if any, only in little incidents in the class room or the common room. But every one knew that he meant well. The students have now issued an appeal to the students, old and new, and to Gujarat to contribute to the purse they intend to raise for

Acharya Kripalani's Gandhi Ashram, Benares. However narrow may be Gujarat's outlook, or however lacking in politeness or warmth it may be, according to Acharya Kripalani, it will, we hope, prove that it can never be accused of ungratefulness.

The following is a condensed summary of Acharya Kripalani's speech as edited by him:

"It is now five years and a half since I came to your lovely land. I had come for a year only. But my stay was prolonged owing to unavoidable circumstances. I had no intention of becoming a Gujarati. I was already a citizen of three provinces—Bihar, U. P. and Sindh. Even a more ambitious man than myself would have been satisfied with this. But how could the single atom of an individual resist the attraction of such a great province? Gujarat has great virtues—robust common sense, business acumen, industry and thrift. I could not fail to mark the determination and doggedness of your character. If the crawling order had been issued in Gujarat I have no doubt that some weak, emaciated, contemptible-looking Bania would have resisted it even at the point of the bayonet. This tenacity of character attracted me, also your great *ahimsa*. Nowhere in the world do birds, beasts and fish roam about with greater freedom and less fear. I was also attracted by the emotional side of your nature. To a superficial observer you appear cold and unemotional. This is because of your inexpressiveness and want of sentimentalism. You did not, however, deceive me long. I knew behind what appeared a hard or unattractive exterior was the sweet kernel of abiding affections, the proof of which you have given during these last few days. All this coupled with the little service I rendered to you made me one of you, I believe, and my experience has confirmed the belief, that nothing draws man closer together than this disinterested service. All this brought me nearer and nearer to you so that for some time I have been feeling like a Gujarati. I am proud of the fact.

"You will therefore this evening allow me to exercise the

privilege of indulging in a little innocent criticism. But why should I need your indulgence when I am already one of you?

"I find that we Gujaratis lack a breadth of vision found in some other people of India. Everything here is on a moderate scale. Our *poles* are narrow, our houses small, our doors and windows small, our roofs low, our rivers streamlets, our mountains hillocks. The very men and women are short in stature. Another defect of ours is our coldness, want of sociability, and politeness of expression, which keep individuals and groups divided in air-tight compartments. Yet another blemish of our character is a subtle cruelty in spite of our non-killing. These are some of our glaring defects. May these defects be not the rank growth of modern over-commercialism which marks us from other provinces of India? These are harsh words, but I have used them, so that by marking off the defects and drawing attention towards them I may not have to repeat what I have just said.

"It has been our effort in these institutions to preserve and advance what is great and good in Gujarat, and eliminate what is weak and unworthy. We have also tried to reflect here the great personality of Gandhi. I know that he is too complex and many-sided to be exhaustively represented by us. I believe his is a unity in trinity and this trinity is represented by three groups and three institutions in Ahmedabad. One face of this trinity is in the Ashram at Sabarmati which represents his great *tapasya* and *samyama*. It represents his untiring energy and industry. Above all in the Ashram he tries to reach the footstool of his God, where rest the humble, the lowliest and the lost. All this is typified in the charkha.

"The second and the opposite face of this trinity is at the other end on the opposite side of the Sabarmati. It is represented by Sjt. Vallabhbhai who is a host in himself and an institution. He represents Gandhi's politics, his robust commonsense, his firm grasp of the essentials, his spirit of ready compromise so necessary in politics.

"In between these two is the central face of the great

trinity. It is in our Vidyapith. Here we represent the master in his learning, full of reverence, his great culture informed by his great humility. We represent his catholicity, tolerance, and charity, his ready understanding and reconciliation of opposite and apparently conflicting points of view. Here we delight with him in his merry, open and contagious laughter, his love of poetry, music, art, flowers and children. Here we try to keep the ancient ideal of poverty of the scholar and the teacher. Ours is an aristocracy of learning wrapped in rags. But the rags are not unpleasant because they represent voluntary renunciation. It is a poverty that does not impoverish but enriches, ennobles, and elevates. It accepts all the good things of the world and even its luxuries if they come in the course of its business, but disdains hankering after them. It refuses to bend the knee to insolent power or insolent riches.

"We occupy the central position touching the other two faces of the trinity. Thus we perform a function of unification. Our fundamental work is that of advancement of learning and culture, but we do not hesitate to leave our books when occasion demands or when we feel that the other two faces do not perform their function properly. You will therefore find us often in the city attending political meetings, joining processions, and demonstrations. Also when some constructive work has got to be done we do not lag behind. This was evidenced by our efforts in flood relief here and in distant Sindh. It was therefore no accident that placed me at the head of this institution. Essentially I am a man of books, a student, but when occasion has demanded I have not hesitated to close my books and participate in political propaganda and march off to jail. My Ashram in which I do Khadi work in Benares is the symbol of the master's charkha.

"The ideas I have kept before you this evening have steadily guided me in the conduct of these institutions. I hand them on to my successors. I hope they will carry on and develop them. Whatever changes they may introduce in the present re-construction I hope they will not go against the traditions already established. If they touch these they will not only be destroying the Vidyapith but also impoverishing Gujarat. Let them do what they can, but they must preserve what already is there because it is good and when weighed in the balance has not been found wanting.

"Now I would like to address a few parting words to my pupils. I want to have a heart-to-heart talk with them. In your address you have assured me that you have seen my love even in my anger and wrath. I in turn assure you that I have never doubted yours even when you have been refractory and rebellious. Rebellion is the privilege of youth and however it might have been inconvenient to me at the time, I was not agitated because I knew that in your worst moods you would not over-step the bounds of decency and decorum. I never doubted your love, it has been greater than I deserved. Mine has been the joy and profit; and when today accounts have to be squared, I declare myself bankrupt, knowing full well that in this land of commerce the laws of bankruptcy are not unknown. As if the burden of your love was not heavy enough already, you have during these last few days made it heavier still. I have not failed to mark the clouds that have overcast your countenances, nor the repressed tears that have moistened your eyes. My task of leave-taking is, therefore, heavy and sad.

"A parting word of advice—I will not preach to you any copy-book maxims of morality, I would only charge you to keep the traditions of this institution intact. Above all, keep the three silences which we have always observed. First the silence in the prayer class which I have never entered but with a sense of joyful peace. Alas! that it should be so necessary today to preach silence to the descendants of those who kept it for years without break. Even our places of worship are not free from irrelevant and confusing sounds. It is a humiliation but I say it, as I have said it often, continue to observe the silence of the Christian Church in your prayer class. Decorate it with pictures and flowers. Let the incense continue burning and see to it that its sanctity is preserved. The second silence that has become a tradition with us is the one that we observe at the first notes of music. That is the only way to appreciate music and mark our sense of gratitude to the musician who lifts us to the World of Ideas. Third is the silence with which we listen to the most boring and unpopular speaker, one which you are observing just now. Let these three silences not mark you here only but carry them with you and spread them throughout Gujarat. You hardly know how much sweeter public life would be and how orderly our meetings would be if these three silences were observed, even as they are here.

"It was always my effort to direct the Mahavidyalaya to live a common family life. Continue these efforts till your institution becomes a real Ashram. You remember that I had abolished all holidays except national days, the week-ends and the long vacations. You have re-introduced them but keep them as few as possible. They might have been once the symbol of our religion and culture, but today they represent our lethargy and want of vitality. Above all I charge you to keep the spirit of mirth and joy that is the privilege of youth. Carry in afterlife your ideals, hopes and aspirations intact. Remember, however heavy the burdens that life imposes, they are yet light. Dismiss with a smile the follies of others and if you can, try to smile at your own. Wherever your lot be cast, I assure you life is worth living even on the rack and the cross."

M. D.

16th February, 1928

ON THEIR TRIAL

By M. K. Gandhi

What happened to the students during the Rowlatt Act agitation is repeating itself now. During those precious days one of them wrote to me that he felt like committing suicide because he was rusticated. A student now writes:

> 'The students of . . . of . . . . heard the mother's call and responded to it. We observed *hartal* on the 3rd. For this courageous deed of ours, we are being fined Rs. 2 per head. The poor students are losing their freeships, half-freeships and scholarships. Please write to Mr. . . . the Principal or advise him through *Young India*. Tell him we are no criminals, we have committed no crime. Tell him we listened and responded to the mother's call, we saved her, to our utmost, from dishonour. Tell him we are no cowards. Please come forward to our aid."

I cannot follow the advice to write to the Principal. If he is not to lose his 'job' I suppose he has to take some disciplinary measures. So long as educational institutions remain under the patronage of the Government, they will be, as they must be, used for the support of the Government, and the students or the teachers who support anti-Government popular measures, must count the cost and take the risk of being dismissed. From the patriot's standpoint, the students did well and bravely in making common cause with the people. They would have laid themselves open to the charge of want of patriotism, if not worse, if they had not responded to the country's call. From the Government standpoint, they undoubtedly did wrong and incurred their severe displeasure. The students cannot blow hot and cold. If they will be with the people's cause, they must hold their scholastic career subservient to the cause and sacrifice it when it comes in conflict with the interests of the country. I saw this quite clearly in 1920 and subsequent experience has confirmed the first impression. There is no doubt that the safest and the most honourable course of the student world is to leave Government schools and colleges at any cost. But the next best course for them is to hold themselves in readiness to be thrown out whenever a conflict occurs between the Government and the people. If they will not be, as they have been elsewhere, leaders themselves in the revolt against the Government, they must at least become staunch and true followers. Let their facing of the consequences be as brave as was their response to the nation's call. Let them not humiliate themselves, let them not surrender their self-respect in trying to re-enter colleges and schools from which they may have been dismissed. The bravery of their response will be counted as bravado, if it succumbs on the very first trial.

I hear that during the days preceding the *hartal* the students discarded foreign cloth and very largely patronised Khadi. Let it not be said of them that this was but a passing show and that they have on pressure from without or temptation from within discarded Khadi as quickly as they discarded foreign cloth. To me foreign cloth for this country means foreign Government. I wish this was accepted as a self-evident proposition.

16th February, 1928

MY HEALTH

BY M. K. GANDHI

It is a matter of great sorrow to me that my health should cause anxiety to many friends. Hitherto I have allowed Mahadev Desai subject to censorship to write whatever he has wished about my health, seeing that the break-downs important or unimportant occurred whilst I was travelling, and were supposed to be due to fatigue, and because those who were in charge of me during the travels had a responsibility about my bodily condition. But circumstances have now altered. I am having a respite from travels and onerous public duties. I am taking part only to the extent that I wish in re-organising some of the activities in Gujarat specially educational, for which I am perhaps predominantly responsible. I have therefore felt called upon to take up what has been a hobby of a life-time, namely dietetic experiments. They are to me as important as many of the most important activities which have engrossed me from time to time, and it was in the course of these experiments that the present so-called break-down has occurred. The alarming registrations of doctor's instruments have had no response in my own feeling. But I have accepted the statement of medical friends that very often blood pressure patients feel no evil effects, although they may be stealthily present in the body, and must therefore be guarded against. Happily, however, even these instruments registered last Sunday a very great improvement, a fall from 214 mm. systolic to 178 mm. and a rise from 120 mm. diastolic to 118 mm. I am also taking the rest prescribed by Dr. Haribhai Desai and his medical companions, and carrying on my dietetic experiments under their observation and guidance. Dr. Muthu who seems to have made a special study of dietetics is also kindly guiding me by correspondence.

Having given all this information, I would implore newspaper correspondents to curb their pen and kindly to forget me and my health for the time being. And I would ask anxious friends not to worry about my health, accepting my assurance that I am in no hurry to die and that therefore I shall be taking all the care of my body that is humanly possible for me, and is consistent with the ideals to which the body is dedicated, and which I hold to be more precious than the body. Let the friends rest assured, that if the nation has any use for this body of mine, it is because a serious attempt has been made for many a long year to hold it in trust for those ideals. I would ask them also to share my belief, which I hold even at the risk of being dubbed a fatalist, that not one hair of any one's body can be touched without His will, and that when he has no use for our bodies. He defies all the care, attention and skill that money, prestige, patriotism, friendship and what not can summon to one's assistance. This belief does not mean, that I do not want to take advantage of the assistance that medical friends all over India ungrudgingly and most generously render to me. I take that assistance gladly and faithfully. For God has given me no inkling of his intentions, but He has imposed upon me the duty of taking care of the body consistently with other more imperative obligations which, in my opinion, He has imposed upon me in common with the rest of humanity.

16th February, 1928

AN EYE-OPENER

Sir Chunilal Sankaleshvar Mehta has sent to the *Navajivan* a most interesting account of the progress which the spinning wheel has achieved among the Raniparaj people in Surat District I summarise the report below:

The following table shows the number of various apparatus of the spinning and weaving industry sold to the Raniparaj people from the Vedchhi Ashram from year to year.

Name of article	Number sold in St. 1980-81	St. 1982	St. 1983
Spinning wheels	388	70	441
Spindles	466	103	607
Carding bows (small)	75	14	
" (large)	14	25	23
Handgins	23	14	16
Handlooms	1	3	1

The above table shows the sales from Vedchhi centre alone; but the total sales from different centres were much larger, as can be seen from the following:

Name of article.	Number Sold in St. 1983 from Vedchhi	Bartad	Bardoli	Total.
Spinning wheels	441	126	45	612
Spindles	607	200	50	857
Carding bows (large)	23	2	7	32
Handgins	16		14	30
Handlooms	1		1	2

No one should imagine that these poor folk take away all these things as pieces of idle and ornamental furniture to embellish their houses, as some of us do. The following figures of yarn brought to the various centres for weaving tell their own tale:

Year	Vedchhi	Sarbhon	Bardoli	Madhi	Total.
	Pounds of yarn brought to				
St. 1980	163				163
„ 1981	830				830
„ 1982	2,102	211	375		2,688
„ 1983	4,760¼	2,048½	1,006¾	523½	8,339

This total of 8,339 pounds of yarn was made up by 1,062 families, scattered in 119 villages, out of which 49 families spun from 20 to 30 pounds, 14 families from 30 to 40 pounds and 8 families over 40 pounds each.

The number of spinning families advanced from 320 in Samvat 1982 to 1,062 in 1983, and the number of families producing over 20 pounds of yarn, which was 24 in 1982, increased to 71 in 1983. The Total output of yarn increased from 2,736 pounds in 1982 to 8,339 pounds in 1983.

And the beauty of it is, that all these spinners are busy cultivators who in several cases till many more *bighas* of land than the pounds of yarn they spin.

Among these spinners, the palm must perhaps be awarded to Ranchhodbhai Chimtabhai of Tokarfaliyun, who with a total family strength of 26 members (12 adults and 14 children) tilled 81 *bighas* of land, cut grass from 45 *bighas* of fallow land and spun 76 pounds of yarn during 1983.

Ranchhodbhai introduced the spinning wheel into his home only last year, and yet he proved himself to be the champion as soon as he entered the lists.

The story of how he came to accept the gospel of the wheel makes instructive reading. His village Tokarfaliyun is only a mile away from Vedchhi where wheels were introduced as early as 1980. He saw that the Vedchhi people had taken to spinning and friends pressed him to do likewise. But he was afraid that spinning might be detrimental to cultivation, and therefore held back. However at a meeting held in Gopaldev he heard that one Somabhai Babarbhai tilled 50 to 60 bighas of land and simultaneously spun 57 pounds of yarn. Somabhai's was not an isolated case, but there were many other farmers who tilled large holdings and spun 25 to 30 pounds of yarn at the same time. This set Ranchhodbhai a-thinking, and he purchased one wheel to begin with. He found that spinning was incredibly easy and was admirably adapted to serve as a recreation for the family during their leisure hours. To cut a long story short, he is now the proud possessor of 1 handgin, 1 carding bow and 12 wheels, and the champion spinner among his people, with a dozen spinners under his roof. The yarn was spun by Ranchodbhai's family mostly at night, and when he was asked how they could take up the wheel after a day of hard work on the farm, he replied, that spinning was as pleasant a diversion for them as reading papers or stories was for some people, and that the wheel now lulled them gently to sleep, whereas formerly they for some time every night used to lie awake in bed before sleep was good enough to approach them.

In Samvat 1982 Ranchhodbhai spent Rs. 140 on the clothing of the family. But in 1983 thanks to the wheels he spent only Rs. 56 (Rs. 30-8-0 per cotton plus Rs. 20-13-0 for weaving charges plus Rs. 4-11-0 for cloth bought from the bazaar), thus effecting a saving of Rs. 84.

And yet unfortunately for the country still there are skeptical arm-chair critics who shake their wise heads and entertain philosophic doubts as to the infinite possibilities of the spinning wheel.

The Raniparaj were entirely new to weaving as to spinning. Such of them therefore as take to weaving are paid at somewhat higher rates than ordinary weavers. Thus last year there were 21 weavers belonging to families of cultivators who earned total wages amounting to Rs. 1,731-4-0, the average monthly earnings being Rs. 12. One of them earned as much as Rs. 19 per month. A young cowherd of the age of 15 earned Rs. 69 in six months.

A cultivator, Mangabhai, who also took to weaving, earned Rs. 75 in eight months as weaver. With a family strength of 8 members (himself, wife and six children) he tilled 19 *bighas* of land, spun 17 pounds of yarn and earned as a weaver an average monthly wage of over Rs. 9 for 8 months from Kartik to Jyeshtha, showing that a farmer can take not only to spinning during his leisure hours but also to weaving.

A conference of the Raniparaj was held last year at Rupvada where the qualification for membership of the Reception Committee was that the candidate should be weaving cloth woven from yarn spun in his own home, and there were as many as 1,152 persons who satisfied this stringent test.

If we examine the balance sheet of the Raniparaj so far as their spinning and weaving activities are concerned, we find on the credit side Rs. 9,122 (the value of Khadi woven) plus Rs. 820-12-0 (the value of cotton seed) plus Rs. 1,731-4-0 (earned as weaver's wages), total Rs. 11,674. On the debit side we have Rs. 4,170 (the value of cotton stocked) plus Rs. 2,280 (weaving charges), total Rs. 6,450. Thus there was a clear gain of Rs. 5,224. This sum will be multiplied several times when there are spinners in all the 110 villages, not only in 25 or 30 of them as at present, and when all the spinning families put their heart into the industry, for many of the 1,062 spinning families spun only 2 to 5 pounds of yarn each, when they could have spun many times as much.

What has been done in a small section of it can be done throughout the Raniparaj district. Thus the harvest is great but the labourers are few. What we want is an army of skilled and devoted workers. The Ashrams at Bardoli and Vedchhi are training up Raniparaj youths with a view to supply that need.

V. G. D.

23rd February, 1928

FIGHT SQUARE

BY. M. K. GANDHI

Translation of an article published by Sr. Shankar Dattatreya Dev, Editor of the *Swarajya*, on pages 4 and 5 of that paper dated 15th September 1927, and headed 'At least wage a religious War.'

"*The King who does not protect (his subjects) after saying 'I will protect you,' should after uniting be killed like a rabid and diseased dog.*"

Mr. Vinayakrao Bhuskute has given elsewhere in the *Swarajya* detailed information from the beginning about the events that have been taking place at Telegaon. An account of the riot that took place at Sholapur on the occasion of the immersion of Ganapatis this year has also been published in news-papers. If the accounts of the happenings at both these places are read carefully, the outstanding fact that strikes the mind is that in both the cases the Government is more to blame than the Musalmans. The vacillating and unjust policy alone of the Government is wholly responsible for the quarrels that took place between the Hindus and Musalmans over the religious rights of the former at Telegaon, Sholapur and other places in India, during the last two or three years, and it was only on account of this attitude of partiality that Muslim community is encouraged and prompted to encroach upon the religious rights of the Hindus. *This apparently vacillating and unjust conduct of Government is not due to (any) misunderstanding or ignorance, but there is methodical political motive at the bottom of that policy. As Hindu Moslem quarrels are the sole justification for British rule the Government can never sincerely wish that they should be made up. Their interest does not lie in this. It is true that protection of religion is the principal duty of the King; and it is a fact that the King of England and Emperor of India still appends to his name the title of "Defender of the Faith," but in India this title of his cannot possibly have a meaning. The re-*

sponsibility which this title entails cannot include responsibility for protecting the religion of others. As the religions of the Indians and the British Government are different, the latter cannot possibly take pride, nor believe that they have been discharging their duty, in defending the religion of Indians. Similarly they will not think of spreading their own religion also on the strength of the sword as that is not the aim of their policy. *As economic plunder is the principal aim of the English policy, they think that their main duty so far as the subjects are concerned is to maintain peace in the country in order that they may carry on that plunder without let or hindrance. Peace is to be maintained in the country not because the Government feels devotion or pride for the religion of the subjects, nor because it regards the property of the subjects as sacred, but because it may enable it to plunder their property.* This is the explanation of why the Government tramples under foot the old religious practices in the name of peace. *For this peace not only will the Government be prepared to trample under foot the religion of the subjects, it will not and does not hesitate even to sacrifice the lives of the subjects. General Dyer sacrificed 500 Indian lives to this Goddess of peace and this is just the reason why the British Nation praised him for that meritorious deed.* The Government spends 66 crores of rupees on the army and 15 crores on the police for maintaining peace in the country not with a view to safeguarding and promoting the worldly and spiritual welfare of the subjects, but for its own interests. I think that the sooner the Indians impress upon their minds this fact and take to the path of self-reliance to protect and elevate their religion and their interest, the better will it be (for them).

If the Indians,—this (term) includes Hindus, Musalmans and all other communities—want to safeguard their religion and interest, they should establish Swaraj. *If the existing system of administration does not protect our religion or property or has become unfit to do so, then to ignore it and to set to work to create independent means for that (purpose) is the true and effec-*

tive remedy. This is the duty of the King or system of rule established in the country. And if for any reason that (King) or that (system) does not or cannot do this duty, then the real remedy for this is to establish another King or another system in place of them. There will be no protection to religion so long as there is anarchy in the country. The present Government is deliberately creating this anarchy. Therefore, the subjects should establish their own Government and remove this anarchy. To remain quiet taking consolation in the belief that if the King or the system of administration does not protect the religion of the subjects, God will punish him or it, and he or it will go to hell, is not only suicidal fatalism making the subjects dependent, weak and cowardly, but to do so is to exhibit deep ignorance of realities. The Emperor of India or Bureaucracy has no fear of hell. It is a different question whether the idea of hell is or is not in their religion. Here their rule is not based on righteousness but on considerations of profit. *Then how can they be reformed by a threat of hell? There is only one way of reforming them and it is just that which our ancestors have indicated in the shloka quoted at the top of (this) article. It is the duty of the subjects not to disregard the conduct of the King who has fallen from his duty but to punish him and if the Indians need any education at present, it is about this duty and not about fatalism. The way to punish the King is to refuse to recognise his existence and by establishing our own Government to begin to protect our religion through it.* In the present circumstances only this is the one remedy and I do not think this is an impossible thing to happen if the sensible leaders among the Hindus and Musalmans will take it into their minds. In my opinion, to achieve this end the two communities should whole-heartedly agree mainly to the following stipulations (lit. things). The Indian Swaraj that is to come in future will not belong either to the Hindus or the Musalmans or to any caste or sub-caste, but will belong to all. As this Swaraj will be made up of peoples of different religions, these belonging to each constituent religion must recognise the other constituent religions. From this point of view, women and places of worship belonging to other people must be held sacred by every follower of a religion and (the followers of every religion must proclaim that it is irreligion to practise outrage on them. While following a religion, the guiding principle (lit. motto) must be that one's religion is one's own (concern). From this point of view, as an attack made by one's own co-religionists on another religion is irreligious, the follower of every religion must consider it to be his duty to resist that attack The right of propagating one's religion must be recognised by others But violent methods in propagating a religion must be made a religious and legal offence

I think the question of protecting our religion will certainly be solved if sensible leaders in both the communities will agree to these (principles) and act accordingly, but (along with this) the question of Swaraj also will be solved. Still if the people in the two communities do not wish to solve this question by pacific measures in this way and insist upon solving it by (a trial of) their strength, I do not think even that will cause much harm, provided that even while this question is thus being solved the two sides should take certain things for granted and act accordingly. *For us to be prepared to take in our (own) hands the duty of protecting our religion is simply tantamount to issuing a proclamation that we do not recognise the existing system of* administration. And even from this point of view this step will prove very beneficial. If any one comes in the way of Hindus and Musalmans purging their minds of their animosity it is the present Government. Therefore, the third party that comes in the way of our vomiting out this long-standing animosity must be got rid of, and for this purpose the Hindus and Musalmans must first be united at least on this point. *Similarly, when the very existence of the Government is ignored, it would be against principle to carry before Government (complaints about) the happenings resulting from this war.* In my opinion the Courts of the English are banned to warring Hindus and Musalmans. If they will not thus ban them, it will have to be said that their devotion to religion and their animosity are not genuine, and that it is all a sham. Lastly both sides should act in this war in such a way that neither side would have occasion to say, "This is not a righteous war." This war should take place not only after giving a previous warning, but after the end of one battle up to the beginning of another, warriors on both sides should place before their eyes the conduct of the warriors of the Mahabharat (as described) in the Bhishma Parva (Chapter). No one should inflict a blow on the back of another and none should attack a solitary individual catching him in a lonely place. Judged from this point of view the attack made on Mr. Kulkarni Vakil at Sholapur is irreligious warfare and in my opinion our Musalman brethern cannot too strongly condemn it. *In conclusion I want to say only this that if it is impossible to solve this question by pacific measures, if the two sides have no faith in this course, then it is not irreligious to solve it by (an appeal to) force.* If that will not happen this quarrel will not be settled to the end of time and besides causing destruction of our religion will perpetually impose slavery of others upon us.

Sd. SHANKAR DATTATRAYA DEV.

[The foregoing is dealt with below. The headline 'Fight square if you must' is in my opinion a more correct rendering of *Nidan Dharma yuddha Kara* instead of 'At least wage a religious war' in the authorised translation. M. K. G.]

23rd February, 1928

REMINDING OF OLD TIMES

BY M. K. GANDHI

Sjt. Shankarrao Dev and Sjt. V. B. Harolikar were convicted the other day at Poona under Section 124-A and sentenced to undergo imprisonment for two years with hard labour. There were two charges against them, waging war against the King (Section 121) and attempting to excite disaffection against the Government established by law in British India (Section 124-A). Sjt. Dev as editor of *Swarajya* wrote the article which was the subject-matter of the offence and Sjt. Harolikar was the publisher. I print elsewhere the authorised translation of the offending article as produced before the court by the prosecution. Though it admits of improvement, it cannot be called an unfair presentation of the original.

The accused will not be defended by counsel though free assistance was volunteered by Dadasaheb Karandikar and other lawyers of distinction. Friends advised them to be defended. They were told that everybody nowadays sought legal advice without any slur being cast on them. But these non-co-operators were adamant. They did not care what others did. They were non-co-operators on principle and therefore did not wish to listen to any advice based on prudential considerations. I knew Sjt. Dev in Yeravda. He with Sjt. Dastane had undertaken a severe fast from which it was difficult for me to wean them. I tender my congratulations to these friends on their firmness in abiding by their own convictions. For I am convinced that of such will the Kingdom of Swaraj be made. They have undoubtedly brought Swaraj nearer by their crystal-like sacrifice. Let no one think that such solitary individual sacrifice has no place in national up-building, or that it does not produce great consequences. Indeed it is the purest sacrifice alone that will count in the end. It lays the surest and the purest foundation of Swaraj.

The article is undoubtedly written to promote disaffection against the existing Government. To promote such disaffection is the bounden duty of every nationalist. Every Congressman is I hope an avowed enemy of the existing Government. We have no quarrel with men, but if we are worthy of Swaraj, we must destroy the existing system of Government by all legitimate and peaceful means. The recent debate in the Assembly on the Statutory Commission was an object lesson in disaffection in which all parties, be it said to their eternal credit, whole-heartedly joined. The late Harchandrai Vishandas risked his life in travelling to Delhi for the sake of registering his vote in favour of disaffection. One daily comes across stronger articles than Dev's in point of disaffection. His is a reasoned appeal to Hindus and Musalmans to disown the protection of a Government that enslaves the country and if fight they must, fight fairly, squarely, honourably. I have read the article more than once and whilst I may not use the same language there is nothing in the argument that I cannot adopt. A prejudiced critic may cavil at the verse quoted from Mahabharat. But read together with the context its meaning is clear. We have no King. We have a rule masquerading under the sacred name of law. Rulers are many. They come and go. The rule abides. But it is a corrupt, mischievous, soul-destroying rule which has to be ended at any cost. The cost that Dev and people like him are prepared to pay has to be consistent with their creed of non-violence. They seek to establish the rule of real law not by killing other people, however misguided or cruel they may be, but by being themselves killed if need be in the attempt. This is the necessary limitation imposed upon them by their very conception of Swaraj. It is therefore most difficult for me to understand why these two innocent workers were singled out for prosecution, or shall I call it, persecution. If they are fit for imprisonment, Lala Lajpatrai and company are surely fit for transportation, if nothing worse. If it be said that the Assembly gives members privileges for statutory crimes which ordinary mortals outside do not enjoy, there is then perhaps no one who is guilty of such calculated and deliberate disaffection towards the 'Government established by law' as I am. The whole of my being is worked in order to achieve the destruction of this Government and to that end to spread disaffection as wide as possible, and I think I can lay a fair claim to having a somewhat larger audience than Dev and Harolikar. But real consistency, justice and courage are hardly to be expected of governments that are based upon exploitation sustained by violence.

23rd February, 1928

HANDLOOM *v.* SPINNING WHEEL

Apropos of the contention often thoughtlessly advanced that the handloom is the only thing worth preserving and that it can only be preserved through the use of mill-spun yarn, Sjt. C. Balaji Rao writes:

> "An effective answer to those who, in order to belittle the charkha, would exalt the handloom, is given here. 'Lord Curzon was voicing the opinions of his departmental scientific advisers when he declared at the Delhi Durbar that it was inevitable that the handloom should be superseded by the powerloom, just as the hand punkah was being superseded by the electric fan.' "

Of course Lord Curzon's dictum need not be accepted as a conclusive answer if the longevity of the handloom can be sustained through mill yarn or any other means save the spinning wheel. And these pages I hope are daily making it clear that handspinning can save the handloom in spite of the prediction of Lord Curzon. Indeed if the wheel regains its ancient status in our national life, the handloom and many other domestic industries must revive automatically.

M. K. G.

23rd February, 1928

THE ORIGIN OF IT

By M. K. Gandhi

I observe that newspaper paragraphs have been going round that I have predicted my own death by the 12th of March next and that as a consequence I am in a despondent mood. It is also stated that I am my own astrologer. I would have passed over this delicious morsel of news but for the fact that many anxious friends have taken it seriously and have therefore been upset. If the enquiring friends had only followed my advice never to depend upon newspaper paragraphs but always to ascertain, at their source, the truth of statements, seen in the press, they would have been spared all that anxiety. The correspondent who set the news in motion could also have spared the enquirers considerable anxiety if he had been good enough to test the truth of the statement made by him. But if the correspondents became more scrupulous about statements they may make, their occupation would be largely gone. I may then state for the information of friends that I am not an astrologer, I know nothing of the science of astrology and that I consider it to be a science, if it is a science, of doubtful value to be severely left alone by those who have any faith in Providence. Nor am I in a despondent mood, despondency being foreign to my nature. What precisely, however, did happen was this. When I was convicted six years ago and was asked what I thought about the prospects of Swaraj, I said that it was highly likely that there was the hand of God in the limit of six years and that during that time either we should win Swaraj or that I should die and that six years' time was long enough time for the country to win her freedom. This statement was based upon an observation of the state of things as then prevailed in India. I never attached any importance to it beyond this that I should myself leave no stone unturned to contribute so far as an individual could to the attainment of our freedom. The statement was on a par with the conditional statement made by me in 1920 about attainment of Swaraj within one year. That statement has served the purpose, if of nothing else, of giving satisfaction to my critics of laughing at my folly and to me that of seeing a tremendous effort being made by the country during that eventful year. I did not hesitate to say at the end of the year, when the Congress was held in Ahmedabad, that whilst we had not been able to achieve statutory Swaraj, the freedom that politically-minded India gave itself and the unity that seemed to exist among the various communities amounted to substantial Swaraj, and that if the people had carried out the conditions mentioned by me at Calcutta and Nagpur, they could have even attained statutory Swaraj within the year. But even as I remained unaffected in spite of the failure to attain statutory Swaraj within the year specified, so do I remain unaffected in spite of the approaching termination of six years which, by the bye, is not the 12th of March but the 17th of March next. Not only am I not preparing for the imminent approach of the dissolution of my body, but I am making every effort to put it in as good order and condition as is possible, and have already fixed some provisional appointments for the coming summer and the rainy season. After all the relevant portion of my talk six years ago twice repeated to friends was the attainment of India's freedom. Nothing depends upon the death of an individual, be he ever so great, but much depends upon the freedom of India. Let us therefore all forget individuals and concentrate upon attaining that precious freedom which will never be showered upon us from Downing Street or elsewhere, but which can be ours for the taking any day even inside of the 17th of March. No great preparation save a mental revolution is necessary for us,—Hindus, Musalmans, Parsis, Sikhs, Christians and Jews and others to feel as one indivisible nation and as having a common stake in the country, nor is more than a mental revolution required for Hindus to forget that any one is to be considered superior to any other and to regard the so-called 'untouchables' to be their own kith and kin, nor is much effort required if we but make the resolve to achieve *complete* boycott of foreign cloth. I repeat what I have said so often at the risk of exciting laughter, that if we achieve this triple programme, no power on earth can prevent us from attaining our birthright. It is for us to work out our own salvation as it is in us to compass our own undoing.

1st March, 1928

STUDENTS' NOBLE SATYAGRAHA

By M. K. Gandhi

In referring to the universality of Satyagraha I have time and again observed in these columns that it is capable of application in the social no less than in the political field. It may equally be employed against Government, society, or one's own family, father, mother, husband or wife, as the case may be. For it is the beauty of this spiritual weapon that when it is completely free from the taint of *himsa* and its use is actuated purely and solely by love it may be used with absolute impunity in any connection and in any circumstances whatever. A concrete instance of its use against a social evil was furnished by the brave and spirited students of Dharmaj (in Kheda District) a few days back. The facts as gleaned from the various communications about the incident received by me were as follows:

A gentleman of Dharmaj, some days back, gave a caste dinner in connection with the twelfth day ceremony of the death of his mother. It was preceded by a keen controversy about the subject among the young men of the place who shared with a number of other local inhabitants their strong dislike of this custom. They felt that on this occasion something must be done. Accordingly most of them took all or some of the following three vows:

1. Not to join their elders at the dinner or otherwise partake of the food served on that occasion.

2. To observe fast on the day of the dinner as an emphatic protest against this practice.

3. To bear patiently and cheerfully any harsh treatment that might be accorded to them by their elders for taking this step.

In pursuance of this decision quite a large number of students, including some children of tender age, fasted on the day on which the dinner was given and took upon themselves the wrath of their so-called elders. Nor was the step free from the dangers of serious pecuniary consequences to the students. The 'elders' threatened to stop the allowances of their boys and even to withdraw any financial aid that they were giving to local institutions, but the boys stood firm. As many as two hundred and eighty five students thus refused to take part in the caste dinner and most of them fasted.

I tender my congratulations to these boys and hope that everywhere students will take a prominent part in effecting social reform. They hold in their pocket as it were the key to social reform and the protection of their religion just as they have in their possession the key to Swaraj—though they may not be aware of it owing to their negligence or carelessness. But I hope that the example set by the students of Dharmaj will awaken them to a sense of their power. In my opinion the true *shraddha* of the deceased lady was performed by these young men fasting on that day, while those who gave the dinner wasted good money and set a bad example to the poor. The rich, monied class ought to use their God-given wealth for philanthropic purposes. They should understand that the poor cannot afford to give caste dinners on wedding or on funeral ceremonies. These bad practices have proved to be the ruin of many a poor man. If the money that was spent in Dharmaj on the caste dinner had been used for helping poor students, or poor widows, or for Khadi or cow protection or the amelioration of the 'untouchables' it would have borne fruit and brought peace to the departed soul. But as it is, the dinner has already been forgotten, it has profited nobody and it has caused pain to the students and the sensible section of the Dharmaj public.

Let no one imagine that the Satyagraha has gone in vain because it did not succeed in preventing the dinner in question from taking place. The students themselves knew that there was little possibility of their Satyagraha producing any immediate tangible result. But we may safely take it that if they do not let their vigilance go to sleep no *shethia* will again dare to give a post-mortem dinner. A chronic and long-standing social evil cannot be swept away at a stroke, it always requires patience and perseverance.

When will the 'elders' of our society learn to recognise the signs of the times? How long will they be slaves to custom instead of using it as a means for the amelioration of society and the country? How long will they keep their children divorced from a practical application of the knowledge which they are helping them to acquire? When will they rescue their sense of right and wrong from its present state of trance and wake up and be *mahajans* in the true sense of the word?

Translated from Navajivan by P. L.

1st March, 1928

FOREIGN PROPAGANDA

BY C. R.

Before the non-co-operation movement, Indian political activity largely consisted of propaganda in Great Britain. A great deal of money, comparatively, was spent on it and was considered well spent. When Gandhiji took up the guidance of our national affairs there was a change of outlook. A grasp of the essentials of national strength was the first result of his programme and it marked all our political thought at the time. We understood the natural laws that governed the sanctions needed for the non-violent enforcement of national demands. An almost exclusive spirit of self-reliance was the natural consequence. The cultivation of favourable opinion in foreign parts including Great Britain was valued at its correct worth and distinct efforts to that end were practically given up, and opposed vigourously whenever the question was raised. So intense was the work in India, so marked were the results that the tables were soon turned, and instead of Indians going to do propaganda in Great Britain and foreign parts, India attracted numerous foreign visitors; and the British Government was forced to undertake counter-propaganda in foreign parts. In India itself the Government had to give up its self-confidence and organise its own propaganda among the people in order to resist or at least postpone the effects of the national upheaval.

With the stoppage of aggressive non-co-operation, however, there has been a reversion in Indian thought. Slowly but steadily the cry for foreign propaganda is gaining volume again. The internal situation also, namely, the difficulties in the way of united national action, has naturally led people to turn to easier outlets of activities abroad. To those who still hold to the creed of non-co-operation and who look to emancipation only from within, this turn of the national gaze and energy to East and West is a symptom of growing weakness and a cause for anxiety. The vision is bound to be clouded and constructive efforts are bound to be prejudiciously affected by the growing tendency to this diversion. Not only does it divert attention but some of the best workers will be drawn bodily into this channel of pleasanter though futile work.

Pre-non-co-operation foreign propaganda was mostly propaganda in Britain. But one of the permanent results of the efforts of these eight years is loss of faith in Britain. The last vestiges of faith that stuck to the British Labour party have been also destroyed. The present harking back to foreign propaganda is therefore not for propaganda in England, but for the cultivation of contacts and friendship with other foreign nations. We are told that it is very desirable to develop intimate association with the German and Russian people. We are told that the Latin races of Europe present a favourable field for propaganda. France, Italy, Spain and Portugal are mentioned. Even Scandinavia is not forgotten, being important neutral soil. We are told again that the need of the hour is to link India up with other countries suffering under like imperialistic exploitation. We are assured that the hope of India is a federated Asia rising against Western domination. This change of attitude in regard to foreign propaganda had naturally its echo in the proceedings of the All-India Congress Committee where foreign affairs dominated the atmosphere, and many resolutions were adopted calculated to form a basis for international friendships.

It would be narrow-mindedness, indeed, and show us to be lacking the spirit of culture and humanity to refuse to have dealings with other nations if we were better circumstanced. But what would be civilisation and culture and broad-mindedness under favourable circumstances would be mere helplessness under existing conditions and would lead to nothing beneficial. Friendship with other nations can grow and be beneficial only if as in personal friendships it is not cultivated on the mere expectation of advantages all on one side. If we seek honourable friendship with others there must be something for us to give them while we seek something from them. If we are in effect truly unable to help others and only ask for something at their hands it would not conduce to mutual esteem; nor can a healthy alliance grow. If we are able really to help others, it must be by a supreme effort of national assertion which can and must, if well directed, produce far more marked results at home. The nations, whose friendship we go to woo, must find something to learn or something to gain from close association with us. If we have going on amidst us some movement of dynamic value, some revolutionary effort or some great constructive activity worthy of copy or study on others' part we would be seeking friendship on honourable, if not equal, terms. But we cannot be ever living either on the capital of our ancient culture or on the history of the Gandhian movement.

The link of mere friendship of slavery is not likely to be a real or useful bond. Why do we turn to Russia, China or Turkey? It is not simply the greatness of the past history of these nations that attracts us. If that alone were offered we would hardly be interested. But it is because we believe that there are great movements now going on in those countries which furnish matter for useful study or admiring observation, that some of our people go to those countries. Similarly if we seek international friendship with such nations, we should have something to offer to them of value. Otherwise we would only be beggars and should expect to be treated no better.

But then, it may be said, this is to ignore world politics. There are wars coming on. The nations of the world are ever seeking to subvert one another's plans, and India is an important piece on the board. We are not so helpless internationally, as we may be internally in our own affairs. This needs clearing up and plain talking. Are we in for a war and the formation of alliances with those likely to fight England, or do we expect other countries to go to war over us? If the powers abroad go to war, they do it with gunpowder and ships. Are we ever likely usefully to participate as a nation in such a war? Is it contemplated that India and other slave nations in the East may enter into a treaty, sometime in the future, to rise in revolt helping each other against the common foe? Is India to expect under any contingency arising in a world-war to render active assistance to a belligerent power against England? What, to put only one argument, is the chance of our ever achieving anything in this way? Is it practical politics of the remotest kind, disarmed as we are?

We do not want arms, it may be said: we can do a great deal by passive resistance. The only weapon in our hand is non-co-operation with the British Government during a war or peace. Here we come back to the old position. The Indian fight against England if it is to be by non-violent means depends entirely on its own strength and can never be converted into an international affair. In a non-violent struggle it is not easy, if at all possible, to obtain any material help from abroad. It must be conceived and organised and fought only on a basis of complete self-reliance.

Non-material moral help we can get from foreign countries. This we shall do not by any propaganda foreign or domestic but exactly in the measure that we do solid constructive work and develop internal strength.

[I have no desire to start any hot controversy over the question of foreign propaganda, but I publish the foregoing as it summarises the views of many workers who hold them in no sense weakly because they do not express them in public. If the pure non-co-operation of 1920 is not witnessed on an extensive scale at the present moment, it is most decidedly going deeper with some and everything that is happening today in the land goes to strengthen their belief. But they cannot make themselves felt by being vocal in season and out of season. On the contrary they feel that they serve the cause of Swaraj better by observing silence where they cannot serve by speech and helping humbly and actively wherever they can. M. K. G.]

1st March, 1928

CHAOS v. MISRULE

By M. K. Gandhi

An esteemed friend writes:

"It is not often that I intrude upon your expressions of political opinion. But a sentence of yours in a recent editorial, repeating a heresy uttered by you long ago, compels me to ask you whether you have measured your words with the care that one expects of an expounder of moral issues. You declare that you would accept chaos in exchange for freedom from the English yoke. That an Indian should desire and work for freedom from any foreign yoke is perfectly natural, normal and healthy. That any one in his senses should exchange any kind of orderly government for chaos is simply incomprehensible, for the one implies some sort of discipline, whether imposed or stimulated, whereas the latter is the very negation of self-discipline. Chaos is a word that may find a place in the vocabulary of the Deity. In the mouth of a human being it is meaningless, and is just as much a dangerous exaggeration and hallucination as is the word 'independence,' against which you properly gird. Moreover, it seems to me and you yourself have recognised it so often, that wisdom lies in refraining from acts and words calculated (though not intended) to mislead the ignorant, who will undoubtedly give it a connotation that you have not contemplated. Every wild man will emphasise the term without reference to your condition of non-violence. If non-violence be, as you claim it to be, creative, purposeful and divine in its nature; then chaos cannot be its consequence or characteristic. If you have used the term with deliberation, then I should comment that you have rendered no service to mankind, who need rather a reminder, that they should acquire the cosmic vision, rather than the chaotic one, to which they are already prone. If you have fallen into a mere looseness of language under the urge of a deep and noble emotion, I hope, upon reflection, you will find a way to make clear your real meaning."

There is no mistaking the earnestness running through the letter. And I have so much regard for the friend's views, that if I could have suited mine to his, I would gladly have done so.

But I must say that my choice was deliberate. Chaos means no rule, no order. Rule or order can come, does come out of no rule or no order, but never directly out of misrule or disorder masquerading under the sacred name of rule or order. My friend's difficulty arises, I presume, out of his assumption that the present Government of India represents 'some sort of discipline whether imposed or stimulated.' It is likely that our estimates of the existing system differ. My own estimate of it is that it is an unmitigated evil. No good therefore can come out of this evil. I hold misrule to be worse than no rule.

Nor need my words cause any confusion in the minds of the ignorant or the violent, For I admit my correspondent's contention that chaos can be the result only of violence. Have I not often said in these pages that if I were compelled to choose between this rule and violence I would give my vote for the latter though I will not, I could not, assist a fight based on violence? It would be a matter for me of Hobson's choice. The seeming quiescence of today is a dangerous form of violence kept under suppression by greater violence or rather readiness for it. Is it not better that those, who, out of a cowardly fear of death or dispossession, whilst harbouring violence refrain from it, should do it and win freedom from bondage or die gloriously in the attempt to vindicate their birthright?

My non-violence is not an academic principle to be enunciated on favourable occasions. It is a principle which I am seeking to enforce every moment of my life in every field of activity. In my attempt, often frustrated through my own weakness or ignorance, to enforce non-violence, I am driven for the sake of the creed itself to countenance violence by way of giving mental approval to it. In 1921 I told the villagers near Bettiah that they had acted like cowards in that they had instead of resisting the evil-minded *amlas* left their wives and homes on their approach. On another occasion I expressed myself ashamed of a priest who said he had quietly slipped away and saved himself when a ruffian band had entered his temple to loot it and break the idol. I told him that if he could not die at his post defending his charge non-violently, he should have defended it by offering violent resistance. Similarly do I hold that, if India has no faith in non-voilence, nor patience for it to work its way, then it is better for her to attain her freedom from the present misrule even by violence than that she should helplessly submit to a continuing rape of her belongings and her honour.

Look at the shameless manner in which, for sustaining the spoliation of India, British statesmen (?) are setting one party against another. They have suddenly discovered the 'untouchables,' for they seem to fear that the Hindu-Muslim dissensions alone might not prove enough security for retaining possession of the 'most glorious diadem in the British Crown.' They are trying to set the helpless princes against the people. Sir John Simon finds it necessary to play the same game. The penetrating intellect he is said to possess does not penetrate the very thin veil that covers the frauds that are set up for his edification and he finds nothing seriously amiss in the Indian atmosphere. This sort of 'orderly discipline' has unmanned and unnerved the people as nothing in their previous history has ever done.

My own position and belief are clear and unequivocal. I neither want the existing rule nor chaos. I want true order established without having to go through the travail of chaos. I want this disorder to be destroyed by non-violence, *i. e.*, I want to convert the evil-doers. My life is dedicated to that task. And what I have written in the previous paragraphs directly flows from my knowledge of the working of non-violence which is the greatest force known to mankind. My belief in its efficacy is unshakeable, so is my belief unshakeable in the power of India to gain her freedom through non-violent means and no other. But this power of hers cannot be evoked by suppressing truth or facts however ugly they may for the moment appear to be. God forbid that India should have to engage in a sanguinary duel before she learns the lesson of non-violence in its fulness. But if that intermediate stage, often found to be necessary, is to be her lot, it will have to be faced as a stage inevitable in her march towards freedom and certainly preferable to the existing order which is only so-called but which is like a whited sepulchre hiding undiluted violence underneath.

1st March, 1928

TOLSTOY CENTENARY

BY. M. K. GANDHI

Mr. Aylmer Maude than whom there is no better English authority on Tolstoyan literature writes:

"Knowing your interest in Tolstoy, I am sending you copy of a circular just issued to members of the Tolstoy Society, as well as copy of a letter by Bernard Shaw.

"We are anxious that this Centenary Edition should find a place in public libraries, and also that its publication should enable us to give assistance to members of Tolstoy s family, who are in distress since the Russian Revolution.

"Should you have an opportunity of mentioning the Edition to librarians or members of the committee of any of your Indian libraries, the Committee of the Tolstoy Society would feel greatly indebted to you."

I take the following from the printed notice of the Tolstoy Society:

"After negotiation with other publishers here and in America, arrangements have finally been made with the Oxford University Press to produce a Crown 8vo 21-volume Centenary Edition of Tolstoy's works, limited to 1,000 sets, to be issued in three instalments in 1928, 1929, and 1930, and to be followed, if sufficient subscribers desire it, by 14 more volumes to make the edition complete. A prospectus will be issued later and the first delivery of volumes will be in August.

"This arrangement enables your Committee to release guarantees that were kindly promised when we aimed at a more expensive publication. The price will be 9 guineas for the 21 volumes, and 6 guineas for the 14 additional volumes, with no necessity to pay more than 3 guineas in any one year. Members placing their orders through our Secretary will receive a discount of ten per cent.

"There will be an Introduction to each work."

The Secretary is Miss L. E. Elliott, Ladywell House, Great Baddow, Chelmsford, England.

Any one can become a member of the Tolstoy Society by paying at least £ 1-1-0 and an associate by paying a minimum subscription of 2s. 6d.

1st March, 1928

KHADI NEAR MEERUT

BY M. K. GANDHI

Dr. Ray gave me soon after his recent visit to Meerut an account of his impressions. I take the following from his letter:

"During my recent visit to Meerut I learnt something about Khadi, which was in the nature of an agreeable surprise to me. I was taken to a village 20 miles north of the town where the peasants are comparatively prosperous, as owing to the irrigation from the Ganges canal they raise three or four crops in the year and yet the womenfolk do not disdain to ply the primitive time-honoured charkha. In almost every house I visited the mother, the daughter, and sometimes the daughter-in-law were found basking in the sun and spinning 10 to 12 count yarns. The coarse cloth woven in the village itself is used by the local people and ready-made slivers hawked about. In the fields also side by side with the standing crops there are patches of cotton cultivation. The march of 'civilisation' has not yet fully overtaken the unfortunate villagers, but they have begun to taste of it: for the *pagris* invariably and the *dhotis* sometimes, are of finer Bilati cloth. I exclaimed: Oh for a Meerut Jamnalal Bajaj to finance and a Satish Babu to organise the neglected, and, I am afraid, dying home industry—an industry upon the revival of which depends the salvation of the hungry millions of India. The Benares Gandhi Ashram with the help of a local band of devoted, sacrificing workers is doing its level best but funds and proper organisation are both badly needed."

The hum of the wheel need not die either in the Punjab or elsewhere in India, if we would be true to our trust. The band of workers from the Benares Ashram who attracted Dr. Ray's attention are working in and near that district to put Khadi on a stable footing. Now that the parent of the Ashram, Acharya Kripalani, is in the midst of his workers, there should be redoubled zeal on their part and greater support and appreciation from the public.

8th March, 1928

WAR AGAINST WAR

BY M. K. GANDHI

A correspondent writes:

"My excuse for writing this is that the autobiographical chapter about your attitude towards war as a follower of *Truth* and *Ahimsa* has apparently stirred the thoughts of many, and abler people would be writing to you about it. But I wish to present some aspects that have struck me. Is it not a fundamental doctrine that to the true disciple of *Truth* and *Ahimsa*, there can be no tampering with bad things even though one cannot resist them? War is a necessary evil as some say, but that is no excuse for supporting it in the hope that after it there will come to the world a realisation of the wickedness of waging war. It cannot be. On the contrary, the callousness of man is increased further in intensity and the feeling about the sacredness of life is destroyed. The anarchist could argue just as you do and say: 'We cannot stop European aggression and terrorism. We cannot resist terrorism by mass force. But if we can only demonstrate to them the wickedness of such methods by using them against them, they will see the folly of their attitude and we shall become free, and we shall also save the world from terrorism. So long as *himsa* is resorted to by our rulers and so long as we hate terrorism, what is the harm in using these weapons provided we do not allow them to obsess us?' Has the Great War actually done any good to the nations and particularly to the victors? Materially, morally, and socially they have lost heavily as a result of the victory. Their moral standards have all been upset and the strife after the life of the moment, and the disregard for truth and honesty in international dealings is becoming more and more apparent every day. Can any good come out of a war, however 'righteous' it may be? Are we not bound to oppose it and suffering for the cause rather than in any way acquiesce in it either passively or actively? Do you not believe that the pacifists served the cause better than those who actively engaged in the War? What you say might represent the state of your mind in 1914 when you thought there was a sense of justice in the British mentality. Do you now feel that it was right? If another war was declared tomorrow, would you volunteer your help to England in the hope that you would be making things better after the war? I know I have not presented the case in the best way but you can understand what it is that I am trying to tell you, and I shall be glad to have your reply."

I agree with the correspondent that he has not presented his case 'in the best way,' but he does represent a type of readers who will not read carefully even writings that are meant to be serious, simply because they happen to be found in a weekly journal. If readers like the correspondent will re-read the chapter in question they will be able to deduce from it that

1. I did not offer my services because I believed in war. I offered them because I could not avoid participation in it at least indirectly.

2 I had no status to resist participation.

3. I do not believe that war can be avoided by taking part in it even as I do not believe that evil can be avoided by participation in it. This however needs to be distinguished from sincerely helpless participation in many things we hold to be evil or undesirable.

4. The anarchist's argument is irrelevant as his participation in terrorism is deliberate, voluntary and preconceived.

5 The War certainly did no good to the so-called victors.

6. The pacifist resisters who suffered imprisonment certainly served the cause of peace.

7. If another war was declared tomorrow, I could not with my present views about the existing Government assist it

in any shape or form; on the contrary I should exert myself to the utmost to induce others to withhold their assistance and to do everything possible and consistent with *Ahimsa* to bring about its defeat.

8th March, 1928

PREM MAHAVIDYALAYA

BY M. K. GANDHI

This creation of Raja Mahendra Pratap has a proud record and is one of the very few pre-non-cooperation institutions that were created and have lived without Government aid, recognition or affiliation. Like all such undertakings it has had to pass through many vicissitudes but has come out scatheless through them all. Recently it celebrated its anniversary. Dr. Ansari presided on the occasion. The report before me states, that 'the proceedings began with a *takli* demonstration and hoisting of the national flag by Dr. Ansari and singing of the flag-song by the volunteers of the Hindustani Seva Dal followed by *Bande Mataram*.' The report then proceeds:

> Principal Gidwani followed with his report in which he gave an account of his stewardship of the institution from 1st July 1926 when he took charge up to date. The report disclosed rather a gloomy state of things, so far as the financial position is concerned, the cash reserve being only Rs. 7,000 and the annual deficit Rs. 10,000. While urging the trustees to secure more efficient management of the trust property, and to make energetic efforts to secure support from the District Local Board, the Mathura and Brindaban Municipalities and the general public, for the immediate future he pointed out the stern necessity of retrenchment.
>
> "During the period under report, Principal Gidwani has carried out radical changes in the Prem Mahavidyalaya, effecting substantial reduction in expenditure without sacrificing efficiency, while he has at the same time in-

creased the usefulness of the institution by adding a tailoring department, a dyeing department, a painting class, a book-binding department, and restarting the Vidyalaya Press and the *Prem* as a monthly magazine, financing all these new activities from the savings made by severe retrenchment in other departments. With the changes already introduced and the changes proposed in the report the institution will assume the character of a school of arts and crafts and a cottage industries institute. The report lays great emphasis on the necessity of providing more suitable and extensive accommodation for the institution in more healthy environment and makes an appeal for two lakhs for necessary buildings and equipment. The support of Mahatma Gandhi is confidently expected, for, as Principal Gidwani said, 'the Prem Mahavidyalaya has a proud record of absolutely unaided independence from its very start through all its chequered career of 18 years. Dignity of labour is its watchward and spinning and weaving fit in naturally with our scheme. Every student is clad in *shuddha* Khadi and spins daily on *takli* or charkha. We sent volunteers to far off Sindh to help the flood-stricken people and when the call came we contributed our quota to the prisons for patriots. And above all Bhangis and Chamars receive instruction side by side with Brahman boys. If these features are retained and ideals of social service are prominently placed before students for their future careers, I know of no educational institution that answers more to the standards set up by Gandhiji and which has greater claim on his assistance.' Principal Gidwani concluded with an exhortation to the students to remember that the 'Prem Mahavidyalaya is not only a school or a factory, it is a temple of Love, a garden of youth, a shrine of Freedom which Raja Mahendra Pratap had in mind.' "

Principal Gidwani had every reason to anticipate my support for an institution for which he was able to claim so much. The reader may not know that Principal Gidwani is going to

Karachi to join his new post under its Municipality. Sjt Jugal Kishore's services have been loaned to the trustees by Acharya Kripalani's Ashram at Benares. But it is understood that though Sjt. Jugal Kishore will act on behalf of Acharya Gidwani, the latter will continue to be interested in the Mahavidyalaya and guide its destinies in so far as it is possible.

8th March, 1928

A STATE KHADI CENTRE

By C. R.

Badanwal is a village six miles south-east of Nunjungud in Mysore, where the Mysore Government has a handspinning centre. About fifty villages are served by this centre. An enterprising Tirupur merchant did some Khadi work in this area, independently for some time, and later with financial assistance from the All-India Spinners' Association. Private agency was, however, not found satisfactory and the work was taken up under the direct management of the Karnatak branch of the All-India Spinners' Association. When Syts. Shankarlal Banker, Gangàdharrao Deshpande and myself went round in Mysore province on a Khadi tour preliminary to Gandhiji's arrival, we had opportunities to meet the Director of Industries and Commerce and the Second Member of Government in charge of Development, and exchange ideas in regard to Khadi work. Our proposals that the Mysore Government should undertake rural reconstruction work in the form of the revival of the handspinning industry were so well received, and they showed such a keen desire to undertake practical work in that direction, that we suggested their taking over the Badanwal centre under their own management and we offered to assist them in the task of development by lending the services of men with practical experience in Khadi work in the A.I.S.A. service. The proposals were accepted and as a result there has been, from the 1st of November 1927, a Government Khadi production centre at Badanwal.

One of the oldest and best of the self-sacrificing Khadi

workers in Karnatak, Syt. Siddu Rao Pujari has been temporarily deputed to do the work of organisation and development, and Syt. S. V. Rajaram Iyengar is in charge. The latter is one of the finest products of the spirit of sacrifice and patriotism that is moving young Mysore. He gave up his career and course in the Tata Institute of Science to join the A. I. S. A. Khadi service and he has now been lent to the Mysore State for working the centre.

The Director of Industries and I visited Badanwal last week. We went round the villages and visited the homes of spinners and weavers. We found the work going on most satisfactorily. There is promise of great expansion. The results so far achieved have successfully demonstrated the value of the handspinning movement as a means of giving productive occupation to large numbers of peasant families in rural areas. The Lingayat population which forms the bulk of agriculturist labourers as well as the Adikarnatakas have taken to handspinning like fish to water. The old wheels and gins and carding bows which had been put away for some years have received new life. Every day some more of them are being taken down from the lumber heap, repaired and set to work. As we went round the houses we saw a new atmosphere of industry, a spirit of confidence, and a cheerful activity among young and old.

"We won't sell our cotton hereafter," said one. "This girl has been learning to spin," said another pointing to her bashful daughter-in-law. "This girl has no time for she does the cooking and the household work," said another mother-in-law. "Look at my yarn. Is it not good?" asked another woman. "After I began to spin since the arrival of this old man, I have an untorn *sadi* to wear after many years," said an old woman. "We make what we want for salt and kerosene oil," said another in answer to the Director's enquiry as to what she earned by the wheel. "We shall all spin. There will be more wheels this year," said another. "We shall wear only this cloth henceforth," said a village Patel

It was pleasant to see that the untouchables in these villages were clean and lived in airy big houses, unlike their brethren in other parts of the country. They live on the most friendly terms with the Lingayats and are treated much better than the people of the same class in other places. They weave Khadi now and have no seasonal unemployment. If only the drink shops were removed, their condition would be much better and leave very little cause for complaint. For some time the toddy shop had been closed and these people then built tiled roofs for their huts; but the shop has come again,' complained an old ryot.

In some respects the Badanwal centre is unique. In the first place this is the only Khadi production centre in India managed by a State agency. This is again the only centre within a stone's throw of a railway station. At Narasambudi station in the Chamrajnagar-Nunjungud line the booking office is on one side of the line and Syt. Rajaram's Ashram consisting of four picturesque white-washed straw-roofed mud huts are on the other side of the line, in the same field with the Station Master's quarters. There are other special features also to be noted by a Khadi worker. The spinners stock their cotton, grown on their own fields, or paid in kind as wages for work done on the land, or bought in the village. The local cotton is a fine variety of Nadam with lint percentage 20 per cent. and nearly as good in staple as Karunganni, ranging from 5/8" to ¾". There is good black soil in the area on which cotton is raised. But it is never continuously put under cotton crop, so that the cotton is free from disease. The cotton crop, too, is not so extensive as to invite the export trade to crush the cottage industry. The women gin and card their own cotton. This increases the family earnings more than mere spinning could do, and makes the work clean and easy. The weavers are all untouchables. Of the 44 villages now spinning, the yarn in 26 is from 6 to 8 counts at present, and that in 18 villages from 10 to 15 counts and of good twist. The wheels as well as gins are exactly the same shape and size as those used by the Tamil Nadu peasantry. In fact even the carving on the old wheels is the same pattern. On the Khadi map the Badanwal area and the Coimbatore area would be contiguous and form part of old Kongunad. The bows are hand-bows stringed with double guts and are plied with the thumb, round which a little cotton lint and a narrow bit of cloth are wound for protection. The yarn is sold in *kalus* (Kanarese for *kalis* in Tamil). These are round balls of yarn and not the cross-hanked *kalis* of Tamil Nadu. Syt. Pujari is trying to introduce the cross-hank. Each *kalu* weighs about 13 tolas and is given away for four annas. 6½lbs. of cotton takes four hours to gin, yielding 1.3 lbs. of lint and 5 lbs. of seed, 1/5 lb. being wastage. The seed is valuable fodder for the milch cows and buffaloes. Nunjungud butter and ghi are famous in those parts. The carding and slivering of this 1.3 pounds of lint takes another four hours' work; and one pound of carded cotton takes about 12 hours to spin, .3 lb. being wastage in carding. Thus starting with 6½ lbs. of cotton worth 12 as., the product of 20 hours' spare time home labour in which the aged, the infirm and the immature take part is seed worth five annas and yarn sold for twelve annas, Re. 1—1—0 in all. With slightly finer spinning the yield is better. In some villages the yarn is delivered in warped lengths and paid according to length.

The weavers are paid at the same rates as in Tamil Nad. They weave enough to earn about three rupees eight annas per week on each loom. There are now five hundred wheels in this area and the number is expected soon to reach one thousand. There are now 16 looms and the number will increase as the spinning extends. The Bangalore Khadi Vastralaya is buying up the produce and part of it is also sold locally. The Mysore Government is placing orders on this Khadi centre for its store purchases for uniforms and hospitals. The results have so far given such satisfaction that the present Government investment of Rs. 3,500 is to be increased to Rs. 15,000 to provide for the expansion that is immediately expected. In Syt. Pujari's language the revival of this cottage industry in this part of the Mysore state (a) enables the agriculturists to convert their raw material to as near a degree to finished goods as they can without extra expenditure and thus add to their income; for every maund of seed cotton worth Rs. 3, if they sell as raw product, they make Rs. 4—4—0 of seed and yarn; (b) gives an opportunity to them to get their cloth made with the least possible cost and save their cloth expense; (c) offers an opportunity to the needy, the aged, the infirm and the cripple and to the women who would not like to leave their homes in search of employment to convert idle hours into active work and enable them to keep the wolf from the door; and (d) finds work for the Adikarnatakas in their own villages and thus prevents emigration as also lightens pressure on agricultural land.

Syt. Pujari has sent an exhaustive report of work done until 31st January 1928 to the Director of Industries and Commerce in Mysore enclosing complete statement of accounts and other useful appendices giving information as to weavers' and spinners' earnings. The Director is printing the report and intends to place the same before the Economic Conference and move for an increased grant.

Mrs. Rajaram lives in the mud-hut with her husband. She cooks for him and shares in the work even going round with him to the villagers like a true Khadi wife. Syt. Pujari calls himself the father and is head of the young people's household. Few blood connections are as happy. The bond of self-sacrifice and service and common ideals can be as strong as that of blood.

15th March, 1928

WHAT CAN OUR MILLS DO?

BY M. K. GANDHI

Everybody is anxious that at this critical juncture in our history, we should be able to exhibit some real strength. It is becoming more and more realised that such strength can be developed and shown only through boycott of foreign cloth as distinguished from British cloth. In this boycott it is possible for our mills to play an important, indeed, a decisive part, if they wish.

Some day or other they will have to choose between this alien Government and the people. There is no doubt that to a large extent they are dependent for their existence upon the toleration if not the goodwill of the Government. Thoreau told the truth when he said that possession of riches under an evil Government was a sin and poverty was virtue. The riches of the rich are always at the disposal of the Government of the day whether it is good or bad.

But if the mills are dependent for their existence on the toleration or goodwill of the Government, they are no less so on the toleration or goodwill of the people. They can afford to ignore the people only so long as the latter remain ignorant, supine or disunited. But the past seven years have not been lived in vain by the nation. The mass awakening that has taken place will never die. No one can tell when and how the people will show their strength.

But the mills occupy a privileged position. By showing a little courage, a little consideration for the true interests of the nation and by exercising a little self-sacrifice they can serve both the Government and the people. They can convert the Government and advance the people's cause.

This is how in my humble opinion they can do it.

They can standardise their prices taking the lowest average of a number of top and lean years.

They can come to terms with the leaders organising boycott as to the quantity and quality of cloth required for the nation.

They can refrain from manufacturing those varieties that can be easily and immediately produced by Khadi organisations thus freeing their energy for manufacturing more of the varieties they can at the present moment more easily manufacture than the Khadi organisations.

They can limit their profits to a minimum and let the surplus if any be devoted to the fulfilment of the boycott, or if that be unnecessary, to the improvement of the condition of the labourers.

This would mean all-round honesty, perseverance, mutual trust, a voluntary and honourable triple alliance between labour, capital and the consumer. It would mean capacity for organisation on a vast scale. And if we are to attain boycott of foreign cloth through non-violence, we shall have some day or other to fulfil the tests just enumerated by me.

In my humble opinion we are eminently fitted for the task. The organisation required for the purpose is not unfamiliar to us. The only question is, have we the will? Have the mill-owners enough vision, enough love of the country? If they have, they can take the lead.

Let me redeclare my own faith. For boycott to be swiftly brought about a combination between Khadi and truly indigenous mills is desirable, but not absolutely necessary. I use the words truly indigenous, because we have bogus mills in India which are Indian only in the sense that they are located in the country but whose shareholders, whose management, whose spirit are mainly, when not wholly, foreign. But if the indigenous mills cannot or will not lead or join the national movement, I am convinced that Khadi alone can achieve the boycott if the politically-minded India has the will, the faith and the energy required for the purpose. We have not enough horse-power expressed through steam engines, oil engines or electricity, but we have an inexhaustible reservoir of man-power lying idle and pleading to be used, and essentially qualified for the purpose. Oh for a faith that would see and use this supply of living power!

15th March, 1928

HOW TO DO IT?

BY M. K. GANDHI

Notice has already been taken in these pages of the West Khandesh Zilla Mandal of which Sjt. Shankarrao Dev is the founder, president and guardian angel. This Mandal has village reconstruction as its principal activity, and has become convinced that spinning must be the centre of every activity connected with reconstruction, if it is to prosper and respond to the deep poverty of the masses. All its work is as thorough as it can be made. Sjt. S. V. Thakkar has been training himself for some time before settling down in a village for reconstruction service. He has been travelling, together with Sjt. Balubhai Mehta in those centres where such activity is going on. The brief report he has presented to the president of his Mandal is worth reading. I therefore reproduce the main part of it for the guidance of those who do this work.

I beg to submit herein a brief account of the work done by me during the second year which commenced from the 1st April, 1927.

"But before doing so I must, by way of introduction to the same, give in short the gist of the interviews which the Mandal had with Gandhiji during and after his memorable visit to this district in the middle of February 1927. This introduction is essential inasmuch as the said interviews with Gandhiji have contributed to give a definite shape to the future activities of the Mandal in general, have been of invaluable service as a source of inspiration for myself, and have brought the Mandal in touch with the All-India Spinners' Association.

"On the advice of Gandhiji, this second year was, by me spent by me in getting myself trained in the technique of ginning, carding, spinning, weaving, etc., in visiting some centres of Khadi production and village organisation, and in fixing upon a particular village as the centre of my future activities.

"The work of visiting the centres of Khadi production

and village organisation practically commenced even before the year under report began, and under the very eyes and guidance of Gandhiji. During the month of March 1927, Gandhiji was kind enough to give me the invaluable opportunity of accompanying him, with my wife, during his visit to the Raniparaj people round about Bardoli and to their Conference at Khanpur which was indeed of a very unique nature. This short tour made a deep and lasting impression upon our minds, as to how highly potential Khaddar work can be in contributing to the economic, moral, religious and social elevation of the down-trodden masses of India.

"As noted above, the second year of the Mandal, *i.e.*, the year under report commenced from the 1st of April 1927. The first fortnight of this year had unfortunately to be spent in attending to some domestic ailments. The Satyagrahashram at Wardha was selected as the place for receiving technical instruction which, under the direction of Sjt. Vinobaji Bhave, was gone through by me, along with my wife to some extent, from the 19th April 1927 to the 19th August 1927 with the break of a fortnight in between 21st May and 4th June. All the processes prior to warping, sizing and weaving were gone through. This training has been directly helpful in introducing me to the rudimentary technique of the art and has also been indirectly helpful in arousing in me a confidence regarding self-sufficiency in point of cloth. The latter benefit though an indirect consequence of the training, is perhaps of far more significance to a propagandist and a village organiser than the former. On finishing this elementary training we were advised by Sjt. Vinobaji to visit the Sawali centre in the Chanda District which we did with great advantage.

"Sheth Jamnalal Bajaj happened to come down to Dhulia soon after our arrival from Wardha, and the opportunity was taken by the Mandal of talking to him about the general plan of the village organisation work, and of consulting him about the intended tour throughout India to visit various centres of Khadi production and village organisation. He chalked out a programme of the tour and was kind enough to give letters of introduction to the heads of the particular centres and institutions, which he directed us to visit.

"This extensive tour engaged us from the 16th September 1927 to the 20th January, 1928. During this tour we had to pass through Karnatak, Tamil Nad, Andhra, Orissa, Bengal, Bihar, U. P., Rajaputana and Gujarat. The diary of the tour along with a concise and brief report of the impressions formed on visiting various institutions ashrams and centres has been already submitted. It is fortunate that this work which began with the benediction and under personal guidance of Gandhiji may be said to have practically ended after interviews with him during our stay at the Sabarmathi Satyagrahashram from the 15th to the 18th of January 1928. Gandhiji was delighted to find how deeply and indelibly impressed we were with the all-round potentiality and beneficence of Khadi, which, as the tour has convinced us, must necessarily be the cornerstone of any edifice of village organisation work.

"It may also be stated here that an opportunity was taken during this tour of receiving training in the elements of warping, sizing, weaving etc., during our stay at Hemnivas weaving school near Bijolia.

"On returning from the tour, the natural work and responsibility that engaged and is still engaging me has been the selection of a particular village whereon I have to concentrate all my energies hereafter. The work of selection has been found to be of prime importance and hence requires great caution and care. However, a suitable centre in a favourable locality will soon be fixed upon and it is hoped that work will be commenced in right earnest on the coming Hindu New Year's Day or on the Rama-Navami Day, *i.e.*, on the 22nd or the 29th of March 1928, from which auspicious day the third year of my humble services will be said to have commenced."

22nd March, 1928

CHARKHA A PROVED WANT

By M. K. Gandhi

Akbarpur in U. P. is a little place where Professor Kripalani's Khadi band worked for seven years. For reasons into which I need not go, this band had to withdraw from Akbarpur. Pandit Jawaharlal Nehru describes the touching scenes that followed the withdrawal and how the centre had somehow to [k]ept up. The following from his letter to the All-India [Spi]nners' Association will be read with interest.

"I have told you already that the Gandhi Ashram has left Akbarpur. We have taken charge temporarily because we felt that pending your decision we ought to carry on. If we had not taken charge there would have been a break and it would have been more difficult to start afresh. Besides on sentimental grounds also it was a little difficult to abandon the place. It has been a well-known centre for so many years and a large number of weavers and others are intimately connected with it. To leave it suddenly would have had a bad effect on the whole neighbourhood and upset the economy of a great number of poor households who were dependent on it. Indeed, we were told that some touching incidents were witnessed when the Gandhi Ashram announced that they were closing up. Many old women spinners who used to sell their yarn at a distant centre, finding this centre closed, trudged up many miles to headquarters and wept when they found that their yarn was not to be bought. Many weavers with their wives and families came up to the Akbarpur Office and said they would perform *Satyagraha*. For seven years they had been working for the Ashram and now they were being left in the lurch. You will realise how difficult it was for us to refuse to take charge under these circumstances. But, of course, sentimental considerations cannot decide the question. Akbarpur possesses some marked advantages and at the same time a very great disadvantage. As a weaving centre it is famous and even now some of the finest weaving in India is done at Tanda in the neighbourhood. Unhappily this fine weaving—called Jamdani work—is done with foreign yarn. On the other hand, there is very little spinning done near Akbarpur and if the centre is to be worked it will be necessary to bring yarn from elsewhere. The Gandhi Ashram, I believe, used to get their yarn chiefly from across the border in Bihar, also from Muzaffarnagar. For us it will be easier to get it from the Northern Districts of the U. P.—Moradabad, Bijnor, etc. The cost of sending the yarn is not great."

If Khadi became as current as *ghee* or grain there could never have been a thought of withdrawing from any centre. If we had funds and workers we would have representatives not only in 1600 villages but in 7,00,000 villages. This is no impracticable ambition, when we remember the fact that there are at least two representatives of the alien Government in each of these villages. If any one before the British advent had suggested any such thing, he would have been laughed out of court. But reflection should show that the restoration of the wheel in every one of the villages is not half as laughable as the hope of imperial Britain being represented in the republican villages of India would have been in the 17th century. What the women near Akbarpur are reported to have said demonstrates what a felt want the charkha fills or can fill in every village of this ancient land. It is no credit to our patriotism that the able weavers of Akbarpur have to fall back upon foreign yarn for their far-famed *jamdani* which it was their pride nearly half a century ago to weave out of yarn spun by the sacred hands of their own sisters living next door to them. It won't be long before the spinners in our villages are able to spin as fine and as strong yarn as any foreign yarn now infesting our market.

22nd March, 1928

CAN IT BE TRUE?

BY M. K. GANDHI

The President, Arya Samaj, New Delhi writes:

"The Baghat State is situated in the Simla Hills and its ruler is an enlightened Hindu chief. The capital of the State is at Solon which is noted for its salubrious climate. The population of the State is about ten thousand and mainly consists of Rajputs, Kanets and Brahmans. The other tribes are Kolis, Chamars etc. who are regarded as menials. Although the Kolis chiefly live on agriculture yet the social disabilities to which they are subject are numerous. Briefly stated they are the drudges of the caste-Hindus. Moved by the inhuman treatment which these people suffer at the hands of their Hindu brethren, the Arya Samaj, Simla, brought them into their fold with a view to raise their status in life and invested them with the sacred thread, inasmuch as by occupation they are Vaishyas. Since the time of their formal purification they have given up the evil habits of meat-eating and drink and have shown strong resentment at their being addressed as Achhuts. This seems to have given umbrage to the caste-Hindus who challenged tho right of their being invested with the sacred thread. A summary trial was consequently held on the 6th January, 1928 by the Chief of the State himself and on the subsequent day on the plea of antiquity and customs, the poor Kolis who were ten in number were sentenced to undergo six months imprisonment in addition to a fine of Rs. 200 each. No opportunity was given to these unfortunate persons to defend themselves, nor permission was given to the Pandit of the Arya Samaj who happened to be present on the occasion to explain the point of view of the Arya Samaj in this matter. It is now reported that they are being coerced in the jail to take off their sacred thread."

The information contained in the foregoing seems to me to be unbelievable. The Kolis can in no way be considered to be untouchable or to be of the suppressed or the depressed classes. If they are their own farmers, according to the definition of the different *varnas*, they are born *vaishyas* and have every right to wear the sacred thread. But assuming that they have no right in religion, I was totally unprepared for the news that the wearing of the sacred thread would be considered a crime punishable in law in any State. Equally unthinkable it is that the unfortunate men who thought that they had passed through some desirable or meritorious religious ceremony were denied even the right of defending themselves and producing their witnesses. And, if the statements about the punishment and farcical trial are true, I should not at all wonder if the sacred thread had been forcibly taken off their persons. I would invite the president of the Arya Samaj to send further details, if any, in corroboration of the charges brought by him against the Baghat State and I would invite the State authorities if they wish to send me their version of the incident which I shall gladly publish.

22nd March, 1928

FOREIGN CLOTH BOYCOTT—SOME QUESTIONS

BY M. K. GANDHI

A friend intimately connected with mills and desirous of having our mills contributing their full quota to the foreign cloth boycott movement asks:

> 1. "On what basis do you want prices standardised? For remember all mills are not alike. Some are bad, some are good; some use more sizing than others, have more reserve than others; Bombay mills make less profits than up-country ones. These differences are illustrative of many others that might be stated."

The one general answer that may be given is 'where there's

a will there's a way.' The mills will contribute their quota only when they get rid of inertia, think 'furiously,' and that too in terms of the nation, not merely the pockets of shareholders directors or agents. But by way of making my position in this matter clearer I may say that all the mills who will join the boycott movement will have to pool all the differences and arrive at a standard price which would at least mean a large slice off from the present profits of at least some mills. If their patriotism is sound and progressive the flourishing ones will cover the losing ones, avoidable differences will be avoided. In the scheme I have in view the mills need never lose in the aggregate and they must not profit at the expense of the buyer.

2. "Only some mills will undertake not to manufacture Khadi. But what about those that only spin low counts? What is your test of Khadi?

This is a matter of *common* honesty and arrangement between Khadi organisations and mills At present I am sorry to have to say that even some good mills are not ashamed to label their cloth 'Khadi' simply in order to take an illegitimate advantage of the growing Khadi atmosphere in the mofussil. If a workable arrangement is come to, I expect that there will be a line of demarcation for the time being between the cloth to be manufactured by Khadi centres and mills. The manufacture of cloth will be controlled as it often is in times of war. What in a war based on violence we do by compulsion, in this war based on non-violence we shall do by choice. Our ability voluntarily, *i.e.* merely under pressure of public opinion, to arrange boycotts etc., will be the outward but indispensable test of our non-violence if we have any in us.

3. "How will profits be regulated? You know as well as I do that prices of cotton fluctuate with irritating irregularity."

This assumes our inability to control the cotton market. Surely if the largest manufacturers of the country combine in the patriotic effort, they will control the cotton market. America rules our cotton prices because we stupidly, thoughtlessly, and selfishly send out our cotton. But boycott means that we shall control the movement of cotton, as we shall control many other things, if we are to achieve complete boycott, as we must, if we have developed the true national spirit and have confidence in ourselves and the nation.

4. "If you lay much stress upon honesty, perseverance, mutual trust etc., you are doomed"

As I have no bayonet at my command and would not have it even if I could command it, I must press for the qualities which the friend fears are at a discount. I do not share his fear—what is more I have patience enough to wait for the development of those qualities if they are not available in sufficient measure today. For this nation will never come to her own unless we exhibit them as a nation. I know too that we shall take much longer to discipline ourselves for violence, fraud and the like than we shall for truth and non-violence and all that they imply.

The friend then draws my attention to the following omissions in my previous article:

(a) The mills that join the scheme may not use foreign yarn or foreign artificial silk as many now do.

(b) They may not insure with foreign companies.

(c) They may not import foreign cloth and label it 'Swadeshi.'

I had assumed that (a) and (c) were a foregone conclusion. I should not care to insist on (b) if the insistence would hamper the proposed joint venture. Much as I should like indigenous insurance enterprise, I am convinced that it is the foreign cloth that blocks the way as nothing else does. If we can put this Himalayan obstacle out of the way, we shall easily cope with hillocks.

22nd March, 1928

DIFFERENCE STATED

BY M. K. GANDHI

Dear Mr. Gandhi,

May I again thank you for allowing me to stay with you in the Ashram a few weeks ago?

While there I read in *Young India* of January 19th the account of the meetings of the International Fellowship, and had several discussions with members of the Ashram on the subject. I wonder if you will kindly print this letter of mine giving the thoughts it suggested to me.

1. I think there is some confusion of thought in going on from the admission that "all religions contain truth" (which I feel most of us frankly and gladly admit) to say that "all religions are true." The latter statement takes us a great deal too far, for it would mean that the simplest and crudest forms of primitive belief in magic, idolatry, spirit-worship etc. are as good as the great higher religions of the world *e.g.* Judaism, Islam, Hinduism, Christianity, Buddhism.

And surely that is not true? We can see at a glance that it is not. Your own words at the top of column 2 p. 22* seem to admit as much. If we believed that, we should be quite content to leave our backward savage brethren to go in their blindness. And common humanity, even apart from any sense that we possess more light in any special higher religion, will not allow us to leave them so.

2. Surely a more correct account is to say that each religion, higher or lower, does contain indeed some light and truth, mixed up more or less with darkness and error. And it is the plain duty of every man and woman to search and test, by the power of the moral conscience that God has given him or her, wherein the clearest light and truth shines.

And further it is his *moral responsibility*, as a free spirit, in co-operation with God's Spirit, so to search and examine and

* See Page 566.

test; and not to excuse himself by any slack vagueness from this stern call to clear and brave thinking. And if his thinking leads him to some fuller light, surely, that same moral responsibility must lead him to try to help others to see the truth he has learnt and free them from this or that element of falsity in their religion.

God is one. His light and truth are one. But there have been and are many degrees and varieties of men's understanding of them. We are all called upon to think more and think clearly, lest we miss something of what He reveals.

3. I am very much attracted by your illustration of the smell of a rose. We will all admit that the real proof of the truth of a religion is the fragrance of real spirituality, love, joy, peace, that may emanate from those that hold to that religion. And without that our creeds and professions and preachings of it, even our worship and prayers, will not lead anyone to see that we have "a secret of the Lord" with us.

But does it follow from this that we cannot impart a share of what we rejoice in to others in any other way than as the smell of a rose imparts itself? The answer to this comes, I think, out of the succeeding paragraphs.

4. The word Christianity suggests a system or code of beliefs and practices, rather than a Living Way, as the first Christians thought of it. The word "proselytize" has gathered round it associations of *tabligh* and *sangathan* etc. of an unfortunate kind. Even the word "Conversion," though it is so good, meaning the turning of a man's heart to God as he has found Him, has not escaped giving a wrong impression sometimes.

But, to put it quite simply, if a man comes to see in Jesus Crucified and Risen God's Truth and Love and Power manifested in a way he does not find anywhere else; and if, so finding and seeing, he falls in love with Jesus, and knows that He is his Saviour and King through life and through death; and if he feels how much others need Him also; ultimately can he do less than come out and confess Him, and take his place on His side clearly and openly and finally, and help his fellows to share in his new-found treasure, even if it means suffering for His sake?

5. The break with the old home and brotherhood which so often results from a man's or a woman's open confession of Christ as Lord, has been very distressing to both sides. But it would be remembered that in almost all cases it is the old home and brotherhood which has forced this on, and not the 'convert.' He has not sought this, but has been driven by their opposition into this position of acute separation and over-againstness.

Christ does call men to take up the Cross and follow Him, whatever it cost; to place themselves under His banner, join His fellowship of faithful servants, however you like to express it. But it is not in order that they may form yet another exclusive community, fighting for its own rights, striving for *tabligh* of its own numbers; but simply in order that they may become a leaven within the whole lump, gradually transforming those around them by the influence of their faith and life, a regenerating force for the whole nation, a fellowship of service of the whole.

How far we of Christ's brotherhood have failed to be this, you and we, alas, know. But nevertheless that is clearly what He means us to be.

13-3-28 Yours Sincerely,
Cambridge mission W. F. IRELAND

[I gladly publish the foregoing It was made clear at those meetings of International Fellowship that I had meant the principal religions of the world and I had maintained that all were true more or less and that all were necessarily imperfect. Here, therefore, there is agreement. But Mr. Ireland's letter leaves on the mind the impression that there is a fundamental difference between him and me regarding conversion, no matter by what name it is called. Let me extend the analogy of fragrance, faulty as all analogies are in their very nature. The rose imparts its fragrance not in many ways but only one. Those who have not the sense of smell will miss it. You cannot feel the fragrance through the tongue or the ear or the skin. So may you not receive spirituality except through the spiritual sense. Hence have all religions recognised the necessity of that sense being awakened. It is a second birth. A man with intense spirituality may without speech or a gesture touch the hearts of millions who have never seen him and whom he has never seen. The most eloquent preacher if he has not spirituality in him will fail to touch the hearts of his audience. Therefore I venture to think that most of the effort of modern missions is not only useless but more often than not harmful. At the root of missionary effort is also the assumption that one's own belief is true not only for oneself but for all the world; whereas the truth is that God reaches us through millions of ways not understood by us. In missionary effort, therefore, there is lack of real humility that instinctively recognises human limitations and the limitless powers of God. I have no feeling that from a spiritual standpoint I am necessarily superior to the so-called savage. And spiritual superiority is a dangerous thing to feel. It is not like many other things which we can perceive, analyse and prove through our senses. If it is there, I cannot be deprived of it by any power on earth, and it will have its effect in its own due time. But if in matters of medicine and other natural sciences, I feel my superiority over others, a thing of which I may be legitimately conscious and if I have love for my fellow-beings, I would naturally share my knowledge with them. But things of the spirit I leave to God and thus keep the bond between fellow-beings and myself pure, correct and within limits. But I must not carry this argument any further.

My first feeling was not to publish Mr. Ireland's letter but to send a brief reply to him privately. But my regard for him has prompted me to comply with his wish without any ado knowing full well that this is not a matter which admits of any conclusive argument especially from my side and in view of the position herein described by me.

29th March, 1928

A CREEPER IN PERIDINIYA

A couple of miles from Kandy, itself a natural garden, are situated the Peridiniya Botanical Gardens, renowned to be perhaps the best in the world, and when we were in Kandy during the Ceylon tour in November last, we made up our minds to devote some time to a visit to this beauty spot. It is vast in extent and it would take a botanist to enumerate the multitudinous varieties of trees, plants and creepers that one finds there. This floral kingdom seemed very much like a human or animal kingdom and perhaps there was more harmony in it than in the other two. For the giant and the dwarf, the elephant and the ant, and the carnivorous and the vegetarian among them seemed to live there in perfect amity, and if one invited you to its most cooling shade, the other invited you to appreciate the beauty, the fragrance, or the weird form and colour of its flowers. And if there were many destined to live a day or at best a season, there were some that had lived for ages and could reveal in their hoary limbs a nation's history to a wizard who could unlock their secrets. There were huge rugged palms that reminded one of tall nude red Indians, as there were majestic eucalyptuses reminding one of perfect Greek statues, and there were some that had outgrown the 'semi-barbarous' state and were draped in luxuriant vegetation. For the first time in our lives we saw the tree that yields the familiar mace and nutmeg. The ground underneath was covered over with pear-shaped fruits, some of them split into two and exposing a rich crimson arillus draping the dark nut within. With the curiosity of children we picked pocketfuls of them and moved on wondering how little we knew of things so familiar.

We now came to an expansive lawn and as we were treading on it carelessly, we found numerous shrubs closing their leaves and shrinking from us as though from one who had outraged their modesty. We sat down and for several minutes watched the little leaves close and droop, sometimes at the merest puff of a breath, and wondered at their strange sensibility

But we moved on, and now a graceful human form clad in Tamil *sari* attracted Sjt. Rajagopalachari's attention. We had watched the trees and lingered near the mimosas, but we had not the power to commune with them. Sjt. Rajagopalachari hurried towards this sylvan beauty, confident that he would be able to hold converse with her even if she was a human mimosa.

She did not shrink from us as she would have done had she met us in the land of her birth. But she took care to tell us that she was an 'untouchable.' She hailed from a village very near Salem and Sjt. Rajagopalachari and his daughter took no time in winning her confidence. In a little while we found them plunged into intimate conversation about how she had happened to come there, what she was doing and whether she had anything like a home.

She felt as though she had met a full brother and sister and there was a touch of pathos in her voice although her face was ever smiling. She had come in search of work, possibly with a *kangany* recruiting labour for the plantations, but she had happened to find work in the Gardens and lived in a hut close by. 'Are you quite happy?' 'Yes,' she said, but there was a strange sadness in her tone.

She was earning some seven annas a day and her husband a trifle more than she, and they were apparently happy. And what could be happier than to sweep the garden grounds and to tend and water the little plants and live in those glorious surroundings with her husband? She was as clean and tidy as any one of us, her single-piece garment was as clean as our clothes and there was an ineffable grace and manner about her which any upper class girl would covet.

Sjt. Rajagopalachari's mind went back for a moment to the tea plantations we had visited a few days before. His heart had sunk within him as he contemplated the conditions under which the thousands of Tamil labourers were working for their European employers. 'Khadi may not give them as much as eight annas a day,' he had said to himself, 'but Khadi would certainly prevent their moral ruin.' In fact some of the self-introspecting ones had confessed to him, 'If we had employment at home, giving us no more than Khadi can give, we would not venture out to these strange lands to earn a few more coppers and damnation into the bargain.'

'This girl is certainly better off than they,' concluded Sjt. Rajagopalachari, 'better off both materially and morally, and Khadi would not have made her happier.' He had argued, quite vehemently, with the labourers on the hills that they were no better for having come to that distant land. They were cut off from their homes and surroundings. Some of them had left their wives and children at home, and were leading immoral lives. Some of them had come under the grip of drink. Why not go back home and help in Khadi production rather than in the production of tea and work their own as well as others' ruin? But he saw no occasion to argue in a similar way with the girl. She was there with her husband and happy. Whereas he could promise the plantation labourer employment and clean and respectable living, he could not promise her those things. She would be no happier if she went back home, she would be again an outcast and might fail to find employment, for all that Sjt. Rajagopalachari might like to do for her.

But we passed on. We now came across a three years old baby rolling on the lawn, quite happy with himself. He got up and greeted us with a smile. We did not know that he was the child of her whom we had met a short while ago, until the proud mother came running and met us again, and held up the baby before us, as though wanting us to admire the 'Madonna with her child.' We had a pleasant chat again, Sjt. Rajagopalachari feeling more convinced than before that by no possible argument could he tempt her back to her old home. The baby completed if there was anything wanting in that picture of domestic felicity.

We talked mechanically away, about her new home, her baby, her husband. At the mention of the last word, however, a shadow crept over her face, casting another shadow over the mental *picture* of felicity we had drawn of her surroundings. Her freedom of speech left her for a moment, and with deep sorrow she gave out her secret. Whether it was because she did not want us to go away with a wrong impression of her, or because she felt that she must not keep the truth from us, heaven-born Brahmans, I cannot say. But she now told her tale of woe. She had been married in the land of her birth, and her good man was not her lawfully wedded husband, but one with whom she had been tempted to come away from a life of poverty and misery. That was the canker that seemed to be consuming her heart and casting a blight on all the happiness that the comfort and beauty of her surroundings could give her. Fugitive moments of self-introspection made her pine for the old days of hardship and poverty, but of innocence. The heart of the Hindu wife within her seemed to revolt against what she in the depth of her being 'knew to be a wrong. She seemed to forget all the indignities and insults that were her daily lot in India and pined to get back home.

Sjt. Rajagopalachari moved away from the scene silent and speechless, through the very uprush of feelings that had choked him. He sighed within himself and his thoughts went back to the potency of the spinning wheel.

Would not the charkha have prevented the wrong? Perhaps. But it seemed to be a monstrous tragedy that a human being, with such a keen sense of right and wrong, should be regarded as untouchable and driven to a course from which there seemed to be no escape. M. D

29th March, 1928

THE DOCTRINE OF FRIGHTFULNESS

In answer to a question but by a member of the late Hunter Committee, General Dyer admitted that Jallianwalla was designed to create frightfulness. In making the admission the late General enunciated no new doctrine. Indeed "the ablest

Civil Service in the world" has laid the foundation of its greatness on frightfulnesses.

In pursuance of this well-known policy, according to the information received at the time of going to press it appears that summary steps are now to be taken against the farmers of Bardoli in order to compel submission. For eight preliminary notices of forfeiture have been served upon certain Satyagrahis of Bardoli. The names of these seem to have been carefully chosen, for all of them happen to be banias of note. The choice has been so made presumably because banias, who have the reputation of being weak and timid are expected to yield under notices of forfeiture. What can be more natural, officialdom would argue, than that banias weakening, the others must follow suit. Satyagrahis need not be surprised at this first show of frightfulness. They have been repeatedly told to expect forfeitures and worse. Let them now show their strength if they have it in them.

M. K. G.

29th March, 1928

THE NATIONAL WEEK

BY M. K. GANDHI

The national week comes upon us with seasonlike regularity and has found us more or less wanting since after 1922. The 6th April to 13th April should be regarded as days of privilege, introspection, intense national activity and self-purification. These precious seven days should be days of stock-taking and heart-searching. The morning of 6th April 1919 found an India awakened to a sense of her dignity. Hindus, Musalmans and others composing the nation felt themselves united like blood brothers as they are in reality, if they would but recognise themselves as sons of the soil.

6th of April 1919 found an India endowed with a true spirit of Swadeshi which culminated in Khadi and which is now feeding according to the latest figures over 90,000 poor spinners.

The spirit thus awakened continued to advance during 1920 and 1921 and we seemed to be within an ace of statutory Swaraj.

But the Swaraj did not come and there was a set-back. Apparently since then there has been only an ebb. Hindus and Musalmans are flying at each other's throats.

Instead of Swadeshi we have the cry for boycott of British goods pending settlement as if support of Japanese goods including Japan's cheap calico can ever be a substitute for Swadeshi, *i. e.*, Khadi, exclusive of all foreign cloth. After much research, reasoning and experience, we seemed in 1920-21 to have come to the conclusion that the only practical effective and necessary Swadeshi was Khadi, not pending any settlement but for all time or such time as we could discover a better and more paying occupation for the starving millions. I have seen no new argument in support of boycott of British goods only as distinguished from foreign goods. No new situation has arisen to warrant the belief that boycott of British goods is a practical proposition and that the use of foreign cloth other than British is not almost equally detrimental to the best interest of India.

Would that those who are supporting the cry of boycott of British goods will seriously think over their programme, and if necessary, revise their plan and join the Khadi movement with the whole-hearted conviction that it and it alone can bring about complete boycott, not merely of British cloth but of all foreign cloth.

But whether they do so or not, I am sure they do not make of support of foreign cloth other than British cloth a matter of principle. And if I am right in my supposition, let them support the sales of Khadi during the national week. If they will but study the progress of the Khadi movement during the past seven years that it has been going on, they will discover that the charkha has more potency than they have ever dreamt of. It is potent enough, if it receives the whole-hearted and active support of politically minded India, to bring about boycott of foreign cloth even without the assistance of our mills. With the active and organised support of the latter, boycott of foreign cloth becomes a much easier proposition. Indeed the mill-owners hold the trump card if only they would play it for the sake of the nation. They have at their disposal a ready-made extensive organisation, which, if they devote it to the service of the nation, can simplify the campaign of boycott and arm the nation with the power it so much needs.

And why will not Hindus and Musalmans recall those precious seven days and shed all fear, mutual distrust and weakness?

Let me not forget the so-called untouchables, the classes that we, Hindus, have been guilty of suppressing. Shall we not have the vision to see that in suppressing a sixth (or whatever the number) of ourselves, we have depressed ourselves? No man takes another down a pit without descending into it himself and sinning in the bargain. It is not the suppressed that sin. It is the suppressor who has to answer for his crime against those whom he suppresses.

29th March, 1928

BOYCOTT AND STUDENTS

BY M. K. GANDHI

The principal of a college writes:

"The promoters of the boycott movement are dragging the students into their movement. It is obvious that no one will attach the slightest value to the part the students play in this political propaganda. When the students leave their schools and colleges and join any demonstration, they mingle with the rowdies of the place and have to be responsible for all the outrages of the badmashes and often receive the first blows from the policeman's batons. They, besides, incur the displeasure of the school and college authorities whose punishment they have to submit to; they further disobey their guardians who might refuse to finance them further, which spells their ruin. I can understand youth movements which aim at doing such constructive work as teaching the ignorant peasants, spreading knowledge of sanitation etc., during holidays; but to see them turn against their own parents and teachers and walk along streets in questionable company and help the breaking of law and order is a sorry spectacle. May I request you to advise the politicians not to draw the students from their legitimate work to make their demonstration *more effective?* In fact, they are detracting from the value of their demonstration by so doing, as it is likely to be easily put down as the work of inconsiderate boys led astray by selfish and foolish agitators.

"I am not against their learning modern politics. It will be a good thing if the teachers would collect and bring to their notice newspaper utterances for and against any pending question of the day and teach the students to draw their own conclusions. I have tried the scheme with success. In fact no subject is taboo to the students, as Bertrand Russell and others advocate students should be taught even sex questions. What I am dead against is the students being used as tools for purposes which serve not themselves or those who so use them."

The correspondent has written in the hope of my condemning the participation by the student world in active political work. But I am sorry to have to disappoint him. He should have known that in 1920-21 I had not an inconsiderable share in drawing students out of their schools and colleges and inducing them to undertake political duty carrying with it the risk of imprisonment. I think it is their clear duty to take a leading part in the political movement of their country. They are doing so all the world over. In India where political consciousness has till recently been unfortunately confined in a large measure to the English-educated class, their duty is, indeed, greater. In China and Egypt it was the students who have made the national movement possible. They cannot do less in India.

What the principal might have urged was the necessity of students observing the rules of non-violence and acquiring control over the rowdies, instead of being controlled by them.

29th March, 1928

MACAULAY'S DREAMS

BY M. K. GANDHI

A friend sends me the following quotation from Macaulay's 'Life and Letters.'

> "On the 7th March 1835 Lord William Bentinck decided that 'the great object of the British Government ought to be the promotion of European Literature and Science among the Natives of India;' two of the orientialists retired from the Committee of Public Instruction; several new members, both English and Native, were appointed; and Macaulay entered upon the functions of President with an energy and assiduity which in his case was an infallible proof that his work was to his mind."
>
> "Our English Schools," said Lord Macaulay, "are flourishing wonderfully. We find it difficult,—indeed in some places impossible,—to provide instruction for all who want it. At the town of Hooghly fourteen hundred boys are learning English. The effect of this education on the Hindoos is prodigious. No Hindoo who has received an English education ever remains sincerely attached to his religion. Some continue to profess it as a matter of policy; but many profess themselves pure deists, and some embrace Christianity. It is my firm belief, that if our plans of education are followed up, there will not be a single idolater among the respectable classes of Bengal thirty years hence. And this will be effected without any

efforts to proselytise; without the smallest interference with religious liberty; merely by the natural operations of knowledge and reflection. I heartily rejoice in the prospect."

I do not know whether Macaulay's dream that English-educated India would abandon its religious belief has been realised. But we know too that he had another dream, namely to supply through English-educated India clerks and the like for the English rulers. That dream has certainly been realised beyond all expectation.

29th March, 1928

PEACE AMIDST STRIFE

By M. K. Gandhi

Before now I have shared with the reader some of the beautiful things that a friend sends me from time to time for my Monday silence. I am tempted to share with him the following further instalment which has been lying with me in my jacket for a long time. All but the last two are extracts from Buddhistic writings. The last but one is from Emerson and the last of all is a Hindu proverb.

Like a beautiful flower full of colour, without scent, the fine words of him who does not act accordingly are fruitless.

A mind unshaken by life's vicissitudes, unstirred by grief or passion, is the greatest of all blessings.

There never was, there never will be, a man who is always praised, or a man who is always blamed.

As a solid rock is not shaken by the wind, so wise men falter not amidst blame or praise.

Let us live happily, then, not hating those who hate us.

Let us live free from hatred among men who hate.

Let us live happily, then, free from ailments among the ailing,

Let us dwell free from afflictions among men who are sick at heart.

Let us live happily, then, free from care among the busy.

Let us dwell free from yearning among men who are anxious.

Let us live happily, then, though we call nothing our own.

We shall become like the bright Gods, who feed on happiness.

The greatest prayer is patience.

Never in this world does hatred cease by hatred.

Hatred ceases by love: this is always its nature.

Reverence and lowliness
Contentment and gratitude,
The hearing of the Lord at due season
This is the greatest blessing.

As a mother, even at the risk of her own life, protects her son, her only son: so let a man cultivate good-will without measure among all beings.

Let him cultivate good-will without measure toward the whole world, above, below, unstinted, unmixed with any feeling of differing or opposing interests. Let a man remain steadfastly in that state of mind all the while he is awake, whether he be standing, walking, sitting or lying down. This state of heart is the best in the world.

By rousing himself, by earnestness, by restraint and control, the wise man may make for himself an island which no flood can overwhelm.

As the bee—injuring not
The flower, its colour, or scent—
Flies away, taking the nectar:
So let the wise man dwell
Upon the truth.

Ye taught my lips a single speech
And a thousand silences.

Even Buddha was once a cart-horse, and carried the loads of others.

29th March, 1928

ON FASTING

By M. K. Gandhi

The reader is familiar with the letters of a Polish professor from which I have published extracts from time to time in these columns. In one of his letters referring to my fasts he writes:

> "According to my experience, if the bowels are kept perfectly clean by enemas, it is quite easy to fast 15 days, not very much more difficult than to fast 10 days. But this refers to me, and I have a normal weight of 80 kilograms, which in fasting goes down to 70. Your case is different and if I look at your picture, I have the impression that you ought not to fast over *7 days*.
>
> "In fasting I take no food whatever, but plenty of distilled water—2-3 litres every day with a little fresh lemon juice if necessary. I take my weight of the naked body every day and the loss is usually ½ kg. or a little more than one English pound a day. I have taken these fasts since 1907 every year four to seven times, I mean every year 40-60 days of fasting, divided into periods of 3, 7, 10 or 15 days according to indications of the general state and subjective need. Fasting is at certain times a need for me, and then every food is unpleasant. So I have within the last 20 years experience of over 100 fasting periods of different lengths — the shortest 3 days, the longest 16 days. My weight now, after more than 3 months without fasting, is 80 kilograms, and I long to take a long fast. . . . I fast generally before undertaking a long lecturing tour. The intensity of work is not lessened by fasting, rather increased. Now I feel exhausted, tired, sleepy, because I have been travelling more than 100 days and could not fast. . . . As I have no leisure for bodily exercise, I am liable to have too much weight whenever I do not fast. Very likely this deficiency of bodily ex-

ercise and also insufficient mastication account for excess of weight. By nature and inheritance I am not a spare eater. It needed a long training to reduce the amount of food taken and even now, at the age of 65 it happens that I eat too much if the food pleases me.

By clearing the bowels, I understand introducing through the rectum water, of which only a part is secreted by the kidney, while the greater part after a short time is expelled by the rectum. The water flows from an irrigator, at about 100 centimetres height. I take this enema with the naked body in a warm bath. I should not think it advisable to drink so much water. I introduce into the bowels first 1 litre water and after having got rid of it, several times in succession 2 litres and then 3—4 litres until the water is transparent, clean. . . . The effects of fasting are not only increased bodily activity, but also spiritual enlightenment, if we fast for a purpose, in order to obtain a result. Whenever I have a moral or intellectual difficulty, I fast. If I have a struggle against an adversary, I fast. Once I had a difficulty with a printer who delayed my work in order to print other more profitable things. By fasting I succeeded in changing his mind. I have found fasting and prayer efficacious in most difficulties with men and things."

I publish this as being of use to the reader who is interested in such researches. The physical and moral value of fasting is being more and more recognised day by day. A vast number of diseases can be more surely treated by judicious fasting than by all sorts of nostrums including the dreadful injections—dreadful not because of the pain they cause but because of the injurious by-products which often result from their use. More mischief than we are aware of is done by the drug treatment. But not many cases of harm done by fasting can be cited. Increased vitality is almost the universal experience of those that have fasted. For real rest for body and mind is possible only during fasting. Suspension of daily work is hardly rest without the rest that the overtaxed and overworked digestive apparatus needs in a multitude of cases.... The moral effect of fasting, while it is considerable, is not so easily demonstrable. For moral results there has to be perfect co-operation from the mind. And there is danger of self-deception. I know of many instances in which fasting undertaken for moral results has been overdone. To a limited extent it is a most valuable agent if the person fasting knows what he is doing. There was considerable force in the warning given by the Prophet against his disciples copying his fasting over and above the semi-fasts of *Ramzan*. 'My Maker sends me food enough when I fast, not so to you,' said the Prophet. Of what use is a spiritual fast when the spirit hankers more after food, the longer the body is starved?

5th April, 1928

REMEMBER THE 'UNTOUCHABLES'

By M. K. Gandhi

Within two days of the publication of this issue, the National Week will be on us. We used at one time in the processes of self-purification to picket liquor dens. I am reminded of those days as I go through the following paragraph from an address received from the members of the Coimbatore Adi-Dravida Association:

> "When the National Congress included the removal of untouchability in its creed, it was thought that all impediments to the progress of our community numbering over 60 millions of Hindus would be removed in no time, but years have rolled on since without giving us even a ray of hope in this respect. Perhaps it has only resulted in the benign Government passing pious G. O's throwing open all public roads, wells and institutions to the members of our community. The old order has not changed even to a small extent, and even our souls are despised by the other Hindus so that we are not allowed to

worship in temples the one God, the ruler of the destinies of men and nations. The churches and mosques have their doors wide open to receive us and the missionaries in charge of them extend us a hearty welcome. The Government tempts our young men by locating liquor shops in or near our *cheries*, the living quarters of our community. If industrial institutions took the place of such shops and if social workers befriended us instead of abkari contractors, we have no doubt that our progress would be assured in a very short time. We, therefore, earnestly appeal to you for help to organise industrial schools in or near our living quarters to save our community from ruin."

We need not consider during the National Week what the Government has done or not done, but we are bound to consider what we have done and what we can do. Whilst there is no doubt that public opinion against untouchability has been strengthening day by day, public action still remains weak. We have not even been able to induce the keepers of public temples to throw their doors open to the suppressed classes nor have we been able to replace a single liquor den with an industrial school or a refreshment room where instead of the fiery liquid, they can receive health-giving nutritious drinks and other refreshments in clean surroundings.

5th April, 1928

BAGHAT STATE AND SACRED THREAD

By M. K. Gandhi

With reference to my note* about the treatment of Kolis in Baghat State, the President of the Arya Samaj, New Delhi, writes:

"*Apropos* of your note which appeared in *Young India* of 22nd March in regard to the position of Kolis in the Baghat State, you have very kindly given to me an opportunity to send further details in corroboration of the char-

* See page 659

ges brought by me against the Baghat State. I am equally glad to learn that simultaneous opportunity has been offered to the State authorities, if they wish, to send in their version of the incident. I am not aware whether the Baghat State officials receive copies of your esteemed weekly, but for their convenience I have sent to them under a registered cover the relevant excerpt from *Young India* dated the 22nd March 1928 to enable them, if they care, to contradict the charges levelled against them.

"As far as I am concerned I enclose for your kind perusal a copy of the correspondence which has passed between me and the State authorities. The only reply which I have so far received from the State officials is their letter of the 13th January 1928. Notwithstanding my repeated reminders I have as yet received no further answer to my letter of the 16th January. I may however mention that attempts have also been made to secure an interview with the Chief of the State but to no purpose. I therefore leave it to you to judge for yourself whether any further proof is required in support of the charges which I have brought against the State. The change in the position which has occurred since I last wrote to you on the subject is that the Kolis in question were released on the specific condition that if again they wore the sacred thread they would be punished with a fine of Rs. 500 each. This has greatly frightened these men and like the burnt child who dreads the fire, no good counsel from outside has now any meaning for them.

"I further attach for your perusal a cutting from the *Tribune* dated the 18th January 1928 which is from the pen of a correspondent and contains more truth than fiction. It will be observed therefrom that the only fault of the Kolis concerned was, that in consequence of the propaganda of the Arya Samaj for the uplift of the so-called depressed classes in the Simla Hills, they had taken the sacred thread as an emblem of Hinduism and had simultaneously with the purification " given up several evil habits and taken to religious ways. All this desire to improve their social conditions by means which unthinking orthodoxy prohibits for 'untouchables' brought on their heads the wrath of the Ruler of the Baghat State, even though these people gave a very good account of themselves in the Rana Saheb's Court in regard to their knowledge and observance of Hindu religious practices. I am not used to stronger language than the facts justify, but I respectfully submit that if the Rulers of some of the States are too narrow-minded to initiate measures for the removal of the great curse of untouchability from Hindu society, they should, at any rate, refrain from placing serious and utterly unjustifiable obstacles in the way of those who are carrying on the humane work of upliftment of the so-called depressed classes. I hope that a further note from your pen may make the Rana Saheb see the utter unwisdom and injustice of his action in this matter and may persuade him to take the earliest opportunity of undoing it."

The president is no other than Rai Saheb Lala Ganga Ram the well known philanthropist and public worker of Delhi. Lala Ganga Ram's letter seems to leave little doubt about the correctness of the allegations made in the previous letter published in these pages. I had hoped that his informants had exaggerated the happenings in Baghat State and that it had not treated as a crime the wearing of the sacred thread by the so-called untouchables. I have before me a copy of the letter written to Lala Ganga Ram by the Prime Minister of the State. It runs:

"In reply to your letter dated 10th January, 1928, I regret that the State is unable to supply you the copy of the judgment, as Arya Samaj is not a party to this suit."

I cannot help remarking that the reply is in extremely bad taste. It is a bad copy of some English officials' laconic and stereotyped replies which they ordinarily send to correspondents who ask inconvenient questions. But these estimable gentlemen as a rule respect rank and status and do not crudely invent things to suit their replies. The Prime Minister of Baghat State has dared to ignore Lala Ganga Ram's status in society (I mean apart from his title) and for the sake of insulting him has imagined what Lala Ganga Ram has never said in his letter. For he never asked for a copy of the judgment in the case nor claimed to be party in the case against the unfortunate Kolis.

This is essentially a matter of the Hindu Maha Sabha to take up. I do not know whether the Sabha countenances the wearing of the sacred thread by the so-called untouchables. Whether it does or not, it cannot possibly approve of coercion being used against those who choose to wear it. Immediately the thread becomes a monopoly carrying with it a punishment for its breach, it will cease to be sacred. It was sacred because and when the wearers were men of learning and piety. It will soon become a mark of degradation, if the alleged example of Baghat State proves infectious.

5th April, 1928

SHASTRI'S SELF-DENIAL

The decision of the Right Honourable Shrinivasa Shastri to remain in South Africa beyond his term will gladden the hearts of the Indian settlers as it has pleased and eased the minds of those here who are interested in the South African question and who have been anxiously following the course of events in that sub-continent. Familiarity in Sjt. Shastri's case instead of making the Europeans indifferent or lukewarm has made them look to the Agent General as their friend and peacemaker. By his punctilious impartiality combined with firmness wherever necessary Sjt. Shastri has inspired them with trust as well as respect. The grateful Indians have not been slow to discover and appreciate the worth of this distinguished countryman and they were urging him to prolong his stay, if it was at all possible. Let them now demonstrate their affection and appreciation by becoming united and by being correct in the observance of all their part of the agreement. I tender my congratulations to Sjt. Shastri on his self-denial. For I know how anxious he was to return home at the end of his term.

M. K. G.

5th April, 1928

A MILL-OWNER ON BOYCOTT

BY M. K. GANDHI

An Ahmedabad mill-owner writes:

"I have been closely following your articles re foreign cloth boycott and am desirous of offering a few suggestions with some of my fears in organising the boycott. I believe that if the mills of India join your scheme in the boycott of foreign cloth we shall have achieved a success not only in boycott but in getting a ready market for the goods already accumulated in the mill warehouses. The mills can join this movement with double gain of serving the nation and safe-guarding the shareholders' interests. For the shareholders could be assured of a regular dividend, instead of a fat dividend one year and no dividend the next. Not only will the profits be regulated but as the goods will find a ready market, not much interest or warehousing charges will be incurred. This will be a direct saving in the cost of manufacture. The mills should under this organisation manufacture cloth with such size only as may be necessary for weaving purposes, and thus a considerable national waste will be saved. Again only that sort of cloth should be manufactured which may be decided upon by the controlling board and all such pieces should be stamped with a stamp of the Boycott Committee so that no mill can pass off any cloth under standard or foreign.

As regards artificial silk, I cannot understand how any objection should be raised, if we are to use foreign dyes and sizing materials.

"The aim of the boycott ought to be on the lines of replacing foreign cloth as far as mills are concerned. You ask the mills not to manufacture Khadi and that too rightly, which in other words means that they should make such cloth only as would replace foreign cloth not at present replaced by Khadi. Artificial silk yarn is made from wood pulp and is a cheap luxury which in my opinion should not be boycotted because it helps to replace foreign manufacture. Of course those mills using foreign yarn should not be called Swadeshi. But, what would you call a mill using foreign cotton? Is the cloth made from it Swadeshi? Cotton fluctuations, unless they are wild, do not make any difference in the prices of cloth. No change has taken place in cloth prices since cotton has risen from Rs. 339 to Rs. 375. Your friend need not be afraid on this score. But, at the same time Indian mills are unable to control the cotton prices as long as America rules the world cotton prices. Yes, if, as you say, the export of cotton is controlled, the fluctuations will not be so big. However, to attain that state nothing seems to be possible before we have swaraj and to get it we have to boycott foreign cloth from now. Therefore cotton fluctuations are likely to abide and they will play their part in the present scheme of boycott.

"Now coming over to the question of your trust in the honesty of the mill-owners I must remark that you are too sanguine. Need I remind you of the fate of the Ahmedabad Mills Tilak Swaraj Fund and the threats held out on many occasions regarding its disbursement? Take it from me that you will certainly be doomed, if you are going to join hands with us without the strictest guarantees.

"If the boycott is to succeed, you will only take those

mills whose agents are genuine and reliable. Even if you have one dozen good mills to join you, good propaganda can be made and believe me that the others will soon mend their ways.

"It seems to me that if anything important is to be done it should either be put off till you return from Europe if you are going there, or you should decide not to go to Europe, and take up this question, because I believe and many join me in my belief that your presence is necessary to conduct the proposed joint movement."

The letter is refreshingly candid. I wish that the other mill-owners would take the view that this correspondent takes of the possibility of standardization of prices and necessarily therefore of cloth. It is refreshing too to find that fluctuations of cotton prices do not much affect prices of cloth. And I would add in spite of the correspondent's view to the contrary, that it is possible to control cotton prices if it is possible for us to boycott foreign cloth. For prices of our cotton are dominated by America only because we export large quantities of cotton and that too to the market for which America also caters. If we consider it to be possible as it has proved to be possible to appeal successfully to the patriotism of the buyer of cloth it is equally possible to make a successful appeal to that of the grower of cotton. Indeed the importance of foreign cloth boycott is derived from the knowledge that for it to succeed all the component parts of the nation have voluntarily to join the movement. It cannot succeed unless there is willing and hearty co-operation from the vast mass of the village population. My faith in the movement persists because I know the masses to be sound. Only the classes block the way because of their want of faith. If they will only shed their fear and their unbelief and lead the movement, the masses will follow. *And this boycott is the only thing in which it is possible for the masses actively to join without having to make much sacrifice.*

I do not share the view of the correspondent that artificial silk may be used with impunity in the manufacture of cloth in our mills. His comparison of foreign dyes and foreign size with artificial silk is hastily made. Just now we contemplate boycott only of foreign cloth not of dyes and size. All foreign yarns therefore, whether silk, wool or cotton, natural or artificial, must be taboo; or if foreign artificial silk yarn may be used with impunity why not foreign cotton or wool or natural silk yarn?

But with foreign cotton it is a different thing. We need not exclude from use foreign cotton, for it is a raw product. What we *must* boycott for the sake of the starving masses living in enforced idleness for at least four months in the year is *foreign yarn and cloth which the masses can spin and weave in their cottages.*

The indigenous mill cloth too would be intolerable if it displaced these masses without finding for them an equivalent industry. The mills have a place in the economy of national life only to the extent that they supplement the national industry of handspinning in millions of our cottages. They will be a hindrance if they compete with them and supplant them. Their natural tendency no doubt is to supplant both the village spinner and the village weaver. It is only when the mill-owners, mill-agents and their shareholders become truly national and conduct their affairs not to exploit the masses but for their benefit first and their own profits after, that they will be able to appreciate and not merely to join but to lead the boycott movement. That, if they take a long view of the matter, they have nothing to lose and much to gain has been made clear by the foregoing letter. Indeed it is a self-evident proposition. Boycott of foreign cloth, if it is the best assurance of steady work for the masses, is also an equal assurance to the mills of steady profits in the long run.

But the history of the mill industry at least during the past seven years of the mass movement does not fill one with much hope of the mills rising to the occasion and realising their duty to the nation. Instead of looking upon Khadi with favour and fostering it, our mills have entered into an unfair, unpatriotic and illegitimate competition with Khadi. The following are the figures of Khadi manufactured by our mills during the respective years:

	1925	1926	1927
Lbs.	2,28,87,970	2,72,36,337	3,39,77,851
Yards	6,50,48,487	7,43,13,280	9,43,80,368

They have sold this enormous quantity of coarse cloth as Khadi and have not hesitated in some cases shamelessly to use the charkha label etc. with the deliberate purpose of exploiting the Khadi atmosphere created by Congress organisations. It gives one pain to have to say that the mills that thus manufactured coarse cloth and palmed it off as Khadi did a distinct disservice to the nation.

If their eyes are now opened and if only to do belated reparation for the grave wrong done by them to the nation, they will head or at least join the boycott movement on the terms suggested by me or others equally effective.

This painful discovery of the figures has however a bright side to it. It is a revelation even to an optimist and Khadi expert like me of the hold that Khadi has acquired over the people. It shows that a much larger number than we are aware of has in obedience to the nation's call changed their taste and preferred to buy and use coarse cloth instead of the fine cloth they used to wear before. They have undoubtedly often paid higher prices than they used to. They have bought mill Khadi largely under the mistaken belief that it was genuine and that it had the imprimatur of the Congress. An ardent lover of the masses has in these figures and my legitimate deductions therefrom much food for thought and equal cause for hope. As for my feared visit to Europe, I may assure the correspondent that I do not propose to visit Europe if an effective scheme of boycott materialises in the very near future.

5th April, 1928

AFRICANS AND INDIANS

Dinabandhu Andrews when he was here recently drew my attention to what the poet had written in the press in connection with a movement in the Transvaal said to be going on, on behalf of Indians to isolate themselves from the Africans and wanted me to give my opinion on it. I do not think that any importance need be attached to the alleged movement. For I feel that it has no bottom. Indians have too much in common with the Africans to think of isolating themselves from them. They cannot exist in South Africa for any length of time without the active sympathy and friendship of the Africans. I am not aware of the general body of the Indians having ever adopted an air of superiority towards their African brethren, and it would be a tragedy if any such movement were to gain ground among the Indian settlers of South Africa. Needless to say, I entirely associate myself with the opinion so forcibly expressed by the Poet condemning the movement. If, as has been stated on behalf of the leaders of the so-called movement, 'it is humiliating to the Indian sentiment and to the Indian national honour and civilization to think that our Agent-General is trying to bring us down to such a low level,' it will ill befit us to repudiate such a sentiment when it is expressed by the South African whites in respect of ourselves. And what is more, the South African whites are able to translate their contempt and prejudice against us into action whereas ours towards the South Africans can only react against ourselves.

M. K. G.

5th April, 1928

WOMEN AND JEWELS

BY M. K. GANDHI

A lady doctor in Tamil Nadu sends a letter accompanying her gift referred to in it. As the letter, in my opinion, enhances the value of the gift and is likely to serve as an example to others, I compress its contents as follows, omitting the names of the donor, the Raja and the place:

> "Just a few lines to tell you that I sent you yesterday a parcel of diamond ring and a pair of ear-rings which were given to me about 12 years ago in remembrance of service in the palace . .. when the heir was born to the Raja. It grieved me much when I came to know that the Raja did not have even the courage to invite you to his place when you passed by and I was told that it was due to fear of the Government. You can imagine my feeling when after your visit I looked at these jewels which before used to travel with me. Now when I looked at them, bitterness rose in my breast and then it turned into deep sympathy for the starving millions about whom you spoke when you were here. I said to myself, 'Are not these jewels made out of the people's money? And, what claim have I to keep them as my own?' I then made up my mind to send them on to you. You could use them for Khadi service and so help some of the starving millions, I feel sure that it is a better use to make of them than that they should remain in a corner of my box. A friend has valued them at Rs. 500. They are therefore insured for that amount. I only hope that some generous person will give you more than the actual price, knowing the circumstances in which these things are being sent to you. You may make what use you like of this letter."

It is remarkable how we imagine fears even when there is no cause. There are many Rajas who have openly and willingly supported Khadi and there-through the cause of the poor from whom, after all, as my correspondent correctly puts it, they derive their riches. It is true that Khadi has a political significance; but we have not yet come to the stage when support of Khadi can be safely declared by the Government to be criminal. Every philanthropic movement can be turned to political use, but it would be a sad day when on that account it is boycotted even as to its philanthropic aspect. But it is only fair to state that the Raja to whom reference has been made by the lady doctor is not the only one who is afraid of supporting Khadi or showing ordinary courtesy to a public servant like me. It is well however, that the Raja's boycott of me has stimulated the gift. But I would like all the sisters who may chance to see this note to realise that it is not necessary to be able to emulate the fair donor to have occasions like the one that set her athinking about her duty to the starving millions. Surely it is easy enough to realise that so long as there are millions of men and women in the country starving for want of food because of want of work, the sisters have no warrant for possessing costly jewels for adorning their bodies or often for the mere satisfaction of possessing them. As I have remarked before now in these pages if only the rich ladies of India will discard their superfluities and be satisfied with such decoration as Khadi can give them, it is possible to finance the whole of the Khadi movement, not to take into consideration the tremendous moral effect that such a step on the part of the rich daughters of India will produce upon the nation and particularly the starving masses.

5th April, 1928

KARVE JUBILEE

BY M. K. GANDHI

It gives me joy to publish the following appeal by Sjt. V. M. Joshi, President of Karve Jubilee Committee:

"Professor Karve, who will see his 71st birthday on the 18th of April next, is not only a founder of institutions like the Widows' Home and the Indian Women's University but is in himself an institution. His name is honoured not only in Maharashtra but in the whole of India, not only by the rich (to whom by the bye this appeal is addressed) but also by the poor (for whose daughters and sisters he has been selflessly and zealously working for more than thirty years), not only by this or that political party but by *all* parties, not only by the heterodox but also by the orthodox section of the people. This unique position he did not attain in a day, nor without the difficulties and the trials which are the inevitable lot of all who attempt to do something good and great, against the prejudices and deep-rooted sentiments of the common people, especially when these attempts are not backed by wealth or position. Himself a poor man, without much help or even appreciation from the rich during the first decade of his work, hated and calumniated by the uneducated for his heterodoxy in educating the widows and supported very lukewarmly by the educated because of what they considered to be his cowardice in not going as far as they wanted him to go, he has succeeded after years of strenuous, patient and self-abasing work in converting his enemies into admirers and his lukewarm sympathisers into zealous adherents. Men of his stamp are rare anywhere, but especially in a country like India which, through the conjunction of a number of circumstances, does not, or cannot recognise and encourage its heroes. That such a man should be among us for many a year to come is naturally the wish of all who know him or have heard of him (which means practically the whole of literate India), and one of the best ways of prolonging the lives of such men is to let them feel by our actions that after all we *do* recognise their worth and that we are desirous of helping forward causes they have so selflessly made their own. Some of his friends and admirers have already started a Fund with a view to instituting scholarships in his name, the scholarships to be utilised for the education of helpless widows. It is hoped that the aristocracy as well as the intelligentsia will gladly help forward this movement and enable the organizers of this Fund to announce on his seventy-first birthday the collection of a sum which will gladden him on that day and add to the health, enthusiasm and optimism which he still retains, thanks not only to his regular and temperate habits but also to the invigorating and energising nature of noble thoughts and aspirations, coupled with unblemished character."

Professor Karve is not an ordinary man who is satisfied if he satisfies an indulgent public which, if it proves itself exacting and imperious at times, issues a certificate of merit ninety-nine times out of hundred if some little service is rendered to it during recreation hours. Prof. Karve has obeyed a master that is never generous, never indulgent and ever exacting though invariably just. This master is his own conscience. His self-effacement, his single-minded devotion to duty, his exhaustless energy, his honesty in all circumstances, his faith in the midst of opposition, his irrepressible optimism are a national asset of the first magnitude. There may be two opinions about the work to which he has devoted his great gifts but there can be only one opinion about the gifts themselves. And the latter are any day far more valuable and lasting than the work itself. The organisers of the Jubilee have set before themselves a very modest task to collect Rs. 25,000 to be presented to Prof. Karve for his work. It is a sum that should readily come forth from the numerous men and women who have come under the influence of this giant among silent and selfless workers or who have profited by his labours of a lifetime.

12th April, 1928

PLACE OF KHADI

BY M. K. GANDHI

Lovers of Khadi have been writing to me energetically warning me against coquetting with mill-owners in the vain hope, as they call it, of securing their active co-operation on terms beneficial to the nation in the prosecution of the campaign of boycott of foreign cloth. I appreciate their warning.

Some of them are tried and experienced workers in the Khadi movement. But I do not give up hope of the mill-owners some day or other coming round to the national view. After all as an out-and-out believer in the method of non-violence, I may not let a single opportunity slip of converting the mill-owners to the nationalistic view, even as I may not pass by a single occasion of converting Englishmen to the Indian view of India's good. After all if we are to win our freedom by non-violent means, we shall have to knock at the doors of those who put obstacles in its way and plead with them to remove them. And even as in a bloody revolution those who are supposed to stand in the way are made to pay the last penalty whether they are countrymen or otherwise, so in a non-violent revolution are they, whether countrymen or foreigners, required to face Satyagraha, if they will not listen to reason and will obstinately stand in the way.

I therefore see no harm in having stated the conditions on which mill-owners can co-operate with the nation. It would have been wrong not to have done so. And if they accept the terms I know that Khadi (*i. e.*, the masses) has nothing to lose. For if the mills work not for exploiting the masses as they now do, but for serving them, they will supplement the products of the cottage spinning wheel and the handloom and not supersede them as they now do. There is no doubt, that if they hesitate to accept the terms stated by me, they will do so because the logical consequence repels them even as the logical consequence of Englishmen really becoming servants of the nation repels them. I would therefore ask Khadi-lovers not to be afraid of my so-called 'coquetting.' If we are strong in our faith, if Khadi has the inherent vitality we claim for it, if it is the need of the masses, and if we persist in our effort with them, they will not fail to realise it. Khadi will fail only when Khadi-lovers falter in their faith or if their faith is based on a mere shadow, *i. e.*, if there is no grinding poverty among the masses, if they have no leisure hours during the year, or if, though they have spare hours, the spinning wheel is not the most suitable and practicable occupation conceivable for many millions.

It is because of the implicit faith I have in Khadi in terms of the propositions just stated and of the strength born of that faith that I am 'coquetting' with the mill-owners. It is quite likely, it is perhaps now practically certain, that no immediate goodwill come out of these negotiations. But they will serve for further action or guidance if we have not meanwhile already achieved boycott of foreign cloth.

It is therefore profitable to inquire even at the risk of repetition what place Khadi has in any scheme of boycott. In my opinion, boycott of foreign cloth is both necessary and feasible only because it affects and benefits the masses and can be achieved only if they co-operate. Boycott of foreign cloth would have but a temporary value if it could be obtained solely by the indigenous mills. And I hold it to be impossible in the near future to enforce the boycott through the single agency of mills. In my opinion, it is Khadi alone that has made such boycott a practical proposition. Indeed it is so practical that if politically-minded India were to take up the sales of Khadi, it is possible to manufacture in a year all the Khadi that may be required by the nation even though there may be not a single yard of mill calico foreign or indigenous available. I affirm this on the basis of the assumption that the villages will mostly manufacture their own Khadi and the organised centres will manufacture for those who are not selfspinners. Experience of past seven years shows that if there is a sudden famine of cloth in the country and if the masses are encouraged they have sufficient skill and the indigenous machinery for manufacturing their own Khadi. No doubt a revolutionary change in the mental outlook and sartorial tastes of politically-minded India is necessary. I have no doubt that if the bulk of them do not respond now, they will have to do so when they realise that Khadi has become irresistible. And to make it irresistible Khadi-workers have to work away with steadfastness, honesty, scientific skill and precision. I have 'coquetted' with mill-owners and discussed the possibility of immediate boycott of foreign cloth in association with them, in order to show that if they mean it they can give themselves the privilege of serving the nation at the same time that they serve themselves. Meanwhile let none doubt that Khadi is silently and imperceptibly revolutionising the national taste and will bring about the boycott in its own good time, if it is not anticipated by some such combination as I have ventured to suggest.

12th April, 1928

BREACH OF PROMISE?

BY M. K. GANDHI

When I was in Berhampur, Ganjam District, last year, I was taken to a temple which I was told was open to all including the so-called 'untouchables'. I was accompanied by some 'untouchable' friends. A few weeks after I received a letter that the trustees had declared prohibition against the entry of 'untouchables.' I was loath to believe the statement. I, therefore, inquired and here is the reply to my inquiry:

> "With reference to your letter dated 22—3—'28, I beg to state that the so-called 'untouchables' are still excluded from the Raghunath temple at Berhampur, and Sr. T. Jaganaikulu Naidu, Retired Nazar, Dt. Court, Ganjam, the trustee of the temple who invited you, is putting more restrictions than before you visited the temple as for the so-called untouchables who approach to offer their pooja to Raghunath. The leaders of the town are quite indifferent to this question even though appeal was made by the Patitapavan Mission through the press and the platform. The so-called untouchables are slowly losing faith in the movement of untouchability carried on by the Congress. A note from your pen may now awaken them to their responsibilities."

If the information is correct, it is a clear breach of promise by the trustees—a promise that was publicly made not merely to me but to the public of Berhampur through me. I wonder whether the trustees have any defence or explanation to offer. The 'untouchables' have undoubtedly a clear case for offering Satyagraha in this case. I do hope however that the public of Berhampur will redeem their self-respect by insisting on removal of the bar, if the bar does as a matter of fact exist.

12th April, 1928

SOUTH AFRICA INDIANS

By M. K. Gandhi

The following letter dated 24th February, 1928, addressed on behalf of the Minister of the Interior to the Secretary, South African Indian Congress, records the concession granted by the Union Government regarding the alleged fraudulent entries:

"I have the honour to acknowledge receipt of your letter dated the 6th January, 1928, in which you convey to the Honourable the Minister of the Interior the following resolution passed at the eighth session of the South African Indian Congress, held at Kimberley in January 1928:

'That this eighth session of the South African Indian Congress in conference assembled as representing the Indian Community of South Africa hereby assures the Union Government on its own behalf and also on behalf of its constituent bodies, *viz.*, the Transvaal Indian Congress as representing the Indian Community of the Transvaal, the Cape British Indian Council as representing the Indian Community of the Cape Province and the Natal Indian Congress representing the Indian Community of Natal, that it will stand by and will generally honour the Agreement arrived at between the Indian and Union Governments at Cape Town, in the spirit in which it has been conceived and declares as it has always done that it will not tolerate any illicit entry of Indians into the Union.'

"In view of this assurance, and as an act of grace to

mark the appointment of the Right Honourable V. S. S. Sastri, P. C., as the first Agent of the Government of India in the Union, the Union Government has been pleased to refrain from the full enforcement of Section 10 of Act 22 of 1913 as amended by Section 5 of Act 37 of 1927, in the case of an Indian who proves to the satisfaction of the Minister of the Interior that he entered a Province of the Union other than the Orange Free State prior to the 5th July 1924, subject to the following provisions;

"(a) Every Indian who has illicitly entered the Union must apply on his own behalf or through the South African Indian Congress or a body affiliated thereto in the Transvaal to the Commissioner for Immigration and Asiatic Affairs, Pretoria, and in the Cape and Natal Provinces to the Principal Immigration Officers at Cape Town and Durban respectively, and shall furnish such particulars as may be required by these officers. Such application must reach the officers mentioned on or before the 1st October, 1928. Indians who are in possession of registration certificates or certificates of domicile or other documents authorising them to enter, reside or remain in the Union or any Province thereof, obtained by fraudulent representations made by them or on their behalf, must apply for the Protection Certificate or authorisation to retain the documents in their possession referred to in paragraph (b) hereof.

"(b) If the Minister is satisfied that an applicant comes within the terms of this concession he will direct that a Protection Certificate be issued to the applicant in the prescribed form or authorise him to retain the documents illegally obtained. No application will be entertained from any individual whose case does not fall within the terms of this concession.

"(c) The Protection Certificate or the documents he has been authorised to retain under pargraph (b) above will preserve to the holder all the rights enjoyed by him.

at the date of the commencement of Act 37 of 1927, *viz.*, 5th July, 1927, and the holder will be regarded as having entered the Province concerned in terms of Section 25 of Act No. 22 of 1912; but if he has not already brought his wife and (or) children to the Union such wife and (or) children will not be admitted.

"(d) An Indian whose entry into the Union or any Province thereof was illegally made, and who, after the 1st November 1928, is not in possession of a Protection Certificate or who has not been authorised to retain his documents in terms of paragraph (b) above will be dealt with in accordance with the Law irrespective of the date of his entry.

"(e) The Minister reserves the right to apply the provisions of the Immigration Law in the case of an Indian who illicitly entered the Union prior to the 5th July, 1924 and who has after that date been convicted of a deportable offence.

You are authorised to publish this letter if you so desire."

If the condition regarding wives and children in clause (c) of the letter is not over-strictly enforced the concession should work well.

19th April, 1928

OFF THE TRAIL

BY M. K. GANDHI

Remarkable are the attempts made by and on behalf of the Government to befog people's minds and take them away from the main point by raising side issues and discovering or professing to discover flaws in evidence produced in support of the main point. It does not suit the Government to admit that its history is a history of the ruin of India's industries and India's manhood. One of such recent attempts is to discredit the oft-told story in the press and on the platform about the cutting off by the weavers of their own thumbs in order to escape the East India Company's myrmidons who sought to compel them to wind silk. If the weaver has no thumb he cannot do the work expected of him. And the way the history has been discredited is by digging out the credentials of William Bolts on the strength of whose evidence the late Ramesh Chandra Dutt first made the statement regarding the cutting off of thumbs. The writer of the refutation is not able to say that William Bolts gave false evidence, but he says that Williams Bolts had no character to keep and that therefore his evidence is not worthy of credence. And he further says, that he was a dismissed servant of the Company under its resolution which described him as 'a very unworthy and unprofitable servant of the Company, his conduct has been distinguished by a tenacious adherence to those pernicious principles relative to the rights of inland trade, in which he appears to have been so conspicuously oppressive.' Who does not know the tricks of pettyfogging lawyers to discredit witnesses by proving their bad character as if a man with a bad character was ever incapable of making a true statement? I make bold to say that whatever the character of William Bolts, his testimony about the cutting off of thumbs need not be discredited unless it can be otherwise disproved, and there has been nothing brought forward to show that that testimony is unworthy to be believed. On the contrary, what is more likely than that weavers in order to escape harrowing and continuous oppression would once for all render themselves physically unfit to do the work imposed upon them under unbearable punishment? After all the evidence of William Bolts is only part of the story of the ruin of India's industries told by Ramesh Chandra Dutt with such deadly effect and supported by the evidence of a variety of witnesses, the cumulative effect of whose evidence becomes irresistible. The main point is whether the industry was or was not ruined with the greatest deliberation. If it was, it makes little difference if the evidence of one witness is rejected and it will lie ill in the mouth of the criminal to say that out of a hundred witnesses one has told an untruth. But as I have said in this instance, there is nothing relevant brought forward to show that William Bolts' testimony is not to be believed. Let me however put before the reader a few relevant extracts from Dutt's first volume on the *Economic History of India*. He says:

> "It will appear from the facts stated in the last two chapters that large portions of the Indian population were engaged in various industries down to the first decade of the nineteenth century. Weaving was still the national industry of the people; millions of women eked out the family income by their earnings from spinning; and dyeing, tanning, and working in metals also gave employment to millions. It was not, however, the policy of the East India Company to foster Indian industries. It has been stated in a previous chapter, that as early as 1769, the Directors wished the manufacture of raw silk to be encouraged in Bengal, and that of silk fabrics discouraged. And they also directed that silk-winders should be made to work in the Company's factories, and prohibited from working outside 'under severe penalties by the authority of the Government.' This mandate had its desired effect. The manufacture of silk and cotton goods declined in India, and the people who had exported these goods to the markets of Europe and Asia in previous centuries began to import them in increasing quantities."

So much was the importation of silk and cotton goods from England stimulated by these methods that whereas in 1794 it was £ 156, in 1813 it rose to £ 108,824. In 1813 the Company's charter was renewed and important evidence was taken at the enquiry prior to renewal. "In respect of Indian manufactures," says the author, "they—the Commons—sought to discover how they could be replaced by British manufactures, and how British industries could be promoted at the expense of Indian industries."

The commercial policy of England is thus described by Henry St. George Tucker:

> "What is the commercial policy which we have adopted in this country with relation to India? The silk manufactures and its piecegoods made of silk and cotton intermixed have long since been excluded altogether from our markets; and of late, partly in consequence of the operation of a duty of 67 per cent., but chiefly from the effect of superior machinery, the cotton fabrics, which hitherto constituted the staple of India, have not only been displaced in this country, but we actually export our cotton manufactures to supply a part of the consumption of our Asiatic possessions. India is thus reduced from the state of a manufacturing to that of an agricultural country."

Here is another testimony of the same character by H. H. Wilson:

> "It is also a melancholy instance of the wrong done to India by the country on which she has become dependent. It was stated in evidence (in 1813) that the cotton and silk goods of India up to the period could be sold for a profit in the British market at a price from 50 to 60 per cent. lower than those fabricated in England. It consequently became necessary to protect the latter by duties of 70 and 80 per cent. on their value, or by positive prohibition. Had this not been the case, had not such prohibitory duties and decrees existed, the mills of Paisley and Manchester would have been stopped in their outset, and could scarcely have been again set in motion, even by the power of steam. They were created by the sacrifice of the Indian manufacture. Had India been independent, she would have retaliated, would have imposed prohibitive duties upon British goods, and would thus have preserved her own productive industry from annihilation. This act of self-defence was not permitted her; she was at the mercy of the stranger. British goods were forced upon her without paying any

duty, and the foreign manufacturer employed the arm of political injustice to keep down and ultimately strangle a competitor with whom he could not have contended on equal terms."

According to Thomas Munro "the Company's servants assembled the principal weavers and placed a guard over them until they entered into engagements to supply the Company only."

The author then proceeds:

"When once a weaver accepted an advance he seldom got out of his liability. A peon was placed over him, to quicken his deliveries if he delayed, and he was liable to be prosecuted in the courts of justice. The sending of a peon meant a fine of one anna (about 1½ d.) a day on the weaver, and the peon was armed with a rattan, which was not unoften used to good purpose. Fine was sometimes imposed on the weavers, and their brass utensils were seized for its recovery. The whole weaving population of villages were thus held in subjection to the Company's factories. . . . The control under which the weaver population was held was not merely a matter of practice, but was legalised by Regulations. It was provided that a weaver who had received advances from the Company, 'shall on no account give to any other persons whatever European or Native, either the labour or the produce engaged to the Company;' that on his failing to deliver the stipulated cloths, 'the Commercial Resident shall be at liberty to place peons upon him in order to quicken his deliveries;' that on his selling his cloths to others, the weaver 'shall be liable to be prosecuted in the *Dewani Adalat*;' that 'weavers, possessed of more than one loom, and entertaining one or more workmen shall be subject to a penalty of 35 per cent. on the stipulated price of every piece of cloth that they may fail to deliver according to the written agreement;' that 'landlords and tenants are enjoined not to hinder the Commercial Residents or their officers from access to weavers;' and that they 'are strictly prohibited from behaving with disrespect to the Commercial Residents of the Company'."

Is it to be wondered at if weavers living under such intolerable restraint broke loose from it by cutting off their own thumbs? To revive an industry that was thus deliberately destroyed and which supplemented the resources of millions of people is the sacred duty of every Indian who loves his country and should be considered a privilege by every Englishman who would repent of the grave wrong done to a great country by his ancestors. But instead of repentance, we see a painful persistence in the policy initiated 150 years ago and an equally painful effort made by every means possible to bolster up the wrong.

19th April, 1928

SERVICE OF THE SUPPRESSED

BY M. K. GANDHI

The servant of the suppressed serves both himself and the society, as the oppressor ultimately oppresses himself, and the engineer is always hoist with his own petard.

We were on the point of being pariahs of the world, having treated the bulk of our brethren as untouchables. We are however likely to escape that catastrophe, as the Hindu society is trying to remove this blot in various ways and in many provinces. By far the biggest and most successful of these efforts is perhaps the one conducted by Anasuyaben in Ahmedabad.

I addressed two meetings last month, one under the auspices of the Sweepers' Mahajan and the other a gathering of the children of the Labour Union schools. Most of these children belonged to the suppressed classes. I take the following from the report that was read at the meeting:

"The bulk of the labourers are ignorant, illiterate, badly housed, and in the grip of pernicious customs and vices. Infant marriages are still common amongst them, and 50 per cent of the infants die within a year of their birth. They are also heavily indebted and have to pay as much as 75 per cent. interest. And yet, they are not an inconsiderable portion of the city population, looking to their number and the office they perform. The prosperity of the great mill industry of the city depends largely on them, and hence welfare work amongst them is most essential. The Labour Union is trying to serve them in various directions, but education would seem to be the very basis of the whole effort. Here is a brief account of the educational work that is being done.

"There are at present 10 day schools with 699 students, 75 of whom are girls. 183 of these are Patidars, 60 Musalmans, 456 belong to the various untouchable communities. They are taught up to the Gujarati fourth standard, and special attention is paid to inculcating principles of sanitation, hygiene and temperance. As a result many of them who were never used to bathing and washing regularly do so now. Manual training is compulsory and almost all the students know *takli*-spinning. Carding is also taught in the higher classes and so the schools have for the most part their own slivers. There is a steady improvement in speed, children in the higher classes spinning 100 yards an hour. A successful effort has been made in interesting the children in wearing Khadi, three day schools having all their children Khadi-wearing. The other schools are also trying to follow suit. The schools have stimulated a desire for education and there is a steady improvement in the number on the rolls as well as in attendance. In fact the demand for schools is too great to cope with.

"In order that the children may begin their training in clean and healthy habits from their very boyhood we have a Montessori school also with 50 children, 22 of whom are girls. These spend all their time between 7 a.m. to 5 p.m. in the school. The school has had a most salutary effect on their habits. We wish we could dot all the mill areas with a number of such schools.

"For grown-up boys of promise and character we have been having an Ashram since 1921, the selection being limited to 25, and attention is concentrated on bringing them into very close contact with teachers of culture and character who live all the 24 hours in their midst. All the processes of cloth-making from carding to weaving are taught them, and it is expected that the Ashram will turn out good workers for social reform in their own communities.

"The desire for education has been catching, so much so that the workers in the mills also have asked for schools for themselves. We have 16 night schools with 612 students, 36 Patidars, 100 Musalmans, and 576 belonging to the untouchable communities. The school hours are from 7-30 p.m. to 9-30 p.m. The schools have had a wholesome influence in weaning the students from drink. There is a library and a reading room in each of the two mill areas.

"The expenditure on education was Rs. 33,620 last year, out of which Rs. 6,250 were contributed by the Mill-owners' Association, and Rs. 5,658-4-8 were contributions from various donors. For this we are grateful to all the donors.

"There are in all 45 teachers in the day schools and 38 teachers in the night schools. They take a lively interest in their work and are affecting the lives of the workmen for the better."

I do not know of workmen's children elsewhere receiving education under such orderly and careful organisation and in such numbers.

The mill-owners ought to welcome the enterprise. On the contrary they are reported to threaten to stop the monetary help they are at present giving. I do hope not only that it is a false alarm, but that they will yearly add to their contributions. In doing so I should humbly think they will be doing nothing beyond what they owe to their workmen.

A noteworthy feature of the enterprise is the large contribution of the workmen themselves towards the expenses, the ultimate aim being to conduct these schools wholly at their own expense. This of course presupposes their economic betterment, a stimulation in them of the desire for sacrifice and for the education of their children. In the meanwhile the mill-owners and other philanthropists should keep the enterprise going.

The sweepers' meeting was remarkable for the things it brought to light. I heard them sing their songs with flawless pronunciation. They were comparatively unlettered, but no one who listened to their songs could say that they belonged to the suppressed classes. But they are indebted, underpaid, and addicted to drink. Most of them beg and live on leavings from plates given to them by Hindus of higher castes. Their condition makes the conclusion irresistible that we the so-called high caste Hindus are responsible for their failings, and only the inherent strength of Hinduism is responsible for their good points. Hinduism has helped them to retain some of their culture in spite of the oppression they have laboured under. They would never have been reduced to their present state if we had regarded them as our own kith and kin.

Anasuyaben may carry on welfare work among them, but who will look to their housing? I have seen the hovels they live in. It is the duty of the mill-owners and the Municipality to provide them with better houses, and even if the former fail in their duty the latter may not do so, for better housing is essential as much for the health of the city as for that of the workmen.

I addressed a third meeting which was full of painful experience. There is a suppressed class night-school under the Gujarat Vidyapith conducted by the students of the Vidyalaya. They take considerable pains over the school, which until a short time ago had a very large attendance of *dhed* children.

The teachers thought of the sweepers' children and induced the sweepers to send their children to the school but as soon as these came most of the *dheds* withdrew their children from the school! The teachers therefore turned to me to find a way out of the situation. So I went there. Very few *dhed* parents attended the meeting. One of them whom I tried to tackle said frankly taking his stand on the traditional religion: "How may a *dhed* touch a sweeper?" 'But if the touch of the sweeper pollutes the *dhed*, why should the higher castes touch the *dheds*?' I asked. 'We never ask them to do so,' he quickly rejoined, and floored me.

This is how we are hoist with our own petard. If untouchability had been allowed to go on unchecked, each one of us should have considered the other untouchable and we should have been doomed. But thank God, in spite of the orthodox *dheds* and *banias* and *brahmans*, the snake of untouchability is breathing its last.

The teachers, of course, ought to adhere to their resolve. They should not be angry with the *dheds*, but neither should they let go a single sweeper boy for the sake of *dhed* boys. Let them shower all their love and attention on the sweeper boys, and there their duty ends. Their determination and faith will melt the hearts of the *dheds*, who, as soon as they find the sweepers' children growing in cleanliness and character, will not help sending their own children too. The anti-untouchability worker has to begin at the lowermost rung of the ladder. There are, I know some 'reformers', who are apt to think: 'Better reform and serve our own castes before we reform and serve the *dheds*.' This way of thinking betrays impatience and ignorance, impatience because we fight shy of obstacles, and ignorance because we forget that all other reform of Hinduism is nothing worth until the main reform, *viz.*, the removal of untouchability is achieved. This blot poisons the whole system, even as a drop of arsenic would poison a tankful of milk. Remove this and you open the door for other reforms, retain this and you render other reforms nugatory. The disease of a consumptive unless the root cause is tackled remains just the same whether you remove or do not remove a few abscesses on his body.

(Translated from Navajivan, M. D.)

19th April, 1928

NATIONAL WEEK AT SATYAGRAHASHRAM

The readers of *Young India* are now familiar with the way in which the National Week is celebrated at the Satyagrahashram, Sabarmati. This year too, like the previous years, was one of fasting, prayer and intensive work. Last year marked a new departure in that the women and girls took their first lessons in scavenging during the Week. This year the services of the sweeper have been entirely done away with, and so what was unusual last year was absolutely usual this year. The inmates of the Ashram did the extra intensive spinning over and above their normal work, only the school being closed to allow the children to do their extra carding and slivering for the extra spinning.

The weekly spinning shows an advance over last year, so far as the adult inmates are concerned. The youngsters and children would seem to have somewhat slackened, though individual efforts in all cases show an advance over the previous year, which in its turn was better than the year before last.

Unlike previous years the practice of having some wheels running day and night during the whole week was practically discontinued, it being thought the process ultimately became a feat of physical endurance rather than one of spiritual advance. A number of wheels were therefore run this year for 16 hours by several groups of inmates, some being worked for a day or two for 16 hours by single individuals.

Three youngsters, however, with irrepressible zeal, plied their wheels for 24 hours on the last day, if only to keep the yearly tradition going. The results were creditable, but none of them could approach Keshu Gandhi's record of last year, either in point of quantity or quality. Here are the results:

Name	Yards	Hours	Test	Evenness	Count
Navin	13,481	23	53	87	14
Kanti	12,266	23	55	89	18
Gulab	11,000	22	56	87	15

Keshu Gandhi's last year's record was 15,748 yards in 23 hours, his yarn being stronger than that of this year's competitors. One of the youngsters took it into his head to card cotton for all the 24 hours one day, and performed the feat quite successfully to the astonishment of many. Carding involves more physical exertion than spinning, and even a professional carder finds it difficult to be at his bow for over 10 hours. This youngster was at his for 22½ hours, having carded and slivered 220 tolas of cotton!

I now tabulate the results of the Week's spinning, placing them side by side with the two preceding years:

	1928		1927		1926	
	Yds.	Average per day	Yds.	Average per day	Yds.	Average per day
Adult men	3,29,992	610	2,54,630	589	2,49,943	640
„ women	2,69,520	792	1,58,272	658	2,02,685	846
Youngsters	4,00,044	1,353	4,07,289	1,696	3,16,013	1,449
Children	50,210	433	59,945	624	47,032	465
	10,50,366	812	8,80,136	869	8,15,673	858

The number of spinners this year was 172 out of 182, as against 135 last year and 134 in 1926, there being this year a large number of non-members come to spend some time at the Ashram. This circumstance probably accounts for the superiority of the results of 1926 over this year's. But individual spinning broke all previous records as will be seen from the following table:

HIGHEST WEEKLY SCORE IN YARDS

1928	1927	1926
23,208	26,536	22,840
19,488	18,848	13,600
40,512	27,856	22,992
10,912	10,368	9,708

Expressed in terms of yards of cloth, taking the yarn to be on average of 14 counts, it may be said the youngster who did over 5,000 yards every day spun enough to make two *dhotis* of 5 × 50" and the whole yarn produced during the week was sufficient for 358 yards of cloth of 36 inches width. That gives an average of 2 square yards for each.

I hope the reader will permit me to conclude with a personal note. Ordinarily I do not exceed 225 yards an hour. The week's intensive work found me spinning some time at the rate of 525 yards an hour and normally at the rate of over 450 yards an hour. I admit the wheel was a better one, but I should attribute the very sudden jump in the speed to continuous work and concentration. As it is during the first three hours I spun at the rate of not more than 300 yards, but the speed gradually increased and from the second day it never fell below 450 yards. I am also inclined to think that the fact that most of us managed to spin from two to three hours a day besides attending to our normal work, is an ample demonstration of the fact that no one should find it difficult to find at least one hour a day for sacrificial spinning. Apart from the sacrificial value of the spinning, I can safely say that it is possible for a man or woman to produce at the end of the year 30 yards of cloth of 50" width, if he or she made a point of religiously spinning for an hour a day. I take the speed to be 350 yards or 10,000 yards per month, and 20,000 yards of 15 to 20 counts of yarn is enough for a *dhoti* or *sari* of 5 × 50".

M. D.

26th April, 1928

MY BEST COMRADE GONE

BY M. K. GANDHI

He whom I had singled out as heir to my all is no more. Maganlal K. Gandhi, a grandson of an uncle of mine, had been with me in my work since 1904. Maganlal's father has given all his boys to the cause. The deceased went early this month to Bengal with Sheth Jamnalalji and others, contracted a high fever whilst he was on duty in Bihar and died under the protecting care of Vrajakishor Prasad in Patna after an illness of nine days and after receiving all the devoted nursing that love and skill could give.

Maganlal Gandhi went with me to South Africa in 1903 in the hope of making a bit of a fortune. But hardly had he been store-keeping for one year, when he responded to my sudden call to self-imposed poverty, joined the Phoenix settlement and never once faltered or failed after so joining me. If he had not dedicated himself to the country's service, his undoubted abilities and indefatigable industry would have made him a merchant prince. But in a printing press he easily and quickly mastered the secrets of the art of printing. Though he had never before handled a tool or a machine, he found himself at home in the engine room, the machine room and at the compositor's desk. He was equally at ease with the Gujarati editing of the *Indian Opinion*. Since the Phoenix scheme included domestic farming, he became a good farmer. His was I think the best garden at the settlement. It may be of interest to note that the very first issue of *Young India* published in Ahmedabad bears the marks of his labours when they were much needed.

He had a sturdy constitution which he wore away in advancing the cause to which he had dedicated himself. He closely studied and followed my spiritual career and when I presented to my co-workers *brahmacharya* as a rule of life even for married men in search of Truth, he was the first to perceive the beauty and the necessity of the practice, and though it cost him to my knowledge a terrific struggle, he carried it through to success, taking his wife along with him by patient argument instead of imposing his views on her.

When Satyagraha was born, he was in the forefront. He gave me the expression which I was striving to find to give its full meaning to what the South African struggle stood for, and which for want of a better term I allowed to be recognised by the very insufficient and even misleading term 'passive resistance.' I wish I had the very beautiful letter he then wrote to me giving his reasons for suggesting the name *Sadagraha* which I changed to *Satyagraha*. He argued out the whole philosophy of the struggle step by step and brought the reader irresistibly to his chosen name. The letter I remember was incredibly short and to the point as all his communications always were.

During the struggle he was never weary of work, shirked no task and by his intrepidity he infected every one around him with courage and hope. When every one went to gaol, when at Phoenix courting imprisonment was like a prize to be won at my instance, he stayed back in order to shoulder a much heavier task. He sent his wife to join the women's party.

On our return to India, it was he again who made it possible to found the Ashram in the austere manner in which it was founded. Here he was called to a newer and more difficult task. He proved equal to it. Untouchability was a very severe trial for him. Just for one brief moment his heart seemed to give way. But it was only for a second. He saw that love had no bounds and that it was necessary to live down the ways of 'untouchables', if only because the so-called higher castes were responsible for them.

The mechancial department of the Ashram was not a continuation of the Phoenix activity. Here we had to learn weaving, spinning, carding, and ginning. Again I turned to Maganlal. Though the conception was mine, his were the hands to reduce it to execution. He learnt weaving and all the other processes that cotton had to go through before it became Khadi. He was a born mechanic.

When dairying was introduced in the Ashram he threw himself with zeal in the work, studied dairy literature, named every cow and became friends with every cattle on the settlement.

And when tannery was added, he was undaunted and had proposed to learn the principles of tanning as soon as he got a little breathing time. Apart from his scholastic training in the High School at Rajkot, he learnt the many things he knew so well in the school of hard experience. He gathered knowledge from village carpenters, village weavers, farmers, shepherds and such ordinary folk.

He was the Director of the Technical Department of the Spinners' Association and during the recent floods in Gujarat, Vallabhbhai put him in charge of building the new township Vithalpur.

He was an exemplary father. He trained his children,—one boy and two girls, all unmarried still,—so as to make them fit for dedication to the country. His son Keshu is showing very great ability in mechanical engineering all of which he has picked up like his father from seeing ordinary carpenters and smiths at work. His eldest daughter Radha eighteen years old recently shouldered a difficult and delicate mission to Bihar in the interest of woman's freedom. Indeed he had a good grasp of what national education should be and often engaged the teachers in earnest and critical discussion over it.

Let not the reader imagine that he knew nothing of politics. He did, but he chose the path of silent, selfless constructive service.

He was my hands, my feet and my eyes. The world knows as little of how much my so-called greatness depends upon the incessant toil and drudgery of silent, devoted, able and pure workers, men as well as women. And among them all Maganlal was to me the greatest, the best and the purest.

As I am penning these lines, I hear the sobs of the widow bewailing the death of her dear husband. Little does she realise that I am more widowed than she. And but for a living faith in God, I should become a raving maniac for the loss of one who was dearer to me than my own sons, who never once deceived me or failed me, who was a personification of industry, who was the watchdog of the Ashram in all its aspects— material, moral and spiritual. His life is an inspiration for me, a standing demonstration of the efficacy and the supremacy of the moral law. In his own life he proved visibly for me not for a few days, not for a few months, but for twenty-four long years,—now alas all too short,—that service of the country, service of humanity and self-realisation or knowledge of God are synonymous terms.

Maganlal is dead, but he lives in his works whose imprints he who runs may read on every particle of dust in the Ashram.

26th April, 1928

A MORAL STRUGGLE

BY M. K. GANDHI

I am a husband aged 30. My wife is about the same age. We have five children, of which two are fortunately dead. I know the responsibility for the rest of our children. But I find it difficult, if not impossible, to discharge that responsibility. You have advised self-restraint. Well, I have practised it for the last three years, but that is very much against my partner's wish. She insists on what poor mortals call the joy of life. You from your superior height may call it a sin. But my partner does not see it in that light. Nor is she afraid of bearing more children to me. She has not the sense of responsibility that I flatter myself with the belief I have. My parents side more with my wife than with me and there are daily quarrels. The denial of satisfaction to my wife has made her so peevish and so irritable that she flares up on the slightest pretext. My problem now is how to solve the difficulty. The children I have are too many for me. I am too poor to support them. The wife seems utterly irreconcilable. If she does not have the satisfaction she demands, she may even go astray or go mad or commit suicide. I tell you, sometimes I feel that if the law of the land permitted it, I would shoot down all unwanted children as you would stray dogs. For the last three months I have gone without the second meal, without tiffin. I have business obligations which prevent me from fasting for days. I get no compassion from the wife because she considers I am a humbug. I know the literature on birth-control. It is temptingly written. And I have read your book on self-restraint, I find myself between the devil and the deep blue sea."

The foregoing is a faithful paraphrase of a heart-rending letter from a young man who has given me his full name and address and whom I have known for some years. Being afraid to give his name, he tells me he wrote twice before anonymously hoping that I would deal with his communications in the pages of *Young India.* I receive so many anonymous letters of this type that I hesitate to deal with them, even as I have considerable hesitation in dealing with this letter, although I know it to be perfectly genuine and know it to be a letter from a striving soul. The subject-matter is so delicate. But I see that I may not shirk an obvious duty claiming as I do claim a fair amount of experience of such cases and more especially because my method has given relief in several similar cases.

The condition in India, so far as English-educated Indians are concerned, is doubly difficult. The gulf between husband and wife from the point of view of social attainments is almost too wide to be bridgeable. Some young men seem to think that they have solved it satisfactorily by simply throwing their wives overboard, although they know that in their caste there is no divorce possible and therefore no re-marriage on the part of their wives possible. Yet others, and this is the far more numerous class,—use their wives merely as vehicles of enjoyment without sharing their intellectual life with them. A very small number,—but daily growing,—has a quickened conscience and are faced with the moral difficulty such as my correspondent is faced with.

In my opinion, sexual union to be legitimate is permissible only when both the parties desire it. I do not recognise the right of either partner to compel satisfaction. And if my position is correct in the case in point, there is no moral obligation on the part of the husband to yield to the wife's importunities. But this refusal at once throws a much greater and more exalted responsibility on the husband's shoulders. He will not look down upon his wife from his insolent height but will humbly recognise that what to him is not a necessity is to her a fundamental necessity. He will therefore treat her with the utmost gentleness and love and will have confidence in his own purity to transmute his partner's passion into energy of the highest type. He will therefore have to become her real friend, guide and physician. He will have to give her his fullest confidence and with inexhaustible patience explain to her the moral basis of his action, the true nature of the relationship that should subsist between husband and wife and the true meaning of marriage. He will find in the process that many things that were not clear to him before will be clear and he will draw his partner closer to him if his own restraint is truthful.

In the case in point I cannot help saying that the desire not to have more children is not enough reason for refusing satisfaction. It appears almost cowardly to reject one's wife's advances merely for fear of having to support children. A check upon an unlimited increase in the family is a good ground for both the parties jointly and individually putting a restraint upon sexual desires, but it is not sufficient warrant for one to refuse the privileges of a common bed to the other.

And why this impatience of children? Surely there is

enough scope for honest, hard-working and intelligent men to earn enough for a reasonable number of children. I admit that for one like my correspondent who is honestly trying to devote his whole time to the service of the country it is difficult to support a large and growing family and at the same time to serve a country, millions of whose children are semi-starved. I have often expressed the opinion in these pages that it is wrong to bring forth progeny in India so long as she is in bondage. But that is a very good reason for young men and young women to abstain from marriage, not a conclusive reason for one partner refusing sexual co-operation to the other. That co-operation can be lawfully refused, it is a duty to refuse when the call for *brahmacharya* on the highest ground of pure religion is imperative. And when such a call has clearly come it will have its healthy reaction upon the partner. Assuming, however, that it does not produce such reaction in time, it will still be a duty to adhere to restraint even at the risk of losing the life or the sanity of one's partner. The cause of *brahmacharya* demands sacrifices no less heroic than say, the cause of Truth, or of one's country. In view of what I have said above, it is hardly necessary to state that artificial control of birth is an immoral practice having no place in the conception of life that underlies my argument.

26th April, 1928

TO EUROPEAN FRIENDS

BY M. K. GANDHI

It is not without deep sorrow that I am now able to announce that the much talked of visit of mine to Europe is not to come off this year at any rate. To those in Austria, Holland, England, Scotland, Denmark, Sweden, Germany and Russia who had sent me kind invitations, I can only say that their disappointment will be no greater than mine.

Somehow or other I dread a visit to Europe and America.

Not that I distrust the peoples of these great continents any more than I distrust my own; but I distrust myself. I have no desire to go to the West in search of health or for sightseeing. I have no desire to deliver public speeches. I detest being lionised I wonder if I shall ever again have the health to stand the awful strain of public speaking and public demonstrations. If God ever sent me to the West I should go there to penetrate the hearts of the masses, to have quiet talks with the youth of the West and have the privilege of meeting kindred spirits—lovers of peace at any price save that of Truth.

But I feel that I have as yet no message to deliver personally to the West. I believe my message to be universal but as yet I feel that I can best deliver it through my work in my own country. If I can show visible success in India, the delivery of the message becomes complete. If I came to the conclusion that India had no use for my message, I should not care to go elsewhere in search of listeners even though I still retained faith in it. If, therefore, I ventured out of India, I should do so because I have faith, though I cannot demonstrate it to the satisfaction of all, that the message is being surely received by India be it ever so slowly.

Thus whilst I was hesitatingly carrying on the correspondence with friends who had invited me, I saw that there was need for me to go to Europe, if only to see M. Romain Rolland. Owing to my distrust of myself over a general visit, I wanted to make my visit to that wise man of the West the primary cause of my journey to Europe. I therefore referred my difficulty to him and asked him in the frankest manner possible whether he would let me make my desire to meet him the primary cause of my visit to Europe. In reply I have a noble letter from him through Mirabai (Miss Slade) wherein, he says, that in the name of truth itself, he will not think of letting me go to Europe if a visit to him is to be the primary cause. He will not let me interrupt my labours here for the sake of our meeting. I read in his letter no false humility. I read in it a most genuine expression of truth. He knew when he wrote his reply that my desire to go to Europe to meet him was not for a mere courteous discussion but in the interest of the cause as dear to him as to me. But evidently he was too humble to bear the burden of calling me merely so that in furtherance of the common interest we might by mutual talks understand each other better. And I wanted him to shoulder that very burden, if he felt that truth required us to meet each other face to face. His reply, therefore, I have taken as a clear answer to my prayer. Apart from this visit, I felt within me no imperative call.

I have taken the public into my confidence, as against my wish, the fact that a visit to Europe during this season was under serious contemplation was published in the papers. I regret my decision but it seems to be the correct one. For whilst there is no urge within to go to Europe, there is an incessant call within for so much to do here. And now the death of my best comrade seems to keep me rooted to the Ashram.

But I may say to the many friends in Europe, that next year, if all is well and if they still will have me, I shall try to undertake the postponed tour, under the strict limitations mentioned by me and this I shall do whether I am ready to deliver my message or not. To see my numerous friends face to face will be no small privilege. But let me conclude this personal explanation by saying that if ever I am privileged to visit the West, I shall go there without changing my dress or habits, save in so far as the climate may require a change and self-imposed restrictions may permit. My outward form is I hope an expression of the inward.

26th April, 1928

FOUR MONTHS' WORK

BY M. K. GANDHI

The Vaishya Vidyashram Sasavane which started the constructive programme in right earnest last year has sent the following report of work during four months ending Chaitra:

"We started with carding and spinning. During the four months under report we added ginning and weaving. We have to import cotton from Central Provinces and Gujarat. We have recently purchased 784 lbs. of unginned cotton from Wardha, and the whole of it will be converted into Khadi by the boys themselves. The Khadi department is under Sr. Kane, one of the teachers. He received his training at Satyagrahashram during the last vacation. We have engaged the services of a weaver on Rs. 25. The boys have formed a committee of eight to look after the whole work.

"Half an hour's spinning on the wheel is compulsory for boys of the 5th to the 10th class. Forty wheels are at work. Spindles and other accessories we have to get from Ahmedabad and Bardoli. 40 lbs. of yarn was spun during the period under report. The lowest count was 6 and the highest was 20. The usual speed is 250 yards and the highest speed is 560 yards.

"Boys of the lower classes spin on the *takli*. Their speed ranges from 75 to 100 yards.

"The upper class boys who spin on the wheels do their own ginning and carding. All the three varieties of bows are used. The highest rate is 16 tolas an hour. 60 lbs. was carded during the period under report.

"Weaving has been started only recently. We had 50 lbs. spun during the first half year ready for weaving. There are 3 fly shuttle looms working, one for *dhoti*, one for towels and one for ordinary cloth. Some boys have learnt weaving. During the four months under report 200 yards or 85 rupees worth of Khadi was woven, and the whole has been sold.

"All the teachers of the school are members of the A. I. S. A., and 15 boys are members of the Juvenile Branch B Section.

"The number of habitual Khadi wearers amongst

students is 75 per cent. of the total number and is daily increasing."

The foregoing resume of four months' increasing work is proof, if proof be still necessary, of what earnest effort can do. Where the wheel is reported to have failed, it was not the wheel that failed, but the wheel masters that failed because they had no faith. School-boys all the world over will respond to honest endeavour as the boys of the Sasavane Ashram have done. And from the figures that are published from time to time in these columns, any one who cares can work out an arithmetical calculation showing how many children working say at least one hour per day at the wheel or the *takli* can spin enough yarn to clothe the whole nation. Oh for an imagination that will visualise the simple beauty of the wheel as a sure solvent of the economic distress of the country!

3rd May, 1928

MAGANLAL GANDHI

[In these days of their trial Gandhiji and the Ashram have been recipients of numerous telegrams and letters of sympathy. Needless to say that they have made the cross more bearable, and on behalf of the Ashram I publicly express my gratefulness to all those friends, as it is impossible to reply to all of them individually.

Numerous have been the spontaneous tributes paid to the memory of dear Maganlalbhai. It is some comfort to find that though he was not at all in the limelight his work was appreciated by all alike who agree that his death is a national loss which is irreparable. I wish I could publish all those tributes. I am afraid I can find room for only a few. M. D.]

HIS MATCHLESS TAPASYA

I was stunned by the telegram about the untimely and sad death of Maganlal. Single-handed he managed the Ashram in your absence and alone gave to it its outer form.

The Ashram, the whole of Gujarat, nay the entire country, will be the poorer for the loss.

He was the very soul of the Khadi movement. His loss is indeed irreparable.

How I miss him today. When he went to Calcutta he came to take leave of me. I was loath to give it for I needed him here badly. But when he promised not to stay a day longer than necessary I let him go. I cannot still believe that he is gone. He captured me from the moment I visited the Ashram, and I felt like a blood brother towards him. If there was one person whom I found immersed in work, no matter when I went to the Ashram, it was he. I never found him free. He had an iron frame, but, for the last two or three years, it had begun to betray marks of overstrain and much mental worry.

He built up the Ashram. He took up your burden and toiled tirelessly under it and during the two years you were in jail the entire responsibility fell on his shoulders. It was easy for you to keep all the elements together. Your very personality compelled deference and obedience, but for any one else it was a veritable crown of thorns. But Maganlal wore it manfully, by dint of his self-effacement and austere penance.

As an outsider I could only now and then look in and tried to lighten his load by a word of cheer or sympathy. He felt much relieved.

No one's *tapasya* equalled his, and he was the only person who made an incessant effort to carry out entirely all your principles. You sowed the seed of Khadi, but it was he who from its germination watered and nursed and tended it with watchful care.

For me his help was invaluable in connection with public work in Gujarat. The part he played in flood relief work was simply wonderful. It is a pity he did not live to finish the building of Vitthalpur which he had planned.

It has often occurred to me that today your principles are not making sufficient headway in the country because your co-workers are so imperfect and it almost seems that it is God's will that you should be born again with all your co-workers to complete your mission. May it not be that He has called away Maganlal to prepare the way? His will be done.

VALLABHBHAI PATEL

NO ONE LIKE HIM

Satishbabu and I got out at Barrackpur from the North Bengal Express to go to Sodepur sending Jamnalalji straight on to Calcutta. At Barrackpur we picked up a Bengali paper and saw what we expected least in our wildest fancies—the passing away of Maganlalbhai. I would not believe it until I spelled out the Bengali characters with my own eyes.

In the midst of life we are in death indeed. What a blow to Bapu!

There was no one like Maganlalbhai in the whole circle of Khadi men. I had got to like him beyond measure, straight as an arrow in character, simple as a child, so sweetly reasonable and so gentle that he could bear even with my cynicism and the deplorable weakness for ridicule I so often displayed. It is a terrible loss to us all. Babu may be the Ashram's grandfather. But Maganlalbhai was like an eldest son and what loss is so great and what sorrow so keen to a mother as the death of one's first born? Maganlalbhai was so truly Bapu's right hand and he is gone. No one can replace him. Where is the faith, the discipline, the unalterable purpose, the simplicity of character, the balance and the purity? C. R.

ONE TRUE STEADFAST SOLDIER

Yesterday in the paper I read of the passing away of Maganlalbhai and could hardly believe my eyes. So has gone out of the struggle one true steadfast soldier, better than whom there are few amongst our people. I see that strong, clean, manly face and figure going about silently with flashing eyes and that bright smile lighting up the face when occasion arose, and all the time one felt that the fire of your ideals burnt brightest because he never showed it. I know what place he occupied in your heart and though I feel like bringing a drop of water into the ocean, I feel that you will understand my feeble attempt to tell you that I am aware of the shadow that must pass over those sad world-embracing eyes of yours, though your soul is quite sure that you are one with him across the barriers.

NARGIS CAPTAIN

SEVERE LOSS

Your telegram telling of Maganlal's death came this afternoon. From Chhaganlal I had heard of his illness, but I thought his rugged constitution would carry him through safely.

I am exceedingly sorry. He was the first Indian friend I had after coming to this country and a finer friend no one could ask for. I did love him much. Such charm, tact, kindness, cheerfulness, humility, steadfastness, persistence, enthusiasm, earnestness, carefulness, intellectual curiosity and zeal and candour, understanding, breadth of mind and of sympathy, faith! He was a fine strong man. We will all miss him greatly, and the loss to the Khadi movement is severe.

GOVIND (Richard Gregg)

3rd May, 1928

CLERKS *v.* WORKINGMEN

BY M. K. GANDHI

Sheth Ranchhodlal Amritlal has sent me the following scheme of Industrial Insurance for clerks:

> " Workingmen's condition, their wages, their needs etc. are a constant subject of enquiry in these days in this as well as in foreign countries, but no one seems to take any interest in the welfare of the clerks supposed to belong to the middle classes. These clerks are considerably worse off than workingmen. In a family of four to six members there is only one wage-earner who starts life with 30 rupees a month and ends with 60. Much of his misfortune is due

to the social status of which he is the victim. On the death of the single bread-winner his wife and children are reduced to a plight very near starvation. To say nothing of his ever becoming rich, the clerk's life is one long-drawn-out agony of anxiety as to how to keep body and soul together. A trifling increment of Rs. 2 or Rs. 3 tempts him to change masters now and then, and he has hardly a record of long unbroken service in one firm.

"The following measures are suggested for the betterment of the clerks' lot:

1. Service to be as permanent as possible.
2. Cheap grain and cloth shops to be provided by the employers.
3. Free medical aid.
4. Houses at cheap rent.
5. Provision of education for their children.
6. Loans at moderate rates of interest.
7. Insurance schemes making provision for dependents after the death of the employee.

"The first six would seem to be eminently easy to introduce, but the seventh should be also no less easy and beneficial. The Ahmedabad New Cotton Mills Company is seriously considering the scheme and a concrete step is likely to be taken immediately.

"The industrial insurance scheme would seem to be very effective. Under it every clerk of the mill would have his life insured for Rs. 1,500, trifling fractions of the monthly salary being charged as premium, somewhat as under:

"No premium for clerks drawing under Rs. 50 p m
For those drawing Rs. 51 to 75 Re. 0-15 p.m.
For those drawing Rs. 76 to 100 Rs. 1-6 p.m.
For those drawing Rs. 101 to 150 Rs. 1-8 p.m.
For those drawing Rs. 151 to 250 Rs. 2-0 p m.
For those drawing over Rs. 251 Rs. 2-4 p.m.

"In addition to this the mill will pay a bonus of

Rs. 1,200 annually which will be distributed to the members of the family of the clerk deceased during the year. It has been ascertained that the average annual mortality is 1 among 60, so that each deceased's family is likely to get an extra Rs. 1,200. How this sum is to be utilised and distributed to the members of the deceased's family will be decided by the Insurance Board, but in no case will any part of it be permitted to be applied to post mortem dinner or other questionable expenses.

"I hope all the mills in the country would follow suit."

I understand little of insurance, but I take it that in this age of insurance any scheme of industrial insurance devised for the benefit of the clerical workers would be to their good. Only an insurance expert can offer helpful criticism of the scheme, and I take it that Sjt. Ranchhodlal has framed the scheme in consultation with some large-hearted expert.

There cannot be two opinions as to the fact that mill-owners, no less than other business and commercial firms, ought to take a paternal interest in the welfare of their employees. The relations between the employer and the employee have been up to now merely those of the master and servant, they should be of father and children. I therefore welcome the scheme.

Medical relief should not, in my opinion, be free. It should be genuine, prompt and cheap. Free aid is likely to undermine their independent spirit. Sometimes free aid is rendered perfunctorily and sometimes it is abused, from both of which evils the clerks should be saved.

The main grievance of the clerk and the workingman is low pay and indifference to his welfare. The measures suggested in the scheme will be a direct and simple redress of the grievance, and I welcome them.

The condition of clerks is in certain respects, undoubtedly much more pitiable. I have a vivid picture of their condition before my mind. It was given to me in 1915 in Calcutta by the Marwadi Clerks' Association. It was a tragic tale of their helplessness. The number of clerks is small, their power of endurance and their capacity for union is feeble. Whereas the clerk is the only earning member of his family, practically all the members of the workingman's family are wage-earners. The clerks must bestir themselves to improve their own condition. They must unite, and must educate their dependents, especially their wives, to engage in some gainful occupation. They have lost all self-confidence and are helpless. Those who are honest, competent in their work, conscientious and hard working need not despair of finding a suitable situation.

True social economics will teach us that the workingman, the clerk and the employer are parts of the same indivisible organism. None is smaller or greater than the other. Their interests should be not conflicting but identical and interdependent.

(Translated from *Navajivan* by M. D.)

3rd May, 1928

NECESSITY OF DISCIPLINE

By M. K. Gandhi

Some workers in the Khadi service write:

"By Head Office circular dated the 20th ultimo, we the workers of this Head Office were notified to come punctually at 6.30 and leave the office at 10 in the morning and to attend at 2 and leave at 6.30 in the evening. Some of us who reside two miles off from the Ashram felt it very difficult to go and come in the hot sun especially in these days of the year. As it injured our health due to irregularity of meals, we requested the Secretary to change the time which he flatly refused to do. Anyway, though we tried to be punctual, sometimes we went a few minutes late and were marked absent. Now, when we were marked absent we again wrote to him explaining our difficulties and requested him to change the time so as to suit us and we requested him also to cancel the previous absences marked owing to late-coming. We received no reply to our notice. So we refrained from going to the office. Though he himself resides just a furlong from the Ashram, even having a departmental cycle, he could not be punctual in this respect; but we were required in an authoritative manner to be punctual. You say, 'Khadi is sacred service to '*Daridranarayan*.' If it signifies so much sacredness, why should this inferiority and superiority prevail among workers in the same field?"

Here there is an obvious confusion of ideals. Distorted notions of superiority and inferiority have given rise to indiscipline in almost all the national organisations. Many people think that to abolish distinctions of rank means passport to anarchy and licence. Whereas the meaning of abolition of distinctions should be perfect discipline,—perfect because of voluntary obedience to the laws of the organisation to which we may belong, *i.e*, the laws of our being. For man is himself a wonderful organisation and what applies to him applies to the social or political organisations of which he may be a member. And even as, though the different members of the body are not inferior to any, they are voluntarily subject to the control of the mind, whilst the body is in a healthy state, so have the members of an organisation, whilst none is superior or inferior to any other, to be voluntarily subject to the mind of the organisation which is the head. An organisation which has no directing mind or which has no members co-operating with the mind suffers from paralysis and is in a dying condition.

The correspondents who have signed the letter I have reproduced do not realise that if they do not accept the elementary discipline involved in giving regular attendance, that Khadi office of which they are members cannot work profitably to its purpose, *i.e.*, service of *Daridranarayan*. Let them realise that the voluntary discipline of a Khadi office should be much stricter than the compulsory discipline of a Government office. If the chief of the Khadi office concerned does not attend always in time, it is highly likely that he is engaged in Khadi work even when he is not at his office. For whilst the staff has fairly regular hours the chief has no hours of recreation. If he is honest and realises the responsibilities of his high office, he has to work day and night in order to make Khadi what it should be. It is one thing to come into a going concern, totally another to enter a newly formed organisation intended to be the largest of its kind in the world. Such an organisation requires the vigilant, intelligent and honest watch not of one worker but of thousands. These workers have to come into being by belonging to the existing organisations and imposing on themselves the hardest discipline of which they may be capable.

3rd May, 1928

THE MEANING OF VOLUNTARY POVERTY

BY M. K. GANDHI

Sjt. Chhaganlal Joshi is the Secretary to the Managing Committee of the Satyagrahashram, Sabarmati. He had a University scholarship for post-graduate study in economics and ever since he gave up that scholarship to take part in the Non-co-operation movement he has been in the Ashram. About a fortnight ago he had a summons from a first class magistrate to appear as witness in a criminal case. The policeman who came to serve the summons behaved most carelessly. He came shouting for Chhaganlal Joshi. This I heard and directed him to Sjt. Chhaganlal Joshi. He gave him the summons. Sjt. Chhaganlal asked him to wait until he had read it, but 'take it if you care' he said and went away.

Sjt. Chhaganlal read out the summons to me. He seemed to be knowing nothing about the case, and he did not know what to do. He had no time of his own, nor had he any money for railway fare. For all his time and money belonged to the Ashram, as every member is supposed to have given his all to the Ashram. The money in possession of the Ashram is all public money ear-marked by the donors for the purpose for which it exists, and could certainly not be utilised for railway fare to respond to a summons. And so Sjt. Chhaganlal Joshi was in the predicament of the pauper of Orissa, the only difference being that whilst the latter could receive and use for himself whatever others gave him, the former could not use a donation except for the purpose of the Ashram. Herein lies the beauty as well as the restraint of voluntary poverty.

What then would an Orissa pauper do if he was served with a summons as in this case? The policeman had not cared to explain to him the meaning of the summons, nor to pay him the railway fare to enable him to go to the court. In the present case the magistrate's court was some miles away from Ahmedabad near a station on the Prantij line. The Orissa pauper would be absolutely helpless and would not know what to do.

So Sjt. Chhaganlal decided to sit still and suffer the consequences. Otherwise his voluntary poverty would have no meaning, nor could he serve the poor if he did not behave like them.

This inevitable inability to respond to the summons was interpreted by the magistrate as contempt of court and he issued a warrant of arrest against Sjt. Joshi. The man serving the warrant said: 'We will not arrest you, if you promise to attend on the due date.'

'I would willingly promise,' said Sjt. Joshi, 'provided I get the railway fare and allowance.'

The man had no authority to make the payment and so he produced Sjt. Joshi before a first class magistrate in Ahmedabad. The latter had no time to go into the case. Sjt. Joshi explained how he failed to obey the summons, but the magistrate trained in the traditions of the bureaucracy said:

'I am afraid I can do nothing. I am prepared to release you on bail, and you may if you like agitate later on.'

If he was prepared to give bail, without getting the fare and the allowance, why should he not have obeyed the original summons?

The sun was blazing overhead when Sjt. Joshi was ordered to proceed to the police station. He refused any longer to walk and the policemen in charge were compelled to hire a carriage. Ultimately Sjt. Joshi was taken to Talod under a full police escort and produced before the magistrate. The moment the magistrate saw Sjt. Joshi he realised his mistake, paid him the fare and allowance and released him on parole.

It is reported that this simple act of courage had a very good effect on the people of Talod who were greatly delighted.

Those who have accepted voluntary poverty can by acting in the manner of Chhaganlal Joshi easily hasten the end of the injustice and tyranny that seems today to be the lot of the poor.'

The thoughtless discourtesy of the magistrate in the case was remarkable. He issued the summons without the least inquiry and having done so did nothing to provide the man summoned with the wherewithal to obey the summons. I am told that it is not the practice to pay the witnesses' railway fare and allowance in advance. If that is the case, it means terrible hardship for the poor. The issue of warrant in the case betrayed the magistrate's criminal negligence. He had no evidence of the proper service of the summons.

He did not care to inquire whether Sjt. Joshi had at all received the summons. One can only imagine what terrible injustice lies hidden in this Government's department of 'justice.'

It is difficult to say what would have happened in Talod, had Sjt. Chhaganlal been the dumb pauper of Orissa. What a shower of abuse he might have received and how fiercely the magistrate might have bullied him! The man who had been so much sinned against might have been branded as a sinner.

Though the Government is responsible for this reckless

and insolent behaviour towards the poor, one cannot help observing that the Indian officials who behave in this fashion have absolutely no excuse to do so. It is possible that this high-handedness was there even in pre-British days. But a wrong does not become right if it can be proved to be pre-British. And if even Indian officials do not mend their ways, those who have accepted voluntary poverty ought to correct them through Satyagraha.

(Translated from *Navajivan* by M. D.)

10th May, 1928

CAPITAL AND LABOUR

BY M. K. GANDHI

At the request of Sheth Kasturbhai the agent of the 'Raipur Manufacturing Company' Gandhiji performed the opening ceremony of a creche for the benefit of the infants of the mill-hands working in the company's mills. In his introductory speech in which he expatiated on the duties of the mill-agents towards the mill-hands, Sheth Kasturbhai said that it was his visit to Messrs. Lever's Port Sunlight in England that had stimulated his interest in starting some welfare work among his mill-hands. The building was erected at a cost of Rs. 25,000. Gandhiji in declaring the institution open said:

"Perhaps it is quite appropriate that this creche is being opened by one who calls himself a labourer, though let me confess to you that it was not without some hesitation that I accepted the invitation when it was brought to me by Sheth Kasturbhai, not because I did not like the object, but because I was so pre-occupied, and nothing would have pleased me better than that you should have got this function performed by some one more deserving than myself preferably, a mill-owner. But my regard for Sheth Kasturbhai prevailed and I had to yield.

"When I established my Ashram in Ahmedabad the consideration which weighed with me was not merely that it was the capital of Gujarat, nor that it was a busy commercial centre but that it was a great centre of textile industry and I felt that I could reasonably count on the help of the mill-agents and be able to render some service to the city. Today I am glad to be able to say that these expectations of mine have not been altogether unfulfilled. Though I have a recollection of some bitter experiences I have also a number of sweet recollections of my relations with the mill-owners. I have not yet given up hope of Ahmedabad. I still expect great things of it. It has much to accomplish yet, and among other things, speaking as a labourer myself, and as one who has tried to enter into the innermost feelings of the working class I say that Ahmedabad has much to do yet towards the amelioration of the condition of the labouring class.

"My connection with the labour of this place is not of yesterday. It is as old as my first coming to this city, and so I make bold to tell you that you have not yet done your part towards your labouring population. In some cases the labourers have not been provided with even the primary amenities of life. There are exceptions, however. Some mill-owners have made some effort in the direction, and the present one is an instance in point.

"The sentiments about the welfare of the mill-hands that Sheth Kasturbhai has just now uttered before you reflect credit on him and the city of Ahmedabad. Sheth Kasturbhai was delighted with Port Sunlight, and rightly. But Port Sunlight cannot be our ideal. Messrs. Lever Bros. represent to my mind the minimum standard that an employer must do for his employees. To do less would be a discredit. But we cannot afford to rest content with that. We must think in terms of our own civilisation, and if the picture presented to us in the Mahabharat and the Ramayan of the social conditions prevailing in the ancient times be correct, our ideal would seem to go much farther than Port Sunlight. I have read a lot of literature about Port Sunlight, and I am an ardent admirer of their welfare work, but I maintain that ours is a higher ideal. In the West there is still a watertight division between the employer and the employees. I know it is impertinent to talk of our ideal, while the curse of untouchability still stalks through the land. But I should be untrue to myself and be failing in my duty to you, if I did not place before you what I regard as the highest ideal. The relation between mill-agents and mill-hands ought to be one of father and children or as between blood-brothers. I have often heard the mill-owners of Ahmedabad refer to themselves as 'masters' and their employees as their servants. Such loose talk should be out of fashion in a place like Ahmedabad which prides itself on its love of religion and love of *ahimsa.* For that attitude is a negation of *ahimsa,* inasmuch as our ideal demands that all our power, all our wealth and all our brains should be devoted solely to the welfare of those who through their own ignorance and our false notions of things are styled labourers or 'servants'. What I expect of you therefore is that you should hold all your riches as a trust to be used solely in the interests of those who sweat for you, and to whose industry and labour you owe all your position and prosperity. I want you to make your labourers co-partners of your wealth. I do not mean to suggest that unless you legally bind yourselves to do all that, there should be a labour insurrection. The only sanction that I can think of in this connection is of mutual love and regard as between father and son, not of law. If only you make it a rule to respect these mutual obligations of love, there would be an end to all labour disputes, the workers would no longer feel the need for organising themselves into unions. Under the ideal contemplated by me, there would be nothing left for our Anasuyabens and Shankarlals to do; their occupation would be gone. But that cannot happen until there is a single mill-hand who does not regard the mill in which he works as his own, who complains of sweating and overwork, and who therefore nurses in his breast nothing but ill-will towards his employers.

"And where is the difficulty?

"You have told us and it is recognised everywhere that the mill-owners stand only to gain by doing all this. Messrs. Lever Bros. lost nothing by doing all that they did. They felt so encouraged that they even tried to create another Port Sunlight in Natal. As our experience gradually broadens we are beginning to see more and more clearly that the more we give to our workers the more we stand to gain. From the moment your men come to realise that the mills are theirs, no less than yours, they will begin to feel towards you as blood-brothers, there would be no question of their acting against the common interest and the need for having a heavy supervisory establishment over them."

"You have given me credit for keeping the city of Ahmedabad free from a labour upheaval such as Bombay is at present passing through. Well, I cannot quite disclaim that credit, for does any one among you for a moment doubt that things would have been otherwise here, but for the work that Shrimati Anasuyaben and Sjt. Shankarlal have been doing? It is true perhaps that you the mill-owners of Ahmedabad are more tactful than the Bombay mill-owners. In case of an upheaval you do not employ hooligans to crush your men as some employers in the West do, and I fancy that you have deliberately abjured that weapon of suppressing the aspirations of labour. My critics tell me that this is all moonshine, and that you would not hesitate to resort to such means, if you could. But I believe that they are mistaken and I want you to prove by your conduct that they are mistaken. I hope you will help to bring near the time when the sort of work that Sjt. Banker and Shrimati Anasuyaben are doing would be rendered needless and pending that consummation give them all the help, all the encouragement that they need in their work.

"Now perhaps you understand why I have dared to appropriate a little credit for the peace that prevails here today. It belongs not to me but to Shrimati Anasuyaben and Sjt. Shankarlal Banker. They live, move and have their being among the labourers, which I am unable to do. If you aid the efforts of these friends you will find there will not be much need left for erecting creches like this one or for providing medical relief. I do not wish to detract from the merit of these efforts of yours, but I ask you whether any well-to-do man would care to send his children to a creche like this. Our endeavour should be to bring about a state of things under which there would be no occasion for a mill-hand's baby to be torn from his mother, and when a factory hand's child would receive the same opportunities for education that our own children have." M. D.

10th May, 1928

MAGANLAL GANDHI

Letters and telegrams—now from friends in South Africa—are still coming in. Even those who but slightly knew him testify to his selfless work and his unostentatious way. Pandit Motilalji who never knew him intimately gives in a few sentences a vivid impression which was as true about him at the time of his death as at any time of life. "I did not know him very intimately," he says, "but he made a deep impression on me the first time I saw him some years ago. He came one night with two or three others from some eastern district, stayed with me for a day or so and then left. He and his companions refused all the little comforts that we could provide, preferred to sleep on the floor and eat the coarsest food. He struck me as the very picture of earnestness." It is as 'the very picture of earnestness' that he lives and will live in the memories of us all. Those who had the privilege of a close contact with him, however brief, were struck with his supple body which worked without rest and without haste, as also with his character which was 'steel-true and blade-straight.' "My beloved brother Hanumantrao used to say," writes Sjt. Ramaswami who mourns Maganlalbhai's loss as much as he mourned his brother's three years ago, "Maganlalji was a veritable dynamo in the Ashram, knowing no fatigue or surfeit for work, always expecting similar assiduity from his co-workers."

For us, members of the Ashram, it is not possible, at the present moment, to take the gauge of the loss. Every day that passes brings home to us a deeper realization of it. It is not so much the loss of the actual work he was doing—we shall somehow muddle through, as we must—but the loss of the living inspiration that he used to be for us. His life was an inspiration, that in a certain sense, no other life can give us. His presence was our security. He was the noblest representative of Gandhiji and the Ashram. Both were safe in being judged through him.

The *shraddha* ceremony was in keeping with the solemnity of the death of Maganlal Gandhi.

On the *shraddha* day Keshu, who was advised to perform the *shraddha* ceremony in the orthodox style, the chip of the old block as he is, came and said to Gandhiji: '*Shraddha* is a rite of faith. I should disdain to do anything for my father in which I have no faith. Far be it from me to seek to propitiate the departed spirit with untruth or hypocrisy. I should love to do so by doing the work in which he lived and moved and had his being.' Gandhiji's joy knew no bounds. It was agreed that for the three days of the *shraddha* the children should early morning recite the whole of the Bhagavad Gita, the book that inspired and guided the departed, and all in the Ashram who felt like joining them should do so, and in order that all might be privileged to take part in this last rite to the deceased it was decided to have, for those three days, as many wheels running for twelve hours of the day, as it was possible.

It is gratifying to note that Maganlalbhai's aged parents who have thought and lived all their lives in the orthodox way blessed the truthful son's decision and whole-heartedly joined in its fulfilment. It was a pleasure and a privilege and a supreme solace to see the sevent-five year old father sitting in rapt meditation for the hour and a half during which the children recited the Gita. And the stricken widow, no less bred up in the orthodox tradition than her husband's aged parents, accepted the decision gladly and joined in the act of consecration. During the afternoons, instead of cries and sometimes shrieks of grief and agony that are heard in the so-called orthodox Hindu households during the first few days of mourning, Maganlalbhai's house was filled with the melodious recitation from Tulsidas' Ramayan in which his widow and her mother, his mother and his brothers' wives and Kasturba took part. The *shraddha* was thus, we are thankful to say, worthy of the great departed soul.

The greater *shraddha* has yet to come. It can come only if God wills it to make us worthy of our inheritance. May it please Him so to ordain is our heartfelt prayer. M. D.

0th May, 1928

A LIVING EXHIBITION

The Sixth Raniparaj Conference was held in Puna, a little village in Mahua Taluka (in Baroda territory). Puna is a little hamlet with a beautiful rivulet running by, and its claim to have the Conference held there was based on the earnestness of its residents who some time ago made a grant of two *vighas* of land and some material to build a hut with and above all on its Khadi atmosphere. The hut now houses a Khadi Ashram.

It is remarkable that in spite of all the workers being engaged in Satyagraha which is now in full swing, the people managed to hold this Conference unaided and made it a complete success. It is an index of the silent work of the past four or five years.

It was with the greatest difficulty that Sjt. Vallabhbhai had to find one day out of his precious time in Bardoli for these simple people. But he could not do otherwise. There is an indissoluble bond of attachment between them and him.

Five thousand Khadi-clad Raniparaj men and five hundred

women attended the Conference. All these were the covenanters, but those out of the fold whom the Satyagraha campaign has drawn towards their abstemious brethren also mustered strong. For these last there could not be a better education than this Conference.

Before Sjt. Vallabhbhai proceeded to address the Conference he had received a message to say that Sjt. Ravishankar was arrested. That gave him the cue, and he gave an impassioned speech on the part they could play in the campaign. I shall extract just two sentences: 'That you who have the courage to risk your lives in climbing the toddy tree, shooting straight up to the sky without a branch or a stump to afford a foothold,—that a daring people like you should be afraid of people who fight shy of that adventure is incomprehensible. Send your children to our Ashrams to learn the lesson of fearlessness, and at the same time you learn at home the lesson of abstinence from drink and that of self-spinning.'

There were the usual resolutions about Khadi and giving up of drink and of heavy brass and stone ornaments, and a resolution on the part of the people of the Taluka not to help Government in any way in their work of crushing the spirit of the people and putting down Satyagraha.

But the best thing about the Conference has yet to be told. It was the little Khadi Exhibition which was in certain respects of a unique character.

The first was the cotton section. There were two heaps of cotton, one of the usual cotton people keep for marketing,—cotton picked half-raw, and mixed with dry leaves or soiled by earth. The other was a heap of very carefully picked mature cotton from fully opened bolls. There were two volunteers demonstrating by their hand-gins the difference between the two.

The second was the carding section. There were different carding bows exhibited here, and the different processes shown, the results of carding with a thick gut, a thin gut and a medium gut also exhibited, and by the side of these a sample of cotton cleaned and combed and carded with the hand, with all its fibres absolutely separated, resembling a transparent autumn cloud.

The third section was the spinners' section. That did not contain different wheels, as one might expect, but there were spinners, good, bad and indifferent, spinning with slivers, good, bad and indifferent, and showing how good carding is of the essence of good spinning. With the different samples of yarn was also shown the Khadi turned out of them, again a speaking testimony to the absolute necessity of good carding. Then there were spinners busy at their wheels with elaborate history-tickets giving interesting details thus: 'Here is a big landowner who finds time to spin and makes all the members of the family spin and has thus made his house self-contained from the point of view of cloth;' 'Here is a little girl who cards so beautifully and spins her own hand-made slivers. If she can do it, why not you?' And again; 'Some of these women are over sixty and seventy. If they can spin, why not you?'

The fouth section contained hanks of yarn spun by Sjt. Vallabhbhai during the spare moments of the Satyagraha campaign.

The fifth section showed the cloth values of different qualities of yarn, and exhibited the various spinning accessories.

The sixth was the weaving section. Here were two youngsters busy at their looms, with their history-tickets. One of these was a son of well-to-do Raniparaj parents, educated for three years at the Vedchhi Ashram. He had during a particular period done Rs. 200 worth of weaving, over and above his household work. The other youngster was weaving a fine piece of cloth. The ticket showed that he was a cowherd a year ago, tending the cattle of a Raniparaj landlord. This landlord was converted to Khadi, and with him his children and his servants including this cowherd boy. His success at the loom was amazingly rapid and speech and look and lustrous eyes made one suspect for a moment the truthfulness of the history ticket,

The last section contained three eloquent equations:

I maund cotton = 7 rupees.

I maund cotton = 2 mill *dhotis*.

I maund cotton = 6 handspun and handwoven *dhotis* 1927 lbs. of good cotton seed best suited for sowing.

This living exhibition was arranged in little huts with walls of handmade thatching, and was perhaps less expensive than the Conference arrangements, and demonstrated more eloquently than a hundred speeches on Khadi what a revolution Khadi has brought about in the life and outlook of these simple, ignorant, guileless people.

M. D.

10th May, 1928

MILL CLOTH v. KHADI

BY M. K. GANDHI

A friend writes in effect:

> "Several Congressmen are now-a-days advocating the use of indigenous mill cloth side by side with Khadi. There is a movement to give mill cloth a place in Congress Khadi shops. Will you not give your clear opinion on this point? I know what it is but all Congress workers do not. They would like to have your guidance especially in view of your recent articles on the part the indigenous mills may play in the boycott movement."

The Congress resolutions on Khadi are unequivocal. For those therefore who wish to respect them there is no course open but to avoid the use of cloth manufactured in our mills. But in these days of growing anarchy, it is idle to quote Congress resolutions either to support or to oppose particular conduct on the part of Congressmen.

Let us therefore re-examine the question of Congressmen optionally using indigenous mill cloth in the place of foreign cloth, or hawking such mill cloth. We know the experience of Bengal. The Swadeshi movement of Bengal during the partition days suffered a check because of the greed and dishonesty of mill-owners. They inflated prices and even sold foreign cloth in the name of Swadeshi. There is no warrant for the belief that they would behave better on this occasion. Indeed the facts about spurious Khadi that I have brought to light show that the mills will not be slow to exploit the Swadeshi spirit for their own benefit as opposed to the larger benefit of the consumer.

But even if the mills were to play the game, Congressmen will not need to use mill cloth or to advertise it. The mills playing the game means their advertising and selling Khadi, their assimilation of the Khadi spirit, their recognition of the predominance of Khadi over mill cloth.

It must be definitely realised that mills alone even if they wished cannot in our generation displace foreign cloth. Therefore there must be in the country an agency, that would devote its attention, so far as boycott of foreign cloth is concerned, exclusively to Khadi propaganda. That agency has been the Congress since 1920. Khadi production and Khadi propaganda act at once as a check upon the greed of mills and also, strange as it may appear, as an indirect but very effective encouragement to mills in their struggle against foreign competition. Exclusive devotion to Khadi on the part of Congressmen enables Khadi to find a foothold and enables mills effectively to carry on their operations where the Congress has as yet no influence worth the name. Hence it is that the mills have never resented the Khadi propaganda. On the contrary many of their agents have assured me that they have benefited by the Khadi propaganda inasmuch as it has created an anti-foreign cloth atmosphere enabling them to sell their comparatively coarser count cloth. Stop exclusive Khadi propaganda, play with mill cloth and you kill Khadi and in the long run you kill even mill cloth, for it cannot by itself stand foreign competition. In a competition between indigenous and foreign mills the one disturbing factor of healthy mass sentiment will be wholly wanting, if there was no Khadi spirit.

Last but not least the inestimable value of Khadi consists in its capacity for tremendous mass education, mass uplift and substantial relief of growing starvation. Whereas mill cloth affords no work and no financial help to the masses, every yard of Khadi means so much work and money to the masses who are being doubly ruined for want of work and wages. Therefore for every patriotic lover of the country there is no escape from exclusive use of and propaganda of Khadi.

10th May, 1928

MORE OF MILL-OWNERS' GREED

BY M. K. GANDHI

The figures I gave the other day of spurious Khadi manufactured by our mills were for nine months only. I have now obtained them for ten months. Here are the magic figures:

Figures of the production of Khadi, Dungri or Khaddar for ten months, April to January.

	1925-26	1926-27	1927-28
Lbs.	2,58,22,442	3,11,95,169	3,70,36,206
Yards	7,32,44,238	8,54,31,611	10,30,61,072

This shows that they manufactured one crore yards per month meaning at least 20 lakhs of rupees worth of Khadi per month. This means a year's output of genuine Khadi. This is taking money directly out of the mouths of the poor people through a movement that was designed for helping the starving millions. Baseness could go no further. The mill-owners could have served the country if they had made common cause with Khadi and helped it directly instead of trying to kill it by unfair and dishonest competition. Their action is on a par with that of merchants who sell to a gullible public artificial *ghi* claiming it as genuine product. Like the Government they have traded on the ignorance of the people and like all their predecessors in kind they will find, if they do not retrace their steps, that they played the trick once too often. It is possible to fool some people for all times but it is not possible to fool all the people all the times. It should not be necessary for capital to be dishonest for its growth.

10th May, 1928

DEADLY, MARCH OF CIVILISATION (?)

> "Although at the time of writing (1917) foreign cloths are being imported to a certain extent into the Shan States, it is the custom for all Shan women to weave cloth for their own garments and those of their families. . . . The cotton from which the cloths are made is grown locally and prepared by the women. . . In Shan villages nearly every house has a loom made sometimes of bamboo, sometimes of heavy wood, and generally kept on the ground in the open space beneath the living rooms. The raw cotton is prepared by drying the bolls in the sun, extracting the seeds by passing them through the usual small two-roller gin and then opening it out by catching the partly cleaned cotton up from the revolving basket in which it is placed, by means of an instrument shaped like the bow of a violincello. After the cotton fibres have been separated in this way they are made into slivers and wound round a stick about 8 ins, long and ¾ in. thick, from which the cotton is converted into thread by a form of spinning jenny." From *Burmese Textiles* from the Shan and Kachin Dt. Notes from Bankfield Museum, by Laura E. Start. 1917."

But for the hypnotic spell under which the intoxicating education of our times drives us to live, we would consider it a sacrilege to deprive people of their own existing honourable occupation in the distant, vague and often vain hope of bettering their fleeting material condition. If civilisation means change of form merely without regard to substance it is an article of doubtful value. And yet that is what the foregoing paragraph sent by Sjt. Balaji Rao means. Under the guise of the civilising influence of commerce the innocent people of Burma are being impoverished and reduced to the condition of cattle. As Sjt. Madhusudan Das has pointed out, people who merely work with cattle and forget the cunning of the hand by giving up handicrafts are impoverished not only in body but also in mind.

M. K. G.

17th May, 1928

SUPPRESSED CLASSES AND BAGHAT STATE

After all the Rana Saheb of Baghat did receive on the 5th instant a deputation on behalf of the Arya Pratinidhi Sabha, Punjab, consisting of Rai Saheb Lala Ganga Ram, Pandit Chamupati, M. A., Dewan Ram Sharan Das of Ludhiana, Pandit Dharmavir, Vedalankar, aad Lala Shankar Nath, Advocate, Simla, to discuss the situation that had arisen out of the recent attitude of the State in the matter of wearing of the sacred thread by Kolis, reclaimed by the Arya Samaj.

The deputation has been permitted to issue the following agreed statement of what happened at the interview :

> "The members of the deputation thanked Rana Saheb for the cordial hospitality extended to them, and explained the position of the Shastras and the Arya Pratinidhi Sabha in this behalf. His Highness gave a patient hearing to their representation and assured them that his State gave perfect liberty to all well-established religious societies to propagate their religion among his subjects, The members expressed their gratitude for the courtesy with which their representation was heard and the encouraging reply vouchsafed to them and withdrew."

The agreed statement betrays too much caution and great timidity on the part of the State. The State would have gained in public estimation by a frank confession of the wrong done to the suppressed classes and the insult offered to a great religious organisation. However let us be thankful for small mercies. The wrong and the insult will be forgotten if the letter and the spirit of the promise made by the Rana Saheb are fulfilled.

M. K. G.

17th May, 1928

MAGANLAL GANDHI MEMORIAL

BY M. K. GANDHI

The Council of the All-India Spinners' Association passed the following resolution at its meeting on the 12th instant:

> "Resolved that a Khadi Museum be organised in memory of the late Sjt. Maganlal K. Gandhi and that an appeal be made for rupees one lakh for this purpose, the location of the Memorial and other details of the administration to be decided by the Council."

The numerous messages of condolence sent to me from all parts of India and distant South Africa show the place that the deceased found in the affections of the public. A silent worker so good and popular as the deceased deserves a memorial. The Council of the All-India Spinners' Association after deep consideration came to the conclusion that there could be no better memorial to the deceased than that a Khadi Museum be established at some suitable place. The deceased himself had conceived the idea and as was his wont had utilised a room in the Satyagrahashram for a miniature museum. But the manner in which Khadi has progressed requires a permanent and commodious building and a collection worthy of the deceased and the movement. Such a museum cannot cost anything less than one lakh of rupees. Hence the minimum amount of one lakh fixed by the Council. A Khadi Museum to be a house of serious study and instruction is capable of limitless expansion. With one lakh of rupees the Council hopes only to make a modest yet substantial beginning and give permanent shape to the scheme the deceased had in view. In accordance with the response the public may make the Museum may have a full set of books dealing with the past and the present of cotton culture, the specimens of the finest to the coarsest Khadi produced in the past and in the present, the specimens of spinning wheels, handgins, carding bows and handlooms from the most ancient obtainable to the most modern. There may be a plot of ground attached to the Museum where experiments can be made in cotton growing to suit not the world market and the princes of exploitation but the humble villager. This latter was being done by the deceased at the Satyagrahashram. The cotton grown at the Ashram has become very popular with spinners. Home-grown cotton which is well picked and which does not need to undergo the devitalising process of pressing saves immense labour and time for the carder and enables the spinner to draw a stronger thread. These and many other things can be done at the proposed Museum if the response is liberal and exceeds the minimum fixed by the Council.

The machinery to give effect to the scheme is to be the All-India Spinners' Association which is a growing organisation of men determined upon doing solid and constructive work.

The venue of the Museum is not fixed as the Council has a choice of more places than one. Sabarmati naturally occurs first to the mind. And if it is found to be otherwise the most convenient spot, no doubt it will be chosen by the Council. It hopes to make the Museum as businesslike as was the deceased himself. No false sentiment will therefore be allowed to weigh with the Council in the choice of the venue.

All subscriptions will be acknowledged in these columns. Payments may be made either to the Secretary, Sjt. Shankarlal Banker, Mirzapur, Ahmedabad, or to Sheth Jamnalalji Bajaj, 395 Kalbadevi Road, Bombay, or to the Manager, Satyagrahashram, Sabarmati.

17th May, 1928

KHADI IN HYDERABAD STATE

It is a matter for joy that the Princes of India are recognising the place of Khadi in national economy. The latest comer in the line is the Hyderabad State. The Department of Industries in the Nizam's dominions recently sent its inspector to study the technique of Khadi at the Satyagrahashram and sent also two young men to learn the various processes. The young men were not able to finish the course, as the climate and perhaps the life at the Ashram did not agree with them. The point is that a beginning has been made, the inspector Moulvi Mohomed Ali was full of enthusiasm and he seemed to realise as never before the importance of the spinning wheel. Let me hope that the Department of Industries will keep in touch with the Technical Department of the A. I. S. A. and organise the charkha work in Hyderabad in a proper businesslike manner, as it is being done in Mysore, where the other day the Dewan, Mr. Mirza Mahomed Ismail personally inspected the Khadi work being done through the suppressed classes. Sjt. Pujari who escorted the Dewan tells me that he admired the work and appreciated the fact that besides being a supplementary occupation for the peasantry the spinning wheel seemed to give substantial uplift to the suppressed classes.

M. K. G.

24th May, 1928

HISTORY OF SOUTH AFRICAN SATYAGRAHA

Sr. S. Ganesan, the enterprising publisher of Madras, has now brought out a translation from the original of my History, if it may be so called, of Satyagraha in South Africa. The translation has been carefully made by Sr. Valji Govindji Desai. The volume is well printed, is bound in Khadi, covers 511 pages and is rightly dedicated by the publisher to the late Maganlal Gandhi. The book contains 50 chapters and covers practically the whole of the period of my stay in South Africa. Those numerous readers who are following *The Story of My Experiments with Truth* cannot afford to be without this volume, if they will rightly understand the implications of truth as they have occurred to me and the very wonderful and matchless force which I have called or rather which Maganlal Gandhi called 'Satyagraha,' otherwise rendered as 'love-force,' 'soul-force,' 'truth-force,' as distinguished from the force connoted by the term 'passive resistance.' Satyagraha is not conceived as a weapon merely of the weak. It is the strongest force that one can possibly imagine or wish for and is a complete substitution for brute force. Those who will understand how the former worked in South Africa in the face of all odds should possess this volume.

M. K. G.

24th May, 1928

ANDREWS' TRIBUTE

[From the tribute sent by Dinabandhu Andrews, to the memory of Maganlal Gandhi, with whom he had come in close contact, I take the following omitting personal references. M. K. G.]

His humility was so great that he was able almost entirely to efface himself with regard to everything he achieved. No one practised more than he did the command not to let the left hand know what the right hand did, in all his deeds of unselfish loving kindness.

He never concealed anything and was the soul of purity and truth. All the rigorous simplicity of the Ashram he practised in his own person. No one kept more true and faithful to its ideal than he did. He never relaxed its rules in his own favour for a single moment. Even in times of illness he practically tried to keep his own life up to the Ashram standard. He was hardest with himself and tenderest with others.

I have said in the public press, that his greatest characteristic was his humility. This was true of him at all times. In the South African Satyagraha struggle, he had the hardest work of 'carrying on,' while most Phoenix settlers were in prison. It was always the same. Although it would have been easy for him to have come forward, he invariably kept in the background. He was ready to do the most menial work, while others got the full credit for any success. He had a gift for keeping out of sight, while doing the vital and essential things. Of all men I have ever known, he had realised most the words of the Bhagavad Gita:

'Thy right is to the work, but never to the fruit.' This humility was so profoundly deep in his own character, that very few indeed realised what a tower of strength he was.

There is a beautiful phrase in the Book of Isaiah, which speaks of a noble human character in that period, as being, 'like the shadow of a great rock in a very weary land.' Numbers found shelter in the rock-like strength of Maganlalbhai.

His unswerving purity of heart comes uppermost to my mind when thinking of his character. He never swerved for a moment in carrying out what he knew to be the truth. The Sabarmati Ashram ideal is not an easy one to practise in its entirety; and it would have been easy for one, with so many responsibilities as Maganlalbhai upon his own shoulders, to have eased a little his own personal burden of strict fulfilment. But he never did this. He kept the Ashram ideal, in letter as well as in spirit. Few realised at what a cost this was done, and how unceasing was the sacrifice.

His tenderness comes up next to my own mind,—especially his compassion for those whom the world despised. His love for the 'untouchables' was nothing less than a passion. One of my last happy memories of him was a day in the flooded area, in the Kheda district, where he was building the new model village. I watched him that day, dealing with all sorts and conditions of men and women; and my mind went back to similar scenes of tenderness I had witnessed, during the

Satyagraha struggle in South Africa, when he ministered to the needs of the indentured labourers, including the women and the children, serving them with never-tiring patience.

Last, I would mention his perfect genius for everything practical connected with the peasant life of India, down to its smallest detail, more particularly for cotton cultivation, spinning and weaving. He was the main inspirer of all the vast improvements which have been made in the last few years in Khadi. Without him, the whole movement would never have reached the practical efficiency that wins our deep admiration today. He might truly describe himself as a 'farmer and Weaver.' The strength that this gave to the Ashram, in its early construction period and to the whole Khadi programme was quite incalculable.

But, however magnificent his achievement of these practical things, his true greatness lay in his humility and pure goodness. His spirit abides. It is not lost. It has won immortality.

It was a pure joy to me to read in *Young India* about the *shraddha* which Keshu had performed, such as his father loved. My words will reach Keshu and tell him, that the life work of his father must now be carried on by the son.

24th May, 1928

BUYING MERIT

By M. K. Gandhi

A correspondent draws my attention to the institution of lotteries in Goa for the purpose of supporting hospitals. The correspondent tells me that lakhs of rupees are spent by people in British India in these lotteries in the vain hope of suddenly becoming rich without effort and yet gaining heavenly merit. Here is an extract from an advertisement sent by the correspondent:

"Behold the sick. He that giveth to the poor lends to

God. Then why not help our poor by staking a rupee at this drawing? It is a comely way of exercising charity." The advertisement contains a portrait of a hoary-headed reverend gentleman.

It would be interesting to know the condition of the hospitals built with the monies gained from these lotteries. Meanwhile it is worth while to examine the ethics of founding charitable institutions with monies collected by an appeal to man's greed, enhancing it by a promise of merit if the purchaser of such a lottery ticket should fail to get the tempting prize or prizes as lakhs of purchasers must fail.

As it is, the haste to be rich without working and waiting for the happy day pervades the atmosphere. Every one who spends a rupee on the race course or in a lottery ticket erects the pyramid of his hope on the foundation of the ruin of a multitude of such hopes of men and women having equal right with the few lucky (?) winners of prizes. It is difficult, however, to single out the lottery system for criticism, when the gambling spirit possesses even those who are ranked among the most respectable. The share market is nothing but a feverish gamble. And yet who is free from that fever? Every man who finds himself rich in a day by manipulating the share market knows that the sudden accession of wealth means desolation of many a widow's home. Only the relatives of the widows who bought shares had no doubt almost the same kind of hope that the clever speculator of our imagination had.

Cotton, rice and jute are, strange as it may appear, objects of such speculation. The system of lottery is but a crude extension of the same gambling spirit. It is no doubt good to treat the lottery as disrespectable, but it is better to make the acquaintance of the spirit that is common to the lottery and the share market and thus deal with the root cause of the disease rather than its worst symptom. It is, therefore, to be wished that the worst symptom will enable us to reach the root cause and deal effectively with it.

But it is a far off hope. Let not my mention of the pervasive nature of the disease make a single person connected with those lotteries seek justification for his participation in the lottery system.

And the caution is all the more necessary when the lottery is in connection with a charitable institution. Surely, it is bad enough to want to be rich without deserving, but it is positively wrong to connect charity with a gamble. Those who throw away rupees in lotteries must not think that they gain merit even whilst they are hoping to satisfy an unlawful ambition. We may not hope to serve God and Mammon at the same time.

And why do the Christian conductors of the Goan hospitals degrade religion by exploiting the evil tendency of human nature? Do they imagine that they please God by attempting to support a hospital by making lakhs of people morally diseased? Are they not robbing Peter to pay Paul? What will it profit them to heal a few bodies if at the same time they wound a thousand times more souls?

24th May, 1928

TRUE AND FALSE INDUSTRIALISATION

By. M. K. Gandhi

"I cannot accept a merely territorial definition of national wealth. Hoards buried under the earth or in the coffers of a few millionaires are not national wealth. That alone is national wealth which is equably distributed among the millions," said C. R., addressing a typical gathering of intellectual and critical men at Poona.

"You cannot distribute wealth equably *after* producing it. You won't succeed in getting men to agree to it. But you can so produce wealth as to secure equable distribution before producing it. That is Khadi.

"Like a good father claiming that family property should be divided equally among all his children, we want that Agriculture and Cloth must be treated as ancestral family assets in

India and should belong to the millions. Both are ancient industries in which all can take part, and almost everywhere, in the homes of the millions. So these are assets for equal division. We do not object to industrialisation. We object only to false and unfair industrialisation. Have true industrialisation. Do not rob the poor millions of the only means of honourable life and call it industrialisation! Invent and organise a thousand other forms of industrialisation if you can, other than agriculture and cloth-making, which must belong to all and not be monopolised by captains of power industry. No father would object to any member of the family claiming his self-acquisition. So also let capitalists build up special industries. But Agriculture and Cloth must be left untouched as common property, for it is the only asset for the poorer members of the nation.

"'Let the poor go to the mills,' you may say. But no one, who has seen the pitiable condition of the strikers now in Bombay, can fail to see what happens to the poor man who leaves his home for a factory city. After years of toil, the one lakh and odd men now dismissed from the mills at Bombay have not enough in their pockets to pay their fares home, and wish to go in deputation to the Governor for free railway passes. They have saved nothing and have acquired the evil habits of improvidence, drink, gambling, and a loose attitude towards moral restraints. The peasants of India, men and women, are gentle, industrious and good folk, semi-starved and illiterate, but possessing a culture of which any nation may be proud, and to turn such a people into victims of vice is not a good national programme.

"For all these years of capitalistic industrialisation, we have secured work in the textile power industry including all the net-work of gins and presses in the smaller towns to 4 lakhs of men and women. This is not much when more than 2,000 lakhs of souls wait outside. Look at the other picture. In four years, by dint of hard work and public support, we have given supplementary work in their own homes to one lakh of people.

It is not a bad record for the Spinners' Association. Insignificant, you may say; and I agree that it is but a small achievement. It is small, but only as a seed is small. A big tree will grow out of this seed, under which, as under the Indian banian tree, an army can rest. While you cannot infinitely multiply or successfully manage your factories, we can multiply the charkha almost infinitely and make it into a spreading tree to give shelter to all the peasantry in this vast country of ours."

24th May, 1928

SPINNING IN MUNICIPAL SCHOOLS

The Secretary, Khadi Board, Jalgaon, sends me a well-prepared tabulated report of *takli* and charkha spinning in its Municipal schools. The report covers the period between 15th June 1927 and 15th February 1928. 149 girls and 126 boys were spinning either on the *takli* or the wheel. The time allowed was from 25 minutes to 50 minutes per day. The total output was 4,48,000 yards. The maximum speed on the *takli* was 125 yards per hour and on the wheel 325 yards. This is a creditable record. What has been possible in the Jalgaon Municipal schools is possible in all the Municipal schools. It can be shown that if the nation willed it, it could get all the yarn it needs through its school-going children and teach them self-respect and self-reliance during their scholastic life, a period which some falsely think is one of irresponsibility and indulgence. I note that only boys spinning on the wheels do their own carding. The implication is that the others do not. It is being more and more realised that the secret of good spinning is not merely good but perfect carding. This can be attained only if every one cards for himself or herself. If it is learnt truly it is easily learnt. Another suggestion I venture to offer is that no time should be lost in turning all the yarn spun into Khadi and for that purpose either one of the promising boys should be trained or one of the teachers should learn the art of weaving. Failing that the local weaver should be induced to weave such yarn.

M. K. G.

31st May, 1928

UNTOUCHABILITY IN THE SOUTH

Though untouchability appears in its worst and crudest form in the extreme south, that is Kerala, not much, at least not enough, is being done by the reformers in the south to stamp out the evil. They will not even finance the movement to the extent that is necessary and possible for them. When therefore, I started collections during my visit to Calicut amongst the people locally, I was glad to find that the South Indian colony in Bombay signified their intention of making a much more substantial collection than was made in Calicut and giving it to me when I passed through Bombay. In continuation of their promise a deputation came to me in Bombay during my recent visit and assured me that they had not forgotten it but that they were waiting for a favourable season for making the collections. One of them now writes: "Many a young man with meagre salary is wasting his money in races and other city inducements, and if only we could wean them from their present tendencies, much could be expected of them for their own benefit as well as for the benefit of the city of Bombay." I hope that this reform movement will take deep root amongst the South India young men. I would advise them not to wait for a 'favourable season.' For any time is a favourable season for doing good work or begging or giving in a good cause. No cause can be better than the cause of the 'untouchables,' the 'unapproachables' and the 'invisible.' If the young men from the south living in Bombay will only deny themselves some of the costly luxuries such as smoking, races, visits to teashops etc., there will be a fat collection. Every religion enjoins the setting apart of a certain portion of one's income for charitable purposes. Unfortunately, young men nowdays in most cases have given the go-by to religion. But if the practice of invariably allocating a certain portion of one's income to charitable purposes can be revived, causes such as those of the untouchables need never wait for a 'favourable season.'

M. K. G.

7th June, 1928

THE ONLY CURE FOR UNEMPLOYMENT

BY M. D.

Those who argue that by industrialising India we may be able to tackle the problem of India's appalling unemployment do not know that far from being a cure for unemployment industrialisation is one of the direct causes of unemployment and constitutes a menace which is attracting the attention of thinkers and economists. Mr. Brailsford in an illuminating article in the *New Leader* shows how in the republic of increasing wealth and prosperity '*the ultra-modern civilization is victimised by its own progress.* Day by day it can turn out more wealth. Day by day it does turn out more wealth. But it has not learnt the secret of distributing it.' He goes on to refer to the 'bread lines,' *i.e.*, the queues of the destitute who wait outside the doors of the soup kitchens and the offices of charitable societies, ever lengthening out until they block the streets and impede the traffic and analyses the extent of this destitution and its causes:

"The most careful attempt to guess at the extent of the unemployment was published this week by an unofficial institution known as the Labour Bureau. It started from the known figures of the decline in employment in certain industries, and then guessed at the figures in the rest, while deducting—again by guess-work—an estimate for those who may have quitted factories to find work in such thriving careers as the promotion of instalment buying by house to house canvassing, or in the service of every man's motor car. The result can only be a guess, but I believe it is a conservative guess; I have heard able economists arguing for a much higher figure. The chances are that, at this moment, there are at least four million unemployed in this prosperous republic. That means ten per cent. of the occupied population, a high figure for a contented nation to carry. It is, relatively to population, at least the equivalent of our own figure.

"What is the explanation? The odd thing about it is that some of the usual signs of depressed trade are absent. There has been no 'slump' in prices. 'The volume of business,' declares the National City Bank, 'is distinctly above the average.' The index of prices compiled by the Federal Reserve Board, which seems to include the last perfections of statistical ingenuity, shows over a long period an almost uncanny stability. From the beginning of 1923 onward, month by month, this index of the general price level—as compared with 1913—has never fallen below 168, nor risen above 173. It has been all but absolutely steady round the figure 170. One might not be surprised, under these conditions, if special circumstances were to produce severe unemployment in some group of trades, but ought not a steady general level of prices to mean a fairly steady general level of employment? Evidently it does not.

"The explanation is, I think, evident when one turns to the available statistics, which in their way are highly instructive. They have been analysed by a skilful economist, Professor S. H. Schlichter, in the *New Republic*, the one paper which has persistently and ably sought to rivet attention on this crisis. The statistics enable us, over a wide range of manufacturing industries, to measure both production and employment. *The significant fact is that while output has increased, employment has declined.*

"The figure 100 means the average of factory output and factory employment in the period 1923—25.

"During the first ten months of 1927 the index of factory output rose to 107.

"In the same period the index of factory employment fell to 95.

"In other words, with 5 per cent. fewer employees the factories turned out 7 per cent. more goods.

"It is not difficult to read the meaning of these figures. There has been no slump. But the American process of ever-increasing mechanical efficiency is taking its own course.

The restless substitution of mechanical processes for human labour is on the march."

As Professor Soddy, putting it in a different way, has said, 'None of the world's real problems centre today around the mere provisions of wealth. The difficulties arise rather in getting rid of even a small part of what can be made without fighting for the privilege of either making or selling it."

Let us now look at another picture comparable in vividly poignant pathos to some of the pictures of poverty given under a series of articles 'Face to face with the Pauper' in *Young India*. A writer in the *Spectator*—no Radical but a Conservative paper—gives a pen-picture of appalling destitution in a Welsh town.

"Let us tap at the door of Mr. Jones's cottage, and see for ourselves what the family is doing Mrs. Jones is none too glad to see us, poor woman, for she gave the children their weekly dose of physic last night 'and the bedroom's something awful—you can't go in'. So the bedroom, which we shall never see, is worse than this front room!

'It is a small dark place, largely filled by a table on which a litter of white-enamel breakfast cups and plates still stand at noontide. Part of one wall has peeled off its plaster. There are polished brass ornaments on the mantelpiece, and a large number of hangings and decorations, while the rugs on the floor are filthy and moth-eaten. Pictures and knickknacks are strewn on walls, dresser, mantelpiece. One would sweep all these things away if one could and burn or bury them, and then attack the walls with a pail of sanitary distemper.
This is not a typical miner's house, however. Even the friends I have come with are surprised—startled would be more accurate. 'She is such a good, clean woman,' they said to me afterward, 'but she is getting ill from worry and over-work.' I don't know what will happen to her.'

"Perhaps she will have rest in the hospital. She is ash-gray with dark rings under her eyes, and complains of a pain in her back. With a tiny baby to nurse and three children and a hungry husband to provide for, she has o leisure or peace.

"Mr. Jones has been unemployed for four ars, with a few spells of work. His family supports itself thirty one shillings a week. Rent is 7s. 6d. a week for two oms. Last night from nine until seven this morning he was wking at an outcrop, and won two sacks of coal as the reward ohis labour. That is the only exercise he takes. He never goes out except to the coal-pit or the outcrop. At the moment is sitting by the fire, dandling the baby, whose already dark air proclaims his race. Its very brown eyes fix my eyeglass in astonishment, then twinkle with the greatest good humour as it waves a fat hand in my direction. It is accustomed to bright, clean things. Only in the last day or two has a change come over the home. What will be its life during the next few weeks, with a sorrow that I sense hanging over the house? What will it grow? A miner? A millionaire?

"Mrs. Jones is scrubbing an older boy's face. John Thomas is about six: he wants to stare at us, and does, although the soap keeps getting in his eyes. Robert and Doreen, aged nine and ten, stand rather shamefacedly at bay; they know we have come at an inopportune moment, and dislike our intrusion. They know how proud their mother is to keep the house clean. And now—it is different. Something is going to happen; they don't know what, and I don't know. But the Jones *Menage* cannot long continue in its present disorder. Mr. Jones, however, chats away cherfully enough. . . . Mrs. Jones is still scrubbing John Thomas's face, absent-mindedly lathering it over and over again. His clothes are dirty and in rags. One heel is off his boots, and soles of both are worn thin. His face is already burnished like the brass on the mantelpiece; the rest of him remains unwashed. This morning the family breakfasted on bread and margarine and tea with no milk. There is some very unpleasant-looking bacon for dinner—nothing else. For supper bread and margarine and tea again. It is a cold, wet day with terrific wind. I should go mad in a week.

cooped in that cold valley, with the house walls crumbling, the children restless and uneasy, my wife wilting before my eyes. But Mr. Jones is inured to hardship and discomfort; he lives in hope of better times."

Well, this is the condition to which machinery of increased efficiency and more output succeeds in reducing the workingman. It is a picture of comparative unemployment, the American picture is of those who have no work at all and are cast on the mercy of society. If factories are thus already a menace to those employed in them how can they be expected to help the unemployed outside?

It is the restless substitution of mechanical processes for human labour that constitutes the menace, and the only cure lies in reversing the process. Khadi has proved itself to be an effective cure for unemployment outside industrial areas. The time is fast coming when industrialists may have to cry halt and pause to consider whether it may not be a solution for the increasing unemployment within the industrial areas themselves.

M. D.

7th June, 1928

CASH v. CREDIT

BY M. K. GANDHI

The Secretary, All-India Spinners' Association, writes as follows:

> "The credit sales of the provincial branches of the Association amount to Rs. 1,54,488-13-8½ representing 15 per cent. of the capital invested in these branches, and this is in spite of the resolution passed by the Council putting a ban generally on credit sales. This is largely due to the misgivings of our workers. They fear that the sales will go down if credits are completely stopped. The fear is groundless. The Tamilnad has done away with all credit sales, and it after all shows the largest sales amongst

all the Khadi depots throughout India. "You may inform our various branches and the public that past experience shows that Khadi work loses through these credit sales as well by reason of the purchasers making default as by reason of the locking up of capital which is none too large."

I entirely endorse the warning uttered in the foregoing letter. So long as Khadi remains an infant national industry requiring delicate nursing and protection from the public, there should be no credit sales in Khadi depots. We must simply rely upon the support of a patriotic public and if we cannot command cash sales, we may regard the disinclination to pay cash as a sign that Khadi does not enjoy the benefit of public protection. But my own personal experience throughout my extensive wanderings has shown that people gladly pay cash for Khadi when they require and receive credit in respect of their other purchases. To pay cash for Khadi that the people want is the least protection that Khadi is entitled to. Managers of sale depots must not be afraid of losing custom if they do not give credit. They must rely upon their ability to carry on propaganda in their neighbourhood in favour of Khadi for commanding cash sales. And in no case are they warranted in giving credits in spite of instructions from headquarters to the contrary. Discipline demands that if they have no confidence in themselves to carry on Khadi depots successfully without being able to give credit, they should give such notice to the head office and ask to be relieved of their charge. The head office should be trusted to know what is best on the whole for turning Khadi into a business proposition as quickly as possible.

7th June, 1928

INDIANS IN SOUTH AFRICA

BY M. K. GANDHI

Two very important cases have been decided recently by the Transvaal Provincial Division of the Supreme Court of

South Africa. One of them, S. B. Medh v. Immigrants Appeal Board, though important in itself, affects only a few special cases of Indians who received exemption certificates under the Smuts-Gandhi Settlement as being educated Indians. It was contended by the Union Government that the exemptions were not complete. I need not go into greater detail. The Court has now found that the exemptions were complete in the sense submitted on behalf of the appellant.

The other case, Daya Purshottam *v.* Immigrants Appeal Board, has far-reaching consequences for the Indian settlers. The judgment in this case lays down that section 5 of Act 37 of 1927 does not possess retrospective effect. Hence certificates obtained by fraudulent means do not become cancellable at the will of the Immigration Board or the Immigration Officer. If this judgment stands, holders of certificates even though they were originally tainted will remain undisturbed. This is a great victory for the settlers. I have no desire to see fraud in any shape or form protected. But the case of these settlers is not one of ordinary fraud. In many cases, at least up to 1914 the Asiatic Office was a corrupt department and it made it practically impossible for *bona fide* entrants to enter unless they resorted to some crooked means so as to satisfy the greed of the Asiatic officers. Where Government officials are privy to fraud, it ill-becomes that Government to punish the helpless victims.

Cables from the South African settlers tell me that the Government are appealing against the two decisions. I venture to suggest to the Union Government that it would be more in keeping with their conciliatory attitude and the spirit of the new understanding that they do not seek to deprive the Indians of the advantage the two appeals give them. The judgment in the first appeal protects only a few individuals. And in their case there is no question of fraud. The judgment in the second appeal protects a fair number of those who are already in the Union. It will be no serious calamity for the Union to have to absorb a few more Indians than the Government had counted upon. The Union Government should remember that these appeals are very expensive affairs, especially for the poor Indians. It is hardly fair for an organised powerful Government to take successful citizens through appellate courts and thus exhaust them into submission or worse. It may be well to possess a giant's strength, but it is admittedly wrong to use it against dwarfs.

The settlers will do well not to set much store by their success in these two appeals. They have in Sjt. Shastri a great friend and adviser. Let them press their suit as much as ever before him but having done so let them abide by his advice. He will use in their behalf all the influence he has acquired with the Union Government. I welcome their cables. I appreciate the trust they repose in me. But my power to help them from this distance and in the changed circumstances I found myself in 1920 is much too limited to be of value. Their strength therefore lies in their unity, moderation and reliance upon one who is not merely Agent General for the Government of India but is their true and powerful friend and guide.

21st June, 1928

NATIONAL *v.* ALIEN EDUCATION

In the course of his inaugural address to the students of the Vidyalaya and the Vinayamandir which opened after the summer vacation on the 11th instant, Gandhiji delivered an address which is condensed below:

" I trust you have given careful thought during your vacation to the fundamentals recently adopted by the Vidyapith. As I have repeatedly said our strength does not lie in numbers. Not that we ignore them, but the fewness need cause no worry to us. Our real strength lies in a correct understanding, acceptance and practice, so far as it is humanly possible, of these fundamentals. If the students who have remained loyal to the Vidyapith live up to its creed, we are sure to achieve through them the goal that we have set before us, namely, Swaraj

What is needed is sincerity of purpose and fearless pursuit of the principles. I want you to put your teachers at ease and to assure them that you will be loyal at all hazard to the principles for which the Vidyapith stands. Truth and *Ahimsa* constitute the keystone of our arch, and those who have no faith in these have no place here.

"Let us understand some of the obvious distinctions between Government institutions and the national. One of our students has gone to jail in Bardoli and many more will go. They are the pride of the Vidyapith. Much as they may desire to do likewise, can students of Government institutions dare to do so? It is not open to them to go to Bardoli and help Vallabhbhai, as it is to you. They can only give secret sympathy. What is literary training worth if it cramp and confine us at a critical moment in national life? Knowledge and literary training are no recompense for emasculation.

"Again there is a world of difference between our method of teaching and theirs. For instance, we may not teach English in the way they do. We may give a working knowledge of that language, but we may not, without committing national suicide, neglect the mother tongue, and make English the vehicle of our thought. In this national institution we strive to correct the pernicious practice. We must learn all our subjects through the Gujarati language. We must enrich it and make it capable of expressing all shades of thought and feeling. In no other country do we find the state of things we do here. We have paid dearly for having all these years learnt everything through the medium of the English language. We have strayed from the path of duty.

"Then take the teaching of economics. The present system obtaining in Government institutions is vicious. Each country has its own economics. German text-books are different from the English. Free trade may be England's salvation. It spells our ruin. We have yet to formulate a system of Indian economics.

"The same about History. A Frenchman writing a History of India will write in his own way. The Englishman will write it quite differently. The descriptions of battles between the English and the French will differ with the writers who have described them. Indian History written from original sources by an Indian patriot will be different from that written by an English bureaucrat though each may be quite honest. We have grievously erred in accepting English estimates of events in our national life. Here, therefore, there is a vast field for you and your teachers for original research.

"Even our teaching of a subject like arithmetic will also be different. Our teacher of arithmetic frames his examples from Indian conditions. He will thus simultaneously with the teaching of arithmetic teach Indian geography.

"Then we are putting a special emphasis on manual and industrial training. Do not make the mistake of imagining that this training will dull your wit. It is *not* by making our brains a storehouse for cramming facts that our understanding is opened. An intelligent approach to an industrial training is often a more valuable aid to the intellect than an indifferent reading of literature."

21st June, 1928

A NOBLE SOUL GONE

As I am writing for *Young India*, I have a wire from Nilkanth Babu advising me of the death at Sakhigopal of Pandit Gopabandhu Das who was one of the noblest among the sons of Orissa, the land of sorrows and tears. Gopabhandu Babu had given his all to Orissa. I heard of him and his sterling character and steadfastness when Sjt. Amritlal Thakkar was sent to Orissa in 1916 to distribute relief to the famine-stricken. Sjt. Thakkar used to write to me how Gopabhandu Babu braved inconvenience and disease in struggling to help the helpless. He gave up his practice and his membership of the Legislative Council during the Non-Co-operation days and never wavered. What was more for him was to stake the existence of his dearest creation, the Satyavadi School. He braved the taunts of some of his closest friends and persisted to his eternal honour in what they considered to be his folly. His one ambition in life was to see dismembered Utkal united and happy. He had lately become a member of Lala Lajpatrai's society and was planning to make Khadi an efficient vehicle for the economic relief of poverty and flood-stricken Orissa. The country is the poorer for the death of Pandit Gopabhandu Das. Though he is not in our midst in the flesh, he is in our midst in the spirit. Let that noble spirit guide the workers of Orissa, let his death result in a larger dedication to service, greater effort, greater self-effacement and greater unity among the scattered workers who are too few for the national requirements. I tender my condolences to the relatives and the many disciples of the deceased patriot. M. K. G.

21st June, 1928

A SHAME UPON YOUNG MEN

A correspondent sends me a newspaper cutting showing that recently in Hyderabad, Sindh, the demand for bridegrooms has been increasing at an alarming rate, an employee of the Imperial Telegraph Engineering service having exacted Rs. 20,000 as cash dowry during betrothal, and promises of heavy payments on the wedding day and on special occasions thereafter. Any young man who makes dowry a condition of marriage discredits his education and his country and dishonours womanhood. There are many youth movements in the country. I wish that these movements would deal with questions of this character, Such associations often become self-adulation societies, instead of becoming, as they should be, bodies representing solid reform from within. Good as the work of these bodies is at times in helping public movements, it should be remembered that the youth of the country have their reward in the public appreciation they get. Such work, if it is not backed by internal reform, is likely to demoralise the youth by creating in them a sense of unwarranted self-satisfaction. A strong public opinion should be created in condemnation of the degrading practice of dowry and young men who soil their fingers with such ill-gotten gold should be excommunicated from society. Parents of girls should cease to be dazzled by English degrees and should not hesitate to travel outside their little castes and provinces to secure true gallant young men for their daughters. M. K. G.

21st June, 1928

A TRIBUTE

In a letter to Mahadev Desai thus writes Mr. H.S.L. Polak about the death of Maganlal Gandhi :

> "I can fully enter into your appreciation of the disaster that has befallen the Ashram by Maganlal's sudden passing. It was as though I had lost an own brother. You, of course, know far better than I how tremendously important he was to the life and purposes of the Ashram, and how much he symbolised its ideal and practical character. It seems incredible that this dear, cheerful, smiling brother, with whom I had exchanged so close and affectionate an embrace on my last day at the Ashram, should have passed in the physical form from among us so suddenly. He has died, as gallantly as any knight of old, on the battlefield.
>
> "Maganlal and I, as you know, worked closely and always harmoniously at Phoenix, Indeed, cheerfulness and harmony were the keynotes of his character, and a supple courage that adapted itself to meet the needs of each new trial. Of late years we met only upon my occasional visits to India, and then only, for brief periods, but I always felt refreshed and stimulated by this renewal of an old and affectionate comradeship.
>
> "He has left a noble and shining example for us all, and I feel very sure that, though he be absent really in the

flesh, his spirit will move among you perhaps more really than if he had remained in the form that was so familiar and dear to us."

Many of us in the Ashram are realising the truth of the last observation.

28th June, 1928

THE DOOM OF PURDAH

BY M. K. GANDHI

A reasoned appeal signed by many most influential people of Bihar and almost an equal number of ladies of that province advising the total abolition of the *purdah* has been just issued in Bihar. The fact that over fifty ladies have signed the appeal shows that if the work is carried on with vigour, the *purdah* will be a thing of the past in Bihar. It is worthy of note that the ladies who have signed the appeal are not of the anglicised type but orthodox Hindus. It definitely states:

> "We want that the women of our province should be as free to move about and take their legitimate part in the life of the community in all particulars as their sisters in Karnatak, Maharashtra and Madras in an essentially Indian way, avoiding all attempts at Europeanisation, for while we hold that a change from enforced seclusion to a complete anglicisation would be like dropping from frying pan into fire, we feel that *purdah* must go, if we want our women to develop along Indian ideals. If we want them to add grace and beauty to our social life and raise its moral tone, if we want them to be excellent managers at home, helpful companions of their husbands and useful members of the community, then the *purdah*, as it now exists, must go. In fact no serious step for their welfare can be taken unless the veil is torn down and it is our conviction that if once the energy of half of our population, that has been imprisoned artificially, is released, it

will create a force which, if properly guided, will be of immeasurable good to our Province."

I know the evil effects of the *purdah* in Bihar. The movement has been started none too soon.

The movement has a curious origin. Babu Ramanandan Mishra, a Khadi worker, was desirous of rescuing his wife from the oppression of the *purdah*. As his people would not let the girl come to the Ashram, he took two girls from the Ashram to be companions to his wife. One of them, Radhabehn, Maganlal Gandhi's daughter, was to be the tutor. She was accompanied by the late Dalbahadur Giri's daughter, Durgadevi. The parents of the girl wife resented the attempt of the Ashram girl to wean young Mrs. Mishra from the *purdah*. The girls braved all difficulties. Meanwhile Maganlal Gandhi went to see his daughter and steel her against all odds to persist in her efforts. He took ill in the village where Radhabehn was doing her work and died at Patna. The Bihar friends therefore made it a point of honour to wage war against the *purdah*. Radhabehn brought her charge to the Ashram. Her coming to the Ashram created additional stir and obliged the husband who was already prepared for it to throw himself in the struggle with greater zeal. Thus the movement having a personal touch promises to be carried on with energy. At its head is that seasoned soldier of Bihar, the hero of many battles, Babu Brijkishor Prasad. I do not remember his having headed a movement that has been allowed to die.

The appeal fixes the 8th of July next as the date on which to inaugurate an intensive campaign against the system which puts a cruel ban on social service by one half of Bihar humanity and which denies it freedom in many cases and even the use of light and fresh air. The sooner it is recognised that many of our social evils impede our march towards Swaraj, the greater will be our progress towards our cherished goal. To postpone social reform till after the attainment of Swaraj is not to know the meaning of Swaraj. Surely we must be incapable of defending ourselves or healthily competing with the other nations, if we allow the better half of ourselves to become paralysed.

I therefore congratulate the Bihar leaders on their having earnestly taken up the struggle against the *purdah*. The success of such a reform especially, as of all reform generally, depends upon the purity of the workers. A great deal will rest with the ladies who have signed the appeal. If, notwithstanding their having given up the *purdah*, they retain the original modesty of India's womanhood and show courage and determination in the face of heavy odds, they will find success quickly awaiting their effort. The campaign against the *purdah* if properly handled means mass education of the right type for both men and women of Bihar.

5th July, 1928

THE CURSE OF FOREIGN MEDIUM

BY M. K. GANDHI

The spirited plea on behalf of the vernaculars as media of instruction of Nawab Masood Jung Bahadur, Director of Public Instruction, Hyderabad State, recently delivered at the Karve University for Women, has evoked a reply in the *Times of India* from which a friend sends the following extracts for me to answer:

> 'Whatever is valuable and fruitful in their writings is directly or indirectly the result of Western culture. . . . Instead of sixty, we can go back a hundred years and yet say that from Raja Ram Mohan Roy down to Mahatma Gandhi, every one of the Indians who have achieved anything worth mentioning in any direction was or is the fruit directly or indirectly of Western education'.

In these extracts what is considered is not the value of English as the medium of higher instruction in India but the importance and influence of Western culture to and on the persons mentioned. Neither the Nawab nor any one else has disputed the importance of the influence of Western culture. What is resented is the sacrifice of Indian or Eastern culture on the altar of the Western. Even if it could be proved that Western culture was superior to Eastern, it would be injurious to India as a whole for her most promising sons and daughters to be brought up in Western culture and thus become denationalised and torn from the people.

In my opinion, whatever reaction for the better the persons named in the extracts had upon the people at large was due to the extent they retained their Eastern culture in spite of the adverse influence of the Western. I regard as adverse the influence of Western culture in this connection in the sense in which it interfered with the full effect that the best in Eastern culture might have produced on them. Of myself whilst I have freely acknowledged my debt to Western culture, I can say that whatever service I have been able to render to the nation has been due *entirely to* the retention by me of Eastern culture to the extent it has been possible. I should have been thoroughly useless to the masses as an anglicised, denationalised being knowing little of, caring less for and perhaps even despising their ways, habits, thoughts and aspirations. It is difficult to estimate the loss of energy caused to the nation by her children being obliged to resist the encroachments of a culture which, however good in itself, was unsuited for them whilst they had not imbibed and become rooted in their own.

Examine the question synthetically. Would Chaitanya Nanak, Kabir, Tulsidas and a host of other reformers have done better if they had been attached from their childhood to the most efficiently managed English schools? Have the men named by the writer of the article in question done better than these great reformers? Would Dayanand have done better if he had become an M. A. of an Indian university? Where is among the easy-going, ease-loving English-speaking rajas and maharajas brought from their infancy under the influence of Western culture one who could be named in the same breath as Shivaji who braved all perils and shared the simple life of his hardy men? Are they better rulers than Pratap the intrepid? Are they good specimens of Western culture, these Neroes who are fiddling in London and Paris whilst their Romes are burning? There is nothing to be proud of in their culture which has made them foreigners in their own land and which has taught them to prefer to waste the substance of their ryots and their own souls in Europe to sharing the happiness and miseries of those over whom they are called by a higher power to rule.

But the point at issue is not Western culture. The point at issue is the medium of instruction. But for the fact that the only higher education, the only education worth the name has been received by us through the English medium, there would be no need to prove such a self-evident proposition that the youth of a nation to remain a nation must receive all instruction including the highest in its own vernacular or vernaculars. Surely, it is a self-demonstrated proposition that the youth of a nation cannot keep or establish a living contact with the masses unless their knowledge is received and assimilated through a medium understood by the people. Who can calculate the immeasurable loss sustained by the nation owing to thousands of its young men having been obliged to waste years in mastering a foreign language and its idiom of which in their daily life they have the least use and in learning which they had to neglect their own mother tongue and their own literature? There never was a greater superstition than that a particular language can be incapable of expansion or expressing abstruse or scientific ideas. A language is an exact reflection of the character and growth of its speakers.

Among the many evils of foreign rule this blighting imposition of a foreign medium upon the youth of the country will be counted by history as one of the greatest. It has sapped the energy of the nation, it has shortened the lives of the pupils. It has estranged them from the masses, it has made education unnecessarily expensive. If this process is still persisted in, it bids fair to rob the nation of its soul. The sooner, therefore, educated India shakes itself free from the hypnotic spell of the foreign medium, the better it would be for them and the people.

5th July, 1928

OUR TOBACCO BILL

A correspondent who is interested in a variety of reforms asks what the nation pays for her tobacco bill. I find that we pay for unmanufactured tobacco and cigarettes 213 lakhs of rupees per year. The cost is increasing every year. The import of unmanufactured tobacco which was 1¼ million lbs. in 1923 rose to 5 million in 1927. There was a corresponding increase in the import of cigarettes. If the references I have consulted are reliable, we do not export any of our own tobacco. Therefore the value of that considerable crop has to be added to the figures quoted above. If every smoker stopped the dirty habit, refused to make of his mouth a chimney to foul his breath, damage his teeth and dull his sense of delicate discrimination and make a present of his savings to some national cause, he would benefit both himself and the nation.

M. K. G.

5th July, 1928

AN AMERICAN TRIBUTE

By M. K. Gandhi

One of the many American friends who visit and sometimes stay at the Ashram writes thus to Mrs. Maganlal Gandhi:

"The memory of the two days I spent in 1925 at the Ashram, and particularly in your hospitable home, stays with me like a benediction. I shall always feel it to have been a privilege beyond price to have been permitted to come so closely into contact with Mr. Maganlal Gandhi, whom I have always considered one of the rarest and most beautiful souls I ever met. Though so true an Indian, he had a sympathy and understanding broad as life itself. He seemed the very embodiment of that spirit of Satyagraha which I had come to know through the writings of Mahatma Gandhi, in *Young India*. Strength, purity and sweetness radiated from him like perfume from a flower.

"The faultless English, his perfect diction, his brilliant conversational powers showed the rare qualities of his mind, which, added to his urbanity of manner, and gracious tact, would have qualified him to shine in any social gathering. But one felt in his presence not only that particular brightness and charm; there was something more; something deeper; a personal sanctification that could mean nothing less than that every gift, every ability, every part of his being had been laid upon the altar, consecrated to God for the highest purpose to which man as a human being can aspire. Not that he talked religion or stressed piety—even the tone of his voice showed the same practical, efficient man of affairs that he was about the Ashram; but religion was the spring from which the current of his life flowed, and the sanctity which emanated from his presence was the sanctity that comes from surrender of self—the constant habit and purpose of living and doing for others.

"You will pardon me, Madam. These are no idle words meant simply to be complimentary, which I am writing. A hundred times since my return from India, when speaking or thinking of what I saw and felt there, I have tried to put into words the impression which was made upon me by that remarkable man, your revered husband. It was worth going round the world to have met him alone, when one considers all that his life means to India from the support which he gave and still continues to give to the work of the great Mahatmaji.

"But I am well aware that words of commendation for the dear departed, whatever their sincerity, or the sympathy they seek to convey, are of little avail in assuaging grief like yours. I must remind you however, that the potency for good of a soul like that of Mr. Maganlal Gandhi cannot wholly leave the sphere of its usefulness here on earth. It abides in a thousand tangible ways and will be there to comfort you, even though the bodily form be removed by death. But more truly than in any other way he will be with you in your children,—your two beautiful daughters and your son, who will take up the work and carry it on—the great work to which the life of your revered husband was so nobly consecrated." M. K. G.

12th July, 1928

EDUCATION FOR SERVICE.

A friend sends the following interesting extract from *The Service of Motherhood* by M. E. D. Smith:

"Our educational methods have been far too slipshod. It has, for instance, been too much the practice at our universities to let the young men learn if they choose but if they find study distasteful, then to allow them to idle their time away almost at their own pleasure. It seems strange that it should have been overlooked what a wrong was thereby being done to the nation, for wrong it assuredly is, since every member of a nation is born into it to serve not to be a mere passenger. For the slack methods pursued by certain of our educational heads are much to blame. Blind to the needs of the hour and dwelling in an atmosphere of aloofness and self-complacency, they have failed to appreciate the real aim and the vital importance of education. Let us hope that in the future it will be accounted as great a disgrace to omit to take advantage of opportunities for learning as it now is for a soldier to desert his post."

Be it remembered that this is said of national education as of national military service. It will be as wrong to serve in an army of hirelings drilled and paid to crush the spirit of their kith and kin as it would be to belong to an educational institution designed to subserve the purpose of a foreign domination.

M. K. G.

19th July, 1928

SPINNING IN SAWANTWADI

[The following report prepared by Sjt. S. P. Patwardhan has been lying in my file for some time. It will be read with interest by the general reader and with profit by Khadi workers.

M. K. G.]

THE TASK

The task before the Sardesai Charkhalaya is a little different from and more difficult than that before many other production centres. The Sawantwadi state lies to the south of the Ratnagiri District and is bounded on the other three sides by the Kolhapur state, the Belgaum District and the Goa Territory. It is a small state with a population of two lacs and a revenue of nearly six lacs. The Konkan produces no cotton except small quantities of *devkapas*, a perennial variety, with a long, white staple. There are traces—or rather old folk tell us—of wheels having been plying in certain parts but spinning was never universal. Before the construction of the Southern Mahratta Railway cotton beyond the Ghats used to go out through the creeks and ports of the Konkan. Plenty of cotton was thus available, at these places, and women—so far as we know, Musalman women—used to card and spin in their leisure hours and sell their yarn to local weavers. With the construction of the railway, the cotton from Belgaum, Satara and other districts went directly to Bombay and the supply of cotton being thus cut off the wheels fell into disuse. This was about forty years ago. Many old women are still living who used to spin as young girls. But the industry has hardly left any traces behind. The art which was once known by many, has now been entirely forgotton. The task before the Khadi worker.

is therefore one of the *creation* of a new, rather than the *revival* of an old, tradition.

There need be no doubt, however, that the spinning wheel has a place, that nothing else can fill, in the economic life of the Konkan. The land is proverbially poor, and there is enough leisure with the working classes, not to say anything of the 'white professions' (*pandharpeshas*). The people are intelligent and industrious and *devkapas* can easily supply the needs of each household. Cotton can also be imported from beyond the Ghats from a distance of nearly seventy miles. What is needed is a training up of the masses in the arts of ginning, carding, spinning and perhaps also weaving, because families of caste weavers are few and far between. The processes must not only be learnt but must form part of the daily life of the people. This is an uphill task that requires constant work for many a year to come.

The Sardesai Charkhalaya has accordingly been trying to popularise spinning in a variety of ways. To train school children to card and spin, to encourage the working classes to earn a few coppers by spinning, to induce the middle classes to spin for home-consumption and the higher classes to spin as a sacrament, to point out to the spinners the advantages of growing their own cotton, to demonstrate the various processes to thousands of spectators at the annual village fairs etc.,—these methods have been tried during the last ten months with varying success.

Kamler, seven miles from Sawantwadi, was recommended to us as a suitable centre to start the activities of the Charkhalaya, the main attraction being a number of small weaving factories, successfully going on for the last dozen years and more, and worked by agriculturists, who are not caste weavers. They all weave mill yarn but it was believed that the looms had prepared the ground for the spinning wheel. Experience, has, if at all, given the lie to that belief however.

Spinning was started in five primary schools in the neighbouring villages. The idea was that the schools would react on the general public and would at any rate send out so many children trained in spinning. At His Highness' instance spinning was later extended to all the girls' schools in the state and a few more schools have also been taken up in response to the demand of the school teachers or the village people.

Most of the schools are spacious enough to allow a dozen wheels being worked besides *taklis*. Our idea also is to popularise the wheels through the students and so the student is introduced to the wheel as soon as he has spun 2500 yards on the *takli*. The following table will show the schools, the date when spinning was introduced, and the number of students spinning on the takli and the wheel respectively,

School	Date when spinning was introduced	No. of students spinning *takli*	wheel
1. Akeri	August '27	26	30
2. Jharap	September '27	25	Nil
3 Vajrat	October „	21	8
4. Mangaon	November „	33	15
5. Sawantwadi English Girls' School	March '28	28	5
6. Sawantwadi Marathi Girls' School	„ „	44	5
7. Sawantwadi Urdu Girls' School	„ „	24	Nil
8. Kudal	„ „	37	2
9. Banden	April '28	25	Nil
10. Mangaon (Talivada)	„ „	16	„
11. Math	„ „	19	„
12. Humras,	„ „	20	„
13. Maduren English School	„ „	8	„
	Total	316	65

Spinning is done as a rule for half an hour every day, though the students in their eagerness sometimes take their *taklis* home for spinning with the permission of the teacher

Nearly 50 lbs. of yarn was thus spun in the schools up to the end of April 1928. In three of the schools the bigger boys do carding also.

This item of our work has been successful and popular beyond all expectation. All the children show the greatest liking for the work and most of them pick up the art in a couple of days. This liking is not a mere child-like love of novelty. It has been sustained through months. During the ensuing year the authorities have decided to start spinning, if possible, in all the primary schools of the state, and to hold a teachers' training class for that purpose within a few weeks' time.

A charkha competition was held among the boys and a *takli* competition among the girls at the end of last April. The results were creditable enough as will be seen from the following table:

Winner	Age	Yards	Count	Test (approximate)
No. 1	20	470	17½	50
No. 2	11	375	17	50
No. 3	6	475	9¼	32

The youngest boy spun quickest but his low test and count assigned him a lower rank. Extra time was given for hanking.

Among girls, the highest, a girl of 8, spun after only six weeks' practice, 134 yards of count 20. Five more girls spun over 100 yards each and ran a close race, the prizes being divided between all of them.

We have however not been able to do much yet by way of serving the poor. We are situated in a village where the looms supply whole-time work to nearly a hundred men and leisure-time work under their own roofs to dozens of women. It is only the 'untouchables' who have no admission to these weaving factories that have been profiting by charkha spinning. A dozen of these 'untouchable' boys from two localities do card ing and spinning in their leisure time and are glad to earn a few coppers. We pay them a bit more than the standard wage, *viz.*, six pies for each hank of 500 yards. Some of them do carding also and earn more, the rate being two annas per pound of carefully prepared slivers. Malaria has been the curse of many of these villages during the last twentyfive years and more; and the work in one of the untouchable quarters has been stopped during the last few weeks, almost all the boys having been laid up with malaria. The little that has been accomplished, however, points to the vast possibilities of work in this direction at any rate among 'untouchables.' Half a dozen women and children from the higher castes also spin for wages but not with the regularity and the earnestness of the 'untouchables.'

The idea placed before the middle classes is to spin for home consumption. About twenty families have thus been spinning for their own needs. Seven families thus got Khadi to the extent of 160 yards woven out of their own yarn at the Charkhalaya and seven more have sent in their yarn. The Charkhalaya charges half rates (*i. e.*, 1½ pies per *vishi* of 160 threads) from those who bring yarn of their own spinning enough for a warp of 18 yards.

The Revenue Minister of the state introduced two charkhas in his own home at the very start. Gandhiji presented a nice folding wheel to Her Highness the Maharani-Saheb. But even before that could be done she ordered an ordinary wheel from us, took lessons from our representative, and picked up the art in a couple of days. Her Highness' example proved contagious. Three of the state sardars and some of the high officials have introduced charkhas in their homes and these charkhas have been yielding regular instalments of yarn to the Charkhalaya.

On the 1st of May we held a small Exhibition of the activities of the Charkhalaya for the main purpose of giving to His Highness, the officials and the sympathetic public an idea of the work that is being done. It was opened by His Highness. The following passage from the address delivered by His Highness on the occasion is worth noting:

> "Mr. Patwardhan and his co-workers deserve to be congratulated on the silent, steady, earnest and disciplined manner in which they have been working. If the promoters of other institutions will imitate them we shall be spared the unpleasant sight of many an institution coming to an abrupt end immediately after they are started. Let us hope that the citizens of this state will profit by the example of Mr. Patwardhan's sacrifice, sincerity and method of work."

19th July, 1928

BY-PRODUCTS OF KHADI

By M. K. Gandhi

On the 14th instant the Gandhi Ashram conducted by Sjt. C. Rajagopalachari near Tiruchengodu in Tamil Nadu had a free dispensary opened by Dr. Ray. From the report read at the meeting it appears that round the Khadi as the centre, removal of untouchability and drink evil, rural sanitation and medical relief have sprung up. The Ashram serves 175 villages among which annually 45,000 rupees are distributed through Khadi. Removal of untouchability is done through the personal service of the 'untouchables' exactly on the same terms as the rest. The Ashram now proposes as soon as funds permit to dig 5 wells and build cottages for them. They need Rs. 10,000, five being for five wells. The wells are a sore need as the 'untouchables' 'have to go long distances and suffer many humiliations and hardships to get their daily pot of water.' In 19 months the Ashram gave medical relief to 28,095 men and women. The need for expansion became so great that they had to build a proper dispensary at a cost of Rs. 5,000. It was to open this that Dr. Ray travelled all the way to the Ashram. The hospital cost Rs. 200 per month which was supported from Khadi work. But now the need for donations is felt. I must give in its own language the report of sanitation work:

> "The people are very conservative in their habits and are impervious to new ideas. Under these conditions we thought our campaign for sanitation should begin with the children. A children's bathing scheme was started on 18-2-1928 under which all the children in the neighbourhood below twelve years were offered an oil-and-soap-nut bath on Saturdays and a soap bath on Tuesdays. The doctor and other members of the Ashram attend to this work personally, oiling and removing the vermin from the children's hair and rubbing them down clean and tidy. Only the untouchables have taken advantage of the scheme. At first a very large number of these children came and it was a happy sight to see them being bathed and made clean and tidy. But many of them have later stopped away as the novelty wore off. Only about twenty children are regularly attending every week. We hope, however, that if we persist, a large number will take advantage of the scheme."

Such are the few among the many by-products of Khadi. Let scoffers take note. And let friends help the Ashram which is slowly but surely penetrating the masses through their real service by making them self-reliant and self-supporting.

26th July, 1928

CROWN OF THORNS

BY M. K. GANDHI

The Congress crown has ceased to be a crown of roses. The rose petals are year by year falling off and the thorns are becoming more and more prominent. Who should wear such a crown? Father or the son? Pandit Motilalji, the weather-beaten warrior or Pandit Javaharlal Nehru, the disciplined young soldier who by his sterling worth has captured the imagination of the youth of the country? Sjt. Vallabhbhai Patel's name is naturally on everybody's lips. Panditji says in a private letter that he as the hero of the hour should be elected and the Government should be made to know that he enjoys the fullest confidence of the nation. Sjt. Vallabhbhai is however out of the question just now. His hands are too full to allow of his attention being diverted from Bardoli. And before December comes upon us he may be a guest in one of His Majesty's innumerable prisons. My own feeling in the matter is that Pandit Javaharlal should wear the crown. The future must be for the youth of the country. But Bengal wants Motilalji to guide the Congress barque through the perilous seas that threaten to overwhelm us during the coming year. We are torn within and are encircled by an enemy that is as unscrupulous as he is powerful. Bengal has special need of an older head and one moreover who has proved a tower of strength to her in the hour of her trial. If India as a whole has no easy time before her, Bengal has still less. There are a thousand reasons why Panditji should be chosen to wear the crown of thorns. He is brave, he is generous, he enjoys the confidence of all parties, Musalmans acknowledge him as their friend, he commands the respect of his opponents and often bends them to his view by his forceful eloquence. He has moreover deep down in him a spirit of conciliation and compromise which makes him an eminently worthy ambassador of a nation that is in need of and is in the mood to take an honourable compromise. It is these considerations which actuate even the dare-all Bengali patriot to want Pandit Motilal Nehru as the helmsman for the coming year. Let the impatient youth of the country wait a while. They will be all the stronger for the waiting.

26th July, 1928

A TRIUMPH OF JUSTICE

BY M. K. GANDHI

There is in Wardha a well-known and very well decorated shrine dedicated to Shri Lakshminarayan. It was built by Sheth Jamnalalji's grandfather. It is a private temple made accessible to the public. Jamnalalji has been endeavouring to have this temple available to the so-called untouchables also, as he has been trying with great success to have wells in Wardha made accessible to them and generally to procure for them all the facilities available to the other classes. He had difficulty with the trustees in bringing them round to his view that this select temple should be thrown open to those whom blind orthodoxy has suppressed. Success has at last attended his effort. On the 17th instant the trustees unanimously passed the following resolution:

> "Whereas the question of admitting the so-called untouchables inside the temple of Shri Lakshminarayan has been before the Committee on several occasions and they have been unable to come to a firm decision till now; and whereas, the most representative body in India, namely, the Congress has insisted upon the removal of untouchability; and whereas the Hindu Mahasabha has considered it necessary and just that all public temples should be made accessible to the so-called untouchables; and whereas the well-known leaders of public opinion in India have expressed the same opinion, the trustees hereby resolve, regard being had to the foregoing facts and after full consideration of the religious and the social condition of the country, that the above named temple dedicated to Shri Lakshminarayan in Wardha be declared open to the 'untouchables' and that the managing trustee, Sheth Jamnalal Bajaj, be authorised to enforce this resolution in such manner as may appear to him to be best."

Accordingly a printed notice was widely circulated in

Wardha that from the 19th instant, that is two days after the resolution, the temple would be declared open for the 'untouchables.' It is stated that although there was no organised effort made beyond circulating the foregoing notice, nearly 1,200 men and women and children including 'untouchables' visited the temple without the slightest untoward incident having occurred. It is most significant that in an important centre like Wardha a celebrated temple could be flung open for the 'untouchables' without orthodoxy raising its voice of protest or some people in the name of Sanatana Dharma creating a disturbance at the time of 'untouchables' trying to cross the sacred and hitherto forbidden threshold of a Hindu shrine. It is a striking demonstration of the tremendous headway that the movement against untouchability has made. It shows too what quiet determination and persistence can do to create healthy public opinion in favour of a genuine movement for reform. I congratulate Sheth Jamnalalji and his fellow trustees on the bold step that they have taken and hope that this example will be followed all over India,

---

26th July, 1928

PURDAH IN BIHAR

By M. K. Gandhi

The organised demonstration against the purdah that was held in many important centres in Bihar on the 8th instant was, a Bihari friend's letter tells me, successful beyond the expectations of the organisers. The *Searchlight* report of the Patna meeting opens thus:

> "A unique spectacle was witnessed at the mixed meeting of ladies and gentlemen of the 8th July held at Patna in the Radhika Sinha Institute on Sunday last. In spite of heavy rains that fortunately stopped just at the time of the meeting, the gathering was unexpectedly large. In fact half of the spacious hall of the Radhika Sinha Institute was crowded with ladies, three fourths of whom were such

as had been observing purdah a day before, nay, an hour before."

The following is the translation of the resolution adopted at the meeting:

"We, the men and women of Patna, assembled hereby declare that we have today abolished the pernicious practice of purdah, which has done and is doing incalculable harm to the country, and particularly to women, and we appeal to the other women of the province, who are still wavering, to banish this system as early as they can and thereby advance their education and health."

A provisional committee was formed at the meeting to carry on an intensive propaganda against purdah and for the spread of women's education in the province of Bihar. A third resolution advised the formation of Mahila Samitis in every town and every village of the province. And a fourth resolution was passed to the effect that Mahila Ashrams should be started at different places where ladies might stay for certain periods and receive a training so as to become 'good' wives' 'worthy mothers' and 'useful servants' of the country. Over 5,000 rupees were promised on the spot for the purpose and I see many ladies among the donors, giving anything between Rs. 250 and 25. The paper publishes reports of similar meetings in several places in Bihar. If the campaign is well organised and continued with zeal, the purdah should become a thing of the past. It should be noted that this is no anglicising movement. It is an indigenous conservative effort made by leaders who are conservative by nature and are yet alive to all the evils that have crept into Hindu society. Babu Brajakishore Prasad and Babu Rajendra Prasad who, from far-off London, is keenly watching and supporting the movement, are no westernised specimens of Indian humanity. They are orthodox Hindus, lovers of Indian culture and tradition. They are no blind imitators of the West and yet do not hesitate to assimilate whatever is good in it. There need therefore be no fear entertained by the timid and the halting ones that the movement is likely to be in any shape or form disruptive of all that is most precious in Indian culture and especially in feminine grace and modesty so peculiar to India's womanhood.

2nd August, 1928

SELF-SUPPORT IS SELF-RESPECT

By M. K. Gandhi

The suggestion has often been made in these columns that in order to make education compulsory or even available to every boy or girl wishing to receive education, our schools and colleges should become almost, if not wholly, self-supporting, not through donations or State-aid or fees exacted from students, but through remunerative work done by the students themselves. This can only be done by making industrial training compulsory. Apart from the necessity which is daily being more and more recognised of students having an industrial training side by side with literary training, there is in this couuntry the additional necessity of pursuing industrial training in order to make education directly self-supporting. This can only be done when our students begin to recognise the dignity of labour and when the convention is established of regarding ignorance of manual occupation a mark of disgrace. In America, which is the richest country in the world and where therefore perhaps there is the least need for making education self-supporting, it is the most usual thing for students to pay their way wholly or partially. Thus says the *Hindustanee Student*, the official bulletin of the Hindustan Association of America, 500 Riverside Drive, New York City:

> "Approximately 50 % of the American students use the summer vacation and part of their time during the academic year to earn money. 'Self-supporting students are respected,' writes the bulletin of the California University. With reasonable diligence a student can devote from 12 to 25 hours per week (during the academic year) to outside work without seriously interfering with college

work of 12 to 16 units (credits) involving 36 to 48 hours a week. . . . . 'A student should have some sort of practical knowledge of the following: carpentry, surveying, drafting, bricklaying, plastering, autodriving, photography, manchine-shop work, dyeing, field work, general farm work, instrumental music and so on.' Such common work as waiting on table for two hours, etc., is available during the academic year, which relieves a student from expenses for board. A partially self-supporting student by working during the summer vacation may save up from $ 150 to 200. Kansas, N. Y. University, Pittsburg, Union University, Antioch College offer 'cooperative' courses in Industrial Engineering by which a student can earn one year's tuition fees working in industrial plants for which he also receives credit for his practical experience.

"The University of Michigan has under consideration the opening of similar cooperative courses in Civil and Electrical Engineering. One year more is required to graduate in engineering by pursuing cooperative courses."

If America has to model her schools and colleges so as to enable students to earn their scholastic expenses, how much more necessary it must be for our schools and colleges? Is it not far better that we find work for poor students than that we pauperise them by providing freestudentships? It is impossible to exaggerate the harm we do to India's youth by filling their minds with the false notion that it is ungentlemanly to labour with one's hands and feet for one's livelihood or schooling. The harm done is both moral and material, indeed much more moral than material. A free scholaship lies and should lie like a load upon a conscientious lad's mind throughout his whole life. No one likes to be reminded in after-life that he had to depend upon charity for his education. Contrarily where is the person who will not recall with pride those days if he had the good fortune to have had them when he worked in a carpentry-shop or the like for the sake of educating himself mind, body and soul?

2nd August, 1928

INDIAN SHIPPING

The tragic history of the ruin of the national village industry of cotton manufacture in India is also the history of the ruin of Indian shipping. The rise of Lancashire on the ruin of the chief industry of India almost required the destruction of Indian shipping."

It will be remembered that in 1923 the Indian Mercantile Marine Committee was appointed in order to explore among other things the means of encouraging indigenous shipping 'by a system of bounties, subsidies etc.' Its timid and over-cautious recommendations provide for the reservation of the coastal traffic for Indian shipping. Sjt. Sarabhai Haji now seeks through two bills to secure legislative effect for the recommendations of the Committee. One bill aims at the abrogation of unhealthy monopolies and the other aims in five years at the passing of all the tonnage of the coastal traffic into the hands predominantly of Indians. Both the bills are necessary and both should pass without delay or difficulty. I am an out-and-out protectionist. I hold that every country, especially a poor country like India, has every right and is indeed bound to protect its interest, when it is threatened, by all lawful protective measures and to regain to such measures what has been wrongfully taken away from it. I have my doubts about anything substantial being done under the existing system through legislative effort. But I take up the same position that I have always maintained regarding organised industries such as mills. I should welcome and support all action that would protect them against foreign aggression or free them from foreign competition especially when the latter is grossly unfair as it is in the case of foreign shipping and foreign piecegoods. I therefore wish Sjt. Sarabhai Haji every success in his very moderate effort. He might quite justly have gone further than he has.

M. K. G.

9th August, 1928

KHADI IN CENTRAL INDIA

The non-political aspect of the All-India Spinners' Association has gone a great way in popularising Khadi and Khadi work in the States of Rajputana. Individual effort in the direction has been there ever since 1921, but it had not borne fruit, for want of technical knowledge and organisation.

But the establishment of the Spinners' Association in 1926 encouraged me to make a start again with Khadi hawking in Malwa. I wanted Sheth Jamnalalji to tour some of the favourable tracts, but as he was not available, I contented myself with hawking Khadi in Indore and Gwalior. I was fortunate in having a fine response, some of the State officials having purchased Khadi. The Deputy Prime Minister, Sardar Kibe, is a more or less habitual Khadi wearer. The Prime Minister and the President of the Council even encouraged me to open a Khadi centre in the State, which however could not be done for want of workers. But a Khadi bhandar could be opened thanks to the efforts of Sjt. Babubhaiya Date. It had a monthly sale of Rs. 100, without any effort on our part.

The Regency Council in Gwalior also sent me encouraging letters, inviting Jamnalalji to confer with the Minister for Industry and Commerce as to the organisation of Khadi centres in the State. Unfortunately Sheth Jamnalalji has not yet been able to make time to go to Gwalior.

My hawking in Ujjain has resulted in the opening of a Khadi store there under the supervision of Sjt. Pustake. It has a steady monthly sale of Rs. 100 and we are now thinking of extending it.

In 1927 as a result of the efforts of Sjt. Pustake, the Gwalior Council resolved to appoint a commission to report on the possibility of introducing subsidiary cottage industries amongst the agriculturists of the State. The commission has toured various parts of the State and collected evidence, and its labours are not yet finished. I had the honour to be examined by the commission on behalf of the Rajasthan Charkha Sangha. In the course of my evidence I stated that there was no subsidiary occupation for the agriculturist save carding and spinning, and suggested that in those parts of the State where there were two harvests the voluntary spinning system should be introduced, and where there was only one harvest and the agriculturist had considerable spare time at his disposal a regular production centre should be opened. The commission visited the Satyagraha Ashram and conferred with Gandhiji and Sjt. Shankarlal Banker. Gandhiji suggested three cottage industries, *viz.*, spinning, cattle-breeding and dairying. The first of the three could be organised by the agriculturist himself with the encouragement and help of the State, but the other two could be done only by the State.

The suggestion, so far as I can say, appealed to the commission whose report is now awaited with anxious interest. The late Maharaja of Gwalior has himself borne testimony to the fact that for at least four months in the year the agriculturist has no work, and no one who has given evidence before the commission has yet been able to suggest a better subsidiary occupation than spinning.

The Gwalior friends were so much interested in Khadi that they expressed a desire to have a Khadi exhibition at the time of the All Maharashtra Literary Conference. The exhibition was a great success, the students of the Satyagraha Ashram having gone there to demonstrate the various processes. The number of visitors every day exceeded 500 and the total sale exceeded Rs. 4,000. The sardars and the State officials, and even Her Highness the Maharani extended their sympathy to Khadi. The Dowager Maharani honoured the exhibition by her visit and the Vice-President of the Council and the Ministers for Commerce and Industry and for Finance also visited the exhibition and gave their active support by purchasing Khadi. Much of the credit for this success is due to the Chief Medical Officer of the State, Major Phatak, and Sardar Saheb Angre, who is anxious to make his whole jagir self-sufficient in respect of cloth. He has also decided to grant a scholarship to a student who is being sent to learn all the processes of Khadi manufacture.

Another encouraging feature is the introduction of *takli* spinning in several boys' and girls' schools of the Gwalior State. About 800 students in Malwa are spinning on the *takli*, and the head-masters of the schools are evincing a keen interest. Better results can be achieved if the Education Department appoints a specially trained teacher to supervise the teaching of carding and the adoption of a uniform type of *takli* in every school.

Gwalior and Indore are the two biggest states in Central India. Gwalior is now leading and Indore too, we hope will not lag behind, and both completely organised will set an example to the rest of the states in Central India.

HARIBHAU UPADHYAY

(Condensed from the original in *Hindi Navajivan* of May 10, 1928, by M. D.)

16th August, 1928

THE NEHRU REPORT

BY M. K. GANDHI

Pandit Motilal Nehru and his colleagues deserve the highest congratulations for the very able and practically unanimous report they have been able to bring out on the question that has vexed all parties for the past long months. The report is well got up, accessible in book form and printed in bold type. No public man can afford to be without it. It is signed by Pandit Motilal Nehru, Sir Ali Imam, Sir Tej Bahadur Sapru, Sjt. M. S. Aney, Sirdar Mangal Singh, M. Shuaib Qureshi, Sjt. Subhash Chandra Bose and Sjt. G. R. Pradhan. About M. Shuaib Qureshi's signature however there is the following note at the end of the report:

"Mr. Shuaib Qureshi was unfortunately unable to be-present at the last meeting of the Committee when the draft report was considered. The draft however was sent to him and he has informed us that in regard to the recommendations contained in Chapter III he is of opinion that one third seats in the Central Legislatures should be reserved for Muslims." Further, he says, 'I agree with the resolution adopted at the informal conference of July 7th but do not subscribe to all the figures and arguments produced in its support."

The report covers 133 pages, appendices 19 pages. The report is divided into ten chapters, of which four deal with the communal aspect, reservation of seats, redistribution of provinces and Indian States. The seventh chapter contains the final recommendations of the Committee. I must not attempt to summarise the report, if only because it has come into my hands at the moment of sending the last article for *Young India*. I have not even the time to study the report in full beyond having a cursory glance through it. But the great merit of it is that All Parties Conference Committee has at last been able to produce a unanimous report bearing weighty representative signatures. In the matter of the constitution the main thing was not to present perfect recommendations but to secure unanimity for the recommendations that might in the circumstances be considered the best possible. And if the practical unanimity arrived at after strenuous labours by the Committee is sealed by the Conference about to meet at Lucknow, a tremendous step will have been taken in the direction of constitutional Swaraj as distinguished from what might be termed organic Swaraj. For if the country arrives at a workable unanimity about the questions that have been agitating it for years, the next thing would be to work for the acceptance of our demands. And we have arrived at such a step in the country's history in our evolution that if we can assure real unanimity about any reasonable proposal, there should be no difficulty in securing acceptance. I hope therefore the Conference will meet at Lucknow with a fixed determination to see the thing through and that the members who will be there will not engage in a critical examination of the report with a view to tear it to pieces but with the determination of arriving at a proper settlement. And if they will approach the report in that spirit they will endorse the recommendations, except for valid reasons which would appeal to any sane persons. In thus commending this report to the public, I tender my congratulations to Pandit Motilal Nehru without whose effort there would have been no Committee, there would have been no unanimity and there would have been no report.

16th August, 1928

OUR GAOLS

BY M. K. GANDHI

In spite of my two years in Indian gaols, I see that others who have been in them for much shorter periods than I have more knowledge of their working than I. The Satyagrahi prisoners who were recently discharged tell me of the many hardships which can be avoided if there is some consideration shown to the prisoners as human beings. The experiences of a Satyagrahi prisoner in the Surat gaol are that the prisoners are all cooped up in a small ill-ventilated and ill-lighted room, the food served is hardly digestible and not much facility given to the prisoners for keeping themselves clean.

The prisoners at the Sabarmati Central Prison give me more details. The flour issued is gritty, the *dal* is pebbly and often contains animal dirt. The Satyagrahis were inclined to excuse the gaol authorities for this defect saying it was the fault of the prisoners who had to do the cleaning and the grinding. I am unable to adopt the view. I feel that the authorities are bound to attend to the cleaning of foodstuff either by having it done outside or by effective supervision. It is futile to expect the prisoners especially in the way they are kept to do this or anything well or conscientiously. Instead of taking the most important work of cooking through them, it would be better and more economical to have the cooking and the preparatory work done through reliable agency and take from the prisoners other tasks of a more remunerative nature and involving no danger to health.

Nor was clean food indifferently cooked the whole of the complaint on this head. A kind of dry fermental stinking cabbage was rationed as green vegetable. From what the friends described I could gather that this cabbage was a kind of human silage copied from cattle silage, cabbage being revitalised by subjecting it to high fermentation. If the information given to me is correct, I can only say that the prison authorities are playing with prisoners' lives entrusted to their care.

Among the prisoners discharged were three in a weak condition ; one a student who had completed his full term was discharged in a precarious condition. His condition was so far gone that in spite of all the loving attention being bestowed upon him by the Mahavidyalaya professors and students and skilled medical assistance, he is not yet out of danger. I was informed that for several days in spite of his fever he was kept on coarse *jowari* bread for a time. I should not at all wonder if this indigestible bread caused intestinal inflammation.

I shall be glad to publish any explanation that the authorities may have to give in regard to these allegations.

I know that conditions being as they are prisoners may not expect the comforts of home life. I know too that Satyagrahis may not grumble at their lot which in a way is of their own seeking. Nevertheless even a Satyagrahi whether he complains or not should receive human treatment and should get food that is suited to his constitution and that is, above all else, clean and cleanly prepared.

23rd August, 1928

ALL EYES ON LUCKNOW

BY M. K. GANDHI

The Nehru Committee report has rightly attracted universal attention. All the leading Indians who have spoken upon it have blessed it. The critics have been obliged to write about it with marked restraint and often involuntary admiration. It has set every one thinking.

All eyes are naturally therefore centred on Lucknow where Dr. Ansari has invited the All Parties Conference to meet. A report that has compelled such attention is bound to draw a large and representative gathering.

What will the Conference do? It will be easy enough to render the proceeding of the Conference nugatory and reduce to nothingness the labours of the Nehru Committee. Musalmans may destroy the great edifice built by patient effort on the ground that they have not got all they wanted. Hindus may vow never to yield an inch and thus make an advance impossible. Political theorists may pick big holes in the report. But they will all be wrong if they approach the report from their individual stand-points. We shall not easily get again anything so good as the report bearing the representative signatures it does.

Let all therefore approach the report from only one standpoint, *i. e.*, the national. There is room enough under the constitution devised by the Committee for all to rise to their full height. Every legitimate interest has its protection guaranteed if it has enough vitality in itself for expansion. The franchise is the broadest possible.

Of course the impatient extremist will be dissatisfied. Let him know that the report represents the largest common measure possible for parties often representing opposite views. It will be anti-national to resist to the breaking point what is offered by this representative report.

Apart however from the standpoint of expediency, I venture to suggest that the report satisfies all reasonable aspirations and is quite capable of standing on its own intrinsic merits. All therefore that is needed to put the finishing touch to the work of the Nehru Committee is a little forbearance, a little mutual respect, a little mutual trust, a little give and take and much confidence not in our little selves but in the great nation of which each one of us is but a humble member.

23rd August, 1928

HINDI-HINDUSTANI

BY M. K. GANDHI

That Sir T. Vijayaraghavachari should deliver a public lecture at the Hindu High School in Triplicane, Madras, on the 'place of Hindi in Indian Education' is a sign of the times and proof of the efficacy of the work done by the Hindi Prachar Office in Madras which has carried on Hindi propaganda for the last seven years. The lecturer had no difficulty in showing that the fact that of the 300 million people of India 120 millions spoke Hindi and 80 millions more understood it and that Hindi was the third most widely spoken language in the world 'was by itself a strong reason for every one learning Hindi.' The learned speaker rightly thought that 'six months would be a sufficient period for learning the language well.' He contended that 'the place of Hindi in Indian Education must be compulsory. It ought to be a compulsory language in school, college and university.' He concluded: "We are all eagerly looking forward to the day when we shall all be Indians first and Madrasis or Bengalis next. That day will be hastened if Madrasis, who are the worst offenders in this respect, begin to learn Hindi in larger numbers." The people of the South have every facility afforded to them through the Hindi Prachar Office of learning Hindi. Surely, if we have real love of India, as we have of our respective provinces, we would all learn Hindi without delay and avoid the humiliating spectacle of carrying on our proceedings in the popular assembly i. e., the All-India Congress Committee predominantly, if not often wholly, in English." Let me repeat once more what I have often said that I do not contemplate the suppression of provincial languages by Hindi but addition of Hindi to the former so as to enable provinces to establish a living contact with one another. This must result also in enriching both the provincial languages and Hindi.

23rd August, 1928

A WAGE INVESTIGATIC

Much has been said about the little return that spinning gives. Little, no doubt it is. Its place in rural life is not by itself, but *along with work in field and home.* It is just the 'little' addition that is badly needed to make decent life possible for the humble and home-loving folk, such as the vast population of India are. If one is not satisfied with this 'little,' the alternative is to abandon home and field. Therefore to give up this 'little' is to give up much, perhaps all. For, too often, is the whole soul lost when man or woman leaves the village home and goes to town or city slum, or to the tea or rubber garden abroad.

But it is worth while to know what exactly is the actual proportion, and the results may be an eye-opener to many. There is a Railway station of growing importance in the South Indian Railway line in Salem district, named Sankagiri. It is one of the big *pan* export stations, and the Railway Company is adding extensive buildings to the station. I asked about wages paid, and learnt that for full-time adult labour, the men get four annas each, and the women two annas. It is summer now and the days are long and the full daylight is saved by the gang-drivers. The coolies leave their hamlets at not later than half past five in the morning, gulping their drink of cold porridge before that. They work hard the whole day with an interval for the midday meal. The sun hangs on long in the evening and the people are let off only near seven o'clock until when there is bright daylight. They reach home about half-an-hour later. Thus their working day is really fourteen hours counting the interval and the time taken to and from the place of work. For 12 good solid hours they certainly work and an adult woman is paid 2 annas for this at a Railway centre.

Twelve miles from this place we have a spinning centre where women spin 12 to 14 counts of yarn at 300 yards per hour. Allowing sufficient time for carding and preparing slivers, and taking only five days a week for spinning, at the rate of the working hours shown above, a woman could spin 20,000 yards in a week and earn eleven annas wages at the rate at which we pay for 12 to 14 counts. This may be compared with fourteen annas which she might earn if she joined the contractor's gang at the building works. Thus a woman earns no more than 27% extra by hiring herself out for outside day labour, i.e., the charkha at home can give her more than three fourths of what can be earned as a coolie, if we take the working hours demanded in the latter case. And this is where big works have been started by a big Railway administration.

C. R.

23rd August, 1928

THE FUTURE OF KHADI

By C. R.

Every one that sleeps under the stars in the open wakes up at a particular hour long before dawn and then he hears the lowing of the cattle and a slight disturbance among the birds nestling in the trees. Some one has said that this is probably due to a periodic and universal influence of the stars. One night, as I thus woke up and lay in my bed, drinking in the serene beauty of the spangled sky, the still small voice within me began to have a talk.

"You have lived and bustled all these years," said the Voice. "Your time is well nigh up. What have you achieved?"

I was lost for a while in thought. "It is a sad confession but I have to admit that I have done but little, with all the talents God gave me and the time I have had. Why, I have not even arranged my affairs as I should."

"No, no," said the Voice. "That is not what I am wanting to know. What have you done by way of making the world a better place for men and women?"

"Yes," said Ego which now got ready for discussion. "There is something to my credit here. I have helped the revival of a lost industry in these villages. Thousands of spinning wheels are now alive and humming. The women in almost all the cottages are spinning and they earn a few copper pieces every week, where before they were without work, and these extra copper pieces help the half-starved families to get a few more mouthfuls of food. It is a permanent good I have helped to bring about, which must be remembered after I pass away."

"Ah!" said the small voice. "Are you sure of that? You talk of permanent good. After you and others who are working here for Khadi cease to do so, who will keep it up?"

"I expect," said Ego, "new men will join the ranks of Khadi service and keep the work going. The cause is great and good, and there is humanity enough among men."

"Do you think," asked the Voice, "that the All-India Spinners' Association will be a permanent institution ever furnishing capital and managing the business?"

"I rather think so," said Ego.

"No," said the Voice. "That can't be. That is not how Khadi can become a permanent industry of the land. The Association's part in the work must be only preliminary and can't go on for ever: its hope must be that the people in general will give up other cloth and take to Khadi so that everywhere weavers will ask for handspun, and peasant families everywhere will spin, as they now keep cows and sell milk and *ghi.* There is no Association for the production and distribution of *ghi,* though lard or Cocogem may be better organised and cheaper and even cleaner, made odourless and packed in attractive cases.

"You say that unless the people make Khadi their own interest, all our association-work may come to a standstill some time?" asked Ego.

"Yes, I fear so," answered the Voice. "All your work in producing 24 lakhs worth of handspun cloth every year and running depots to dispose of it will come to nothing, unless one day the people, through the traders and the weavers, make it their own interest. You are now but like a foreign mission among the people."

I sank in thought; and Voice and Ego merged and became as one, as it happens wherever the latter is humbled. The silent stars seemed to confirm the littleness of human endeavour.

Everything depends on the soul of the people. Will they look on the poor spinners with the eyes of brothers and sisters, and see the beauty, the patriotism, the humanity, and the urgency of Khadi, and make it their own business? Otherwise the life of Khadi will be, as the Lancashire and our own mills people like to think, only as long as Gandhi's frail life. Up, my dear people! It is in your hands to make the good work a reality. Cast your eyes on your starving brothers and sisters, whom civilisation keeps far away from you, even so as to let you forget them altogether,—though you cannot live a single day without their toil and sweat. Give them honest work, such as they can do and you can give, and this is Khadi. Patriotism consists not in building castles in the air based on mere love of power but in remembering the life of your people, their joys and their sorrows while you are going through your daily routine of eating, dressing and enjoying family life. Then will there be harmony of life in our country, and happiness and freedom. Do not think that the work of the Spinners' Association is like that of some foreign proselytising mission. You must make it your own deepest concern and place it on the solid foundation of a whole people's daily life.

30th August, 1928

BRAHMO SAMAJ'S CONTRIBUTION TO HINDUISM

[Speaking on the 20th August at the Ahmedabad Prarthana Samaj on the occasion of the celebration of the centenary of the foundation of the Brahmo Samaj, Gandhiji delivered an address of which the following is a condensed translation. M. D.]

I do not think I am at all fitted to say anything on this great occasion, but I consented to come because of the great esteem in which I held the late Ramanbhai and because I could not resist Shrimati Vidyagauri. I am unfit to say anything today for many reasons. I have read nothing of or about Raja Ram Mohan Rai. What I know about him is based on what I have heard from his admirers. I do not claim to have studied the history of the Brahmo Samaj either. I made a desperate effort to read something today, something from a brochure on Ram Mohan Rai that we have in our library, but I could not find a moment for it. I therefore contented myself with the prayer that God might give me the right word to acquit myself of the task.

Although, then, I cannot claim to have studied the history of the Brahmo Samaj, I do claim to have a close connection with the members of the Brahmo Samaj extending over several years. It dates as far back as 1896 when I first visited Calcutta. In 1901 I came in contact with several eminent members of the Brahmo Samaj through Gokhale and Dr. P. C. Ray. I used to visit occasionally the Samaj Mandir, and listen to the sermons of the late Pratap Chandra Mozumdar. I also came in touch with the late Pandit Shivanath Shastri.

These experiences were enough to convince me that the Brahmo Samaj has rendered a great service to Hinduism, and that it has rescued the educated classes of India, especially Bengal, from unbelief. I have always regarded it as a movement essentially designed for the educated classes. Though religion in India sometimes takes the form of superstition, wooden formalism and hysterics, I cannot escape the conviction that a man cannot long remain an unbeliever in India. But the faith of the educated class in the early part of the nineteenth century was in danger and it was Ram Mohan Rai who came to their rescue. I have heard that he had come under the influence of Christian missionaries and Kaka Saheb told me that he had made a deep study of Persian and Arabic. There can be no question about his scholarship or about his catholicity. He made a deep study of Hinduism, especially the religion of the Vedas, and then allowed himself to be influenced by the essential principles of Christianity and Islam. As a result he saw that there was for him no escape from inaugurating a new movement to liberalise the existing Hinduism which had been overgrown with superstitious weeds. Sacrifice of animals and social evils were flourishing in the name of Hinduism. How could the educated class tolerate it? It was open to Ram Mohan Rai to rest content with individual dissociation from the evils. But he was a reformer. He could not afford to hide his light under a bushel, he gave public expression to his views, secured a following and founded the Brahmo Samaj in 1828.

But it would have languished, had not a man of great spiritual gifts like Maharshi Devendranath Tagore joined it. It is for the future historian to estimate the Tagores' contribution to the intellectual and spiritual life of Bengal, India, and even the world. Ravindranath Tagore's contribution in the direction has been stupendous. We cannot adequately estimate it, even as men living in the valleys of the Himalayas cannot adequately visualise their sublimity. And the Tagores received their inspiration from the Brahmo Samaj. The

Brahmo Samaj liberated Reason, and left room enough for Faith. There was once a danger of the Brahmo Samaj severing its tie with Hinduism or the religion of the Vedas: but the Maharshi's *tapasya* and knowledge rescued the Brahmo Samaj from that catastrophe. It is due to him that the Samaj remained part of Hinduism.

One may not measure the contribution of the Brahmo Samaj from the number of its adherents. The Brahmos are indeed very few but their influence has been great and good. The service of the Brahmo Samaj lies in its liberalising and rationalising Hinduism. It has always cultivated a toleration for other faiths and other movements, it has tried to keep the fountain source of religion pure and to hold up the ideal of pure worship of the Supreme Being.

Not that there is nothing for me to criticise in the Samaj: but this is not the occasion for it. My desire is to place before you whatever is best in the Brahmo Samaj. Let this celebration awaken the religious instinct in you. True religion is not narrow dogma. It is not external observance. It is faith in God, and living in the presence of God; it means faith in a future life, in truth and *ahimsa*. There prevails today a sort of apathy towards these things of the spirit. Our temples appear today to be meant only for the simple and the ignorant. Few visit real temples of God. Let the educated class take up the work of reform in this direction.

We have rightly honoured Vallabhbhai over the Bardoli victory. But you may not know his greater victory. Vallabhbhai realised his *Vallabha* (God) in Bardoli. He saw that nothing but faith in God could keep together the thousands of men and women bound to their pledge. It is through religion that he found his approach to the hearts of those simple illiterate men and women.

I am inundated with letters from young men who write frankly about their evil habits and about the void that their unbelief has made in their lives. No mere medical advice can bring them relief. I can only tell them that there is no way but that of surrender to and trust in God and His grace. Let us all utilise this occasion by giving the living religion in our lives the place it deserves. Has not Akhobhagat said,

Live as you will, but so
As to realise God.

30th August, 1928

EUROPE GOERS BEWARE

By M. K. Gandhi

Now that so many people have begun to go to Europe and the interest India and Indians has since the days of Non-co-operation grown, there is a growing demand on their time on the part of European public bodies and political parties. Not one of us was however prepared for what befell Babu Rajendra Prasad. Rajendra Babu went to London some months ago to fulfil an important legal engagement. Having finished his case he did a bit of travelling on the Continent and among other things attended the War Resisters' Conference in Vienna. Prompted by a stranger, he accepted another engagement in the neighbourhood. There was some days ago in the *Bombay Chronicle* a cable to the effect that a meeting at which Babu Rajendra Prasad was speaking on peace was broken up by Fascists and that he was seriously assaulted. In the absence of any cable from Rajendra Babu, I refused to believe in the assault. The same day that I saw the press cable, I had a cable from Rajendra Babu asking for a message for the Youth Conference in Holland. This removed all suspicion about the assault; but by the last mail I received a letter from Austrian friends, a professor and his wife, containing a graphic description and confirmation of the assault reported in the press. I reproduce below the relevant portion of the letter which moreover contains a warning important for all who visit the Continent :

"Though very rejoiced at your letter of introduction

of Mr. Rajendra Prasad I was terrified by a postscript of one——whose name we had never heard before at the backside of your letter. In your kind letter there was no word about any meeting, but at the back, this Mr.——wrote, 'Comrade Raj. Pr. will speak at the Steinfelder Sale, and requests you to meet him there.' I was very much astonished and terrified. For, in the 'Steinfelder Sale,' which is a beerhouse, there was on the same day a meeting of 'International Women's League for Peace and Freedom.' I did not know this league. This letter came into our hands at 9 in the morning of the 1st August, and we tried the whole forenoon to find out whether this meeting guaranteed security, but we could not find in any directory or telephone-book any address or name of the members of this league. So we went to the station to fetch brother Prasad, to take him with us to our home. Mr. Prasad did not know the circumstances of this meeting and did not know enough of this Mr.——. He agreed with this Mr.——to speak at the meeting in which were concentrated from the surroundings and the town the followers of war and violence in order to disturb this women's meeting. Not knowing anything——and myself went there with Mr. Prasad to satisfy his obligation. Mr.——was not at the meeting, no one was there of the women's Committee, the hall was full of smoke, the tables full of beerglasses, men were yelling——here was no one of that Committee though it was already quarter of an hour later. Going to the Women's Committee table, we were suddenly attacked even before the beginning of the meeting, and though guarding him with our own bodies, we could not prevent brother Prasad from being injured. After our injuries we came to know: (1) that he was taken to be one——, the name of whom we had never heard, who had to speak at this meeting; (2) that Mr.——was an anarchist and editor of an anarchistical newspaper! We are very sorry at all this. Not only because of our wounds—

fortunately my double quilted Khaddar-hat and my hair-knot caught up many of the blows with wooden laths and chairs and glasses, nevertheless, brother Prasad was slightly hurt on the head, on the forehead and upon one hand, and — was injured with a chair-leg on the cheek under one eye. This small wound of — and a small wound on the forehead of Mr. Prasad could be dangerous for the eyes, perhaps also a stab with a knife which I caught up with my hand and which was soon healed. I do not know whence I had the strength to hold up so many blows in order to make a way out through perhaps a thousand men beating us three, and insulting me because I was protecting the men, I had only one hand to hold up the blows, with the other hand I held Mr. Prasad whom . . . . and myself had between us . . . . trying to save his Gandhi cap which was finally lost. Our hands and feet were covered with blue spots, and for two days I had a slight commotion in the brain. All were crying: 'Slay him down,'—it was dreadful. . . . We have kept the good brother in our home and dressed his wounds. On the next day he felt well, and we travelled with him by railway one hour before leaving him. The next day we received a letter from him reporting that he was feeling well, and that the doctor had examined his small wounds and fortunately found these all right. Today he is staying at Monsieur Romain Rolland's in Villeneuve, to whom I have written an explaining letter. Now I beg you to say to all Indian brothers, who are starting for Europe or staying there, not to be implicated in any strange movement. Your principles of Non-violence etc. are torn from their setting and misused by political parties. The Indian brothers are too good and too credulous; for instance: we have heard; when one European says to an Indian brother, that he (the European) is a vegetarian, the Indian brother in his goodness believes that this European is a follower of your principles in the whole, but such a European can be also an Anarchist etc. I entreat you to warn the Indian brothers against having intercourse with strange people."

These friends deserve the warmest thanks of the relatives and the numerous friends of Rajendra Babu for their bravely defending his person at peril to their own lives. The incident shows the essential identity of human nature and it shows that gentleness, self-sacrifice and generosity are the exclusive possession of no one race or religion.

But it is the warning contained in the letter which is much the most important part of it. There is no doubt that there is a desire on the part of all sorts of Continental parties to exploit for their own purposes Indian visitors, especially if they happen to hold a position in the public life of India. It is therefore a good thing to bear in mind the Shakespearian warning, "Give thine ear to every one, thy voice to none." There must be on the part of Indian visitors an estimable desire to advertise the Indian cause by speaking to European audiences. It is as well however to know that exemplary self-restraint in everything will advertise the Indian cause much better than any amount of public speaking. Character is any day more eloquent than speech.

30th August, 1928

TORTURE OF BULLOCKS

An English lady writes:

"I am much distressed and perplexed by the habitual torture of bullocks by the inhabitants of this country, chiefly Hindus, who call themselves protectors of the cow! The sight of the dislocated mutilated tail joints of the over-burdened creatures toiling along roads is one never to be forgotten by a visitor to this country. The way the hands of the drivers, made filthy by cruelty, grasp and twitch the very backbone of the shrinking creatures at the tail socket, when the tail itself is a broken twisted abomination, is a sight which brings shame on the Hindu religion. Can you do nothing through your paper *Young India* on behalf of these creatures, as also on behalf of the tormented fowls carried by the legs head down for miles to their destruction? I enclose a picture of English oxen at work. The Indian has adopted the motor car for himself, why not the harness for his bullocks?"

Whilst it is true that this fair visitor to India has indulged in a hasty generalisation by accusing the inhabitants of India of habitual torture of bullocks,—for it is not every inhabitant, not even every tenth man who ill uses bullocks,—there is no doubt that some drivers in the cities are guilty of the practice referred to in the letter, and there is no doubt also that the passer-by goes his way totally oblivious of the torture and there is truth too in the statement about the inhuman carrying of fowls. It is possible to say of us who talk about *ahimsa* that we strain at a gnat and easily swallow a camel. We would be agitated if a rabid dog was shot, but we are indifferent, if not willing, witnesses to the cruelties such as are mentioned in the letter I have reproduced. We seem to think that we have fully carried out the doctrine of *ahimsa* so long as we do not actually kill. In my opinion this is a travesty of *ahimsa*. Every act of injury to a living creature and endorsement of such act by refraining from non-violent effort wherever possible to prevent it is a breach of *ahimsa*. Here there is work for religious organisations that would be faithful to their convictions to conduct a crusade against cruelties to lower animals practised in the cities. The change from the yoke to the harness is undoubtedly desirable.

30th August, 1928

A KHADDAR CLAD HIGH SCHOOL

Dr. P. B. Datta of Chittagong sends the following interesting report of a High School in which all boys and teachers have been using Khaddar for the last four years:

"Durgapur High School (P. O. Bhardvajhat, Chittagong) is in the district of Chittagong and is situated 40 miles north of the town of the same name. Durgapur is a fairly large village with an area of about three square miles and a population of nearly 3,500 souls. The school was started on the 1st of January, 1908 and was a successful institution from the very beginning. In 1912 a Co-operative Credit Society was started in the village mainly through the efforts of the school teachers. This Society has now a working capital of Rs. 29,000 (entirely subscribed by the local people) and is one of the best managed rural Societies of Chittagong.

"About the year 1922 a Khadi producing organisation was started at Mahajanhat, about 7 miles from Durgapur. A few months later Acharya Prafulla Chandra with Satish Babu of Khadi Pratishthan came to see it. Boys flocked to hear the Acharyadeva and caught their first inspiration of Khaddar. A small but sincere group of boys began to use Khaddar and a small Khaddar store was started to supply their needs. Nearly a year later (perhaps in 1923) Gandhiji with a large number of followers visited Mahajanhat Khadi Pratishthan and boys of Durgapur flocked to see and hear him. By this time the use of Khaddar had became almost universal amongst Durgapur schoolboys without any compulsion whatever—teachers of course showing the way.

"When the use of Khaddar became almost universal the Managing Committee stepped in to give the movement their official support. The use of Khaddar was made obligatory for students and teachers in the Managing Committee meeting of 14th July, 1924. It was ordered that from 15th August, 1924 nothing but full Khaddar dress shall be allowed in the school. As all teachers and most of the boys had already taken to Khaddar, the order really affected only a few boys. They also very soon adopted Khaddar and are wearing the same for the last four years. When the school sits at 11 A.M. it is a real pleasure to see three hundred boys trooping into school fully clad in Kaddar. Now after four years' wearing of Khadi we find that it has done no boy (or his parents) the slightest harm but has done much positive good. Parents now do appreciate that the use of Khaddar has been on the whole economical and has curtailed a good deal of unnecessary expense. It has inculcated amongst the boys a sense of plain living and patriotism. Villages surrounding Durgapur constitute the most important Khaddar producing area in Bengal. There are branches of the Calcutta Khadi Pratishthan and Comilla Abhoy Ashram in the village itself besides several other Khadi organisations within a radius of six miles.

"Agricultural activities of the school are also worth mentioning. A small experimental farm was attached to the school in 1919. Most of the boys come from cultivator families and therefore agriculture has been introduced in middle standards. It is also in contemplation to maintain a Goshala and a small workshop, but financial stringency stands in the way. The school is already under a heavy debt incurred for acquiring necessary lands for agricultural demonstration farms.

"There are thousands of high schools all over India. What has been possible at Durgapur is surely possible in many other privately managed schools."

M. K. G.

30th August, 1928

THE MORAL SIDE OF CITY MILK SUPPLY

Much has been said about the milk supply of Indian cities from the economic, sanitary and social point of view, but the moral side has been entirely neglected.

The milk trade is in the hands of ignorant and poverty-stricken city *govals* who have no conscientious scruples about what they do. The only aim before them is to get as much money as possible.

Nature has created milk in the udders of cows for their young ones and it is through human efforts that the milk flow has increased to such an extent that he can get *surplus milk* for his own use, but what do we find in the ordinary cow-stable? Mothers with half starved calves or whose calves have been killed by long starvation, so as to get as much milk as possible. To produce a good quantity of milk requires special energy on the part of the cow and this should be furnished in the form of extra rich food, but the poor animal gets barely enough to keep body and soul together. The maltreatment and the abnormal ways of life the animal has to lead indicate how wrong it is to use this milk. There is always a cry amongst the farmers working round about big cities that the *govalis* use the field crop of the poor farmer or some times cut away his crop for animal feeding. This is one of the reasons why ordinary farming is being given up gradually. The city people do not know that the milk they take is thus tainted with crime.

Does the *goval* really benefit in the end? Probably not. The bulk of his income is snatched from him by the Ghanchi and the city milk dealer who is both money-lender and middleman and squeezes the last drop of blood from the *goval.* The Ghanchi manipulates the milk in more ways than one and the thing that reaches the customer is generally a dirty unwholesome, watery milk-like substance.

Could this state of things be remedied and how? Let every consumer make it a point to get his supply only from an honest source. The extra cost will be more than balanced by the purity of milk. But the honest source has to be created. The rich people of the cities should band together and count no cost too great to get expert advice and open one or more dairies where the rich and the poor can get pure milk on equal terms even as all get postage stamps on the same terms irrespective of their status. With a little philanthropy the problem is not beyond solution. The city people owe it to the babies, if to none else, that there is an abundant supply of good and cheap milk available for every baby in their cities.

Y. M. PARNERKAR

6th September, 1928

HELP UTKAL

BY M. K. GANDHI

Sjt. Niranjan Patnaik who represents the All-India Spinners' Association in Utkal writes a letter from which I take the following:

"For some months past the selling work of the Utkal Branch of the All-India Spinners' Association has not been quite satisfactory. Production work is going on quite well, the present rate of production being about Rs. 4,000 a month. At your suggestion we have started two new centres in the more distressed areas,—at Aul in Cuttack district and Tihidi in the Balasore district,—these two centres have now on their rolls nearly 300 spinners and their yarn production up to date has come to nearly 9 maunds (1 maund=82 lbs.) most of which is 12s to 15s and some even 20s. The sales, however, are low. Last year we sold on an average Rs. 2,741 per month; during the current year though we sold nearly Rs. 20,000 worth a few weeks before and during your visit to the province, there was a fall subsequent to that. That is, though the current year's average monthly sale would be nearly Rs. 3,500, the sale during the last few months went down even below Rs. 2,000 per month. The result is that our Khadi stock is now nearly Rs. 40,000. Last year our gross profit was 10.3 per. cent, and our prices this year also are fixed on that basis. I take a typical variety of production and show below what relation the cost of production bears to sale price:

"Shirting piece 10 yds. × 45 inches: This weighs 4 lbs. 28 *tolas* and contains about 26 threads per inch of 8s and 9s,

1. Cost of cotton 5 lbs.	Rs. 2—8—0
2. Spinning wages (allowing reduction of 2½ *tolas* per lb.)	1—4—9
3. Weaving wages @ 3 as. per yd.	„ 2—9—6
4. Washing	„ 0—3—0
5. Freights, from spinning centre up to sale depot (last year's basis)	„ 0—4—8
Primary cost of production	Rs. 6—4—2
Sale price @ Re. 0—10—9 per yd.	„ 6-11—6
Difference	Re. 0—7—4

"This hardly allows an anna in the rupee for establishment charges of production centre, sale or for supervision. During your last visit to Utkal you asked us not to worry over the question of sales but to put our energies solely in production work. I have requested the Secretary of the All-India Spinners' Association to help us to sell our stock. If you consider that the matter might usefully be mentioned in the columns of *Young India* kindly help us."

Having faith in Khadi and faith in the people I did tell Niranjan Babu during my Utkal tour last year that he should concentrate on production. It was not possible to see those blank eyes of skeletons and stand still when one had work for them. The reader will be surprised to learn that Utkal Khadi is not cheaper than Khadi from the other provinces except perhaps Gujarat. The reason is that the people being more helpless than elsewhere, every new introduction carries more cost than it would in ordinary circumstances. The tendency however is to bring down the prices as efficiency and production grow. Meanwhile appeal must be made to the philanthropy and patriotism of the people to take up this Khadi and thus help the paupers of Orissa. The analysis of cost given in the letter shows that the bulk of the money goes directly into the pockets of the poor people. Only Rs. 0-7-4 out of Rs. 6-11-6 go towards part payment of overhead charges which too after all pay the middle class workers who man the Khadi service. Thus in Khadi production there is no overlapping. It means pure addition be it ever so slight to the wealth of the country and a fresh avenue of honourable employment for honest middle class young men without the necessity of their having to pass through English schools and produce at least matriculation certificates if not higher. There are two ways of helping to clear the surplus stock, either by buying the Khadi for personal use or by paying a bounty towards reduction of the price of the Khadi so that it could be sold at cheaper rates to poor local people. I hope those who understand the condition of Orissa and appreciate the value of Khadi in national economics will adopt one of the two courses suggested by me. The address of the head office of the Utkal Branch of the All-India Spinners' Association is Swaraj Ashram, Berhampur, B. N. Ry.

6th September, 1928

AFTER LUCKNOW

BY M. K. GANDHI

The most brilliant victory achieved at Lucknow following as it does closely on the heels of Bardoli makes a happy conjunction of events. Pandit Motilalji is today the proudest man in India and has every reason to be so. But even he could have done nothing if every one had not conspired to make the proceedings a success. It would have been easy for the Hindus or the Musalmans to block the way. The Sikhs could have done likewise. But no one had the heart to destroy the patient labours of the Nehru Committee. Little wonder that Pandit Malaviyaji the irrepressible optimist said that Swaraj would be attained in 1930.

The honours for the happy result must however be shared with Pandit Nehru by Dr. Ansari. His invisible help was much greater than his visible and tactful guidance of the proceedings at Lucknow. He was ever at the beck and call of the Nehru Committee. He used all his unrivalled influence with the Musalmans in disarming their opposition. Hindus could not resist his transparent honesty and equally transparent nationalism. The Liberals led by Sir Tej Bahadur Sapru lent a weight to the Conference which it would otherwise have lacked. I join Dr. Besant in her wish that they would re-enter the National organisation. They need not lose their identity even as the Hindu and Musalman organisations do not lose theirs.

The mention of the Liberals brings us to the future work. There is still much diplomatic work to be done. But more than the diplomatic work is that of forging the sanction. Pandit Jawaharlal Nehru truly observed that whether it was Dominion Status or Independence, a proper sanction would be necessary if the national demand was to be enforced. Bardoli has shown the way, if the sanction has to be non-violent. The Congress creed has non-violence as its integral part. There is no denying the fact that non-violence had receded in the background before Bardoli. But even as the Nehru report has made a unanimous demand possible, Bardoli has brought back the vanishing faith in non-violence.

If then we are sure of the sanction, we need not worry whether Swaraj is otherwise spelt Dominion Status or Independence. Dominion Status can easily become more than Independence if we have sanction to back it. Independence can easily become a farce, if it lacks sanction. What is in a name if we have the reality? A rose smells just as sweet whether you know it by that name or any other. Let us therefore make up our minds as to whether it is to be non-violence or violence and let the rank and file work for the sanction in real earnest even as the diplomats must work at constitution-making.

6th September, 1928

AHIMSA IN EDUCATION

[For some time past Gandhiji has been following the practice of giving weekly talks to the students of the Gujarat Vidyapith. He used on these occasions to invite questions from students and teachers which he would answer. Before their interrogatories could be exhausted, however, he had to take up the reading of *Hind Swaraj* with them at their request. But as some of the questions received by him are of general interest he proposes to deal with them in the pages of *Navajivan*. The substance of one is given below. M. D.]

One of the questions put to me was as follows:

"The moment one begins to talk of *ahimsa*, a series of trifling questions are mooted, *e.g.*, whether it is permissible to kill dogs, tigers and wolves, snakes, lice, etc., and whether one may eat brinjals or potatoes. Or else the questioner engages in a disputation over the question of maintaining an army or of offering armed resistance. Nobody seems to trouble to inquire how the principle of *ahimsa* should be worked out as part of education. Will you kindly shed some light on this question?"

This is not a new problem. It has been discussed threadbare in these columns off and on in one shape or another. But I know that I have not succeeded in making it absolutely clear to my readers. The task, I am afraid, is beyond my capacity. But I should be thankful if I could succeed in contributing somewhat to its solution.

The introductory part of the question shows that questions betraying a narrow outlook are often put. By unnecessarily exercising ourselves over conundrums about the justifiability of man's killing creatures and animals of a lower order, we often seem to forget our primary duties. Every one of us is not faced every day with the question of killing obnoxious animals. Most of us have not developed courage and love enough to practise *ahimsa* with regard to dangerous reptiles.

We do not destroy the vipers of ill-will and anger in our own bosom, but we dare to raise futile discussions about the propriety of killing obnoxious creatures and we thus move in a vicious circle. We fail in the primary duty and lay the unction to our souls that we are refraining from killing obnoxious life. One who desires to practise *ahimsa* must for the time being forget all about snakes etc. Let him not worry if he cannot avoid killing them, but try for all he is worth to overcome the anger and ill-will of men by his patient endeavour as a first step toward cultivating universal love.

Abjure brinjals or potatoes by all means, if you will, but do not for heaven's sake begin to feel yourself self-righteous or flatter yourself that you are practising *ahimsa* on that account. The very idea is enough to make one blush. *Ahimsa* is not a mere matter of dietetics, it transcends it. What a man eats or drinks matters little, it is the self-denial, the self-restraint behind it that matters. By all means practise as much restraint in the choice of the articles of your diet as you like. The restraint is commendable, even necessary, but it touches only the fringe of *ahimsa*. A man may allow himself a wide latitude in the matter of diet and yet may be a personification of *ahimsa* and compel our homage, if his heart overflows with love and melts at another's woe, and has been purged of all passions. On the other hand a man always overscrupulous in diet is an utter stranger to *ahimsa* and a pitiful wretch, if he is a slave to selfishness and passions and is hard of heart.'

Whether India should have an army or not, whether or not one may offer armed resistance to Government,—these are momentous questions that we shall have to solve one day. The Congress has in its creed already furnished an answer to them in part. But important as these questions are, they do not much concern the man in the street, they do not touch the aspect of *ahimsa* with which an educationist or a student is concerned. *Ahimsa* in relation to the life of a student stands quite apart from these questions of high politics. *Ahimsa* in education must have an obvious bearing on the mutual relations of the students. Where the whole atmosphere is redolent with the pure fragrance of *ahimsa,* boys and girls studying together will live like brothers and sisters, in freedom and yet in self-imposed restraint; the students will be bound to the teachers in ties of filial love, mutual respect and mutual trust. This pure atmosphere will of itself be a continual object-lesson in *ahimsa.* The students brought up in such an atmosphere will always distinguish themselves by their charity and breadth of view, and a special talent for service. Social evils will cease to present any difficulty to them, the very intensity of their love being enough to burn out those evils. For instance the very idea of child-marriage will appear repugnant to them. They will not even think of penalising the parents of brides by demanding dowries from them. And how dare they after marriage regard their wives as chattel or simply a means of gratifying their lust? How will a young man brought up in such an environment of *ahimsa* ever think of fighting a brother of his own or a different faith? At any rate no one will think of calling himself a votary of *ahimsa* and do all or any of these things.

To sum up. *Ahimsa* is a weapon of matchless potency. It is the *summum bonum* of life. It is an attribute of the brave, in fact it is their all. It does not come within reach of the coward. It is no wooden or lifeless dogma, but a living and a life-giving force. It is the special attribute of the soul. That is why it has been described as the highest *dharma* (law). In the hands of the educationist therefore it ought to take the form of the purest love ever fresh, an ever gushing spring of life expressing itself in every act. Ill-will cannot stand in its presence. The sun of *ahimsa* carries all the hosts of darkness such as hatred, anger and malice before himself. *Ahimsa* in education shines clear and far and can no more be hidden, even as the sun cannot be hidden by any means. One may be sure that when the Vidyapith is filled with the atmosphere of this *ahimsa,* its students will no more be troubled by puzzling conundrums.

(Translated from *Navajivan*)

6th September, 1928

LIMITS OF SATYAGRAHA

BY M. K. GANDHI

A correspondent impatient to stop the marriages of aged men with young girls writes:

> "This evil requires drastic remedies. Twenty-five young men of character should form themselves into a band of Satyagrahis, proceed to the place of the marriage eight or ten days before the event and plead with both the parties, with the heads of the caste organisation, and with all concerned. They should parade the streets with suitable placards condemning such marriages and produce an atmsphere of opposition to the proposed marriage. They should persuade the people of the town or village to declare a peaceful boycott against the parties to the marriage, and court arrest or whatever other punishment that comes to them.
>
> "Thus the Satyagrahi band would soon become a power in the locality, and these marriages would be a thing of the past."

The suggestion looks attractive, but I am afraid it cannot be of use on more than one occasion. Where lust and cupidity join hands the slaughter of the innocents becomes almost impossible to avoid. As soon as lustful old candidates for brides and the greedy parents get scent of the invasion of the Satyagrahi band, they will evade the band by performing the wedding secretly, and they will find enough priests and wedding guests to help them in the ceremony. The readers of *Navajivan* may be aware of an incident that happened some time ago. The old man in that case feigned contrition, and successfully threw dust into the eyes of all by a hollow public apology. The reformers were delighted, but before they had finished congratulating themselves the old man managed to get secretly married. What happened in one case may happen in many cases. We should therefore devise other means to grapple with the evil. I have an idea that it may be easier to reach the greedy father of the bride than the slave of his lust. There is a great necessity for cultivating public opinion in the matter. The parents who readily sell away their girls, out of cupidity, should be sought out and pleaded with, and caste organisations should be persuaded to pass resolutions condemning such marriages. Evidently such reforms cannot be carried out all at once by the same band in large areas. Their field must needs be circumscribed. A Satyagrahi band in Cape Comorin will not be able to prevent a monstrous marriage in Kashmir. The reformers will have therefore to recognise their limitation. We may not attempt the impossible.

Love and *ahimsa* are matchless in their effect. But in their play there is no fuss, show, noise or placards. They presuppose self-confidence which in its turn presupposes self-purification. Men of stainless character and self-purification will easily inspire confidence and automatically purify the atmosphere around them. I have long believed that social reform is a tougher business than political reform. The atmosphere is ready for the latter, people are interested in it, and there is an impression abroad that it is possible without self-purification. On the other hand people have little interest in social reform, the result of agitation does not appear to be striking, and there is little room for congratulations and addresses. The social reformers will have therefore to plod on for some time, hold themselves in peace, and be satisfied with apparently small results.

I may here throw out a practical suggestion. The most effective means of creating an atmosphere against the marriages of aged persons with young girls is to create public opinion against the actual marriage and to set in motion a peaceful social boycott against the aged bridegroom and the greedy father of the bride.

If a successful boycott can be carried out even in one

single instance, parents will hesitate to sell their daughters and old men will hesitate to run after young brides.

It will not be easy to wean lustful old men from their lust. They may be therefore induced to marry old widows, if they must marry. In Europe old men easily seek out old widows.

In conclusion, we must be clear about our objective in opposing these marriages. It cannot be our object to wean old men from their lust; if it is we will have first to deal with lustful young men. But that is a tall order. Our objective can be only to save young girls from the clutches of lustful old men and the cupidity of their parents. The reformer must therefore address himself to carrying on a crusade against the sale of brides. It is the bride's parents who have to be reached. Let the Stayagrahi therefore chalk out the field of his activities, have a census of all girls of a marriageable age living in that area, let him get into touch with their parents, and awaken them to a sense of their duty towards their daughters.

Let not the reformer go outside these limits if he wants to achieve success. The scheme proposed in the correspondent's letter easily transgresses these limits.

(Translated from *Navajivan* by M. D.)

6th September, 1928

OUR POVERTY

BY M. K. GANDHI

It is to be hoped that the reader has followed the carefully and ably written articles of Prof. C. N. Vakil which he recently contributed to this journal on the problem of India's poverty. Prof. Sam Higginbottom sent me a circular letter propounding the following four questions :

I. What are the tests of poverty?

II. Whether India is richer or poorer today than 25 years ago or a longer period?

III. Is poverty in India general or confined to particular groups?

IV. Causes and remedies.

As a layman I could but give my evidence on the questions without carrying conviction to a critic. I therefore had the important and pertinent questions circulated among economist friends with a request to answer them in some detail if they could make time for the purpose. Prof. Vakil promptly responded with the articles to which I have drawn attention. The series is really not concluded. When I came upon the last chapter dealing with the remedies, I observed that it admitted of re-writing with a view to fuller and more accurate treatment. I am now trying to induce Prof. Vakil to re-write the chapter if he can possibly find the time and has the inclination. If he does send me anything the reader may expect a further instalment. Meanwhile he may regard the series as concluded.

The articles show clearly and I venture to think conclusively that India is poorer today than 25 years or a longer period ago and that the poverty is general and not confined to groups. Prof. Vakil has applied two tests for proving his proposition. He has shown that though during the past 40 years our average income has increased in the ratio of 1 to 2.74 (and he has accepted top figures in every case) the cost of living has increased in the ratio of 1 to 3.78, in other words we are poorer today to the extent of 2/7 than we were 40 years ago. He then examines the population figures and arrives at the same conclusion by showing that whilst the population has increased the capacity for coping with the increase has not only not kept pace with the increase but has probably deteriorated.

Prof. Vakil has enumerated the following six causes for this growing poverty:

1. Not enough work for the vast mass of the agricultural population during the off season.

2. The social system which imposes the burden upon one person of supporting a large family.

3. The presence of a large number of able-bodied beggars miscalled *sadhus*.

4. Enervating climate.

5. Resignation to fate and consequent want of determination to fight against poverty.

6. Faulty educational syste....

Whilst these are contributory causes of more or less value, with the exception of the first none seems to me to go to the root of the matter. There is no doubt enough in the chapters to show that foreign exploitation of India is a cause of poverty. But in collecting the causes the Professor has evidently felt some delicacy about mentioning what is obviously a primary cause. This exploitation is a hydra-headed monster taking a variety of shapes to suit given occasions. The marine, the military, the currency, the railway and the revenue policy of the foreign Government is directed deliberately to promote an exploitation such as the world has never before witnessed. Poverty of India will never be removed so long as the exploitation continues unabated. Even the spinning wheel or any other subsidiary occupation that may be provided for the millions of peasantry will bring only partial relief, if the terrible drain as Dadabhai Naoroji called it is not stopped. He, therefore, who would explore the remedies for removing poverty has to tackle first the question of stopping the continuous drain.

13th September, 1928

MY ATTITUDE TOWARDS WAR

By M. K. Gandhi

Rev. B. de Ligt has written in a French journal called *Evolution* a long open letter to me. He has favoured me with a translation of it. The open letter strongly criticises my participation in the Boer War and then the great war of 1914 and invites me to explain my conduct in the light of *ahimsa*. Other friends too have put the same question. I have attempted to give the explanation more than once in these columns.

There is no defence for my conduct weighed only in the scales of *ahimsa.* I draw no distinction between those who wield the weapons of destruction and those who do Red-Cross work. Both participate in war and advance its cause. Both are guilty of the crime of war. But even after introspection during all these years, I feel that in the circumstances in which I found myself I was bound to adopt the course I did both during the Boer War and the great European War and for that matter the so called Zulu 'Rebellion' of Natal in 1906.

Life is governed by a multitude of forces. It would be smooth sailing, if one could determine the course of one's actions only by one general principle whose application at a given moment was too obvious to need even a moment's reflection. But I cannot recall a single act which could be so easily determined.

Being a confirmed war resister I have never given myself training in the use of destructive weapons in spite of opportunities to take such training. It was perhaps thus that I escaped direct destruction of human life. But so long as I lived under a system of Government based on force and voluntarily partook of the many facilities and privileges it created for me, I was bound to help that Government to the extent of my ability when it was engaged in a war unless I non-cooperated with the Government and renounced to the utmost of my capacity the privileges it offered me.

Let me take an illustration. I am a member of an institution which holds a few acres of land whose crops are in imminent perils from monkeys. I believe in the sacredness of all life and hence I regard it as a breach of *ahimsa* to inflict any injury on the monkeys. But I do not hesitate to instigate and direct an attack on the monkeys in order to save the crops. I would like to avoid this evil. I can avoid it by leaving or breaking up the institution. I do not do so because I do not expect to be able to find a society where there will be no agriculture and therefore no destruction of some life. In fear and trembling, in humility and penance, I therefore participate in the injury inflicted on the monkeys, hoping some day to find a way out.

Even so did I participate in the three acts of war. I could not, it would be madness for me to sever my connection with the society to which I belong. And on those three occasions I had no thought of non-cooperating with the British Government. My position regarding that Government is totally different today and hence I should not voluntarily participate in its wars and I should risk imprisonment and even the gallows if I was forced to take up arms or otherwise take part in its military operations.

But that still does not solve the riddle. If there was a national Government, whilst I should not take any direct part in any war I can conceive occasions when it would be my duty to vote for the military training of those who wish to take it. For I know that all its members do not believe in non-violence to the extent I do. It is not possible to make a person or a society non-violent by compulsion.

Non-violence works in a most mysterious manner. Often a man's actions defy analysis in terms of non-violence: equally often his actions may wear the appearance of violence when he is absolutely non-violent in the highest sense of the term and is subsequently found so to be. All I can then claim for my conduct is that it was, in the instances cited, actuated in the interests of non-violence. There was no thought of sordid national or other interest. I do not believe in the promotion of national or any other interest at the sacrifice of some other interest.

I may not carry my argument any further. Language at best is but a poor vehicle for expressing one's thoughts in full. For me non-violence is not a mere philosophical principle. It is the rule and the breath of my life. I know I fail often, sometimes consciously, more often unconsciously. It is a matter not of the intellect but of the heart. True guidance comes by constant waiting upon God, by utmost humility, self abnegation by being ever ready to sacrifice one's self. Its practice requires fearlessness and courage of the highest order. I am painfully aware of my failings.

But the Light within me is steady and clear. There is no escape for any of us save through truth and non-violence. I know that war is wrong, is an unmitigated evil. I know too that it has got to go. I firmly believe that freedom won through bloodshed or fraud is no freedom. Would that all the acts alleged against me were found to be wholly indefensible rather than that by any act of mine non-violence was held to be compromised or that I was ever thought to be in favour of violence or untruth in any shape or form. Not violence, not untruth but non-violence, Truth is, the law of our being.

13th September, 1928

ON TOLSTOY'S BIRTHDAY

M. D.

Tolstoy lives and will live not because of the monumental works of art that he has left us, but because through whatever he has done or written, he has held aloft for all time the never-fading light of Truth. To a critic who scrutinises the pages of his life, it looks like a stupendous failure, possibly a huge shipwreck. But the thing that survived the shipwreck was Truth and his ever-wakeful pursuit of Truth—"the heroine of my writings, she whom I love with all the forces of my being, she who always was, is, and will be beautiful, is Truth." In a sense his life was one unending misery, an unbroken tide of resolutions broken, of hopes unfulfilled. "Eternal Being! Let a single man tell me, if he dare: I was better than that man!" he exclaims and yet coupled with this humility was in him that defiance which can spring only out of a relentless pursuit of Truth: "I say it loudly and fearlessly: Whosoever could believe me a dishonest man is himself a man to be suppressed"—an epitaph that should satisfy the most ambitious of us. Even his failures arose out of his quenchless pursuit of Truth, because he never shrank from the conclusions that rigorous logic, which in other words was rigorous devotion to truth, brought him to. At the end of all his great works, *What shall We do Then?* or *Kreutzer Sonata*, he might have said as he said in the Epilogue to the latter work, "My own conclusions terrified me at first, and I was tempted to reject them." But the conviction always rings clear in every page of his books as of his life: 'It was impossible for me to refuse to hear the voice of my reason and my conscience.'

It may not be inappropriate, on the day when multitudes of people are thinking of him, to take an excerpt or two from some of his pages written with his heart's blood, and live with them for a quiet moment:

"What do I want? To live with God, according to His Will, with Him. What is wanted for that? One thing only is wanted: To preserve the talent given to me, my soul, given to me not only to preserve but to make it grow. I know for myself what is needed: to keep *what is animal in me in purity what is human in humility, and what is divine in love*. What is wanted for preserving purity? Privations, privations of every sort. Humility? Humiliation. Love? The hostility of men. When and how am I to keep my purity without privations, my humility without humiliation, and my love without hostility? 'And if you love those that love you, that is not love, but love ye your enemies, love ye that hate you.' One sorrow approaches humiliation and hostility, and these thoughts have revived me. Another sorrow is privation, suffering—the very thing that is needed for the growth of the soul. That is how one must look at it."

Or take this leaf from a letter written just before his death: 'You ask whether I like the life in which I find myself. No. I don't like it. I don't like it because I am living with my own people in luxury, while there are poverty and want around me, and I cannot help the poverty and want. For this I do not like my life. I like it in that it is in my power to act, and that I can act, and that I do act in the measure of my strength in accordance with the teaching of

Christ, to love God and my neighbour. To love God is to love the perfection of goodness and to approach it as far as one can. To love one's neighbour is to love all people alike as one's brothers and sisters. It is this, and this alone, that I am striving for, and since little by little, however poorly, I am approaching it, I do not grieve, but only rejoice. You ask me too, if I rejoice, at what do I rejoice, and what joy do I expect? I rejoice that I can carry out to the measure of my strength the task set me by my Master; to work for the setting up of that Kingdom of God to which we are all striving."

And as I think of Tolstoy, I think of a kindred spirit, who throughout his brief life on earth tried "to carry out to the measure of his strength the task set him by his Master," with as quenchless a pursuit of Truth as the great veteran, and possibly with a greater measure of success. I mean, of course, Maganlal Gandhi, who, had he been in the flesh, would have blushed at, and remonstrated against, being mentioned in the same breath as Tolstoy. And as I think of him, I have before me a letter written by him which I must share with the readers of *Young India*, a letter which is so wonderfully reminiscent of Tolstoy and which like most of the master artist's letters would

"arouse the sensual from their sleep
Of death, and win the vacant and the vain
To noble raptures."

Here is the letter:

"I have gone through the same ordeal as you, though circumstances were more favourable. But I can easily put myself in your position. What I say is not by way of advice, but is a leaf from my experience, which might save one like you from shipwreck.

"Man ought not to assume that woman is inferior to him. It behoves him to adore her. It is only that attitude of mind that purges our heart of passion. Man when he is swayed by passion forgets the wretched plight to which he is reduced. But woman understands him, and allows herself to be affected by his poiselessness. Before a man who retains his poise and is not swayed by passion she responds without fail to his purity. Woman is by nature passive, man active. It is man who uttered the calumny that woman is the root of all evil; on the contrary, it is we men who are the root of evil and if we root the evil out of our hearts there is no fear.

"If you have the courage to plead with your wife, ask her to abjure all ornaments, coloured and gaudy clothes. If her object is only to please you, tell her that coarse spotless Khadi is enough to please you. But if her ornament and her fineries are intended to attract the world, tell her plainly it is none of a chaste woman's concern. A woman gaudily bedecked is like the delicacies displayed in a confectioner's shop. They attract, as they are meant to attract, passers-by. They attract flies too. But the pollution rendered by these insects is harmless as compared to the pollution that a lustful eye creates. A woman gaudily bedecked invites the pollution or goes about with the pollution. Of what worth is outward beauty before the natural beauty of a pure heart and soul?

"Having said this I may mention a few details which help to keep the mind and body pure. I need not expatiate on the necessity of plain and simple fare. For you are living a life of purity. But I would ask you to try to give up salt for a few months. You may have lime as a substitute.

"And do you desire to have children? Does your wife desire them? I would suggest to you to adopt a friend's or a relative's baby. Shower all your love on the baby, and sublimate all your passion into pure energy for the upbringing of that baby. This is a divine state—I shudder to write this but the experience of sages points to that as the condition of supreme bliss. It is also common experience that as soon as a baby is born, the passions of the parents, if they are not dominated by lust, gradually begin to cease, and with a little endeavour man can easily get free from the shackles of the flesh by concentrating all his energy on the upbringing of the baby. If therefore you can realise that it is no part of your duty to add to the number of slaves in the country, you will also realise that it is better and more serviceable to adopt a baby and nurse him to liberty. I have hardly the fitness to say all this, but I say it because I see it as clear as daylight. Pray think of the truth regardless of the unworthiness of the man telling it.

"If however you cannot restrain for good the desire for offspring, keep it in abeyance until you have fitted yourself for the act of procreation by a course of *brahmacharya* in thought, speech and action extending over a few years."

And as I read the words so crudely translated I have before me Maganlal's truthful look, the look which like Tolstoy's went 'straight to the heart,' through those eyes 'which pierce you through.' M. D.

20th September, 1928

PRISON TREATMENT

BY M. K. GANDHI

The Director of Information in his communique dated 12th September, 1928, has attempted a reply to the article in *Young India* of 16th August regarding the food served out to prisoners at the Sabarmati Central Jail. He boldly says that these statements are incorrect. It is perfectly clear from the communique that he has not made the inquiry himself but his opinion is based upon the statement supplied to him by the very parties who are accused of neglect. It is unnecessary for me to refute the statement that the health statistics in the prisons of India compare favourably with the statistics of the population living outside. This is an admitted fact, for the simple reason that the laws of sanitation are undoubtedly better enforced in the prisons than outside. But better sanitation does not prove more humaneness or more consideration for the prisoners. My point is that there is absence of the human touch about the whole of the prison system. And it seems to me to be wholly beside the point to mention that the general health of the inmates of prisons is better than outside, and I claim that even this statement becomes untenable when applied to the class of prisoners from whom Satyagrahis are drawn. It was open to the Director to say, if he had so chosen, that the Satyagrahis knew that there would be no humanity to be found inside the prison walls. Statements such as I made in the article in question had point, because the claim is often made that the prisoners in Indian prisons are treated humanely and that as much consideration as is possible to give to prisoners is given in these jails.

With regard to the specific statements made in the Director's communique I can only give extracts from the statements made by the released prisoners, every one of whom I hold to be far more reliable than all the jail authorities put together. The statements were made by the Satyagrahis on their discharge from the jail in reply to my request about the treatment, and when I saw with my own eyes the shattered constitution of Sjt Chinai whom I knew to be in possession of excellent health and when I saw a Vidyapith lad Dinkar suffering from an obstinate fever which, but for extraordinarily good nursing and able medical aid he had the good fortune to receive after being discharged from the prison, might have proved fatal.

I shall take the first extract from the statement made by Sjt. Sanmukhlal, a well known man of Valod who got dysentery twice as a result of bad food:

> "The greens served out were wretched beyond description. . . . *Luni* simply stank in one's nostrils so much so that I had to discontinue taking it. When it was exhausted, radishes and a hotchpotch of dry leaves like those of cabbage etc, were substituted in its place with the result that soon after many prisoners began to suffer from bowel complaints in large numbers. But nobody could muster sufficient courage to lodge a complaint about it with the Superintendent. I even heard from some prisoners that

one of the prisoners was given bar-fetters for several months for making such a complaint.

"Things improved a little after some time.

Pumpkin and onions and later *turiya* and *gowar* were introduced in the vegetable fare; the *gowar* and *turiya* were hard and stringy being over-ripe, but even so were picked out and regarded by the prisoners as a delicacy."

"The *juwar* bread was only half-baked and so full of grit that it could hardly be chewed and had to be swallowed. This was especially the case when the grinding stones of the flour mills were freshly dented. As a result of this food I got dysentery, almost half of our number sharing the same fate with me."

Sjt. C. L. Chinai in his statement repeats the same story :

"The food did not agree with me and I began to get stomach-ache and finally had diarrhoea, sometimes getting as many as 30 or 35 motions in a day Whenever I took the greens they invariably gave me diarrhoea. Thus I began fast to lose my weight. When I complained about it to the doctor he said that I should give up taking the greens if I wanted to keep fit, which I did and from that time till the end remained on bread and water only. I did not complain about it to the Superintendent because he never paid any heed to the complaints of the prisoners regarding food. I even heard that there had been cases of prisoners being punished for making such complaints. Therefore nobody dared to take the matters before the authorities."

Even Sjt Ravishankar Vyas with his iron constitution was driven to say in his statement:

"The greens consisted of dry, tough, leathery leaves with an admixture of pumpkin. To eat it was to court certain stomach-ache."

Sjt. Chinai was given hard labour beyond his capacity and consequently he had attacks of giddiness, but for twenty days he could not get the medicine that he needed. He lost over

20 lbs. in weight during his incarceration. Similarly, Govind Gosain who was already in a poor state of health when he was sentenced came out of jail in such a weak condition that he could scarcely keep steady on his legs.

I have given only the briefest extracts from the statements in my possession. If the authorities are serious, I shall have much pleasure to send them all the statements and any further proof that they may need. Refutations such as the Director of Information has made, I feel sure, carry no weight with the public, certainly do not improve the condition of the prisoners, nor make for humaneness in the prisons. The first condition of humaneness is a little humility and a little diffidence about the correctness of one's conduct and a little receptiveness. One misses all the three in the Director's refutation.

20th September, 1928

A LETTER FROM SIMLA

Though we have been here for some days we are feeling like fish out of water. 'Three strange animals' is how the President of the Assembly described us to a friend and Sjt. Ghanshyamdas Birla, my host, was reminded of the Urdu expression *kababmen haddi* (lit. bone in the fritters) as he saw us having our lunch in the Cecil Hotel with some friends who had invited us. And he was perfectly right. Sjt. Vallabhbhai, Swami Anand and I were by no strength of imagination 'outsiders' in Bardoli, but we were certainly 'outsiders' in that Hotel and are so in Simla. The President wanted his brother to have some rest and we followed him as part of his Bardoli camp followers.

'Why all this expense for such a brief session? You don't seem to think of the tax-payer at all,' said the Younger Patel to the elder. The elder, whose power of repartee is as great as the younger's, replied: 'You didn't think of the tax-payer when you started the Bardoli campaign! What a lot of expense in six months!' Let the tax-payer arbitrate between the two brothers' but to help him I might place a little more evidence before him. The Assembly Members all get their first class double fares and Rs. 20 daily allowance during the session of the Assembly. The allowance is regarded as inadequate in certain quarters and an M. L. A. was seriously arguing the other day; 'The Cecil charges as much as Rs. 10 per day if you stay the whole month and Rs. 14 for a shorter period. There are other expenses of course, including the inevitable rickshaw costing Rs. 5 per day. How is one to live?' The one who was thus addressed being far more practical gave the disgruntled friend a bit of his mind: 'But who asks you to stay in the Cecil? Some of our friends from the South live in huts on the Cart Road and improvise their little kitchens and they even save something at the end of the session. And you are quite able-bodied. Why must you have the rickshaw?'

I am told that every season about 25,000 people come up to Simla from Delhi—they have to, they are part and parcel of the Simla gods. If the gods come, the lesser ones and still lesser and their families also must come to Simla—as, for instance, some one might say, we followed Sjt. Vallabhbhai! But what a tremendous charge on the resources of the poor country?

To go to Simla with the Speaker's brother and to avoid going to the Assembly was beyond me, though a confirmed non-co-operator. So I went. The Speaker simply rules the Assembly, not because he is an autocrat,—no autocrat would be tolerated by an autocratic Government,—but because of his wonderful independence, powerful personality and consummate tact. 'Impartially unfair' was the compliment he earned from Sir Charles Innes and he is living up to his reputation. The other figure that arrested my attention was Pandit Motilal Nehru. It delighted my heart to see Pandit Motilalji, revered by all on the opposition benches and dreaded by the other side.

But leaving the great ones aside, let me talk about the humble folk. In a luminous passage Cardinal Newman asks: "Can anything be more marvellous or startling unless we were used to it, than that we should have a race of beings about us whom we do see, and as little know their state, or can describe their interests or their destiny, as we can tell of the inhabitants of the sun and moon? It is, indeed, a very overpowering thought, when we get to fix our minds on it, that we periodically use—I may say hold intercourse with—creatures who are as much strangers to us, as mysterious, as if they were the fabulous unearthly beings, more powerful than man, and yet his slaves which Eastern superstitions have invented. We have more real knowledge about the angels than about the brutes; they have apparently passions, habits and a certain accountableness; but all is mystery about them. We do not know whether they can sin or not, whether they are under punishment, whether they are to live after this life; we inflict very great sufferings on a portion of them, and they, in turn, every now and then, retaliate upon us, as if by a wonderful law."

Cardinal Newman was thinking of the brute creation, but one may ask the same question here as regards our own fellowmen whom we do not regard as any better than brutes. How many that ride the rickshaws on the steep hills of Simla care to know of the life the rickshaw coolies lead, of the conditions under which they live or of their feelings! A Ghanshyamdas Birla may pay his rickshawmen double or treble the scheduled rate, get them to spin during their leisure hours, and a Pandit Malaviyaji may exclaim every moment he rides a rickshaw, *bada pap karna padta hai* (what a sin we have to commit), and get off his rickshaw whenever they have to climb a difficult ascent. But what of the rest? A rickshaw coolie's wage does not come to more than seven annas a day and those who ride on their backs like the Old Man of the Sea are hardly content with Rs. 20 a day! What a tragedy! And what of the numerous other coolies on the hill? Where do they sleep, what do they get to eat, do they live with their women or children, what is the effect on their lives of this drudgery on the hill? 'Did you ever stop to inquire,' asked Sjt. Vallabhbhai at a meeting where he was forced to speak, 'did you ever inquire what is the death rate among these coolies who really are the children of the soil whom you have ousted?'

They talk so much of whether or not a necessity has been made out for a particular bill. They had one day better discuss whether a necessity has been made out for the whole Government and legislative machinery to go to Simla. They can get through more work, we are told; do they? Do they get through better work? Do they legislate better on the heights of Simla? And what shall we do under Swaraj?

M. D.

20th September, 1928

HOW I DISCOVERED THE SPINNING WHEEL

BY M. K. GANDHI

A friend who has been studying the All-India Spinners' Association organisation after having studied a centre in Karaikudi (Tamilnad) writes:

"This (Uttukuli) is a heavy production centre for handspinning and weaving. I have half picked up this work here. There are about a thousand spinners. I have gone about the villages and met many of them in their own little cottages. Every day that passes makes me marvel the more as to how you discovered the spinning wheel. I am very much tempted to ask if you could not kindly tell in the pages of *Young India* when and how exactly you re-discovered the wheel. It is so little and so big at the same time. It reminds me of the rain drops—each so tiny by itself but together 'the mighty ocean.' Nothing is more wrong than to think that you have asked India to spin and that India has begun to spin driven to do so by you. The truth is rather that the millions in the villages have driven you to it—to be their agent for disposing of all their yarn. I am daily watching crowds of old women and girls coming with their yarn. They come with smiling faces, their precious yarn clutched to their hearts. And Khadi is retouching slowly into life just those vital parts of our national being that have been touched almost into death by this most soulless of exploitations. I realise now as never before the truth of your words when you said that the world will some day accept Khadi as the noblest of your works."

He is right when he says that the toiling starving millions drove me to it. It was in London in 1908 that I discovered the wheel. I had gone there leading a deputation from South Africa. It was then that I came in close touch with many earnest Indians—students and others. We had many long conversations about the condition of India and I saw as in a flash that without the spinning wheel there was no Swaraj. I knew at once that every one had to spin. But I did not then know the distinction between the loom and the wheel and in *Hind Swaraj* used the word loom to mean the wheel. This is what I have said in the concluding chapter of the booklet:

> "We will get nothing by asking; we shall have to take what we want, and we need the requisite strength for the effort and that strength will be available to him only who
>
> * * *
>
> 2. "if a lawyer, will give up his profession and take up a hand-loom (spinning wheel):
>
> * * *
>
> 8. "although a doctor, will take up a hand-loom (spinning wheel)
>
> * * *
>
> 10. "if a wealthy man, will devote his money to establishing handlooms (spinning wheels), and encourage others to use hand-made goods by wearing them himself;"

The words are as true today as they were in 1908 when the booklet was written. Today not only are lawyers, doctors and others spinning by way of sacrifice but they are also organising the movement. But alas, they are yet far too few for the purpose of waking the millions from their helpless lethargy. The vast majority are still standing aside. They seem to be waiting for a catastrophe greater than the one that is happening in front of them. They seem to await the simultaneous destruction of millions to produce in them a shock that would move them to action. Be that as it may, there is no organic Swaraj until the starving millions feel its glow. They will not feel it until the living contact is established between them and us the vocal class who literally bleed them in order that we may live.

But to return to the wheel. Though the wheel was discovered to the mental vision in 1908, it saw work only in 1918 after three years' patient and strenuous effort. The first Khadi vow (very much adulterated to suit the fashionable sisters of Bombay) was taken in 1919. The wheel found a place in the Congress programme in 1921. The history of the movement since then is an open book still being written in the lives of the two thousand odd organisers and nearly seventy thousand spinners in whose lives the wheel has brought a ray of hope. Were we not under the hypnotic and desolating spell of the city civilisation, we would realise through our hearts that only a little combined, conscious and honest effort in the shape of work is required to take the wheel to every cottage in India. Multiply the return of one wheel by say one hundred million and the result will convince the most confirmed unbeliever of its potency. But probably he will refuse to be willing and say, 'What you say is true as an arithmetical problem, it is wholly untrue as a practical proposition.' You can only take a willing horse to the trough. But a true spinner must have unlimited patience. He does not give in. The answer to the question propounded by the friend therefore perhaps should be, 'The wheel is still being discovered.' I know that it shall be one day, for there are some in this country who are prepared to pay for the discovery with their lives.

20th September, 1928

TOLSTOY AND THE YOUTH

[Last week there was time only to give the barest outline of Gandhiji's message on Tolstoy delivered to the Youth League of Ahmedabad in the Satyagrahashram on the Tolstoy Centenary day. The following is a condensed translation of the message. P.]

Personally I do not believe in the *shraddha* ceremony as commonly understood among us in India, and although I remember having performed *shraddha* at a time, I have given up the practice long since, for, as I wrote to a correspondent recently in reply to a question of his, I believe that the only true way of celebrating the *shraddha* of one's ancestors is constantly to ponder over and translate into daily life their good qualities. I might have neglected the observance of this great *shraddha* but for the insistence of Dr. Hariprasad, your President, that I should speak to you on this occasion. He told you just now that like Dattatreya, I had many *gurus* of whom Tolstoy was one. I wish I could claim the honour.

I have called Gokhale my political *guru*. But in spiritual matters, I am sorry to say, I have not yet found any one to whom I could completely surrender myself and whose opinion I could implicitly and unquestioningly accept as I could Gokhale's in politics. Perhaps I am not yet ripe for a spiritual *guru* because I believe that the spiritual *guru* comes to you of himself, in fact seeks you out when you are ready for him.

But while thus the little throne within has remined vacant, next to the late Rajachandra, Tolstoy is one of the three moderns who have exerted the deepest spiritual influence on my life, the third being Ruskin. It was forty years back when I was passing through a severe crisis of scepticism and doubt that I came across his book *The Kingdom of God is within you*, and was very deeply impressed by it. I was at that time a believer in violence. Its reading cured me of my scepticism and made me a firm believer in *ahimsa*. What has appealed to me most in Tolstoy's life is that he practised what he preached and reckoned no cost too great in his pursuit of truth. Take the simplicity of his life, it was wonderful. Born and brought up in the midst of the luxury and comfort of a rich aristocratic family, blessed in an abundant measure with all the stores of the earth that desire can covet, this man who had fully known all the joys and pleasures of life turned his back upon them in the prime of his youth and afterwards never once looked back.

He was the most truthful man of this age. His life was a constant endeavour, an unbroken tide of striving to seek the truth, and to practise it as he found it. He never tried to hide truth or tone it down but set it before the world in its entirety without equivocation or compromise, undeterred by the fear of any earthly power.

He was the greatest apostle of non-violence that the present age has produced. No one in the West, before him or since, has written and spoken on non-violence so fully or insistently and with such penetration and insight as he. I would even go further and say that his remarkable development of this doctrine puts to shame the present day narrow and lop-sided interpretation put upon it by the votaries of *ahimsa* in this land of ours. In spite of India's proud claim of being the *karmabhumi* the Land of Realisation, and in spite of some of the greatest discoveries in the field of *ahimsa*, that our ancient sages have made, what often goes by the name of *ahimsa* among us today is a travesty of it. True *ahimsa* should mean a complete freedom from ill-will and anger and hate and an overflowing love for all. For inculcating this true and higher type of *ahimsa* amongst us, Tolstoy's life with its ocean-like love should serve as a beacon light and a never-failing source of inspiration. Tolstoy's critics have sometimes said that his life was a colossal failure, that he never found his ideal, the mystical green stick, in whose quest his entire life was passed. I do not hold with these critics. True, he himself said so. But that only shows his greatness. It may be that he failed fully to realise his ideal in life, but that is *only* human. No one can attain perfection while he is in the body for the simple reason that the ideal state is impossible so long as one has not completely overcome his ego, and ego cannot be wholly got rid of so long as one is tied down by shackles of the flesh. It was a favourite saying of Tolstoy that the moment one believes that he has reached his ideal his further progress stops and his retrogression begins and that the very virtue of an ideal consists in that it recedes from us the nearer we go. To say therefore that Tolstoy on his own admission failed to reach his ideal does not detract a jot from his greatness, it only shows his humility.

Much has been often sought to be made of the so-called inconsistencies of Tolstoy's life; but they were more apparent than real. Constant development is the law of life, and a man who always tries to maintain his dogmas in order to *appear* consistent drives himself into a false position. That is why Emerson said that foolish consistency was the hobgoblin of little minds. Tolstoy's so-called inconsistencies were a sign of his development and his passionate regard for truth. He often *seemed* inconsistent because he was continuously outgrowing his own doctrines. His failures were public, his struggles and triumphs private. The world saw only the former, the latter remained unseen probably by Tolstoy himself most of all. His critics tried to make capital out of his faults but no critic could be more exacting than he was with regard to himself. Ever on the alert for his shortcomings, before his critics had time to point at them he had already proclaimed them to the world magnified a thousandfold and imposed upon himself the penance that seemed to him necessary. He welcomed criticism even when it was exaggerated and like all truly great men dreaded world's praise. He was great even in his failures and his failures give us a measure not of the futility of his ideals but of his success.

The third great point was the doctrine of 'bread-labour,'*

* Tolstoy adopted the phrase from the Russian peasant. Bondrieff and insisted that it should be interpreted literally.

viz., that every one was bound to labour with his body for bread; and that most of the grinding misery in the world was due to the fact that men failed to discharge their duty in this respect. He therefore regarded all schemes to ameliorate the poverty of the masses by the philanthropy of the rich while they themselves shirked body labour and continued to live in luxury and ease as hypocrisy and a sham, and suggested that if only man got off the backs of the poor, much of the so-called philanthropy would be rendered unnecessary.

And with him to believe was to act. So in the afternoon of his life, this man who had passed all his days in the soft lap of luxury took to a life of toil and hard labour. He took to boot-making and farming at which he worked hard for full eight hours a day. But his body labour did not blunt his powerful intellect, on the contrary, it rendered it all the more keen and resplendent and it was in this period of his life that his most vigorous book *What is Art?* which he considered to be his master-piece was written in the intervals saved from the practice of his self-chosen vocation.

The choice before our youth today lies between the way of self-restraint and the way of indulgence and ease, the one leading to salvation and freedom, the other to utter destruction. They are at the parting of the ways. Literature, full of the virus of self-indulgence served out in attractive forms, is flooding this country from the West and there is the greatest need for our youth to be on their guard. The present is for them an age of transition of ideals and of ordeals and the one thing needful for the world, its youth and particularly the youth of India in this crisis is Tolstoy's progressive self-restraint, for it alone can lead to true freedom for themselves, the country and the world. It is we ourselves, with our inertia, apathy and social abuse, that more than England or anybody else block our way to freedom. And if we cleanse ourselves of our shortcomings and faults, no power on earth can even for a moment withhold Swaraj from us. The test for the youth lies before them and that is to win their diploma from the university of life, with its snares and pitfalls and ordeals, without which their academic degrees will be in vain. The three essential qualities of Tolstoy's life mentioned by me are of the utmost use to the youth in this hour of the world's trial.

The Youth League has very rightly set before itself the ideal of service of country. But that service is not possible unless it is rooted in love or *ahimsa*. *Ahimsa* is not mere non-killing. A person who remains smugly satisfied with the non-killing of noxious life but has no love in his heart for all that lives will be counted as least in the Kingdom of Heaven. True love is boundless like the ocean and rising and swelling within one spreads itself out and crossing all boundaries and frontiers envelops the whole world. This service is again impossible without bread-labour, otherwise described in the Gita as *yajna*. It is only when a man or woman has done body labour for the sake of service that he or she has the right to live The Gita says that anybody who eats without performing *yajna*, in Tolstoy's language bread-labour, is a thief, 'eats sin.' But body-labour becomes *yajna* only when it is undertaken in a spirit of service not of indulgence as it may easily become when it is done only to develop the animal in man. A man who adopts service as his ideal will go on curbing his carnal appetites more and more and though, as in the case of Tolstoy, the attainment of full self-restraint seem always as far away as ever he will never cease to persevere in it and regard such perseverance as the *summum bonum* of life. Firhad in his quest of Shirin wore away his life in breaking rocks, shall we do less for our Shirin of Truth, without which service is not?

27th September, 1928

'STARTLING CONCLUSIONS'

BY M. K. GANDHI

William R. Thurston, according to the publisher's preface, was a Major in the United States army, which he served for nearly ten years. And, during these years, he had varied experiences in several parts of the world, including China. During his travels he studied the effects of marriage laws and customs, as a result of which he felt the call to write a book on marriage. This book which is called *Thurston's Philosophy of Marriage* and was published last year by the Tiffany Press, New York, contains only 32 pages of bold type, and can be read inside of an hour. The author has not entered into an elaborate argument but has simply set forth his conclusion with just a dash of argument to support his conclusions which the publisher truly describes as 'startling.' In his foreword, the author claims to have based his conclusions on "personal observation, data obtained from physicians, statistics of social hygiene and medical statistics," compiled during the war. His conclusions are:

1. "That Nature never intended a woman to be bound to a man for life, and to be compelled to occupy the same bed or habitation with him, night after night, in pregnancy and out, in order to earn her board and lodging, and to exercise her natural right to bear children.

2. "That the daily and nightly juxtaposition of the male and female, which is a result of present marriage laws and customs. leads to unrestrained sexual intercourse which perverts the natural instincts of both male and female, and makes partial prostitutes of 90% of all married women. This condition arises from the fact that married women have been led to believe that such prostitution of themselves is right and natural because it is legal, and that it is necessary in order to retain the affections of their husbands."

The author then goes on to describe the effects of 'continual unrestrained sexual intercourse' which I epitomise as follows:

(*a*) "It causes the woman to become highly nervous, prematurely aged, diseased, irritable, restless, discontented, and incapable of properly caring for her children."

(*b*) "Among the poorer classes it leads to the propagation of many children who are not wanted."

(*c*) "Among the higher classes, unrestrained sexual intercourse leads to the practice of contraception and abortion." "*If contraceptive methods, under the name of 'birth control' or any other name, are taught to the majority of the women of the masses, the race will become generally diseased, demoralized, depraved and will eventually perish.*" (The italics are the author's.)

(*d*) "Excessive sexual intercourse drains the male of the vitality necessary for earning a good living." "*At present there are approximately 2,000,000 more widows in the United States than there are widowers. Comparatively few of these are war widows.*" (Italics are the author's.)

(*e*) "The excessive sexual intercourse incident to the present married state develops in the minds of both male and female a sense of futility." "*The poverty of the world today, and the slums of the larger cities are not due to lack of profitable labour to be performed, but to excessive, unrestrained sexual intercourse, resulting from present marriage laws.*" (Italics are the author's.)

(*g*) "Most serious of all from the standpoint of the future of the human race is sexual intercourse during pregnancy."

Then follows an indictment of China and India into which I need not go. This brings us to half of this booklet. The next half is devoted to the remedy.

The central fact of the remedy is that husband and wife must always live in separate rooms, therefore necessarily sleep in separate beds, and meet only when both desire progeny, but especially the wife. I do not intend to give the changes suggested in the marriage laws. The one thing common to all marriages throughout the world is a common room and a common bed, and this the author condemns in unmeasured terms, I venture to think, rightly. There is no doubt that much of the sensuality of our nature, whether male or female, is due to the superstition bearing a religious sanction that married people are bound to share the same bed and the same room. It has produced a mentality, the disastrous effect of which it is difficult for us living in the atmosphere generated by that superstition, properly to estimate.

The author is equally opposed, as we have already seen, to contraceptive methods.

S. Ganesan, the enterprising publisher of Madras, has obtained the permission of the author to reprint the booklet for circulation in India. If he does so,* the reader can possess a copy at a trifling price. He has secured also the rights of translation.†

Many of the other remedies suggested by the author are, in my opinion, not of practical use to us, and in any case require legislative sanction. But every husband and wife can make a fixed resolution from today never to share the same room or the same bed at night and to avoid sexual contact, except for the one supreme purpose for which it is intended for both man and beast. The beast observes the law invariably. Man having got the choice has grievously erred in making the wrong choice. Every woman can decline to have anything to do with contraception. Both man and woman should know that abstention from satisfaction of the sexual appetite results not in disease but in health and vigour, provided that mind co-operates with the body. The author believes that the present condition of marriage laws 'is responsible for the greater part of all the ills of the world today.' One need not share this sweeping belief with the author to come to the two final decisions I have suggested. But there can be no doubt that a large part of the miseries of today can be avoided, if we look at the relations between the sexes in a healthy and pure light and regard ourselves as trustees for the moral welfare of the future generations.

* Since Published: Price 12 annas.

† Tamil Translation Published. Price 4 annas

27th September, 1928

KHADI WORK IN BIJOLIA

[The following is a summary of an elaborate report prepared for the Khadi workers by Sjt. Jethalal Govindji, the indefatigable worker who has specialised in the self-help method of Khadi production. Sjt. Jethalal Govindji swears by his method. Whether one agrees with him or not, one cannot help admiring the single-minded zeal with which he has worked out his method. His exclusive absorption in his self-imposed labours is worthy of emulation. It is the spirit that defies defeat. The experiences of such a worker cannot but be of value to every national servant. M. K. G.]

Man should be self-contained in the matter of food and clothing. Realisation of this ideal should result in eliminating the 'middleman' who lives on the economic exploitation of the cultivator.

With this end in view we chalked out the following programme: (1) to teach the farmers to do their own ginning, carding, and spinning and also to weave their yarn in their own homes: (2) to bring within their easy reach the instruments needed for the purpose and to teach them to manufacture the same themselves and (3) to help those who could not do their own carding or weaving to get their cotton carded and their yarn woven and to enable the people in general to purchase Khadi on the occasion of weddings, festivals etc.

The argument we adopted in approaching the people in this connection will be found outlined in the appendix at the end.

In this way we organised work among 5,500 people or to put the same in terms of output, 66,000 square yards weighing over 320 maunds of Khadi were maunfactured from self-spun yarn as a result of our effort. To this must be added about 25 p. c. more Khadi manufactured from yarn spun for wages. To do this we needed little capital, no stores, no hawkers, only a little demonstration workshop till the people had learnt the art of self-help in cloth.

Over 1,000 spinners spin for themselves, about 300 for wages. The count spun ranges from 4 to 10. The coarseness of count need cause no worry as the people want coarse Khadi. They will soon spin finer counts when they need fine Khadi.

The economic condition of the people is far from satisfactory. The slightest failure of crops would bring at least 60 p. c. of the people face to face with starvation. And yet before we went there they thought nothing of borrowing to buy their cloth.

Khadi tradition had not altogether died out here when we started our work. A few dilapidated old wheels could still be found here and there on which they spun 1 to 2 counts. And even this was being replaced by machine-made coarse cloth, We had to fight the superstition that (1) it was not possible to spin finer than 2 counts, (2) it was inconsistent with a farmer's dignity to spin, (3) it was cheaper to buy mill cloth than to have it woven from homespun, and (4) it was hopeless to fight against fate. To counteract the evil, we started a house to house propaganda and demonstrated the possibilities of the wheel by spinning in their presence.

It is necessary here to mention a discipline that we had laid upon ourselves. We made it a point to 'live and move and have our being' in Khadi alone and refused to interest ourselves in or talk about any other topic except Khadi. This conserved our energy and our self-evident earnestness compelled attention.

There were no doubt scenes of squalor, dirt and disease, vice and corruption, political and social degradation. We refused to be moved by them believing that if we could interest the people in their economic welfare through the only means open to them the rest would follow.

I must say that it stands to the credit of my co-workers that by dint of this discipline, by their ceaseless house to house propaganda and infinite patience and forbearance even in the face of rebuffs and insults that were very often their lot, they succeeded in revolutionising the mentality of the people. No weather was too inclement for their work. It gives me a thrill of joy even today to recall how in the biting cold of the winter mornings, in the blazing noon-day summer, or in the soaking rains and in the soft ankle-deep slush and mire of the rainy season, they would go about from village to village visiting people in their homes, carrying their thick, coarse *chapatis* with them in their haversacks. I am sure our life during the first two years must have excited the envy of even the peasants.

The result was all that one could wish. The ignorance, prejudice, laziness, apathy and despair of the people were at last replaced by self-confidence. With the hope of improvement in their economic condition, far-reaching psychological and spiritual changes began to come upon those who took to the wheel.

It would have been impossible for us—some three or four persons in all as we were—to achieve all these results if we had followed the usual methods of work. But we had so organised our programme that all that we had to do was to persuade people to learn the various processes themselves and to give them practical instruction—there was thus no investment of funds or special machinery for the production and sale of Khadi to tax and bother us. And as we had no monetary dealing with the people our motives always remained above suspicion.

Two difficulties stood in our way in the initial stages of our work.

1. The self-spinners would send their yarn to the village weaver. Now if the weaver was careless or unscrupulous and adulterated their yarn or substituted with inferior yarn, the self-spinners would be naturally discontented. We combated this difficulty by assuring the people that we would see to it that the weavers kept and wove the yarn of each individual separately.

2. The rates charged by the professional weavers were prohibitive. I realised my mistake which was due to inexperience and haste to achieve the end. I saw that a cultivator took about a month to spin sufficient yarn for an instalment of cloth. And

since he was naturally anxious to wear only the cloth produced from his own yarn he could at the most allow the village weaver one month's time to weave it into cloth by which time the next instalment of yarn would be ready.

As most of the spinning is done by the cultivator in his slack season and there is hardly any yarn ready for the weaver when the agricultural operations are going on in full swing most of the weaver's work must be crowded into one season. And so unless he can find some supplementary occupation to fall back upon he will be confronted every year with a season of unemployment. The weaver's supplementary occupation can only be cultivation of the soil. I therefore realised that we must induce each spinning family to set apart one of their members for weaving. And we have succeeded in thus preparing a few families already. Had I discovered this truth earlier we would have saved much time, trouble and worry.

3. A third difficulty now cropped up. We found that high dyeing and printing charges again put an unnecessary burden on the self-spinners. We are trying to revive indigenous dyeing. But for want of skill, we are at present relying on the prepared dyes. I know that our work is incomplete till we enable every family to do its own dyeing and printing.

The test that a weaver has to pass through in our weaving school before he can get a certificate in weaving is that he should be able to finish and submit to the examiners three pieces of cloth consecutively, all the processes anterior to weaving that cotton has to undergo being also performed by the candidate himself. If however he should be unable to finish all the three pieces unaided, he must do an extra piece in order to obtain the necessary certificate. We have thus prepared 90 weavers.

Satisfactory though the result is, we are not yet able to say that foreign or mill cloth has been banished altogether from Bijolia. Marriage brings fresh additions to existing families. They bring with them their taste for foreign cloth and need conversion. But this I can confidently claim that the method of self-help advocated here is the cheapest; the quickest and probably the most durable. We do not now expect to leave here more than one or two workers, who will attend to the repairs and such other difficulties that must crop up for some time to come.

APPENDIX

1. Man must somehow provide himself with food and clothing. But his harvest may fail and to earn wages locally may not be always possible. It is then that the spinning wheel comes to the rescue as an unfailing friend and helper.

2. If a cultivator sets out to purchase his cloth greater part of his produce would have to go to defray its cost and he would be left with hardly sufficient corn to eat and he will consequently be driven into debt.

3. Again what a topsy-turvydom! The unemployed cultivator sets out in the slack season to purchase cloth from the sowkar and thus as it were provides him with a living! Can anything be more perverse?

4. More satisfaction can be had from the bread obtained by baking half-anna's worth of flour at home than by purchasing four annas worth of fritters in the bazar.

5. The cloth bill of a farmer swallows up 4 to 5 times the amount of all the taxes that he has to pay. But while for the latter there is at present no help the former could all be saved if only he wills it.

6. The drain on the farmer's purse caused by the purchase of cloth is so insidious that his debt often runs into three figures before he is aware of it and yet the satisfaction which he gets from it is so inconsiderable.

7. Handspun and handwoven cloth is far more durable and lasting than mill cloth.

8. Spinning does not interfere with the agricultural work of the cultivator since it has to be done only during leisure time after the harvest is gathered in.

9. God made day for work and night for sleep, but no

time for idleness.' One must therefore never be idle and if there is no other work to do one must spin.

10. An idle man's brain is the proverbial devil's workshop. Idleness dulls the intellect and ruins man.

11. If the farmer had not to go to the petty cloth dealer to purchase cloth he would be saved from the baneful effect of moral and economic exploitation by the middlemen.

12. Where there is a will there is a way.

13. Nobody is born omniscient or all-wise. Every one lives to learn.

14. We (Khadi workers) are always ready to help.

15. Every man makes his *chapati* thin or thick according to his requirement or taste, similarly one can produce fine or coarse Khadi according to one's requirement.

16. Just as we can cook *dal* or vegetables just as we please and when we please if we have our own kitchen, so can we prepare *dhotis, saris,* shirts etc. according to our requirements, if we run our own spinning wheel and loom.

17. When we run out of bread, we do not go straight to the baker's shop to purchase *chapatis* but purchase grain from the bazar and make it into bread in our own home. Similarly when we are in need of clothing, the right thing to do would be to purchase raw cotton if we do not grow it and make it into cloth in our own homes.

18. If a farmer performs all the processes involved in the manufacture of cloth in his own home, he gets his cloth for the price of cotton.

19. A farmer who purchases his cloth from the bazar is like a leaky vessel which can never be filled even if you milk a hundred cows into it.

20. Carding is like grinding of flour. It is always done best at home.

21. Cotton should be stocked like grain for the whole year.

22. All the members of the family must take part in the

production of cloth whenever they have leisure just as they take part in agriculture.

23. The cultivator has his special season, the spinner and the weaver have the whole year for their season.

24. A hired worker never works with the same zeal as the one who works for himself.

4th October, 1928

'THE FIERY ORDEAL'

BY. M. K. GANDHI

[The killing of an ailing calf in the Ashram under circumstances described below having caused a great commotion in certain circles in Ahmedabad and some angry letters having been addressed to Gandhiji on the subject Gandhiji has critically examined the question in the light of the principle of non-violence in an article in *Navajivan*, the substance of which is given below. P.]

I

WHEN KILLING MAY BE AHIMSA

An attempt is being made at the Ashram to run a small model dairy and tannery on behalf of the Goseva Sangha. Its work in this connection brings it up, at every step, against intricate moral dilemmas that would not arise but for the keenness to realise the Ashram ideal of seeking Truth through the exclusive means of *ahimsa*.

For instance some days back a calf having been maimed lay in agony in the Ashram. Whatever treatment and nursing was possible was given to it. The surgeon whose advice was sought in the matter declared the case to be past help and past hope. The suffering of the animal was so great that it could not even turn its side without excruciating pain.

In these circumstances I felt that humanity demanded that the agony should be ended by ending life itself. I held a preliminary discussion with the Managing Committee most of whom agreed with my view. The matter was then placed before the whole Ashram. At the discussion a worthy neighbour vehemently opposed the idea of killing even to end pain and offered to nurse the dying animal. The nursing consisted in co-operation with some of the Ashram sisters in warding the flies off the animal and trying to feed it. The ground of the friend's opposition was that one has no right to take away life which one cannot create. His argument seemed to me to be point-less here. It would have point if the taking of life was actuated by self-interest. Finally in all humility but with the clearest of convictions I got in my presence a doctor kindly to administer the calf a quietus by means of a poison injection. The whole thing was over in less than two minutes.

I knew that public opinion especially in Ahmedabad would not approve of my action and that it would read nothing but *himsa* in it.

But I know too that performance of one's duty should be independent of public opinion. I have all along held that one is bound to act according to what to one appears to be right even though it may appear wrong to others. And experience has shewn that that is the only correct course. I admit that there is always a possibility of one's mistaking right for wrong and *vice versa* but often one learns to recognise wrong only through unconscious error. On the other hand if a man fails to follow the light within for fear of public opinion or any other similar reason he would never be able to know right from wrong and in the end lose all sense of distinction between the two. That is why the poet has sung:

> " The pathway of love is the ordeal of fire,
> The shrinkers turn away from it."

The pathway of *ahimsa*, that is, of love one has often to tread all alone.

But the question may very legitimately be put to me: Would I apply to human beings the principle I have enunciated in connection with the calf? Would I like it to be applied in my own case? My reply is yes; the same law holds good in both the cases. The law of *ethha pinde thathha brahmande* (a with one so with all) admits of no exceptions, or the killing of the calf was wrong and violent. In practice however we do not cut short the sufferings of our ailing dear ones by death because as a rule we have always means at our disposal to help them and because they have the capacity to think and decide for themselves. But supposing that in the case of an ailing friend I am unable to render any aid whatever and recovery is out of the question and the patient is lying in an unconscious state in the throes of fearful agony then I would not see any *himsa* in putting an end to his suffering by death.

Just as a surgeon does not commit *himsa* but practises the purest *ahimsa* when he wields his knife on his patient's body for the latter's benefit, similarly one may find it necessary under certain imperative circumstances to go a step further and sever life from the body in the interest of the sufferer. It may be objected that whereas the surgeon performs his operation to save the life of the patient, in the other case we do just the reverse. But on a deeper analysis it will be found that the ultimate object sought to be served in both the cases is the same, *viz*., to relieve the suffering soul within from pain. In the one case you do it by severing the diseased portion from the body, in the other you do it by severing from the soul the body that has become an instrument of torture to it. In either case it is the relief of the soul within from pain that is aimed at, the body without the life within being incapable of feeling either pleasure or pain. Other circumstances can be imagined in which not to kill would spell *himsa*, while killing would be *ahimsa*. Suppose for instance, that I find my daughter—whose wish at the moment I have no means of ascertaining—is threatened with violation and there is no way by which I can save her, then it would be the purest form of *ahimsa* on my part to put an end to her life and surrender myself to the fury of the incensed ruffian.

But the trouble with our votaries of *ahimsa* is that they have made of *ahimsa* a blind fetish and put the greatest obstacle in the way of the spread of true *ahimsa* in our midst. The current (and, in my opinion, mistaken) view of *ahimsa* has drugged our conscience and rendered us insensible to a host of other and more insidious forms of *himsa* like harsh words, harsh judgments, ill-will, anger and spite and lust of cruelty, it has made us forget that there may be far more *himsa* in the slow torture of men and animals, the starvation and exploitation to which they are subjected out of selfish greed, the wanton humiliation and oppression of the weak and the killing of their self-respect that we witness all around us today than in mere benevolent taking of life. Does any one doubt for a moment that it would have been far more humane to have summarily put to death those who in the infamous lane of Amritsar were made by their torturers to crawl on their bellies like worms? If any one desires to retort by saying that these people themselves today feel otherwise, that they are none the worse for their crawling, I shall have no hesitation in telling him that he does not know even the elements of *ahimsa*. There arise occasions in a man's life when it becomes his imperative duty to meet them by laying down his life; not to appreciate this fundamental fact of man's estate is to betray an ignorance of the foundation of *ahimsa*. For instance, a votary of truth would pray to God to give him death to save him from a life of falsehood. Similarly a votary of *ahimsa* would on bent knees implore his enemy to put him to death rather than humiliate him or make him do things unbecoming the dignity of a human being. As the poet has sung:

"The way of the Lord is meant for heroes,
Not for cowards."

It is this fundamental misconception about the nature and scope of *ahimsa*, this confusion about the relative values, that is responsible for our mistaking mere non-killing for *ahimsa* and for the fearful amount of *himsa* that goes on in the name of *ahimsa* in our country. Let a man contrast the sanctimonious horror that is affected by the so-called votaries of *ahimsa* at the very idea of killing an ailing animal to cut short its agony with their utter apathy and indifference to countless cruelties that are practised on our dumb cattle world. And he will begin to wonder whether he is living in the land of *ahimsa* or in that of conscious or unconscious hypocrisy.

It is our spiritual inertia, lack of moral courage—the courage to think boldly and look facts squarely in the face that is responsible for this deplorable state of affairs. Look at our *panjrapoles* and *goshalas*, many of them represent today so many dens of torture to which as a sop to conscience we consign the hapless and helpless cattle. If they could only speak they would cry out against us and say, "Rather than subject us to this slow torture give us death." I have often read this mute appeal in their eyes.

To conclude then, to cause pain or wish ill to or to take the life of any living being out of anger or a selfish intent is *himsa*. On the other hand after a calm and clear judgment to kill or cause pain to a living being with a view to its spiritual or physical benefit from a pure, selfless intent may be the purest form of *ahimsa*. Each such case must be judged individually and on its own merits. The final test as to its violence or non-violence is after all the intent underlying the act.

II

WHEN KILLING IS HIMSA

I now come to the other crying problem that is confronting the Ashram today. The monkey nuisance has become very acute and an immediate solution has become absolutely necessary. The growing vegetables and fruit trees have become a special mark of attention of this privileged fraternity and are now threatened with utter destruction. In spite of all our efforts we have not yet been able to find an efficacious and at the same time non-violent remedy for the evil.

The matter has provoked a hot controversy in certain circles and I have received some angry letters on the subject. One of the correspondents has protested against the 'killing of monkeys and wounding them by means of arrows in the Ashram.' Let me hasten to assure the reader that no monkey has so far been killed in the Ashram, nor has any monkey been wounded by means of 'arrows' or otherwise as imagined by the correspondent. Attempts are undoubtedly being made to drive them away and harmless arrows have been used for the purpose.

The idea of wounding monkeys to frighten them away seems to me unbearable though I am seriously considering the question of killing them in case it should become unavoidable. But this question is not so simple or easy as the previous one.

I see a clear breach of *ahimsa* even in driving away monkeys, the breach would be proportionately greater if they have to be killed. For any act of injury done from self-interest whether amounting to killing or not is doubtless *himsa*.

All life in the flesh exists by some *himsa*. Hence the highest religion has been defined by a negative word *ahimsa*. The world is bound in a chain of destruction. In other words *himsa* is an inherent necessity for life in the body. That is why a votary of *ahimsa* always prays for ultimate deliverance from the bondage of flesh.

None, while in the flesh, can thus be entirely free from *himsa* because one never completely renounces the will to live. Of what use is it to force the flesh merely if the spirit refuses to co-operate? You may starve even unto death but if at the same time the mind continues to hanker after objects of the sense, your fast is a sham and a delusion. What then is the poor helpless slave to the will to live to do? How is he to determine the exact nature and the extent of *himsa* he must commit? Society has no doubt set down a standard and absolved the individual from troubling himself about it to that extent. But every seeker after truth has to adjust and vary the standard according to his individual need and to make a ceaseless endeavour to reduce the circle of *himsa*. But the peasant is too much occupied with the burden of his hard and precarious existence to have time or energy to think out these problems for himself and the cultured class instead of helping him chooses to give him the cold shoulder. Having become a peasant myself,

I have no clear cut road to go by and must therefore chalk out a path for myself and possibly for fellow peasants. And the monkey nuisance being one of the multitude of ticklish problems that stare the farmer in the face, I must find out some means by which the peasant's crops can be safeguarded against it with the minimum amount of *himsa*.

I am told that the farmers of Gujarat employ special watchmen whose very presence scares away the monkeys and saves the peasant from the necessity of killing them. That may be but it should not be forgotten that whatever efficacy this method might have, it is clearly dependent upon some measure of destruction at some time or other. For these cousins of ours are wily and intelligent beings. The moment they discover that there is no real danger for them, they refuse to be frightened even by gun shots and only gibber and howl the more when shots are fired. Let nobody therefore imagine that the Ashram has not considered or left any method of dealing with the nuisance untried. But none of the methods that I have known up to now is free from *himsa*. Whilst therefore I would welcome any practical suggestions from the readers of *Navajivan* for coping with this problem let the intending advisers bear in mind what I have said above and send only such solutions as they have themselves successfully tried and caused the minimum amount of injury.

4th October, 1928

MISTAKEN HUMANITY?

By M. K. Gandhi

Sjt. Jamshed Mehta is rightly accepted as the truest man of Karachi. Almost every good public movement there claims him as its own. He devotes practically the whole of his time to public movements. He is one of the best representatives of theosophy. His honesty and independence are as unquestioned as his patriotism. When therefore such a man commits an error of judgment or runs counter to public opinion, his friends feel sore at heart. Sjt. Jamshed Mehta who is the President of the Karachi Municipality seems to me to have committed an error of judgment. Though a lover of Khadi he recently felt called upon to move on behalf of an absentee member a resolution about Khadi which drew forth very strong opposition from the members. Another matter was his attitude about a product that has been introduced from Europe into India as vegetable *ghee*.

Many common friends have drawn my attention to the controversy that has been going on in Karachi on these topics and invited me to express my own views on them, I suppose in the hope that they may either influence the President who knows my regard for him, or if they do not influence him, may at least prevent some of the Karachi public from being misled into wrong action owing to what the correspondents consider to be the erroneous views of the popular President. Whether my views produce any such influence or not, the opinion on these questions of Sjt. Jamshed Mehta deserve a patient and respectful examination.

I

He tells me that he moved the Khadi resolution in order to test the feeling of the Municipality and withdrew it when he saw that the members were opposed to it. I copy the resolution and the argument from the local press:

> "This Corporation resolves to cancel its resolution No. 304 dated 2nd July, 1924, because compulsory purchase and use of handspun and handwoven Khaddar *in all cases* has frequently resulted in pure waste of Municipal money in different departments of the Municipality."
>
> "In moving the above resolution, the President at the outset assured the house that he himself was actually in favour of popularising the use of Khadi but during the last three years the Corporation had spent no less than one lakh of rupees for encouraging this cottage industry but his honest opinion was that the poor menials wearing Khadi supplied by the Corporation were undergoing great hardships. The Councillors were doing great injustice to

themselves and to the rate-payers by spending such an enormous amount on Khadi which did the wearers little good. It was really a cruelty to ask the sweepers to wear this heavy cloth and go in the streets. Moreover white Khadi became dirty soon and poor peons had to spend lot of money for washing. The colour was tried but found useless. The Corporation could give only two suits and they had to suffer much for keeping them clean. The President emphatically observed: 'I tell you it is really a cruelty. We have spent nearly a lakh of rupees but Rs. 85,000 is really wasted. Our purpose has not been served. Unless and until we give them a better and lighter Khadi of a superior quality at double the present cost, we should not think of giving Khadi suits. The stuff we are now giving our peons is enough to bring tears in one's eyes.'"

Let us examine this argument. In judging the Municipal employees as he did by his own standard, I feel that the President has done the employees and the cause of Khadi a serious injustice. His judgment is very like that of a delicate lady judging the appetite of her weather-beaten guests by her own or like that of an ant measuring out a few particles of flour to the elephant and feeling that she had meted out to her guest an exact measure—we know that the measure in each case would be false. The delicate lady and the ant would be right in their measure if they had guests of the same species finding themselves in the same circumstances.

In the Karachi case, the measure adopted by the President is wrong because the Municipal employees have not been delicately brought up like the mover of the resolution. The President's measure is doubly false first because the sweepers do not need the same fineness in their dress material as the President and secondly because they do not want the same style of dress which educated Indians have from fear, ignorance or ambition imitated from the rulers. I venture to suggest that the Councillors should revise their notions of decency and equip their employees with garments of a style in keeping with the climate and the manners of the country. They need not then fear to use the coarsest Khadi. And they will save Municipal money, promote the comfort of the employees, revive true art and will at the same time serve the poorest of their countrymen whom they cannot reach save through Khadi. If the President would do unto the employees as he would that they should do unto him, let him for a moment step into their shoes and see how he would feel and his measure would be right.

But assuming that the employees must have an unnatural uniform in order to suit Municipal vanity, it is not difficult to pick up fine Khadi now-a-days if the Municipality will pay the price, nor is it impossible to have khaki coloured Khadi for the purpose.

The cheapest and the most patriotic method will be to train the girls and the boys of the Municipal schools and for the Councillors to train themselves to spin fine yarn and have it woven locally. The other citizens will then copy the patriotic and industrious example of the Councillors and if say one-third Karachi devotes only half an hour to philanthropic spinning, there would be many times more than enough Khadi to clothe the employees.

One valid objection may be taken to this course being adopted, namely that Khadi thus produced will not support the paupers in whose interest it has been recommended to public corporations. Whilst the objection is sound so far as it goes, it must not be forgotten that if any city takes up spinning in the manner suggested by me, it will be very substantial though indirect service of pauper India in that the moral effect of such sacrificial spinning will be so pervading that there will be produced a spinning atmosphere that would make the irresponsive masses take to it for supplementing their present income which is admitted to be altogether inadequate for human sustenance. Where the average daily income is less than seven pice, the addition of even one pice per day will be a princely addition.

But this may be treated as counsel of perfection not worthy of consideration by practical businessmen. Anyway I know that the idealist President will not dismiss my suggestion quite so summarily. But for those who will not seriously and scientifically organise home-spinning in the manner suggested, I submit that no expense incurred for Khadi need be considered as waste, no discomfort suffered on its account too much, when it is borne in mind that every pice spent upon Khadi goes directly into the pockets of the needy and that even of this at least 85 per cent. goes into the pockets of the poorest artisans including the semi-starved spinners.

But says the President: "Why not supply the employees with uniform made of Swadeshi mill cloth and save over sixty per cent. of the price paid for Khadi?" This is an argument I had least expected from Sjt. Jamshed Mehta the friend of the poor. Surely, if every Municipality gave a bounty of 60 per cent. to Khadi, it would not be wrong to do so assuming that it had the power so to do.

And I have repeatedly shown in these pages that there can be no comparison between Khadi and mill cloth even as there can be none between the home-made *chapati*, however costly it may be and troublesome to make, and cheap easily prepared machine-made biscuit. Mill cloth needs no protection or patronage from the public in the sense that Khadi does. Indian mill cloth gets preference as it ought to when Khadi is unavailable at any cost, when machine-made cloth becomes a necessity and when the choice lies only between foreign cloth and Swadeshi mill cloth. Khadi it is clear must displace both. Khadi has no established market like mill cloth. It has not even become as yet a bazar article. Every yard of Khadi bought means at least eighty five per cent. in the mouths of the starving and the poor ones of India. Every yard of mill cloth bought means more than 75 per cent. in the pockets of the capitalists and less than 25 per cent. in the pockets of the labourers who are never helpless, who are well able to take care of themselves, and who never starve or need starve in the sense that the helpless millions starve for whose sake Khadi has been conceived. Indeed I should be surprised if the Municipal employees whose supposed discomfort owing to wearing coarse Khadi has moved the humanitarian Sjt. Jamshed Mehta to action would not, if they were informed of the great national importance of Khadi, themselves prefer it to Swadeshi mill cloth however comfortable the latter may be to wear. Khadi in my opinion is cheap at any cost *so long as it functions to find work for and through work feed the millions.*

II

Sjt. Jamshed Mehta is not only a humanitarian, he is an ardent vegetarian and dares to incur the wrath of friends for the sake of his principles. He has somehow come to the conclusion that the product known as vegetable *ghee* which enterprising foreign manufacturers have introduced into the Indian market is preferable to what passes as genuine *ghee* but what is according to him almost always adulterated with animal fats. Though I yield to none in my enthusiasm for vegetarianism and personally always avoid the bazaar *ghee* and would, if I could get some medical encouragement or could summon sufficient strength of mind, avoid even goat's milk *ghee*, I could never bring myself to use the chemically doctored vegetable product which is generally palmed off on the gullible public as *ghee*.

So far as I have been able to examine medical authorities, they show that there is no effective vegetable substitute for *ghee* or animal fats, these being rich in vitamin A which they say is absolutely necessary for a person to keep in good health. We therefore arrive at this (for vegetarians) painful conclusion that whilst fat adulterated *ghee* is bad from the vegetarian standpoint, from the medical it is harmless. The only proper course for jealous food reformers like Sjt. Jamshed Mehta is to move heaven and earth to ensure a never failing supply of pure *ghee* and to that end I invite him to join the Goseva Sangha if he has no other and more expeditious method of reaching the common goal. Let him municipalise the milk and *ghee* supply of Karachi and run an efficient Municipal dairy. Vegetable *ghee* deserves only to be boycotted at all cost. For it is itself often adulterated and unlike adulterated *ghee* equally often injurious to health being chemically treated and in almost every case it is worthless as a food. In this country which abounds in oil seeds, the fresh seed oils are infinitely superior to the prepared vegetable fats whose basis is mostly cocoanut. Every one in India can prepare for himself good vegetable *ghee* from an undried cocoanut which can be procured cheap in any bazar.

11th October, 1928

GOD IS

BY M. K. GANDHI

Correspondents often invite me to answer in these pages questions about God. That is the penalty I have to pay for what an English friend calls the God stunt in *Young India*. Whilst I am unable to notice all such questions in these columns, the following compels an answer:

> "I read your *Young India* of 12-5-'27 p. 149* where you write, 'I think it is wrong to expect certainties in this world where all else but God that is Truth is an uncertainty.'
>
> "*Young India* p. 152**: 'God is long-suffering and patient. He lets the tyrant dig his own grave only issuing grave warnings at stated intervals.'
>
> "I humbly beg to say that God is not a certainty. His goal ought to be to spread truth all round. Why does He allow the world to be populated by bad people of various shades? Bad people with their unscrupulousness flourish all round and they spread contagion and thus transmit immorality and dishonesty to posterity.

* Gandhiji's Autobiography, Vol. I. Page 582.

** See Page 178 *Infra*.

"Should not God, omniscient and omnipotent as He is, know where wickedness is by His omniscience and kill wickedness by His omnipotence there and then nip all rascality in the bud and not allow wicked people to flourish?

"Why should God be long-suffering and be patient? What influence can He wield if He be so? The world goes on with all its rascality and dishonesty and tyranny.

"If God allows a tyrant to dig his own grave, why should He not weed out a tyrant before his tyranny oppresses the poor? Why allow full play to tyranny and then allow a tyrant, after his tyranny has ruined and demoralised thousands of people, to go to his grave?

"The world continues to be as bad as it ever was. Why have faith in that God who does not use His powers to change the world and make it a world of good and righteous men?

"I know vicious men with their vices living long and healthy lives. Why should not vicious men die early as a result of their vices?

"I wish to believe in God but there is no foundation for my faith. Kindly enlighten me through *Young India* and change my disbelief into belief."

The argument is as old as Adam. I have no original answer for it. But I permit myself to state why I believe. I am prompted to do so because of the knowledge that there are young men who are interested in my views and doings.

There is an indefinable mysterious Power that pervades everything. I feel it, though I do not see it. It is this unseen Power which makes itself felt and yet defies all proof, because it is so unlike all that I perceive through my senses. It transcends the senses.

But it is possible to reason out the existence of God to a limited extent. Even in ordinary affairs we know that people do not know who rules or why and how he rules. And yet they know that there is a power that certainly rules. In my tour last year in Mysore I met many poor villagers and I found upon inquiry that they did not know who ruled Mysore. They simply said some god ruled it. If the knowledge of these poor people was so limited about their ruler I who am infinitely lesser than God than they than their ruler need not be surprised if I do not realise the presence of God the King of kings. Nevertheless I do feel as the poor villagers felt about Mysore that there is orderliness in the Universe, there is an unalterable Law governing everything and every being that exists or lives. It is not a blind law; for no blind law can govern the conduct of living beings and thanks to the marvellous researches of Sir J. C. Bose, it can now be proved that even matter is life. That Law then which governs all life is God. Law and the Law-giver are one. I may not deny the Law or the Law-giver, because I know so little about It or Him. Even as my denial or ignorance of the existence of an earthly power will avail me nothing, so will not my denial of God and His Law liberate me from its operation; whereas humble and mute acceptance of divine authority makes life's journey easier even as the acceptance of earthy rule makes life under it easier.

I do dimly perceive that whilst everything around me is ever changing, ever dying, there is underlying all that change a living power that is changeless, that holds all together, that creates, dissolves and recreates. That informing power or spirit is God. And since nothing else I see merely through the senses can or will persist, He alone is.

And is this power benevolent or malevolent? I see it as purely benevolent. For I can see that in the midst of death life persists, in the midst of untruth truth persists, in the midst of darkness light persists. Hence I gather that God is Life, Truth, Light. He is Love. He is the supreme Good.

But He is no God who merely satisfies the intellect, if He ever does. God to be God must rule the heart and transform it. He must express Himself in every the smallest act of His votary. This can only be done through a definite realisation more real than the five senses can ever produce. Sense perceptions can be, often are, false and deceptive, however real they may appear to us. Where there is realisation outside the senses it is infallible. It is proved not by extraneous evidence but in the transformed conduct and character of those who have felt the real presence of God within.

Such testimony is to be found in the experiences of an unbroken line of prophets and sages in all countries and climes. To reject this evidence is to deny oneself.

This realisation is preceded by an immovable faith. He who would in his own person test the fact of God's presence can do so by a living faith. And since faith itself cannot be proved by extraneous evidence, the safest course is to believe in the moral government of the world and therefore in the supremacy of the moral law, the law of truth and love. Exercise of faith will be the safest where there is a clear determination summarily to reject all that is contrary to Truth and Love.

But the foregoing does not answer the correspondent's argument. I confess to him that I have no argument to convince him through reason. Faith transcends reason. All I can advise him to do is not to attempt the impossible. I cannot account for the existence of evil by any rational method. To want to do so is to be coequal with God. I am therefore humble enough to recognise evil as such. And I call God long-suffering and patient precisely because he permits evil in the world. I know that He has no evil in Him, and yet if there is evil, He is the author of it and yet untouched by it.

I know too that I shall never know God if I do not wrestle with and against evil even at the cost of life itself. I am fortified in the belief by my own humble and limited experience. The purer I try to become, the nearer I feel to be to God. How much more should I be, when my faith is not a mere apology as it is to-day but has become as immovable as the Himalayas and as white and bright as the snows on their peaks? Meanwhile I invite the correspondent to pray with Newman who sang from experience :

Lead, kindly Light, amid the encircling gloom,
Lead Thou me on;
The night is dark and I am far from home,
Lead Thou me on;
Keep Thou my feet, I do not ask to see
The distant scene; one step enough for me.

11th October, 192

'WHAT ARE WE TO DO?'

BY M. K. GANDHI

Two weeks ago I wrote in *Navajivan* a note on the tragedy in Godhra, where Sjt. Purushottam Shah bravely met his death at the hands of his assailants, and gave the note the heading 'Hindu Muslim Fight in Godhra.' Several Hindus did not like the heading and addressed angry letters asking me to correct it. I found it impossible to accede to their demand. Whether there is one victim or more, whether there is a free fight between the two communities, or whether one assumes the offensive and the other simply suffers, I should describe the event as a fight if the whole series of happenings were the result of a state of war between the two communities. Whether in Godhra or in other places there is today a state of war between the two communities. Fortunately the countryside is still free from the war fever which is mainly confined to towns and cities, where, in some form or other, fighting is continually going on. Even the correspondents who have written to me about Godhra do not seem to deny the fact that the happenings arose out of the communal antagonisms that existed there.

If the correspondents had simply addressed themselves to the heading, I should have satisfied myself with writing to them privately and written nothing in *Navajivan* about it. But there are other letters in which the correspondents have vented their ire on different counts. A volunteer from Ahmedabad who had been to Godhra writes:

"You say that you must be silent over these quarrels.

Why were you not silent over the Khilafat, and why did you exhort us to join the Muslims? Why are you not silent about your principles of *ahimsa*? How can you justify your silence when the two communities are running at each other's throat and the Hindus are being crushed to atoms? How does *ahimsa* come there? I invite your attention to two cases:

"A Hindu shopkeeper thus complained to me: 'Musalmans purchase bags of rice from my shop, often never paying for them. I cannot insist on payment, for fear of their looting my godowns. I have therefore to make an involuntary gift of about 50 to 75 maunds of rice every month.'

"Others complained: 'Musalmans invade our quarters and insult our women in our presence, and we have to sit still. If we dare to raise a protest, we are done for. We dare not even lodge a complaint against them.'

"What would you advise in such cases? How would you bring your *ahimsa* into play? Or even here would you prefer to remain silent?"

These and similar questions have been answered in these pages over and over again, but as they are still being raised, I had better explain my views once more at the risk of repetition.

Ahimsa is not the way of the timid or the cowardly. It is the way of the brave ready to face death. He who perishes sword in hand is no doubt brave, but he who faces death without raising his little finger and without flinching is braver. But he who surrenders his rice bags for fear of being beaten is a coward and no votary of *ahimsa*. He is innocent of *ahimsa*. He, who for fear of being beaten, suffers the women of his household to be insulted, is not manly but just the reverse. He is fit neither to be a husband nor a father, nor a brother. Such people have no right to complain.

These cases have nothing to do with the inveterate enmity between Hindus and Musalmans. Where there are fools there are bound to be knaves, where there are cowards there are bound to be bullies, whether they are Hindus or Musalmans. Such cases used to happen even before the outbreak of these communal hostilities. The question here therefore is not how to teach one of the two communities a lesson or how to humanise it, but how to teach a coward to be brave.

If the thinking sections of both the communities realise the cowardice and folly at the back of the hostilities, we can easily end them. Both have to be brave, both have to be wise. If both or either deliberately get wise, theirs will be the way of non-violence. If both fight and learn wisdom only by bitter experience, the way will be one of violence. Either way there is no room for cowards in a society of men, *i.e.*, in a society which loves freedom. Swaraj is not for cowards.

It is idle therefore to denounce *ahimsa* or to be angry with me on the strength of the cases cited. Ever since my experience of the distortion of *ahimsa* in Betiah in 1921 I have been repeating over and over again that he, who cannot protect himself or his nearest and dearest or their honour by non-violently facing death, may and ought to do so by violently facing death, may and ought to do so by violently dealing with the oppressor. He who can do neither of the two is a burden. He has no business to be the head of a family. He must either hide himself, or must rest content to live for ever in helplessness and be prepared to crawl like a worm at the bidding of a bully.

I know only one way—the way of *ahimsa*. The way of *himsa* goes against my grain. I do not want to cultivate the power to inculcate *himsa*. As *ahimsa* has no place in the atmosphere of cowardice prevailing today, I must needs be reticent over the riots we hear of from day to day. This exhibition of my helplessness cannot be to my liking. But God never ordains that only things that we like should happen and things that we do not like should not happen. In spite of the helplessness, the faith sustains me that He is the Help of the helpless, that He comes to one's succour only when one throws himself on His mercy. It is because of this faith that I cherish the hope that God will one day show me a path which I may confidently commend to the people. With me the conviction is as strong as ever that willy-nilly Hindus and Musalmans must be friends one day. No one can say how and when that will happen. The future is entirely in the hands of God. But He has vouchsafed to us the ship of Faith which alone can enable us to cross the ocean of Doubt.

(Translated from *Navajivan* by M. D.)

18th October, 1928

THE TANGLE OF AHIMSA

By M. K. Gandhi

My article 'The Fiery Ordeal' has brought down upon me the ire of many an incensed critic. Some of them seem to have made the violence of their invective against me a measure of their solicitude for *ahimsa*. Others, as if to test my capacity for *ahimsa*, have cast all decorum and propriety to the winds and have poured upon me the lava of their unmeasured and acrimonious criticism, while still some others have felt genuinely grieved at what seems to them a sad aberration on my part and have written to me letters to unburden their grief to me. I have not the time to reply to all the letters that have been sent to me, nor do I feel it to be necessary. As for the acrimonious letters, the only possible purpose that they can serve is to provide me with some exercise in forbearance and non-violence. Leaving aside such letters therefore I shall here try to examine some arguments that I have been able to glean from other and soberly written communications.

I am always prepared to give my best consideration to letters that are brief and to the point and are neatly written out in ink in a clear legible hand. For I claim to be a humble seeker after truth and am conducting *Navajivan* not merely to teach but also to learn.

To come now to the objections and the counsels addressed to me by my correspondents they may be summed up as follows:

1. You should now retire from the field of *ahimsa*.

2. You should confess that your views about *ahimsa* are imported from the West.

3. You must not express views even when they are correct if there is a possibility of their being misused.

4. If you believe in the Law of *karma* then your killing of the calf was a vain attempt to interfere with the operation of that law.

5. What warrant had you for believing that the calf was bound not to recover? Have you not heard of cases of recovery after the doctors have pronounced them to be helpless?

Whether I should retire or not from the field of *ahimsa*, or for the matter of that from any other field, is essentially and solely for me to judge. A man can give up a right, but he may not give up a duty without being guilty of a grave dereliction. Unpopularity and censure are often the lot of a man who wants to speak and practise the truth. I hold it to be the bounden duty of a Satyagrahi openly and freely to express his opinions which he holds to be correct and of benefit to the public even at the risk of incurring popular displeasure and worse. So long as I believe my views on *ahimsa* to be correct, it would be a sin of omission on my part not to give expression to them.

I have nothing to be ashamed of if my views on *ahimsa* are the result of my Western ideas, nor am I prepared to anathematize everything that comes from the West as inherently evil. I have learnt much from the West and I should not be surprised to find that I had learnt something about *ahimsa* too from the West. I am not concerned what ideas of mine are the result of my foreign contacts. It is enough for me to know that my views on *ahimsa* have now become a part and parcel of my being.

I have publicly discussed my views in the matter of the calf, not necessarily because I believe them to be correct, but because they are to the best of my knowledge based on pure *ahimsa* and as such likely to throw light on the tangled problem of *ahimsa*.

As for the problem of the monkeys, I have discussed it publicly, because I do not know my duty in the matter, and I am anxious to be enlightened. Let me assure the readers that my effort has not been in vain and I have already received several helpful suggestions from my correspondents. Let me further assure them that I would not proceed to the extreme length of killing unless I am absolutely driven to it. It is because I am anxious to be spared this painful necessity that I have invited suggestions for dealing with these persistent and unwelcome guests.

I firmly believe in the law of *karma*, but I believe too in human endeavour. I regard as the *summum bonum* of life the attainment of salvation through *karma* by annihilating its effects by detachment. If it is a violation of the law of *karma* to cut short the agony of an ailing animal by putting an end to its life, it is no less so to minister to the sick or try to nurse them back to life. And yet if a man were to refuse to give medicine to a patient or to nurse him on the ground of *karma*, we would hold him to be guilty of inhumanity and *himsa*. Without therefore entering into a discussion about the eternal controversy regarding pre-destination and freewill I will simply say here that I deem it to be the highest duty of man to render what little service he can.

I admit that there was no guarantee that the calf would not recover. I have certainly known cases that were pronounced by doctors to be hopeless and were cured afterwards. But even so I hold that a man is bound to make the utmost use of his reason, circumscribed and poor as undoubtedly it is, and to try to penetrate the mists of ignorance by its light and try to act accordingly. And that is precisely what we do in countless cases in our every day life. But strangely paradoxical as it may seem, it is nevertheless a fact that the moment we come to think of death the very idea frightens us out of our wits and entirely paralyses our reasoning faculty, although as Hindus we ought to be the least affected by the thought of death, since from the very cradle we are brought up on the doctrines of the immortality of the spirit and the transitoriness of the body. Even if it were found that my decision to poison the calf was wrong, it could have done no harm to the soul of the animal. If I have erred I am prepared to take the consequences of my error, but I refuse to go into hysterics because by my action I possibly cut short the painful existence of a dying calf say by a couple of hours. And the rule that I have applied to the calf I am prepared to apply in the case of my own dear ones as well. Who knows how often we bring those we love to a premature end by our coddling, infatuation, wrong diagnosis or wrong treatment? The letters that I have received from my correspondents more than ever confirm me in my conviction that in our effusiveness over matters like this we forget the elementary duty of kindness, are led away from the path of true love, and discredit our *ahimsa*. The fear of death is thus the greatest obstacle in the way of our realising the true nature of *ahimsa*.

(Translated from *Navajivan* by P.)

18th October, 1928

SASTRI'S WORK

BY M. K. GANDHI

A graphic letter received this week from an eye-witness describes the now famous Klerksdorp incident of which the South African press is full. Though nothing remains or needs to be said from the political standpoint after the full, free and frank apology from the Union Government, too much cannot be said of Sjt. Sastri's generous and courageous behaviour in the face of a plot which might have proved fatal in its result. The letter before me shows that this true son and representative of India stood his ground without the least nervousness even when the lights were put out by the party that had come led by the Deputy Mayor to break up the meeting he was addressing. And when the firing of an explosive had made the meeting hall too suffocating for the audience, Sjt. Sastri went outside, and as if nothing untoward or serious had happened, finished his speech without even referring to the incident. Popular as he had already become among the Europeans of South Africa before this incident, his cool courage and generous behaviour raised him still further in their estimation.

And as he wanted no fame for himself (few men would be found shier than Sjt. Sastri of fame), he turned his popularity to the advancement of the cause he has represented with such singular ability and success. During his all too brief stay in South Africa he has immensely raised the status of our countrymen in that part of the world. Let us hope that they will by their exemplary conduct show themselves worthy of him.

But Sastri's contribution to the solution of the difficult and delicate problem of South Africa does not rest merely upon what was after all an accident. We know nothing except through the results of the inner working of the ambassador's office in which he had to exhaust all his art of a diplomacy that comes from a conviction of the correctness of one's cause and that spurns to do or countenance anything wrong, mean or crooked. But we do know how unsparing he has been in the use on behalf of his cause of the gifts of eloquence, scholarship, both English and Sanskrit and great and varied learning with which nature has lavishly endowed him. He has been delivering to large and select audiences of Europeans lectures on Indian philosophy and culture which have stirred European imagination and softened the hard crust of prejudice which has hitherto prevented the general body of Europeans from seeing anything good in the Indian. These lectures are perhaps his greatest and the most permanent contribution to the Indian cause in South Africa.

It must be a serious problem for the Government of India to choose Sjt. Sastri's successor. He has persistently withstood all pressure to prolong his stay in South Africa.

Letters from South Africa show me how our people dread Sjt. Sastri's impending departure. It will be a calamity if a worthy successor is not found to continue the mission so successfully inaugurated and represented by Sjt. Sastri. Tradition has, I hope, been set up at the Viceregal Lodge of treating the office of India's Agent in South Africa as neutral ground which the Government and popular parties may jointly tread. It is to be hoped that the successor to be chosen will be one who will commend himself equally to the Government and the people, and who will truly represent not merely the Government of India but the people as well.

18th October, 1928

A CONUNDRUM

BY M. K. GANDHI

Some fiery champions of *ahimsa*, who seem bent upon improving the finances of the Postal Department, inundate me with letters full of abuse, and are practising *himsa* in the name of *ahimsa*. They would if they could prolong the calf controversy indefinitely. Some of them kindly suggest that my intellect has suffered decay with the attainment of sixtieth year. Some others have expressed the regret that the doctors did not diagnose my case as hopeless when I was sent to the Sassoon Hospital and cut short my sinful career by giving me a poison injection in which case the poor calf in the Ashram might have been spared the poison injection and the race of monkeys saved from the menace of destruction. These are only a few characteristic samples from the sheaf-fuls of 'love letters' that I am receiving daily. The more I receive these letters the more confirmed I feel in the correctness of my decision to ventilate this thorny question in the columns of *Navajivan*. It never seems to have struck these good people that by this unseemly exhibition of spleen they merely prove their unfitness to be votaries or exponents of *ahimsa* and strike it at the very root. I turn however from these fulminations to one from among a batch of letters of a different order that I have received and I take the following from it:

> "Your exposition of the ethics of the 'calf-incident' has cleared up a lot of my doubts and shed valuable light on the implications of *ahimsa.* But unfortunately it raises a fresh difficulty. Suppose, for instance, that a man begins to oppress a whole people and there is no other way of putting a stop to his oppression than proceeding on the analogy of the calf, would it not be an act of *ahimsa* to rid society of his presence by putting him to death? Would you not regard such an act as an unavoidable necessity and therefore as one of *ahimsa?* In your discussion about the killing of the calf you have made the mental attitude the principal criterion of *Ahimsa.* Would not according to this principle the destruction of proved tyrants be counted as *ahimsa,* since the motive inspiring the act is of the highest? You say that there is no *himsa* in killing off animal pests that destroy a former's crops; then why should it not be *ahimsa* to kill human pests that threaten society with destruction and worse?"

The discerning reader will have already perceived that this correspondent has altogether missed the point of my argument. The definition of *ahimsa* that I have given cannot by any stretch of meaning be made to cover a case of manslaughter such as the correspondent in question postulates. I have nowhere described the unavoidable destruction of life that a farmer has to commit in pursuit of his calling as *ahimsa.* One may regard such destruction of life as unavoidable and condone it as such, but it cannot be spelt otherwise than as *himsa.* The underlying motive with the farmer is to subserve his own interest, or, say that of society. *Ahimsa* on the other hand rules out such interested destruction. But the killing of the calf was undertaken for the sake of the dumb animal itself. Any way its good was the only motive.

The problem mentioned by the correspondent in question may certainly be compared to that of the monkey nuisance.

But then there is fundamental difference between the monkey nuisance and the human nuisance. Society as yet knows of no means by which to effect a change of a heart in the monkeys and their killing *may* therefore be held as pardonable, but there is no evil-doer or tyrant who need be considered beyond reform. That is why the killing of a human being out of self-interest can never find a place in the scheme of *ahimsa*.

To come now to the question of motive, whilst it is true that mental attitude is the crucial test of *ahimsa*, it is not the sole test. To kill any living being or thing save for his or its own interest is *himsa*, however noble the motive may otherwise be. And a man who harbours ill-will towards another is no less guilty of *himsa* because for fear of society or want of opportunity, he is unable to translate his ill-will into action. A reference to both intent and deed is thus necessary in order finally to decide whether a particular act or abstention can be classed as *ahimsa*. After all intent has to be inferred from a bunch of correlated acts.

(Translated from *Navajivan* by P.)

25th October, 1928

'DEATH IS REST'

When I am overwhelmed with correspondence betraying in every line fear of death and consequent travesty of *ahimsa*, it refreshes me to come across the following beautiful dialogue a friend sent me on Maganlal Gandhi's death:

"Tzu Kung said to Confucius,—'Master, I am aweary, and would fain have rest.'

"'In life,' replied the sage, 'there is no rest.'

"'Shall I then never have rest?' asked the disciple.

"'You will,' said Confucius. 'Behold the tombs which lie around; some magnificient, some mean. In one of these you will find rest'.

"'How wonderful is Death' rejoined Tzu Kung. 'The wise man rests, the worldly man is engulfed therein.'

" 'My son,' said Confucius, 'I see that you understand. Other men know life only as a boon; they do not perceive that it is a bane. They know old age as a state of weakness; they do not perceive that it is a state of ease. They know Death only as an abomination; they do not perceive that it is a state of rest.

" 'How grand,' cried Yen Tzu, 'is the old conception of death! The virtuous find rest; the wicked are engulfed therein. In death each reverts to that from which he came. The ancients regarded death as a return to, and life as an absence from, home. And he, who forgets his home, becomes an outcaste and a byword in his generation.

It is not reproduced to defend the infliction of death *penalty* on any living being or thing. But it is given here to show that death is *not* a terror *in all circumstances* as many correspondents contend and that it may be a deliverence in certain cases, especially when it is *not inflicted as a penalty but administered as a healing balm.* 'Death is but a sleep and a forgetting,' says the English poet. Let us not seek to prop virtue by imagining hellish torture after death for vice and *houris* hereafter as a reward for virtue in this life. If virtue has no attraction in itself it must be a poor thing to be thrown away on the dung heap. Nature, I am convinced is not so cruel as she seems to us, who are so often filled with cruelty ourselves. Both heaven and hell are within us. Life after Death there is, but it is not so unlike our present experiences as either to terrify us or make us delirious with joy. 'He is steadfast who rises above joy and sorrow,' says the Gita. 'The wise are unaffected either by death or life. These are but faces of the same coin.

M. K. G.

25th October, 1928

TRUE HOLIDAY MAKING

A correspondent invites me to warn those who care against turning during the forthcoming Divali holidays good money into fireworks; bad sweets and unhygienic illuminations. I heartily respond. If I had my way I should have people to do house cleaning and heart cleaning and provide innocent and instructive amusements for children during these days. Fireworks I know are the delight of children, but they are so because we the elders have habituated them to fireworks. I have not known the untutored African children wanting or appreciating fireworks. They have dances instead. What can be better or healthier for children than sports and picnics to which they will take, not bazar-made sweets of doubtful value but fresh and dried fruit? Children both rich and poor may also be trained to do house cleaning and whitewashing themselves. It will be something if they are coaxed to recognise the dignity of labour if only during holidays to begin with. But the point I wish to emphasise is that at least a part, if not the whole, of the money saved by doing away with fireworks etc., should be given to the cause of Khadi, or if that is anathema, then to any other cause in which the poorest are served. There cannot be greater joy to men and women and young and old than that they think of and associate the poorest of the land with them in their holidays.

M. K. G.

25th October, 1928

HOW WE LOST INDIA

By M. K. Gandhi

It was at Jalpaiguri just before Deshabandhu's death that I said to a mercantile audience in reply to an address from the merchants that we had lost India through merchants and that we should regain it also through them. If illustrations of the truth of this statement were wanted, a striking one is furnished by the following circular letter from a mercantile association to other similar bodies:

> "As you are aware, trade in Manchester piece-goods and yarn has much gone down in recent times and is still showing a marked tendency to decrease. It has been noticed that businessmen are not taking as keen an interest in this trade as they used to do formerly. As a result of this indifference, our countrymen are steadily losing what was as it still may be a source of great profit and income to them. The Marwari community, along with other commercial communities, being very greatly interested in the piece-goods and yarn trade, my Committee adopted a resolution in their meeting of the 7th instant, to fully investigate into the causes of its depression with a view to taking definite steps for the rehabilitation of this important branch of trade.
>
> "As the matter is one of general interest, my Committee consider it advisable to meet the representatives of different public bodies interested in the trade in a conference in order to take concerted action if possible.
>
> "If this proposal meets with the acceptance of your chamber, as my Committee hope it will, they will be glad to arrange for a conference of representatives of the different public bodies as soon as possible. The favour of an early reply is therefore solicited."

The circular is dated 19th July, 1928. I do not know the outcome of the effort. We are however just now not concerned with its result. The fact that there should be in our midst respectable bodies of merchants engaged in devising means for sustaining the trade in Manchester yarn and piece-goods, at a time when the whole country is trying to boycott *all foreign* cloth, is a portent which should be taken notice of by every national worker.

Enough evidence has been adduced from time to time in these pages that India is held by the English for their commerce and that by far the largest imports consist of piece-goods. Surely no committee or commission is required to prove that so long as this exploitation of our country is permitted by us, India will be held by the British by every means at their disposal. What we need therefore above all is not so much conversion or expulsion of the British residents or rulers as the conversion of our own merchant princes and their dependents who are selling their country for their own interest.

Nor need our merchant princes ruin themselves for the sake of the country. India will want all the quantity of the cloth and yarn that they are now importing. They have but to apply their undoubted ability to the manufacture of this quantity in our seven hundred thousand villages. In doing so they will naturally benefit themselves. I admit that they will have to give up commercial gambling, speculation and palaces out of all proportion to their surroundings, and be satisfied with an income bearing some relation to the condition of those for whom and with whom they would trade. In other words, instead of taking part as they are now doing in bleeding the villages, they would be making some tardy return to those on whom their prosperity has depended. The story of the belly and the members has an eternal application. The toiling millions are the belly. The merchants and others are the members. They must wither if the belly is starved. Those who have eyes can see that the belly has been shamefully starved for a long enough period. The withering of the members must follow soon as night follows day. Let us then repent before it is too late.

25th October, 1928

JAIN AHIMSA?

By M. K. Gandhi

A Jain friend who is reputed to have made a fair study of the Jain philosophy as also of the other systems has addressed me a long letter on *Ahimsa*. It deserves a considered reply. He says in effect:

"Your interpretation of *Ahimsa* has caused confusion. In the ordinary sense of the term *himsa* means to sever life from body and not to do so is *Ahimsa*. Refraining from causing pain to any living creature is only an extension of the original meaning which cannot by any stretch of language be made to cover the taking of life. You would not understand me to mean from this that I regard all taking of life as wrong in every possible circumstance; for I do not think that there is any ethical principle in this world that can be regarded as absolute and admitting of no exception whatever. The maxim, '*Ahimsa* is the highest or the supreme duty' embodies a great and cardinal truth but it does not cover the entire sum of human duties. Whilst therefore what your have termed 'non-violent killing' may be a right thing it cannot be described as *Ahimsa*."

I am of opinion that just as life is subject to constant change and development, the meanings of terms too are constantly undergoing a process of evolution and this can be amply proved by illustrations from the history of any religion. The word *Yajna* or sacrifice in the Hindu religion for instance is an illustration in point. Sir J. C. Bose's discoveries are today revolutionising the accepted connotations of biological terms. Similarly if we will fully realise *Ahimsa* we may not fight shy of discovering fresh implications of the doctrine of *Ahimsa*. We cannot improve upon the celebrated maxim, '*Ahimsa* is the highest or the supreme duty' but we are bound if we would retain our spiritual inheritance, to explore the implications of this great and universal doctrine. But I am not particular about names. I do not mind whether the taking of life in the circumstances I have mentioned is called *ahimsa* or not, so long as its correctness is conceded.

Another poser mentioned by this friend is as follows:

"I have been unable to follow you in your description

of the imaginary killing of your daughter in the hypothetic circumstances described by you. It may be right to kill the ruffian in such a case, but what fault has the poor daughter committed? Would you regard the pollution of the poor victim as a disgrace to be avoided by death? Don't you think that in such circumstances even if the poor girl for fear of public ignominy and shame begs to be put out of life, it would be your duty to dissuade her from her wish? As for me, I do not see the slightest difference between a case of dishonour, and a case in which one has had one's limbs cut off by force."

My reason for putting my daughter to death in circumstances mentioned by me would not be that I feared her being polluted but that she herself would have wished death if she could express her desire. If my daughter wanted to be put out of life because she was afraid of public scandal and criticism I would certainly try to dissuade her from her wish. I would take her life only if I was absolutely certain that she would wish it. I know that Sita would have preferred death to dishonour by Ravan. And that is also what, I believe, our Shastras have enjoined. I know that it is the daily prayer of thousands of men and women that they might have death rather than dishonour. I deem it to be highly necessary that this feeling should be encouraged. I am not prepared to admit that the loss of chastity stands on the same footing as the loss of a limb. But I can imagine circumstances in which one would infinitely prefer death even to being maimed.

The third poser runs:

"I cannot understand why the idea of wounding a few monkeys in order to frighten away the rest instead of straightaway proceeding to kill them off should be regarded as intolerable by you. Don't you feel that the longing for life is strong even among the blind and the maimed animals? Don't you think that the impulse to kill a living creature because one connot bear to see its suffering is a kind of selfishness?"

The idea of wounding monkeys is unbearable to me because I know that a wounded monkey has to die a lingering death if left to itself. And if monkeys have to die at all by any act of mine, I would far rather that they were killed summarily than that they were left to die by inches. Again it beats my comprehension how I am practising *ahimsa* by thus wounding the monkeys instead of killing them outright. It might be a different thing if I was prepared to erect a hospital for wounded monkeys. I concede that the maimed and the blind would evince a longing for life if they have some hope of getting succour or relief. But imagine a blind ignorant creature, with no faith in God, marooned in a desert place beyond the reach of any help and with a clear knowledge of his plight and I cannot believe that such a creature would want to continue its existence. Nor am I prepared to admit that it is one's duty to nurse the longing for life in *all* circumstances.

The fourth poser is as follows:

"The Jain view of *ahimsa* rests on the following three principles:

'No matter what the circumstances are or how great the suffering, it is impossible for any one deliberately to renounce the will to live or to wish another to put him out of pain. Therefore the taking of life cannot in any circumstances be morally justified.

'In a world full of activities which necessitate *himsa*, an aspirant for salvation should try to follow *ahimsa* by engaging in the fewest possible activities.

'There are two kinds of *himsa*—direct such as that involved in agriculture, and indirect as that involved in the eating of agricultural produce. Where one cannot altogether escape from either, a votary of *ahimsa* should try to avoid direct *himsa*.'

I would earnestly request you critically to examine and discuss these three Jain principles of *ahimsa* in *Navajivan*. I notice that there is a vital difference between your view of *ahimsa* and that of the Jains. Whereas your view of *ahimsa* is based on the philosophy of action, that of the Jains is based on that of renunciation of action. The present is an era of action. If the principle of *ahimsa* be an eternal and universal principle untrammelled by time and place, it seems to me that there is a great need to stimulate the people's mind to think out for themselves as to how the principle of *ahimsa* that has so far been confined to the field of renunciation only can be worked in present day life of action and what form it will take when applied to this new environment.'

It is with the utmost reluctance that I have to enter into a discussion of these principles. I know the risks of such discussion. But I see no escape from it. As for the first principle I have already expressed my opinion on it in a previous portion of this article. It is my firm conviction that the principle of clinging to life in *all* circumstances betrays cowardice and is the cause of much of the *himsa* that goes on around us and blind adherence to this principle is bound to increase instead of reducing *himsa*. It seems to me that if this Jain principle is really as it is here enunciated it is a hindrance to the attainment of Salvation. For instance a person who is constantly praying for salvation will never wish to continue his life at the expense of another's. Only a person steeped in ignorance who cannot even remotely understand what salvation means would wish to continue life on any terms. The *sine qua non* of salvation is a total annihilation of all desire. How dare, then, an aspirant for salvation be sordidly selfish or wish to preserve his perishable body at all cost? Descending from the field of salvation to that of the family, one's country, or the world of humanity, we again find innumerable instances of men and women who have dedicated themselves to the service of their family, their country or the world at large in entire disregard of their own life and this ideal of utter self-sacrifice and self-abnegation at present is being inculcated throughout the world. To hang on to life at all cost seems to me the very height of selfishness. Let however nobody understand me to mean that one may try to wean another even from such sordid egoism by force. I am adducing the argument merely to show the fallacy of the doctrine of will to live at all cost.

As for the second, I do not know whether it can at all be described as a principle. But be that as it may, to me it represents a truism and I heartily endorse it.

Coming to the third principle in the form in which it is enunciated by the friend, it suffers from a grave defect. The most terrible consequence of this principle to me seems to be this that if we accept it then a votary of *ahimsa* must renounce agriculture although he knows that he cannot renounce the fruits of agriculture and that agriculture is an indispensable condition for the existence of mankind. The very idea that millions of the sons of the soil should remain steeped in *himsa* in order that a handful of men who live on the toil of these people might be able to practise *ahimsa* seems to me to be unworthy of and inconsistent with the supreme duty of *ahimsa*. I feel that this betrays a lack of perception of the inwardness of *ahimsa*. Let us see, for instance, what it leads to if pushed to its logical conclusion. You may not kill a snake but if necessary, according to this principle, you may get it killed by somebody else. You may not yourself forcibly drive away a thief but you may employ another person to do it for you. If you want to protect the life of a child entrusted to your care from the fury of a tyrant, somebody else must bear the burnt of the tyrant's fury for you. And you thus refrain from direct action in the sacred name of *Ahimsa*! This in my opinion is neither religion nor *Ahimsa*. So long as one is not prepared to take the risks mentioned and to face the consequences, one cannot be free from fear and so long as a man has not shed all fear he is *ipso facto* incapable of practising *Ahimsa*. Our scriptures tell us that *Ahimsa* is all-conquering, that before it even the wild beasts shed their ferocity and the most hard-hearted of tyrants forget their anger. Utterly inadequate and imperfect as my own practice of *Ahimsa* has been it has enabled me to realise the truth of this principle. I cannot once more help expressing my doubt that Jainism subscribes to the third principle of *Ahimsa* as enunciated by this friend. But even if the Jain doctrine is just as it is stated by the friend, I must say, I for one cannot reconcile myself to it.

Now to come to the question of renunciation versus action: I believe in the doctrine of renunciation but I hold that renunciation should be sought for 'in' and 'through' action. That action is the *sine qua non* of life in the body, that the Wheel of Life cannot go on even for a 'second' without involving some sort of action goes without saying. Renunciation can therefore in these circumstances only mean detachment or freedom of the spirit from action, even while the body is engaged in action. A follower of the path of renunciation seeks to attain it not by refraining from all activity but by carrying it on in a perfect spirit of detachment and altruism as a pure trust. Thus a man may engage in farming, spinning, or any other activity without departing from the path of renunciation provided one does so merely for selfless service and remains free from the taint of egoism or attachment. It remains for those therefore who like myself hold this view of renunciation to discover for themselves how far the principle of *ahimsa* is compatible with life in the body and how it can be applied to acts of every day life. The very virtue of a *dharma* is that it is universal, that its practice is not the monopoly of the few, but must be the privilege of all. And it is my firm belief that the scope of Truth and *ahimsa* is world-wide. That is why I find an ineffable joy in dedicating my life to researches in truth and *ahimsa* and I invite others to share it with me by doing likewise.

(Translated from *Navajivan* by P.)

1st November, 1928

CONDOLENCES

M. K. G.

I tender my respectful condolences to Mrs. S. R. Das and her family on Sjt. S. R. Das's death. Though I had little in common with the deceased in politics, I could not but recognise his phenomenal generosity and his open-heartedness. Many do not know how this great man beggared himself so that no worthy cause might knock in vain at his door.

1st November, 1928

MORE ABOUT AHIMSA

By M. K. Gandhi

I

A correspondent writes:

> "I have read your article 'The Fiery Ordeal' over and over again but it has failed to satisfy me. Your proposal about the killing of monkeys has taken me aback. I believed that a person like you with his being steeped in *ahimsa* would never swerve from the right path even though the heavens fell. And now you say that you might kill off the monkeys to protect your Ashram against their inroads. May be that my first impression about you was wrong. But I cannot describe to you what a shock your proposal about the killing of the monkeys has given me, and may I also confess, how angry it has made me feel against you? Would you kindly help me out of my perplexity?"

I have received several other letters too in the same strain. I am afraid people have formed an altogether exaggerated estimate of me. These good people seem to think that because I am trying to analyse and define the ideal of *ahimsa* I must have fully attained that ideal. My views regarding the calf and the monkeys seem happily to have shattered this illusion of theirs. Truth to me is infinitely dearer than the 'mahatmaship' which is purely a burden. It is my knowledge of my limitations and my nothingness which has so far saved me from the oppressiveness of the 'mahatmaship.' I am painfully aware of the fact that my desire to continue life in the body involves me in constant *himsa*, that is why I am becoming growingly indifferent to this physical body of mine. For instance I know that in the act of respiration I destroy innumerable invisible germs floating in the air. But I do not stop breathing. The consumption of vegetables involves *himsa* but I find that I cannot give them up. Again, there is *himsa* in the use of antiseptics, yet I cannot bring myself to discard the use of disinfectants like kerosene etc. to rid myself of the mosquito pest and the like. I suffer snakes to be killed in the Ashram when it is impossible to catch and put them out of harm's way. I even tolerate the use of the stick to drive the bullocks in the Ashram. Thus there is no end of *himsa* which I directly and indirectly commit. And now I find myself confronted with his monkey problem. Let me assure the reader that I am in no hurry to take the extreme step of killing them. In fact I am not sure that I would at all be able finally to make up my mind to kill them. As it is friends are helping me with useful suggestions and the adoption of some of them may solve the difficulty at least temporarily without our having to kill them. But I cannot today promise that I shall never kill the monkeys even though they may destroy all the crop in the Ashram. If as a result of this humble confession of mine, friends choose to give me up as lost, I would be sorry but nothing will induce me to try to conceal my imperfections in the practice of *ahimsa*. All I claim for myself is that I am ceaselessly trying to understand the implications of great ideals like *ahimsa* and to practise them in thought, word and deed and that not without a certain measure of success as I think. But I know that I have a long distance yet to cover in this direction. Unless therefore the correspondent in question can bring himself to bear with my imperfections I am sorry I can offer him but little consolation.

II

Another correspondent writes :

"Supposing my elder brother is suffering from a terrible and painful malady and doctors have despaired of his life and I too feel likewise, should I in the circumstances put him out of life ?"

My reply is in the negative. I am afraid some of my correspondents have not even taken the trouble to understand my article. In propounding their conundrums they forget that whilst I have certainly compared the case of an ailing human being with that of an ailing calf and recommended the killing of the former in exactly similar circumstances, in actual practice such a complete analogy is hardly ever to be found. In the first place the human body being much more manageable in bulk is always easier to manipulate and nurse; secondly man being gifted with the power of speech more often than not is in a position to express his wishes and so the question of taking his life without his consent cannot come within the rule. For I have never suggested that the life of another person can be taken against his will without violating the principle of *Ahimsa*. Again, we do not always despair of the life of a person when he is reduced to a comatose state and even when he is past all hope he is not necessarily past all help. More often than not it is both possible and practicable to render service to a human patient till the very end. Whilst, therefore, I would still maintain that the principle enunciated regarding the calf applies equally to 'man and bird and beast', I should expect an intelligent person to know the obvious natural difference between a man and an animal. To recapitulate the conditions the fulfilment of *all* of which alone can warrant the taking of life from the point of view of *Ahimsa* :

1. The disease from which the patient is suffering should be incurable.

2. All concerned have despaired of the life of the patient.

3. The case should be beyond all help or service.

4. It should be impossible for the patient in question to express his or its wish.

So long as even one of these conditions remains unfulfilled the taking of life from the point of view of *ahimsa* cannot be justified.

III

A third correspondent writes:

> "Well, the killing of the calf is all right so far as it goes. But have you considered that your example is likely to afford a handle to those who indulge in animal sacrifices and thus accentuate the practice; do you not know that even those who commit these deeds argue that the animals sacrificed gain merit in the life to follow?"

Such abuse of my action is quite possible, and inevitable so long as there are hypocrisy and ignorance in this world. What crimes have not been committed in the world in the sacred name of religion? One therefore need not be deterred from doing what one considers to be right merely because one's conduct may be misunderstood or misinterpreted by others. And as for those who practise animal sacrifice, surely they do not need the authority of my example to defend their conduct since they profess to take their stand on the authority of the Shastras. My fear however is that proceeding on my analogy some people might actually take it into their head summarily to put to death those whom they might imagine to be their enemies on the plea that it would serve both the interests of society and the 'enemies' concerned, if the latter were killed. In fact I have often heard people advance this argument. But it is enough for my purpose to know that my interpretation of *Ahimsa* affords no basis whatever for such an argument, for in the latter case there is no question of serving or anticipating the wishes of the victims concerned. Finally even if it were admitted that it was in the interest of the animal or the enemy in question to be summarily dispatched the act would still be spelt as *himsa* because it would not be altogether disinterested.

The fallacy is so obvious. But who can help people who seeing see not, or are bent upon deceiving themselves?

(Translated from *Navajivan* by P.)

1st November, 1928

AHIMSA BY THE CARD?

While following Gandhiji's articles on *ahimsa* in *Young India* and the storm of criticism and protest that it has raised among the orthodox Hindu circles, I am strongly reminded of an illuminating article by Professor Jacks in which he discusses the fallacy of what he calls 'morality by the card' that I happened to read some years back in his book *The Alchemy of Thought*. Gandhiji's action in killing the calf has been criticised first on the ground that although to all appearance the calf was past all hope and all help there was no absolute guarantee that it would not recover and secondly because although one might feel that in a position like that of the calf one would only feel grateful if one is put out of pain it was by no means certain that the calf itself wished it at that moment, and that in the absence of this certain knowledge, it was wrong to kill it. The thesis which Prof. Jacks advances in his book is just the reverse of this. He holds that this demand for a 'safe conduct' is the very negation of morality, that the sphere of morality lies just in the hinterland between certainty and doubt. "What ought to be done," he says, "can (in the region of morality) never be demonstrated in the sense in which we can demonstrate the answer to any scientific problem, the essence of morality being not the mere registration in action of a demonstrated result but the willingness to go beyond the proof and to take risks in a realm where no proof is to be had." Morality that seeks to safeguard itself against all possible risks of error by asking for 'formal guarantees' is a very poor and sordid affair without any lustre of virtue or heroism about it. "There is indeed no surer means of degrading the conscience," says Prof. Jacks, "than to treat it as a problem requiring an answer. . . . A man who delays the use of his conscience until he can wholly understand the nature of that impulse which bids him act,—such a man, we do not hesitate to say, is approaching that point of immoral neutrality, that dead centre of the will, at which he will cease to have any conscience at all."

There may be wrongs to be redressed, and no infallible guidance is obtainable. "What is one to do in the circumstances?" he asks. And the reply that he gives is identical with that given by Gandhiji. "It remains for me," he says, "either to make an experiment or do nothing. I will make an experiment based on the fullest knowledge I can obtain, but on a clear understanding with myself that this knowledge is fallible. I will lay down my life to carry this experiment through, even though I may be told on the Judgment Day that the enterprise is vain. For the sake of right I will run the risk of being *ad hoc* in the wrong," He does not minimise the risks of such a course. He admits, that 'many a Columbus has set sail into the West and never come back.' But he holds that it is by men who have thus dared that the moral progress of the world has been achieved.

He then goes on to sketch forth in vivid detail the dangers of prescriptive morality. A society that is based on such a system of ethics may be "conspicuously clean, but it will be weak on the side of courage, faith and enterprise; having inherited a certain level of moral excellence it will remain stationary at that level, its temper will be essentially legal and conservative and perhaps timid; will occasionally degenerate towards a Pharisiac pride; it will discourage originality and be afraid of it; it will produce no more new types; out of its bosom no Columbus will set sail into the West—perhaps to be heard of no more. It will honour those who have set great examples in the past, but it will fail of high deeds through not perceiving that the only way to morally imitate an old example is to set a new one," Who can read the above pen picture without recognising some of the most conspicuous traits of our present day Hindu orthodoxy featured in it?

And the reason for this inevitable decay is not far to seek. Beyond the group of morality summed up in the ten 'Don'ts' lies a vast host of positive duties, of tremendous moral tasks. "In this group of tasks, which constitutes the life business of of every man who 'is perfect in the works of the law' the safe conduct of scientific guidance is not to be had. And a person who always seeks for 'safe conduct' becomes blind to the existence of such tasks and incompetent to deal with them when discovered by others. What, therefore, is required is imagination, creativeness, initiative, and that heroic willingness to trust oneself to the unknown without which the work of the Moral Will cannot be done."

Lessing, the searcher after truth, once said that if God holding truth in His right hand and in His left the ever-living desire for it although on condition of perpetual error left him the choice of the two, he would humbly seize His left hand and beg its contents for himself. As in the case of truth so in that of *ahimsa* its essence lies in a ceaseless ever-active desire to search for it, in an unflagging striving of the soul to come nearer to its ideal; than in the mechanical observance of a set of categorical 'shalls' and 'shall nots' however perfect it may be.

Much of the prevailing confusion about *ahimsa* arises because it is forgotten that *ahimsa* is not merely a negative virtue or a dead neutrality which as Dante has pointed out may at times be the most heinous of sins but a dynamic quality of the soul known to us as love. And the measure of one's love is the amount of risk that one is prepared to undergo for its sake. To quote Prof. Jacks' once more, "Love has always been the fulfilling of the law, and love is ahead of all definiteness and independent of all formal guarantees." '*Ahimsa* by the card,' thus according to the canons of morality set forth by Prof. Jacks, is a self-defeating proposition—a hopeless contradiction in terms. Placed as man is in a world which is 'red in tooth and claw' the path that a votary of *ahimsa* has to tread is often dim and dark and he finds himself confronted at every step with dreadful dilemmas, awful riddles of the Sphinx which mock us as it were by baffling all solution and yet to refuse to solve which would spell death for the principle of *ahimsa*. The spirit of experimental research, the capacity and willingness to take risks requiring faith and courage are thus the first thing needful for any approach to the ideal of *ahimsa* as in fact they are for all morality and a person, who regards *ahimsa* as if it were a deal in 'gilt-edged' securities only, knows not what *ahimsa* means.

P.

1st November, 1928

'FREEDOM TO THE FREE'

Whilst we are cutting one another's throats in the name of religion and some of us running to the Statutory Commission in the vain hope of getting freedom, a friend sends me the following from James Allen to remind us that even in the land of so-called freedom, the real freedom has still to come. Here is the passage:

> "All outward oppression is but the shadow and effect of the real oppression within. For ages the oppressed have cried for liberty, and a thousand man-made statutes have failed to give it to them. They can give it only to themselves; they shall find it only in obedience to the Divine Statutes which are inscribed upon their hearts. Let them resort to the inward freedom, and the shadow of oppression shall no more darken the earth. Let men cease to oppress themselves, and no man shall oppress his brother. Men legislate for an outward freedom, yet continue to render such freedom impossible of achievement by fostering an inward condition of enslavement. They thus pursue a shadow without, and ignore the substance within. All outward forms of bondage and oppression will cease to be when man ceases to be the willing bond-slave of passion, error, and ignorance."

The outward freedom therefore that we shall attain will only be in exact proportion to the inward freedom to which we may have grown at a given moment. And if this is the correct view of freedom, our chief energy must be concentrated upon achieving reform from within. In this much needed work all who will can take an equal share. We need neither to be lawyers, nor legislators to be able to take part in the great effort. When this reform takes place on a national scale no outside power can stop our onward march.

M. K. G.

1st November, 1928

IN TEN YEARS?

BY M. K. GANDHI

Professor C. N. Vakil's instructive articles* published in these pages are supplementary to the series he recently wrote on poverty* and should be read together. I coaxed him to give the reader something more definite on remedies of poverty than what he had done in the article which I ventured to withhold and which he expanded into the four articles above referred to. I do not think that the programme sketched by the learned Professor can be finished in ten years. Perhaps it is impossible to devise a ten years' programme of improvement to cover a vast and impoverished country like ours.

Let us however glance at Professor Vakil's remedies for India's central disease. He rightly says that the problem is how to increase production of wealth and how to distribute it equitably among the people, principally therefore, I presume, among the starving millions. To this end the learned writer

1. would recast small uneconomic holdings,

2. would pay off the debts of the ryot through mortgage and co-operative banks,

3. would revise the revenue law and graduate the land tax so as to bring it in a line with the income-tax leaving a minimum of income from land free of tax,

* Omitted in this collection.

4. would re-employ the population displaced through the recasting of uneconomic holdings by bringing under the plough cultivable waste, *i.e.*, 23 p. c. of the total area available and by nationalising and thus developing large industries,

5. would draw small and large capital by putting the banking system on a basis more in keeping with the requirements of the country than it is now,

6. would improve labour conditions so as to avoid war between capital and labour,

7. would deal with such social abuses as child marriages etc. which give rise to over-population and unfit progeny,

8. would radically reform the educational system so as to spread education among the masses and have it answer the needs of the people,

9. and would cut down the military expenditure and stop the drain from the country by manning the services with indigenous talent.

This is not an unattractive programme. But as I was re-reading the articles, the question continued to force itself upon me, 'Who will bell the cat?' There is hardly an item here which can be tackled without Government aid. And a Government that is admittedly based on exploitation of the governed will not and cannot, even if it will, undertake the proposed changes with the despatch necessary to create an immediate impression. It can undertake irrigation schemes costing crores, it will not undertake sinking wells costing lakhs. What therefore Professor Vakil wants first is a summary programme of Swaraj and having been chiefly instrumental in getting it, he can command the appointment of a commissioner of banishment of poverty department.

This however is a heroic remedy and Pandit Motilal Nehru and the co-signatories to his report are the men to tackle it. Our author's was but to place a scheme before any government that would deal with the most pressing problem before the country.

But I had hoped that the learned Professor, especially when he wrote for *Young India,* would have examined the one sovereign remedy that has in season and out of season been advocated through these pages and has, so far as it has gone, been tried with no inconsiderable success. True, the Professor has hidden the tiny wheel in a little unseen arc of his circle of suggestions. I claim for it not a point in a circumference but the centre from which can radiate innumerable other things including many the learned writer has in view. But the fact is, whereas it was possible for him with patient research carried on in a well-stocked library to write convincing essays to prove India's deep and deepening poverty, it was impossible without a close study of a group of villages with an open and receptive mind to spot the seat of the disease and to know the capacity of the patient to bear the remedy, A Gregg took a year of reading and living among the villagers to know the remedy and prove its worth with a freshness of outlook all his own. The cardinal facts to realise are that there is already terrible, forced unemployment among the toiling millions in that they have no work for at least four months in the year. Once that is realised surely it follows that not a moment should be lost in bringing work to these millions so as to utilise their idle hours. The other fact to realise is that if the average income of the inhabitant of this land is seven pice per day, *i.e.,* less than two English pennies per day, at the present rate of exchange, the average income of the toiling millions must *ipso facto* be much less. He, who adds two pice per day to their income and that without any great capital outlay, makes a princely addition to their income and in addition revives the dying hope within the breasts of these millions. The further merit of this programme is that it is now in operation without Government aid. But it needs much greater encouragement and admits of infinite expansion. P. has shown elsewhere* in this issue of *Young India* what America wrought through the wheel during those times of her Revolution. I invite the economists of India to study

* See page 905

the movement on the spot. They have nearly two thousand villages to select from for their study and let them then condemn the movement if they can, or give it not a niggardly place that prudence or patronage can grudgingly afford but the central place it deserves.

1st November, 1928

A LEAF FROM AMERICAN HISTORY

"You say, sir, that the people are propagating large quantities of flax and cotton, and they are provided with weavers, who have already wove several large pieces of cloth of a useful sort whereof they sold divers, and some they made use of in their own families. . . . . They must expect no encouragement for setting up manufactures which may interfere with those of England."

These were the instructions sent by the authorities in England to the Governor of Georgia in 1775 and he was advised to discourage all manufacturing of textile goods on the grounds that it might occasion 'complaints here.' The Americans had begun more and more to manufacture their own clothing and England wanted all the American cotton for the use of her own spinners and weavers. Not only that, even in the production of food-stuffs all the surplus must go to the 'mother country.'

The way in which the American colonists met this affront forms a most fascinating chapter in history and might well be adopted by us as an object-lesson.

In India her own rulers conspired with the foreigner to crush the indigenous spinner and weaver and the greedy middleman joined hands with the foreign trader to dump down foreign goods upon the hapless Indian masses and the process is still going on. America had no tradition of spinning and weaving reaching back to dim antiquity, but having raw materials close at hand and being far removed from England, the American people gave the only effective reply that a freedom-loving people could give to cruel laws imposed upon them. They disregarded them and set themselves to learn to spin and weave in grim earnest. Spinning and weaving schools were established everywhere in pursuance of the programme. A movement was started in New England and the South to promote economy and house-hold industry. Spinning tournaments were organised. To excel in the use of the wheel became the pride of every lass and matron. The 'Spinning Bee' became a popular social function and was celebrated sometimes in the Town Hall and again in the village manse; "the women bringing with pride their wheels and flax for the contest, while cake and wine and tea were generously supplied by the gallant gentlemen who danced attendance on them." Societies for encouraging home manufactures were formed notwithstanding instructions from England and the ministers delivered sermons to the women on the necessity of economy. Weaving parties called the young people together and 'while they talked and laughed some were carding cotton, some were spinning and some were weaving.'

It was not long before the effects of this movement began to make themselves felt in England. As the American fabrics gained in excellence and the spinners and weavers in America proceeded from the manufacture of coarse goods to the finer stuffs coming within effective range of competition of the finer fabrics of England, "a cry went up from the manufacturers in England and the pressure became heavier and heavier affecting every colony from Massachussets to Georgia." This, however, only stiffened the resolve of the colonists to become completely independent of England in the matter of their clothing.

As early as 1640 the courts of Massachussets and Connecticut had promulgated two orders to increase the cultivation of flax. Orders were now issued to prepare lists of colonists who were skilful in carding cotton, spinning and weaving and requiring that boys and girls be taught to spin. Every family was required to spin a certain quota of flax or to pay a fine and prizes were instituted for the best spinners and weavers.

In the meantime hand-made goods had reached a high stage of perfection in Europe and were very much in request among the wealthier classes of America, who imitated the styles set in London and thus helped to send larger and large sums of money out of the country for the purchase of foreign fineries. As the restrictive laws against the colonists were made more and more stringent and affronts accumulated the sentiment against the use of British luxuries grew with it and to put a stop to the drain, the weavers of New England now took to importing cotton from the West Indies because the long staple cotton from the West Indies was much better suited for the manufacture of fine cloth than the short fibre of the colonies. The industry made such a rapid headway that presently there was hardly any cotton left to be exported to England.

In his evidence before a Committee of the House of Commons in 1766 that desired to ascertain whether the colonies could really clothe themselves without the aid of England, Benjamin Franklin alluded not only to the increasing manufacture of wool in addition to linen, but said of the people in the populous state of Virginia, "their winters are short, and very severe; *and they can very well clothe* themselves with linen and cotton of their *own raising for the rest of the year.*" And in 1786 Jefferson was able to report that in the four southernmost states . . . the poor were almost entirely clothed in cotton winter and summer. "In winter they wear shirts of it and outer clothing of cotton and wool mixed In summer their shirts are linen but the outer clothing cotton. *The dress of the women is almost entirely of cotton manufactured by themselves*, except the higher class, and even many of these wear a good deal of homespun cotton. It is as well manufactured as the calicoes of Europe."

When the Revolutionary War broke out the people of America found themselves driven to rely entirely on their own resources for all the manufactured goods. This gave a great impetus to both the cultivation of cotton and the manufacture of cotton goods, and increased the demand for wool and linen.

In 1775 the Assemblies of both South Carolina and Virginia exhorted the people to cultivate more cotton and flax. At the same time societies were organised for the purpose of encouraging home manufacturing. Women refused to wear the silk imported from England; congregations of men and women would come together, 'and while they spun and wove and carded, the minister preached to them the necessity of economy in the home."

Every farmer's daughter, we are told by a historian, was taught not only to weave as well as to spin, but to weave better and to spin finer. The sound of the loom and the buzz of the spinning wheel in every farmer's home told of the industry. Men and boys who were not in the army learnt the art. Legislators encouraged it, and requested families to supply enough clothing for the soldiers in the field. Vast quantities of homespun cloth were made on the plantations. Hundreds of yards were made annually at Mount Vernon, the home of Washington, and it is told of Martha Washington: "That she always carefully dyed all her worn silk and gowns and silk scraps to a desired shade. After ravelling them with care, she wound them on bobbins, and had them woven into chair and cushion covers. To a group of visitors she one time displayed a dress of a red and white striped material, of which the white stripes were ravelled chair covers and silk from the General's worn-out stockings." That the instance of Martha Washington was not an isolated one but reflected the general spirit that prevailed among the *elite* is evidenced by a contemporary's comment on this incident, that this dress 'in all probability was as pretty as that stolen from Mrs. Benjamin Franklin.'

A special feature of the movement was spinning demonstrations that were held to mark events of national importance. In 1789 on hearing of the adoption of the constitution between 30 and 40 young ladies met at the house of a certain minister, taking their wheels with them, and spent the day in spinning. At the close of the day a prize was given to the best spinner, 'after which the minister delivered a profitable discourse.' A favourite text for such occasions was taken from Exodus xxxv, 25: "And all the women that were wise-hearted did spin with their hands, and brought that which they had spun, both of blue and of purple, and of scarlet, and of fine linen."

It is again related that 43 ladies met on a certain day in the State House of East Greenwhich, Rhode Island, and spent the day in "spinning and while they spun, the young gentlemen waited on them and served wine and cake."

A powerful movement was set on foot to prevent the importation of British manufactures into America and Non-importation societies sprang up everywhere. The seaport towns were urged to join the movement. Societies for the encouragement of home manufactures were also organised on a large scale. The members of the society formed in Delaware pledged themselves to appear on the 1st of January of each year clothed in home-spun goods and the graduates of Harvard College in Massachusets stood up to take their degree clad in New England black cloth. Young society women no longer thought it a disgrace to wear home-manfactured clothes and they became proficient in the art of spinning. "Priscilla being none the less attractive to the John Aldens of the day by reason of her use of the wheel, to excel in which was the pride of every lass and matron." Young men took special pride in being seen in home-spun stockings that came above the knees, and home-made jeans. Politicians boasted of the fact that they cared only for home-manufactured goods, and held up to ridicule those who still bought their goods in London. Washington's army was nicknamed 'The Homespuns', an epithet, however, which they regarded as a compliment and adopted with pride. When George Washington stood forth to take the oath of office, as the first President of the United States, he was, we are told, clad from head to foot in garments the material for which was made in America, a large part being made at Mount Vernon; and John Adams, on his way to take the oath as Vice-president, was presented by the society of Hartford with a roll of cloth made from the Hartford looms.

The boycott of British cloth proved so effective that the imports from England to all the colonies fell off to a very serious extent, showing a decline from £ 2,378,000 worth of goods in 1768 to £ 1,634,000 worth in 1769. Yet it was not the economic loss inflicted on England as a result of the boycott so much as the spirit of self-help, co-operation and unity that the organisation of home-manufacturing engendered among the American people—"the women grew to love their looms as companions in the conflict, and they wove their prayers and love into cloth"—that told in the end. And we have the testimony of men like Cassie Hardwick and Prof. Brooks that if the colonies in 1775 had been as dependent on England for food, clothing, and shelter, as in the few years just after the first settlements, there would have been no Revolutionary War, "for there would have been but little, if any, independent political thinking."

What the Americans claimed was the right to make their own clothes, to exchange where they pleased their own surplus foodstuffs, to sell where they pleased and to buy where they pleased, and when the mother country tried to interfere with this elementary right it roused the national sentiment of self-respect to such a pitch that they forthwith resolved to throw off the humiliating foreign yoke and to declare their complete independence of Great Britian. An illustration of the temper of the times is furnished by the replies which Benjamin Franklin gave to his questioners who were considering the repeal of the Stamp Act when he appeared before a Committee of the House of Commons in 1776.

"What used to be the pride of Americans?" Franklin was asked.

"To indulge in the fashions and manufactures of Great Britain," he answered.

"What is now their pride?" he was next asked.

"To wear their old clothes over again, till they can make new ones," he replied.

While Franklin the pioneer in thought was uttering these

memorable words in England, George Washington, the hero of action, was trying to give to the idea a practical shape on his estate in Virginia. The entries in the records of his weaving establishment show that in 1767 he manufactured clothing goods for 28 different persons besides himself and Mrs. Washington, making a total of 1556 yards, of which about 300 yards were of cotton, including "cotton striped, cotton-plain, cotton-filled, cotton-bird-eye, cotton-Jumpstripe and Cotton-India dimity;" while his summary of the production for 1768 shows that he spun and wove for his own use (including his plantation) 815¾ yards of 'linen,' 355¼ yards of woollen, 144½ yards of linsey and 40 yards of cotton—"thus demonstrating his complete independence of England in the matter of clothing."

Not that arm-chair critics were lacking even then whose sole pastime was to indulge in destructive criticism, but the American colonists had the good fortune to have at the helm of their affairs hard-headed practical men and their sound commonsense prevailed against the sceptical counsels of these academic do-nothings. It was argued against the development of home manufactures that it would give a setback to agriculture. The reply which George Washington gave to this argument was characteristic of him. Writing to Lafayette in 1789 he said, "Though I would not force the introduction of manufactures. . . . to the prejudice of agriculture, yet I conceive much might be done in the way by women, children, and others, without taking one really necessary hand from tilling the earth." In another letter written the same year he said. "No diminution in agriculture has taken place at the time when greater and more substantial improvements in manufactures are making than were ever known before in America. I hope it will not be a great while before it will be unfashionable for a gentleman to appear in any other dress (except homespun). Indeed, we have already been too long subject to British prejudices."

Would that our public men and intellectuals caught a

spark of the spirit of these illustratious soldiers of freedom and adopted a leaf from their diary! P.

8th November, 1928

THE INEVITABLE

BY M. K. GANDHI

"Thanks. Assault unprovoked and deliberate. Recieved two severe injuries but not serious, one on left chest, other on shoulder, other blows warded by friends. Satyapal, Gopichand, Hansraj, Mohammad Alam, others received blows and injuries. No cause for anxiety.—Lajpatrai."

This was the prompt reply Lalaji sent me upon my wire to him of congratulations and enquiry. Lalaji earned the title of Punjab Kesari, *i.e.*, the Lion of the Punjab, when most of the present generation were in their teens. All these years he has survived the title. For whatever may be said of him or against him, he still remains the unchallengeable leader of the Punjab and one of the most beloved and esteemed leaders in all India. He has been president of the National Congress, enjoys a European reputation and is one of the few public men who think aloud at the risk of being often misunderstood and more often being considered indiscreet. He remains incorrigible; for he cannot harbour anything in his breast. He must speak out just as he thinks. When therefore, I read the headline 'Lalaji assaulted' and discovered how and why, I could not help saying: 'Well done! Now we shall not be long getting Swaraj.' For whether the revolution is non-violent or violent, there is no doubt about it that before we come to our own, we shall have to learn the art of dying in the country's cause. Authority will not yield without a tremendous effort even to non-violent pressure. Under an ideal and complete non-violence, I can imagine full transformation of authority to be possible. But whilst an ideally perfect programme is possible its full execution is never possible. It is therefore the most economical thing that leaders get assaulted or shot. Hitherto obscure people have been assaulted or done to death. The assault on Lala Lajpatrai has attracted far greater attention than even the shooting of a few men could have. The assault on Lalaji and other leaders has set the politically minded India athinking and it must have perturbed the Government. I am loath to think that the local Government as a body knew anything of the contemplated assault. If they did and the assault was part of a deliberate plan as in the days of yore, it is so much the worse for the Government. Then of course the Government can only pretend perturbation. I would not mention such a possibility in ordinary circumstances, but holding the view that I do about the Government, —the view being based on experience,—whilst I should be sorry, it would not surprise me if a discovery was made that the assault was part of a deliberate plan. I admit that the provocation, *viz.*, the very fact of the boycott, no matter how peaceful, was quite enough without the fraudulent story concocted by the police. I call the police version fraudulent because I would any day trust Lalaji's word against a host of interested witnesses that the police can bring to its assistance. If I was not convinced that this system of Government is based on force and fraud, I should not have become the confirmed non-co-operator that I am. Indeed Lowes Dickinson in his essay *War, its Causes and Cure* has shown from sufficient evidence that a war cannot be conducted without fraud. *Pari passu* this Government of ours which professes to hold India by the sword and whose foundations were laid in fraud cannot be sustained without either, except when it undergoes transformation and is based upon popular will and confidence.

Nor are we to think that the Punjab incident is to be the last of the barbarities committed during the pendency of the Statutory Commission. The boycott of the Simon Commission is a continuing sore for the Commission and the Government. Sir John Simon and his colleagues cannot be contemplating this boycott with equanimity. They have not the courage to acknowledge defeat. The boycott itself has been given additional momentum by the unprovoked assault on the Punjab leaders. The Government will therefore feel itself bound to suppress the boycott by any means that it can command. The Punjab incident therefore I regard as the first trial of strength, the strength of non-violence against violence. Lalaji had no difficulty in restraining the vast crowd behind him in spite of the police provocation. And if throughout the stay of the unwelcome Commission in India, this non-violent policy can be successfully and efficiently carried out, the Government will find much of its occupation gone and the people would have had a striking demonstration of the effectiveness of mass non-violence. The moral therefore I would have national workers to draw from this incident is not to be depressed or taken aback by the assault, but to treat it as part of the game we have to play, to turn the irritation caused by the wanton assault into dynamic energy and husband it and utilise it for future purposes.

8th November, 1928

FACT AND FICTION

BY M. K. GANDHI

A friend has sent me a cutting from the *Pioneer* purporting to be a report of an interview with me and I have seen a press message in the Bombay papers giving a summary of a further report. Both have grieved me. It would have been nice if Mr. Wild, who is the author of these reports, had submitted proofs to me before publishing his reports. The late Mr. Saunders of the *Englishman* used to send to interviewed persons proofs for correction or confirmation of the interviews taken by his reporters. I wish that his very laudable and desirable practice was universally followed. It was all the more necessary for Mr. Wild to follow the practice as he had come to the Ashram as an honoured guest sent by his chief and as he had taken no notes while he was interviewing me. Whilst clever reporters have been known to recall from memory an accurate substance of what they had heard without taking notes, even the cleverest will fail to reproduce in full the very words of his victim if he will take no notes. Mr. Wild has been guilty of sins both of omission and commission. He omitted to send me proofs and although he took no notes, he has professed to reproduce my own words. The result is a series of unfortunate misrepresentations. In many respects the reports are a travesty.

I do not however propose to examine the reports in detail. I would content myself with correcting one mischievous representation. Mr. Wild makes me say that "there is not a man in India today whom he (I) can name as a national leader." I could never be guilty of making such a false, arrogant and impertinent statement. Fortunately for India, she has not one but scores of national leaders who are able to give a good account of themselves and who need no certificate from me or any one else. Probably Mr. Wild has confused the question of successor with leaders. I was taken aback when he put me the question about successor. For I have never thought of successors. I believe that a successor will come without effort when one is needed. But a successor even a poor scavenger or spinner may have. He need not be a leader. Once when I was called upon to name a successor I named Gulnar, the daughter of Maulana Mahomed Ali. But she is no longer now fit to occupy the coveted place. But she is no more a baby. My notions of successor remain as primitive now as they were seven years ago when the question was first put to me

---

8th November, 1928

HANDICAP OF MAHATMASHIP

BY M. K. GANDHI

The difficulties and afflictions of a 'mahatma' are no less serious and very often much more serious than those of misters and shriyuts, not excluding knights and baronets. More than once in my life have I had to battle against these difficulties and afflictions created by unfriendly critics and not unoften through misunderstanding on the part of friends who will not take the trouble of ascertaining the true situation after personal inspection but will unhesitatingly accept as gospel truth any rumour that may appear in print.

Now what has appeared in the press about the Satyagraha Ashram was wholly unauthorised. When one important change in the Ashram was adopted, opinion was divided as to whether without giving a trial to the great change, we were called upon to take the public into confidence. I yielded to the express wish of some of my trusted co-workers not to announce the change. When I accepted their advice, I knew the consequence. I knew that nothing happening about anything connected with me could escape the attention of newspaper reporters. The published report is altogether misleading.

Here are the plain facts:

The constitution of the Ashram has not suffered any vital change except in its name. The reported change about *brahmacharya* for which I have received from some quarters undeserved congratulations and for which anxious friends have shown nervous concern was never made. I did leave it absolutely free to my co-workers to make whatever change they wished. After full deliberation among themselves over the proposal to relax the *brahmacharya* vow and at the discretion of the Managing Committee to admit married people unprepared for the observance, they came to the unanimous conclusion that the change could not be made. I must deal at a future date with the reasoning behind this very important decision.

The other reported change relates to the introduction of spices in the Ashram. In the beginning, the Ashram had only one joint board when the food was prepared without spices. Later when many families joined the Ashram separate kitchens were set up for them and they were free to use spices. But it was decided some months ago to revert to the joint kitchen We tried for some time to do without spices but as I held the joint kitchen to be an important thing for corporate life and as many, if they had separate kitchens, would revert to spices, it was decided to have two varieties of food in the joint kitchen, spiced and unspiced. We want to give all the assistance and freedom the womenfolk need. Many of them have come to the Ashram because they are the wives of their husbands. They have not yet been able to argue out all the *pros* and *cons* of everything they do.

The real change in my opinion is the change in the name. It has caused the original founders of the Ashram many an anxious night. We claim to be votaries of unadulterated truth and so new possibilities of the definitions of fundamental truths have dawned upon us. The name Satyagraha Ashram was adopted deliberately and with the intention of giving the fullest effect to its meaning. But the progressive realisation of the meaning of the name made us conscious of our unworthiness to bear it. And so we resolved upon voluntary self-suppression and we chose a name in keeping with the evolution of the corporate life at the Ashram. If the Ashram has done nothing else, it has at least demonstrated the necessity and usefulness of labour undertaken not for self only but for the whole nation. Therefore the name Udyoga Mandir, I felt, more answered our present evolution than Satyagraha Ashram. The co-workers accepted the suggestion though not without considerable hesitation. 'Industrial Home' is a poor rendering of the original as Dominion Status or even Independence is a poor substitute for Swaraj which alone can signify the great mass longing of India as an individual nation. We do not take up any industry that comes our way. We select only such as we must carry on as a consecration, *yajna* (sacrifice) or a *kurbani*. An industrial home connotes a conglomeration of industries which may appeal to some but which have no universal application. The word 'Mandir' has sacred associations and so has 'Udyoga' read in the light of the Bhagavad Gita. I must therefore invite friendly critics with the poetic instinct to present me with an English expression that will exactly fit in with the expression Udyoga Mandir. Till I get some good equivalent it must remain untranslatable.

But the Satyagraha Ashram does not entirely disappear. Whilst it divests itself of its external activities and allows the use of the ground on which the Ashram stands to the Udyoga Mandir,—the possession to be resumed at will,—the Ashram retains the open prayer ground and therefore its most life-giving activity, hoping some day to be able to reabsorb the activities now surrendered. The name Satyagraha Ashram has so many sacred associations, that only the hope of reverting to it intact has reconciled us to the change of name to the extent indicated.

There is one thing more which I may not omit. It has been openly stated, more secretly whispered, that Mahadev Desai has been appointed chairman of the Managing Committee owing to the inmates having lost confidence in me and as a concession to weakness. This is altogether untrue. The Managing Committee, if the reader will recall the previous description of the Ashram in these pages, was appointed long ago. I ceased for a long interval officially to guide its deliberations. Then at the invitation of the Committee, I took up the active guidance. But when the change in name came, the responsibility of the chairman seemed to be eased a bit. Hence I withdrew and Mahadev Desai became chairman once more. The virtual control of the Ashram however still remains with me and will continue to do so, so long as I continue to deserve the affection of my comrades.

15th November, 1928

AS EVER

BY M. K. GANDHI

The Punjab Government's communique over the unprovoked assault on Lalaji and other leaders exculpates the police from all blame which means that the old policy of excusing the police and the military, no matter how they act, continues to reign supreme as ever. This is not to be wondered at. So long as the Government remains irresponsive and irresponsible to the popular will, so long must it be subservient to the police and the military.

The departmental inquiry proposed by the Government is a further eyewash. It is preposterous to expect Lalaji and the other leaders to stultify themselves by leading evidence before a committee which the people have every reason to distrust. If the Government had been really anxious to know the truth about the incident, they would have appointed a representative committee of a judicial nature which would inspire public confidence and whose findings would command respect. I congratulate Lala Lajpatrai and his friends on having decided not to lead evidence before the departmental committee. Lalaji has thrown down the challenge. He courts a libel action and undertakes to prove a case which the Government had the hardihood summarily to brush aside.

But the question that arises from this incident is much larger than the mere demonstration of the truth of Lalaji's version. For the public, so long as the Government do not prove otherwise beyond doubt, Lalaji's version stands. The larger question is how are the people to remedy the evil of irresponsible Government. The assault and the bolstering are but a symptom of the great disease of bondage. I wish that we could all seriously deal with the root of the evil rather than set about cutting off the branches which sprout forth like Ravan's heads as soon as they are cut off. In other words we have to develop sufficient strength to resist the main disease.

I dare not enter into the question of remedies. My own remedy is well known. My purpose just now is not to insist upon its acceptance or the acceptance of any particular remedy. I simply plead that it is up to all the leaders of public opinion seriously to concentrate upon finding an expeditious and effective remedy for dealing with the evil of foreign domination.

15th November, 1928

KARACHI SWEEPERS

With reference to the discussion that took place recently in the Karachi Municipality on the question of Khadi wear for its employees, the President of the Sweepers' Union has now sent me the text of a resolution passed by the Sweepers' Union. It runs as follows:

> "The Union notes with regret the discussion *re* Khadi uniforms in a recent Municipal meeting and, thanking sincerely the President of the Karachi Municipality for the solicitude shown by him for the sweepers, most respectfully and humbly begs to draw his attention to the fact that as agriculturists sweepers have been wearing Pankorun, *i.e.*, Khadi for a long time and that the Khadi uniforms are not at all inconvenient to them. On the contrary they (the sweepers) appreciate the national sentiment signifying the use of Khadi and sympathise with their brothers and sisters, who get much needed supplementary income by spinning and doing other processes. This Union therefore urges on the Municipality to continue Khadi uniforms in future."

I wonder whether this resolution was passed only by half a dozen sweepers or whether it was known and explained to all the sweeper employees of the Municipality. The secretary informs me that it was fully explained to the sweepers before the resolution was passed. It is a resolution which I can gladly commend to all the Municipal employees. No compulsion superimposed upon them about Khadi or anything else can possibly last; but if an educative propaganda such as has been carried on amongst the sweepers of Karachi were to be carried amongst the employees of Municipalities throughout India and if they were to ask for Khadi uniforms, no Municipality will be able for any length of time to resist such a demand. I therefore congratulate the Sweepers' Union upon their resolution.

M. K. G.

15th November, 1928

'GOD IS'

Having read this article in *Young India* (11-10-1928) a reader sends the following bracing quotations from Emerson:

> "A little consideration of what takes place around us everyday would show us, that a higher law than that of our will regulates events; that our painful labours are unnecessary and fruitless; that only in our easy, simple, spontaneous action are we strong and by contenting ourselves with obedience we become divine. Belief and love—a believing love will relieve us of a vast load of care. O my brothers, God exists. There is a soul at the centre of Nature, and over the will of every man, so that none of us can wrong the universe.
>
> "The lesson is forcibly taught that our life might be much easier and simpler than we make it, that the world might be a happier place than it is; that there is no need of struggles, convulsions, and despairs, of the wringing of the hands and the gnashing of teeth; that we miscreate our own evils. We interfere with the optimism of nature."

If we would but have a little faith we would see God and His love everywhere about us. M. K. G.

15th November, 1928

GREENS AND DIETETIC AHIMSA

A friend writes from Calcutta:

"You have observed in one of your previous articles on dietetics that it is undesirable to cook the greens since cooking destroys their vitamin contents. Now the Jains believe that all vegetable fare with the exception of ripe fruit contains countless germs invisible to the eye which by setting up putrefaction give rise to a variety of diseases unless the vegetables are cooked. Jain *sadhus* do not even take water unless it is previously boiled. This view is thus in direct contradiction to your view. Which of these views can be correct? Would you throw some light on the matter?"

I have already expressed my opinion on this point in *Navajivan*. If one may take ripe fruit without cooking I see no reason why one may not take vegetables too in an uncooked state provided one can properly digest them. Dieteticians are of opinion that the inclusion of a small quantity of raw vegetables like cucumber, vegetable marrow, pumpkin, gourd etc. in one's menu is more beneficial to health than the eating of large quantities of the same cooked. But the digestions of most people are very often so impaired through a surfeit of cooked fare that one should not be surprised if at first they fail to do justice to raw greens, though I can say from personal experience that no harmful effect need follow if a *tola* or two of raw greens are taken with each meal provided one masticates them thoroughly. It is a well established fact that one can derive a much greater amount of nourishment from the same quantity of food if it is masticated well. The habit of proper mastication of food inculcated by the use of uncooked greens therefore, if it does nothing else, will at least enable one to do with less quantity of food and thus not only make for economy in consumption but also automatically reduce the dietetic *himsa* that one commits to sustain life. Therefore whether regarded from the viewpoint of dietetics or that of *ahimsa* the use of uncooked vegetables is not only free from all objection but is to be highly recommended. Of course it goes without saying that if the vegetables are to be eaten raw extra care will have to be exercised to see that it is not stale, over-ripe or rotten, or otherwise dirty.

M. K. G.

15th, November, 1928

THE STUDENTS' INTERROGATORIES

[Before Gandhiji commenced reading *Hind Swaraj* with the students of the Gujarat Vidyapith they had addressed him a string of questions for answer. As some of these questions are of general interest Gandhiji has dealt with them in the columns of *Navajivan*. The following assortment out of them will be found useful by the readers of *Young India*. P.]

BOLSHEVISM

Q. What is your opinion about the social economics of Bolshevism and how far do you think they are fit to be copied by our country?

A. I must confess that I have not yet been able fully to understand the meaning of Bolshevism. All that I know is that it aims at the abolition of the institution of private property. This is only an application of the ethical ideal of non-possession in the realm of economics and if the people adopted this ideal of their own accord or could be made to accept it by means of peaceful persuasion there would be nothing like it. But from what I know of Bolshevism it not only does not preclude the use of force but freely sanctions it for the expropriation of private property and maintaining the collective state ownership of the same. And if that is so I have no hesitation in saying that the Bolshevik regime in its present form cannot last for long. For it is my firm conviction that nothing enduring can be built on violence. But be that as it may there is no questioning the fact that the Bolshevik ideal has behind it the purest sacrifice of countless men and women who have given up their all for its sake, and an ideal that is sanctified by the sacrifices of such master spirits as Lenin cannot go in vain: the noble example of their renunciation will be emblazoned for ever and quicken and purify the ideal as time passes.

UNDER SWARAJ

Q. What in your opinion ought to be the basis of India's future economic constitution? What place will such institutions as savings banks, insurance companies etc. have in it?

A. According to me the economic constitution of India and for the matter of that, the world should be such that no one under it should suffer from want of food and clothing. In other words everybody should be able to get sufficient work to enable him to make the two ends meet. And this ideal can be universally realised only if the means of production of elementary necessaries of life remain in the control of the masses. These should be freely available to all as God's air and water are or ought to be; they should not be made a vehicle of traffic for the exploitation of others. Their monopolization by any country, nation or group of persons would be unjust. The neglect of this simple principle is the cause of the destitution that we witness today not only in this unhappy land but other parts of the world too. It is this evil that the Khadi movement is calculated to remedy. Savings banks and insurance companies will be there even when the economic reforms suggested to me have been effected but their nature will have undergone a complete transformation. Savings banks today in India though a useful institution do not serve the very poorest. As for our insurance companies they are of no use whatever to the poor. What part they can play in an ideal scheme of reconstruction such as I have postulated is more than I can say. The function of savings banks ought to be to enable the poorest to husband their hard earned savings and to subserve the interests of the country generally. Though I have lost faith in most Government institutions, as I have said before, savings banks are good so far as they go but unfortunately today their services are available only to the urban section of the community and so long as our gold reserves are located outside India they can hardly be regarded as trustworthy institutions. In the event of a war all these banks may become not only utterly useless but even a curse to the people inasmuch as the Government will not scruple to employ the funds held by these banks against the depositors themselves. No Government institution can be depended upon to remain loyal to the interest of the people in emergency, if they are not controlled by and not run in the interests of the people. So long therefore as this primary condition is absent banks are in the last resort additional links to keep the people in chains. They may to exist but it is well to understand where we are in respect even of such harmless looking institutions

FOREIGN v. SWADESHI

Q. What is your opinion about the importation of foreign goods other than cloth into India? Are there any foreign commodities which you would like to see immediately laid under prohibition? What do you think should be the nature of India's foreign trade in the future?

A. I am more or less indifferent with regard to trade in foreign goods other than cloth. I have never been an advocate of prohibition of all things foreign because they are foreign. My economic creed is a complete taboo in respect of all foreign commodities, whose importation is likely to prove harmful to our indigenous interests. This means that we may not in any circumstance import a commodity that can be adequately supplied from our own country. For instance I would regard it a sin to import Australian wheat on the score of its better quality but I would not have the slightest hesitation in importing oatmeal from Scotland, if an absolute necessity for it is made out, because we do not grow oats in India. In other words I would not countenance the boycott of a single foreign article out of ill-will or a feeling of hatred. Or to take up a reverse case, India produces a sufficient quantity of leather; it is my duty therefore to wear shoes made out of Indian leather only, even if it is comparatively dearer and of an inferior quality in preference to cheaper and superior quality foreign leather shoes. Similarly I would condemn the introduction of foreign molasses or sugar if enough of it is produced in India for our needs. It will be thus clear from the above that it is hardly possible for me to give an exhaustive catalogue of foreign articles whose importation in India ought to be prohibited. I have simply inculcated the general principle by which we can be guided in all such cases. And this principle will hold good in future too so long as the conditions of production in our country remain as they are today.

15th November, 1928

SOLDIERS OF KHADI

The students of the Charkha Sangha Khadi Vidyalaya, Sabarmati, availed themselves of the presence of Sjt. C. Rajagopalachar who had come to the Ashram on a flying visit, to have from him a 'talk' on the work before them of which the following is the gist:

'If you compare the texture of the cloth that you produce here on your looms with the Khadi that you are wearing and which you have purchased at some Khadi depot, you will probably find that the latter is much superior to that which you weave here. People may rightly expect that in a central institution like the All-India Spinners' Association Technical Department where you have come to get your training the best spinning and weaving must be found. But let me warn you that when you go out to work among the people as organisers and teachers you will find that you have as your pupils men and women who are much better spinners and weavers than you are. This is but natural. It is not an easy thing to take to an occupation which is not your ancestral or family occupation and become as good in it as those who are born to it. I therefore warn you to be humble. If you forget humility and think when you go out of this institution to work among the people that you know all, you may stumble and get into a wrong hole.

'For the same reason I would caution you to make yourselves as near to perfect spinners and weavers as possible while you are here. Here with first class instruments you may produce fine results and think that you have mastered the various processes to perfection; but you will be greatly mistaken if you think so. I have seen many a young man trained at institutions like yours and full of confidence cut a very sorry figure when he has sat down to spin at a crude country wheel. The thread breaks at every turn and the women laugh at the new arrival. A part of your training therefore must be to get be regarded as an unavoidable evil and therefore to be suffered used to tools which are in use among the people with whom you have to work. You must be able to produce good yarn on shaky old type wheels such as you find among the villagefolk; you should be able to card with primitive bamboo bows with thick guts and no *atmas*, as well as on your nicely made elastic correctly strung bows. Or the village folk will have no confidence in you and then you cannot effect any reforms. A part of your training must be to be able to do well under the conditions in which the peasants among whom you have to work live.

'So much for the technical side of your training. But your task among the people will not be merely to give them technical assistance. You will have to look after quite a number of other things too; you must become centres of a better life in the villages where you work and it is here that the routine, the discipline and restraints under which you live here will be useful. The greatest of these restraints as I have already pointed out to you is humility. Do not develop self-righteousness. Pride of any kind, including the pride of humility itself, is bad. Real humility you will not be able to cultivate unless you learn to think that even among the unlettered village folk, often ignorant and superstitious, there may be sterling quality that you might well emulate. Secondly you must learn to observe the restraint that you are observing here not in a mechanical way to be followed by a reversion to old habits as soon as possible, but you must put your mind into them and cultivate taste for them so that they might grow to be as second nature with you. If when you eat food without condiments and spices, you all the time keep thinking of the absent spices, you will not really make headway.

'Then I have another warning to give you. Khadi work is a great and vast thing and individual workers can only take a very small part in it—so small a part indeed that it may hardly afford you a perspective of the whole. If I may use a simile, Khadi work is like a mighty river. A sightseer may from the top of a hill be able to have a view of its beautiful course as it winds its way through the valleys below down to the sea, but the fish in the river cannot have that glorious view. It is at once their limitation and privilege. Surely you do not want to be a mere outside spectator of Khadi work, you will then have to be satisfied with what little inconspicuous part may be assigned to you in it. You may have to miss all those beautiful and inspiring things in connection with what may be called real Khadi work. You may be put in charge of a sale depot and all you will have to do will be to learn the catalogue of prices by heart, to keep your shop in proper trim, to make out the bills properly and be nice and persuasively polite to every customer. Or you may be a mere auditor asked to sift accounts and pick holes and do nothing else. You may find the work dull, monotonous even irksome and be tempted to throw it up. But you must not give way to that feeling. Many a soldier during the Great War remained cooped up in a trench and never saw anything else. Many a soldier merely marched to and fro and waited and saw no fighting. Yet it was soldiers such as these who were content to remain at their posts, that helped to win the war. Similarly, you must be prepared to merge your personality entirely in the plan of the whole and be content to stick to your post in the battle and not complain that you were not able to take the fullest part in the battle.

'You should also bear in mind that not only have you to become technical experts in respect of carding, spinning and weaving, you must also learn to be businessmen. It is not enough that you are honest, you must be good clean accountants, and keep everything tidy and nice. Every one of you will be dealing with public funds, and so business habits, accuracy and perfect integrity are essential.

'Then you must master the arguments in favour of Khadi for you have to persuade all sorts of people to adopt it. And in your arguments with the people you must never exaggerate, for if you do so, you won't be able to convince. It does not require much argument to persuade people to give up foreign cloth. Your greatest difficulty will be in making them prefer Khadi to

Indian mill cloth. Briefly the argument against mill cloth is that it will not solve the problem of unemployment in the villages. Even if the whole of India were to take to Indian mill cloth it will not provide work to the peasants in the villages. If you want to protect the cow you have got to use cow's milk and prefer it to buffalo's milk. Similarly if you want to save the villagers from starvation and squalor you must only use the cloth manufactured by them from start to finish and not mill cloth. I hope you will all learn your work well and go out to your centres and serve the great cause.'

P.

22nd November, 1928

FROM FACTORIES TO FORTS

At the close of the first quarter of the 18th century the English factory at Madras, one hundred years after its establishment, still retained its essentially commercial character. Fort St. George was a fort only in name being occupied more with the management of its investment than with military operations. It carried on business with the Indian merchants either for providing a sufficient number of bales of Indian cloth for exportation to Europe, or for disposing of broad cloth, iron and other articles of home produce which had been imported from England. The story of these commercial transactions as revealed from the consultation books of the factory at this period constitutes one of the saddest chapters if also the most instructive of Indian history. It brings out in vivid detail the process of the transition from 'factories to forts and forts to territorial sovereignty' and shows that the foundations of the British economic imperialism in India were laid not by a natural process of economic evolution but by violence and a gross betrayal of the people by perfidious rulers. In proof of my statement let me turn to the following entries in the consultation books of the Fort St. George, relating to the year 1726 as supplied to us by J. Talboys Wheeler in his *Madras in Olden Times*.

"Thursday, 6th June, 1726. The Ware-house keeper reported to the Board, that the chintzes being brought from painting (dyeing) had been examined at the Sorting Godown and that it was the general opinion of the Sorters that both the cloth and paintings were worse than the musters; wherefore they had resolved, if the Board approved thereof, to allow the merchants only 35 pagodas per corge, instead of 40 for the cloth; and the painter 47½ pagodas per corge, instead of 60, which they used to have. This being approved, the merchants were called in and told the resolution of the Board."

"The Native merchants," observes Mr. Wheeler, "appear to have submitted this time to the reduction very quietly." In what circumstances it is not mentioned, but a clue is afforded by the significant admission that follows, *viz.*, that when the Company again desired to make a contract with the same merchants, 'it was not found so easy to deal with them'!

How this diffidence was overcome will be seen from the minutes of the following transaction; it begins with oily diplomacy and ends with the proverbial 'pound of flesh':

"Saturday, 11th Feb. 1727. The President represented to the Board, that the Merchants having received no *tasharief* according to custom at signing the contract with the Company the preceding two years insisted upon their being now *tasharief-ed* for the three contracts." An order was therefore issued to the Ware-house keeper to deliver 'seven pieces of scarlet cloth for that use.' The following curiously one-sided 'sight-unseen' contract was thereupon signed by the Chetty merchants:

"1. That the Merchants should receive all woollen goods expected upon the next shipping from England at 30% advance on the invoice prices, but the goods should remain in the Company's Ware-house *to be released only on payment of their price in full.*

"2. That the Merchants should supply the Company 30,000 bales of cloth by a certain date but *should on no account demand any payment on their behalf in advance* beyond 20,000 pagodas which they would have to pay to the weavers as earnest money.

"3. In case of non-compliance with the contract the Merchants would have to pay a penalty of 20% for all the bales that they might deliver short of the number agreed upon '*unless* it shall be manifestly made to appear that the *troubles in the country have hindered them* in which case any *shortage within 500 bales* of the contracted figure would be exempted from penalty.'"

But it was easier to get such a designedly iniquitious and unfair contract signed than to get it executed, for on Monday, 14th July, 1729, we find the following:

"The President represented to the Board 'that notwithstanding the indulgence given to the merchants in February last they had nevertheless been very backward in bringing the cloth, and that unless some further measures were taken to oblige them to bring cloth,' he feared, 'we shall be very much disappointed in the quantity necessary for the despatch of our ships. . . .' Accordingly the following terms were agreed to be proposed to them;

"That they should provide and deliver 17 hundred bales of calicoes by the 20th of June next in consequence of which they should have broad cloth at 35 p. c. on invoice price. But if they did not comply and deliver the said 17 hundred bales . . . they should pay 10 p. c. more for the broad cloth. In order to do which they should be advanced 15 thousand pagodas without interest till the 20th June next."

The merchants however rejected these proposals alleging that the great drought in the country, and dearness of cotton made it very difficult to provide cloth. "Whereupon they were told, it was a favour to them that was designed thereby that they had incurred a penalty of 20 thousand pagodas by their non-compliance of last contract; that they were now . . . asked to provide only three hundred bales more than they were obliged to by their old contract etc.

"But they still urged difficulty of providing cloth, the

scarcity and famine and dearness of cotton which made the weavers turn their hands to other work and retire into other countries where grain was to be got, which arguments they insisted on so strenuously that the Board dismissed them with an assurance that they would sell the broad cloth at outcry and insist on the performance of the last contract, or the penalty due for the breach thereof."

The terms however must have been found by the Company to be absolutely unfeasible for even they were forced, on the 31st of July, to "wholly forgive them the penalty of the last contract;"—not however till they had made them to enter into a fresh contract "to deliver by the 20th of January 17,000 bales with the usual provision of penalty in the event of non-compliance and to receive all the Company's cloth at 35 p. c."

And so the tangle goes on deepening. It is the familiar old story, once a slave always a slave.

II

So far, as we have seen, the Company had at least to entice the merchants into its parlour before they could be fleeced and if the merchants subsequently suffered one could at least say that they had their own greed and indiscretion to thank for their trouble, but as a result of the episode that was enacted next the entire artisan population of Karnatak was at a stroke reduced to the position of bond-slaves to the foreign exploiter without any hope of redress or succour. Nabob Saadatulla Khan, was the ruler of Karnatak and Imam Sahib, Bakshi (paymaster) to the Nabob, a courtier with a peculiar weakness for 'palm-oil' was supposed to have great influence in the court. The English factors of Fort St. George having come to know that "the French had wrote a letter of condolence to Nabob on the death of his wife and that the letter written by their President on that occasion, being unaccompanied by a present, had remained undelivered," it was agreed that '6 bottles of Rose water and a piece of broad cloth be sent to the Nabob to accompany the letter.'

At the same time the President took an opportunity to

represent to Imam Sahib about "the ill state of the Company's investment and to beg his countenance and assistance in advancing it," care of course having been taken to propitiate him before-hand with a suitable present. The effect was magical as will be seen from the following excerpts from the correspondence that passed between the President, the Nabob and Imam Sahib:

"'From the Nabob, Saadatulla Khan Bahadur to the President:'

" . . . Your present . . . I have sent through means of Imam Sahib orders to the several Havildars of Town where you provide your goods, to give you all the liberty possible, to serve you only, and not to permit any hindrance whatever."

"'From the Imam Sahib to the President:'

" From the time I left Your Honour nothing has run in my mind so much as your goodness . . . I have made my request to him (Nabob) . . . The following circular order has been issued:

It is my will, you give strict order to all the merchants in your parts to sell goods as are proper to the Governor of Madras only to his people, and that they immediately deliver whatever cloth they have ready to his Gomastas. What they refuse you permit them to sell anywhere. Take care that none buy such goods in your parts but his people; for this is my strict command: and take penalties from your merchants to perform the same.'"

Armed with this instrument the Company now proceeded with their task with a systematic ruthlessness. Forcible seizure of goods at prices arbitrarily fixed, compelling the spinners and weavers to enter into contracts impossible of fulfilment with stipulations for heavy penalties in case of non-fulfilment with the deliberate puropose of keeping him enslaved, preventing the merchants and artisans from entering into engagements with any but themselves even though others offered better terms, writs of attachment and arrest against those who proved recalcitrant became the order of the day and a regime of oppression ond exploitation was set up for which there is probably no parallel in history.

Let us now see how the exigencies of these commercial operations reacted on the course of political developments.

III

Confronted with the question, 'how to provide the purchasing power' without having to import bullion from home, since Europe at this time hardly produced any manufactured goods that could be sent to the East in return for the Eastern commodities that were so much in request in the West, except 'toys' and inconsiderable quantities of longcloth, the Dutch Governor Coen had suggested the expedient of 'developing' the Company's possessions and investing all available capital in 'principal means of production—many thousands of slaves.' His plan was vetoed by the Dutch Government but was taken up by the English. This in its turn necessitated the acquirement of political sovereignty. But the experiment could hardly be tried so long as there was a powerful central Government in existence. But thanks to the civil strife that set in at the dissolution of the Moghul Empire a suitable opportunity for it soon presented itself and the incubus of political slavery was added to that of economic servitude. The fact, however, which specially deserves to be noted here is that long before this event took place entire populations of artisans and workers that everywhere constitute the strongest bulwark of a nation's freedom had already been brought under a system of capitalistic slavery. Having been accustomed to swallow the camel of economic exploitation for generations they could hardly afford to strain at the gnat of political subjection when in its turn it presented itself. P.

22nd November, 1928

LONG LIVE LALAJI

BY M. K. GANDHI

Lala Lajpatrai is dead. Long live Lalaji. Men like Lalaji cannot die so long as the sun shines in the Indian sky.

Lalaji means an institution. From his youth he made of his country's service a religion. And his patriotism was no narrow creed. He loved his country because he loved the world. His nationalism was international. Hence his hold on the European mind. He claimed a large circle of friends in Europe and America. They loved him because they knew him.

His activities were multifarious. He was an ardent social and religious reformer. Like many of us he became a politician because his zeal for social and religious reform demanded participation in politics. He observed at an early stage of his public career that much reform of the type he wanted was not possible until the country was freed from foreign domination. It appeared to him, as to most of us, as a poison corrupting every department of life.

It is impossible to think of a single public movement in which Lalaji was not to be found. His love of service was insatiable. He founded educational institutions; he befriended the suppressed classes; poverty wherever found claimed his attention. He surrounded young men with extraordinary affection. No young man appealed to him in vain for help. In the political field he was indispensable. He was fearless in the expression of his views. He suffered for it when suffering had not become customary or fashionable. His life was an open book. His extreme frankness often embarrassed his friends, if it also confounded his critics. But he was incorrigible.

With all deference to my Musalman friends, I assert that he was no enemy of Islam. His desire to strengthen and purify Hinduism must not be confounded with hatred of Musalmans or Islam. He was sincerely desirous of promoting and achieving Hindu Muslim unity. He wanted not Hindu Raj but he passionately wanted Indian Raj; he wanted all who called themselves Indians to have absolute equality. I wish that Lalaji's death would teach us to trust one another. And we could easily do this if we could but shed fear.

There will be, as there must be, a demand for a national memorial. In my humble opinion no memorial can be complete without a definite determination to achieve the freedom for which he lived and died so nobly. Let us recall what has after all proved to be his last will. He has bequeathed to the younger generation the task of vindicating India's freedom and honour. Will they prove worthy of the trust he reposed in them? Shall we the older survivors—men and women—deserve to have had Lalaji as a countryman by making a fresh, united, supreme effort to realise the dream of a long line of patriots in which Lalaji was so distinguished a member?

Nor may we forget the Servants of People Society which he founded for the promotion of his many activities all designed for the advancement of the country. His ambition in respect of the Society was very high. He wanted a number of young men all over India to join together in a common cause and work with one will. The Society is an infant not many years old. He had hardly time enough to consolidate this great work of his. It is a national trust requiring the nation's care and attention.

CONDOLENCES FROM OVERSEAS

'Anavil Yuvaks' send me the following message from Port Louis, Mauritius:

"Deeply regret Lalaji's death. Irreparable loss national cause. Tender heartfelt condolence bereaved family."

Transvasal Khatri Mandal, Johannesburg, sends the following:

"Khatri community deeply mourns death great patriot Lalaji. Kindly convey message condolence to bereaved family."

Patidar Society, Johannesburg cables:

"Patidar community mourns death great patriot Lala Lajpatrai. Kindly convey Society's condolence to bereaved family."

22nd November, 1928

SOME MORE POSERS IN AHIMSA

BY M. K. GANDHI

Letters in connection with the calf incident still continue to pour in. But I have had my full say already and such letters as needed a reply I have already answered. I however feel in duty bound to deal with some posers addressed to me by some correspondents. Not to do so might lead to consequences not warranted by my action.

I

One of them writes :

> "My baby is four months old. It fell ill a fortnight after its birth and there seems no end of its ailment in sight. Several *vaidyas* and doctors have tried their skill upon him, but in vain; some of them now even decline to administer any medicine to him. They feel, and I feel with them, that the fate of the poor thing is sealed. I have a big family to maintain and I feel myself reduced to sore straits as I have an accumulation of debts. Nor can I any longer bear to see the terrible sufferings of the baby. Would you kindly tell me what I should do in the circumstances?"

It is clear that this friend has not been reading *Navajivan* carefully or he would not have asked this question. There would be no warrant for taking the life of the baby even if all the doctors in the world were to pronounce the case to be hopeless because it would always be possible for its father to nurse it. He can soothe the baby in a variety of ways, its size unlike the calf's being manageable. It is only when every possible avenue of service however small is closed and the last ray of hope of the patient surviving seems extinct that one is justified in putting him out of pain, and then too only if one is completely free from the taint of selfish feeling. In the present case, not only is the service of the ailing baby possible, but the main consideration that, on the father's own admission, weighs with him is the personal inconvenience involved in nursing the baby. Largeness of the family or one's pecuniary difficulty can never serve as a justification for putting an end to the life of an ailing patient and I have not the slightest doubt that in the present instance, it is the bounden duty of the father to lavish all his love and care on his suffering baby. There is however one thing more which he can do; if he has sense enough to see it, he should resolve forthwith to lead a life of perfect self-restraint and further stop procreating irrespective of whether his present baby survives or not.

II

Another friend writes in the course of a Hindi letter:

"I am the manager of . . . . *goshala*. There are in my charge some 500 head of cattle. They are all utterly useless for any purpose and are simply eating their head off. Out of these from 350 to 400 animals on the average are constantly at death's door, destined to die off one by one in the long end every year. Now tell me what am I to do?"

As I have already explained, giving the short shrift, from considerations of financial expediency, can never be compatible with non-violence. And if it is a fact that not a day passes in this *goshala* without some animal or other dying painfully in the manner of that calf in the Ashram, it makes out a strong case for closing the *goshala* at once for it betrays fearful mismanagement. The calf in the Ashram was reduced to such piteous plight only as the result of an accident but daily instances like this should *ipso facto* be impossible in a well managed institution. The duty of the management in the present case is thus clear. It is incumbent upon them and upon the organisers of all similarly placed institutions to devise the most effective means of nursing and ministering to the needs of diseased and ailing cattle. I would also recommend to them for careful study and consideration my description of an ideal *panjrapole* and the way it ought to be managed that I have given more than once in these pages.

III

Writes a Kanbi friend:

"There is a grazing ground for the cattle near our village. It is overrun by a herd of deer about five to seven hundred strong. They work havoc upon all our cotton saplings. We are in a fix. We can easily get rid of them by employing professional watchmen who would kill them for the venison they would get. What would be your advice to a man in my condition? Again when insect pests attack our crops the only way to deal with them is to light a fire of hay which means making a holocaust of the insect pests. What course would you suggest in these circumstances?"

This question is of a different order from the other two questions; it falls under the category of the monkey question, not the calf question. I am unable to guide any one in the path of *himsa*. In fact no person can lay down for another the limit to which he may commit *himsa*; this is a question which everybody must decide for himself according to the measure of his capacity for *ahimsa*. This much however I can say without any hesitation that to use the analogy of the monkeys to justify the killing of the deer would only betray a laziness of thought and lack of discrimination; the two cases are so dissimilar. Besides, I have *not* yet decided to kill the monkeys, nor is there any likelihood of my doing so presently. On the contrary it has been and shall be my ceaseless anxiety to be spared that painful necessity. Moreover there is quite a number of ways of keeping off the deer from the fields which would be impossible in the case of elusive creatures like monkeys. Whilst therefore reiterating what every farmer knows from his daily experience also to be true, *viz.*, that destruction of small insects and worms is inevitable in agriculture' I am unable to proceed any further, but must content myself by stating generally that it is the sacred duty of everybody to avoid committing *himsa* to the best of one's power.

IV

Still another friend writes:

> "You say that an absolute observance of *ahimsa* is incompatible with life in the body, that so long as a man is in the flesh he cannot escape the commission of *himsa* in some form or other as the very process of our physical existence involves *himsa*. How then can *ahimsa* be the highest virtue, the supreme duty? Would you set forth as the highest religious ideal a code of conduct which is altogether impossible of being fulfilled in its completeness by man? And if you do, what would be the practical worth of such an ideal?"

My humble submission is, that contrary to what this writer says, the very virtue of a religious ideal lies in the fact that it cannot be completely realised in the flesh. For a religious ideal must be proved by faith and how can faith have play if perfection could be attained by the spirit while it was still surrounded by its 'earthly vesture of decay'? Where would there be scope for its infinite expansion which is its essential characteristic? Where would be room for that constant striving, that ceaseless quest after the ideal that is the basis of all spiritual progress, if mortals could reach the perfect state while still in the body? If such easy perfection in the body was possible all we would have to do would be simply to follow a cut and dry model. Similarly if a perfect code of conduct were possible for all there would be no room for a diversity of faith and religions because there would be only one standard religion which everybody would have to follow.

The virtue of an ideal consists in its boundlessness. But although religious ideals must thus from their very nature remain unattainable by imperfect human beings, although by virtue of their boundlessness they may seem ever to recede farther away from us, the nearer we go to them, still they are closer to us than our very hands and feet because we are more certain of their reality and truth than even of our own physical being. This faith in one's ideals alone constitutes true life, in fact it is man's all in all.

Blessed is the man who can perceive the law of *ahimsa* in the midst of the raging fire of *himsa* all around him. We bow in reverence before such a man; he lays the whole world under debt by his example. The more adverse the circumstances around him, the intenser grows his longing for deliverance from the bondage of flesh which is a vehicle of *himsa* and beckons him on to that blessed state which in the words of the poet

"Even the Great Masters saw only in a trance
Which even their tongue could not declare,"

a state in which the will to live is completely overcome by the ever active desire to realise the ideal of *ahimsa* and all attachment to the body ceasing man is freed from the further necessity of possessing an earthly tabernacle. But so long as that consummation is not reached a man must go on paying the toll of *himsa*, for *himsa* is inseparable from all physical existence and it will have its due.

(Translated from *Navajivan* by P.)

22nd November, 1928

FALSE TO HIS DHARMA

The intelligentsia of India are behind those of no other country in talents or power of understanding. They should use their talents and all their new knowledge to enquire into the causes of the appalling poverty of the rural population and discover and work out remedies. Until a more satisfactory solution is found it is their sacred and urgent duty to examine, and if found even in a measure good, try the remedy of Khadi. If they find that hand-spinning is the only supplementary cottage industry that can be taken up by large masses of people normally engaged in agriculture whose time is available for other work during a great part of the year, they are bound to carry that conviction into practice and protect the Khadi industry themselves and call upon the State and people to do likewise. Any other course would be country to *dharma.* In the course of a lecture delivered by Mr. P. J. Thomas, University Professor of Economics in Madras, the problem of rural reconstruction was approached with commendable warmth of feeling. The professor did not mince matters despite the thoroughly official auspices under which he spoke. His Excelleney the Governor of Madras occupied the chair and among those who were present to lend importance to the meeting were the Vice-Chancellor of the University, the principals of three big colleges, at least one minister in charge of a portfolio of Government, and the head of the Department of Agriculture.

"In the India of the present day," the professor said, "the problem urgently needing our attention is the appalling poverty and distressing backwardness of our teeming population. Such poverty and backwardness exist both in the countryside and in the town; in the country, it is due to the unremunerative character of agriculture, our predominant occupation; and in the towns where poverty is no less intense and perhaps even more poignant, it is connected mainly with the decay of our handicrafts and the slow progress of our manufacturing industries." "The neglect of agriculture and the countryside is," he warned, "bound to disintegrate civilizations and ruin kingdoms. The invention of the steam engine gave a phenomenal advantage to machine industry and made industrial countries wealthy and powerful, but today such countries are in a pitiable plight owing to various new developments."

Mr. Thomas pointed out, that our "agriculturists are almost entirely petty peasants cultivating small holdings. The entry of India into the welter of world economy caused by all the recent changes in long distance transport has in various ways worsened the position of the Indian agriculturists." In tracing the causes of the miserable condition of the people of India, Mr. Thomas did not, happily, forget 'the loss of supplementary income from domestic' handicraft due to the competition of machine industry. But, alas, beyond mentioning it, he did not care to examine it further or utter a single suggestion about it. It is truly remarkable, this conspiracy of silence on the part of Commissions and even University professors. Yet Mr. Thomas' words are emphatic and suggestive enough. "If the Indian economist does not whole-heartedly give his attention to these pressing problems, he will be false to his *dharma* and unworthy of his profession, for it is his duty to study the economic evils of the community and to suggest suitable remedies." C. R.

29th November, 1928

WHO SHOULD WEEP?

[I have before me notes of Acharya Kripalani's speech delivered at Jabalpur at a public meeting from which I take the following striking extracts to show what the British people have lost through Lalaji's death. Though the vast majority of them are today ignorant of Lalaji's genuine friendship towards them, a day will come when they will realise what service patriots like Lalaji have rendered to them. M. K. G.]

"But there is another party which should participate with us today in this our immense loss though it may be unconscious of what it has lost. Our rulers have a vast empire at stake. And in Lalaji they have lost a friend true and sincere, a friend who helped them even every time that he was punished and insulted by blind and intoxicated authority.

"It was in the Partition agitation days that Lalaji was deported without trial by the Government and yet when he returned he resisted the overtures of the so-called extreme wing of the Congress politicians. He helped the Moderates headed by Phirozeshah and Gokhale. Though he was injured the most yet he turned the left cheek to the nominal Christians who no more remember the virtues of their master. When the great War broke out, Lalaji proved his loyalty again. He was at the time in America and was not allowed to return, as long as the War lasted and for a period afterwards. Yet while the War was going on and the fate of the Empire was trembling in the balance, Lalaji forgot the injury to himself and from America blessed the so-called opportunity given to Indians to fight side by side with the British. He welcomed the opportunity given to India for service to the Empire based upon injustice.

"Once more during the Non-co-operation movement he was sent to jail on a charge which could not bear the light of law and justice. But when he was discharged from jail he again helped his persecutors. He pleaded for entry into the Councils for what is called discriminate support.

"This attitude of friendship to the powers that be lasted up to the last. A fortnight before his tragic passing away he was insulted, he was humiliated, not only he but the entire nation in his person, and that in most brutal and wanton fashion. Yet only five days after the incident he went to Delhi when his wounds were hardly healed, to plead with those of the younger generation whose warm blood would be satisfied with nothing less than complete independence for their suffering motherland. And then a week afterwards came the end hastened by the last favours of the masters whom he served according to his lights up to the last. Well therefore might the British people weep, and weep they would were they not dazzled and blinded by the pride of power.

"If even after the departure of such trusty Indian friends, tried and true, the Englishmen persist in their obstinacy, a time may come when the Indian generations to be will vow eternal enmity to England. It may even be the kind of enmity that Christians vowed and carried out through centuries against the Jews for the Christ who was crucified. It is quite possible that their domination may come to be viewed as a crucifixion of a whole nation and might rouse the worst passions of the generations yet unborn. Let therefore the Empire take thought and take heed, make up while yet there is time for the night cometh when the die will have been cast and retreat and compromise will be out of the question."

29th November, 1928

LALAJI MEMORIAL

BY M. K. GANDHI

I invite the attention of readers to the appeal for five lakhs issued over the signatures of Dr. Ansari, Pandit Malaviyaji and Sjt. Ghanshyamdas Birla. Signatures have been purposely restricted to those only without whose signatures no memorial can be considered truly national. There was great difficulty in choosing other names. Nor was there time enough to consult all the parties whose names should appear, if some of them might. After all if the prestige of Lalaji's name is not enough to induce the public to subscribe liberally, no names however many or distinguished they may be are likely to fetch subscriptions. The only assurance therefore the public need have in respect of memorials such as this is that the appeal must be from those whose names are a guarantee of good faith and honest administration. The three signatories are more than ample guarantee of these essentials.

I hope that the response will be quick and generous. It is to be wished that all those who have come under Lalaji's benign influence will send in their mite. The Memorial will gain in weight for small subscriptions making up the total of five lakhs. If we can collect five lakhs from five lakhs men and women, this collection by itself will be substantial propaganda for Swaraj. And if the minimum sum fixed by the signatories to the appeal is made up principally of small subscriptions, no pressure will be felt by any one during these hard times. If monied men have a special duty in such matters, the others are not on that account absolved from their duty of contributing according to their ability.

I suggest therefore to the various associations and societies that they make immediate collections from all on their rolls or under their influence. We have at least 27,00,000 students in high schools and colleges. They can always save from their pocket money enough to make a very substantial sum. Nor should the suppressed classes lag behind in tendering their quota.

We often waste time and energy in debating and wrangling over a multitude of suggestions and rehearse many possible improvements. Let such critics remember that perfection is not possible in human undertakings. Let us therefore try to do well things even though we may think of better things so long as what is presented to us for acceptance is not open to any fatal objection and especially when it comes from tried and trusted leaders.

Any subscriptions sent to the *Young India* office will be acknowledged in these columns.

APPEAL FOR FIVE LAKHS

To

The Citizens of India.

It is but meet that there should be a national memorial to the revered memory of a patriot so brave, so great and so self-sacrificing as Lala Lajpatrai. We the undersigned have therefore taken it upon ourselves to make an appeal to the generous public for funds which we hope will meet with universal response. If we expect large donations from the rich, we know that Lalaji's spirit would find the greatest solace from the coppers of the poor. We propose to announce later the exact manner in which the funds will be used, but we constitute ourselves as trustees for the funds with power to associate others with us in their administration. We may, however, generally state that we shall use them for the advancement of Lalaji's many political activities to which he so nobly gave the best part of his life. We shall naturally bear in mind his great creation and the instrument of his operations—the Servants of the People Society.

We have fixed the sum of Rs. 5,00,000 (five lakhs) as the minimum that a grateful country should give to Lalaji's memory. Regard being had to the bad times through which we are passing, we have chosen the lowest sum consistently with Lalaji's all-India greatness and the cause to which the monies are to be devoted.

Subscriptions should be sent to Sjt. Ghanshyamdas Birla, 8, Royal Exchange Place, Calcutta, who has kindly consented to act as Secretary and Treasurer for the fund.

M. A. ANSARI
MADAN MOHAN MALAVIYA
GHANSHYAMDAS BIRLA

26th November, 1928

29th November, 1928

GOOD IF TRUE

Dr. Satyapal sent me on 22nd November, 1928 the following telegram:

> "Lala Lajpatrai's death causes irreparable loss to Punjab. I offer my most humble and affectionate salutations to the great departed leader at this deplorable and critical juncture. I on my behalf and of other friends who differed from Lalaji assure friends who were offended for differing from Lalaji that we hereby sink all differences and resolve starting with a clean slate. We bear no ill will, we have no prejudice and we offer our hearty co-operation in all political movements started by Lalaji and we place ourselves unreservedly at the disposal of such friends. We offer hearty invitation to all these friends who have remained away from the Congress to join hands with us vigorously to pursue the campaign of Swarajya, for which Lalaji lived and died. Henceforth in sacred memory of Lalaji we resolve to present a united front, even if it be possible by our complete surrender."

It reflects great credit upon its authors, if the sentiments expressed in the telegram are heartfelt. I am obliged to utter this note of warning because I have known so many such death-bed repentances that one is never sure whether they are heartfelt or whether they are due to the impulse of the moment, or what is worse, outward pressure. The authors will never be able to bury the hatchet if inside their heart they feel that their opposition to Lalaji was justified and warranted by circumstances and dictated by no selfish consideration or other unworthy motives but by the purest patriotism. If such was the case there would be no cause for repentance. One can only be just to the memory of a dead man, one cannot wipe from one's memory the wrong he might have really done. Repentance pre-supposes conviction of one's own error. If then the authors feel that on the whole they wronged Lalaji in his lifetime or that the motive for their opposition was mixed then the repentance is genuine and should last. Subject to this reservation, I tender my congratulations to Dr. Satyapal and his companions on this patriotic message and hope that there would be a strong, sustained and united effort in the Punjab to carry on the mission bequeathed by Lalaji. In many respects it is possible for the Punjab to give the lead to the whole of India, if only the Punjab wills it, and if party feeling and communalism disappear in that land of five rivers. If the Punjab press, instead of indulging in vituperation and innuendoes as a portion of it deos, will but educate public opinion along right lines, I have no doubt that the rest of India will follow. Nothing can be a greater monument to the memory of Lalaji than that the Punjab should lead all India along the right path.

M. K. G.

29th November, 1928

A BLOT ON BOMBAY'

BY M. K. GANDHI

Sjt. Nagindas Amulakhrai of Ghatkopar Sarvajanik Jivadaya Khata has sent to the President, Municipal Corporation, the following reasoned letter on the question of milk supply to Bombay:

"1. Newly calved buffaloes of the best breed giving utmost quantity of milk are brought to Bombay with their young ones and sold from Grant Road Station yard to supply daily want of the cattle owners who have to purchase them to replace those which go dry after one milking period (9 to 12 months) is over. The owner has to pay about Rs. 300 per head for a fresh buffalo while he receives only about Rs. 60 per head for his dry one.

"From a letter addressed by the Municipal Commissioner of Bombay to the Corporation dated the 15th December, 1924, the following statement of facts is very important:

"'The high price at which milk is being sold in Bombay at present and the increase in the price with which we are being threatened are entirely due to the faulty system of stabling animals in the heart of a big city. The main causes of this high price of milk are:

(1) the costly feeding of animals, and

(2) the heavy depreciation on the initial cost of the animals.

"'As regards the first, the milch cattle in Bombay are fed on highly nitrogenous and expansive foods in order to maintain them in good milking condition, under the artificial condition in which they are kept. This kind of feeding would not be necessary if they were kept in more natural surroundings. Further, forage has to be imported into the city, many miles away from where it is grown, and both the cost of transport and the cost of storing it in a place like Bombay, where storage expenses are very high, add to the cost of feeding.

"'The second and more important reason is the heavy depreciation on the initial cost of the animals. Under the present system, owing to various considerations, arising out of the unnatural conditions under which the animals are kept in the city, the cattle owner has no other option but to sell his animal to the butcher when it gets dry. The difference between the price he so receives, and the original price is very great, and this difference goes into the cost of the milk.

"'This can be avoided, if animals are kept under more natural conditions and given a chance to bear calves again and live out their life. Of recent years the initial cost of the milch animals imported into Bombay has increased considerably, without a corresponding increase in the price fetched by the animals when they run dry. This is one more reason for the present high cost of milk and unless measures are taken to do away entirely with the present city stables, the dangers of a further increase in the cost of milk will continue to exist.

"'Apart from these local considerations, the premature slaughter of useful animals brought to Bombay results in a constant drain on one of the natural resources of this country. But for the existing system of town stabling, few valuable animals, if any, would find their way to the slaughter houses.'

"This pernicious system of keeping stables in the city further leads to the loss by death of thousands of valuable calves and young buffaloes which are left by the owners to starve in the open exposed to all the inclemencies of weather, as they would not feed them with any part of their mother's milk and certainly not rent a stall in order to accommodate them.

"Doctor Harold Mann, D. Sc., Director of Agriculture, Bombay Presidency, in his report on milch cattle stables in Bombay in the year 1919 stated as follows:—

"'The collection of animals housed together, the accumulation of dung even for a few hours, the smell which cannot be avoided when large numbers of animals are packed in a confined space in a thickly populated area, the collection of milk in large quantities in the dusty and possibly disease-infected air of towns, all these tend towards the lowering of the standard of milk produced, lead to the creation of a nuisance in the neighbourhood and may result in the possible dissemination of disease by means of the flies, which inevitably follow cattle stables.'

"I give below a statement showing the number of buffaloes slaughtered at the Bandra and Kurla Municipal Slaughter Houses along with the number of calves both of cows and buffaloes tortured to death in the city of Bombay and brought to Tardeo flats for disposal from 1st April 1919 to 31st March 1928:

Year ending 31st March	Buffaloes slaughtered at Bandra	Kurla	Total	Newly born young calves tortured to death.
1920	10,240	6,782	17,022	16,558
1921	10,241	6,282	16,523	18,394
1922	11,536	7,408	18,944	22,086
1923	11,009	8,205	19,214	20,564
1924	11,396	7,705	19,101	19,981
1925	11,248	10,416	21,664	21,733
1926	11,420	8,442	19,862	18,271
1927	10,912	8,754	19,666	20,097
1928	10,800	9,722	20,522	19,270

"It does not reflect any credit to the Bombay Municipality, representing the best intellect of the country, to import best breed of cattle from outside Bombay and to slaughter them at the rate of 20,000 per year, although capable of bearing calves again and again for a long time and torturing to death all their calves—about 20,000 every year. Even in America and Europe no milch cattle that are likely to bear calves again are ever allowed to be slaughtered.

"Mr. W. Smith, Imperial Dairy Expert, Bangalore, in the Dairy Journal of April, 1927, states: 'Fresh milk is 75% cheaper in London than in our capital cities which is a serious state of affairs when we consider the earning power and the consequent spending power of the workman in Bombay as compared with the earning power of his London confrere.'

"Considered purely from an economic point of view the poor of Bombay of all religions and creeds suffer immensely for want of milk which is responsible for the increasing high infant mortality in Bombay.

"Such constant drain on the cattle wealth of the country and the destruction of the dry cattle and their calves by Bombay has made cattle stock very scarce in the whole country and a buffalo which could be had for Rs. 60 in 1903 costs now Rs. 300 which state of affairs directly affects the milk supply of Bombay.

"From the letter of the Municipal Commissioner No. H. 80-C dated the 10th August, 1928, it appears that Bombay used to consume about 23,000 gallons of milk per day in the year 1923, which may correctly be taken at 6,000 maunds per day in the year 1928 and the maximum rate of milk in the year 1903 was Rs. 5 per maund which in the year 1928 is Rs. 15 per maund. The daily loss accordingly for the year 1928 owing to the dearth of milk over the same quantity in 1903 is Rs. 60,000 per day amounting to Rs. 2 crores and 19 lacs for the year.

"The Superintendent of Markets in his letter No. M. 1143-C dated the 24th September, 1927, states that the maximum number of buffaloes slaughtered per day at Bandra is 33 yielding 16,5000 lbs. of beef and at Kurla 18, yielding 10,800 lbs., in all 27,300 lbs. of the value of Rs. 6,825 per day at four annas per lb. (first class rate). Taking the same ratio of dearness as that of milk the loss per day in buffalo beef in the year 1928 over that in 1903 is Rs. 4,550, *i e.*, Rs. 16 lacs and 50 thousand for the whole year. This gives clear idea as to how much Bombay will gain by making arrangements for protection and how much it loses by the slaughter as at present.

"Bombay Municipality does feel for the daily havoc and therefore does not issue licenses for over 16,000 buffaloes in Bombay stables and has not allowed new stables to be built for many years but that is not an effective preventive for the slaughter nor the right means for the increase of cheap milk supply. Obviously the only way to get cheap milk in the city of Bombay is on one side to stop the slaughter of dry cattle and on the other side to breed them and to rear the young stock. Thus supply of milk can be added from two different directions and the cost of milk production very much cheapened without having to send them up-country and purchase fresh ones every year.

"It behoves the greatest city of India to make provision for its own regular milk herd of about 36,000 animals in about 100 stables with about 400 acres of fodder and pasture land at different places near Bombay for the milk supply.

"Bombay by its conduct as at present has disgraced itself and has created a blot on its good name. All citizens feeling proud of Bombay as well as the Municipality should now immediately take active steps to efface the blot and to remove the stables from the heart of the city and to start Municipal cattle breeding and dairy farms near Bombay. The Municipality is further requested to encourage individual efforts by getting all convenience for their transport of milk from suburbs to Bombay at convenient times and at nominal rates of season tickets with no luggage pass fares, and of carriage of all kinds of animal feeds and animals from and to the suburbs and for grazing and fodder growing land facilities in the suburbs within and without Municipal limits so that cattle owners may be induced to remove their stables from the heart of the city."

Bombay has been called Bombay the beautiful. If Bombay means merely Malabar Hill and Chowpati and beauty is to be referred only to the exterior, then Bombay is certainly beautiful. But if the heart of Bombay is penetrated, like most of our cities it is ugly both in appearance and reality. The indifference of city fathers to the milk supply of their city is truly criminal and the facts carefully compiled in the foregoing letter do constitute a 'blot' on Bombay the beautiful. But it seems to me to be useless merely to blame the members of the

Municipality. They are after all what the voters make them. If Bombay is to have a cheap supply of pure milk the education of the voters should be undertaken on a wide scale. They should be taught never to vote for any candidate who does not pledge himself to secure a proper milk supply for the city in the quickest possible time. In the language of Blatchford milk should be treated like postage stamps. It should not be left to private enterprise but should be the first care of every Municipality.

29th November, 1928

HAND-SPINNING IN MYSORE

BY M. K. GANDHI

No state in India has so systematically encouraged hand-spinning as the State of Mysore. I have before me a copy of the note prepared by Sjt. C. Ranganatha Rao Sahib, the Director of Industries in Mysore, for submission to the State Sub-committee constituted to consider the question of hand-spinning. I give the note below in full:

> "An attempt is being made at Badanval, a village seven miles south of Nanjangud, to test by intensive work the practicability of introducing hand-spinning as a subsidiary occupation to our agriculturists. Badanval and the villages round about are favourably situated for carrying out such a test. The raiyats here grow a local variety of cotton and a large majority of them are very poor. There is no subsidiary occupation worth the name and the agriculturist has plenty of spare time except when he is actually employed on field work. The spinning of yarn by hand had died out less than 20 years ago and several old women well remembered the days when they were employed in spinning yarn in their girlhood. The spinning wheels were still stored up in their attics and the occupation was only given up because there was no demand for the yarn

There were a few Adikarnataka weavers plying their trade but they were using mill yarn.

"It was decided to make an intensive experiment here. A scheme for the purpose was obtained from the Secretary of the All-India Spinners' Association who not only lent an officer trained in this work, but also undertook to sell the finished goods.' A working capital of Rs. 3,500 was sanctioned for the purchase of raw cotton and giving advances to spinners, weavers, etc. A grant of Rs. 1,725 was sanctioned towards out-right expenditure required to meet the charges on account of establishment and it was expected that in the initial stages the operations would involve a loss of Rs. 500 and separate provision was made for meeting this loss. The working capital was subsequently increased by Government to Rs. 10,000.

"The special organiser sent by the All-India Spinners' Association started work on 1st November, 1927. Sixty-two spinners, mostly Adikarnataka weavers were willing to restart working their charkhas if raw cotton was advanced to them and an undertaking was given that the yarn made would be purchased. When they found that the special organiser actually meant business, spinning spread rapidly to the surrounding villages. The average output of yarn for the first three months was about 500 lbs. and the number of charkhas had increased to 398 at the end of this period. The production during the succeeding three months was 740 lbs. and the number of charkhas rose to 560. By the end of June 1928, the number of charkhas had risen to 1,000. The total weight of yarn spun up to the end of August 1928 for the ten months since the commencement of operations in the centre was 7,744 lbs. and the price paid for this yarn is Rs. 6,711. After spinning had become fairly established, advances of raw cotton were discontinued and the spinners were required to buy their own cotton. Advances of money were also discontinued in May 1928. The cotton spun in the early months was very coarse, the count ranging from 6 to 8 and was purchased at the rate of four annas per ball of 13 *tolas*. The purchase by weight was also discontinued with a view to induce the spinners to spin higher counts and the purchase at present is effected mostly by length. The count of yarn spun at present varies from 10 to 13.

"The average production of a spinner per month working during spare time is about 2 lbs. and her daily earnings varies from ¾ to 1 anna a day. Small as this amount would seem, there are 1,000 spinners who find it worth while to earn this wage by putting three or four hours of work at the wheel daily.

"Along with the introduction of hand-spinning in the centre, arrangements were made with some of the looms at Badanval to weave the yarn into cloth. At first only towels could be made with the yarn. As finer yarn was produced, sheets, coatings, and turban cloth were made. There are at present 62 looms engaged in weaving the yarn produced at the centre. All varieties of goods are made. By the end of June 1928, about 9,200 yards of Khadi weighing 3,083 lbs. and valued at Rs. 3,741 had been made. The value of the production during the months of July and August 1928 amounted to Rs. 3,372 giving an average of Rs. 1,686 per month.

"The total sales by the end of June amounted to Rs. 3,777 of which Rs. 714 was sold through the Stores Purchase Committee and the balance to the general public. The Stores Purchase Committee have since placed an order for about 15,000 yards of double thread coating cloth and 600 turbans with the centre and about half the production is absorbed by Government departments at present.

"Careful statistics are maintained of the earnings of weavers. It is found on an average they weave about 62 yards of cloth a month and earn about Rs. 7 during the period. They work from two to three hours a day.

"A balance sheet was struck at the end of June 1928.

It was found that the working capital had suffered no diminution and it had on the other hand increased by Rs. 152. The provision of Rs. 500 to meet any loss that might occur had proved unnecessary.

"But the issues involved at present are of such vital importance that the gain or loss of a few rupees in the initial stages of this experiment is of no moment. If Rural Reconstruction is to be achieved in the future, work must be found for the people living in our villages, work such as they can do and such as can profitably employ their idle time. The Agricultural Commission recognise the urgent need for a subsidiary occupation for the Indian agriculturist but are vague in their recommendations as to what this occupation should be. They make no reference to hand-spinning presumably because the earnings in this occupation are so slight. But the irony of the situation is, the insignificant income yielded by hand-spinning is large enough for a large proportion of our village folk to induce them to strive for it. There is no occupation that is so easily learned as hand-spinning and that interferes so little with the main avocations of life. In the absence of a more paying occupation it seems a folly to reject hand-spinning simply because in the eyes of the dwellers in towns the wages of the hand-spinner are so inconsiderable. Hand-spinning should not be encouraged and cannot be established wherever a more profitable subsidiary occupation can be started. But in centres where no other alternative occupation is available, hand-spinning should be given a chance. The experience in working the charkhas for ten months at Badanval has shown that with larger wheels and with cotton of longer staple, finer yarn can be spun. Improved charkhas are being introduced and the new variety of cotton introduced by our Agricultural Department will be sown at Badanval during the ensuing season. One of the greatest obstacles in spinning finer counts on the spinning wheel is the fact of the cotton not having been suitably carded before the slivers are made. This will soon be remedied as a suitable carding machine is being made at the Government Weaving Factory. After these improvements are introduced there is every prospect of the spinner making yarn of 25 to 30 counts and the industry being thoroughly established."

After the note was read, the Sub-Committee resolved:

"1. that the work now carried on at Badanval should be continued on the lines indicated in the note.

"2. that a copy of the note may be sent to the Deputy Commissioners, with a request to select suitable centres in their districts where work on similar lines may be organised.

"The Sub-Committee was of opinion that the District Economic Superintendents should be asked to visit Badanval and be made responsible for organising similar work in one centre in each district, the services of Spinning Demonstrators trained at Badanval being utilised for such work."

I congratulate the Director and the Sub-Committee on the thoroughness with which they are handling this very important national supplementary cottage industry. Naturally the Director is cautious in his note. Equally naturally every step taken in organising hand-spinning is being taken with deliberation and due thought. The result is that even from the very commencement the Department has been able to avoid loss on capital. The Department did not disdain to profit by the labours of the All-India Spinners' Association or to accept the technical assistance offered by it. It is quite clear from the report that the field to be covered by the wheel is vast enough to engage the attention of many workers in the field. I hope that the experiments that are being carried on to perfect a village carding machine will succeed. The machine to be of value will have to be such as to be capable of being worked by the villagers. My own humble opinion is that it is not possible to improve upon the carding-bow now in use in our villages. The Technical Department of the All-India Spinners' Association tried to introduce small changes in the original bow, but the foundation seems to be incapable of alteration, if we bear in mind the purpose for which the bow is intended. What is more, if the cotton to be carded is good, well-picked and well-cleaned, carding with the bow becomes an incredibly easy, simple and quick process and capable of being undertaken by even delicately built men and women. And my own experience is that no more than five minutes need be given to carding and sliver-making for an hour's spinning of thirty counts. Half a *tola* of thirty counts gives 320 yards, fine average speed for a good spinner. To card half a *tola* of cotton will not require more than five minutes for a tolerably good carder. And if the thousand spinners whom the Director mentions could be coaxed to learn carding, they could prepare their own slivers and add a little more to their earning per hour, because it will be possible to give spinners who are their own carders a little more wage than to those who spin with slivers prepared for them.

Whilst tendering my congratulations to the Mysore State upon its zeal on behalf of the poorest raiyats, I venture to remind the well-to-do citizens of Mysore and also the officials that Khadi will not find an abiding place in the homes of the people of Mysore unless these two classes adopt Khadi for their own wear. They now know that it is possible to get as fine Khadi as they wish to possess. Let them not confuse the minds of the unsophisticated villagers by leading them to think that the so-called higher classes are not prepared to practise what they preach. Let them remember the words of the Bhagavad Gita:

'The simple folk imitate the action (not the speech) of excellent men.'

6th December, 1928

THE LION OF THE PUNJAB

It is difficult to express my feelings of Lala Lajpatrai, after reading the eulogies in the English and vernacular papers. He is not dead. His spirit, his message is with the nation.

The British Lion and the Lion of India came to grips more than once. 'Incorrigible' as Mr. Gandhi says he was. His desire to see the 'yoke' eased or removed was so intense, that words poured out regardless of any consequences to himself. He was fearless, if sometimes not quite just in his denunciations of the foreign rule. In the Legislative Assembly last February, his voice vibrant with the deep indignation and emotion he felt, he told us what he thought in unmistakable terms. He did everything with intensity, burnt himself out so to speak with the fire and zeal for freedom for his country. He seemed to leave himself no time for personal ease or rest. In Lahore when I met him in March 1927, in the house of a friend, he sat very silently in a chair in a deep despondency and melancholy as an Aura and when he spoke his voice was gentle and weary and he sighed. The words he then spoke for me alone and I will keep them sacred. It was just a gentle message from an Indian to an Englishwoman.

May I venture to give a message to India? Revere this great son and in token of his memory make up communal differences.

Do not criticise and handicap national leaders, cherish and help them while they are in your midst. The orations and elegies after they pass on will not be necessary. India, make up communal differences. The Great God is the Father of all. In universal love may East and West find a solution to the unrest and trouble. Only by love can we vanquish the differences now existing.

In memory of the Lion who can roar no more may I entreat you to live in brotherly love? Muslims, Hindus and Christians all followers of the Great Masters who have trodden this earth.

Indians, countrymen of the great soul Lalaji, lend me your ears. Let his memorial be:

Peace and good-will to all men irrespective of colour and creed. His soul rest in peace.

EMMA HARKER

6th December, 1928

'HER EYES AS OUR EYES'

[Mr. N. M. Bell is the joint Editor of a tiny monthly called the *International Sunbeam* published at 2 shillings per annum at 59, Mary's Road, Christchurch. He has favoured me with a copy of his monthly which contains the following interesting article. M. K. G.]

India sees life through different windows than we do; but her eyes are as our eyes, and she has the same desires as we have.

Total world disarmament, the only material safeguard of peace, should be the outward and visible sign of that inward mental disarmament on which alone outward peace can rest secure. So long however, as one people is actually subjecting another to itself by superior military might, even the very first step towards this inward mental disarmament has not been taken.

What has this got to do with India? Everything.

When the Russian delegates made their historic proposals for total world disarmament before the Special Disarmament Committee of the League of Nations, what really prevented Great Britain from agreeing? India. In India are some 70,000 British troops and some 1,40,000 native levies, costing some £ 70,000,000 a year keeping some 350,000,000 Indians subject to British rule. When the Egyptians make their periodic attempt to secure peaceably the independence of their country from British domination, what prevents Britain from granting their request? India. The Suez Canal is the main route to India.

Disarmament would mean to Great Britian the loss of the 'brightest jewel' in the British imperial crown, and the end of her empire generally as distinct from the British Commonwealth of Nations, the bonds of which are racial and sentimental, and not military. It is a disagreeable saying, but true, that *empires rest on armaments.*

Of all the books I have recently read on India, none have impressed me so much as Fielding-Hall's *The Passing of Empire.* Here we have a District officer giving the result of his twenty years' experience in Burma. And what is the conclusion of the whole matter according to him? *India must govern herself.*

The old Village Communes must be re-established, with their Council of Elders and a Headman, not as now the agent of the Government, but the official representative of the village. Then District Councils must be formed out of the Village Councils and Provincial out of District.

"The Indian who has entered the Civil Service is really in an impossible position": the English will not meet him as a social equal; he is separate from his own people. The present land laws are bad; the whole "Court procedure wrong from top to bottom;" "the perspective of the Indian penal code is wrong"; and all because it is based on English law and "the records of our courts in England is the most brutal and bloody in history." "Humanity and justice," he cries, "are the only studies that I care for. Law is mainly a denial of both."

India should govern herself. But here is the crux of the whole matter. The "*British mercantile and other interests would refuse to give Indians any appreciable control of their own affairs.*"

5th December, 1921

ITS GORY CAREER

By M. K. Gandhi

The certificate granted by the Punjab Government to the police seems to have emboldened the Lucknow police to outdo the Punjab police in the free use of the baton and the spear.

The Lucknow police seem according to Pandit Jawaharlal Nehru to have even used brickbats in order to disperse an utterly innocent crowd. Granted that the processionists were defying orders supposed to be legal, the police, I hold, were not justified in charging the processionists unless injury on the part of the latter to person or property was imminent. I rely implicitly on Pandit Jawaharlal's narrative. According to it the crowd was orderly and well behaved. It was not out to do any harm to anybody. Its motive was known to be a peaceful demonstration against the entry into Lucknow of a Commission that has been imposed upon the people against their will. The exercise by the police of punitive powers in such circumstances was arbitrary, uncalled for and brutal. The behaviour of the crowd in the face of this provocation and in the face of a cowardly assault upon their chosen leader Pandit Jawaharlal Nehru and his companions was amazingly exemplary. Their self-restraint was as great as their leaders. I claim that no crowd outside India would have retained the calmness that the Lucknow crowd did.

But this calmness is probably mistaken for cowardice by the brave Commissioners who under the protecting wing of an armed police seem to be bent upon continuing their blood-red progress. Innocent blood was spilt in the Punjab and severer injuries seem to have been inflicted by the police in Lucknow on an equally innocent crowd. Two men are said to have been so badly injured as to be in danger of losing their lives. Difficult as the conduct of the English Commissioners is to understand, that of their subordinate Indian colleagues is still more difficult to understand. They do not seem to perceive the widening gulf between them and the people whom they are supposed to represent and whom (some of them flower of the nation) they are content to see trampled under horses' hoofs, charged with batons and driven with spearheads like cattle for the heinous offence of daring to demonstrate against this unwelcome Commission.

Well did the enraged father and patriot Pandit Motilal

Nehru give a warning to the Government, that "if a violent disturbance takes place in this city or any other part of the country, the responsibility for that would fall upon such officials as misbehaved themselves for the last three days at Lucknow." My fear is that the Government do not mind, if they would not actually welcome, such a disturbance. If a disturbance takes place, they will have another opportunity of showing the red claws of the British Lion and of terrorising a docile people into abject submission to their imperious will.

For if the Government do not desire an outbreak of violence on the part of the people and if the Commission will persist in their peregrinations, they should notify to the latter that they should instead of going from place to place summon witnesses to a central place and finish their work. But such wisdom and consideration for popular will are hardly to be expected of the Government.

The duty before the people is clear, to continue their non-violence in the face of the gravest provocation. Then one may safely regard these great demonstrations as so many lessons in non-violence preparatory to the final struggle in which people will willingly and valiantly lay down their lives without the slightest retaliation. That day is fast coming, faster than most of us imagine. So far as I can see, sacrifice of precious lives will have to be made before we come to our own, whether in a struggle wholly non-violent or predominantly violent. I am hoping and praying that non-violence will be maintained even up to the last heat.

6th December, 1928

A GOOD BEGINNING

BY M. K. GANDHI

Subscriptions for the Lalaji Memorial have begun well with Sjt. Ghanshyamdas Birla heading the list with Rs. 15,000 at Wardha. The fact that a strong provincial committee has been formed in the Punjab and had at the time (1st instant) of writing this already had Rs. 25,000 on their list also augurs well. I wish all the provinces will follow suit and fix their own minimum and set about collecting that sum. Whilst I suggested a method of finding one's quota on the basis of population, it was obviously not intended to apply to those provinces, districts or cities which could bear a far larger proportion. It would be ridiculous for instance for Bombay to fling at the treasurer of the fund its quota on the basis of population. Its quota can only be fixed according to its world-wide name and fame. Unfortunately we have in our country terrible contrasts. There are the submerged not tenth but fifth who are living in semi-starvation and who can therefore give nothing. Their burden has to be shouldered by the cities and the other prosperous areas.

The rapidity with which the subscriptions for the memorial are collected will be a measure of people's earnestness about preserving the memory of the Lion of the Punjab whose roar we shall hear no more. But let us remember that even twice the amount asked by the distinguished signatories to the appeal will not meet the requirements of the present day. Evidence is daily gathering round us that if we are to vindicate national honour which was stabbed when Lalaji was so brutally assaulted, we have to devise some means of hastening the advent of Swaraj. One such means and the mildest is to finish the work that Lalaji was doing. He had undertaken to popularise the Nehru report. Surely an effort in this direction is worth making and is quite feasible. To secure unanimity of approval for the report is but a step in the national march. By itself it will not give even dominion status. But we shall surely need unanimity about some demand of ours before we devise common action to enforce the demand.

In my humble opinion any discussion on the respective merits of dominion status and unadulterated independence is irrelevant to our present purpose. Everybody seems to agree that if we get dominion status, it would be a long step in the direction we want to go. But the independence group seem to argue that it is certain that we are never going to get dominion status and that since dominion status is not our final goal, why waste national energy on a fruitless errand and why not straightway work for independence pure and simple? There would be considerable force in the argument if the attainment of dominion status was an impossibility and if unanimity on independence was possible. As it is, if we can take action for independence with a fair chance of success, the same action plus unanimity which the Nehru report has made possible on the issue of dominion status should surely make its attainment more possible than that of independence. All therefore I plead for is not cessation of independence propaganda on the part of those who are enamoured of the enchanting formula but whole-hearted support for dominion status even as a stage in their progress. I claim that the two are in no way incompatible provided of course dominion status for India does not mean something quite different from what it means for South Africa or Canada. Memory of Lalaji and reason then demand consolidation of public opinion on the Nehru report, and that now. For let it be borne in mind that that report is not a permanent or final document. It is a compromise the best attainable which representatives of most parties have endorsed. If public opinion cannot be now focussed upon it, all the effort spent upon it will be reduced to nought and the great document will be out of date and out of place. Its value depends purely upon its immediate acceptance by all the great national organisations.

6th December, 1928

HOW TO MEET BASE INNUENDOES

BY M. K. GANDHI

"What should a public worker holding a responsible position in public life do if he is subjected to dishonest and malicious innuendoes or is falsely accused of misappropriation of public funds? Should he bring an action for libel against his calumniator in a law court? Will it not be his duty as a responsible public worker to do so, and is it not likely that if he fails to do so some unwary people would be deceived? And if one may in no circumstance bring an action in a law court is there not a real danger that unscrupulous persons might take shelter behind a brazen silence and defy public scrutiny into their malpractices while pretending to follow your advice? Again if recourse to law courts must be ruled out altogether does it not follow that some other remedy against the evil of unrestrained libel should be found?"

These are some of the questions arising out of the case of a prominent public worker that I have been called upon to answer. My reply is that slander and misrepresentation have always been the lot of public men. The way to overcome the opponent is by non-resistance and that is the remedy needed in the present case. Nor is a successful action in the law court by any means a conclusive proof of a man's innocence, for do we not meet every day instances of scoundrels who use the certificates of law courts as a cloak to hide their sins and to continue with impunity their practices? Again can any penalty that a law court may inflict stop the poison of evil tongues from spreading? Would not what was said openly before be now, for fear of penalty, propagated secretly and in whispers and thus be rendered all the more insidious? My advice, therefore, generally speaking, is that one should take no notice of baseless and malicious imputations, but pity the calumniator and always hope and pray for his ultimate conversion. As for the public it can always take care of itself against dishonest servants. Corruption will be out one day however much one may try to conceal it, and the public can, as it is its right and duty, in every case of justifiable suspicion, call its servants to strict account, dismiss them, sue them in a law court, or appoint an arbitrator or inspector to scrutinise their conduct, as it likes. Therefore instead of suing one's calumniator in a law court for false allegations of corruption, the best and the only right course would be for the public to prevent actual corruption from taking place by maintaining a sleepless vigilance and for the servant to keep the public on the *qui vive*.

If this course is found to be insufficient and some further action is felt to be necessary, the author of a libel can be called upon to bring his charge before a *panchayat*. The aggrieved party can offer at the same time to appear before it to vindicate its position. Of course this remedy would be useless when the calumniator is an altogether unscrupulous person. For he will never agree to appear before the *panchayat*. But where allegations are made by respectable persons offering to produce evidence in support, reference to a *panchayat* would be found to be most useful.

"But what about the villain who fakes a silent *hauteur* to mask his villainy?" one may ask. My reply is that if the people are vigilant and wide awake such a person will not be able to maintain his mask for long, while, if on the other hand they allow their vigilance to go to sleep not all the law courts in the world will be able to prevent the practice of villainy. For we daily see how law is unable to touch gentlemen rascals dressed in spotless white, and going about in motor cars. The fact is, as Carlyle has observed, that the fool and the scoundrel go always hand in hand. Where there is one the other is bound to be. But a true and just man need not worry on that account. Let him remember and ponder over what Dadu has sung:

"My reviler is like a respected and
dear brother unto me.
He labours for my good for nothing,
And helps to purge me of my countless sins
And comes to my aid without
expectation of reward.
He loses his own soul but that of
others he saves;
He is my dear friend—my saviour;

Oh Ramdev, pray to God for his
long life—may he live for ever.
My reviler is my greatest benefactor, says Dadu,
For he brings home to me my littleness."

It is enough if one is true to one's own self: one can then safely let the 'turbid streams of rumour flow.'

(Translated from *Navajivan* by P.)

6th December, 1928

RELIGIOUS EDUCATION

BY M. K. GANDHI

A student of the Gujarat Vidyapith writes:

"What concrete form ought religious instruction to take in the Vidyapith?"

To me religion means truth and *ahimsa* or rather truth alone, because truth includes *ahimsa*, *ahimsa* being the necessary and indispensable means for its discovery. Therefore anything that promotes the practice of these virtues is a means for imparting religious education and the best way to do this, in my opinion, is for the teachers rigorously to practise these virtues in their own person. Their very association with the boys, whether on the playground or in the class room, will then give the pupils a fine training in these fundamental virtues.

So much for instruction in the universal essentials of religion. A curriculum of religious instruction should include a study of the tenets of faiths other than one's own. For this purpose the students should be trained to cultivate the habit of understanding and appreciating the doctrines of various great religions of the world in a spirit of reverence and broad-minded tolerance. This if properly done would help to give them a spiritual assurance and a better appreciation of their own religion. There is one rule, however, which should always be kept in mind while studying all great religions and that is that one should study them only through the writings of known votaries of the respective religions. For instance, if one wants to study the Bhagavata one should do so not through a translation of it made by a hostile critic but one prepared by a lover of the Bhagavata. Similarly to study the Bible one should study it through the commentaries of devoted Christians. This study of other religions besides one's own will give one a grasp of the rockbottom unity of all religions and afford a glimpse also of that universal and absolute truth which lies beyond the 'dust of creeds and faiths.'

Let no one even for a moment entertain the fear that a reverent study of other religions is likely to weaken or shake one's faith in one's own. The Hindu system of philosophy regards all religions as containing the elements of truth in them and enjoins an attitude of respect and reverence towards them all. This of course presupposes regard for one's own religion. Study and appreciation of other religions need not cause a weakening of that regard; it should mean extension of that regard to other religions.

In this respect religion stands on the same footing as culture. Just as preservation of one's own culture does not mean contempt for that of others, but requires assimilation of the best that there may be in all the other cultures, even so should be the case with religion. Our present fears and apprehensions are a result of the poisonous atmosphere that has been generated in the country, the atmosphere of mutual hatred, ill-will and distrust. We are constantly labouring under a nightmare of fear lest some one should stealthily undermine our faith or the faith of those who are dear and near to us. But this unnatural state will cease when we have learnt to cultivate respect and tolerance towards other religions and their votaries.

(Translated from *Navajivan* by P.)

6th December, 1928

'FAULT OF MAN'

BY M. K. GANDHI

"I know it is very easy of us to give advice; but only those who live amongst the nuisance can realise how destructive monkeys are, and as one who has suffered some small loss at their small, mischievous hands I can sympathise.

"And yet is it the fault of man or monkeys—this impasse? Why do monkeys come into the cities, near the dwelling places of men, risking, poor wretches, their lives, and the lives of their dearly loved babies for food?

" Said an official to me just recently at Mt. Abu: 'The monkeys are too dreadful a nuisance, and yet we are not allowed to shoot them. They get worse and worse every year, I wonder why.'

"And yet the reason is obvious. From every jungle-tree, Jamboo, Karenda and Bod, we see man, with perfect disregard for everything but his own selfish purposes, stripping the trees of their fruit *to the last berry.*

"The Bhils of Abu take down hundreds and hundreds of baskets, one sees them rotting at Abu Road.

"The sahibs' butlers have learnt to make Karenda jam, it costs only the sugar and the picking.

"Man encroaches ruthlessly on the rights of animals and birds, but punishes with severity any encroachment by them on *his* supreme rights.

"Do the gods treat men thus? I see in the misery that presses on man not the arrogance of the rich and mighty to them retribution in kind, for there is no greater coward than your real bully, but the awful reckoning due to this continual encroachment on the privileges of bird and animal.

"It is nature's retribution: a retribution that has already come to the sailors on ships who shot the 'Stormy

Petrel' whose appearance warned them of storms, shot them to extinction. Men destroyed birds in thousands and saw their dear ones in the grip of the malarial mosquito whose larvae are now too many for man's scope."

Thus writes a fair correspondent who is a lover of bird and beast. Unfortunately for me she adds to my difficulty, does not solve it. Knowing the wrong done by my kind, am I to give up agriculture and seek the cave, or am I to prevent the monkeys' encroachment? The natural consequence of her reasoning which I do not deny is that the monkeys should have full play of my garden, in other words I should grow for them what my fellowman has robbed them of!!!

13th December, 1928

THE PITFALLS

BY M. K. GANDHI

Describing the incidents of Lucknow in a private letter Pandit Jawaharlal Nehru writes:

"An incident which took place yesterday morning might interest you. I have not mentioned it in my statement. Soon after the mounted and foot police had driven us back near the station, a young man whom I took to be a student, came to me and said that he could bring me two revolvers immediately if I wanted to use them. We had just experienced the baton and *lathi* charges and there was a great deal of anger and resentment in the crowd. I suppose he thought that it was a favourable moment to make the offer. I told him not to be foolish. Soon after I found out quite casually that this particular person was known to be in the C. I. D."

Pandit Jawaharlal was safe as he has no secrets. If he finds any use for revolvers in his scheme for the freedom of the country, he will not need the offer from an outsider to lend him one. He will carry it himself openly and use it effectively when in his opinion the occasion has arrived. So he was safe from the blandishments of the C. I. D. And what applies to Pandit Jawaharlal applies in a measure to all Congressmen. For happily the Congress politics abhor secrecy. Congressmen have ceased to talk with closed doors; they have shed the fear of the C I. D.

But the C. I. D. will not be itself if it does not have emissaries whose business among other things it is to expose people to temptations and entrap them in the nets prepared for them. It is difficult to imagine an occupation more debasing and degrading than this, and yet it has been reduced to a science by the chief governments of the world and has attracted to it some of its cleverest brains. Britain takes perhaps the first place in this occupation. Lying in the C. I. D. is cultivated as a fine art. Ponsonby's *Falsehood in War Time* gives a painful record of lying on the part of all the powers that were engaged in the pastime of mutual destruction on the false plea of philanthropy. It is a black record of crimes committed by the nations of whom Britain was not the least but probably the greatest offender. She could have stopped the War if she had been less greedy and less selfish.

Wherever you turn in India you encounter pitfalls. To me every institution—be it the most philanthropic—run by and in the name of the Empire in India has an unmistakable taint about it. That we run to and hug most or some of them is no test of their goodness. It is test of our helplessness, short-sightedness or selfishness. We have not the courage to sacrifice much in order to save ourselves from criminal participation in sustaining an Empire which is based on fraud and force, and whose chief, if not one, aim is to prepetuate the policy of ever-growing exploitation of the so-called weaker races of the earth.

In a way the C. I. D. is the least dangerous of the traps so cleverly laid by the builders. Those whose exterior is attractive are really the most dangerous of all. We often fall into one of these enticing but deadly traps, before we hardly know where we are. It was for some such reason that the Romans said: 'Beware of the Greeks, specially when they bring you gifts. When an enemy comes to you bearing the look of philanthropy, he is to be most dreaded. Would that the youth of the country learnt this simple truth and avoided the pitfalls into which they daily fall even whilst they are cursing the Empire and hoping to deliver the country from the intolerable yoke which is not only ruining the nation economically but is also causing unfathomable moral mischief.

13th December, 1928

JUSTICE RUN MAD

BY M. K. GANDHI

I reproduce elsewhere* in this issue the first instalment of a sample of the translation of the Tamil songs of the late Bharati, the Tamil Poet, whose songs were the other day confiscated by the Madras Government acting under instructions, or, it is perhaps more proper to say, orders from the Burma Government. The Burma Government it appears in its turn suppressed these songs not by any order of court but by executive declaration. It appears that under that declaration the books of this popular Tamil poet which have been in vogue for the last 30 years and which, as appears from the evidence before the High Court of Madras, were under consideration by the Education Department of Madras for introduction in the school curriculum, are liable to confiscation in any part of India. I must confess that I was unaware of any such wide executive powers being held by provincial Governments. But these are days in which we live and learn. This was no doubt a matter falling under the jurisdiction of the Education Minister. But it is becoming daily more and more clear that these Ministerial offices are a perfect farce, even as the legislative chambers are and that the Ministers are little more than clerks registering the will of the all-powerful I. C. S. Therefore the poor Education Minister could do nothing to save these popular books from confiscation. Probably at the time the confiscation took place, he had even no knowledge, or if he had

* Omitted in this edition.

he was not even told what it was that he was really signing. In due course however the confiscation attracted public attention. Pandit Haribara Sharma of Hindi Prachar Karyalaya and publisher of Bharati's songs, on behalf of his poor widow, could not sit still under the confiscation. He therefore moved the public and the matter was naturally debated in the Legislative Council which condemned the confiscation. Pandit Haribara Sharma even petitioned the High Court for an order to set aside what was clearly an illegal confiscation, and because of some understanding that the order of confiscation will be withdrawn, that the books will be returned and that the Madras Government will make reparation to the poor widow, the petition has been withdrawn, But the wrong still remains. One can only hope that the expectations of Pandit Harihara Sharma will be fulfilled and that the wrong will be remedied by the return of the books. But whatever reparation is made by the Madras Government, the sense of wrong will abide and so will the sense of insecurity created in the public mind by the action of the Madras Government in slavish obedience to the Burma Government.

20th December, 1928

THE ETERNAL DUEL

BY M. K. GANDHI

A friend writes:

" In the article entitled 'The Tangle of *Ahimsa*' appearing in *Young India* of October 11th, you have stated most forcefully that cowardice and *ahimsa* are incompatible. There is not an ambiguous syllable in your statement. But may I request that you tell us how cowardice can be exorcised from a man's character? I notice that all characters are but the sum total of habits formed. How are we to undo our old habits and build the new ones of courage, intelligence, and action? I am convinced that habits can be destroyed, and better and nobler habits can be formed giving birth to a new character in a person. It seems to me that you know prayers, discipline, and studies by which a man can attain a second birth. Won't you kindly tell us about them? Do give us your knowledge and advice in one of the numbers of *Young India*. Please help us by giving an account of the method of praying and working by which a man can recreate himself."

The question refers to the eternal duel that is so graphically described in the Mahabharat under the cloak of history and that is every day going on in millions of breasts. Man's destined purpose is to conquer old habits, to overcome the evil in him and to restore good to its rightful place. If religion does not teach us how to achieve this conquest, it teaches us nothing. But there is no royal road to success in this the truest enterprise in life. Cowardice is perhaps the greatest vice from which we suffer and is also possibly the greatest violence, certainly far greater than bloodshed and the like that generally go under the name of violence. For it comes from want of faith in God and ignorance of His attributes. But I am sorry that I have not the ability to give 'the knowledge and the advice' that the correspondent would have me to give on how to dispel cowardice and other vices. But I can give my own testimony and say that a heartfelt prayer is undoubtedly the most potent instrument that man possesses for overcoming cowardice and all other bad old habits. Prayer is an impossibility without a living faith in the presence of God within.

Christianity and Islam describe the same process as a duel between God and Satan, not outside but within; Zoroastrianism as a duel between Ahurmazd and Ahriman; Hinduism as a duel between forces of good and forces of evil. We have to make our choice whether we should ally ourselves with the forces of evil or with the forces of good. And to pray to God is nothing but that sacred alliance between God and man whereby he attains his deliverance from the clutches of the prince of darkness. But a heartfelt prayer is not a recitation with the lips. It is a yearning from within which expresses itself in every word, every act, nay, every thought of man. When an evil thought successfully assails him, he may know that he has offered but a lip prayer and similarly with regard to an evil word escaping his lips or an evil act done by him. Real prayer is an absolute shield and protection against this trinity of evils. Success does not always attend the very first effort at such real living prayer. We have to strive against ourselves, we have to believe in spite of ourselves, because months are as our years. We have therefore to cultivate illimitable patience if we will realise the efficacy of prayer. There will be darkness, disappointment and even worse; but we must have courage enough to battle against all these and not succumb to cowardice. There is no such thing as retreat for a man of prayer.

What I am relating is not a fairy tale. I have not drawn an imaginary picture. I have summed up the testimony of men who have by prayer conquered every difficulty in their upward progress, and I have added my own humble testimony that the more I live the more I realise how much I owe to faith and prayer which is one and the same thing for me. And I am quoting an experience not limited to a few hours, or days or weeks, but extending over an unbroken period of nearly 40 years. I have had my share of disappointments, uttermost darkness, counsels of despair, counsels of caution, subtlest assaults of pride; but I am able to say that my faith,—and I know that it is still little enough, by no means as great as I want it to be,—has ultimately conquered every one of these difficulties up to now. If we have faith in us, if we have a prayerful heart, we may not tempt God, may not make terms with Him. We must reduce ourselves to a cipher. Barodada sent me a precious Sanskrit verse not long before his death. It means impliedly that a man of devotion reduces himself to zero. Not until we have reduced ourselves to nothingness can we conquer the evil in us. God demands nothing less than complete self-surrender as the price for the only real freedom that is worth having. And when a man thus loses himself, he immediately finds himself in the service of all that lives. It becomes his delight and his recreation. He is a new man never weary of spending himself in the service of God's creation.

20th December, 1928

DINABANDHU'S TRIBUTE

Dinabandhu Andrews writes as follows from Manchester on Lalaji's death:

"The news of the death of Lala Lajpatrai was a very terrible shock to me for it was absolutely unexpected. I reached Birmingham very late on Saturday night and my brother told me about it. Since then I have referred to it and made clear in the *Manchester Guardian* how great the loss must be both to India and to England, and indeed to the world of humanity; for he was the friend of the oppressed in every country and knew no racial barriers. What I am now waiting to hear is how far the death was caused by injuries received at the railway station at Lahore at the time of the boycott of the Simon Commission. This is not at all made clear in the newspapers here, which are very guarded in their utterances, though there is just a hint about it."

I may add that he cabled to me for correct news to which needless to say I sent a suitable reply. M. K. G.

20th December, 1920

LALAJI'S MEMORY

BY M. K. GANDHI

With reference to my note on Dr. Satyapal's telegram which was published in these columns, Lala Dunichand of Ambala writes:

"The publication of Dr. Satyapal's telegram in connection with Lala Lajpatrai's death in *Young India* of November 29, 1928 and your comments thereon have induced me to write this letter to you which I hope you will be able to publish. I am one of those who had been devoted to Lalaji for nearly all their life and it was only during the last elections that serious and even acute differences had arisen between him and myself. I should be offending truth if I were not to say frankly that I and many other Congressmen in the Punjab considered Lala Lajpatrai's activities during the last elections harmful to the interests of the country and it was this honest conviction on our part that had led to the breaking of life-long ties of friendship and devotion and we were never able to reconcile ourselves to the view that he was in the right and we in the wrong. But the blows received by him at the hands of the police and his death shortly after that have naturally and rightly changed altogether my mental attitude towards him and his work. His death has altogether removed any feelings of resentment or hostility that I might have harboured towards him during his life. From the very moment that I received the news of his death my feelings of devotion and veneration for him revived. Now I look upon the sum total of his life work too great to let me entertain any kind of ill-will and his life too sacred to be remembered with anything but feelings of genuine respect. I feel as if quite a different kind of relations have sprung up between him and myself after his death. If the question of our differences with him is viewed in this light, we who differed from him and those who differed from us on account of him can again become comrades in the fight for winning freedom for our country."

This is undoubtedly the correct attitude to take and I hope that everybody who had some differences of opinion with Lalaji will adopt the same attitude and work for the common cause.

20th December, 1928

INDIA'S AMBASSADRESS IN AMERICA

The readers of *Young India* will be glad to share with me the following letter from Mr. R. E. Hume, son of Dr. R. A. Hume of Nagar, regarding the fine work that is now being done by Devi Sarojini Naidu in America:

"You will be pleased, I am sure, to receive this message concerning the successful start of our friend Mrs. Sarojini Naidu in her visit to the United States.

"I heard her at her first appearance in New York City. And I have been testifying that I have never heard either from man or from woman the equal of her platform performance for the beauty and flow of English diction and for the structure and sequence of English sentences. Several times during her sixty minutes of unmemorised discourse I wondered how she would extricate herself from the involved beginning of an elaborate sentence; but she never once failed to complete correctly the subject and verb with which she had proceeded in the sentence.

"However, more beautiful and significant than the grammatical structure of English sentences were the beauty and goodness and truth of her utterances. I rejoice that Mother India is being presented to America in the person of this charming and potent woman, who is perceiving the spiritual side of American life, and who is similarly conveying to the people here the spiritual side of the Indian people. My wife and I have been happy to have had Mrs. Naidu to dinner day before yesterday and to lunch today, along with various American friends. But I am especially happy thus to report to you promptly the very successful realisation of your plan for Mrs. Naidu to visit the United States as an ambassadress from the women and people of India."

30th December, 1928

KHADI IN HYDERABAD STATE

BY M. K. GANDHI

At a Co-operative Conference held the other day in the Hyderabad State, the Finance Minister, Sir Hyder Nawaz Jung Bahadur delivered an address from which a friend sends me the following translation of his reference to the spinning wheel:

> "But the most important thing to which I wish to draw your attention is our home industries. To preserve and help them is the supreme duty of co-operative societies. If co-operative societies could be organised to distribute domestic implements and raw materials amongst the people, it would be a great boon to the country. For the sake of illustration, I would mention spinning and weaving. If they could be revived in our towns and villages, it would be a great achievement. Quite till the other day, spinning and weaving were commonly practised in our homes. Not only in the huts of the poor but also in the homes of the rich and well-to-do, young girls and their matrons used to utilise their leisure time by spinning; and a variety of things for household use, like carpets, sheets, coverlets, table-cloths etc., were prepared out of the yarn thus spun. Respectable widows who have no other means of livelihood used to support themselves and their children by spinning and sewing. By popularising this occupation, you would not only augment the slender resources of the people but by providing them with useful work for filling their spare time save them from falling a prey to many a temptation. I hope that the energetic officials of our Department will make a beginning in this direction this year. I shall carefully go through the next year's report to see how many of us have taken to this good work. . .
>
> "We should never forget that man isolated from society is but an animal. He rises to his full estate which

has been described as 'little less than the angels' only through mutual aid and co-operation with his fellow beings. So long as you stand apart, self-sufficing units, so long as 'I' am 'I' and 'you' are 'you' we are only glorified animals called men. When 'I' and 'you' combine to form 'we', we develop a divine force and the process of developing this force is spelt co-operation."

I congratulate the Minister on his pronouncement and trust that the State of Hyderabad will compete with that of Mysore in the spread of the spinning wheel. Co-operation in spinning is easy and an indispensable thing if Khadi is to be placed on a stable basis. A handspinning co-operative society will start with a cotton depot where bag cotton, not pressed cotton, will be stored for converting into cards. It will have carders, if the spinners do not themselves card in the initial stages. This depot will keep the necessary furniture, *i.e.* hand-gins, carding bows, spinning wheels, accessories and necessary tools with facility for repairs. The depot will be distributing, receiving and selling depot and will distribute cotton or slivers as the case may be. It will receive against cash-payment yarn spun by the members and sell to the members Khadi woven from their yarn or bought from other places. It will sell Khadi at special prices to the spinning members and at ordinary prices to the public. If such societies are formed under Stage patronage and with State aid, partial or in full, there is really no limit to the possibilities of mass co-operation. Only this presupposes a Khadi atmospere among the officials; in other words, the officials must be converts, lovers and trustees of the masses, not their lords and masters, for whom the masses are born to toil and sweat on starvation wages. If the Finance Minister infects his officials with the zeal which his address shows there is a great future for the people of the State. And Hyderabad unlike Mysore is a vast cotton area.

27th December, 1928

UNITY IN THE PUNJAB

BY M. K. GANDHI

With reference to my note in *Young India* on Dr. Satyapal's telegram he has sent me following letter which I welcome :

"I am deeply obliged to you for your letter of 28th November in reply to my telegram and letter, and also for the valuable comments made by you thereon in *Young India*.

"I wish to assure you that every word of that telegram is heartfelt and sincere and is not prompted by any momentary impulse and interested reason, or any outward pressure. It is an expression of the inner feelings of those hearts whose one wish in this world is to establish the dignity and prestige of the Congress in order to make it a powerful and effective organisation to free India. The passing away of Lala Lajpat Rai throws a very heavy burden of responsibilities on the shoulders of the nationalist workers and they cannot afford to have any split in that camp. Guided by this sense of additional responsibility and actuated by the sole desire of making the Congress a compact and successful organisation in our province that offer has been made and I assure you that on our part there will be a genuine, honest and sincere effort to bridge the existing gulf. We shall try our level best to abide by every word of the assurance given in that telegram.

"One point however I want to make quite clear. I have not been able to appreciate the idea of your finding 'repentance' on our part in that telegram. I have read the telegram several times over and still have not been able to find any words which signify any repentance on my part for my having opposed Lala Lajpat Rai during his life time when I felt it necessary to do so. I have not the slightest desire to recall the memory of those days and I wish to draw a curtain on that episode not because I am ashamed of it and not because I am sorry for what I did then; but the sole object in blotting out that episode is to provide a clean slate for future co-operation and harmony.

"I pay my heart-felt tribute to the memory of Lala Lajpat Rai but that does not mean that I subscribe to everything he advocated or championed. I had my acute differences with him and I never concealed them even at the risk of being insulted, abused and stoned. My opposition was always open, honest and straightforward and was based on purely public grounds and I am therefore neither ashamed nor sorry for that opposition nor do I repent of it even for a moment. Lala Lajpat Rai had in his last days of life joined hands with the Congress in the boycott of Simon Commission and had condemned communalism. We all rallied round him as soon as we found him working for the national ideals and he would have found us to be his best friends and most honest supporters if he had lived longer to pursue his activities in this direction.

"I thank you once again for the kindness shown and I wish to assure you that while there is no question of repentance or retraction we are perfectly willing to co-operate with all such friends as on account of our differences with Lala Lajpat Rai have been keeping away from the Congress. We all wish to put our heads together to offer a united front to the forces which are out to destroy nationalism. We will make an honest effort to sink all party differences and to bury all bitterness and rancour of the past in order to secure for our province a prominent position in the first rank of fighters for freedom of India."

27th December, 1928

CURSE OF ASSASSINATION

BY M. K. GANDHI

The assassination of the Assistant Superintendent Mr. Saunders of Lahore was a dastardly act apart from whether it had a political motive behind it or not. Violence being in the air, there will no doubt be silent and secret approbation of the act, especially if it is discovered to have had any connection with the assault on Lalaji and his utterly innocent comrades. The provocation was great and it became doubly great by the death of Lalaji which was certainly hastened by the nervous shock received by him from the disgraceful conduct of the police. Some will insist, not without considerable justification, on ascribing the death even to the physical effect of the injury received by the deceased in the region of the heart. The provocation received also additional strength from the Punjab Government's defence of the police conduct. I should not wonder if the assassination proves to be in revenge of the high-handed policy of the Punjab Government.

I wish however that it was possible to convince the hot youth of the utter futility of such revenge. Whatever the Assistant Superintendent did was done in obedience to instructions. No one person can be held wholly responsible for the assault and the aftermath. The fault is that of the system of Government. What requires mending is not men but the system. And when the youth of the country have the real determination they will find that it is in their power as it is in nobody else's to kill the system.

English books have taught us to applaud as heoric deeds of daring even of freebooters, villains, pirates and train-wreckers. Newspapers fill columns with exciting stories real or in their absence, imaginary, of such deeds. Some of us have successfully learnt this art of applauding as heroic anything adventurous irrespective of the motives or contemplated results behind such deeds.

This cannot be regarded as anything but a bad omen. Surely there is nothing heroic about a cold-blooded robbery accompanied by murder of an innocent wealthy pilgrim carrying treasures for distribution in well-conceived charity. There is equally none in the deliberate secret assassination of an innocent police officer who has discharged his duty however disagreeable its consequences may be for the community to which the assassin belongs. Let us remember that the administrators of the system have held on to the system in spite of previous assassinations. After all the story of the building of the British Empire is not itself wanting in deeds of valour, adventure and sacrifice worthy in my opinion of a better cause. If we may ragard the assassination of Mr. Saunders as a heroic deed the British people would be able to answer this one, I hope, solitary act of so-called heroism with countless such acts enough to fill a volume. But it is time we began irrespective of nationalities to regard deeds with mean motives or meaner consequences with nothing but horror, indignation and disapprobation, no matter how daring they may be. I know that this means a new valuation of such terms as heroism, patriotism, religiousness and the like. No one, I hope, regards the assassinations of Presidents Cleveland and Carnot as reflecting any credit upon the assassins or the nations in whose cause the mad men carried out their evil plans. Islam is not better for the assassination of so many Caliphs or to take a modern instance, for the assassination of the late Swami Shraddhanandji. Nor has Hinduism been ennobled by the frenzied deeds one occasionally reads about of so-called protectors of the cow. The curse of assassination and kindred crimes is not advancing the progress to humanity, religion or true civilisation.

Let the youth of India realise that the death of Lalaji can only be avenged by regaining her freedom. Freedom of a nation cannot be won by solitary acts of heroism even though they may be of the true type, never by heroism so-called. The temple of freedom requires the patient, intelligent and constructive effort of tens of thousands of men and women, young and old. Acts such as we are deploring decidedly retard the progress of this quiet building. When it does nothing else, it diverts the attention of countless builders.

27th December, 1928

A SINDH CURSE

By M. K. GANDHI

The Amils of Sindh are probably the most advanced community in that province. But in spite of all their advance, there are some serious abuses of which they seem to have a monopoly. Of these the custom of *deti-leti* is not the least serious. I have more than once remarked upon it in these columns. My attention was drawn to this abuse during my very first visit to Sindh and I was invited to speak to the Amil friends about it. Though no doubt isolated work has been done in the direction of removing this abuse, no organised effort seems to have been made to end the evil. The Amils are a compact little community. The seriousness of the evil is not questioned by anybody. I have not known a single Amil to defend the vile custom. It has persisted because it is a custom patronised by the educated youth among the Amils. Their mode of life is above the means they can honestly command. Hence they have thrown all scruples to the wind and do not mind degrading themselves by prostituting the institution of marriage for their own base ends. And this one vicious habit has told upon the quality of their national work which otherwise by their intellect and education they are capable of doing to the great benefit of the country.

In order to put an end to this evil, a provisional committee has already been formed now of which Acharya A. T. Gidwani has accepted the presidentship. This is as it should be. When he undertook to go to Sindh from Brindaban it was naturally expected that he would throw himself with zest into all desirable movements that conduce to national well-being. It is to be hoped that the provisional committee will soon become a permanent organisation and under his able leadership the reform which is already belated will make steady progress.

The Secretary, Sjt. Mirchandani, asks me for suggestions. The only suggestion that I can think of just now is that this organisation should create a public opinion against *deti-leti* that would become irresistible. Young educated Amils are able to squeeze the poor parents of marriageable girls only because there is no active public opinion against the custom. There should be work done in the schools and colleges and amongst the parents of girls. The parents should so educate their daughters that they would refuse to marry a young man who wanted a price for marrying and would rather remain spinsters than be party to the degrading terms. The only honourable terms in marriage are mutual love and mutual consent.

27th December, 1928

MILK FOR BOMBAY

By M. K. Gandhi

A friend on reading the artice 'A Blot on Bombay'* in *Young India* (29th November) writes to Mahadev Desai as follows:

> "In the recent issue of *Young India* of 29th November, an interesting article appears under the heading 'A Blot on Bombay' about the milk problem of the Bombay city. The prevalent idea here is that the problem would be solved if the cattle stables in the city be shifted to the suburbs. But any one having an intimate knowledge of the suburbs will be in a position to contradict the statement. Bombay being an island, it is not surrounded by villages. There is very little grazing land in the suburbs; and unless such land is available in plenty, cattle breeding for all the milch cattle of Bombay is out of the question. So long as facilities for cattle breeding to the requisite extent are not available, the slaughter of dry animals and of calves will continue. The cow protection societies in Bombay are merely tinkering with the problem. Its real solution lies in producing milk in rural conditions and exporting it to Bombay in bulk. The city life of Bombay is a product of modern conditions and its problems must

* See page 948.

be solved by modern methods. If milk produced in the country be pasteurised by modern machinery, it can be sent out in a pure condition to a great distance. In my opinion Gujarat alone is in a position to solve the milk problem of Bombay. It is the best milk producing area in the neighbourhood of Bombay. If some important milk producing centres in Gujarat be properly tapped and organised, it would be possible to send out milk to Bombay in large quantity after pasteurising and to supply it to the consumers here at a considerably reduced rate. This can be made possible by starting a company with sufficient capital and Gujarat is quite capable of doing it if the idea is properly put into the heads of the capitalists and the lead is taken by some influential men. The slaughter of cattle and calves in Bombay cannot be prevented by any legislative measures; nor by shifting the cattle stables from the city to the suburbs; it can only be prevented by sending no cattle to Bombay, but by sending only milk in their stead. When cheap milk in plenty is made available in the city, no one, unless he be a fool, will think of bringing cattle to Bombay for selling dear milk and selling dry animals to the butcher for a song. By adopting the above measure, both Gujarat and Bombay will gain; the increased milk trade will increase the prosperity of the peasantry of Gujarat, and the cheap milk supply will give a great relief to the poor of Bombay; and Bombay will perpetually bless Gujarat for the great boon conferred upon her. And above all the cattle slaughter in Bombay will become a thing of the past and every one will wonder why this easy measure of prevention was not taken much earlier."

I am afraid that the writer of the letter has misunderstood the article in question. No one has suggested that the question of the slaughter of cattle in Bombay or of the supply of pure milk will be solved by shifting the stables from the city of Bombay to the suburbs of Bombay. What is required and what has been suggested is that Bombay should bravely face the problem as behoves it. Surely the Gujaratis who are not living in Bombay are not the philanthropists who might be expected to come to the rescue of Bombay and solve one of its tremendous and equally urgent problems. The Municipality of Bombay has to take the initiative and make the move and if need be enlist the sympathy and co-operation of philanthropically inclined Gujaratis. I fear that even if anybody outside Bombay wanted to come to the rescue, he would require special facilities from the Bombay Corporation. But we have not in this country the requisite capacity for private enterprise which would take great risks involved in a big venture that the supply of milk to a large city like Bombay undoubtedly is. Let it be also known that such private effort has been made before now in Bombay and it failed. I think that failure had definite causes. There was not sufficient grit and ability behind those ventures. But I submit that no cost is too great, no enterprise too risky for the Municipality of Bombay to undertake in order to ensure a supply of cheap and pure milk for its citizens and to rid Bombay of stables which are a source of danger to its health and which must be always coming in the way of any radical measure for dealing with malaria and other diseases which are rampant in Bombay. I freely admit that Bombay has to travel outside its radius for the organisation of a vast dairy scheme. But that every city in the world has done for many of its wants.

13th December, 1928

WARDHA LETTER

THIRD CLASS

In accordance with his practice Gandhiji left Sabarmati for a month's sojourn at the Wardha Ashram on the 23rd November. The journey was undertaken when he had hardly recovered from the first shock of Lalaji's passing away. For once he was able to get the better of the solicitude of kind friends and to emulate his palmy days when he used to travel third. The journey was uneventful till we reached Amalner. There Gandhiji was met, with his previous consent, by a group of Khadi workers from the Samarth Udyoga Mandir, Mukti (W. Khandesh). They are trying to organise Khadi production on, what is known, the 'integrated system.' The underlying idea is to develop the internal economics of hand-spinning and hand-weaving by assembling as many processes of cloth manufacture as possible under the same roof to be performed as far as possible by the same family. The system has been tried with great success at Bijolia and would mark a new era in the development of Khadi organisation if it could be successfully introduced elsewhere too. Gandhiji after asking a few questions about the details of their work and emphasising the necessity of self-carding, said to them, "Our scriptures say that 'not to begin any enterprise is the first degree of wisdom but it is folly to give it up after having commenced it.' Now that you have commenced your project after due deliberation I hope you will see it through."

THE WOOD AND THE TREES

The Samarth Udyoga Mandir party was accompanied by Sjt. Shankarrao Dev of Dhulia of Ramdasi literature fame who steals some time every month for doing Khadi propaganda. He travelled with us as far as Jalgaon and engaged Gandhiji in an interesting conversation. The discussion turned on the theme: "Is Khadi really making headway?" "I have no doubt about it," replied Gandhiji, "there are more actual spinners and more genuine Khadi wearers in India today than there were in the 'white cap' days of 1920-21, and as for organised Khadi production it has grown by tenfold at least. But the thing is, we do not see the wood for the trees. Otherwise, where is there another organisation in India which is functioning in nearly 2,000 villages as the A. I. S. A. is doing? It is a compact body, it has influence over the masses because it has established a living contact with them. But the Khadi worker must bide his time. His faith is on trial today. He must refuse to be diverted from his purpose by exciting politics. I have no doubt that the country will remember this perennial source of strength at no distant date. See how one leader after another turns to it for consolation in the darkness of despair. Deshabandhu Das remembered it and declared his faith in it a week before his death, and when a damp fell around the path of Lalaji he too turned to it for strength. You know how he told Mahadev at Simla that he had become a complete convert to Khadi and was learning how to spin? I have no doubt that in its hour of darkness it will be Khadi alone that will come to the nation's rescue."

Situated right in the heart of the cotton area, Wardha is a perfect beauty spot. Gandhiji's room on the upper floor commands a beautiful panorama of open horizons engirdled by a distant line of purple hills while all around lie rich breeze-swept cotton fields with their dark green leaves and silver tongues of snowy fleece gushing out of bursting pods. Here under the sapphire blue sky, clear sunshine and transparent, bracing cool air one would perhaps think that there is a real haunt of peace where a weary spirit may find rest and repose. But one has only to dive a little beneath the surface to discover the tragedy that lies hidden there. For the smiling munificence of the cotton tracts will then be seen to be not a symbol of prosperity but of economic serfdom of the ryot. He is little better than a dairy cow that is made to yield increasing quantities of milk by all unnatural means only to be drained of its last drop for the benefit of its exploiting masters. In spite of bumper crops and the phenomenal rises in cotton prices, according to the settlement report of 1892-94, out of 6,556 proprietors and shareholders of villages, 1,778 or 26 per cent. were in debt. The condition of the tenants was even worse, 15,000 out of nearly 40,000 or 39 per cent. being in a state of indebtedness. In spite of the richest cotton in India at their door step, these people imported European cotton piece goods worth 6 lakhs of rupees in 1904 and Indian piece goods worth another 2 lakhs of rupees, while the number of weavers dwindled from 17,000 in 1891 to 7,000 in 1901, for lack of employment, and the history of famines tells its own tragic tale of the hand-to-mouth life of the people whom a single bad year brings face to face with scarcity and starvation.

A VALE OF PEACE

The only relief that one can find from these oppressive facts is in the atmosphere of 'toil unsevered from tranquillity' of the Satyagrahashram of Wardha. This institution, a glorified edition of its prototype at Sabarmati as Gandhiji once called it, needs no introduction to the readers of *Young India*. It follows the same ideals and principles as its parent institution; only while the latter goes in for bold experiments with the ever present risk of stumbling the former has imposed upon it a voluntary discipline by restricting the field of its experiments. The moving spirit of the Ashram is Sjt. Vinoba Bhave who with his band of young workers has devoted himself to a life of silent and self-effacing service. No one who sees this man of silence would imagine that he is the same silver tongued speaker under the spell of whose luminous eloquence during the Nagpur Satyagraha days even the Government reporters sat open-mouthed and forgot to take their notes. He is an erudite scholar of Sanskrit scriptures. Behind an opaque wall of silence he conceals a big warm heart whose acquaintance if 'slow to begin is never ending.' His one aim in life is to discover and realise the deep spiritual truths buried in our ancient scriptures, and since this can be done only through a process of self-discipline and self-purification in the field of action, he is today dedicating himself to the service of the poorest, the oppressed and the down-trodden in a spirit of renunciation. Naturally the untouchables and the poor spinners and weavers claim him and his companions as their own. In their own way all these workers are the most determined rebels against all current shibboleths and against injustice and oppression wherever found, social or Governmental. But in politics today they have deliberately imposed the discipline of self-suppression upon themselves because they believe that it is only through quiet constructive work that they can bring real freedom to the toiling masses.

AT GRIPS WITH ORTHODOXY

And the patron of the Ashram, Sheth Jamnalal Bajaj is the arch rebel. Some time back he caused a flutter in the orthodox Marwadi community by throwing open the Lakshminarayan temple at Wardha to the so-called untouchables. It was represented to him by friends that the step was premature, that it would strengthen the hands of the reactionaries, and give a set-back to the cause of reform by scaring away those who were slowly veering round to its side. But he preferred to listen to the inner voice rather than counsels of caution. Events have fully justified the wisdom of his step, for whilst the die-hard section of his community has excommunicated him, his action has been hailed throughout India as the death-knell of unreasoning orthodoxy, and an influential portion of his community has not only reconciled itself to the reform but has decided to stand by him through thick and thin.

The excommunication has left him altogether unrepentant and he proved it recently by going a step further by partaking of food cooked by the so-called untouchable boys when recently at Rewadi. It was to understand the motive of this action of his, that a deputation of Agarwal Marwadis waited upon Gandhiji the other day. Sheth Ghanshyamdas Birla who is at present here in connection with Lalaji Memorial Fund and whose opposition to untouchability is known to be no less strong than Jamnalalji's chivalrously offered to act the part of *avocatus diaboli*. "These friends," he said, "are anxious to help Jamnalalji in his work of social reform such as widow remarriage, prevention of child marriage and so forth. They would not even mind Shethji throwing open temples to the untouchables but they feel very strongly about his partaking of food at the hands of 'untouchables.' Since these friends are prepared to go so far they hope that Shethji would at least meet them halfway by giving up dining at the hands of the 'untouchables.'"

"But, how can I do that ?" expostulated Jamnalalji. "In this Ashram I am bound to dine with everybody who comes there and untouchables are freely admitted here."

"We don't mind that," they rejoined. "You may do as you like in the Ashram. The Ashram is a sacred spot and no restrictions need be observed there even as none are at Jagannath Puri".

Gandhiji intervened, "Is your objection religious and fundamental or is it on the score of social tradition?" he asked.

"We are no learned pandits," replied one of them. "Our objection is based on the latter ground."

"In that case," said Gandhiji, "you should bear with Shethji. If you objected to Shethji's dining with such 'untouchables' as were addicted to drink or led unclean lives I could understand you but for lack of moral courage to hold that food is polluted by the mere touch of one born in a so-called untouchable family, though otherwise he may be a pure and righteous man, is a negation of religion. I admit that social tradition should be respected when it is meant for the protection of society even though personally one may not feel any need for following it, but to respect a tradition even when it becomes tyrannous spells not life but death and it should be discarded.

"Jamnalalji has chosen a wider field of service. He cannot exclusively identify himself with any particular community. The world is his family and he can serve his community only through the service of humanity. So let Jamnalalji go his way. One can overcome opposition only by love, untruth by truth, not by compromising truth. See the state of society we are living in, it is full of falsehood, hypocrisy, hatred. Our Panchas should be the Gangotri of our society. But today they have become corrupt. What would be left of the sacredness of the Ganges if its stream were polluted at the very source? Let us therefore try to purify our Panchas, by doing penance, by suffering for right's sake. That is what Jamnalalji is doing. You should give him your blessings even if you cannot follow him.

For a day will come when not only you but even the orthodox section will recognise that by his action Jamnalalji rendered the truest service to Hinduism and the future generation will thank him for it."

The burning appeal coming straight as it did from Gandhiji's heart seemed to go home to his hearers.

LAJPATRAI DAY

The 29th November, the day of national mourning over the loss of Lalaji, was duly observed here. A pillar of strength to the country, for over quarter of a century his life was almost co-terminous with the political and social life of the Punjab. Even those who differed from him considered it a privilege to be opposed by him. And a Musalman friend voiced the feelings of all his critics when he once described him at a time when the communal passions were running high as 'the truest friend and noblest foe.' The inmates of the Wardha Ashram observed the national day after the poor man's way by doing manual labour and contributing the day's wages and denying themselves a week's ration of *gud* the only item of luxury in their ghiless menu. The short address that Gandhiji delivered to the inmates of the Ashram after their evening prayers on that day may be summarised here. "Our scriptures tell us," he said, "that childhood, old age and death are incident only to this perishable body of ours and that man's spirit is eternal and immortal. That being so, why should we fear death? And where there is no fear of death there can be no sorrow over it either. It does not therefore behove us to shed tears over Lalaji's passing away but to emulate and copy his virtues. The central feature of his character was his burning passion for service of the motherland and he began his career with the service of the most down-trooden of his countrymen, *viz.*, the so-called untouchables whilst he was still a youth. It may not be given to everybody to emulate his career in the Assembly which was but a small incident in his career, but all can develop the spirit of sacrifice which ran like a continuous thread through his life. And sacrifice means self-purification. I would like you therefore on this solemn occasion to resolve to make an ever-increasing effort for self-purification. Through it you will be serving yourselves, your country and the world." P.

II

RESULT OF EXPLOITATION

There is quite a motley assemblage of personages here in the Satyagrahashram these days. There is, to begin with, the Sindhi Acharya Kripalani, a professor by vocation, a nomad by instinct and a Khadi worker by choice, going about from place to place with his Khadi samples, canvassing for orders and incidentally delivering addresses to college students in response to invitations and shocking them and their professors into a Khadi sense by his challenging speeches. Then there is a deputation from Lahore come to discuss with Gandhiji several questions of importance regarding the future conduct of the late Lalaji's various activities.

Again there is a big financier, a captain of business spending a few days of privilege and holiday with Gandhiji. Several years back, he had put Gandhiji the question: 'Do you want me or my money for the nation's cause?' 'You,' was the straight reply. 'What task would you assign me if I left off business and joined you?' was the next question. 'The spinning wheel,' replied Gandhiji as he plied his charkha. He is today accompanying Gandhiji on his morning walks, discussing with him the 'inevitability' of Khadi, as also some practical plans of Khadi work. Gandhiji talks to him about the deepening poverty of the masses, their inevitable extermination unless something is done to alleviate their condition and goes on to picture the menace of an industrialised India to the world. 'God forbid that India should ever take to industrialism after the manner of the West,' he observes. 'The economic imperialism of a single tiny island kingdom (England) is today keeping the world in chains. If an entire nation of 300 millions took to similiar economic exploitation, it would strip the world bare like locusts. Unless the capitalists of India help to avert that tragedy by becoming trustees of the welfare of the masses and by devoting their talents not to amassing wealth for themselves but to the service of the masses in an altruistic spirit, they will end either by destroying the masses or being destroyed by them.'

KALI TEMPLE

He next turns to a Khadi worker who is also accompanying him. He must agree to go to Calcutta where he is wanted in spite of his disinclination. "If we could transform Calcutta we should transform the whole of India," he argues. He himself would go there and make it the centre of his activity, but —And he then gives out this sorrowful secret that he has harboured in his bosom all these years of his life. It is the Kali temple. "There lies my difficulty," he says. "I cannot bear the sight of it. My soul rises in rebellion against the cold-blooded inhumanity that goes on there in the name of religion. If I had the strength I would plant myself before the gate of the temple and tell those in charge of it that before they sacrificed a single innocent animal they should have to cut my throat. But I know that for me to do so would be an unreal, a mechanical thing today because I have not yet completely overcome the will to live. And till I can do that I must bear the cross of my imperfect existence."

TIT-BITS

The residence is at last reached and Gandhiji goes to his quarters. Soon after the post arrives bringing all sorts of news. Now it is a national worker seeking advice in connection with his work, now it is an aspiring, struggling soul laying before him an account of its strivings and failures. Gandhiji considers each case carefully and makes a suitable reply, ministering a word of cheer, encouragement or advice as the case may be. To a national worker who has been ordered off to far away Orissa, where at present cholera is raging, he writes:

"And do not be afraid of cholera. . . . Observe proper

precautions. If in spite of all precautions the worst befalls, there is no help for it. There is no place in the world entirely free from danger. . . . But do as the inner voice prompts you."

To another struggling soul he writes:

"With the help of Rama we have got to overcome the ten-headed Ravana of passions within us. Success is bound to be ours if we have faith in Rama and surrender ouselves to His grace. Above all do not lose self-confidence. Avoid indulgence of the palate."

To another he says:

"There is a world of difference between spinning for sacrifice and spinning for recreation. I would advise you to observe a religious silence while spinning. It would give you spiritual peace and if you make it a point always to spin at a particular fixed hour, it will automatically regulate your other appointments too and help you to a well-ordered life."

To still another he writes:

"You may not force the wearing of Khadi on your mother if she is unwilling. But if your faith in Khadi is genuine and strong enough it is bound to prove infectious."

To another correspondent again:

"My sovereign panacea (for communal troubles) is well-known. If either of the parties were completely to purge itself of ill-will and patiently bear any injustice that the other side might inflict a real heart unity between the two was bound to be established in the end. The injustice would come to an end and both sides would become brave. Today they are pitiful cowards."

And so on.

DR. P. C. RAY

The afternoon is the time for visitor. The visitor on this particular day happens to be no other than Dr. P. C. Ray. 'So you have given up taking milk?' he exclaims as soon as he sees Gandhiji and adds something about the necessity of vitamins. "Not given up," replies Gandhiji correcting him, "but only discontinued for the time being. But do not you remember your own words about tooth powders: 'We manufacture tooth powder in our Bengal Chemical Works only for fools, for myself I find chalk powder good enough'? Even so it is with scientific theories, they are implicity believed in by fools only, wise men always take them with a grain of salt. Only today I was reading an article in which the vitamin theory was challenged." The Bengal savant finds the joke too much after his heart to contradict it, and passes on to other subjects, flinging his shafts now at the lawyers who batten on poor people's resources, now on Marwadi 'money bags' whom he would like to see shot, with the exception of, of course, Jamnalalji, who is standing near by with his eye on the time, for the illustrious visitor has to catch the afternoon express, and Sjt. Ghanshyamdas Birla whose princely philanthropy has disarmed even the inexorable doctor. He then lights upon the question of Indianisation. "Indianisation without retrenchment has no meaning," he exclaims indignantly. "The late Mr. Gokhale advocated Indianisation with a view to economising public expenditure but some of our present-day legislators want not levelling down but levelling up, merely a substitution of a brown for a white bureaucracy." Gandhiji addresses himself to say something but the irrepressible savant has already passed on to the youth movement. "In India our youth leagues only assemble periodically, pass some noisy resolutions and then forget all about them. But in China it was a different story. There, at one time, no less than 50,000 lads had gone out to the villages for constructive work during their summer holidays, they mixed with the masses, started evening classes for them and when they returned, made arrangements to continue the work after them. It has always been a puzzle to me how Dr. Sun Yat Sun could proclaim a republic over 400 million people from abroad. But it was this solid constructive work that had prepared the ground for him. When would our youth realise that it is charkha alone that can establish a living contact between them and the masses?"

But the time is now almost up and there are so many things to talk about yet. He appealingly turns his eyes to Jamnalalji, but fails to find a ray of hope there, finally with a heroic effort he gets up, but suddenly remembers that he has forgotten to say a very important thing and hastens to make good the omission. "I am very proud of my chemistry students," he interjects, "I am always in their lap," and suits his action to his words by climbing on the shoulders of Jamnalalji with an agility that a youth of eighteen might envy, and is borne out of the room by Jamnalalji. I wonder, whether in spite of his riches, he ever carried a richer prize in his life.

P.

III

CREED *v.* POLICY

The scene changes. A deputation of the teachers of a national school has come to wait upon Gandhiji. It is one out of a number of national educational institutions that have stood out like islands after the flood-tide of 1920, and have bravely weathered many a storm since then. Gandhiji receives them, while spinning. In the course of conversation one of the teachers lets out that he holds non-violence as a creed only for individual conduct. In the political field he holds to non-violence only as a temporary expedient. Gandhiji starts as at a snake in the grass. 'Are there many other teachers in your school who think like this?' he quietly asks. But his countenance betrays what is passing in his mind. The teacher notices this and tries to explain his position. True, he believes in non-violence in politics only as a policy but a policy is as good as a creed while it lasts, if it is sincerely and conscientiously adhered to. For the time being therefore there is no difference between his position and Gandhiji. As for the future, if he should feel like changing his policy, he would surely obtain the permission of the school authorities first for doing so. But the explanation fails to satisfy Gandhiji. "Don't you see the difference," he remonstrates, sadly shaking his head, "with you non-violence is only an intellectual proposition, with me it is an article of faith, the first and the last. You try to make a distinction between individual conduct and social conduct. I do not see how it is possible. Where is the line to be drawn? And who is to decide where the one ends and the other begins? *yatha pinde thatha Brahmande* 'As with the individual so with the universe.' You say that your abandonment of non-violence would be conditioned by the permission of the school authorities. But let me tell you that in the circumstances postulated by you there should be no room for asking such permission. For then, you would be bound to sacrifice your school at the altar, according to your belief, of your country just as I would my country at the altar of truth and non-violence. And I would honour you for doing so. No, I do not want to blame you. You must follow the light of your convictions I am only trying to view the question from a different angle. There are at present a number of national institutions in the country with truth and non-violence as their creed. I have my eye upon them constantly. For a time is fast coming, it may, as I wrote in *Young India* the other day, come much sooner than most people expect, when the country will be put upon its trial, and will have to make its final choice. I count upon these institutions in that hour to give a good account of themselves. May be a mere handful of workers as we are, we shall have to make a holocaust of ourselves to testify our faith. So far I had believed that I was absolutely safe in your hands. But I now see where I stand. But that need not make you feel unhappy; it is a question for me only to think about."

There is a deep note of sadness in his voice as he utters these words. By the time he has finished speaking, the last sliver of the day's spinning has run to its end. "How much is it?" he askes as the yarn is reeled off the spindle. "290 rounds of 4 feet circumference from 9½ annas weight of slivers." He calculates. 'Well, dividing the former figure by the latter the results is 30.52. So I have spun 30.52 counts today, two counts better than yesterday." And with a gleam of satisfaction on his face he hurries on to the next item of his day's crowded programme.

CENTRALISE SALES

After the evening prayer—it is time that he retired. But there are some Khadi workers waiting to have a little talk in connection with Khadi work. Gandhiji explains to them his policy. 'We must distribute production and centralise sales for the time being,' he tells them. 'We must try the experiment of pooling prices of Khadi produced in various centres to bring down the average.' He then proceeds to give the *raison d'etre*, of the methods: "Look at the figures of mill Khadi. . . . " he points out, "what does it indicate? A revolution in the people's taste. They are prepared to make a sacrifice. They ask for coarse cloth. But they are being foully deceived by the mill-owners who do not hesitate to exploit their patriotic sentiment. Spurious Khadi is being palmed off on them as 'Gandhi' cloth, even my portrait is put upon it. Could there be a greater fraud or a worse betrayal? But the moral for us in this is that we must increase our production. And to do this we must bring about a general reduction in Khadi prices by pooling." He then goes on to utter a prophetic note of warning to mill-owners: "Do they ever think what a fierce resentment it will cause among the masses when they discover, as bound to one day, that they have been betrayed at every step? I should not be surprised, if in a frenzy of anger they should in that event rise against the mill industry in general."

The Khadi workers at last depart. It is now fairly late and he lays down his weary limbs for rest at the end of a seventeen hours' closely dovetailed programme, during which he has been busy with clock-work regularity. He is plunged in deep thought. Suddenly he calls one of his 'nurses' to his side. "You must get my yarn tested for tensile strength tomorrow," he tells him, "and report to me the result. And see that the hanks are properly and neatly made up and tied with a suitable-coloured thread to show off each lea."

P.

9th February, 1928

THE SITUATION IN BARDOLI

By M. K. Gandhi

Readers of *Young India* and *Navajivan* will recall a series of articles written some months ago by Sjt. Narayan Malkani in the former and by Sjt. Narahari Parikh in the latter, about the proposed revision settlement in the Bardoli Taluka of the Surat District. The Settlement Officer who submitted the first report based it on an *ex cathedra* inquiry, without having troubled to take the people into his confidence, and made out that the Taluka had 'advanced in prosperity in the course of the past thirty years.' Objections, as usual, were invited, and they were submitted in shoals, including memoranda by members of the Council. But they were all disregarded though the Government claim to have passed the orders 'after the most careful and exhaustive consideration of petitions, of objections and representations which Government have received from various quarters.' It is out of place here to examine the summary way in which the objections have been disposed of, but an instance or two will serve to illustrate the haphazard and callous way in which the objections have been dealt with. Thus one of the objections was that the Settlement Officer had included abnormal years in calculating the rates based on prices. The Government Resolution scouts the objection, contends that the particular years of abnormal conditions have not been specified, and then naively remarks: 'The effect of a world-wide war cannot be merely to leave the course of affairs simply as it was!' Another objection was the increasing indebtedness of the cultivators. This was based on an exhaustive inquiry made by Rao Bahadur Bhimbhai Naik, M.L.C., who went from village to village collecting statistics. His contention was that, whereas the Revision Settlement Report of 30 years ago showed a debt of 32 lacs, his inquiry went to show that the amount was in the neighbourhood of a crore. As regards this the Government Resolution says: 'No arguments have been advanced in support of the statements that the cultivators are in debt, and their profits are small.' No argument seems to be necessary for Government to assume that the past thirty years have been of increasing prosperity, but the statement based on inquiry made in every village by an M.L.C.,—no non-cooperator—seems to be no argument at all! And then the Resolution proceeds in a strain the recklessness of which is hard to beat: 'If by cultivator is meant the tenant, the statement is irrelevant. If it refers to the landowner who lets his land to a tenant, it is incorrect. If it refers to the owner who cultivates his own land it is clear that he must be making the same rental income as is made by the landlord who lets his land to a tenant, and must be securing the same remuneration for his labour as a tenant receives when he cultivates a landlord's land.' The Resolution closes with a statement that the objections have been based entirely on erroneous ideas, and predicts years of prosperity,—as a result, one wonders, of the enhancement of assessment! Though these objections were overruled, the Settlement Commissioner, far from confirming the Settlement Officer's recommendations, of which the principle was accepted by the objectors but the facts were disputed, brought in a new principle of grouping the villages on the statistics of sales, leases and rental values.' He made a fresh grouping, raising a number of villages to a higher group and thus making them bear the double burden of a higher and an increased rate. The Government have approved the Settlement Commissioner's grouping and taken those villages unawares, with the result that some of them find their rates enhanced by over 60 per cent.

It is to consider the ways and means of resisting the revision settlement that the people of the Taluka held a conference at Bardoli under the presidentship of Sjt. Vallabhbhai Patel. He called a workers' meeting first and conferred with them as to what was to be done. They were anxious not to precipitate matters, and wanted the President to examine and cross-examine the people before he recommended any course of action. So an informal conference of the representatives of villages was called. 79 villages had sent their representatives. Amongst these were men from every community—Kanbis, Anavlas, Kaliparaj and Parsis. They were men with something to lose, and they knew what Satyagraha would mean for them. There were people paying from Rs. 300 to Rs. 500 as land revenue, and there was a Parsi who alone paid Rs. 700 a year. They did not mince matters. Those of five or six villages said they thought it their duty to resist the enhancement, but felt that they must do so by tendering the old rate and challenging the Government to take such action as they desire to recover the balance. The rest were determined that payment of the whole of the revised assessment should be refused, pending the decision of the Government to come to terms. There were two villages of which the representatives described the condition in perfect frankness. 'Are you speaking for the whole of your village?' 'I am,' he said with stubborn determination. 'But if all the rest fall back, what will you do?' 'I will stand alone.' Then came another who was asked the same question. He said: 'My village will stand together, so long as the Taluka stands together, not afterwards.' A third man said; 'We are all determined, Hindus and Musalmans, but I must say that 25 per cent. of the Musalmans are rather shaky.' Then came another who said. 'Sir, if four true people could be found to stand firm, come what might, I am sure of success.' 'What do you mean by four?' 'By four I mean four of the top men.' 'Do you consider yourself to be one of them?' 'No, sir. I am the fifth. I will follow the four.' 'Are there four people who are prepared to risk their last belonging in resisting the enhancement?' asked the President. Immediately four stood up to express their determination. In the meanwhile the representatives of the five villages who thought it advisable to pay up the old rent were confabulating with the rest, and announced their decision to go with the taluka. It was after this that Sjt. Vallabhbhai Patel addressed the Conference. He spoke on the Government Resolution and the general revenue policy of Government, and said that as to the justice of their case he had not the slightest doubt, he was sure that the revision settlement was wrong but he was not sure of their strength. In 1921 they were on the point of being weighed, but unforeseen circumstances intervened, and they had no opportunity of giving a demonstration of their strength. The hour had struck this time, but were they really ready? He asked them to search their hearts and ask themselves if they could carry on a non-violent and truthful struggle for any length of time against a Government who might mobilise all the forces at their disposal, for the question ultimately affected not one taluka, but many talukas and many districts, that is to say, the whole of India. He warned them against coming to a hasty decision and gave them seven days to think the thing over, so that he might in the meanwhile communicate with Government, and see if he could persuade them to reconsider the matter and hold an impartial inquiry in the matter. In the meanwhile volunteer workers have gone forth to the village taking stock of public opinion and they will also return with their report on the 12th of February on which the villagers will meet again.

There were three M. L. C.'s present at the Conference who emphasised the point that they had exhausted every means at their disposal, and as they had failed, they had gladly entrusted their case to one who could take them along the path of non-violent resistance and suffering.

Let us see how the events shape themselves. M. D.

16th February, 1928

BARDOLI DECLARES SATYAGRAHA

I described last week the situation in Bardoli. On return to Ahmedabad, Sjt. Vallabhbhai Patel addressed a letter to H. E. the Governor, inviting his attention to the situation, and to the flagrant injustice of the revision settlement, and suggesting to him "to afford a fair opportunity to the people to place their case before an impartial tribunal clothed with adequate authority." Unless this was done, added Sjt. Vallabhbhai Patel, with all his anxiety to avoid a serious conflict with the Government, he would have no alternative but to advise the people to refuse to pay the assessment and peacefully and quietly suffer the consequences of the refusal.'

To this an acknowledgment was received from His Excellency's Private Secretary who said that the letter had been sent to the Revenue Department for "official consideration and disposal." Until Sunday the 12th instant Vallabhbhai had received no further communication from Government and he accordingly met the people of the Taluka at Bardoli as previously arranged. The people, who had not let the grass grow under their feet, had, in the meanwhile, further discussed the question of non-payment amongst themselves and actually organised taking signatures to a tentative pledge for non-payment. The deliberative meeting this time was very largely attended, more villages having sent their representatives and quite a number of them having sent the pledges duly signed. There was quiet deliberation and sufficient determination in their voices as each stood up to render an account of what his village had done. Their word would have been nothing worth, if they had all mechanically stood up and repeated parrot-like the cry of non-payment. Each told his tale in his own way. '58 men have given their signatures in our village, 12 have not yet. But that does not matter,' said one. 'All excepting the village headman have signed the pledge,' said another, 'but the headman is not hostile to us.' 'Our Patel has already paid up and a Bania from a neighbouring village also, but we never counted on them,' said a third one. 'There is a section among us which is recalcitrant, but we behave as though they were not of us. Our section will never pay, come what may, and trust the rest to the will of God,' said a fourth one. Quite a large majority said: 'All have given their signatures. There is no fear of any one flinching.' Three or four said with pardonable pride: 'Hold *me* responsible for the whole of the village. My village will stand through thick and thin.' Then said Sjt. Vallabhbhai to them: 'I still ask you to think twice before you take the plunge. Do not derive comfort from the feeling that you have as your leader a fighter like myself. Forget me and forget my companions, fight if you feel that you must resist oppression and injustice. Do not take the plunge lightly. If you miserably fail, you will fall not to rise again for several years, but if you succeed you will have done much to lay the foundation of Swaraj. Now I am going to ask you to take charge of the resolution yourselves, *you* will move it and *you* will second and support it. None of us will speak on it. It will be of your own free will and choice.'

After this they met in open conference. Sjt. Vallabhbhai Patel made a brief speech: 'As I told you last time I addressed to H. E. the Governor a letter asking for an impartial tribunal. I have had a reply which is no reply. My letter, I am told, has been sent to the department for consideration and disposal. When they will have finished considering the letter we do not know, neither can we wait for their decision. If the Government had said that pending consideration of my letter they had resolved to suspend the collection operations and asked us also to adjourn our Conference I should gladly have complied. But now I have simply to await your decision. Since I met you last time I have looked up the law to see if in spite of being iniquitous the orders of enhancement satisfied the letter of the law. I have failed to see that they are even within the law. They are in contravention of Sec. 107 of the L. R. Code. The Settlement Officer had based his report on the existing system, and though I have lots and lots of things to say about his report—the principal being that he never troubled himself to visit the villages and hold conference with the villagers as is at present being done in Olpad Taluka,—I must say that he had adhered to the old system. The Settlement Commissioner adopted a different principle and regrouped the villages. In the event of such an alteration, Government are bound to issue a fresh notification but in their hurry to put the revision settlement in force they did no such thing.

'In the circumstances I would in all humility advise you to refuse payment of the whole assessment so long as the Government do not come to terms. You must bear clearly in mind that except your capacity for suffering and grim determination you have nothing to fight Government's brute strength with. The mightiest tyrant must bend if people are determined to put up with suffering. The question today is not of a few lakhs of rupees, but it is a question of self-respect, it is one of the fundamental principles of Government—no taxation without representation. They should do nothing without having had your views in the matter. You have to resist the arbitrary system of fixing the revenue according to Government's own whims and fancies.

'For this you will have to be self-possessed, resourceful and patient. Government will try your strength in various ways, offer various inducements, use insidious means to bring about a division in your ranks. But you will have to adhere to your principle of refusal to pay at all costs and hardships.

'I have suggested a clause in the resolution to the effect that the fight will go on, until Government appoint an impartial tribunal, or revoke the orders of enhancement. Not that we have any doubt that the enhancement is arbitrary, unjust and oppressive, but if we can make Government accept this vital principle of an independent tribunal, it is more than any material gain, temporary or permanent.

'I have nothing more to say. Do what you do with eyes open, with God as witness and fully counting the cost. It is possible that Government might pick up the leading men amongst you first to set an example, Government might first confiscate the lands of those who move the resolution today. If you are sure that those things will leave you unshaken, take up and fight the good fight.'

The following resolution was then moved and seconded and supported by men from different villages and drawn from various communities in the Taluka—Kanbis, Anavlas, Banias, Parsis and Musalmans:

> "This Conference of the people of Bardoli Taluka resolves that the revision settlement in Bardoli is arbitrary, unjust and oppressive, and advises all the occupants to refuse payment of the revised assessment until the Government is prepared to accept the amount of the old assessment in full satisfaction of their dues, or until the Government appoints an impartial tribunal to settle the whole question of revision by investigation and inquiry on the spot."

The first speaker made a very brief speech. Two of those who followed made brief observations and the rest simply supported the resolution.

There were no more speeches, but after recitation of sacred texts from the Koran and of a Hindu hymn and repetition of *Ramanama*,—the whole conference participating,—the resolution was passed in solemn silence.

Volunteers are now being enlisted, and Sjt. Vallabhbhai Patel has already visited some of the villages. M. D.

8th March, 1928

BARDOLI AND GOVERNMENT

By M. K. Gandhi

The illuminating correspondence that has passed between Sjt. Vallabhbhai Patel and the Government of Bombay regarding the assessment in the Bardoli Taluka affords food for reflection to the public worker and reveals in its true light the nature of the Government under which we are living. Vallabhbhai is not unknown to fame or to the Government. They have been obliged to acknowledge his worth as a public worker of great capacity, integrity and industry. They have acknowledged his great work in the Municipality of Ahmedabad. Only the other day he received unstinted praise for his philanthropic services in connection with the floods in Gujarat.

But his work seems to have counted for nothing when they found him engaged in an activity calculated to cause them embarrassment and possibly loss of prestige and what is the same thing to them loss of land revenue. Their prestige they need for the sake of their revenue. They are no believers in empty prestige.

And so in their very first letter in the matter, they thought it becoming to insult Sjt. Vallabhbhai by calling in question his professions of good-will and describing him as an outsider in Bardoli. The last letter emphasises the insult by leaving no doubt that His Excellency the Governor, too, was party to it. Sjt. Vallabhbhai had courteously assumed in his letter that whilst His Excellency might be identified with a policy enunciated in Government communications, he need not be identified with the manner of expression, more especially the insulting language often adopted by civilian secretaries incensed over any the least resistance or independence betrayed by the public in their correspondence with them. That the Governor has chosen to become a party to the unwarranted insult shows how difficult it is for Governors, however well-intentioned and impartial they may be reputed to be as the present Governor is, to escape the bureaucratic coil. 'Pride goeth before destruction and haughtiness before a fall.'

But Vallabhbhai has a back broad enough to bear the wordy insults that the bureaucracy may choose to heap upon him from its safe and entrenched heights My reason for dwelling on the insult is to draw attention to the utterly irresponsible nature of the Government that dares to insult the public worker of the fore-rank.

But let us see for the moment what it is that has upset the Government. Land revenue is a close preserve beyond the pale of law such as it is. The regulation of assessment rests entirely with the executive authority. Every attempt hitherto made to bring it under popular or judicial control has failed. The Government must somehow or other meet the ever-growing expenditure, bulk of which is military. Land revenue lends itself to arbitrary increase as it affects the largest class and a class that has no voice, a class that can be squeezed without wincing There would be an end to irresponsible government if the governed are either allowed to have a say in their taxation or to resist it successfully. Bardoli does not appreciate the increase made in its assessment. Its people approached the Government with petitions and exhausted all the means that are regarded as constitutional to secure redress. Having failed they invited Vallabhbhai to advise them and if necessary to lead them in resisting the Government through Satyagraha.

Vallabhbhai investigated their case and though he found it to be just, sought to approach the Government with a view to save them embarrassment and spare the people prolonged suffering and suggested an honourable course, *i e.* suggested that if the Government did not admit the justice of the people's case, they should appoint an *impartial* tribunal to investigate the case on either side and assured the Government that the people would abide by the decision of such a tribunal. This reasonable suggestion the Government has scornfully rejected.

The public therefore are not called upon to accept the popular version as against that of the Government. They are asked merely to support the demand for the appointment of an *impartial* tribunal and failing such appointment to support their heroic resolve peacefully to resist the assessment and suffer all the consequences of such resistance even including confiscation of their land.

Sjt. Vallabhbhai has rightly distinguished the proposed Satyagraha from the Swaraj Satyagraha. This campaign cannot be properly deemed to be a no-tax campaign launched for the attainment of Swaraj as Bardoli would have done in 1922. This Satyagraha is limited in scope, has a specific local object. Every man has the right, nay, it is his duty to resist an arbitrary unjust levy as the Bardoli assessment is claimed to be by its ryots. But though the object of the proposed Satyagraha is local and specific, it has an all-India application. What is true of Bardoli is true of many parts of India. The struggle has also an indirect bearing on Swaraj. Whatever awakens people to a sense of their wrongs and whatever gives them strength for disciplined and peaceful resistance and habituates them for corporate suffering brings us near Swaraj.

8th March, 1928

THE POLICY OF GRAB

From the correspondence between Sjt. Vallabhbhai Patel and Government regarding the revision settlement in Bardoli Taluka, which has now been published in the press, it would appear that he has erred, if at all, on the side of moderation and understated his case. He has cited extracts from reports of Government officials to reveal the 'grasping, rack-renting, revenue policy of Government,' and confined himself to only two instances. The fact is that the history of land revenue in the Presidency during recent years has been one of calculated flouting of public opinion and insult of members of the Legislative Council, and of unblushing grab. In this connection the Legislative Council Debates for the year 1924 and 1927 are revealing documents. It will be remembered that the Joint Parliamentary Committee appointed to consider the Government of India Bill, 1919, made the following important declaration with regard to the policy that should be followed in revising land revenue assessment:

"They consider that the imposition of new burdens should be gradually brought more within the purview of the legislature. And in particular without expressing any judgment on the question whether the land revenue is a rent or tax *they advise that the process of revising the land revenue assessments ought to be brought under closer regulation by statute as soon as possible.* . . . The Committee are of opinion that the time has come to embody in the law the main principles by which the land revenue is determined, the methods of valuation, the pitch of assessment, the periods of revision, the graduation of enhancements, and the other chief processes which touch the well-being of the revenue-payers."

And in 1924 at the Bombay Session of the Legislative Council the following resolution was passed by a majority of the Council.

"This Council recommends that a committee consisting of official and non-official members of this Council elected by the Council with a non-official majority be appointed to consider the question of bringing the process of revising the land revenue assessment under closer regulation by statute as recommended by the Joint Committee appointed to consider the Government of India Bill, 1919, and to report on the nature and form of legislation that should be undertaken towards that end, and *that no revision be proceeded with and no new rates under any revised settlement be introduced till the said legislation is brought into effect.*"

Government of course opposed the resolution, but seeing that it was carried by a majority, they appointed a committee called the Land Revenue Assessment Committee, in accordance with the first part of the resolution, but ignored the second part we have italicised above. Three years were allowed to roll by, and revision settlement of taluka on taluka was proceeded with and enforced in defiance of the advice of the Parliamentary Committee to introduce legislation as soon as possible, and in defiance of the resolution of the Council reproduced above. Then came another resolution in 1927 which was passed by a majority of 52 against 29, Government again presenting a solid opposition:

"This Council reaffirming the principle of the resolution as amended and carried by it by a majority on the 15th March, 1924, recommends to the Governor-in-Council that *he will be pleased to give immediate effect to it* by introducing the necessary legislation, after taking into consideration the report, the minutes of dissent and suggestions of the members of the Land Revenue Assessment Committee, *and making provision for giving retrospective effect to such legislation* in view of the fact that in many cases new revision settlements were proceeded with and new rates introduced after the resolution of 15th March, *and pending such legislation to issue orders to the revenue authorities concerned not to collect the assessment enhanced in revision after the 15th March, 1924.*"

A year more has elapsed without the necessary legislation having been introduced, and without Government having paid any heed to either of the two resolutions of the Legislative Council. In reply to the most reasonable suggestion that the agriculturists should not be penalised for the procrastination of the Government and that the revenue authorities should be advised not to collect the assessment enhanced in revision, the Revenue Member pleaded '*the present financial conditions of this presidency.*' Government have accused Sjt. Vallabhbhai of making 'perverse misrepresentations.' At the risk of earning the same compliment, we would say that the indecent haste with which Government have proceeded with carrying out the revision settlements in numerous talukas and are proceeding, betrays a determination on their part to frustrate the very object of the legislation when the legislation does ultimately come. For by that time no talukas will be left for the application of the new legislation ! But what can they do? "I should like to point out," said the Revenue Member, "that the revenue for the first 25 talukas for which revision settlements have been carried out already amounts to Rs. 10½ lakhs and I must express surprise that any honourable member of this House should have seen fit to suggest that Government should accept a sacrifice of revenue of this large amount especially in the present financial conditions of this presidency." So Bardoli is only one of the 25 talukas which have suffered under the policy of grab.

SECRECY

But Sjt. Vallabhbhai has evidently left the constitutional aspect of the case to be fought out by the members of the Council whose resolutions have been systematically ignored. He has simply challenged the Settlement Officer's report and the principle on which the Settlement Commissioner has based his report. Let us see the way in which those reports are made available to the public or to be more correct, are kept from the public. Mr. Shivdasani in his speech at the Bombay Session described the thing in careful detail:

"The system which Government follow in making revision settlements is open to several objections. There is not sufficient publicity. Copies of the Settlement Officer's reports are not made freely available to the public. What usually takes place is that one copy is kept at the taluka *kutchery* and the cultivators are expected to know the report and to send in the objections. I say that is not fair. We all know how very backward the villagers are, how very lazy they are, and we cannot expect them to walk 20 miles to the taluka town and to go and see the report which several times is only in English. . . . . As a matter of fact at one stage I was told that in some cases the mamlatdar refused to allow the people to take copies, but even though we take it for granted that people are allowed to take copies, a big report kept in the taluka *kutchery* on a subject which vitally concerns the poor cultivators living in 90 or 100 villages cannot be said to have been made freely available to the public." And Bardoli fared no better. But there is one respect in which Bardoli fared even worse than has been described here. In Bardoli the Settlement Officer submitted the report in October 1925. Usually the report is reviewed in detail by the Collector, but in Bardoli the Settlement Officer's report could not be reviewed, because as the Government Resolution says "the Settlement Officer himself happened at the time to be the Collector during the absence on leave of the permanent Collector." The report has, however, "been exhaustively dealt with by the Commissioner of Settlements, himself a former Collector of the district, and in fact has been practically re-written by him. One wonders what has happened to the report of the Commissioner of Settlements on which Government have mainly relied. To say that he practically re-wrote the report is an euphemism for saying that he rejected the Settlement Officer's report and made his own independent recommendations. We are strengthened in our statement by the fact that the Settlement Commissioner's Report has not been forthcoming, in spite of several members of the Council having asked for a copy. It is not a confidential document, it ought to have been placed before the public and objections should have been invited from the agriculturists, but no such thing was done, and even now the precious document is a sealed book even to the Council members. If Sjt. Vallabhbhai had chosen to be cantankerous, he could have assailed the Government case on the preliminary ground of want of publicity in respect of the Settlement Officer's report, and utter secrecy in respect of the Commissioner's report.

SJT. VALLABHBHAI'S CHALLENGE

But he refrained from doing so, and challenged the Settlement Officer's report which is full of palpable absurdities and contains tables prepared without scrutiny and hence full of uncertain and unreliable data. He has relied on the increase in the value of land, without any reference to the times in which the value had gone up, and without reference to whether the value was due to the trouble taken and cost incurred by the holder of land, as laid down in Sec. 107 of the Land Revenue Code. He has referred to the increase in the gross produce of the land without the slightest regard for a corresponding increase in the cost of production, and in the cost of living. We have a suspicion that the settlement Commissioner felt compelled to reject this part of the Settlement Officer's report and as he could not then support a case for enhancement, he fell back on the tables of leases and sales prepared by the Settlement Officer (Appendices G and H). Sjt. Vallabhbhai Patel has made exhaustive inquiry in the villages and has in the course of his correspondence with Government repeatedly challenged the Settlement Officer's report, and the accuracy of the appendices G and H. The least that the Government can do is to accept Sjt. Vallabhbhai's challenge and order an inquiry.

THE INIQUITY OF IT

And what is the equity of the standard adopted by the Settlement Commissioner? Sjt. Vallabhbhai Patel has cited a number of opinions of Government officials with wide experience of revenue-work in the districts, to show the most mischievous results of adopting the rental value as basis for fixing the assessment. He could have cited many more and demonstrated the absurdity of going by the opinion of a Settlement Commissioner who is obsessed with rental value as a basis for fixing the assessment. Mr. Garrett, Collector of Ahmedabad, said in the course of his answers to the questionnaire of the Revenue Assessment Committee: "But caution is necessary, because free contracts are exceptional. There may be competition among landlords or competition among tenants; rents are then forced up or down. Another point to be noted is that rental statistics must be collected in substantial quantity before they can be used effectively. I entirely disagree with the policy of accepting even scanty data as better than none. Very misleading results may ensue from the use of a few figures. In such cases it may be better to exclude the figures altogether and work on other methods." If the simple fact is borne in mind that 16,315 out of 17,184 landholders in Bardoli have holdings of not more than 25 acres, and 10,379 out of these have holdings of 1 to 5 acres, the iniquity of adopting the rental value as basis would be apparent. With such small holdings, it is not surprising that not more than 5 per cent. of the total cultivated area is leased, and any one can understand the gross injustice of taxing 95 per cent. of the people on doubtful statistics available in the case of 5 per cent. As Mr. Mardhekar, then officiating Collector of Broach, has pointed out. "Non-cultivating classes are few and far between and naturally land leased is not much in each village......If the 'rents' are alone taken as the basis, the assessments must be higher and higher. This would give rise to much agrarian trouble and much discontent." But a Government relying on its arms and ammunition may not fear agrarian trouble and discontent

THE SOLUTION

The solution that Sjt. Vallabhbhai Patel has suggested is simple viz., the appointment of an impartial tribunal to make a thorough investigation into the case. We have another solution which a prestige-ridden government might not disdain to adopt. Assuming that in Bardoli the incidence of the enhanced assessment upon the rent is not above 33 per cent,—it is over 50 as Sjt. Vallabhbhai Patel has pointed out in his letter to the press,—even that is in contravention of the recommendation contained in paragraph 39 of the Revenue Assessment Committee, which lays down, "that the assessment should not exceed 25 per cent. of the profits of cultivation, i e. the gross profits less all the expenses incurred in deriving those profits." There is another recommendation of the Committee:

> "In their opinion there should be a statutory provision that all proposals for revision settlement should be placed before a standing advisory committee consisting of six members, of whom not less than four should be elected non-official members of the Legislative Council, elected by that body itself."

Let Government, if they choose, seek shelter under these recommendations of the Revenue Assessment Committee, and appoint an inquiry, if not in response to the public demand, at least in accordance with the recommendations of the Committee. M. D.

15th March, 1928

HOW THE MACHINE WORKS

"While suggesting a maximum of 50, I would also press for a minimum of 40. Otherwise while the maximum will never be reached in any district, many districts will be unfairly let off their proper burden through the absence of a minimum. Even now many of our districts pay so little that they enjoy a sort of permanent inam or immunity from tax and have their public service paid for and subsidised by less fortunate districts, whose crime is that they already pay a higher proportion and can therefore rarely or never benefit by the enhanced limits."

Since writing the notes on Bardoli, we have been in possession of that precious document which up to now had been kept under lock and key,—we mean the report of the Settlement Commissioner reviewing the Settlement Officer's report. The quotation at the head of the article, reminding one very strongly of the proverbial monkey's anxiety to equalise the shares of the cats, is taken from the dissenting minute appended to the report of the Revenue Assessment Committee, by the same official, whom one may appropriately call the presiding deity of all the settlement transactions in the presidency and of the Government resolution on the report, to which we have referred elsewhere. It is one characteristic of the mentality of the official, and of Government who chooses to think through him.

The report of which the text is now before us justifies our worst fears and knocks the whole bottom out of the Government's case about Bardoli. It would appear from the covering letter of Mr. Jayakar who was the Settlement Officer that he submitted his report in advance to the Settlement Commissioner, and it was 'after being revised in accordance with his instructions in connection with certain paragraphs specially regarding leases, sales, etc.,' that it was again submitted to him for approval, and he then returned it for being officially submitted through the proper channel. We have to bear in mind this fact as we examine that revealing report of the Settlement Commissioner. The 'paragraphs specially regarding leases, sales etc.' are the paragraphs in Mr. Jayakar's report in which he emphasises the point that he has prepared the appendices G and H with the closest scrutiny and having taken care to eliminate all transactions described as uneconomic. This we might safely ascribe to the inspiration of the Settlement Commissioner who was thoroughly dissatisfied with the basis on which the Settlement Officer had proceeded, laid his finger on the only thing that he could set store by—*viz.*, the rental statistics—and suggested to the Settlement Officer to put at least that part of his report in a presentable manner. But let us come to the Settlement Commisioner's indictment of the report of the Settlement Officer. Mr. Jayakar, who by the way is described by the Revenue Secretary in his letter to Sjt. Vallabhbhai as 'an experienced revenue officer who was in charge of the Prant in which Bardoli taluka is contained. 'For a period ranging over ten months he travelled throughout the taluka and inspected each and every village. His inquiries were conducted in the fields and in the villages and after conversation with the cultivators.' We are afraid we must take a long extract but we cannot help it. Here is the indictment:

"We now come to Mr. Jayakar's proposals for fresh rates. I regret to find that he has almost exclusively confined his consideration to the gross value of the produce. Even in his summary of the general conditions in paragraph 57 he confines his notice of the rise in land value and rents to a single instance, and he only says that sale prices have risen steadily, and that the assessment consequently represents a decrease in proportion to the rent. *Here there is no foothold, nothing definite that one can possibly use as the foundation for anything. This is not what one expects in a settlement report.* He then occupies two pages in proving what we all well know that if Government had taken its revenue in kind, then the cash value of the revenue would have increased enormously. He shows that the probable increase in the gross produce of the taluka is something like 15 lakhs, and then only it begins to dawn upon him that perhaps it is all irrelevant, because if the cost of production had increased likewise by 15 lakhs there would be no increase on which any further demand for a share in the rental value could be based. Furthermore if the cost of production had increased say by 17 lakhs and not 15 then there is a case for actual reduction. Now, how is Mr. Jayakar going to determine for us whether the increased cost of production has or has not altogether exceeded the increased value of the produce? He has nothing more to say than that 'this factor cannot certainly be ignored.' In fact he leaves the main gate of the fort wide open. The whole of his conclusions could be rushed and overthrown in a moment without there being in his report a single word of reply by any one who alleges that the cost of production has increased more than the price of the produce. Perhaps now when this is realised it will be seen how exceedingly important it is to base one's settlement proposals *on rentals* and not on gross produce and prices. Rentals of course do take into strict account every item of cost of production as well as value of produce. No man can possibly pay a single anna of increased rent until he had definitely ascertained that the value of the produce at the end of the year is likely to exceed the cost of the production by one anna more than it did previously. I am afraid that almost the whole of Mr. Jayakar's report from paragraph 57 to paragraph 65 is *irrelevant*, and worse than that, *it is positively dangerous as affording no justification for his proposals and suggesting arguments* against them. . . . If you fix settlements with reference to the gross price of produce you are in the worst possible position. The state of mind to which one is reduced is well revealed in the last portion of paragraph 65. When we come to paragraph 66 where Mr. Jayakar makes his final proposals he is of course in this condition He has shown that gross produce has increased enormously so that he is quite sure that the 33 per cent. can certainly be taken on that foundation. At the same time he knows that prices may not be maintained and he does not want to be accused of excess. So he very timidly and without the slightest stated reason at all takes refuge in an increase of 25 per cent. as 'fair and equitable.' If the Government maximum of increase had been 75 per cent. he would probably have said that 65 per cent. was 'quite fair and equitable. The truth is that he is sailing without a compass and without rudder." (Italics ours)

Having thus disposed of the Settlement Officer's report he had certainly to discover some foothold which he could use as foundation for enhancement. And so he turns to '*our one true guide the rental values.*' The value of the Settlement Officer's report, which he has torn to pieces, lies however, says he, 'chiefly in its appendices' And yet let us see what the Settlement Commissioner has to say with regard to one of the two important appendices, viz., appendix G regarding sales: 'Generally, I regret to note that I cannot believe that appendix G has been scrutinised with the care that it required. The number of transactions is very large and any one who will think for a moment will see how impossible it is for transactions which took place between 1901 and 1910 to be scrutinised by a settlement officer in 1925 with any hope of success.' And yet he implicitly accepts the same officer's appendix H of leases and rentals, for otherwise he would have no foothold. Let us now turn to his foothold which, as we will see, is as fatally insecure as the Settlement Officer's. It will be recollected that Sjt. Vallabhbhai has impugned the accuracy and reliability of appendices G and H and challenged an inquiry. . The Settlement Commissioner has accepted appendix H without demur, and fallen into an amazing blunder for which we confess we were not prepared in a report written by an official of the standing of a Settlement Commissioner. But Homer also sometimes nods, and our Homer has not only nodded but blundered to the grievous detriment of the unfortunate peasants of Bardoli. "Mr. Jayakar," he says, "has collected rents for 42,923 acres of dry crop and rice out of a gross area of 126,982. Thus it is clear that at least 1/3rd of the whole taluka and mahal together are actually leased on cash rental and to this must be added the crop shares and produce rent area. I found in going through several villages even some additional areas thus cash leased beyond those he has noted. He had probably not included these rentals, I found, because the transactions were open to some objection. However I think there is little doubt that *at least* half the total area is held by landlords who do not cultivate it." It would be impossible to find a paragraph more full of statistical blunders than this. *Mr. Anderson for the moment forgets that Mr. Jayakar has collected statistics of seven years' leases and has in almost every case multiplied a transaction by the number of years for which it extends. Thus rents for 42,923 acres are really not rents for 42,923 but for something over 6,000 acres.* He next assumes the close scrutiny of the Settlement Officer and arbitrarily adds areas at '*at least half the total area*' as held by the landlords! Well, one may go and ask any agriculturist in Bardoli as to how much of the land is leased, and he will say 5 to 10 per cent. And yet proceeding on this colossal blunder, the Settlement Commissioner has imposed an enhancement on the taluka for which there is not the slightest justification. 'The abundance of the statistics in appendix H,' says he, 'leads one to the conclusion that the quantity of land rented by landlords to tenants must be very large.' Ergo the large mass of landlords must be taxed! But as we have shown in a previous article the proportion of large landlords to the very small ones is extremely small, and it is the vast mass of small landlords who have been punished by a blundering Settlement Commissioner on the strength of statistics which are not only of doubtful value, but which he has fatally misunderstood.

"Bardoli is perhaps almost the only taluka in the Presidency in which for about 30 years there has been no need to resort to any coercive methods or pressure for the recovery of the land revenue." That is the testimony of Mr. Anderson, and it is by wrongfully and blunderingly enhancing the assessment of that taluka that he has thought of requiting them for their law-abiding and peaceful character.

We feel now that the Bardoli case is not merely one for an impartial inquiry. It is one of proved wrong--proved out of the mouths of the prosecutors themselves. No Government with the slightest pretension to decency or fairness can dare to continue the wrong thus proved and exposed. M. D.

15th March, 1928

THE VICIOUS CIRCLE

As regards the solution we suggested in our last article a friend has objected that Government in their resolution of 13th May 1927 on the report of the Land Revenue Assessment Committee of Bombay have declined to accept the recommendations of the Committee referred to in our suggestion. We were sensible of the fact. We could have suggested a better course, viz., that Government should give immediate effect to the resolution of the Legislative Council passed by a majority of 52 against 29 on the 17th March 1927. The most important part of that resolution, so far as the poor agriculturists were concerned, was: 'pending such legislation to issue orders to the revenue authorities concerned not to collect assessment enhanced in revision after the 15th of March 1924.' It would be a straight and manly course to give even belated effect to this part of the resolution; but then it would be a pretty big morsel to stop collections in respect not of one taluka, but of several, and to refund the lakhs already collected. For the matter of that the straightest course would be to accept the moderate demand of the agriculturists of Bardoli. But there comes prestige in the way. It is a vicious circle widening all round. Hence we suggested a safer course, though it would be inconsistent with the resolution on the report of the Revenue Assessment Committee. But Government never made a fetish of consistency.

In the long history of insult of and contempt for public opinion, the resolution on the report of the Revenue Assessment Committee will fill a painful chapter. It will be recalled that the Committee consisted of 22 members, only seven out of whom signed the report without qualification. There was a regular tug of war between the officials and the non-officials, the seven official members appending a joint minute of dissent and six non-official members appending joint or separate minutes. And look at the result. The Government resolution on the report makes short work of almost every important recommendation of the Committee. As regards the basis of assessment, Government, we are told, felt constrained, 'after the fullest deliberation,' to accept the view of the official members of the Committee, 'that rental value must be adopted as the *sole* basis for fixing the assessment.' Take next the question of fixing the maximum percentage of the rental value as the assessment that can be claimed by Government. The Committee decided by a majority that the assessment should not exceed 25 per cent. of the net profits. But here again the Governor-in-Council 'considers that he may appropriately adhere to the present practice of regarding 50 per cent. of the rental value as the maximum limit'—'present practice' meaning, by the bye, the practice introduced by the Settlement Commissioner during the recent settlements! Another important recommendation of the Committee was the appointment of a standing advisory committee to examine all revision settlement proposals. Here again 'the arguments of the official members against this recommendation have been fully set forth in the report, and they have the approval of Government.' There was the question of the subsoil water rate and the non-official members of the Committee were of opinion that the practice of making the subsoil water the subject of assessment should be abolished. Government found that 'the arguments of the official members opposing the abolition of this rate' had not been 'successfully met,' and they were 'unable to accept the recommendation.' Even the most harmless recommendation of the non-official members that the Settlement Officer 'shall have the

65

assistance of two representatives of the cultivators elected by the Taluka Local Board in preparing his settlement' was found unacceptable. 'Government,' we are told, with sickening repetition, 'agree with the arguments of the official members against the proposal and regret that they cannot see their way to accept it.' Why then was this Committee appointed? And how can one with the slightest sense of self-respect agree to serve on a committee knowing that no value would be attached to its recommendations?

Sjt. Vallabhbhai Patel has in his letters to Government pointed out on the authority of opinions of officials 'that rental value was never the basis for fixing the assessment,' and that 'agricultural assessments have never been based entirely on rents in the past.' But Government refuse to accept even this statement of fact and in the resolution on the Revenue Assessment Committee's report 'wish to emphasise that this decision (*viz.* to adopt rental value as the sole basis for fixing the assessment) will merely give legal effect to the existing principle upon which Bombay settlements are already based' It would be impossible to think of a better example of *petitio principii*. The fact as admitted by numerous officials is that the rental value was never the sole basis, an official with that pet obsession appears on the scene and revises all settlements in the terms of his obsession, and Government describe the iniquitous innovation as an 'existing principle' and legalise the wrong.

But one might indefinitely go on multiplying these instances of wrongs and insults and vicious circles. The one object of Non-co-operation was to lay the axe at the root of the whole mischief. The Bardoli Satyagraha is an indication of the desire on the part of the people to try the sovereign remedy in a limited sphere. Our case may be, and is, absolutely unassailable, but it will be nothing worth if we have not the strength to stand by our decision and suffer for it

M. D.

3rd May, 1928

LAWLESSNESS GALORE

Bardoli is now a scene of frantic lawlessness. The men in charge of the operations have thrown all decency to the winds. Fancy, for instance, an official of the grade of Deputy Collector trying to bring pressure to bear on liquor-vendors with the help of excise officers and invading liquor shops and declaring big casks of liquor attached. The story does not end there. The casks could not be removed, so they were sealed and the shop closed and locked. The brave Parsi addressed a strong letter to the Deputy Collector objecting to the procedure and holding him liable for the loss due to the closing of the shop and claiming rent at Rs. 5 per day for leaving the attached casks in the shop. He also stated in the letter that the allegation made by the Collector that undue influence was being brought to bear on those who wanted to pay was entirely false, and that on the contrary he and other Parsi *khatedars* had themselves been victims of undue pressure from Government. It seems the happenings reached the ears of the higher officials who disapproved of this bungling and ordered the shop to be immediately opened. The Deputy Collector's men ran post-haste to the shop and opened it at a late hour in the night, and took the Parsi shopkeeper to task for having addressed that letter. They were angry that he should have dared to contradict the 'badasahib,' and told him that his name would thenceforth be put on the black list.

It may be noted that liquor, from the point of view of Government, is as good cash as currency notes, and they had no right to attach Rs 2,000 worth of it for land revenue amounting to Rs. 300. The casks are still in the shop and though the lock and the sentry have been removed, the shopkeeper refuses to have anything to do with the shop.

The Parsi liquor-sellers are in an unfortunate position, so far as the Satyagraha movement is concerned. They have daily money dealings with Government, and Government do not scruple to credit to the revenue account the money they offer for their permits. In quite a number of cases money sent for a supply of liquor was credited as land revenue. In one case, an item of Rs. 700 was sought to be appropriated to revenue when the man who went to make the payment said that he was not a landholder at all. Then when the official threatened to appropriate the amount to revenue due from some of his relatives, he made no payment and left the place.

Then there are other instances of lawlessness A party with the Mamlatdar at their head proceed to a village at daybreak and declare a herd of buffaloes attached, without stopping to inquire to whom they belong and whether or not they belong to non-agriculturists. What is this but daylight robbery or dacoity?

The Patels are now busy preparing live-stock lists in every village! As to who will identify them and their owners and how, it is difficult to say.

We noted in the last issue that three attachment officers had been appointed to strengthen the hands of the local officials. The Mamlatdar has now been transferred to distant Thana evidently because he has not been found to be doing his job in the proper manner, and a Musalman Mamlatdar appointed in his place, so as to bring pressure on Musalman landholders and if possible, to create a split between them and the Hindus. The Talatis too, it is reported, will be transferred in large numbers to other Talukas, and those from other Talukas will be imported into Bardoli.

The Collector, who visited a few places and who was met by Patels who did not mince matters, has left the Taluka in the safe keeping of the subordinate officials indulging in lawless law.

And yet the result has in no way been commensurate with their zeal. Big benches and bags of grain are attached only to be left where they are for want of porters. Carts are attached and have to be driven by peons. As to the final disposal of what little reaches the Taluka headquarters, they all seem to be in the dark. For forfeiture notices, numbers of which have now been served, the *banias* have ceased to be singled out as targets. For they have been firm as a rock and the same has been the result in case of a prominent Musalman—*viz*, Ibrahim Patel of Bardoli. Thousands of rupees worth of his land will be declared forfeited, but he is absolutely unmoved and is a great moral force in the Taluka. The Patidars' turn has now come, and they have hailed the notices with pride.

Huge meetings are held everywhere, women dressed in Khadi attending in large numbers, laying heaps of yarn before Sjt. Vallabhbhai, as in 1921, and lustily singing the Satyagraha songs.

The first man summoned to take his trial before the magistrate is, we are delighted to note, Sjt. Ravishankar. One cannot think of a nobler sacrifice. He will be tried, it seems, for criminal tresspass and for obstructing Government servants in the performance of their duties. This is how he came to be guilty of the alleged offence. It would appear that three carts were commandeered for removing the kit and luggage belonging to the Deputy Collector. The man to whom the carts belonged came to realise his mistake and went to the *thana* in company with Sjt. Ravishankar to call back his men. One of the cartmen, as soon as he saw his master, said, they were not at all willing to go but they were helpless. Sjt. Ravishankar pleaded with the Mamlatdar that if the men were not willing they should not be forced. He was ordered to leave the *thana*, which he did, the cartman leaving the cart followed him. The other cartmen also ultimately left leaving the carts to be driven by the peons.

One would like to know how this action constitutes criminal tresspass. Obstruction has of course been there, ever since the inception of the movement. All failure on the part of the officials to subdue the Satyagrahis, all failure to attach property and to dispose of attached property, can, of course, be interpreted as obstruction by public workers, and every one of the hundreds of workers in Bardoli can be brought under the penal section. But Sjt. Ravishankar has been singled out for the first honour and well does he deserve it. For with the exception of Sjt. Vallabhbhai, we in Gujarat have no more powerful and successful obstructor of the peaceful type.

That brings me to the very great emphasis being placed on peace and non-violence in all his speeches by Sjt. Vallabhbhai. In a sense we are glad that Government have now sent their C. I. D. reporters to report every one of his speeches, for if they have not realised yet, they will do so now that Sjt. Vallabhbhai has preserved peace and order much better than any of their officials who talk day in and day out of non-violence. At Kadod it seems people of several villages waited in deputation on him asking him not to include Kadod in the movement, without sufficient purificatory penance and guarantees. But Sjt. Vallabhbhai advised patience and tolerance, and said that sincere and genuine regret was sufficient security for their good will and good behaviour in future. Replying to the Collector's libel that there were threats of fire and violence and social boycott, he said in one of his speeches that fire and violence were not in the constitution of the people of Bardoli and that an organisation of society based on wise social boycott was much better and purer than the close corporation of the Indian Civil Service ever relying on brute force. In one of his speeches he said: "Never for a moment think that violence would be of any avail in this movement. No power on earth can beat the British Government in armed force, and they can, if they choose, bombard the whole Taluka. Do not raise your little finger even in face of the greatest provocation. In spite of the right of self-defence which I hold sacred, I say even if you are belaboured, do not hit back. For the slightest shadow of a pretext is sure to be abused by Government, and all the good that we have achieved would be rendered nugatory."

In another speech he said:

"The Collector says that there are people who would pay but who could not do so as there were threats of fire and violence. If there are any people who want to pay, and are afraid to do so for fear of fire and violence, I beseech them to come to me. I will take them to the Mamlatdar myself for the payment of their dues, and will afford them all the protection they may need. But I am sure there is not a single person who wants to pay and cannot pay because of the threats. No movement of this kind if based on coercion and terrorism can endure for such a long time against a Government with unlimited means of terrorism at its disposal. I am sure you will help me to render effectively all the police in the Taluka useless by your peaceful behaviour and leave them without any work."

In another speech full of fine moral fervour he said.

"I may in all humility say that I regard myself as a watchman responsible for the peace of the Taluka. I hold myself responsible to the man who is now watching the movement from his peaceful abode in Sabarmati. I prize more than anything else his name and his work which I cannot allow to be spoiled by a single mistake or error." In yet another speech he exhorted the people to behave towards the Government officials with courtesy and hospitality and to believe that they have no quarrel with them personally. M. D.

The latest news makes the picture of lawlessness still darker. 58 heads of cattle were lifted by a raiding party and driven to the Valod *thana*. The notice affixed at the *thana* simply says; '58 heads of cattle belonging to Rama Govind of Siker and others have been attached for arrears of revenue.' For want of men from the Taluka Pathans have been imported for taking care of the cattle impounded. This is how they are taken care of. one of the buffaloes impounded in Bardoli has died and another is on the point of death Blood-guilt is thus added to lawlessness.

The lifting of the whole herd of cattle in Siker shows that the Bardoli agriculturists are treated as a sort of unlimited liability company, jointly and severally responsible for the arrears of revenue. In a similar way all the khatedars in Isroli have been served with notices of forfeiture, and all the notices in Valod have been made absolute. One of the Valod heroes who has thus lost his valuable property celebrated the event by inviting friends and soldiers of Satyagraha to a party. That shows the unbreakable spirit of the people.

19 owners of carts and conveyances have been summoned to appear before the third class magistrate of Bardoli, for refusing to give their carts on hire for use of Government servants.

Two more cases of misappropriation—for it is nothing less—have occurred. An opium vendor in Bardoli offerred at the *kutchery* Rs. 105 for opium. Rs. 87-15-7 was credited to arrears of revenue and the balance returned. The same thing has happened in the case of a liquor-vendor of Puni, Rs. 42 being misappropriated for revenue out of Rs. 175 tendered by him for toddy

These little instances show that the Satyagraha in Bardoli will demand many more sacrifices, including the refusal by these vendors to purchase or sell the intoxicating drugs, forfeiture of lakhs and lakhs of rupees worth of land, and even a wholesale exodus from the land of terror and crime. That will raise the 'unlimited liability' of the Taluka to the highest pitch, and must in the end enable them to fix an unlimited liability on the whole British Government for all the misdeeds their agents are perpetrating M. D.

17th May, 1928.

THE ONLY ISSUE

By M. K. Gandhi

The Bardoli campaign is going on merrily. At the rate the forfeiture notices are being served, practically the whole of the Taluka of Bardoli should be in Government's possession and they can pay themselves a thousand times over for their precious assessment. The people of Bardoli if they are brave will be none the worse for dispossession. They will have lost their possessions but kept what must be the dearest of all to good men and women—their honour. Those who have stout hearts and hands need never fear loss of belongings.

But forfeiture notices having failed the Government are now adding to them the imprisonment of workers. They are holding mock trials such as we saw during the Punjab martial law days The prosecutor is asking for and the obliging special magistrate is giving deterrent sentences which are all rigorous. These too like dispossession will do good to the willing victims. Suffering willingly undergone never harms the sufferer.

What however goes against the grain is dishonesty and insolence of office. The Commissioner, Northern Division, has written a letter to a correspondent which is full of insulting insinuations and untruths

It is an untruthful insinuation to suggest that the campaign was started by Kheda agitators. It was started by the Bardoli people themselves and the only person whose help and advice they sought was Sjt. Vallabhbhai Patel whom I presume the Commissioner knows somewhat. Whether he can truthfully be called agitator in the sense intended by the Commissioner must be left to the reader to judge.

It is untruthful to say that the officers of the Government are subjected to 'spying, mobbing and other indignities.'

The workers are described as 'the swarm of agitators living on them (the people of Bardoli) and misguiding them' This is an insult for which under better times and if the nation was conscious of its strength the Commissioner would be made to offer a public apology. Let him know that those whom in his anger and intoxication of power he calls a 'swarm of agitators' are honourable servants of the nation giving their free services to Bardoli at considerable sacrifice. Among these, besides Vallabhbhai Patel who is a Barrister, are the hoary-headed Abbas Tyabji, another Barrister, and an ex-Chief Judge of Baroda, Imamsaheb Bawazir who is practically a fakir needing no support from Bardoli, and Dr. Sumant Mehta and his equally cultured wife. Dr. Sumant Mehta who has been ailing for some time has gone to Bardoli at considerable risk to his health These four by the way do not belong to Kheda at all. Then there is the Darbarsaheb of Dhasa and his intrepid wife Bhaktiba who for the sake of their country have sacrificed their estate. They are not living upon the people of Bardoli. There are Doctors Chandulal and Tribhuvandas again not of Kheda. Add to these Phulchand Shah, his wife, and his lieutenant Shivanand (already in gaol). Those again do not belong to Kheda and have for years dedicated themselves to silent service. It is the wail of Bardoli that has called these and others whom I can name. If the Commissioner has any sense of honour about him he will volunteer an apology to these ladies and gentlemen. In fact the Kheda workers are in a hopeless minority among the numerous workers.

The Commissioner pompously trots out the adverse vote of the Bombay Council and conveniently suppresses the two previous votes of the Council that had gone against the Government and that were by them treated as beneath contempt and beneath notice

The Commissioner suppresses the very relevant truth that before resorting to direct action the people of Bardoli tried every means known as constitutional to get redress and hopelessly failed

The Commissioner throws dust in the eyes of the public when he suggests that if the sorely tried people of Bardoli give up their campaign he would gladly investigate the case of any village that may be found to have been wrongly grouped. He suppresses the truth that the point at issue is not the wrong grouping of this village or that the point at issue is the palpably wrong method of assessment.. And *the people of Bardoli do not insist upon their point being accepted but they do insist upon an independent and impartial tribunal being appointed to investigate the justice of their complaint and to abide by the judgment of that tribunal whatever it may be* Here there is no shirking of payment, no question of redress of individual hardship. The question is one of principle. The people of Bardoli deny the right of the Government to dictate without proper investigation any increase in the assessment. Let me add that this is no no-tax campaign launched for any political end. This is a campaign directed towards a well defined specific grievance affecting the people of a whole Taluka.

It is therefore the height of impudence and gross untruth for the Commissioner to say:

"No one is more anxious than I that the poor cultivators should not be ruined by the swarm of agitators who are living on them and misguiding them."

"There are five talukas in Kaira District from which these agitators come, the revision settlements of which have been postponed for 2 years on account of floods. Nearly half a crore of rupees has been advanced by Government in Kaira District for flood relief in the last 7 or 8 months. If they succeed in Bardoli, the recovery of Government assessment and takavi in Kaira District would be imperilled."

If the 'agitators' succeed, it will not be the *takavi* to Kheda that will be in jeopardy. If it is withheld by the borrowers the Government will find the arch-agitator Vallabhbhai Patel to be their unpaid Collector of the loans. What however will happen if the agitators succeed is that the Government officers will not dare to insult honoured servants of the people and utter untruths as the Commissioner, Northern Division, has done and that the people will be able to have some redress against grossly unfair and unjust assessment as the Bardoli assessment is claimed to be.

One word to the people. The Government in their wisdom and in order to emphasise the fact that this rule is sustained by the policy of *divide et impera* have drafted in the midst of an overwhelmingly large Hindu population Musalman officials and Pathan hirelings As Satyagrahis the people can easily checkmate the Government. Let them treat the officials and the Pathans as friends. Let them not distrust or in any the slightest manner fear or molest them They the officials are our countrymen, the Pathans are our neighbours. Ere long the Government will discover their mistake and know that the honour of a Hindu is as dear to a Musalman as to a Hindu and *vice versa*. The people of Bardoli have the chance of demonstrating this in a concrete manner Let them vindicate the law of Satyagraha which is also the law of Love and they will melt even the stony heart of an autocratic Commissioner.

31st May, 1928

BARDOLI ON TRIAL

BY M. K. GANDHI

One may hastily think that the Government is on its trial in Bardoli. But that would be a wrong opinion. The Government has been tried and found wanting scores of times 'Frightfulness' is its code of conduct when its vital parts are affected. If its prestige or its revenue is in danger, it seeks to sustain it either by means fair or foul. It does not hesitate to resort to terrorism and cover it with unblushing untruths. The latest information that Pathans are now being posted in villages with instructions to surround the houses of the villagers day and night need not cause either surprise or anger. The surprise is that they have not yet let loose in Bardoli a punitive police and declared martial law. We ought by this time to know what a punitive police or martial law means. It is evident that by the latest form of 'frightfulness' the Government is seeking to goad people into some act of violence, be it ever so slight, to justify their enactment of the last act in the tragedy.

Will the people of Bardoli stand this last trial? They have already staggered Indian humanity. They have shown heroic patience in the midst of great provocation. Will they stand the greatest provocation that can be offered? If they will, they will have gained everything. Imprisonments, forfeitures, deportations, death must all be taken in the ordinary course by those who count honour before everything else. When the terror becomes unbearable, let the people leave the land they have hitherto believed to be theirs. It is wisdom to vacate houses or places that are plague-infected. Tyranny is a kind of plague and when it is likely to make us angry or weak, it is wisdom to leave the scene of such temptation. History is full of instances of brave people having sought exile in preference to surrender to *zoolum*.

Let me hope, however, that such a step will not be necessary. One hears rumours of intercessions by well-meaning friends. They have the right, it may be even their duty, to intercede. But let these friends realise the significance of the movement. They are not to represent a weak cause or a weak people. The people of Bardoli stand for an absolutely just cause. They ask no favour, they seek only justice. They do not ask any one to consider their case to be true. Their cause is to seek an independent, open, judicial inquiry and they undertake to abide by the verdict of such a tribunal. To deny the tribunal is to deny justice which the Government have hitherto done. The means at the disposal of the people are self-suffering. In such a cause then minimum and maximum are almost convertible terms. Those who rely upon self-suffering for redress of a grievance cannot afford to rate it higher than it actually is. Those therefore who will intervene will harm the people and their cause, if they do not appreciate the implications of the struggle which cannot be lightly given up or compromised.

The public have a duty to perform by the Satyagrahis. The response is already being made to Vallabhbhai's appeal *for* funds. It will be remembered that he refused to make the appeal as long as it was possible to refrain. The imprisonments have made the appeal imperative. I have no doubt that the response will be quick and generous. Equally necessary is the expression of enlightened public opinion. Let the public study the facts carefully and then cover the whole of the land with public meetings. I like the suggestion made by Sjt. Jairamdas that June 12th or any other suitable day should be proclaimed as Bardoli day when meetings representing all parties may be held to pass resolutions and make collections in aid of the sufferers of Bardoli.

7th June, 1928

THE TWO SIDES

BY M. K. GANDHI

The communique of the Government of Bombay on the Bardoli Satyagraha is in keeping with the letter of the Commissioner, Northern Division, which I had the painful duty of criticising only the other day. This communique opens with a repetition of the insult that Sjt. Vallabhbhai and his co-workers are outsiders. Instead of being described as such they are described as 'persons who do not reside there' (in Bardoli). The communique then shamelessly refers to the fact that when the attempt at distraint had failed, the Government resorted to an 'organised attachment of buffaloes and moveable property.' Sjt. Vallabhbhai's publicity department has shown what the attachment of buffaloes has meant. The communique further triumphantly refers to the fact that 'forty Pathans were obtained to assist the Mamlatdar and Mahalkaris in the work of attachment and the care of animals attached.' The publicity department has again shown us what the introduction of Pathans has meant. Even without the assistance of that department, we could have guessed the meaning of this introduction. Whether it is the Government or private people who employ Pathans, people know why the services of these friends are enlisted. Lest, however, the accepted meaning might be attached to the enlistment of Pathans, the communique proceeds: 'Unfounded allegations have been made against these Pathans. Government are satisfied that their conduct has been exemplary in every respect.' Who does not laugh at this explanation? If as the Government contend, the Pathans have been employed in order to replace the *vethias* who are alleged to be under threat of excommunication, it is relevant to ask why Pathans have been chosen instead of *vethias* from other places or some other mild-mannered men. The Government pooh-pooh the notion as incredible that 'five parties, each of five Pathans, working under the eye of a responsible officer of Government, can terrorise a population of 90,000 persons.' Again experience of the people of India shows what one Pathan armed with authority can do in a whole village. It is no doubt humiliating to think that Pathans or anybody else can terrorise large masses of men, but unfortunately it is a fact of daily occurrence in this fear-ridden terror-stricken India. And I would consider the Bardoli struggle to be well fought, even without any further result, if the people of Bardoli shed their fear of men and authority and turn the Pathans into friends.

But the communique is not satisfied with a recital of the coercive measures taken in respect of moveable property; it refers to forfeiture of lands. The Government are not ashamed to own that 'up to date of the communique 1,400 acres of such land have been disposed of under forfeiture notices and that about 5,000 acres more will be disposed of in due course unless the arrears due thereon be sooner paid,' and unnecessarily add that 'such lands once disposed of would never be returned.' There are several other statements in the communique which are open to criticism, but I forbear.

The communique announces some insulting accommodation for those who would pay the assessment on or before the 19th instant. It is for the people of Bardoli to return the only answer open to self-respecting men and women. When they embarked upon this struggle, they knew the cost of resistance. I have little doubt that they will not fail to render a good account of themselves when the last heat of the struggle commences as they did during the opening stages.

In marked contrast to the communique comes the letter addressed to me by Sjt. Vithalbhai Patel announcing a handsome monthly donation of Rs 1,000 so long as the struggle lasts. Throughout his brilliant career as the Speaker of the Assembly Sjt. Vithalbhai Patel has upheld the rights of the people. Occupancy of office has not in the slightest degree made him lose his head or compromise the honour of his country. Whilst he has acted with strict impartiality he has neither hesitated nor been afraid to act on behalf of the people wherever the holding of his office has permitted him to do so. The alien rulers have established a slavish tradition that those who are in the pay of the Government must in all circumstances refrain from showing their sympathy for the people when the latter engage in any fight with the Government, and this even when the Government act in a manner contrary to laws promulgated by themselves. Sjt. Vithalbhai Patel has broken through that unhealthy and slavish tradition and has been able to do so because he has accepted his office not for its honour, not for the salary it brings him, but as he puts it in his letter, as a trust on behalf of those who have elected him to the office. It must be remembered that the Speaker is not a statutory servant of the Crown. He is a popular representative and without taking an active part in political controversies and the like, he has a perfect right to show his sympathy for the people. Having been elected as the Speaker, Sjt. Vithalbhai ceased to be a party man; but he did not and could not cease to be a representative of the combined parties who called him to preside over their deliberations. I therefore tender him my congratulations for the manly stand he has taken up on behalf of the people. If entry into legislative bodies created by the alien Government can be held at all justifiable, he has shown to those who may enter these bodies and accept office the way to act nobly and fearlessly.

I hope that the Bardoli day, that is, 12th June next will be observed throughout India in an earnest and becoming manner. The best way to do so is, wherever, it is possible to suspend all work and devote the day to collection of funds for the Satyagrahi sufferers and for helping Sjt. Vallabhbhai Patel and his band of workers in carrying on the struggle, and have mass meetings where further collections should be made and resolutions passed supporting the demand of the Satyagrahis and condemning the coercive measures of the Government. I do not think that there should be a call for volunteers, because Sjt. Vallabhbhai Patel has already enough for his requirements. Offers have been received from all parts of the country. And if more are required, I have no doubt that there are volunteers ready all over the country. Friends from Maharashtra, Sindh and elsewhere have already sent me messages that Vallabhbhai could rely upon almost an unlimited number. There may be unwarrantable optimism in this language, but after due allowance is made, there is no doubt that enough men and women, if necessary, will be forthcoming when and if the call comes.

21st June, 1928

BARDOLI BUNGLE

BY M. K. GANDHI

The more the Government excuses itself in the Bardoli case, the more it accuses itself. The long letters of H. E. the Governor written to Sjt. Munshi make confusion worse confounded and do not improve its position even in the estimation of a constitutionalist as Sjt. Munshi claims to be

The Governor's letters altogether evade the issue. His Excellency claims that another inquiry has already been made and assures his correspondent that 'there is not one member of Government who is not fully satisfied as to the justice of Government's action and in fact I should use the word generosity.'

This is moving in a circle. If the Government were to make fifty inquiries of the type mentioned in the correspondence, they would not improve matters for it. On the contrary, these inquires would prove its perverse determination to give a stone each time the Bardoli people ask for bread. They do not want a hole and corner inquiry in which they are not usefully and effectively represented and which is not open and independent. They contend that what the Government regards as just, even generous, the people believe to be unjust and oppressive ! They contend, and these columns have attempted to show why, that Mr. Jayakar's and Mr. Anderson's reports are worthless, full of misstatements and errors even of calculation. They undertake to substantiate their contention before an open, impartial and independent committee.

The Government proudly and with fatiguing reiteration tells the public that they accepted neither Mr. Jayakar's rate of assessment, i. e, 30 per cent. increase, nor Mr. Anderson's, i. e, 29 percent. increase (a generous reduction indeed upon 30 per cent), but that they reduced the increase to 20 per cent. And now we are informed by the Governor that this reduction was not only just but even generous. What the people want is not generosity but justice pure and simple, and they submit that even the 20 per cent. increase is unwarranted by facts, unwarranted by the condition of the agriculturists. His Excellency on the other hand protests that if a committee was appointed, it would be found that the increase should have been much higher. If that is the sincere belief of the Government, why does it not accept the very reasonable prayer of the people for the appointment of a proper committee by whose decision they declare they are willing to abide?

When the people challenge the findings of officers of the Government, it is monstrous, it is insulting to throw in their teeth the reports of other officers who base their conclusions upon mere documents often varnished and more often superficial If the Governor is desirous, as he professes to be, of acting on the square, let him accept the honourable offer sealed and sanctified as it is with the sufferings of the people for whom His Excellency makes in his letters profuse avowal of anxious sympathy.

But, declares the Governor, the 'outsiders,' whom the Commissioner N. D. has made famous by his insulting libel, stand in the way of the full flow of that sympathy. If they are in the way of the agriculturists 'who,' the Governor claims to 'know well,' 'would all pay up the assessment as many are now doing, if they are allowed to,' why does he not summarily remove these objectionable tresspassers? The Government has been hitherto always found to be resourceful enough to remove all the 'tall poppies' it has discovered inconveniently in its way. Why then is it leaving alone this (in the elegant language of the Commissioner N. D) 'swarm of agitators from Kheda living on the poor people of Bardoli' and allowing the innocent peasants to become a prey alike to the 'agitators' and the Pathans now to be replaced by the organised police drafted into Bardoli?

The Governor is in such a hurry to justify his 'constitutional' position and discredit Sjt. Vallabhbhai Patel and his faithful companions, that forgetful of his statement in one letter that there were 40 Pathans, in another, he says there were only 25. But of the Pathans I shall have to say more in another article.

The Governor seeks to justify the assessment in Bardoli on the ground that the people of Chorasi who are similarly assessed have not resisted the enhancement. I know nothing of the case of Chorasi. But I do know this that many a wrong has been submitted to before now by the people of India earning for them (in their case) the uncomplimentary title of 'the gentle Hindoo.' It may be that the people of Chorasi are too weak to resist the levy, whereas the people of Bardoli having been under healthy influence for the past six years have found themselves strong and willing enough for sufferings that must be entailed in resisting a Government that has become notorious for its unscrupulousness and frightfulness.

Here is the naked paw. Says His Excellency:

> "Why should Government give up its undoubted right of administration to, as you suggest, the decision of some independent committee? I am anxious to meet the situation in every way that is possible, but no Government would be worth the name of Government which allowed such a thing to happen."

'The undoubted right of administration' is the uncontrolled license to bleed India to the point of starvation. The license would be somewhat controlled if an independent committee were appointed to adjust the points in dispute between the people and the executive authority. Let it be noted that the independent committee does not mean a committee independent of the Government. It means a committee appointed by the Government of men known to be independent of official pressure and authorised to hold the enquiry in the open with the right to the aggrieved people to be duly and effectively represented. But such an open enquiry means the death knell of the secret, autocratic revenue policy of the Government. Where is, in the modest demand of the people, the slightest 'usurpation of the functions of Government?' But even the least check upon the utter independence of the executive officers is enough to send the Government into a fury. And when the British lion is in a fury in British India, God help the 'gentle Hindoo.' Well, God does help the helpless and He only helps when man is utterly helpless. The people of India have found in Satyagraha the God-given infallible *gandiva* of self-suffering. Under its stimulating influence the people are slowly waking up from the lethargy of ages. The Bardoli peasants are but showing India, that weak as they are, they have got the courage to suffer for their convictions.

It is too late in the day to call Satyagraha unconstitutional when truth and its fellow—self-sacrifice—become unlawful. Lord Hardinge blessed the South African Satyagraha and even the all-powerful Union Government gracefully bent before it. Both Lord Chelmsford, the then Viceroy, and Sir Edward Gait, the then Governor of Bihar, recognised its legitimacy and efficacy and an independent committee was appointed resulting in adding to the prestige of the Government and resulting in the ending of a century-old wrong. It was then recognised in Kheda and a settlement, reluctant, half-hearted and incomplete as it was, was made between the Government agents in Kheda and those who were guiding the movement and the people. The then Governor of the Central Provinces condescended to treat with the Nagpur Flag Satyagrahis and released the prisioners and recognised the right claimed by the Satyagrahis. Last but not least Sir Leslie Wilson himself when he was yet untouched by the atmosphere of the 'most efficient service in the world' recognised its efficacy in Borsad and granted the the Borsad people relief.

I wish both His Excellency the Governor and Sjt. Munshi will take note of these facts that have happened within the past fourteen years. Satyagraha in Bardoli cannot now be suddenly declared unconstitutional. The fact is the Government have no case. They do not want their revenue policy to be challenged at an open enquiry. If the Bardoli people can stand the final heat, they will have the open enquiry or the withdrawal of the enhancement. It is their undoubted right to claim for their grievance a hearing before an impartial tribunal.

28th June, 1928

SOME PARALLELS

BY M. K GANDHI

A comparison between the utterances of some of the officials in Bardoli and those during the Satyagraha in Kheda in 1918 reveals the same bureaucratic mind, the same spirit of vindictiveness and tyranny, and the same mendacity. The actual methods employed today are of course unparalleled in lawlessness and brutality, but the mind at the back of them is the same. Mr. Pratt, the Commissioner in those days, was more polite and courteous. He referred to Gandhiji as his 'friend' and 'a pure and saintly character,' and to Sjt. Vallabhbhai as 'Meherban Vallabhbhai Saheb' To Mr. Smart, Sjt. Vallabhbhai and his comrades are 'a swarm of agitators living on the people of Bardoli,' and to the Collector of Surat' they are N.-C-O. leaders who have no land in Bardoli to lose,' and 'false prophets born to make others miserable,'' words used in a *shubha-vachana* (gospel !) issued by Mr. Hartshorne. These different epithets reveal the different culture of those who have used them, though they belong to the same bureaucratic stock. But though their language is therefore different, their argument is the same, their threats are identical and even their misrepresentations bear the same character. Mr. Pratt said: 'You say Mr. Gandhi is fighting for the poor. I ask you to consider who is more solicitous of their interests—Mr. Gandhi or Government? Have you forgotten the famine of 1900? Have you forgotten the many relief works opened and the lakhs of rupees given as *tagavi*?' Mr. Hartshorne today publishes the Leslie-Munshi correspondence with this preface: 'It was because of His Excellency's and his Government's sympathy and solicitude for the afflicted peasants that a crore of rupees were distributed as relief to those afflicted by the floods in Gujarat'

Let us take a sample of misrepresentation. Mr. Pratt said to the Kheda peasants that vows wrongly taken could be broken, even as the Ahmedabad mill strikers had knowingly broken their vow. Now that was a palpable distortion. Mr. Hartshorne in his 'gospel' fares no better. When Sjt. Vallabhbhai asks the brave peasant of

Bardoli to stand firm against rifles and machine guns and prefer to be riddled by bullets and to allow his bones to be manure rather than allow an outsider to put his plough in his field, Mr. Hartshorne says the N.-C.-O. leaders have forgotten all their talk of non-violence and 'are talking of war and bloodshed and firing and bones for manure.' Messrs. Smart and Hartshorne are not tired of repeating that lands worth thousands will be forfeited and sold and will never be returned. Mr. Pratt also said: 'The lands of those who do not pay will be confiscated. Those who are contumacious will get no lands in future. Government do not want their names on their Record of Rights. Those who get out shall never be admitted again.'

It is against this spirit that Kheda fought and Bardoli is fighting a fight unto death.

PUBLICITY

There was no publicity on behalf of Government in the Kheda days. But at the time of the Borsad Satyagraha the Director of Information appeared on the scene, towards the close of the struggle, with a defence of Government extending over six columns of the *Bombay Chronicle*. It received a fitting reply, and within a few days Sir Leslie Wilson remitted the whole of the punitive impost of Rs. 2 lakhs and odd. The Director of Information has now spoken about Bardoli too, after four months of the severest indictment by the Satyagraha publicity office of the Government policy and methods, and not one of his statements bears analysis, as has been amply shown in these columns. But why only in defence of the Pathans, and not a word regarding the numerous allegations of lawlessness that have been made in the Satyagraha publicity leaflets and have now been repeated by intrepid critics of those methods like Sjt. Nariman, Bulabhai Desai and Munshi? The fact is there is not a vestige of defence that they can put forward.

GAME STILL ON

And the process of spoliation is still going on. Here is perhaps the worst case of reckless disposal of forfeited property that has come to light. A buffalo worth Rs. 150 and a young buffalo in calf worth Rs. 60, belonging to Khatedar Ranchhod Gopaldas of Varad have been sold for Rs. 4-8-0 and the same amount credited to his account and receipt for it has been sent to him. The Khatedar has addressed a manly letter to the Mamlatdar returning the amount and the receipt.

THE SATYAGRAHA FUND

The Bardoli Satyagraha Fund, let it be known, is primarily for the prosecution of the Satyagraha. There are about 250 workers posted in different camps in Bardoli, there is a big public kitchen at Bardoli and a publicity office which daily publishes 13,000 copies of its leaflets and distributes them free There are other items of expenditure, *e. g*, petrol, conveyance, postage, etc, and if the struggle is to go on it is likely that more and more funds will be wanted. No relief, let it be remembered, is necessary, at the present moment at any rate, for the afflicted peasant of Bardoli He is too proud to ask for or accept any relief, though I know that some donors do earmark their donations for relief to those who have lost their buffaloes etc. But practically all the amounts received at Bardoli from numerous villages in Gujarat, and all the amounts received at the Ashram from various friends in India, which today total over Rs. 1,50,000, have been given for the prosecution of the Satyagraha.

Some of them are worthy of note The Labour Union of Ahmedabad has sent its first contribution of Rs 500. The Union has issued one anna tickets and the mill hands who are following the struggle week after week have gladly responded. More contributions are coming in and the Union hopes to send more instalments. Another notable contribution is by the students of the Gurukul, Supa, who, true to their traditions, denied themselves milk and ghi for some days, engaged in manual labour, and sent their contribution of Rs. 65 to the fund. The workers gave Rs. 85.

In a letter to Gandhiji sending a contribution of Rs. 250, a friend from Gurukul, Kangdi writes:

"We celebrated the Bardoli Day in a fitting manner. The Brahmacharis earned Rs. 50 by manual labour for two days, *e.g.* repairing portions damaged by the last cyclone, cutting down trees, etc. The Gurukul workers collected from amongst themselves.

Rs. 200. This contribution, it would be interesting to note, includes Re. 1 from a cook who came forward with his contribution, quite unasked."

A third contribution which is worthy of note, from a different point of view, was one amounting to Rs. 2,448-8-0 from the agriculturists of Chorasi—Chorasi, which, though as much hard hit as Bardoli, is said not to object to the enhancement. With one voice the agriculturists who had gathered at Vanjh, where they presented the purses to Sjt. Vallabhbhai, declared that they had exhausted all constitutional remedies and that they had paid the enhanced revenue under protest, as they were not then organised enough for Satyagraha.

M. D.

26th July, 1928

AN APPEAL TO GOVERNMENT

BY M. K. GANDHI

By the time this appears in print probably the Bombay Government would have made its final decision on the Bardoli question. I am framing this appeal on Monday afternoon when probably the Governor is making his statement before the Council. I know too that the appeal will fall on deaf ears. But as a Satyagrahi, it is not for me to yield to my fear but to do what is right in disregard of consequence. As one intimately connected with the movement, it is perhaps my duty to appeal to the Government to desist from a course which has been universally condemned and which, so far as I am able to judge impartially, cannot be defended on any ground whatsoever.

The offer made at Surat is less than what according to reliable rumour had been offered privately. The conditions named by Sjt. Vallabhbhai Patel have been the conditions always contemplated by him and in various ways conveyed to the Government. He has asked for nothing that has not always been done in honourable settlements. If it is acknowledged, as it has been acknowledged even in unexpected quarters, that people of Bardoli and Valod have undergone terrible sufferings for the sake of what to them is a matter of principle, they have not done so merely to have an inquiry by a subordinate revenue official into individual cases which the inquiry proposed by the Government amounts to in fact; nor can the people be expected to forego valuable land which they contend has been wrongly forfeited; nor yet can they as honourable men and women leave in the lurch those who have been wrongly made to suffer. The Government offer means that although the people have done wrong in refusing payment of the enhancement, they would graciously re-open individual cases if the people will cease to do wrong and if they will deposit the very amount which they say is wrongly imposed on them. This is a position which no leader worth the name can possibly subscribe to, when he has no conviction of such wrong on the part of the people and when on the contrary he has the deep conviction that the people are altogether in the right and the Government hopelessly in the wrong

But Sjt Vallabhbhai does not make, like the Government, impossible conditions. He does not ask the Government to own themselves to be in the wrong. His letter reduced to one sentence asks Government to refer the question of right or wrong to a committee of the Government's choice with the only reasonable proviso that it will adequately represent the people. And in making his counter proposal he asks the Government to recognise the natural and logical consequence of such an impartial committee, *viz*, to revert to the *status quo ante bellum.* I venture to suggest that he would be guilty of a gross breach of trust if he asked for or took less. In his proposal there is no humiliation intended or implied of the Government. His reasonableness and anxiety to come to any honourable compromise limits him to the barest minimum. For it is surely open to him to raise the whole question of the revenue policy of the Government and for damages for the terrible losses suffered by the people during the past four months without any fault of theirs.

Two courses are open to the Government—either to bow to the public opinion of all India and accept Sjt. Vallabhbhai's offer or in order to uphold a false prestige to reassert the doctrine of fright-

fulness. If it is not too late, I appeal to the Bombay Government to take the way of truth.

2nd August, 1928

LIMITATIONS OF SATYAGRAHA

BY M. K. GANDHI

Sardar Sardul Singh is an esteemed worker. His open letter advising me to invite sympathetic civil disobedience for Bardoli demands a reply especially because it enables me to clear my own position. If Bardoli Satyagraha were a campaign of lawlessness as the Government paint it, nothing would be more tempting or more natural than sympathetic Satyagraha and that too without the limits prescribed in the Sardar's letter. But the Sardar rightly says: 'I find in prominent Gujarat workers a tendency to allow Bardoli peasants to be kept isolated. This impression has been created in my mind by the reports of Sjt. Vallabhbhai's speeches and your writings. Friends think that any more scruples on this point go beyond the limits of practical politics.'

The Sardar's impression is correct. In order strictly to limit the scope of the struggle to the purely local and economic issue and to keep it non-political Sjt. Vallabhbhai would not let Sjt. Rajagopalachari and other leaders to go to Bardoli. It was only when the Government gave it a political character and made it an all-India issue by their coercive measures that the reins were loosened and Vallabhbhai could no longer prevent public men from going to Bardoli, though where his advice or permission was sought, he said, 'not yet.'

I do not know what Sjt. Vallabhbhai Patel would say to the Sardar's suggestion but I can say, 'Not yet.' Time has not come even for limited sympathetic Satyagraha. Bardoli has still to prove its mettle. If it can stand the last heat and if the Government go to the farthest limit, nothing that I or Sjt. Vallabhbhai can do will stop the spread of Satyagraha or limit the issue to a *bona fide* re-inquiry and its logical consequence. The limit will then be prescribed by the capacity of India as a whole for self-sacrifice and self-

suffering. If that manifestation is to come it will be natural and incapable of being stayed by any agency no matter how powerful. But so far as I understand the spirit of Satyagraha and its working, it is the duty of Sjt. Vallabhbhai and myself to keep to the original limits in spite of the Government provocations which are strong enough even as they are to warrant the crossing of the original boundary.

The fact is that Satyagraha presupposes the living presence and guidance of God The leader depends not on his own strength but on that of God. He acts as the Voice within guides him Very often therefore what are practical politics so-called are unrealities to him, though in the end his prove to be the most practical politics. All this may sound foolish and visionary on the eve of what bids fair to become the toughest battle that India has hitherto had to face. But I would be untrue to the nation and myself if I failed to say what I feel to be the deepest truth. If the people of Bardoli are what Vallabhbhai believes them to be, all will be well, in spite of the use of all the weapons that the Government may have at its command. Let us wait and see. Only let the M. L. C.'s and others who are interested in compromises not take a single weak step in the hope of saving the people of Bardoli. They are safe in the hands of God.

9th August, 1928

ALL'S WELL

By M. K. Gandhi

It is a matter for sincere joy that the settlement has at last been reached over the Bardoli Satyagraha. All's well that ends well I tender my congratulations both to the Government of Bombay and the people of Bardoli and Valod and Sjt. Vallabhbhai without whose firmness as well as gentleness the settlement would have been impossible. The reader will note that the Satyagrahis have achieved practically all that they had asked for. The terms of reference to the Committee of Enquiry are all that could be desired. True there is to be no inquiry into the allegations about

the coercive measures adopted by the Government to enforce payment. But it was generous on the part of Sjt. Vallabhbhai to waive the condition, seeing that the lands forfeited including lands sold are to be restored, the Talatis are to be reinstated and other minor matters are to be attended to. It is well not to rake up old wrongs for which beyond the reparation made there can be no other remedy. The injury into the assessment question will be carried in a calmer atmosphere for the waiver of the clause about the coercive processes.

Let not the Satyagrahis sleep over their well deserved victory. They have to collect and collate material to prove their allegations about the assessment.

And above all, if they are to consolidate their position, they must proceed with constructive work with redoubled vigour. Their strength lies in their ability and willingness to handle this difficult slow and unpretentious work of construction. They have to rid themselves of many social abuses. They must better their economic condition by attention to the charkha. It was the charkha that led to the awakening among them. They must remove the reproach of drink from their midst. They must attend to village sanitation and have a properly managed school in every village The so-called higher classes must befriend the depressed and the suppressed classes. The greater the attention given to these matters, the greater will be their ability to face crises like the one they had just gone through.

The noble band of volunteers who had the privilege of serving under Vallabhbhai deserve the highest praise for their devotion and splendid discipline. The task is not yet finished. Those who can spare time must help the Sardar in his constructive work.

9th August, 1928

GANDHIJI IN BARDOLI

In anticipation of the developments that might take place after the expiry of Monday the 6th Gandhiji shifted to Bardoli on Thursday. "I am going to Bardoli in response to the command of the Sardar," said he on the eve of starting for Bardoli. "Of course

Vallabhbhai often consults me, but does not a commander consult even a private serving under him? I am going to Bardoli not to take Vallabhbhai's place but to serve under him." On coming to Bardoli he maintained the same attitude and has emphasised it at several places to burn the lesson of discipline indelibly on the minds of all engaged in public work.

Peasants from various places came wading through water and mire to pay their respects to Gandhiji. 'We have surrendered our head to the Sardar, not our honour (lit nose),' said a group of them. 'Then you may be sure that your honour is safe,' said Gandhiji. 'But a greater test is still to come. When you have stood the final heat, victory is yours. But tell me one thing. Supposing Vallabhbhai is taken away and others also with him, won't you be cowed down?' 'No fear,' said one of them with firmness. 'Vallabhbhai has done enough to turn our iron into steel, and we know that the only thing we have to do is to be true to our word, even if the very heavens fall.'

Gandhiji was delighted Some friend suggested that he should visit some of the villages. 'Not unless Vallabhbhai wants me to do so' was the reply. It was only at Vallabhbhai's desire that Gandhiji visited Sarbhon and Rayam and met there hundreds of peasants from scores of villages in the vicinity. At Sarbhon he met the redoubtable Talatis who of course were deservedly congratulated. 'But,' said Gandhiji warning them gently, 'you must now keep the high reputation that you have earned. The Talatis in general had acquired a bad name as oppressors of the people. You have by your noble stand washed that away. Let your conduct in times of peace be in keeping with the good name you have earned.' There was no speech—a speech being out of the question in veiw of the general instructions of the Sardar that no one but he should make any speeches. The gathering at Rayam was, however, very large, there were men from many villages all waiting in the sun, a nice, spinning demonstration, hundreds of women and a stream of them laying their contributions at his feet. A speech even by way of excusing himself was therefore necessary. It became another sermon on the importance of discipline. 'I cannot speak as the order of the Sardar is clear,' he said. 'If he had been here and asked me to speak I should have done so. But today I cannot do anything more than congratulate you on your bravery and on your unity. I was glad to see the spinning demonstration, but I cannot even speak about the charkha. It should be a principle with us implicitly to obey the commands or instructions of one whom we have chosen to be our Sardar. I admit I am Vallabhbhai's elder brother, but in public life no matter whether one is father or elder brother of the man under whom one serves, one must obey his instructions. It is not a new law. It used to be a law even in ancient times. It was that spirit of discipline which made such a mighty personality as Lord Krishna humbly serve as Arjuna's charioteer and serve as the meanest of the menials on the occasion of King Yudhishthira's Rajasuya sacrifice. I cannot therefore do anything more than congratulate you. It was Vallabhbhai who made you famous throughout India. But it was Government who made you famous throughout the world. May you achieve even greater things in future."

VALLABHBHAI IN POONA

Never has there been a more strenuous effort than is at present going on to prove the truth of Lord Curzon's phrase that journalism is an art of intelligent anticipation. I shall not enter the lists, but shall confine myself to facts. Vallabhbhai had no hope but it was for the Gujarat members that he went to Poona, as it was on their behalf that he had received the invitation. The headline that a newspaper wag put at the top of his papar 'Vallabhbhai will be guest of Sir Chunilal Mehta on the eve of his arrest?' indicated people's hopes and fears. Thanks to the good-will that has come into our public life since non-co-operation days, a rebel like Vallabhbhai may be Sir Chunilal's guest on the eve of his arrest. On the day he left Poona there was a large crowd at the station mostly composed of students and Congress Committee friends. A prominent member of the station staff requested Sjt. Vallabhbhai for his autograph which was gladly given and then many others took up the hint A Sikh friend went one better by placing his humble contribution before Vallabhbhai and then asking for his autograph, to be given in a copy of *Gita Rahasya* that he had newly purchased.

Everywhere friends and strangers surrounded him, on running trains and on station platforms, and all wished more strength to his elbow. That is an indication of the very wide public interest that the movement has aroused and an inarticulate desire on the part of the public to see it through.

THE INQUIRY

Whatever may be the ultimate issue of the present struggle there can be no mistaking the fact the people are up against a dead wall and that they are fighting for the recognition on the part of Government that a Settlement Officer cannot be the sole arbitrator of the destinies of the people. The fight, like that for the separation of judicial and executive functions, has been an old one, as old as 1873 when in an appeal preferred in the High Court in an assessment suit, the High Court decided the case against the Settlement Officer and in favour of the plaintiff. A storm of agitation raged over the decision and the Bombay Revenue Jurisdiction Act was passed excluding the jurisdiction of the Civil Courts in matters of assessments, and barring all chances for the peasant of seeking an independent tribunal to appeal to against a blundering settlement officer's decision. "My Lord," said the late R. C. Dutt, in his 'Open Letters to Lord Curzon,' "I do not wish to make any reflection against a Revenue Officer. I have been a Revenue Officer myself all through my official career, and I speak from personal knowledge when I state that Revenue Officers endeavour to perform their difficult and onerous duties as justly and conscientiously as a Judicial Officer or as any other class of officers in India. But it will appear from a moment's reflection that in the matter of assessment suits the Revenue Officer and Settlement Officer *are virtually party to the suit*, and it cannot meet the ends of justice if they are made the final judges in such suits The failure of justice which often results from this iniquitable system is" obvious. Now a fight for a repeal of that iniqitous Revenue Jurisdiction Act, or for the introduction of suitable legislation was hardly the Bardoli peasants' business, and certainly not in their non-co-operating leader's line. They therefore confine their demand to the appointment of a judicial inquiry and thus pave the way for ending the iniquity. The disease is old, the remedy applied is new.

M. D

16th August, 1928

A SIGN OF THE TIMES

BY M. K. GANDHI

Bardoli is a sign of the times It has a lesson both for the Government and the people—for the Government if they will recognise the power of the people when they have truth on their side and when they can form a non-violent combination to vindicate it. By such recognition a wise Government consolidates its power which is then built upon people's goodwill and co-operation not merely in act enforced by brute power but in speech and thought as well. Non-violent energy properly stored up sets free a force that becomes irresistible. So far as I have been able to see there is no doubt that the settlement has been wrung from an unwilling Government by the pressure of a public opinion that was ever gathering force in geometrical progression. It is said that His Excellency the Governor was most willing from the commencement to concede the Satyagrahis' demands but that his advisers were equally determined in their opposition. If that is so, whilst it reflects credit upon the Governor, it bodes ill for the Government; for the British Government is not individualistic, it is a powerful organisation capable of working irrespective of individuals. It has persisted without Gladstone and Disraeli, without Kitchener and Roberts. The organisation behind the Government in India is the Civil Service What the Sardar of Bardoli wanted was a change of heart in the Civil Service. What one is told and observes is that the Civil Service is not satisfied with the Settlement. If it was satisfied the persistent campaign of lies carried on about the Sardar and his doings would have stopped. Whilst I was in Bardoli, I constantly heard the complaint through inspired newspaper paragraphs that Vallabhbhai Patel had not carried out his part of the settlement, and I knew that he was carrying it out as fast as he could and had already carried out that part of it about which the complaint was made and before it was made. I can only say that the Government, if it is true that the Civil Service is resisting the settlement, is doomed, assuming of course that the non-violence of Bardoli is an organisation capable of being sustained without particular individuals.

Let us therefore turn to the people of Bardoli. The lesson that they have to learn is that so long as they remain united in non-violence they have nothing to fear, not even unwilling officials. But have they learnt that lesson, have they recognised the unseen power of non-violence, have they realised that if they had committed one single act of violence, they would have lost their cause? If they have, then they will know from day to day that they will not become a non-violent organisation unless they undergo a process of what may be called continuous corporate cleansing. This they can only do by engaging in carrying out a well thought out constructive programme requiring combined effort and promoting common good. In other words before they can claim to have become a non-violent organisation, they must receive education in non-violence not through speeches or writings necessary as both may be, but through an unbroken series of corporate acts each evoking the spirit of non-violence. Sjt. Vallabhbhai Patel knows what he is about. He has set for himself this more difficult task of constructive effort or internal reform. May God grant him therein the same measure of success that has attended the struggle against the Government.

REMEMBER 192

M. K. GANDHI

The following is a condensed summary of Gandhiji's speech at Surat on the occasion of the Bardoli victory celebrations:

'For a Satyagrahi nothing can be truer than to say that no one but God is to be thanked and praised for the triumph of the Bardoli Satyagraha. Indeed we need say nothing more. But I know that that is not going to give us satisfaction, for the conviction has not yet gone home to us that we are but instruments in His hand and He uses us as He wills We have not yet learnt the virtue of surrender to God. Man is yet part man part beast, indeed more beast than man and so his ego is not satisfied with praising God alone. In fact in remembering Him on occasions like this we feel as though we were obliging Him. Following our animal nature therefore we may congratulate our Sardar, his companions and his volunteers and the men and women of Bardoli. Vallabhbhai alone would not have won the battle without the faithful co-operation of his co-workers. But even so should we thank His Excellency the Governor, the officials, and M.L.C.s for their having helped in bringing about a happy settlement. We should be lacking in humility, we should be so much the less Satyagrahis if we failed in our duty to render our thanks to those who were opposed to us.

'The vast gathering of the citizens of Surat, seated before me on wet earth, with so much inconvenience to themselves, reminds me of 1921. I still remember the words I addressed to you in 1921 on this very spot. Possibly some of you also can recall what I said, and I propose to remind you how we have failed to do the things that we decided to do seven years ago. The lesson of Bardoli will have been lost on us if Bardoli and Surat go to sleep over the Bardoli victory after having had victory celebrations and dinners. Vallabhbhai has been telling the Bardoli people that it is easier to fight Government than to fight our own people, for we naturally make,—and should make, if we were men,—mountains of molehills of Government's injustice. But we fight shy as soon as we are face to face with our own drawbacks and shortcomings. I therefore reminded the Bardoli people who had fulfilled the first half of their pledge of the second half, viz., of paying up the old assessment. That I know will be done in the course of a few days. But what next? How will you husband the tremendous stores of energy and enthusiasm that you have brought into being during the Satyagraha campaign? How will you utilise the unprecedented awakening that has come amongst the women of Bardoli? How will you serve them, how will you identify yourselves with them and help to remove their misery? Satyagraha includes civil disobedience, civil resistance to the tyranny of blind authority, but the capacity of resistance presupposes self-purification and constructive work. If I were to ask you to render account of what you have done since 1921 in the direction of self-purification and constructive work I know you and I would have to shed bitter tears.

'I want to tell you that I continue to be what I was in 1921. I have the same inexorable conditions which are a *sine qua non* for peace, prosperity, Swarajya, Ramarajya, or the Kingdom of God that we are hankering after. What right have the Hindus and Musalmans of ease-loving Surat to talk of Swaraj, so long as they run at one another's throats in the name of God, and then run to the courts to seek justice? If you are truly brave, you may fight one another on equal terms, but you may not seek the protection of courts of justice. The English and the German fought on fields of battle, but did not go to law courts. There is some bravery in free and fair fighting, but none in running to law courts. Let the Hindus and Musalmans fight a pitched battle, if they will, let them fight fair and clean and decide their issues. Their names will then go down in history. But this fighting followed by protracted wrangles in law courts, is not bravery. Our present ways are not ways of bravery but of cowardice. True bravery lies in laying down one's life for the sake of religion, in voluntary surrender of non-essentials. That is the lesson of Bardoli, and it will have been lost on us if we lose ourselves in the frenzy of victory celebrations. Until we, who have sprung from the same soil and are children of the same Motherland, though belonging to different faiths, learn to love one another as blood brothers, victories like that of Bardoli will be of no avail.

'Another item, is the purification of Hinduism. Have you purged it of its deepest stain? True Swaraj I repeat is impossible without self-purification. I do not know any other way. Call it my limitation, but then it is the limitation of Satyagraha. If there is any other way, I do not know it, and anything won by means other than those of self-purification will not be Swaraj but something else.

' The third and the last thing in our programme is the duty of men of all religions and all races towards the skeletons of the land. The charkha, I may repeat *ad nauseam*, is the only remedy. I have come across a strong justification of the charkha from a strange quarter. Sir Lallubhai Samaldas in his review of the ponderous Agricultural Commission's Report has shown how the Commissioners have shunned like an untouchable even the mention of the word spinning wheel in the chapter on subsidiary industries. How is it that they have fought shy of a thing which provides the only occupation to the starving millions? I submit that the potency of the spinning wheel lies in that very fact. They might have at least criticised it and even ridiculed it. But no. They could not contemplate with equanimity its infinite possibilities. (A heavy shower of rain) Well I have really done, and need say nothing more.'

22nd November, 1928.

THE PEOPLE'S ADVOCATE

With the inquiry, now proceeding, by the Committee appointed by the Government to investigate and report on the people's complaint that the enhancement of assessment in Bardoli Taluka was unwarranted, the second phase of the Bardoli Satyagraha may be said to have begun. The preliminary argument on behalf of the people was made by the people's advocate Sjt. Bhulabhai Desai of Bombay. The question was mooted whether Sjt. Vallabhbhai might not represent the people before the Inquiry Committee, and Gandhiji decided that some one who had not identified himself with the Satyagrahis should be requested to argue the case on their behalf It was at Gandhiji's request that Sjt. Bhulabhai Desai gladly consented to be the people's advocate. He was kind enough to discuss the case with the people's representatives for some days, gave a good deal of his precious time to study the case and went over to Surat on the 5th instant to open the case. A full report of his argument has already appeared in the papers and I shall not trouble the reader with an elaborate summary of it. But it may be remembered that he took his stand on Section 107 which, he argued, strictly confined the Settlement Officer to a consideration of the profits of agriculture, so far as agricultural land was concerned. A consideration of the rentals may be quite relevant as reflecting the true profits of agriculture, but no conclusion could be based exclusively on the rental values, in fact to rely on them would be strictly illegal especially when in a tract like Bardoli, according to the people, the leased area was very small, and when the statistics of that area collected by the Settlement Officer lacked all scrutiny. The people would therefore lead evidence on the *net* profits of agriculture to be determined by finding out the price of the produce and deducting therefrom the cost of cultivation which included wages on various agricultural operations, seeds, manure, and the cost of stock live and dead.

THE INQUIRY

The actual work of the inquiry began on the 14th instant at Aphwa a village situated within easy distance of Bardoli. The members of the Committee have prepared an elaborate questionnaire to ascertain the conditions of the village. Some of the statistics obtainable from the village records they get from the Talati, the village accountant, and about other details they subject the people to an elaborate examination. In the case in question they went out for a stroll over the paddy fields, making minute inquiries. The inquiries at times reveal a surprising state of things. For instance in Aphwa the people have to keep an acre of ground fallow for every acre in which they planted the particular variety of paddy, so that they might have a ready storage of water in those fallow areas called tanks. What seemed to surprise the members of the Committee was that the fallow areas were subject to the same assessment as the cropped area! They went into careful detail regarding the mode of living and food of the people, inquiring as to how much an agricultural labourer or *dubla* cost the agriculturist. I am glad to note that a cordial spirit prevails between the members of the Committee and the peoples' representatives who often serve as the members' interpreters as the latter do not know the vernacular well enough to put questions to the people. The next day they went to the same village and found another surprise in store for them. They wanted that day to inquire into the rental statistics. The people's representatives had asked for a copy of the detailed statistics prepared by the Settlement Officer and the Committee members too had tried to get at them. They had a copy which could not tally with the Settlement Officer's Appendix H, with the result that the people's representatives had to give their own figures of the total leased area, which also was found to be *less* than the area shown by the Settlement Commissioner. The representatives assured them that so far as the rice area was concerned—and it was a predomimantly rice village—there were practically no rental statistics. The members had to fall back upon the village map to test the truth of the statement, and for about an hour they went on making inquiries about individual occupancies to find that there was no leased area worth the name. I am thankful to say that they examined some of the villagers in minute detail about *jirayat* area some of which was discovered to be leased. There was a lease made in 1922 for an unreasonably high amount. The people's case was that it was an abnormal case. The lessor and lessee were questioned in detail 'Your lease expires next year. Would you offer the same rent if the land was offered to again?' was the question.

'By no means, sir. I would not take it for even half the amount.'

'And what does the lessor say? Do you expect to obtain the same high rent next year?'

'No, sir, I would be lucky if I got even half the amount

'But, supposing you did not?'

'Then I would cultivate it myself.'

'Will the lessee say why he entered into the bargain if it was so unprofitable to him?'

'In expectation of getting rich, as it was a year of abnormal prices. Cotton was Rs. 350 then.'

'But did you do cotton all years?

'No. Two years I did *jowari*.'

'Then it was not for cotton that you took the field on lease.'

'It was after I found that it was an unprofitable affair that I put it under *jowari*!'

And so on and so forth. The members seemed to think that the paucity of the leased area was so great that there were no reliable data to go upon.

A VILLAGER THROUGH THE RACK

The next day they went to Isroli, an adjoining village with entirely different soil conditions—lands cut up by ravines and full of stone and gravel, and a predominantly grass area. The people's representatives put a preliminary question as to the nature of the inquiry and whether if they were satisfied as to the unreliability of the Settlement Officer's statistics they contemplated any action.

'You do not mean to say that we should judge the whole Taluka from Aphwa?'

'We don't, sir, but if you were to find the same condition in many places you would be able to arrive at some conclusion.'

'We should be able to arrive at some conclusion in about a week's time and if we find that Mr. Jayakar's Appendix H is unreliable we should cancel it.'

'We are thankful for the assurance. Another thing we should like to know is whether or not you would go into all the items you have mentioned in your questionnaire. In case you don't we would like to lead evidence on the points you do not go into.'

'You don't expect us to go into all the details in every village? Supposing we were to go into the rentals in every village and ascertained details about every item on our questionnaire, do you imagine what time it would take?'

'We do, but sir, you have to make as full an inquiry as possible.'

It was agreed after some more discussion that the people might submit whatever statements they liked and they would be examined on them.

Then began a detailed inquiry into the existing leases. There were several cases in which extraneous considerations other than the inherent value of the land leased had weighed with the lessees. The members of the Committee therefore heard the people at length and noted down their explanations, cross-examining them in minute detail.

'As regards this rental of Rs. 60 what have you to say?'

'I am allowing the lessee's pair of bullocks to graze free of charge in my field.'

'How much do you allow for that amount?'

'Rs. 30.'

'Rs. 30 for a pair of bullocks to graze in your field? For how many months?'

'Four monsoon months beginning with Jyeshth.'

'Thirty rupees?'

'Yes, and that because I had a man to look after my own three pairs grazing in the same field and I had no extra charge to incur on the lessee's pair of bullocks.'

'Now, will the lessee tell us if he leased a grass field why should he put his bullocks to graze in another field of the lessor?'

'Because, sir, the field, I have leased is a grass field from which one cuts grass. The field in which the bullocks graze is a pasture.'

In another case the explanation for a high rental value was that one of the lessee's fields adjoined the field leased. The lessee was not present on the spot, but the explanation was volunteered by another peasant.

Mr. Broomfield rather indignantly asked, suspecting falsehood: 'Do you know the field?'

'Yes, sir, it is in close proximity, you can see it on the map.'

'What field do you mean?'

'I mean the field leased by so and so!'

'Has he no other leased field in the village?'

'No other, sir.'

The number of the field was ascertained from the records, the number of the field said to be adjoining was also found out and the members of the Committee were satisfied that it was not a random shot that the villager had fired, but that he spoke with knowledge.

But I shall not take the reader through any more detail The work before the Committee is difficult and great, first because they cannot take any data for granted, secondly because they have yet to determine the real basis on which to fix a rate of assessment. So long as the members of the Committee have not definitely made up their minds, the position of the people's representatives is also difficult. But they have decided to collect facts and figures relevant to the inquiry, especially the figures of produce and cost of cultivation, in respect of each and every village and submit them to the members of the Committee.

THE FRUITS

The following pages have been reproduced from "The Story of Bardoli"—by Mahadev Desai.

The fruits of the ordeal through which the peasants of Bardoli passed and after having done so proved to an official committee that their complaints were substantially justified, were many and of a far-reaching nature. However 'incurable' the local Government may be, the revelations made by the Committee opened the eyes of the Central Government. A conference of Revenue Members was at once summoned in Simla where one presumes their attention was drawn to a most damaging passage in the Committee's Report: "The established method of using the statistics is in our own opinion unsound in theory, and however it may work in practice in other districts, is not capable of giving satisfactory results in this part of Gujarat, where leases and sale transactions are affected by such a variety of disturbing factors." However cautious the phrasing of this conclusion, any one could read between the lines. All of them were naturally asked to put their houses in order, but Bombay had to bestir itself betimes. All the settlements directed by Mr. Anderson were based on the "establihsed method" and possibly vitiated like Bardoli. There was a hue and cry in every taluka which was recently settled, with the result that though the Simla Conference did not end in anything definite the Government of Bombay were compelled to declare their intention of introducing legislation of a "sound" and "progressive" character and that pending the legislation the old rates should continue where new settlements had not been already introduced. Whatever the Government may do or may not do, the peasant everywhere is now awake and determined to mend or end the existing unsound and wooden system. That is one of the many far-reaching results of Bardoli.

The material results were not negligible. The enhancement fixed before the Enquiry for both the talukas was Rs. 1,87,492. It was reduced to Rs. 48,648 which means that the two talukas were relieved of a yearly burden of nearly one hundred and forty thousand rupees—if not more, for some of the recommended rates are strictly *illegal* and Government are themselves trying to remedy the illegalities! There are quite a number of minor recommendations in the Report regarding the existing anomalies in assessment and soil classification, apart from the rates. These are bound to result in some small gains for the peasants.

But even materially Bardoli had its repercussions on other provinces. In the Punjab remissions amounting to lakhs of rupees were given, and in the C. P. liberal suspensions of revenue were allowed.

It is impossible to exaggerate the moral results of the victory. It was recognised throughout India and even in the Empire that the peasant who is usually regarded as a "a sack of meal" can organise himself and offer battle to a Government that persists until the last moment that it cannot be in the wrong. If the victory dealt a severe moral blow to British Government, it added to the moral stature of the peasant throughout the length and breadth of India. How it will prepare him for the bigger battle for Swaraj has yet to be seen.

The future is in the hands of God.

GOVERNMENT THREATS

1

LANDS DISPOSED OF WOULD NEVER BE RETURNED

Over the signature of Mr. J. W. Smyth, Secretary to the Government, Revenue Department, the Government of Bombay issued the following notification on 31st May 1928 to the occupants of land in the Bardoli taluka and Valod mahal. The notification was distributed broadcast in Gujarati in the Villages of the Bardoli taluka and was in confirmation of several threats issued already by the Collector:

The occupants of agricultural land in Bardoli Taluka and Valod Mahal with the assistance of persons who do not reside there, combined in February last to refuse to pay the revised assessment. The Settlement Officer had proposed an increase of 30 per cent. The Settlement Commissioner's recommendations involved an increase of

29 per cent Government after the most careful enquiry and the fullest consideration of all the objections raised both by the cultivators and certain members of the Legislative Council fixed the rates at 20 per cent. in excess of those paid during the 30 years' currency of the previous settlement Uptil the middle of April last the Revenue Officers confined their action to notice of demand and attempts at distraint The latter were frustrated by organized evasion, the locking up of houses and threats to the Village Patels and Vethyas of boycott and excommunication.

Government then reluctantly resorted to the forfeiture of land and organised attachment of buffaloes and moveable property. Twenty-five Pathans were obtained to assist the Mamlatdar and Mahalkaris in the work of attachment and the care of animals attached. Unfounded allegations have been made against these Pathans. Government are satisfied that their conduct has been exemplary in every respect They are being employed at headquarters to look after the buffaloes distrained, and also in parties of five to assist in making attachments under the eye of the Mamlatdar and the four Mahalkaris. The notion that five parties each of five Pathans working under the eye of a responsible officer of Government can terrorize a population of 90,000 persons as has been alleged in certain newspapers, is incredible. Nevertheless as soon as the threats to the Vethyas are withdrawn by the non-co-operation leaders and they are allowed to resume their lawful occupations, the necessity for retaining these Pathans will disappear, and they will be sent away.

The non-agriculturist defaulters have been served with notices of forfeiture accompanied by a special warning that their lands would be entered as Government unoccupied waste on expiry of the period of such notice and disposed of to persons applying for the occupancy as opportunity occurred; *and that lands once disposed of would never be returned to them.*

Up to date 1,400 acres of such land have been disposed of and about 5,000 acres more will be disposed of in due course unless the arrears due thereon be sooner paid.

Applicants, Hindus, Mahomedans and Parsis, many of whom

reside in Surat District, are forthcoming for all this land. It is evident that these persons have no apprehensions that the revised assessments are excessive and that they will be unable to pay them.

A very small area of land belonging to agriculturists with large holdings has been similarly dealt with.

Notices of forfeiture of land belonging to other agriculturists have been issued and in some cases proclamations of sale have been made. The area of land so dealt with is very considerable.

Government wish to draw the earnest attention of the cultivators of Bardoli and Valod to the above statement of fact The non-co-operation leaders declared that Government would be afraid to forfeit any land and that if they did, no one would dare to come forward to take up the occupancy. They also said that no one would dare to purchase the buffaloes that had been distrained. These declarations have been proved to be entirely incorrect. They further stated that none of the land revenue would be paid This statement is equally incorrect. Up to the present one lakh of rupees have been recovered by Government towards the realization of the total revenue of the Taluka and Mahal; that is, nearly one-sixth of the revenue has already been paid up. It is to be noted that in the neighbouring Taluka of Chorasi, where the revised rates are higher than in Bardoli and have also been introduced this year, over nine-tenths of the land revenue has been paid up.

Many of the payments in Bardoli and Valod have been received from occupants of all castes and creeds whose names have been kept secret by Government officers, so that they may not be harassed by excommunication, social boycott and fines, with which occupants who pay their lawful dues to Government have been threatened by the non-co-operation leaders.

Government believe that many more persons are anxious to pay and Government wish to give them full opportunity to do so, and so save them from loss of their land. They are therefore informed (i) that the Collector has the power to give exemption from the payment of one-fourth fine which is due from defaulters and that he will exercise this discretion in the case of persons who pay their land revenue on or before June 19 and (ii) that payments may be made through any Government Officer, or by remittance to the Taluka, Mahal or Huzur Treasuries.

YOU WILL REGRET A REINQUIRY!

This is an extract from Sir Leslie Wilson's reply to Sjt. K. M. Munshi, dated May 29th, 1928:

With regard to your remarks about an impartial enquiry, I am convinced myself that no further enquiry could elicit any further facts; and I may point out that an almost impossible position will be reached if, after the fullest enquiry, after the objections to any re-assessment have been received, and after these have all been carefully considered, another enquiry in every case of the re-assessment is to be undertaken. In addition to the consideration given to the Bardoli case mentioned in para 3 above, it is a fact, however, that a further enquiry has been made, for it so happened that Mr. Rieu, the Revenue Member, went on leave, and Mr. Hatch, a very experienced Revenue Officer, took his place. Mr. Hatch has gone through all the papers with an entirely independent mind, and has come definitely to the conclusion, leaving aside rental values altogether (a basis to which objection has been taken) that the increase of assessment proposed by Government is very low, and that Government is more than justified, by the figures of prices, sales, etc. in increasing the assessment as it has done, and that, if any further enquiry were to be made, such enquiry would result in raising the assessment instead of lowering it. I can assure you that there is not one member of Government who is not fully satisfied as to the justice of Government's action—and, in fact, I should really use the word generosity.

GOVERNOR'S ULTIMATUM

In the course of his opening speech H. E. Sir Leslie Wilson said:

Honourable members are aware of the fact that I personally visited Surat as recently as last Wednesday, in the hope that such a settlement might ensue. No settlement was, however, achieved, and it is not possible for Government to delay any longer in making known its final decisions. Government is of opinion, and I feel sure that honourable members will agree, that any announcement on a matter of such importance as this should be made to the elected representatives of the people of the Presidency, more particularly in view of all that has happened during the past few months, and also in view of the vote taken on this question in the Budget Session. Not only is this the proper course, and I have endeavoured since I have been here to act entirely in the most constitutional manner possible. I therefore take this opportunity of putting before this honourable House the views of Government as to the present situation, and the definite and considered decisions of Government, which have been approved by the Government of India.

I say, with intention, that these decisions have been approved by the Government of India, because issues have been raised in Bardoli which have a very wide significance, and indeed it is common ground that this question has become one of all-India importance. So many speeches have been made by public men, and others, during the past few weeks on this subject, that it is not a surprising fact that some confusion of thought arises My Government had always had it impressed upon them that the issue was a very clear one—namely, whether the re-assessment of the land-holders in the Bardoli taluka was a fair or unfair one. If, however, Government is to judge what the issue is on speeches and letters, which have been spoken and written lately, and on actions which have been and are being taken to interfere with the administration of the district, the issue might appear to be a much wider one—and, in fact, one which, in a sentence, is whether the writ of His Majesty the King-Emperor is to run in a portion of His Majesty's dominions, or whether the edict of some unofficial body of individuals is to be obeyed. That issue, if that is the issue, is one which Government is prepared to meet with all the power which Government possesses, and, by the decision of the representatives of the people of the district as to whether they accept or not the conditions which Government lay down before any enquiry can be promised, it will be clearly demonstrated what is the issue before Government and the people of this Presidency, and before the Government of India.

If the only question to be dealt with is the justice or injustice of the re-assessment, then Government is prepared to submit the whole case, after the revenue now due to Government has been paid, and the present agitation entirely ceases, to a full, open and independent enquiry as outlined in the statement which has been published. In making their proposals Government are anxious, above all things that the agriculturists of Bardoli taluka shall be relieved as soon as possible from the unfortunate situation in which they become involved as the result of the campaign against the payment of land revenue, the justice of which has been disputed by some honourable members of this House. I, therefore, on behalf of Government put before honourable members the same proposals I put before those who came to see me at Surat as representatives of the cultivators of Bardoli taluka. Those proposals have been published, and it is not necessary for me to restate them but I must make it quite clear that they are not proposals put forward as a basis for compromise but the definite and final decision of Government. They are fair proposals, and must commend themselves to the mind of any moderate man. They contain certain conditions which must be fulfilled before any fresh inquiry can be promised and these conditions cannot be altered. I will mention one point only with regard to the demand on the part of Government for the payment of the revised assessment. This is obviously a vital condition being a lawful and constitutional demand the repudiation of which is both unlawful and unconstitutional. At Surat I was informed that the condition of payment of the revised assessment would not be accepted and consequently no settlement was possible. I would, however, remind honourable members who are the elected representatives of the people living in Bardoli taluka, that it is their constitutional right to speak on behalf of, and decide in the interests of, their constituents. Those honourable members and the honourable members of this House, must have I am convinced, first of all in their minds the welfare of the agriculturists, and I sincerely trust those interests will be the only ones which will actuate all honourable members in this matter. It is, of course, impossible for the present situation to continue, and a final decision must be arrived at as soon as possible. Government would therefore ask the honourable members concerned to communicate their decision as to whether or no they, on behalf of their constituents, accept or refuse the conditions which must be fulfilled before a fresh enquiry can be set up, to the Honourable the Revenue Member within fourteen days from to-day.

I cannot myself believe that realising the consequences of a refusal—the grave hardship on the agriculturists, the bitterness of feeling which will be engendered, and the inevitable result of any conflict which must ensue between Government and the people concerned—these proposals will be rejected. It is, however, my duty to make it perfectly clear that, if these conditions are not accepted, and consequently a settlement is not secured Government will, in order that there shall be full compliance with the law, take what action they consider desirable and necessary, and will utilise all the powers at their command to ensure that the statutory authority of Government is maintained in every way. Neither the Government of Bombay nor any Government could tolerate a position in which private individuals attempt to put themselves above the law, or take part in organisations which have the effect of inducing others to do so. To permit that is the very negation of Government, and it is not conceivable—whatever may be the consequences—that any Government, worthy of the name of Government in any country, would not take every step in its power to prevent, or to put a stop to any such action.

I have not made these remarks so that they might be considered in any way as a threat. Nothing is further from my mind They are merely statements of fact, but it was my obvious duty both to this honourable House and to the people of Bardoli taluka to make them, so that the position of Government cannot again be misinterpreted or misunderstood.

Indeed, there is no honourable member who will deny that there is a campaign of civil disobedience in Bardoli taluka at the present time, and it is perhaps unnecessary for me to remind honourable members that civil disobedience is an act of lawlessness—however convinced those who are participators in that act may be that their case is just, and lawlessness is none the less lawlessness because it may be fostered or encouraged by persons holding strong convictions, or because its practice may evoke from some men and women qualities worthy of a better cause. Moreover, it would be well that public opinion should clearly realise the inevitable consequences of disregard for law upon the structure of any political society. Once men can convince themselves that it is proper to set at nought the legally constituted executive authority whose duty it is to administer, then it is but a short step to challenge the title of the legislative body whose function it is to make the law, or to impugn the impartiality of the judiciary by whom the law is interpreted. Thus, respect for law is fundamental in every sphere of social life, and to seek to supersede it by the private will of any citizen or body of citizens is to head straight for anarchy.

THE SETTLEMENT DOCUMENTS

The Letters exchanged between the Surat M. L. C.'s and the Government recording the Terms of Settlement

1.

The following letter was addressed by the members of the Legislative Council representing Bardoli Taluka and Surat District to the Hon'ble the Revenue Member.

POONA, 6TH AUGUST 1928.

To

The Hon'ble The Revenue Member,

SIR,

With reference to your letter dated August 3rd 1928, we are glad to be able to say that we are in a position to inform Government that the conditions laid down by His Excellency the Governor in his opening speech to the Council dated 23rd of July will be fulfilled.

Yours sincerely,

Sd. A. M K DEHLAVI
Sd. BHASAHEB (Thakore of Kerwada)
Sd. DAUDKHAN SALEBHAI TYEBJEE
Sd. J. B. DESAI
Sd. B. R. NAIK
Sd. H. B. SHIVDASANI
Sd. M. K. DIXIT

Announcement of the Enquiry

Government thereafter announced the following enquiry:

The enquiry will be entrusted to a Revenue Officer and a Judicial Officer, the decision of the Judicial Officer to prevail in all matters of difference between the two, with the following terms of reference;

To enquire into and report upon the complaint of the people of Bardoli and Valod.

(*a*) That the enhancement of revenue recently made is not warranted in terms of the Land Revenue Code

(*b*) That the reports accessible to the public do not contain sufficient data warranting the enhancement and that some of the data given are wrong;

and to find that, if the people's complaint is held to be justified, what enhancement or reduction, if any, there should be upon the old assessment.

As the enquiry is to be full, open and independent, the people will be free to lead as well as test evidence before it with the help of their representatives including legal advisers.

The following further letters were exchanged between the members of the Legislative Council representing the Bardoli taluka and the Surat district and the Hon'ble the Revenue Member:

Poona, August 7, 1928.

To

The Hon'ble the Revenue Member.

SIR,

Now that the principal point about the Bardoli question is settled satisfactorily we hope and trust that Government will

(*a*) Release all Satyagrahi prisoners,

(*b*) Restore all lands forfeited,

(*c*) Reinstate all Talatis and Patels who resigned their offices.

Yours sincerely,

Sd A M K. DEHLAVI
Sd. DAUDKHAN SALEBHAI TYEBJEE
Sd. BHASAHEB (Thakore of Karwada)
Sd. BHIMBHAI R NAIK
Sd H. B SHIVDASANI
Sd J. B. DESAI
Sd. M. K. DIXIT

The following letter dated 7th August 1928 was addressed by the Hon'ble the Revenue Member to the above members of the Legislative Council:

Gentlemen,

With reference to your letter dated the 7th instant, Government, in exercise of their prerogative, will release all Satyagrahi prisoners and will be pleased to issue orders granting your second request.

The Talatis and Patels will be pardoned if they apply in the proper form.

Yours sincerely,
Sd. J. L. RIEU

N. B—The price paid for the lands which were sold by Government and were transferred to R. B. Naik as stated in para 86 of the Report was about Rs 11,000. or double the assessment in respect thereof. The excess of assessment thus received was also remitted by Government to the individual cultivators with the result that the land was restored to them without their being out of pocket to any extent.

CONCLUSIONS OF THE MUNSHI COMMITTEE

1 In some cases notices of forfeiture were not prepared and affixed according to law; in some cases, notices were affixed at wrong places; some notices were affixed long after the expiry of the period mentioned therein. The number of cases of irregular notices actually put before us is fairly large and drawn from different places in the taluka and indicate that irregularity was not restricted to any small area of the taluka.

2. Over 6,000 notices were issued against khatedars covering the bulk of the lands in Bardoli. These lands were quite disproportionate in value to the assessment recoverable in respect thereof, as the general value of lands in Bardoli according to Government reports is about 50 to 100 times the assessment recoverable therefrom. Such forfeiture is indefensible from either moral or administrative point of view.

3. Lands of the value of over Rs. 3,00,000 were disposed of for Rs. 11,000, under the drastic powers vested in the Executive for

disposal of lands for assessment highly disproportionate in value was totally unjustifiable though technically correct.

4. In many cases proceedings for the distraints and sales of movable properties were illegal or irregular.

5. Numerous cases of breaking open the doors of dwelling houses, spread over different villages, show that the forcing open of doors was by no means the isolated action of a wayward officer but was resorted to as a matter of concerted policy. Doors of houses were broken open without any inquiry as to whether the door attempted to be broken or broken open was that of a khatedar.

6. There are numerous cases in which distraints were levied before sunrise and after sunset. These were a source of great harassment to the villages.

7. Articles such as cooking, vessels, beds, etc., seeds carts, and bullocks which are exempted from attachments were notwithstanding such exemption seized.

8. In numerous cases *japti* officers while levying attachments made no inquiry whether they were attaching the property of a defaulter khatedar or of any other person. In many cases as a matter of fact they seized the property of persons who were not liable to pay any land revenue whatever and the onus of showing that the property did not belong to a khatedar was invariably thrown on the non-khatedars whose property was wrongfully seized. In some cases even while selling the property so seized no attempt was made to find out as to whose property was being sold.

9 In numerous cases articles destrained were sold at gross undervalue and policemen and revenue peons were allowed to make bids and to purchase these articles at the auction sales.

10. The animals destrained were very severely beaten in most cases. While at the *thana* they were not properly looked after in the sense that they were not properly fed or watered.

11. The employment of Pathans for *japti* among a peaceful people was unnecessary and unjustifiable. There is evidence to the effect that Pathans employed were guilty of indecent and improper behaviour and in at least one case, of molestation of a woman. In some cases the Pathans also committed small thefts They were also guilty of ill-treatment of animals.

12 Government invoked the assistance of criminal law to punish the Satyagraha workers and to break the people's movement. In several cases the use of criminal law was unjustifiable and vindictive.

13. Government did not act fairly in appointing a subordinate revenue official as a magistrate to try and dispose of prosecutions which were launched and in installing a court in the heated atmosphere of Bardoli.

14. Government as prosecutors did not lead proper evidence and the process of identification was untrustworthy. The evidence on which these convictions were secured was one-sided and untrustworthy. Most convictions were at best for offences which were merely technical. In many cases the persons present on spot were not called.

15. The Magistrate was wrong in not insisting on better evidence and in some cases has taken an incorrect view of law. In cases even of nominal offences Government asked for deterrent sentences. The Magistrate in most cases agreed with this view and imposed sentences which were out of proportion to the gravity of the offence.

16. The simultaneous and rigorous employment of the processes allowed by the Land Revenue Code and other incidental activities like wholesale forfeiture, sales at gross under-value, disregard of procedure in cases of forfeiture, distraints and sales, the employment of Pathans, harsh treatment of cattle and their sales to butchers, posting of Pathans and police in front of the houses of khatedars for hours together, levying distraints, use of the criminal law and such other measures prove that the processes were worked harshly,

17. These measures were adopted harshly by Government in order to bring the highest possible pressure short of military occupation principally to induce the taluka of Bardoli to give up the Satyagraha movement. Government officials unjustifiably refused to believe that Mr. Vallabhbhai Patel and the Satyagrahis were fighting only a local economic issue. Thus Government adopted measures which were principally directed to the form of the move-

ment as apart from the object thereof; which were drastic and oppressive far beyond the immediate needs of revenue collection which did not regard the technicalities of law with scrupulous respect; which more often than not disregarded the consideration of general well-being towards the classes affected thereby; and which directed to punishing those whom Government wrongly considered as having usurped their authority and to overawing those who had accepted the lead of the so-called usurpers Thus we cannot but come to the conclusion that the measures adopted by Government were punitive and had for their object retribution and not mere revenue collection and as such were vindictive

18. The rigorous employment of coercive measures consolidated the Bardoli taluka leading to the adoption of concerted action to counteract the activities of Government. The official activities led to the resignation of Talatis and Patels and attempts to persuade or threaten the villagers or village officers resulted in the adoption by the people of social boycott against weavers. As a result of official activities all normal work in the taluka was suspended.

19. As a result of the official activities cattle suffered very seriously in health, as will be seen from the following table:

Statistics available from 76 Villages of the Taluka

Total number of buffaloes ..	16,611
Buffaloes suffering illness .	3,801
Total number of bullocks .	13,091
Bullocks suffering illness	442
Inflammation and excoriation of skin ..	960
Pressure sores	92
Ulcerated and worm-eaten ..	2,155
Miscellaneous illness .	1,018
Total number of deaths .	93

20. People also suffered in health. Government Departments failed to take proper precaution to see that no injury was done to to the health of the people as a result of their policy The fact that the incarceration of the people was self-inflicted does not exonerate Government from their responsibility for the well being of the people.

THE ENQUIRY AND AFTER

The following is the text of the correspondence that passed between Sjt. Vallabhbhai Patel and the Government of Bombay in respect of the report Broomfield Committee:

Rectify Errors in the Report

Letter from Sjt. Vallabhbhai Patel to the Hon'ble Sir J L. Rieu, dated Simla, 24th June, 1929:

My colleagues and I have by this time made a careful study of the Broomfield Committee's Report, and we should now like to place before you and through you before H E. the Governor our view in the matter. The feeling that is uppermost in our mind is one of gratification over the fact that the peasants' complaints have been held to be substantially justified but I should be untrue to myself and the peasants, if I disguised the fact that the feeling is not unmixed with one of sore disappointment that the learned Commissioners should by their constructive proposals have done serious injustice to the villagers, which is made all the graver for their complete vindication You will remember what I wrote to you in my letter subsequent to our meeting in Poona last October, and I am bound to say that the constructive proposals of the Commissioners are by no means warranted by the evidence before them. I confess, however, that this injustice, however serious, is not wilful and may be even unconscious, and I therefore do not feel justified to seek any remedy other than that of submitting a representation to the Government pointing out the seriousness of the injustice and requesting them to rectify it by executive action.

I shall now proceed to state as briefly as I can, the grounds on which I characterise the constructive proposals as manifestly unjust. Some of them are general and some apply with particular force to individual cases. I forget for my present purposes the inherent iniquity of the rental theory, and submit my remarks assuming that the theory is sound. The general grounds are these:

1. The Commissioners have based their proposals solely on the rental data, in spite of their clear finding that "the proportion of the whole area of Bardoli taluka covered by the statistics would fall from the alleged figure of one-third to something between one-ninth

and one-tenth" (Para 53 of the Report). This data can by no means be described in the language of the Settlement Manual as 'considerable in volume' so as to entitle the Commissioners to make them a basis for their proposals.

2. The proposals, however, have been based not even on the scanty rental data available in the taluka, but on much scantier data collected by the Commissioners in respect of only 40 out of 137 villages in the Bardoli taluka, and in some cases on the data for one single year. In 17 out of these 40 villages the data according to the Commissioners themselves, were too thin to suggest the normal range of rents.

3. The reason for the enhancement of dry crop rates are in all cases flimsy where they are not vague and the percentage of increase absolutely arbitrary. Here are a few samples of the language used by the Commissioners in justification of their proposals: "Of all the villages in Group I, Sarbhon supplies the best evidence, and shows that some increase of assessment is possible" (Some here meaning 10 per cent.); "The group of villages represented by this and Vadhwania are clearly ripe for some increase in their dry crop assessment" (Some here means 18 8 per cent); "The figures of the group as a whole do not indicate over-assessment."

Thus in Group I, the rental data for one village Sarbhon for one year (1927-28) have been considered to supply the best justification for an increase of 8 per cent. in the dry crop rate, and whilst in the other groups a feeble attempt has been made to set off the dry crop enhancement by a reduction in the rice maximum rates, no such attempt has been made here, though the percentage of rice assessment in the particular village held to afford the best evidence indicated a reduction.

In Group II having in view the circumstances admittedly affecting leasing, one fails to see how "some increase of assessment is possible."

Group III affords an instance of the most arbitrary and capricious increase in the maximum rates. Out of 11 villages 5 villages indicate no data whatsoever (as Appendix E shows) and all of them have been recommended for an increase of 18 per cent. Uva which already bears assessment which is 37 3 per cent. of the rental has been recommended for a similar increase.

Many of the villages in Group IV have been brought down to Group V, because they "do not indicate over assessment," and among which there are "none" in which an appreciable rise of assessment would be justified" and some of which are the "poorest in the whole taluka and Peta" (P. 76) and yet an increase of 8 3 per cent. has been recommended.

4. If the rental data were to be made the sole basis for the assessment, it was incumbent on the Commissioners to collect genuine data for all the villages. The villages inspected by the Commissioners were mostly those which were supposed to have a high rental multiple and it is not unlikely that if other villages had been inspected they would have revealed low rental multiples necessitating a reduction even in the rates. That, however, I admit is problematical. Having found that Mr. Jayakar's statistics failed to afford any reliable evidence of value, and that it was not possible for them to collect correct data affording such reliable evidence in respect of all villages, the least thus the Commissioners could and should have done was to leave the villages they had not inspected and found any data for, undisturbed.

5. 35,611 acres out of the net assessed area in Bardoli are under grass which the Commissioners found "was nowhere exported for sale." The enhancement in the dry crop rates cannot be held to be justified in respect of this large grass area, for any reasons whatsoever.

I now come to some individual cases which have been hit much harder than the rest.

1. By far the most flagrant injustice has been done to three villages Ambach, Vedchhi and Degama, whose dry crop rates have been increased by 33 per cent. All of them are poor Kaliparaj villages. Two of these were inspected and though the pitch of rents was high, as the Commissioners themselves have remarked "in some *savkar* ridden villages such as Ambach and Degama" "the pitch of rents is materially affected," It may be noted that Vedchhi (which was not inspected) and Ambach are the centres of our rural

uplift work in the Kaliparaj area—work which has been favourably noticed by the Commissioners—and the enhancement comes with peculiarly ill grace and as a penalty for the work which might some day raise the villagers from the level of '*savkar*-riddenness'

2. Eight villages—Afva, Akoti, Kantali, Khoj, Palsod, Pardi Kadod, Kuva, Samthan, in Group II have been picked out for special treatment as regards their rice crop rate. Whilst they remain in Group II for dry crop they have been raised to Group I for rice crop. Why 6 villages out of 137 should have different groups for dry crop and rice crop, it is difficult to see. Only 4 out of these were inspected (Afva, Palsod, Pardi Kadod and Samthan), 3 indicated no data, and in Pardi Kadod the data were "affected by the practice of manuring before leasing" Moreover rice is grown mainly for local consumption, and even where it is sold the price is "exactly what it was in 1914" One fails to see, therefore, why this special treatment should have been meted out to these villages. Afva's is the worst case of all inasmuch as a large area of tank lands which grow no rice but are held as reservoirs of water are subject to the same assessment as the rice growing *kyari*

3. The case of five villages (Delwada, Kamalchhod, Orgam, Sejwad, Singod) in Group III which indicated no data whatsoever has been already mentioned as also Uva which is particularly anomalous.

4. A lower group—Group V—has been thought fit to be created for Kaliparaj villages which are the poorest in the taluka The rate however instead of being lowered has been raised by 8 per cent.

But I shall bring my letter to a close. I have confined my remarks to Bardoli. I could speak at the same length about the villages in Chorasi where a high maximum rate already presses too hard on the poor peasantry. The rental data are there no doubt larger in volume, but the other general remarks about Bardoli apply with equal force to the villages in that taluka, and the least the Commissioners could have done was to leave the villages undisturbed. There are in that taluka some cases of particularly anomalous grouping and rating which I am asking Rao Bahadur Bhimbhai to bring to your notice.

To conclude, even the the dry crop maximum rates in both the talukas are capable of considerable reduction and the rice maximum rates of a much larger reduction than has been recommended. But if that is not done, I hope and trust that Government will maintain the old rates in both the talukas in view of the fact that the report apparently opens up the question of all revision settlements made during the recent years, and points to the necessity of deferring consideration of them until legislation laying down the procedure of making revision settlements comes to be passed. But if that did not come, the least that the Government owe to the villages is to remedy the injustice in case of villages which have had to suffer particular hardship.

Should you think it necessary that we should meet, I should be glad to wait on you.

Reminder

Second letter dated Ahmedabad, July 18, 1929, from Sjt. Vallabhbhai Patel to Sir J. L. Rieu

This is to remind you that I am still without even an acknowledgment of my letter of the 24th ultimo. The Government's letter to Mr. Shroff, M. L. C. prompts me to send you this reminder. Whilst I tender my congratulations to His Excellency for the decision conveyed in the letter to Mr. Shroff, I have not been able to follow the exception made in the cases of Bardoli and Chorasi being enhanced, whatever happens to the other places. I appreciate the decision. But if it means that Bardoli and Chorasi cannot receive the benefit, if any of the revisions that may follow the passing of any legislation, you will grant that it would be a serious injustice to the people of the talukas. I contemplate no such result, but I merely wish to point out that the language in which the Government decision is worded is capable of the inference I have drawn. As has been pointed out in my latter of the 24th ultimo, even the enhancement recommended by Messrs. Broomfield and Maxwell has been arrived at in error and that in some cases if that recommendation is carried out, grievous injustice will be done to the ryots. The people are getting some what restive, I have told them that I am in communication with Government. I would therefore like you, in view of the publication of the letter to which I have referred, to expedite your reply, including a clearance of the doubt raised in this letter.

Government's Apologia

Sir J. L. Rieu's reply to the two letters, dated 3, Queen's Gardens, Poona, 21st July, 1929:

Dear Mr. Patel,

I write to acknowledge the receipt of your two letters dated the 24th June and the 11th instant respectively.

I regret the delay which has occurred in replying to the former letter. It was due to the time required for examining the cases of the particular villages referred to therein in order that I might satisfy myself as to the correctness or otherwise of your assertion that 'serious injustice' has been done to the landholders of these villages by the Committee's constructive proposals applicable to them.

This detailed examination having been made, I regret that I find myself unable to concur in your contention. I consider that, in the light of the consideration. I consider that, in the light of the considerations and data brought forward in the Committee's Report, the treatment of the particular villages to which you refer, can be fully justified from the point of view of the interests of their land-holders.

Turning to the more general criticisms advanced in your letter, with reference to your paragraphs (1), (2) and (4) and (4) under this head, I would observe that it is nowhere stated in their Report that the Committee's proposals are based solely on rental data. On the contrary a large part of the Report is directed towards showing why rental data cannot be considered entirely by themselves and how their indication, whether scanty or not, can most safely be used. I would invite your attention more particularly to paragraphs 90 and 122 of the Report.

As regards your paragraph (3), it is expressly mentioned in the Report (para 93) that the figures appearing in the appendices are not repeated in the text. If the figures given in report and its appendices, taken together with the discussion in the former, do not convey to you their intended purport, I am afraid that no further explanation would be useful.

As regards your paragraph (5), grass leases were always noted, as such by the Committee at the time of their inspection, and value was based on them according to circumstances (para 32 of the Report). The fact that grass is not exported for sale does not deprive it of its value any more than, in the case of cereal crops, does the fact that they are consumed locally. The existence of value is demonstrated by the leases themselves.

In conclusion, I would observe that notwithstanding the fact that the Committee's specific proposals entailed a large reduction of the land revenue as determined by the sanctioned revision settlement Government accepted these proposals in their totality unhesitatingly and without reference to the question whether or not the considerations on which this reduction of revenue was based were valid and so acceptable to that extent. In the circumstanees, they consider that they are entitled to expect the same degree of acceptance on the part of the land-holders, and they are not prepared to re-open the whole question of the present settlement as, in justice to themselves: they would have to do if modification of it solely from the point of view of the land-holders, were now introduced in it.

Rectify Palpable Errors

Sjt. Vallabhbhai Patel's reply to the above:

I thank you for your letter of the 21st July. I have no desire to ask Government to re-open the whole question as you have put it, not because the ryots have anything to fear from any such re-opening. But I recognise that there must be some finality in such matters. What I have asked is what is always done even in final awards in arbitration cases, namely, rectification of palpable errors unconsciously committed by arbitrators. My submission is that I have brought to the notice of the Government such errors in a report which is otherwise worthy of high praise for the impartial labours that Messrs. Broomfield and Maxwell have put into the enquiry. But it is a painful injustice when it is brought to their notice only by way of prayer. It is hardly a healthy sign that the ryots should always have to resort to direct action to bring home to Government even cases of apparent injustice and hardship. As I have no desire to put the ryots to the hardships of any further struggle, I must submit to what is in my opinion an obvious injustice.

Your letter is silent—perhaps deliberately—as regards an important point raised in my second letter. May I assume that Bardoli and Chorasi will not be denied the benefit, if any, of the proposed new legislation? I should be thankful to have my assumption confirmed by you.

No Undertaking Possible

Letter dated 8th August 1929, Poona, from Sir J. L. Rieu to Sjt. Vallabhbhai Patel:

I write in reply to your further letter of the 2nd instant.

If I may be permitted to say so, your statement of the case simply begs the question. You contend that Government ought to rectify palpable errors unconsciously committed by the members of the Committee and so redress instances of palpable injustice. This might perhaps be admitted as a purely general proposition, but I fail to see that it has any practical application to the present particular case. Your contention is based on the assumption the justification for which I must decline to admit. And, further you assume that all such errors must necessarily be errors that operate adversely to the interests of the landholders. You overlook the possibility of the existence of similar errors that would operate adversely to the rights of the State. That involves another assumption which I regret I am unable to admit as being valid.

With regard to the point raised in the concluding paragraph of your letter, I think it must be evident both from His Excellency the Governor's pronouncements and from my speech during the debate in the Council on the resolution moved by Mr. Pataskar, M. L. C., that Government are not prepared at present to give an undertaking that the revision settlements of the Bardoli and Chorasi talukas as modified by the acceptance by Government of the Committee's recommendations, will be further revised in the light of such land-revenue legislation as may at some future date be passed by the Council.

I MAY REVIVE SATYAGRAHA

Letter dated Ahmedabad, 14th August 1929 from Sjt. Vallabhbhai Patel to Sir J. L. Rieu:

I must now refrain from entering into further argument with you in connection with what appear to me to be palpable errors in the otherwise estimable report of Messrs. Broomfield and Maxwell. Though the Government did not accept my suggestion that the report should be, in so many words, binding on either party, I know that in this matter of the errors, I dare not enter upon a Satyagraha struggle with the Government. It would be inconsistent with my profession of what to me is a grand doctrine.

With reference to the other part of the letter, I regret the attitude the Government seem to have taken up. As to that my course is absolutely clear and I hereby beg to give the Government notice that should the contemplated settlements arising out of the proposed new legislation be beneficial to Bardoli and Chorasi, if it was made applicable to them, in justice to these poor cultivators, I would be bound to press for retrospective effect being given to such legislation so far as these talukas are concerned, even though it may be at the risk of a revival of Satyagraha.

I take it that you have no objection to our correspondence being made public.

INDEX

A

C

F

G

H

J

K

L

M

N

R

S